Contents

Acknowledgements and Permissions vii
Preface xi

Part One: Busy Being Born . . .

1 1941–59: In My Younger Days 3
2 1960: Sammy Bound for Glory 16
3 1961: Hard Times in New York Town 33
4 1962–3: I Am My Words 50
5 1963: From Town Hall to Carnegie Hall 66
6 1963: Troubled and I Don't Know Why 80
7 1964: On the Heels of Rimbaud 89
8 1964–5: The Ghost of Electricity 100
9 1965: Over Your Shoulder 108
10 1964–5: A Book of Words 118
11 1965: I Accept Chaos 127
12 1965–6: Just Like a Freeze-Out 144
13 1966: A Curious Way to Make a Living 160

Part Two: Learning to Do Consciously . . .

14 1966–7: Evening Things Up 173
15 1968: Drifters, Immigrants, Messengers and Saints 184
16 1969: What's the Matter with Me? 195
17 1970: A Restless, Hungry Feeling 203
18 1971–2: Smooth Like a Rhapsody 211
19 1972–3: Alias What? 222
20 1973–4: Into the Flood 233
21 1974–5: From Renaissance to Reformation 242
22 1975: From the Bottom Line to the Bitter End 257
23 1975: You Come On to Me Like Rolling Thunder 274
24 1976: Hard Reign or Last Waltz? 284

25 1977: Everything Went from Bad to Worse   295
26 1978: Someone's Got It In for Me   314

Part Three: Busy Being Born Again . . .
27 1978–9: Pulling Back on the Reins   327
28 1979: On the Holy Slow Train   337
29 1979–80: Middle of the Road – East Coast Bondage   346
30 1980–82: In the Summertime   359
31 1983: Songs of Experience   372
32 1984: Still Life and Real Live   381
33 1984–5: Burlesques and Benefits   389
34 1985–6: Junco and His Partners in Crime   402
35 1986–7: Down Among the Deadheads   412
36 1987–8: Temples in Flames – Wilburys on the Run   422
37 1989–90: Lord Have Mercy!   433
38 1988–90: The Never-Ending Tour   444
39 1990: The Finishing End?   458

Notes   467
Dramatis Personae   487
A Selected Bibliography   499
A Bob Dylan Sessionography 1961–90   503
Index   537

PENGUIN BOOKS

DYLAN

Clinton Heylin is recognized by fans all over the world as a leading authority on Bob Dylan. Co-founder of *Wanted Man*, the British magazine dedicated to studying Dylan's life and work, he edited the news section of its quarterly magazine, the *Telegraph*, for a number of years. He is also the author of *Dylan: Behind Closed Doors* and *From the Velvets to the Voidoids: A Pre-Punk History for a Post-Punk World*, both of which are published in Penguin. His other books are on musical subjects as diverse as Public Image Limited, Joy Division, Richard Thompson and Sandy Denny.

CLINTON HEYLIN

———

DYLAN ·
BEHIND THE SHADES

PENGUIN BOOKS

For Jill, 'the girl with me behind the shades',
and pretty Penny-O

PENGUIN BOOKS

Published by the Penguin Group
Penguin Books Ltd, 27 Wrights Lane, London W8 5TZ, England
Penguin Putnam Inc., 375 Hudson Street, New York, New York 10014, USA
Penguin Books Australia Ltd, Ringwood, Victoria, Australia
Penguin Books Canada Ltd, 10 Alcorn Avenue, Toronto, Ontario, Canada M4V 3B2
Penguin Books (NZ) Ltd, Private Bag 102902, NSMC, Auckland, New Zealand

Penguin Books Ltd, Registered Offices: Harmondsworth, Middlesex, England

First published by Viking 1991
Published in Penguin Books 1991
Reprinted with a revised sessionography 1992
Reprinted without illustrations 1998
3 5 7 9 10 8 6 4 2

The Acknowledgements on pages vii–ix constitute an extension of this copyright page,
and all lyrics are quoted for review, study or critical purposes.

The moral right of the author has been asserted

Printed in England by Clays Ltd, St Ives plc

Acknowledgements and Permissions

I would like to thank first the editor of the *Telegraph*, John Bauldie, for his generosity with the resources of Wanted Man and for the use of the many important interviews he has undertaken on behalf of Wanted Man.

I would also like to thank all my fellow Wanted Man subscribers who have carried out interviews on behalf of the *Telegraph* and other Dylan-related publications and have thus provided such an impressive archive of Dylan's career. They are: Jonathan Morley, Chris Cooper, Reid Kopel, Markus Wittman, Jorgen Lindstrom, Ake Johnson, Arne Hartelius, Patrick Humphries, Jacques Van Son, Val Lawlan, Spencer Leigh, Brian Wells, Roger Gibbons, Chris Hockenhull, Graham Barrett, Miles, John Hinchey, Stephen Pickering, Wes Stace, Andy Bell and Adrian Deevoy.

Thanks to all those who have given gladly of their time to discuss their association with Dylan, whether to myself or to the people noted above. Especial thanks to Kenny Aaronson, Ira Ingber, Markus Innocenti and Eddie Arno, Al Kooper, Farida McFree, Scarlett Rivera, Rob Stoner, Anthea Joseph, Howie Wyeth and Pete Seeger.

Thanks for general help in putting me in touch with important people in this story and/or for generosity with their archives and hospitality: Mitch Blank, Glen Dundas, Dalton Delan, Susan and Mike Decapite, Raymond Foye, Pete Howard, Bruce Gary, Harvey Kornhaber, Larry Hansen, Steve Keene, Pete Vincent, Rob Whitehouse, Ian Woodward and Paul Williams.

Finally, thanks to my friends Pete Vincent, John Lindley and Steve Shepard, to Dominick Anfuso at Summit and to my enthusiastic editor at Penguin, Tony Lacey, for their comments, opinions and brickbats about the various manuscripts this book has passed through. Whatever the finished version may offer it would have been an inferior book indeed without them.

*

The publishers are grateful for permission to reprint the following copyright material:

British Broadcasting Corporation: for interviews with George Harrison, Robbie Robertson, Bob Dylan and Daniel Lanois.

Chicago Sun Times: for Barbara Kerr–Bob Dylan interview (March 1978).

Contemporary Books, Inc., Chicago, and Omnibus Press, London W1: for Bill Flanagan–Bob Dylan interview from *Written in My Soul* by Bill Flanagan (Contemporary Books, 1986, Omnibus Press, 1990), copyright © 1987, 1986, by Bill Flanagan.

Dallas Morning News: for Pete Oppel–Bob Dylan interview (18–23 November 1978).

Elm House: for Ken Gulliksen interview from *Buzz* (November 1980).

Allen Ginsberg: for interviews in *Rolling Stone*, *Ramparts*, *Telegraph*, *Melody Maker* and on WBAI Radio.

Michael Gross: for *Bob Dylan – An Illustrated History* by Michael Gross, with text by Robert Alexander (Elm Tree Books, 1978).

Los Angeles Times: for Robert Hilburn–Bob Dylan interviews.

William Morris Agency, Inc., on behalf of the author: for *Bob Dylan* by Anthony Scaduto, copyright © 1971 by Anthony Scaduto.

William Morrow & Co., Inc., Publishers, New York, and the author: for *Rock Wives* by Victoria Balfour, Beech Tree, 1986, copyright © 1986 by the author; and Helen Merrill, Ltd: for *Clive: Inside the Record Business* by Clive Davis (Morrow, 1974), copyright © 1975 by the author.

New Musical Express: for Neil Spencer–Bob Dylan interview (15 August 1981).

Playboy magazine: for the 'Playboy Interview: Bob Dylan', conducted by Ron Rosenbaum (March 1978). Copyright © 1978 by *Playboy*. All rights reserved.

Putnam Publishing Group and Warner Books: for *Positively Main Street* by Toby Thompson (Coward–McCann, 1971).

Recording Engineer-Producer: for Rob Fraboni interview (March–April 1974), copyright © 1974.

Sing Out Corporation: for John Cohen and Happy Traum–Bob Dylan interview from *Sing Out!* (10 November 1968), copyright © 1968 The Sing Out Corporation. All rights reserved. The Sing Out Corporation is the publisher of *Sing Out! Magazine*. It is a non-profit organization whose address is Bethlehem, PA 18015, USA. Tel. (215) 865 5366.

Larry Sloman: for *On the Road with Bob Dylan* (Bantam Books, 1978).

Saga Agency, Inc.: for Scott Cohen's 'Interviews with Bob Dylan' from *Spin* magazine (December 1985, February 1986), copyright © *Spin* Magazine.

Straight Arrow Publishers, Inc., for Bob Dylan interview with Kurt Loder and Jann Wenner © 1984, 1969. All rights reserved.

Summit Books, a division of Simon & Schuster, Inc.: for *And a Voice to Sing With* by Joan Baez, copyright © 1987 by Joan Baez.

United Press International: for Bob Dylan interviews from *Photoplay* (September 1978).

USA Today: for Edna Gunderson–Bob Dylan interview (21 September 1978), copyright © 1989, *USA Today*.

University of Texas Press and the author: for Kris Kristofferson from *Peckinpah: A Portrait in Montage* by Garner Simmons.

Wanted Man and John Bauldie: for interviews from the *Telegraph* conducted by John Bauldie or Clinton Heylin. All other interviews © individual interviewers and Wanted Man.

We gratefully acknowledge the following for permission to use extracts from interviews they have conducted for Wanted Man, *Isis* or *Occasionally*: Jonathan Morley, Chris Cooper, Markus Wittman, Jorgen Lindstrom, Ake Johnson and Arne Hartelius.

Every effort has been made to contact copyright holders.

Preface

In the beginning was Scaduto. It was 1971. For five long years Bob Dylan had maintained a public profile that Howard Hughes would have been proud of. Anthony Scaduto's was the first serious biography of the man, at a time when there was little information about his roots, his early life and his dreams of fame. It dutifully recorded his small-town youth in Hibbing, his year in Minneapolis and his early days in New York. By 1965 Dylan had outgrown the former friends Scaduto had talked to and in the final section of his book Scaduto's previously racy style, bereft of any major sources except Dylan's own rewriting of his history in cagey interviews with the author, dissipated into song analysis and speculation.

It was another fifteen years before the publication of the second serious Dylan biography. In that time Dylan had reached the peak of his commercial success, released perhaps his most perfect album, converted to born-again Christianity and embarked on a series of tours all exceeding in scope his mid-sixties touring activities. On 29 September 1986 – the twenty-fifth anniversary of his famous original endorsement of Dylan in the *New York Times* – Robert Shelton published his own, long-awaited biography of his old friend.

Shelton's plans for a book had been first mentioned in the summer of 1966. The volume had been two decades in the making. Not surprisingly, given the level of expectation, it was a profound disappointment. He barely advanced the story beyond Dylan's fabled 1966 motorcycle accident, and much of the chunky tome was filled with pat song analysis and cuttings-file out-takes. Though he filled important gaps in Scaduto's narrative of the early years, Shelton did Dylan a great disservice by interring him in the period he had already spent twenty years trying to live down.

Since Shelton's book there has been one pretender to the title of serious Dylan biographer. In the fall of 1988 Bob Spitz, author of a

previous book on the 1969 Woodstock Festival, published a biography as expansive as Shelton's and as racy as Scaduto's. Yet,
despite conducting many original interviews, Spitz did not advance
Dylan's story. His interviewees were mostly the familiar names
used by Scaduto and Shelton, and his Goldmanesque approach,
excruciating prose style, dubious sense of Dylan's history and – yet
again – virtual exclusion of Dylan's post-accident career resulted in
what one reviewer described appositely as 'a thick, petrified, one-
pound hunk of wood-fibre'.

   Now Bob Dylan is fifty. It is twenty-five years since he fell off
his motorcycle in Woodstock. Yet the history of those twenty-five
years remains untold. Two thirds of this book is devoted to
Dylan's post-accident career. It is my intent to show the full sweep
of his life to date, and his post-accident years actually represent five
sixths of his entire recording career.

   Of course Dylan's rise to fame is an important part of his story
and the first section of *Behind the Shades* deals with the well-
documented pre-accident years. Though Scaduto and Shelton have
given good coverage to this period, I have tried to explore a
particular thread which I find weaving in and out of Scaduto and
Shelton, but rarely overtly: what made Dylan so different from his
contemporaries in Hibbing, in Minneapolis, in Greenwich Village
and among the pop music icons of the mid-sixties? Why did he
continue to grow when others, equally regarded, stagnated? The
ability constantly to reinvent who Bob Dylan was, and is, remains
the primary characteristic of his art. It is the way he unleashes new
works. The process may be subtler now, but it remains apparent. In
the early and mid-sixties it actually seemed as if Dylan had no
control over his chameleon changes, they proceeded at such a
frantic pace. It is likely that Dylan never really knew in those days
how close he was to the precipice.

   How Dylan has coped with the legacy of those amphetamine
years is an equally remarkable story. Like another 'would-be
genius', Orson Welles, he is generally thought to have created his
masterpiece, the *Blonde on Blonde* album, before he was even
twenty-five, and then spent the next twenty-five years twisting in
the wind determined to assert himself as an abidingly creative
artist. But, unlike Welles, he did manage to surpass that youthful
masterpiece with the remarkable *Blood on the Tracks*, and came
close twice more during his so-named religious period.

   If the motorcycle accident represents an obvious demarcation
point in Dylan's career, his religious conversion has been the other

major break with his past. That his post-conversion career has been detailed in a total of less than thirty pages by both Spitz and Shelton does a grave injustice to a major period of Dylan's ever-changing career. Though this period reads as a catalogue of missed chances and poor judgement, the last decade is the story of a very personal battle to construct a world-view that retains his faith in both God and humanity. The struggle has led to its fair share of great Dylan songs. Yet if the story in Part Two of *Behind the Shades* in no way parallels Orson Welles's post-Kane career, Part Three's narrative is rather similar in its repeated hints of revival, the promise of masterpieces often unfulfilled or rendered minor by lack of discipline, poor judgement or the neophobic impulses of others, though the release of *Oh Mercy* and *Under the Red Sky* enables a tinge of optimism to colour the final pages of my book.

How much do the works reflect the man? That was the question I constantly asked myself while writing this book. Of course if the works do not reflect the man, then the story still needed to be told but from a different viewpoint: Why are the works so different from the man? In Dylan's case, though, his works reflect his state of mind.

Dylan's perennial reinventions of himself led me to structure this book around each new guise that he has taken upon himself. In most cases a chapter revolves around a major work or tour introducing a new Dylan (e.g. *Another Side*, *Blood on the Tracks*, *Tarantula*, *Renaldo and Clara*, the Rolling Thunder tours). It is a convenient form to use but it is only a convenience, perhaps the dominant colour in my patchwork, but there will be more besides.

Dylan's career could as easily be divided by his geography. Certain chapters fit neatly into the geographic notion, coinciding with artistic periods as well. Thus his 1960 apprenticeship in Minneapolis marks an obvious divide. His fleeing New York for Durango, and finally settling in Malibu, again marked an important change; while his 'retreat' (1966–9) is often referred to as his Woodstock Period (a slight misnomer, given that he had been spending most of his free time there since 1964). Certain albums have been the product of Dylan's geography. Most of *Another Side* was written in Greece in May 1964, *The Basement Tapes* was written and recorded in Woodstock, *New Morning* was the first product of his return to New York City at the end of 1969, *Blood on the Tracks* was largely composed during a summer on his Minnesota farm, as was *Street-Legal*. Yet ultimately the locale is only a part of what inspires Dylan to his finest moments, certainly not the *raison d'être* of his work.

A credible biography is a bringing together of such strands. It draws from all and distils down to a point of view. With a living artist the picture can never be complete. Dylan surely has many years of creativity left in him. So this book can only be a signpost along the way. Dylan also presents a difficult subject because he has trusted people and they have repaid him accordingly. Many of the most important people in his life have refused to talk about their relationship with him. The voices of his wife Sara Dylan, his ex-manager the late Albert Grossman and his confidants, Victor Maimudes and Bobby Neuwirth are largely absent from this book. Fortunately, most of his important musical collaborators have been less recalcitrant.

Dylan himself cooperated with both Scaduto and Shelton in the composition of their books, freely giving interviews and in Shelton's case suggesting people he should contact. Yet in both cases there was a price to pay. Though neither book could be described as authorized, Dylan exerted his influence upon both. Inevitably this led to a slightly sanitized portrait of the man, particularly in Shelton's book. Spitz, predictably, went to the other extreme and chronicled each and every tale of anyone who had a chip on his shoulder and a grudge to bear. Dylan, like most biographical subjects, is not looking for an accurate portrayal but a favourable one. To quote Orson Welles, 'I don't want any description of me to be accurate, I want it to be flattering. I don't think people who have to sing for their supper ever like to be described truthfully — not in print anyway.'

Dylan's voice, though freely represented in this book, is not the voice of a man presenting an authorized portrait of himself, save perhaps in the few instances where I have drawn from his comments in the *Biograph* booklet. His words have been selected from over two hundred interviews he has given in the last thirty years, from raps he has given at concerts in his more gregarious days, from bio-poems he has written. It is one of the great myths of Dylan lore that his interviews are invariably a stream of put-ons and put-downs. In fact at certain points in his life, notably in 1978 and 1985, he has been very keen to talk about his past in a surprisingly frank and honest manner. Readers will find Dylan's voice represented here on a far greater scale than in previous biographies, but without a concomitant personal influence upon the finished product.

Many of the voices did not offer their version of Dylan for this book, though certainly they were aware they were contributing to a detailed chronicling of his career. Most of the original interviews quoted were conducted over the last nine years, intended for and published in the *Telegraph*, the journal of Wanted Man, the Bob Dylan Information Office. The majority of these were conducted by myself or John Bauldie, my co-founder of Wanted Man and editor of the *Telegraph*. I consider the use of this archive of exclusive interviews to be one of the book's strengths. People treat the idea of talking to a biographer wholly differently from that of talking on behalf of what could be referred to as a cross between a very high-quality fanzine and a critical quarterly.

The use of this impressive archive of interviews I believe enables a far more accurate portrait than the one that would have resulted from the guarded interviews I might have obtained in the guise of biographer. I trust I have performed no disservice to those who freely gave of their time for the purpose of being interviewed about Dylan, and I hope they will share my belief that the result is considerably fairer and more accurate than previous Dylan biographies have been.

I have tried to give each commentator his own voice, rather than provide a second-hand paraphrase of what has been said. I trust the reader will feel a sense of Dylan's many-sided self through his verbatim recollections and the recollections of those around him, a feeling that for me rarely comes through in other accounts of him. Needless to say I have tried to document what I believe really happened, but the reader must be aware that there is much myth-building at stake here and that Dylan's friends and collaborators revel in that process as much as the man himself does. For each brick I pull down, there may well be another put in its place.

Finally I should like to comment on the viewpoint from which this book was written. I hope that readers will find *Behind the Shades* an invigorating mixture of original research, cutting-file hopping and sceptical but informed commentary. What will readily be apparent from the book is that I believe that Dylan is (not 'was') an artistic genius. Though popular art forms have produced few such geniuses, scarcely a handful in the sixty years of mass communication introduced by the talkie era (my own selection, in case you may be curious, totals only four: Fred Astaire, Orson Welles, Bob Dylan and Jimi Hendrix), the notion that popular art cannot by its nature produce them is absurd.

Though a reader who does not share my appraisal of Dylan will still find his story a fascinating one, he will find it hard not to notice an abiding faith in the quality of Dylan's work. This does not mean that I am wholly, or indeed largely, uncritical of Dylan. Indeed, the way that he has (mis)used his talents at points in his career is dealt with at length in *Behind the Shades*. Still, those who are looking for an exposé of a fraudulent sixties icon will be sadly disappointed. After all, 'To live outside the law you must be honest.'

Clinton Heylin, August 1990

Part One:
Busy Being Born ...

Part One:
Busy Being Born

1

1941–59: In My Younger Days

'My country is the Minnesota–North Dakota territory/that's where I was born an learned how t walk an/it's where I was raised an went to school . . . my/youth was spent wildly among the snowy hills an/sky blue lakes, willow fields an abandoned open/pit mines. contrary t rumours, I am very proud of/where I'm from an also of the many blood streams that/run in my roots.' [1963]

At a 1986 press conference a middle-aged, slightly wizened rock & roller insisted, 'I'm only Bob Dylan when I have to be.' Asked who he was the rest of the time, he replied, 'Myself.' In 1986 Bob Dylan was twenty-six years old. His creator, Robert Allen Zimmerman, was forty-five. An inevitable fascination with the roots of this creator of his own mythic persona has meant that the path of Bob Dylan's youth has become a well-worn one. In fact Robert Zimmerman's desire to reinvent himself was only belatedly apparent in his final two years in high school. Prior to his discovery of 'that rock & roll music' the only extraordinary aspect of his youth was its very ordinariness.

Each biographer has filled in progressively more detail, but in essence the story remains the one told by Anthony Scaduto in his 1971 biography, indeed by Toby Thompson in his 1969 articles on Dylan's youth in *Village Voice*: Dylan was born a Jew named Robert Allen Zimmerman on 24 May 1941 in Duluth, Minnesota; he moved with his family to Hibbing, seventy miles away, when not yet seven; by adolescence he had rejected his heritage, formed and disbanded several rock & roll bands and was seeking an escape from the suffocating conformity of his home town; meanwhile he met Echo Helstrom, his original Girl from the North Country, with whom he shared many of his later days at high school, waiting to bust the chains and head down Highway 61, to Minneapolis.

That standard biography tends to deal with Robert Zimmerman's sense of rebellion primarily in terms of a rejection of his Jewish identity rather than a rebuttal of the limits placed on imagination by the bulk of the citizens of Hibbing (Dylan has often talked about the visions he had as a youth and how they sustained him).

This conventional 'bio' underestimates the sense of community he felt as a Jew, at least until well into adolescence. It also fails to emphasize how eclectic he was in his selection of early heroes, musical and celluloid (his catholic influences would be a key factor in his subsequent success), and his own uncertainty about how and when to leave the confines of small-town America.

Most of all, though, it fails to explain why Robert Zimmerman should desire a new identity, should wish to reinvent himself – an integral part of his rejection of Hibbing. When Robert Zimmerman became Bob Dylan, or indeed Elston Gunn or any of his other unknown new identities, it was more an attempt to disavow his small-town background than his Jewish heritage.

The Jewish community in Hibbing in the late forties and fifties was a small community, a minority in an essentially Catholic infrastructure. From an early age Jews were aware of an undercurrent of anti-semitism, which led them to form a close-knit group. The Jews of Hibbing looked to the larger town of Duluth for cultural activities and religious guidance.

Robert Zimmerman's mother, the former Beattie Stone, came from a solid middle-class family, and it was mostly her relatives who resided in Hibbing. His father, Abraham Zimmerman, was himself from Duluth, but had moved to Hibbing at Beattie's bidding in 1947, shortly after she gave birth to Robert's younger brother, David.

Beattie Zimmerman: My grandfather owned the theatres, that would be Bob's great-grandfather. His grandfather on his father's side had a shoe store in Duluth. Then we had an appliance store in Hibbing. We moved back because that was my home town. I was born and raised in Hibbing.

According to Dylan, there was another important reason why the family moved back to Hibbing:

Bob Dylan: My grandfather had come over from Russia in the 1920s. He was a peddler and made shoes . . . My father was a very active man, but he was stricken very early by an attack of polio. The illness put an end to all his dreams ... When we moved from the North of the country two of his brothers, who were electrical fitters, opened a shop and they took him with them so that he could mind the shop. [1978]

His father's electrical-goods store gave Robert Zimmerman a secure, stable environment to grow up in, unlike many on the Minnesota Range. Hibbing's primary economic function came from the huge open-pit mine which provided America with much of its iron ore up to the end of the Second World War. After the war, Hibbing slipped into a steady decline, something which obviously affected the impressionable young Zimmerman, who would store his memories up until a time when they could come out in song.* He later told Chris Welles of *Life* magazine:

Bob Dylan: I was born with death around me. I was raised in a town that was dying. There weren't no need for that town to die. It was a perfectly valid town. [1964]

Not surprisingly in such a small community, Robert Zimmerman was related to most of the Jews in Hibbing. In his own words, 'My grandmother had about seventeen kids on the one side, and on the other side about thirteen kids. So there was always a lot of family-type people around.'

Bob Dylan: When I was young, my life was built around the family. We got together all the time. There weren't many Jews around. [1978]

According to Dylan, at about the time Robert Zimmerman's bar-mitzvah was due, the Jews in Hibbing needed to find a new rabbi.

Bob Dylan: The town didn't have a rabbi, and it was time for me to be bar-mitzvahed. Suddenly a rabbi showed up under strange circumstances for only a year. He and his wife got off the bus in the middle of winter. He showed up just in time for me to learn this stuff. He was an old man from Brooklyn who had a white beard and wore a black hat and black clothes. They put him upstairs above the café, which was the local hangout. It was a rock & roll café where I used to hang out, too. I used to go up there every day to learn this stuff, either after school or after dinner. After studying with him an hour or so, I'd come down and boogie. [1985]

---

* The composition most overtly derived from these childhood memories would be 'North Country Blues', released on his January 1964 album, *The Times They Are a-Changin'*.

Like most Dylan anecdotes, this tale contains its share of inaccuracies. Robert's bar-mitzvah was in the spring of 1954. He could hardly have been playing or listening to rock & roll. Nevertheless it indicates the sense of isolation the Jews in Hibbing felt that they should have only a temporary rabbi residing above a local café.

The only hint of things to come evinced by young Robert before his bar-mitzvah was an early proclivity for writing poetry. Shelton's biography details two poems written at the age of ten to his mother and father, and he was, according to his mother, a prodigious writer of poetry throughout his youth. When talking to TV host Les Crane in 1965, Dylan was at pains to separate his early scribblings from his later songwriting impulses.

Bob Dylan: Well, I started writing a long time ago. You know how you write, you write these insane things down when you really don't know what else to do. That's when I started writing. When I started writing songs – that's a different story. I started writing songs after I heard Hank Williams. [1965]

Rock & roll is generally perceived as having been Robert Zimmerman's first love. However, it was country music which first inspired him. Early in 1955 he discovered 'all sorts of Hanks' as he would later put it.

Bob Dylan: You know, where I'm from I only heard country music from Hank Williams, Hank Snow, Hank Payne. [1980]

His first real idol was Hank Williams. Like many of his later role models – James Dean, Woody Guthrie (whose crippling disease lingered but who was creatively dead by the mid-fifties), Robert Johnson, Arthur Rimbaud – Williams died young, his legacy possibly the most impressive corpus of songs in country music. He was found dead in the back of a car on the way to a gig, on New Year's Day 1953, at the age of twenty-nine.

Bob Dylan: I started singing . . . when I was about ten – ten or eleven – and started out just country and western – Hank Williams, Lefty Frizzell kind of things. [1966]

In September 1955, Robert's second idol, James Dean, was killed in an automobile accident near Paso Robles in California, at the age of twenty-four. If Hank Williams gave him a sound, Dean gave the young Zimmerman an image. A composite of the characters Dean played in *Rebel Without a Cause* and *East of Eden* became the first adopted image of Robert Zimmerman. The teenage angst of Dean seemed to mirror directly their own sense of isolation for Robert Zimmerman and a hundred thousand other teenagers.

Bob Dylan: [I liked James Dean for the] same reason you like anybody, I guess. You see somethin' of yourself in them. [1987]

Bill Marinac: The two of us went to *Rebel Without a Cause* a couple of times. And he kept going, I think he went at least four times. He was one of the first to get a red jacket like James Dean. That was a good film, it made a really big impact on us. I think it was the times. Maybe you had to be there, in a small town in the '50s.

There is nothing profound or revelatory about a teenager searching for identity. Robert Zimmerman in 1955 was fourteen, the archetypal age of rebellion. What made this individual different was that his quest for an identity would be unceasing, going far beyond the simple expedient of finding a comfortable niche in society. Robert Zimmerman aka Bob Dylan would constantly reinvent himself, year in, year out.

In 1956 Zimmerman, along with much of teenage America, discovered rock & roll. Like many of his contemporaries in small-town America, young Robert's connection with this new music was mainly through the radio stations which late at night beamed to outposts of civilization like Hibbing. Much has been written about the sociological impact of rock & roll. Suffice to say, Robert Zimmerman found a new purpose in the music. The lyrics crystallized all his feelings of ambition, rebellion and individual identity while the music made his body move from the groin out. Hibbing no longer represented a frontier to his aspirations.

Bob Dylan: I was never gonna be anything else, never. I was playing when I was twelve years old, and that was all I wanted to do – play my guitar. [1984]

Young Robert would have to wait one more year before he could get his first motorcycle and be mobile enough to attend gigs, taking off at weekends either in his father's car or by bike. Duluth was the closest any live rock & roll act was likely to play.

Yet, if he was unable to see live rock & roll, young Robert could always make his own. At the age of fifteen, as rock & roll music was making its first serious assault on American consciousness, Zimmerman started playing with the Hibbing high school band, consisting of Chuck Nara, Tony Connors, Bill Marinac, Larry Fabbro, John Shepard and now himself, though he quickly aspired to form his own band.

Though Dylan claimed to have played guitar from the age of twelve and piano at some point shortly afterwards, Monte Edwardson, with whom he formed his own first band, said Robert Zimmerman in 1956 played the piano, and came to learn the guitar only when Edwardson showed him the basics some time in 1957.

This makes some kind of sense. The Zimmermans had a piano, which Robert's younger brother, David, had begun to play at a young age, becoming an accomplished musician in his own right. Robert never had the necessary discipline for formal training, but between the ages of twelve and fourteen he started to pound out a rudimentary rhythm on the keys. Even at this stage the rhythm was the thing, melody just a minor incursion.

Val Petersen: When Bobby played the piano he would stand and really pound it. But when David played, he sat and played very nicely.

The chronology of Robert Zimmerman's many teenage bands is a confusing one. It would appear that the first of his own bands was with Bill Marinac, Larry Fabbro and Chuck Nara and was probably called the Shadow Blasters.

Bill Marinac: I had a big old Zenith radio in my basement. My dad had an antenna hooked up to the TV antenna. We'd sit there with our instruments and try to copy the music lines right off the radio. His dad had a hookup like that in their house. Our parents were very understanding.

The Shadow Blasters' only gig of note came in the summer or fall of 1956 when they auditioned for College Capers, a talent contest organized by Hibbing Junior College. The quartet ran through their one Little Richard tune (presumably 'Long Tall Sally'), though Robert was barely audible. Hibbing was not attuned to such hollerin' and the Shadow Blasters did not make the College Capers.

Unlike Zimmerman, Nara, Fabbro and Marinac had no serious musical intentions, and the band disbanded shortly after the College Capers débâcle. By the end of 1956, Robert had formed his second and most famous Hibbing band, the Golden Chords, with Leroy Hoikkala and Monte Edwardson. This band would last until the spring of 1958, debuting at the high school Jacket Jamboree contest early in 1957, at which they were by far the loudest and most raucous band to play. They then began to play regularly at Van Feldt's snack bar and a small barbecue joint called Collier's on Sunday afternoons, these sessions being more like jam sessions with an audience present than full-blown gigs. Nevertheless by this point rock & roll had assumed *bona fide* teenage revolution status and though Hibbing's teenagers may have realized the Golden Chords were no great shakes, they were still the only rock & roll combo they had.

Leroy Hoikkala: He was improvising quite a bit, and he was really good at it . . . He'd hear a song and make up his own version of it.

Their most talked-about show was in February 1958 when they played the Winter Frolic Talent Contest and supposedly received an enthusiastic response from the two hundred and fifty kids packed into the little theatre of the Hibbing Memorial Building, though their brand of music was never going to win the actual talent contest, which was decided by parents and teachers. Even at this point Zimmerman seems to have realized he was doing something different, and somehow threatening.

Bob Dylan: We were just the loudest band around . . . What we were doing, there wasn't anyone else around doing. [The music scene] was mostly horn kind of stuff, jazz – there was one other band in town with trumpet, bass, guitar and drums. Mostly that type of stuff. And you had to play polkas. [1986]

The Chords' 'success', however limited, inevitably meant a degree of notoriety at school. After their debut at the Jacket Jamboree contest, Robert Zimmerman's fellow pupils noted the contrast between his performing self and his introverted nature in class.

George Haben: He would get up [at school] and do songs – imitating Elvis and so on, and it was hilarious! To hear this wild singing coming out of a boy who kept to himself, [who] was really very quiet.

By the summer of 1958, Zimmerman had formed his last Hibbing band, Elston Gunn and the Rock Boppers. According to his then girlfriend Echo Helstrom, it was during that summer Bob Zimmerman ran around to her place and informed her that he had found a stage-name, and it was Bob Dillon. In fact this is extremely

unlikely. Since he had formed a band called Elston Gunn and the
Rock Boppers, and later, according to Bobby Vee, asked to be
called Elston Gunn when he joined Vee's band, it is likely that
Helstrom's memory is faulty. Robert Zimmerman may well have
chosen his first pseudonym, but it was in all likelihood Elston
Gunn. It was probably this band which Helstrom remembers as
being booed at the St Louis County Fair in Hibbing that summer.

Echo Helstrom: Bob was pretty serious about his band and they
practised a lot. It was all a blues sound then . . . Bob sang and played the
piano, and he used to practise with the band in garages around the
neighbourhood. Nobody liked their music much, least of all Bob's voice
. . . He and the band played around town fairly often, at school assemblies,
at the youth club, and at Collier's Barbecue. At Collier's it wasn't so bad
. . . but in the big auditoriums people would laugh and hoot at Bob.

Robert Zimmerman seemed oblivious to such hostile reactions.
He was able to play his beloved rock & roll music and that was all
he asked. In the fall of 1958 he formed a band with his cousin,
based in Duluth. Now that he was mobile, with his own
motorcycle, he could regularly make the seventy-mile trek to
Duluth. The Satin Tones became something of a local success,
playing one song on a local TV station in Superior, Wisconsin,
just over the border from Duluth, recording a session on Hibbing
radio and playing at least one show at the relatively prestigious
Hibbing Armory. However, they disbanded in the spring of 1959,
as Robert began to consider his academic and personal future.
    At the same time as Robert discovered rock & roll, he seemed
to have discovered girls. According to Robert Shelton most of his
early selections were 'plump and large-breasted'. Undoubtedly
Echo Helstrom, a young blonde whom he dated throughout the
summer and fall of 1957 and most of 1958, was the best-known
and probably the most long-standing of his Hibbing girlfriends.
The initial connection was rock & roll, which probably explains
why the relationship was not quite as ephemeral as others.

Echo Helstrom: I met him . . . at the L & B Café in Hibbing. That was
back at the beginning of our eleventh-grade year, 1957 . . . He was
always so well dressed and quiet, I had him pegged for a goody-goody
. . . I mentioned [the song] 'Maybellene' [to him] . . . '"Maybellene",' he
screamed. '"Maybellene" by Chuck Berry? You bet, I've heard it! . . .'
And on and on about Chuck Berry, Fats Domino, Little Richard, Jimmy
Reed – Bob thought he was fabulous, the best!

By the time Robert met Echo Helstrom he was already looking for an escape from Hibbing, and now he rode a motorbike – the image required it. This was after all the post-*Wild One* era, when Brando became the quintessential rebel image, usurping even Dean in the moodiness stakes. While he rode around Minnesota and Wisconsin he felt sure the smitten Echo would be there when he returned. Part of the summer of 1958 he spent at a co-ed camp in Wisconsin, working on ways of impressing the girls. It was here that he first met Judy Rubin, who would later be an important lady in his life, though at this point theirs was an innocent enough friendship. He seemed to perceive camp as just another audience to impress.

Steve Friedman: We went to Camp Herzl together. Louis Kemp also went. It's somewhere about 100 miles south [of Duluth], a co-ed Jewish summer camp. We were all about fourteen, fifteen, sixteen . . . He was the star of the camp. He used to sing just like Jerry Lee Lewis, a dazzling imitation. He'd play a piano while standing up and everything.

Zimmerman was also taking every opportunity through 1958–9 to hitch-hike or ride down to Minneapolis and St Paul to check out the action there. Minneapolis and St Paul were where he wanted to be and it was to the Twin Cities that he was looking to escape as and when the opportunities arose. It was here that he was first able to experience live rock & roll, and he began to realize how parochial Hibbing truly was, though Dylan would later tell a somewhat different and rather embroidered version of his first exposure to rhythm & blues.

Bob Dylan: One of the great lakes is called Lake Superior . . . across the lake is a town called Detroit, and I happened to go to Detroit once when I was about twelve or so, with a friend of mine. We had relatives there. I can't remember how it happened, but I found myself in a pool-hall parlour, where people were comin' to eat all day and play Bingo all night, and there was a dance-band in the back . . . Anyway this was my first time face to face with rhythm & blues. [1980]

Steve Friedman: Sometimes we'd hitch-hike down to St Paul, stay in a lousy hotel and look for live music . . . rock, rhythm & blues – Bob was very into black music.

However, if young Robert felt that he could continue to have his fun and still return to Echo in Hibbing, he finally pushed his luck too far and, in the first semester of his final year at high school, Echo gave him his first rejection slip.

Echo Helstrom: He began taking off every weekend, going down to

Minneapolis or St Paul to listen to music he said, but I knew he was seeing other girls as well.

Echo's beliefs were not unfounded. Robert Zimmerman was developing a roving eye, and was hanging out around the university, which he perhaps already envisioned attending after high school. At a coffee-house on the university campus, the Ten O'Clock Scholar, he met Bonnie Beecher, though they would not develop a lasting friendship until they attended university together that fall.

Bonnie Beecher: Dylan, who was in High School in Hibbing, used to skip school and come hitch-hiking down to Minneapolis, to hang out in the one beatnik spot that we could get to.

They struck up a conversation when Beecher overheard Zimmerman talking to a friend about blues singers. Just as Helstrom had endeared herself to him by sharing a mutual interest in rock & roll, Bonnie first attracted Zimmerman through her interest in blues music.

It is impossible now to do more than surmise what led Robert Zimmerman to start to abandon his love of rock & roll in favour of the black forms on which it was largely based. Possibly his regular trips to bohemian Minneapolis made him realize that rock & roll was not entirely the hip form of music he had thought it was back in Hibbing. It was juvenile. Kids' stuff. According to fellow Hibbing musician Bill Marinac, the change came some time early in 1959.

Bill Marinac: In '59 he started dabbling in [acoustic music] very seriously. We had a jam together, just the two of us, in his house. At that time, he did it on electric guitar. We were talking about . . . [what] if somebody could write lyrics with some social meaning, and could do that in a rock vein. He was already into it.

It should be remembered that the young Zimmerman had always maintained eclectic tastes in music. His first love had not been rock & roll but country music. Zimmerman's love of rock & roll soon extended beyond the white man's sanitized version back to its precursor or rhythm & blues. Jimmy Reed was an early hero. Jim Dandy, a disc jockey from Virginia, Minnesota, who had befriended Zimmerman in the first flush of his enthusiasm for rock & roll in 1957-8, and who was the object of regular pilgrimages by Robert Zimmerman and John Bucklen, Bob's best friend in Hibbing, introduced them not only to the rhythm & blues artists from whose sound Presley and Little Richard derived theirs, but also country blues singers like Son House, Bukka White and Leadbelly. As Bob was developing a purist's feel for the blues, he was turning away from the band mentality required for rock & roll. He was also developing a preference for the guitar over the piano.

In late June of 1959 Robert Zimmerman joined his last rock & roll band. He was staying with some relatives in Fargo, North Dakota, working at the Red Apple Café, when he was offered an opportunity to join Bobby Vee's band. Vee, a Fargo native, had already recorded a single for the local Soma label and was looking to expand his backing band to include a piano player.

Bobby Vee: There was just a rhythm section at that time, and [by adding a piano] we would probably have the ultimate rock & roll band. So we sort of asked around the Fargo area and a friend of ours suggested a guy that had been staying at his house and working at a café as a bus-boy, the Red Apple Café in Fargo. So my brother met with him and they went over to the radio station to use the piano. He sort of plonked around a bit and played 'Whole Lot of Shakin'' in the key of C . . . He told my brother that he'd played with Conway Twitty, so he didn't even want to audition the guy and he got the job.

He was kind of a scruffy little guy, but he was really into it, loved to rock & roll. He was pretty limited by what he could play . . . He liked to do handclaps, like Gene Vincent and the Bluecaps, who had two guys who were handclappers. He would come up [to my mike] and do that every now and then and then scurry back to the piano. He wanted us to use the stage name of Elston Gunn for him.

We went out and played a couple of small jobs in North Fargo, then realized since we didn't have a piano, and weren't in a position where we wanted to buy one and lug a piano around with us . . . we decided to work as a four-piece band again. We told him that we'd decided not to use a piano. And he was a bit disappointed at the time and eventually left Fargo . . . and went down to Minneapolis [and] went to school.

His experience with Vee was the death-knell of his rock & roll dreams, and the beginning of a different kind of dream. Whatever, it would seem that Elston Gunn died when Vee decided he could do without a piano player. Robert Zimmerman would have to reinvent himself again.

Aside from his brief sojourn in Fargo in June, where was Robert Zimmerman in the three months before he started university in Minneapolis? He was rarely in Hibbing and, unlike previous years, he was not at Camp Herzl for much of the summer. Rather this seems to be when Robert's parents sent him to a somewhat different school from Hibbing High (which he graduated from on 5 June).

Though Robert was a member of a large and closely knit Jewish family unit, there is no doubt that as his teens progressed and he channelled his rebellious feelings into rock & roll (and its attendant 'Wild One' image), he and his father became estranged.

Much has been made of Dylan's rejection of his family name. Indeed it has been interpreted as a deliberate rejection of his religious identity, though he would have been hard pressed to disguise his Jewish physicality. It is far more likely that he saw it as a denial of his father. Bonnie Beecher specifically recalls that in the early months of 1960 'there was some conflict about his father wanting him to use the name Zimmerman and Dylan refusing to use the name.' Scaduto cites several sources who knew Dylan in 1960–61 and recall Dylan implying that his father was simply 'too hard to get along with' and that 'he couldn't stand his father'.

It is pertinent to note that the first documented 'alias' Robert adopted was in the summer of 1958, which Echo Helstrom clearly indicates was a period of considerable strife between Robert and his father, Abraham. Indeed Robert was spending much of his time at the Helstroms, where he felt more comfortable.

By seventeen his search for a new identity was no longer just a rejection of small-town myopia but increasingly a repudiation of his father's values. His father was a great believer in the work-ethic and placed great store upon the respect of his fellow citizens. Robert was already separating the world into the hip and the square. Never a great respecter of authority-figures, Robert found it increasingly hard to relate to his father's solid middle-class virtues and mores.

At some point his father decided that a strict regime was required to bring Robert back in line. He was clearly disturbed by Robert's rebellious ways and appears to have genuinely believed his son had psychological problems. He had learnt of a school in Pennsylvania that specialized in dealing with 'difficult' adolescents and, at considerable expense, young Robert was sent there. It is not known how long Robert was in Pennsylvania but it is likely that he drew upon his experiences when writing about the somewhat stricter regime of a reform school in his 1963 composition, 'Walls of Redwing'.

After his time in Pennsylvania, Robert was to continue his education at the University of Minnesota (Dylan would later suggest he attended there on 'a phoney scholarship' though his grades were just about adequate enough to secure him a place on merit). To Robert, Minneapolis represented freedom from both small(town)-mindedness and paternal authority figures. In Minneapolis he could be beyond his parents' command.

He set out for the University of Minnesota in September 1959, where he had secured a place despite his minimal commitment to school work. Minneapolis was another world. All his sojourns in Wisconsin, North Dakota, Duluth, St Paul and Minneapolis were just trial runs. At last he was leaving Hibbing.

Bob Dylan: I left where I'm from because there's nothing there ... When I left there, I knew one thing: I had to get out of there and not come back. Just from my senses I knew there was something more than Walt Disney movies. [1965]

Bob Dylan: I'm not the only one that left there and travelled around ... everybody left there. I don't know really of anybody that stayed there. [1965]

2

1960: SAMmy Bound for Glory

Minneapolis was both excitingly new yet oddly familiar. Having spent many weekends in his final high school year visiting the city, Zimmerman knew a small coterie of fellow Hibbing–Duluth Jews, some of whom were also freshmen at UMinn, including Larry Keegan, one of his longest-standing friends. He also knew at least two girls whom he liked and got along with, both of whom were due to attend the University of Minnesota.

Virtually his first act after setting himself up at Sigma Alpha Mu fraternity house was to go to the Ten O'Clock Scholar to try for a gig. Its owner, David Lee, had recently started using folksingers to entertain the customers, though payment was not one of the perks on offer, simply the opportunity to play to people. According to Lee, when he asked the kid his name, Robert Allen Zimmerman replied Bob Dylan. Though Echo Helstrom later claimed that young Robert had first thought up the Dylan alias in Hibbing, Dylan himself said in 1971, 'It just came to me as I was standing there in the Scholar.' It seems more likely that he would have thought of the name before entering the Scholar. He had after all displayed an early penchant for aliases, and Elston Gunn was hardly the name of a folksinger. Dylan though has continued to insist that it was only in the Scholar that he adopted the name.

Whatever the immediate significance of his new name was, the metamorphosis into 'Bob Dylan' had begun. This process was aided greatly by the people he came to know in Minneapolis, of whom three women were crucial to his development – Judy Rubin, Bonnie Beecher and Gretel Hoffman.

Judy Rubin was the girl he had known the longest – they regularly met up each summer at Camp Herzl. Indeed young Bob had a considerable crush on Judy, and throughout his first fall and winter in Minneapolis he sustained an attempt to become 'serious' with her. In a remarkable unpublished poem he would write nearly four years later in December 1963, Dylan recalled his first Christmas in Minneapolis and how much he missed Judy. This poem corresponds very closely with the events of that Christmas as related to Bob Spitz by Judy Rubin herself, notably her family's hostility towards Dylan and their refusal to treat him as a serious suitor for their daughter's affections:

ring ring her ma answers/her ma hates me/snobby sort . . . wants the best for her daughter/society bitch/bitch of a mother . . . talks down at me when she knows/it's me callin. [1963]

Though Judy attended his gigs at the Scholar, shouting requests and generally encouraging him, she was never in love with him.

Judy Rubin: My parents didn't like him, neither did a lot of my friends, and there were too many things, including drugs, that separated us.

By the beginning of 1960, she finally realized that Dylan was not content to be 'just a friend', and, as she had fallen in love with someone else, their friendship ended. Many years later Dylan would jokingly suggest that Judy Rubin's rejection of him set his ethnic awareness back many years; certainly the fact that he still recalled the break-up suggests the degree of turmoil it produced.

More important to Dylan's development as a performer during his early days in Minneapolis was Bonnie Beecher. According to Shelton, Beecher was Dylan's 'real' Girl from the North Country, and certainly his relationship with Beecher appears to have been the most intimate and long-standing of all his relationships in Minneapolis.

Dylan had met Bonnie, like Judy, before arriving at the University, though in this case they had met on campus, at the Ten O'Clock Scholar. Bonnie was then in her final year at high school, due to attend the university the following academic year. By the time she met Dylan he was already immersing himself in folk and blues music, discussing such matters with Harvey Abrams.

Bonnie Beecher: I didn't know anybody else who knew who Cat Iron was or Sleepy John Estes so I perked up my ears and turned around and I started to join the conversation.

Unlike Judy Rubin, Bonnie did not feel concerned by peer group pressure to disassociate herself from such a 'deadbeat'. In one incident, Bonnie relates how, after Dylan passed out from drink the night before an important exam, she cleaned him up and got him into the exam on time. As well as illustrating a Dylan who, having loosened the bonds around him in high-tailing it to Minneapolis, was experimenting with too much drink, the occasional reefer of marijuana and a lot of late nights, it shows a remarkably self-assured girl.

Bonnie Beecher: I was walking to the building where I had my final and I noticed a crowd standing around. Sure enough, Dylan was lying in the middle of the street and [he was] just a mess, you know. He had thrown up and he was passed out on the street . . . And I remember thinking, 'I could just keep walking . . . I don't have to go in there and say I know this person' . . . But I took a big sigh, knew I was going to be late for my test, and dammit I went in and picked him up. He was barely conscious. I had this ludicrous drunk hanging on me, covered in vomit! I walked him into the ladies' room, cleaned him up. I wanted to take him home, but he said, 'Naw! I have to be at the Music building!'

Bonnie Beecher ended up being kicked out of her sorority house for associating with such dubious company. Certainly she took him under her wing, clearly feeling a need to mother him, a common emotion among those girls who sought Dylan's interest at this time.

Bonnie Beecher: No one would let him even play for dinner. I ended up shoplifting for him, stealing food from my sorority house.

The amount of mothering which Dylan inspired became something of a running joke among his male friends in Minneapolis. He seemed to have no problem endearing himself to most women, even those somewhat older. Clearly Judy Rubin's mother was in the minority. According to Ellen Baker, another girlfriend from his Minneapolis days, Dylan's charm worked on both her and her mother, and he regularly used the Bakers' house as a rather comfortable doss-house. As a useful adjunct to this accommodation, Dylan learnt that Ellen's father had an unsurpassed collection of folk-music literature and records, which he had open access to.

Ellen Baker: He hardly ever seemed to have a place to live. But he liked our house just fine . . . besides having both my mother and me charmed and a free place to stay, he had my father's huge collection of bound folk music to peruse . . . My father was quite a collector. He had old manuscripts, sheet music and folk magazines . . . We'd harmonize old tunes from my father's old records, and songs that were the type Bob was doing then. Not the bluesy stuff he picked up later, but traditional things, sort of A-minorish folky.

For a nineteen-year-old, Dylan seemed remarkably aware of his ability to charm women, and he was not unduly selective when it came to satisfying his more basic urges.

Ellen Baker: Bob was funny about his women. At first he seemed very shy, sort of scared ... but it didn't take long before you found out a good deal of that was an act. Bob was surprisingly amorous, and undiscriminating! He'd see a girl on the street or at a party, and it didn't matter what she looked like or who she was with, if he was in that mood.

He was clearly interested in experiencing as much as life could show a nineteen-year-old would-be beatnik fresh from the backwaters of Hibbing. He did not restrict his sexual adventures to the equally inexperienced women he came across while playing at coffee-houses or parties.

Bob Dylan: I met this woman in a bar. She picked me up. It was horrible. I felt used. I was about nineteen and she was, well, she was old. Really old. God, it's all coming back to me. I'll never forget her red hair ... She was big. I thought she had a lot of experience. I'm not going to tell you her name. Even if I could remember it ... She was wearing a print dress. And a girdle. She made love to me, did it all. I just walked into her room and stood there with my eyes hanging out. She lived in just one room, with a closet, a sink and a window which looked out over the street. She had a dresser with a mirror on top that you can tilt whichever way you want, and a bed with a mattress that sagged clear to the floor in the middle ... That woman was sixty years old and she had filed down her teeth! [1978]

The incident Dylan is referring to here dates from his time in Chicago in December 1960, when he was on his way from Minneapolis to New York.

Apart from acts of immediate gratification, Dylan did manage to establish friendships with women, but only with those who were interested in his type of music. Both Bonnie Beecher and Ellen Baker were very supportive of Dylan in his music-making, and both shared an abiding interest in folk and blues. Bonnie in particular was witness to Dylan's almost pathological interest in getting back to the source of each recording he heard.

Bonnie Beecher: I would go off and find a record – a collection of old blues stuff with a bunch of different artists on – bring it back to Minnesota and we would play it through ...

Harvey Abrams: Dylan was the purest of the pure. He had to get the oldest record and, if possible, the Library of Congress record.

A fellow sorority sister of Beecher's, Cynthia Fincher, was equally intrigued by Dylan. She played banjo, and in the fall of 1960 they would often play together at the Purple Onion pizza parlour. It is her voice that can be heard on the (so-called) First Minneapolis Tape from September 1960, berating him for not playing what she wanted him to.

The other woman Dylan met soon after arriving in Minneapolis was Gretel Hoffman. Dave Whitaker, who would marry her that May much to Dylan's initial chagrin, and would himself become a vital influence on Dylan, said it was Gretel who introduced Dylan to the music of Odetta, who became Dylan's first folk hero.

Bob Dylan: The first thing that turned me on to folk singing was Odetta. I heard a record of hers in a record store, back when you could listen to records there in the store. That was in '58 or something like that. Right then and there, I went out and traded my electric guitar and amplifier for an acoustical guitar, a flat-top Gibson . . . Anyway, from Odetta, I went to Harry Belafonte, the Kingston Trio, little by little uncovering more as I went along. Finally, I was doing nothing but Carter Family and Jesse Fuller songs. [1978]

It sounds here as if Dylan went from playing Little Richard to playing Odetta. In fact the change was considerably more gradual. It was more an uncovering of the layers which formed the basis of the music he loved – rock & roll. The first layer was rhythm & blues. The second was blues. Odetta, whose music formed a bridge between the blues singers he already knew and the myriad forms of 'white' folk music, was a logical development by which he started discovering the ballad tradition, which was the primary element in white man's folk music, and then the more topical songwriters like Pete Seeger and Woody Guthrie.

Bob Dylan: I was singing stuff like 'Ruby Lee' by the Sunny Mountain Boys, and 'Jack o' Diamonds' by Odetta . . . [sometimes I was] part of a duo with Spider John Koerner, who played mostly ballads and Josh White type blues. He knew more songs than I did. 'Whoa Boys Can't Ya Line 'M', 'John Hardy', 'Golden Vanity', I learned all those from him. [1985]

Sadly there is no documentary evidence – recordings or reliable reports – relating what material Dylan was playing when he first started appearing at the Ten O'Clock Scholar in October 1959. However, it seems likely that he was playing a combination of songs by Odetta and Leadbelly, plus some popular traditional folk and blues tunes. At this point he was relatively inexperienced with the acoustic guitar, which he had only begun to play early in 1959, he was playing no harmonica, and he was singing in a sweet, rich voice that sounded like a cross between the country twang of Hank Williams and the more saccharine kind of folk popularized by the Kingston Trio.

Everyone who knew Dylan at this time comments on his voice, and how different it was from what it later became. 'Spider' John Koerner, with whom he started playing in January 1960, says it was 'a pretty voice'. It was this sweet voice which first impressed Terri Wallace when she saw him playing at the Scholar.

Terri Wallace: He had . . . the most beautiful voice, which I was really impressed with. I really thought he had a good singing voice. Which I might add was something of a disappointment after he became well known and I heard the voice that made him famous. It was really disappointing to me because it was so different from the voice that I had first heard coming out of him.

It was not just his friends who witnessed his not-so-gradual development. Also regularly attending his shows at the Scholar was his first small coterie of devotees. Terri Wallace was one of Dylan's earliest fans and regularly attended Dylan's gigs at the Ten O'Clock Scholar in the spring of 1960. Her sister, Karen, would make the first known recording of Bob Dylan. It was Terri who suggested in early spring that Dylan consider playing at the Purple Onion as well as, or perhaps in preference to, the Ten O'Clock Scholar. He had asked for a rise at the latter, where he was now bringing some business in, and was promptly refused. The Purple Onion duly benefited.

Terri Wallace: I met Bob Dylan at the Ten O'Clock Scholar when some friends and I decided that we wanted to try something different . . . this was during the days when Expresso coffee places were the big rage . . . He just reminded me of a little choir boy, he had such a cute little cherub face . . . I remember a pair of brown corduroy pants that he wore almost all the time and I know that he wasn't real concerned with his appearance . . . he had worn them so often he had a rip in the crotch . . . If I remember correctly the Purple Onion had more or less just opened, and he was looking for other places to sing.

The first known Dylan recording, indeed the only pre-Denver

recording definitely extant, was recorded some time around May 1960 at the apartment of Terri Wallace's sister, Karen. On it Dylan's voice matches his contemporaries' descriptions. Yet on 'The Two Sisters', a traditional song collected that year in Alan Lomax's *Folk Songs of North America*, he can be heard singing in Dylanesque tones, 'I'll be true to my luuurve'. The unfamiliarity of this voice even led one major Dylan collector to make the unfounded, and subsequently disproved, allegation that the tape was a fake.

The twenty-seven-song St Paul Tape (as it is generally known) is a useful document for indicating the sort of material Dylan was performing by spring 1960. By this point he had met and played with 'Spider' John Koerner. He had also met Dave Whitaker, who would be a trenchant and galvanizing influence on him. Along with Bonnie Beecher, Harvey Abrams, Gretel Hoffman and Hugh Brown, later his flat-mate, Whitaker began to reshape Dylan's world-view. He and Gretel Hoffman taught Dylan a lot of traditional folk material. Beecher and Abrams stayed more interested in the blues. When Dylan himself came to write his first 'original' composition, it was the blues he turned to. The song was called 'One Eyed Jacks' and it appears on the St Paul Tape. In it he affected a world-weariness that a fifty-year-old bluesman would have been proud of.

Dylan would write in the fall of 1963 that meeting people like Whitaker, Hugh Brown, Harvey Abrams and later Tony Glover was responsible for a key transformation:

Boy Dylan: I'd fell in with a new kind a people there in Minneapolis. I was going t new kinds a parties an thinkin new kinds a things . . . I read into what I was doing an saw myself romantically breakin off all ties with all things of the established order although I'd never really been accepted by that order anyway . . . what I saw connected with the fraternity house summed up the whole established world.

By the spring of 1960, Dylan had been made to feel extremely uncomfortable by his brothers in the Sigma Alpha Mu fraternity house. He had never really fitted in with this rather conventional Jewish lodge. He was reluctant to contribute to fraternity life and did not enjoy being ridiculed by those brothers who knew of his night-time activities down at the Scholar. His departure from the fraternity house was really the end of his formal education. Though he continued to attend lectures intermittently, he was immersing himself more and more in the bohemian lifestyle of his new 'hipper' friends.

Ellen Baker: Bob was serious about his school work for a while. At the very start. He tried very hard, but it wasn't him. He finally decided he just wanted to play the guitar and party.

Dylan was drinking a lot in those days, usually cheap but drinkable wine. Though the milder drugs, pills and dope, were around in 1960, and though he was certainly smoking dope in Minneapolis, it was drinking which gave Dylan the bravado to come on with women, and to conquer his stage fright. He also seemed to have a unique ability to perform when substantially the worse for wear.

Dave Whitaker: One thing I do remember about Dylan was that he always had his guitar in his hands. He'd drink and go on – he used to get really fucking drunk, we all did. But he could always play that guitar when he couldn't even stand up – but he would stand up and play that guitar.

Dave Whitaker was the primary influence in the transformation of Dylan into a hip individual. Dylan later said that meeting Whitaker was the most direct reason for his change of lifestyle. He was 'on this side', met Whitaker, 'and suddenly I was on that side'. He started staying up all night, reading books Whitaker recommended and rap-talking over a bottle of wine till the dawn.

Dave Whitaker: There was a black club we used to go to, and all of these prostitutes were sitting there and you'd come in and there'd be these guys playing the blues. And using drugs. Drugs were coming in. The truckers were using bennies and we used to take four or five and we'd go on for two or three days at a time, drinking beer, playing guitar, and going from scene to scene.

In May 1960, Dylan met Dave 'Tony' Glover, the second important male influence on him in Minneapolis. It was at a party held by the now-married Gretel Whitaker. Though it would be late summer before he and Glover became close, Glover took note of Dylan, who was playing and refused to continue because certain people were not listening to him. Like others, Glover noticed Dylan's insatiable thirst to learn at this time, an incredible way he had of soaking up influences, styles, tunes, though he didn't impress him musically. Glover recalls that Dylan was playing songs by Odetta and Josh White and the occasional Guthrie cover.

Bob Dylan: I can remember . . . if somebody played the guitar, that's who you went to see. You didn't necessarily go to meet them, you just went . . . to watch them, listen to them, and if possible, learn how to do something . . . And usually at that time it was quite a selfish type of thing . . . It wasn't necessarily a song; it was technique and style . . . I certainly spent a lot of hours just trying to do what other people had been doing. [1968]

The speed at which he was metamorphosing may not have been apparent to his Minneapolis friends when he was around every day. Yet, having seemingly vanished during the summer of 1960, by the time he returned he seemed a different singer. This time it was remarked on by just about all his friends.

He had spent a large portion of the summer in Denver, Colorado. Why Dylan went to Denver that summer will in all likelihood remain a mystery. It was hardly a local excursion from Minnesota, being 920 miles from home.

Bob Dylan: [When] I hitch-hiked to Denver I think I went there because I knew a girl whose floor I could sleep on . . . I stayed around Denver for a while, but there was only one coffee-house, and they wouldn't give me a job. But then I met a stripper who worked at a bar called the Gilded Garter, and she bought me some clothes and got me a job playing 'Muleskinner Blues' between strip acts. [1978]

He had not found the girl he intended to stay with. Walt Conley was then playing at the Satire, one of two Denver nightspots Dylan was interested in playing at. In Conley's account in Bob Spitz's biography, Dylan arrived at the Satire telling Conley that an ex-girlfriend from Minneapolis had suggested he look him up. Again according to Conley, he auditioned unsuccessfully at the Satire, and subsequently crashed at his house for three weeks, until Conley managed to get rid of him by getting him a gig at an out-of-town place called the Gilded Garter, in Central City. Within a week Dylan had apparently left the Gilded Garter, having stolen twenty dollars from the owner, and returned to Denver.

This does not accord with Dylan's own version, that he 'met a stripper' who worked there, and she got him the job. It also does not explain how Conley would have known that Dylan was a perfectly competent piano player. That was what the Gilded Garter actually required, it being a touristy honky-tonk joint. Dylan had played guitar and sung at the Satire, but had evidently not played piano. In fact, the only matter Dylan and Conley seem to agree on was that the Gilded Garter gig did not last long. In

October 1961 Dylan told Izzy Young that he lasted a week and a half (though he told Shelton, more plausibly, in 1966 that it lasted 'a few weeks').

Bob Dylan: I played for twenty minutes, strippers worked for forty minutes with a rock & roll band. I'd play for twenty minutes again. Never stopped. One night I was about ready to strip myself. Worst place I ever played. [1961]

Corroboration for at least part of Dylan's story comes from Kevin Krown, a local folksinger he met in Denver. Krown later told Scaduto he met Dylan while 'he was playing piano in this Central City joint' (the Golden Garter) and that 'he was living with this stripper down the road'. If he was living with a stripper, which both Dylan and Krown say he was, it seems surprising that he played the burlesque house for only ten days, particularly as his Minneapolis friends say he was gone most of the summer. Also, despite Conley's insistence that Dylan stayed at his house for three weeks, it is difficult to see how Dylan could have survived for that long without a job. According to Krown, Dylan came to Denver having been offered the job at the Gilded Garter, and his portrait of Dylan contrasts dramatically with Conley's.

Kevin Krown: In those days he had the money, he was the one doing the buying. He had a job and a few dollars and I was broke. He actually gave me a couple of bucks when I was ready to start hitching again.

Quite probably Conley's portrait of Dylan was coloured by his attempts to run off with Conley's record collection before leaving Denver. According to Shelton, they had already fallen out over a girl they were both chasing. Whatever the truth, of the three Dylan biographies to date, only Scaduto's 1971 study correctly places him in Denver in the summer of 1960; Shelton placing him there, totally implausibly, in the summer of 1959 and Spitz placing him there in the fall of 1960 just before he headed for New York.

Krown met Dylan at the Exodus, the coffee-house where according to Dylan 'they wouldn't give me a job'. The Exodus was a prestigious gig, and it would have been a considerable surprise if Dylan had been allowed to play there. However, he did see at least two singers perform at the venue, Jesse Fuller and Judy Collins. The more important at this point in his career would be Jesse Fuller.

Jesse Fuller played guitar and harmonica, his harmonica placed in a metal neck-brace which he blew into between verses. This

style of playing was, in the summer of 1960, considered unorthodox, and clearly intrigued Dylan. Though a couple of uncor-
roborated sources have suggested that Dylan played harmonica
from his early days in Minneapolis, there is no evidence he played
it until after his return from Denver. Indeed close friends comment
on Dylan learning to play harmonica at this point. The connection
with Fuller is no mere coincidence. Dylan told Izzy Young in
October 1961 that he 'met Jesse Fuller in Denver at the Exodus . . .
Jesse was playing downstairs and upstairs was Don Crawford.' He
later told Robert Shelton that he had 'quizzed Fuller' about
playing harmonica using the rack.

Having spent most of the summer in Denver, it was time to
return to Minneapolis. The Dylan that came back surprised his
friends. He had been out on the road, and he had returned to tell
his friends about his adventures, suitably embroidered by his
soaring imagination. Whitaker was one of the first to notice a
change.

Dave Whitaker: The difference had actually happened before . . . going
to New York. He came back [from Denver] with a difference in accent.
He spoke differently. He was more sure of himself really. He had gone to
Denver to the Exodus, and he came back with one song that he used to
play, that was entirely a new level in show business, called 'The Clan' . . .
it was a surrealistic poem . . . someone wrote it and gave it to him.

That someone was Walt Conley (it was his one direct influence
on Dylan). Before the more profound influence Fuller had wrought
upon him could fully flower, Whitaker introduced him to a new
guru, one who would finally provide him with the impetus to
abandon Minneapolis and head for New York's Greenwich Village.

The story of Whitaker introducing Dylan to Woody Guthrie's
romanticized autobiography *Bound for Glory* is well known. It is
important to remember that Whitaker had regularly recommended
books for him to read, books which never appeared on any
university curriculum. One book which Dylan read in 1960 was
Jack Kerouac's *Mexico City Blues*, and in all likelihood Whitaker
encouraged Dylan to read the other Beats, Ginsberg and Ferlinghetti in particular. But it was Guthrie who gave Dylan the
requisite new persona.

Dave Whitaker: My role, as far as Bob was concerned, is that I taught
him to read, turning him on to the world of books . . . For him reading

had always been a painful process outside of his existence. He told me in Oakland, in 1978 . . . 'I never thought of reading books until I met you.' I'd say, 'Bob you've got to read this,' and he'd read it, run around with it. And I gave him *Bound for Glory*, which is the story of these folksingers and how you could earn your living going from place to place, he and Cisco Houston, playing these songs and taking a collection . . . And for days Bob carried it around, and he read it, and he came to me and said, 'Come on Dave, I want to show you something.' And he went and picked up his guitar and he had memorized 'Tom Joad' . . . it's a twenty-minute song! . . . Bob did have this marvellous ability to hear a song once and commit it totally to memory.

The chronology of Dylan's development is very important here. Within a matter of weeks of returning from Denver, already having developed dramatically as a performer, he would become a Guthrie disciple, and shortly afterwards begin to play the harmonica, which within six months would become his trademark. Indeed, Dylan's adoption of the Guthrie persona seems to have come so soon after his return that some old friends thought it was an affectation he had developed while away.

Bonnie Beecher: He came back talking with a real thick Oklahoma accent and wearing a cowboy hat and boots. He was into Woody Guthrie in a big, big way . . . At the time it seemed ludicrous and pretentious and foolish, but now I see it as allowing a greater Bob Dylan to come out.

What is often not considered by those who refer disparagingly to Dylan's adoption of the Guthrie character is that it was a very specific version of Guthrie that he adopted. Dylan was already perfectly conversant with Guthrie. What really appealed to Dylan was the figure Guthrie painted of himself in *Bound for Glory*, a mythological figure. As Whitaker himself said, the story of *Bound for Glory* is 'the story of these folksingers and how you could earn your living going from place to place'.

Many of Dylan's friends had respectable collections of Guthrie's work and on the May 1960 St Paul Tape he had performed four songs credited to Guthrie: 'This Land Is Your Land', 'Who's Gonna Shoe Your Pretty Little Feet', 'The Great Historical Bum' and 'Columbus Stockade Blues'. What he had not yet been performing – and could not have with the sweet style of singing he was using – were Guthrie's talkin' blues, a loose, almost free-verse, song form with a very easy cascading tune and an extended line at the end of every verse to allow a suitably weighted verbal riposte.

It was the talkin' blues that gave Dylan the perfect opportunity to affect an Oklahoma twang to his voice. And that twang became more and more pronounced as he immersed himself totally in Guthrie's *œuvre* and character.

The second earliest recording of Dylan – normally referred to as the First Minneapolis Tape – shows a unique version of the Dylan persona. Recorded probably at the beginning of September, it features a Dylan who had discovered the *Bound for Glory* Guthrie and the talkin' blues form – there are four talkin' blues on the tape, three by Guthrie, one improvised by Dylan about his indolent flat-mate Hugh Brown – but who had yet to fuse it with his harmonica sound. It was this fusion which transformed Dylan from just another Guthrie impersonator. As Harvey Abrams has observed, 'He was the first white performer to combine the Sonny Terry harmonica with the Woody Guthrie guitar.'

On his return to Minneapolis, Dylan had begun to spend a lot of time at Ellen Baker's, playing along to Guthrie records on guitar and/or harmonica:

Ellen Baker: We'd sing Woody's songs all afternoon, play my father's old records . . . and I think it was just about that time that Bob got a har-monica.

Throughout the fall of 1960 he worked at his harmonica playing. Though he still played the Purple Onion, he had another regular gig in St Paul, at the Bastille, a more prestigious locale than the pizza parlour. Sometimes he would play with Cynthia Fincher, who played the banjo; sometimes he would play with 'Tony' Glover. Though Dylan had first met Glover in May 1960, only in the fall did they become close friends. Possibly only at this point did Glover consider Dylan a worthy enough musical companion. Glover and his partner, Dave Ray, were highly respected musicians on the local scene. Glover provided some much needed tutoring on the mouth-harp, though he chooses to underplay his role in Dylan's development.

Glover recollects that Dylan originally had a chord harmonica – that is to say one that can be played in different keys. Though suitable for certain types of traditional music, this type was not of much use when playing the blues, where you were required to blend notes. It also required a degree of musical expertise somewhat greater than the conventional 'blues' harmonica. Glover suggested Dylan utilize a single-key mouth-harp, suitable for playing the blues, and showed Dylan the 'cross-harp' approach, where the harp-player plays in a different key from the one the harmonica is tuned to, a style of playing which Dylan quickly adopted.

The remarkable thing is the pace of Dylan's development as a harmonica player. When he reached New York in January 1961 he was a competent player, indeed most of his early gigs there were as a mouth-harp accompanist. Dylan was an avaricious learner and he had a quality few others have – he genuinely 'didn't give a shit'. Back in Hibbing he had pounded on the piano so loud he broke a pedal. Some hooted, but he was oblivious. Likewise, his harmonica playing early on was a subject of considerable ridicule.

Bonnie Beecher: I got him his first harmonica holder at Schmidt's Music Shop. He would come over to the sorority house . . . And he'd play this harmonica, which he didn't know how to play! And my friends would come in and they would just go, 'Uurgh! Who is this geek?' . . . I wanted him to play guitar, which he could play well and which I knew would impress them, but he just wasn't having any of it. He was saying, 'Naw, I wanna get this – hwang! WHwaongg!' . . . I was mortified, but he didn't give a shit.

When his old friend from Hibbing, Bill Marinac, visited him that fall in Minneapolis he was surprised how far his ex-rock & roller friend had come.

Bill Marinac: After he went down to the university, he had an acoustic and his harmonica. We got together and jammed again. He'd started to write some music. It was really tender, a lot of very good blues, a lot of things about growing up.

Marinac was not the only one to be impressed by Dylan's development. In the fall of 1960 Rolf Cahn came to Minneapolis. A renowned guitarist with his own recordings on Folkways, Cahn apparently informed a few friends on his departure that Dylan was 'the most talented guy around'. Cynthia Gooding also came to town and Dylan played to her at a post-gig party and she was duly 'amazed'.* Gooding would later become friendly with Dylan in New York. So would Odetta, who also came to Minneapolis that fall. Again Dylan played to her and received a favourable response.

Bonnie Beecher: I remember Cynthia Fincher coming running over to my house saying, 'She said that Dylan has real talent and he can make it!'

Such plaudits no doubt reinforced Dylan's consummate faith in

---

* Shelton credits this to 1959 but the 1959 Dylan would hardly have impressed a recognized figure like Gooding.

the value of what he was doing. Certainly some on the Minneapolis folk scene would be very bitter about Dylan after his departure, finding it hard to believe that the untalented runt they had heard in Minneapolis was now the hottest young talent on the New York scene and signed to a contract with Columbia Records. Yet an indication of the way he perceived his own importance can be gleaned from a remark made when he was being taped by Beecher. He informed her that he considered the recording she was making (subsequently lost) to be worth the considerable sum of $200.

Bonnie Beecher: He sits down to make a tape, and he says to me, 'I don't want you ever to let anyone make a copy of these tapes, so that when someone from the Library of Congress asks you for them, I want you to sell them for $200.'

When Dylan finally did decide to head for New York that December, there was a degree of incredulity from certain contemporaries.

Stanley Gottlieb: When he told us he was going to New York, we thought he was crazy. We said, 'You can't make it here; how the fuck are you gonna make it there?'

In fact Dylan had 'made it' in Minneapolis, at least in terms of his ascendancy on the local music scene. He was now considered by many of his peers a noteworthy performer, even if his love for Guthrie covers could be a little wearing at times. He could make no further progress in a mid-West town. Many who would later disparage the 1960 Dylan had seen a lot of him in the spring and early summer, far less of him in the fall, as he worked more frequently in Minneapolis's twin city, St Paul, away from the college campus. They had not seen the startling pace at which Dylan had developed as a performer. Dylan himself knew instinctively that it was time to move on. He had talked about going to New York for so long. The time for indecision had passed.

Bob Dylan: I'd learned as much as I could and used up all my options . . . When I arrived in Minneapolis it had seemed like a big city or a big town. When I left it was like some rural outpost. [1985]

Yet it would appear that — despite the independent self he considered himself to be — he actually returned to Hibbing to tell his parents of his intention to go to New York, a remarkable gesture which debunks the notion that he had wholly cut himself off from his family.

Maurice Zimmerman: Bobby was . . . independent – like when he quit school. Came home from Minneapolis and told his parents he wanted to go to New York, to try and make it on his own. Didn't want any help, just took enough money from his father to get East.

It was almost certainly this occasion that prompted Dylan to ask Bonnie Beecher to crop his now long hair. His concern in avoiding upsetting his parents, while presumably partially motivated by his desire to ensure he obtained the necessary funds to reach New York, also perhaps suggests a respectful son.

Bonnie Beecher: It was an unexpected trip he had to make up to Hibbing and he wanted me to cut his hair 'real short, real short so that she won't know that I wear long hair'. He kept saying, 'Shorter! Shorter! Get rid of the sideburns!' Then in the door come Dave Morton, Johnny Koerner and Harvey Abrams. They looked at him and said, 'Oh my God, you look terrible! What did you do?' And then he went and wrote that song, 'Bonnie, why'd you cut my hair? Now I can't go nowhere!'

Maurice Zimmerman's remarks do not agree with Whitaker's later account, given to both Scaduto and Shelton, that Dylan set out for New York on a whim to visit Guthrie, after being up all night and phoning Guthrie at Greystone Hospital, where he was confined while the hereditary Huntingdon's chorea disease slowly wasted his body away. Though Dylan clearly realized that going to New York would provide an opportunity to visit Guthrie, it would have been an uncharacteristic display of naïvety on his part if he had really travelled to New York specifically or mainly to see Guthrie. It seems more likely that Greenwich Village was his primary destination.

Scaduto is the only biographer to chronicle Dylan's trip from Minneapolis to New York accurately. Both Shelton and Spitz are wildly inaccurate. Spitz claims that Dylan headed straight from Denver to New York, an astonishing claim denied by a mountain of evidence to the contrary. Shelton claims, even more implausibly, that Dylan arrived in New York in December 1960 and spent two months in Times Square hustling as a male prostitute. Shelton bases his tall story on one of Dylan's 'recollections' in 1966 during an all-night flight out of Lincoln, Nebraska. Dylan told a similar story to Adrian Rawlins in Australia a month later. At least it proves that Dylan continued to distort and reinvent his past long after his stories of running away as a child to join the circus had been revealed as a sham. In fact, Dylan's convoluted journey to

New York is well documented, and took in both Chicago and Madison, Wisconsin.

Bob Dylan: I went to Chicago first and stayed there. Then I went up to Wisconsin, which was more or less the same general scene as it was at the school in Minnesota. And from there I went to New York. That was quite a trip. Another guitar player and myself got a ride with a young couple from the campus whose parents were from Brooklyn. They were going there and wanted some more drivers, so we just drove. [1978]

Though Madison lies between Chicago and Minneapolis, not between Chicago and New York, neither Dylan nor Scaduto are mistaken. Having arrived in Chicago around Christmas and having crashed at Kevin Krown's place for a couple of days before moving in with a girl (who may even be the sixty-year-old red-haired woman he later claimed he briefly lived with in Chicago), Dylan decided to give up the idea of New York and return to Minneapolis. Stopping in Madison, whose campus had an active folk scene akin to Minneapolis's, Dylan wrote to the Whitakers informing them of his change of mind.

Marshall Brickman: When I was going to school in Wisconsin, Eric Weissberg and I roomed together. Our apartment was the place where all the folksingers wound up. We were the underground railroad. One day this guy, Bob Zimmerman, came through town on his way from Minnesota [*sic*]. He had a brown suit and tie and played sort of blues on the piano.

Though failing to impress Brickman and Weissberg, Dylan did find a new friend, Danny Kalb, a superb blues guitarist, with whom he played at a local coffee-house. Perhaps surprisingly, he accompanied Kalb on harmonica. He stayed in Madison only a few days, intending to find a ride to Minneapolis. Instead, as luck would have it, he was offered a lift to New York as relief driver for another folksinger, Fred Underhill. So he now found himself completing the journey he had set out on, and Fred proved an invaluable companion. He 'was from Williamstown . . . and he knew New York.' So long, Madison, howdy, Hudson River.

3

1961: Hard Times in New York Town

Bob Dylan arrived in a freezing cold Manhattan on 24 January 1961 and was dropped off uptown with Fred Underhill. They quite probably walked the fifty blocks to the Village – after all this was New York, money was tight, and Dylan had a lot to take in – though he would later claim he took 'a rockin', reelin', rollin' ride' on the subway. They eventually arrived at Greenwich Village and the Café Wha, a fairly seedy 'basket house'. It was Tuesday – hootenanny night – and anyone was allowed to get up on stage and sing a couple of songs. Dylan would later claim that the audience 'flipped', though it seems unlikely that there was a large crowd on a bitterly cold January night. However, the Wha's owner Manny Roth must have been vaguely impressed because Dylan soon began playing there in the afternoons. After his brief set that night, Roth told the few Village stalwarts in attendance that Bob and Fred were looking for a place to crash for the night. The new arrivals did not make the best selection from the few volunteers.

Bob Dylan: My buddy and I . . . picked out this fellow who was with a girl. Then my buddy says to me, 'He doesn't look so hot . . . He looks pretty gay.' And I said, 'He looks OK' – and anyway, he was with a girl. And so we went up with him. And the girl got off at 34th Street, and we got off at 42nd Street! Well, we went in a bar before we went to find this place to stay, and we met his [gentleman] friend 'Dora'. 'Dora' was his friend who stayed with him. And both of us looked, and ran out of the bar. [1961]

It seems unlikely that they really took off at this point. They needed a place to stay and the alternatives were not good. They barely had enough money to eat, let alone stay in a hotel, and they had arrived smack in the middle of what Dylan called the 'coldest winter in seventeen years' (actually the worst in twenty-eight years). So they probably took their chances and spent a warm if worrying night with Dora and his friend.

That first week in New York, Dylan did the rounds of the many folk joints in the Village. He travelled out to New Jersey to the daunting Greystone Hospital to visit Guthrie; he even made it to Howard's Beach to visit Guthrie's family. The first weekend he turned up at Izzy Young's Folklore Center, a small shop which sold an impressive assortment of 'folk' fare on both vinyl and paper, plus assorted acoustic instruments. It also had a back room in which folkies regularly congregated, talked and sang. That first Sunday morning, Dylan was to be heard at the back of the shop running through 'Muleskinner Blues' on auto-harp. J. R. Goddard of the *Village Voice* would later comment on the general reaction.

J. R. Goddard: People looked on in amusement as he began hopping around a bit. He was funny to watch, and anybody with half an ear could tell he had a unique style.

His regular trips to Greystone Hospital were not as important as the weekends at Sid and Bob Gleason's in East Orange, New Jersey. Woody Guthrie was allowed by the hospital to spend each Sunday there in the company of old friends. Congregated there would be figures like Alan Lomax and Ramblin' Jack Elliott. Though initially daunted by such notable company, Dylan's exuberant self-confidence soon flowered and within a couple of weeks he was unselfconsciously playing and talking and laughing, often staying over at the Gleasons for several days at a time.

Dylan soon scouted out those places in the Village where he could get up and play. Initially his only real opportunities were at the basket houses, where acts played without payment from the venue and relied upon donations derived from 'passing the basket' at the end of their set. There were numerous such establishments in the Village at this time, the likes of the Figaro, the Commons or the Wha. After all, America was undergoing something of a folk revival, albeit inspired by the saccharine style of the Kingston Trio, and Greenwich Village was perceived as the centre of a buzzing new scene.

By the beginning of February Dylan was playing regularly at the Commons, Café Wha and even the Gaslight. More upmarket establishments like the Limelight, the Village Gate or Gerde's Folk City remained as yet inaccessible, except on hootenanny nights when amateur talent could attempt to impress a club owner enough to secure a paying gig. At the Café Wha, his first stop in

the Village that cold January evening, he was mostly employed as
a harmonica player rather than as a singer.

Bob Dylan: I worked for Manny [Roth] all afternoons, from twelve till
eight. I worked the day shift back then . . . It stayed open from eleven in
the morning until four in the morning and there was constantly something happening on the stage . . . You never really did get popular
there 'cause people never knew who you were. Nobody was billed on
the outside . . . You passed the basket . . . That's why I started wearing hats.

It was just a non-stop flow of people, usually they were tourists who
were looking for beatniks in the Village. They'd be maybe five groups
that played there. I used to play with a guy called Fred Neil . . . He
would play mostly the types of songs that Josh White might sing. I
would play harmonica for him, and then once in a while get to sing a
song . . . when he was taking a break or something. It was his show, he
would be on for about half an hour, then a conga player would get on
. . . And then this girl . . . used to play sweet Southern Mountain
Appalachian ballads, with electric guitar and a small amplifier. And then
another guy . . . a sort of crooner. Then there'd be a comedian, then an
impersonator. And that'd be the whole show, and this whole unit would
go around non-stop. And you got fed there, which was actually the best
thing about the place. [1984]

Dylan would later suggest, somewhat caustically, that he was
'blowin' his lungs out for a dollar a day'. Certainly it was hard
work and little pay – but it was experience and it allowed him to
join the band of young authentic troubadors who wandered the
streets of the Village. He was a folk musician! When he wrote to
the Whitakers at the beginning of February he told them he was
playing the Commons, where 'people clap for me'. However, his
Minneapolis friends might have had trouble recognizing the man
singing at the Wha as their old buddy. His Okie accent had
become even more pronounced, but in the Village he was considered first and foremost a harmonica player. The man who had
made that awful racket learning to play the harmonica barely five
months earlier had quickly discovered a natural aptitude for the
instrument. He had also – seemingly unconsciously – developed an
unusual way of playing it, a style that was unique amongst his
Village contemporaries.

Bob Dylan: This sounds a little vague, but sometimes, like most of the
time, I would blow out on the harmonica because everybody sucks in.
The proper way to play is like Little Walter or Sonny Boy Williamson
would play – which would be to cross it – and I found myself blowing

out more because nobody was doing that in that area. And that's what
defined that harmonica and guitar sound which I hadn't heard until that
point. I just stumbled on it one day. [1978]

Dylan himself readily admits that there were some conscious
influences involved in his style of playing. If it was Jesse Fuller
who had first impressed him when he saw him in performance
in Denver, he did not forget the music he had heard in Hibbing
and Minneapolis, and the sound that most impressed him when he
listened to his blues records was the sound of Jimmy Reed playing
his mouth-harp. Dylan was synthesizing existing styles, combining
Reed's style of harmonica playing with his own new Guthriesque
drawl and the 'country'-tinged way he had of holding his notes, a
throwback to Jimmy Rogers, the pre-war country singer who
invented the blues yodel.

Bob Dylan: Jimmy Reed blew out instead of sucking in on [the
harmonica]. He had his own style of playing – he'd play like three notes,
sometimes the whole solo would be like three notes. [1989]

In those first few months Dylan was developing at such a pace
that the chronology has become twisted by inconsistent and unreli-
able recollections. Some ex-Village folkies have Dylan writing
prodigiously long before he did. Others omit to recall his days as
a harmonica accompanist or forget the occasions when he played
piano at Gerde's hootenannies.

The furious pace Dylan kept up during those first few months
in New York means that events have become concertina-ed to-
gether in contemporaries' minds. Certainly between February and
September 1961 he steadily rose through the echelons of the small
Village 'folk' community. The landmarks around which accounts
of Dylan's early Village career are usually hung are his two
residencies at Gerde's Folk City. In April he supported John Lee
Hooker, his first sustained paying gig (he had in fact played at the
University of New York Folk Society six days earlier). That first
Gerde's residency moved him off the bottom rung of the ladder.
His September residency, during which he received a rave review
in the *New York Times* and secured a recording contract with
CBS, would signify the end of the first phase of his career. By
then he was considered to be *the* rising star among the new breed
of Village folksingers.

In fact there are several other important dates in Dylan's 1961
calendar. In May he finally had the opportunity to gauge how far

he had come in those six months. He returned to Minneapolis. Those who had envisaged a humbled Dylan coming home after weeks of New York folkies hooting at this unskilled country 'hick' were in for a shock.

Paul Davies: When he came back . . . and played at Kaufman Union on campus . . . he sounded like an Okie. You could hardly understand what he was saying.

The two 'party tapes' which exist from Dylan's May stay in Minneapolis show an artist who has grown beyond the comprehension of those who once knew him. A mythology surrounding that quantum leap was inevitable. How he changed so quickly from the Guthrie clone to a genuine interpreter, capable of powerful harmonica playing and marvellously expressive singing, will never be definitively nailed down. Even Dylan himself was mystified by the process. Indeed, when he attempted to write his first book two years later his initial intention was to base it around his arrival in New York, that point where one road ended and another began.

Of course, Dylan himself would greatly enjoy the growth of a romantic myth regarding the 'change' in him – something like selling his soul to the devil, just as Robert Johnson allegedly did. Perhaps, as Paris unleashed Rimbaud's muse, it was New York itself which released Dylan's.

In May, Dylan also played at an obscure folk festival at a hotel in Branford, Connecticut. He met Bobby Neuwirth there, who would be a regular sidekick for many years to come, and Robert L. Jones, a Boston folksinger. In June he went to Cambridge, Massachusetts, home of the famous Club 47, where he again met Jones, who introduced him to Eric Von Schmidt. He would return in August, again hooking up with Von Schmidt, and this time he would meet folksinger Carolyn Hester and her husband Richard Farina, get to play at the Club 47 at Hester's invitation, and be invited to play harp on the forthcoming session/s for her debut album for CBS. Dylan's Cambridge affiliations were the vital connection which resulted in him meeting the fabled CBS producer John Hammond.

Such simple twists of fate made all the difference. Dylan was also prepared to work at securing his 'lucky break'. Starting in June, he began to work on coaxing Robert Shelton, the *New York Times* folk critic, to review one of his gigs. In July he phoned Shelton to tell him he was playing a week at the Gaslight, but

Shelton considered that strictly small-time. At the end of July, he received a small but favourable mention by Shelton in his review of the twelve-hour Riverside Church concert, at which he performed a four-song set, his first radio broadcast (excluding his Hibbing days), as WRVR-FM broadcast the entire day's proceedings. Finally he convinced Shelton to come down to see the first night of a second Gerde's Folk City residency at the end of September, supporting the Greenbriar Boys.

How was Dylan viewed by his contemporaries during his first six months in New York? The one thing that comes across from all the first-hand accounts of his performances at this time was that he sounded different, in fact unique. Whether you found him interesting depended in part upon how 'purist' your tastes were. Looking back it is easy to forget how divided the early sixties folk scene in New York was. There was a traditional 'purist' side and there was a more 'progressive' side, composed of those more interested in whether a song was good than in its origins on a chicken farm in Alabama.

Bob Dylan: Folk music was very split up, there was a purist side to it. You know, many people didn't want to hear it if you couldn't play the song exactly the way that Aunt Molly Jackson played it. I just kind of blazed my way through all that kind of stuff. [1984]

Even among the more enlightened folksingers there was a purism in the type of music they would allow themselves to assimilate. Folk was good. Blues was fine. The less mawkish kind of traditional country music was just about acceptable. Dylan though was considerably more eclectic. In Hibbing and Minneapolis he had assimilated a hugely diverse amount of music from polkas and country and western, through country blues, rock & roll, rhythm & blues, Mississippi delta blues to Kingston Trio-style folk music, traditional Appalachian music and the politically motivated folk music of Guthrie, Sarah Ogan Gunning and Joe Hill.

In December 1961, Dylan told Robert Shelton, 'I really couldn't decide which I liked the best, country or blues. So I suppose I ended up by becoming a mixture of Hank Williams and Woody Guthrie.' But these were only two figures in Dylan's synthesis. He would later admit to other major influences, observing that 'I combined other people's styles unconsciously . . . I crossed Sonny Terry with the Stanley Brothers with Roscoe Holscomb with Big Bill Broonzy with Woody Guthrie.' Others would notice that his synthesis was not wholly derived from such traditional music forms.

Peter Stampfel: He was doing all traditional songs, but it was his approach! His singing style and phrasing were stone rhythm & blues – he fitted the two styles together perfectly, clear as a bell.

By the end of 1961 Dylan was not trying to become either Woody Guthrie or Hank Williams, but rather himself. By this point the Guthrie phase was fast receding. In December he recorded his Third Minneapolis Tape. The only Guthrie songs amongst the twenty-six titles were 'Ramblin' Blues', his own adaption of 'Sally Don't You Grieve', entitled 'Sally Gal', and Guthrie's obscure quartet of VD songs.

The other major aspect of Dylan's development during those early months in New York was his increasing confidence as a performer. He began to tell long, rambling monologues to his audience, often hilariously disjointed but combining the beat poet's form of rap with his downhome style. Indeed at this point he worked up an astonishing version of Lord Buckley's 'Black Cross', a spoken monologue which told the story of a poor black farmer, Hezekiah Jones, who was hung by white racists for being well-read.

Jack Nissenson: He was always an incredible story-teller. He was distant ... onstage, very into his own thing, but he could do these long, long monologues, with no point, and no punchline – except they kept you in hysterics. Same when you talked to him. He either told you a story, or he said, 'Yeah? Is that right?', as if what you were telling him was the most amazing thing he'd ever heard.

Arthur Kretchmer: On stage he was essentially a funny character. Maybe that isn't what he intended to be, but the audience reaction was one of laughing, not at but with Dylan. I recall him standing up there looking behind the curtains for the words to his next song, or cracking up about something which he was mumbling to himself. He was natural and loose, a real country character, and that is what everybody loved about him ... Sometimes he would play piano, or tell a funny story, or just clown around for a few minutes.

But it would be inaccurate to portray Dylan as being universally accepted by those on the Village scene, or by the numerous tourists turning up in the Village to hear a Kingston Trio style of folk music. Indeed, friends recall that Dylan proved an extremely adept 'house-clearer' whenever the club owners wanted to shift those last few recalcitrant customers.

Happy Traum: Before he made his first album he was even rougher sounding and more off pitch and he didn't tune his guitar ... We used to play in a place called Gerde's Folk City ... we would let him come in and do some songs for the late show ... He'd start playing and if there were ten people in the audience five people would get up and walk out.

Dylan also found it hard to secure gigs out of town, where his unique style of performing was an unknown quantity. The Club 47 in Cambridge repeatedly refused to book him, preferring the dulcet tones of Joan Baez or Carolyn Hester's restrained musings. Dylan seemed to engender wildly contrasting opinions wherever people heard him. Club owners seemed prepared to book him for the sheer joy of seeing him play or go to any lengths to keep him out. Terri Thal, folksinger Dave Van Ronk's girlfriend (and later his wife), took on the part-time responsibility of managing Dylan, and succeeded in obtaining bookings at the Café Lena, in Saratoga Springs, where Lena Spencer, the owner, loved his performance and asked him to return despite much heckling from the audience; and also at a club in Springfield, Massachusetts. But generally he was confined to consolidating his reputation in New York itself.

Terri Thal: We made a tape of Bob and I took it up to Springfield, Massachusetts, where Carolyn Hester and Richard Fariña were playing. The guy who ran that club flipped. We really did a selling job. We went to Boston and I tried to get Manny Greenhill to do a concert with Dave and Bobby, and he turned me down. I went to Cambridge's top folk club, Club 47, and a couple of other places, and they all turned me down. Nobody wanted him.

The tape which Thal is referring to here was a recording made one night at the beginning of September by Victor Maimudes at the Gaslight Café. It featured performances of some six songs by Dylan, including three of his own titles, 'Man on the Street', 'Song to Woody' and 'Talkin' Bear Mountain Picnic Massacre Blues'. The tape, apart from generating out-of-town gigs, was intended to engender interest from record companies. Indeed, Carla Rotolo and Sybil Weinberger tried to interest John Hammond at CBS in the tape, without success.

Dylan had begun writing his own songs, or more accurately his own words to 'traditional' tunes – at this point all of his tunes were wholly derivative. Inevitably most of the songs he had written by September were talkin' blues in the Guthrie vein. It was a form which allowed full rein to his mordant wit and clever turns of phrase. They were more extensions of his story-telling monologues than full-blown songs, but proved extremely popular. 'Talkin' New York', written in May 1961 as he headed for Minnesota, was a sardonic depiction of his early weeks in the Village. 'Talkin' Hava Nagila Blues' mercilessly parodied the type of folksong repeatedly requested by the weekend tourists. 'Talkin' Bear Mountain Picnic Massacre Blues', perhaps the finest of this early trilogy, was a hilarious résumé of a boat trip to the Bear Mountain which had been oversold because of counterfeit tickets.

The most notable of his early compositions, though, was 'Song to Woody', his affecting tribute to his last idol. Dylan actually had the impertinence to lift the tune from one of Guthrie's own efforts, '1913 Massacre', but there can be little doubting the sincerity of the singer's paean. The song was written in February 1961.

Even at this early stage Dylan was aware enough of the need for his own identity to conclude the song with a degree of equivocation. After glorifying those who 'come with the dust', Dylan states he would rather not admit to a desire for 'some hard travellin' too'. He had his own trail of troubles to stride down.

Friends in the Village were not always sure if any song he introduced into his set was an obscure traditional tune he had uncovered or one of his adaptations. In the summer he incorporated a couple of impressive new songs into his repertoire, a plaintive ballad called 'He Was a Friend of Mine' and the more conventional blues of 'Baby Let Me Follow You Down' (aka 'Baby Let Me Lay It on You'). He had in fact just returned from Cambridge, where he had spent a rewarding afternoon with the talented Eric Von Schmidt.

Eric Von Schmidt: Dylan came up once. It was Huck Finn hat time, before his first record ... When we got to my apartment he wasn't much interested in playing; he wanted to listen. So I played 'He Was a Friend of Mine', 'Wasn't That a Mighty Storm', 'Baby Let Me Lay It on You', 'Acne' and a couple of others. It was something the way he was soaking up material in those days.

Dylan was particularly impressed by 'He Was a Friend of Mine', which eulogizes a recently departed friend.

Eric Von Schmidt: He was very impressed by that concept of being able to take the black expression in that kind of song and being able to sing it. He wasn't at that time quite able to handle material that related to the blues, and he was still feeling around for a way to do that.

At this stage in his development Dylan was prepared to 'learn' material from anybody. He soaked up an enormous amount just by listening to contemporaries like Von Schmidt, Mark Spoelstra, Dave Van Ronk and Carolyn Hester. But his attempts to assimilate all forms of acoustic music did not end there. From the summer of 1961 he had access to two very important archives, as well as being able to rely on the expertise of the archives' owners. The first important archive was owned by Robert Shelton, whom Dylan was careful to cultivate as a friend. Sometimes Shelton would even take him along to concerts.

Liam Clancy: Shelton used to bring him to our concerts and tell him, 'Now this is how you have to put a show together!' . . . Do you know what Dylan was when he came to the Village? . . . The only thing I can compare him with was blotting paper. He soaked everything up. He had this immense curiosity; he was totally blank, and ready to suck up everything that came within his range.

Pete Seeger: He didn't have to hear [a song] five times, he'd hear it once and latch right on to it . . . This is the folk process.

More often Shelton would provide him with a place to rehearse and open access to his impressive folk-music collection. Shelton also acted as a useful barometer to indicate whether Dylan was working up something truly original or simply regurgitating old values already reiterated a thousand times by somewhat more authentic troubadors than a middle-class white boy from Minnesota.

Robert Shelton: We used to knock around listening to music together, and that period was interesting because Dylan was listening to every bit of music he could hear. He walked around with his ears hanging out, eager to follow whatever was going on in folk music. He'd come over to my house and play piano and listen to records.

The other important archive belonged to Carla Rotolo. Carla was the dark-haired older sister of a seventeen-year-old golden beauty called Suze. Suze had become a regular attender at Dylan's gigs during his first spring in New York, a companion for the love-struck Sue Zuckerman, though when Suze herself met Dylan at the post-Riverside Church gig party it was Zuckerman's chaperon who interested Dylan. Soon Suze and Dylan together became a regular Village fixture. He found himself flung into his first serious romance since Minneapolis.

Carla was if anything more of a fan of Dylan's music than her sister. It was she who regularly sang his praises to Shelton and, with Sybil Weinberger, tried to tout Dylan's crude audition tape around the record labels. Carla also had another major attraction. She worked for Alan Lomax, the premier living folklorist in America, whose definitive *Folk Songs of North America* had been published the previous year, after years of working on similar folksong anthologies with his father John. Dylan could regularly go round to Carla's and listen to records from her collection, browse through printed material or even call upon Lomax himself (whom he had met at the Gleasons'). Thus he was able to dig out obscure songs like a heartbreakin' blues Lomax's father had learnt from a lady called Dink, known simply as 'Dink's Blues'. It would become one of the highlights of Dylan's fall sets.

His association with Suze also temporarily provided some much-needed stability, though their romance was accelerating at a frightening pace. During his first few months in New York, Dylan had made considerable use of the maternal instincts he seemed to engender in otherwise sane women and which he had utilized so successfully in Minneapolis.

Liam Clancy: Dylan had this image of the lost waif, and all the girls wanted to mother him – he made out like a bandit because he was a lost waif!

Dylan's already noted lack of discrimination, his penchant for 'plump, large-breasted' women and his mock shyness which soon revealed a considerable libido was a successful combination in the Village, where the more bohemian girls could find a previously unsuspected deep desire to mother someone being brought out by this chubby, boyish Huck Finn character. He delighted in showing off his prowess to his male friends, most of whom were more bashful (or maybe just more discriminating) than Dylan was.

Mark Spoelstra: He had a lot of nerve with girls. More than I did. Chasing them, coming on to them, not being intimidated – man, Dylan was remarkable.

Suze temporarily subdued his polygamous instincts, and he finally availed upon her to move in with him in December, a major commitment for both of them. With a steady relationship, the respect of his peers and an increasing repertoire of songs, both original and traditional, it would seem that Dylan's career in the spring and summer of 1961 seemed to be heading in only one direction and that was up. Actually, as indicated by Thal, he was not readily accepted outside the Village. He was also initially unsuccessful in his attempts to secure a recording contract with the well-known folk labels (even his profound ambition did not extend to trying to interest a major label in a young Village folksinger).

Izzy Young: I took him to Moe Asch of Folkways Records, who turned him down immediately. Then I took him to Jac Holzman at Elektra Records. When I asked Jac Holzman about that years later, he said that he doesn't remember me bringing him . . . Then I took him to Vanguard Records. Manny Solomon . . . [later] said, 'Listen, Izzy, I'm glad I didn't put him out on a record, because I don't want a freak on my label.'

Dylan would later say that when he went up to Folkways Records, he thought he'd gone to the wrong address, such was the nature of his reception. Izzy Young was one of the important supporters he acquired that first summer in New York. Young even arranged for him to make his first studio radio appearance, on Oscar Brand's WNYC show, *Folksong Festival*. Dylan apparently performed his two or three songs at the piano, which would have made a unique recording if the appearance had been preserved.

Izzy Young: I had a reputation in New York that I didn't call up people everyday to say, 'Hey, this guy's great.' It was very few times. So I called up Oscar Brand, 'Listen, there's this guy in my store, he writes really good songs, you should really listen to him.' He said, 'OK, send him over.' So I went over to his studio, which was in the Village at the time, and he sang two songs . . . his own songs and he was mumbling. You couldn't understand 'em. I was very embarrassed and Oscar was embarrassed. But, anyway, he put him on the radio.

Young's other venture to boost Dylan's career was a concert uptown at the small 200-seat Carnegie Recital Hall which was part of the Carnegie Hall complex. Young arranged to book the hall, printed up the programmes and attempted to sell the hundred tickets required to break even. Unfortunately, according to Young only fifty-three people attended the 4 November concert, and many of them were friends of Young's and Dylan's, and so had not even paid for their tickets. The performance – the first half of which has been circulating for many years among collectors – seems a trifle hesitant, though Dylan still managed to deliver sensitive versions of Leadbelly's 'In the Pines' and the traditional

'Young But Daily Growin''. Interestingly enough, as Paul Cable has observed, the latter performance proves that Dylan's pre-Guthrie voice had not been wholly lost, and at times he comes eerily close to crossing the years between Minneapolis and Woodstock. Young was bitter when the show was not even reviewed.

Izzy Young: The [Carnegie Recital] concert was never written up, which I could never figure out why, 'cause he was written up in Gerde's. But the write-up in Gerde's was arranged between Al Grossman and Mike Porco, [and] the *New York Times*'s Bob Shelton.

According to Young, Shelton's September review of Dylan in the *New York Times* had been no whim on his part. Shelton had been musing upon how best to introduce Dylan for some weeks before his famous 29 September 1961 review. If originally reluctant to listen to the kid who was so highly thought of by the Van Ronks and Carla Rotolo, when he finally heard him, in June, 'Boom! He went nuts for him,' according to Carla Rotolo. The other Village folkies soon became aware of how much Shelton thought of him, and Shelton, as the *New York Times* folk critic, was a figure of considerable influence. His support caused some animosity towards Dylan in the Village.

Liam Clancy: [Shelton], more than anyone, was responsible for Bob Dylan. He pushed and pushed and pushed. He thought Bobby Dylan was a tremendous poet. He had made a very folkie record at that time with John Hammond that wasn't doing anything, but Shelton kept pushing.

Shelton's first and most famous review certainly provided Dylan with much-needed credibility. Indeed, Suze recollects that Dylan, who had been told by Shelton of the review, raced down to the corner store to buy a stack of copies, one of which he surely sent back to his family in Hibbing, proof that he was making something of himself in the Big Apple. Subsequently Shelton became almost Dylan's unpaid press officer, writing the sleeve notes for his first album, giving him glowing reviews for his October 1962 appearance at the Town Hall with the Travelin' Hootenanny, his solo performance there in April 1963, his guest appearance with Baez at Forest Hills in August of the same year, and his triumphant Carnegie Hall gig in October. Izzy Young even suggests that Shelton's articles were approved by a small coterie of advisers before he ran them.

Izzy Young: At the time, [Dylan] was living at Dave Van Ronk's house, and playing at Bob Shelton's house a lot. That's when I got to know him and that's when I became part of the little mafia around Bob Dylan . . . Bob Shelton was the main mafia. He'd write an article in the *Times* about him being in Mike Porco's place and I'd read the article beforehand and Dave Van Ronk would read the article beforehand, and we would approve it. And then it would be put in the paper.

Even Dylan was caught out by the enthusiastic tone of that first review in September 1961. He had been trying to secure a contract with CBS, and Shelton's review seemed to provide a final endorsement. Though John Hammond subsequently claimed that he signed Dylan to CBS the day before Shelton's review, Shelton recollects Dylan telling him the night of the review that he saw John Hammond that afternoon and that he had offered him a five-year contract with CBS. The standard story, which Shelton reiterates in his own biography, goes like this: Dylan attends Columbia session for Carolyn Hester's first CBS album (held the day of his *New York Times* review), Hammond is impressed by his authentic look and his harp-playing and offers to sign him without even hearing him sing.

There are few plausible aspects to this tale. It would appear that Hammond's decision was largely unaffected by Shelton's review – though the review certainly made it easier for Hammond to get his whim endorsed by the upper echelons of CBS A&R. Hammond had already been told about Dylan by his son, John Hammond Junior, who it seemed recognized an authentic talent as well as his father. Hammond Senior first met Dylan in mid-September at a rehearsal session for Hester's album on which Dylan was to provide harmonica accompaniment, which she held at Ned O'Gorman's apartment on West 10th Street (Spitz dates this rehearsal to 14 September, though he provides no specific evidence).

Carolyn Hester: We began to play and John Hammond just plain liked Bob Dylan. It wasn't that Dylan had written stuff then. He just felt this charisma that Bob had, and I certainly agreed with that.

Throughout the rehearsal Dylan showed his mastery of the harmonica. Hammond was impressed enough to want to hear more. Despite the many repeated stories that he offered him a contract on the spot, Hammond would subsequently insist that he did audition Dylan, asking at the rehearsal if he could come up to Columbia and perform some of his songs for him. It would certainly have been not only unorthodox but profoundly imprudent for Hammond not to have asked Dylan to provide evidence of his ability as a singer.

John Hammond: When I first saw Bob Dylan, it was at a rehearsal of Carolyn Hester's down on West 10th Street and he had on his cap . . . this was before he opened at Gerde's Folk City . . . I liked what I heard of him there so much I asked him to come up to the studio. I didn't know that he did much singing, but I knew that he wrote. So I asked him to come up and I heard some of the things that he did and I signed him on the spot.

Logic suggests that this was a more likely scenario for Dylan's signing to CBS – and it fits in with Shelton's assertion that Dylan had already signed with CBS the night of the 29th (though still requiring the rubber stamp from upstairs) – than the notion that Dylan was signed up on the evidence of his session work for Hester's unstartling debut CBS album the very same day. Hammond can only have signed Dylan as a performer. Despite Hammond's comment that he 'knew that he wrote', apart from 'Song to Woody', and a couple of amusing talkin' blues which would not translate easily to vinyl, Dylan at this point had no really strong original material.

When Hammond and Dylan began to record his debut album, simply called *Bob Dylan* in November 1961, Dylan offered only 'Song to Woody', 'Man on the Street' and 'Talkin' New York' as examples of his own compositions. Dylan would later claim that he 'was still learning language then' and what he was writing he 'was still scared to sing'. He would soon disavow the album as unrepresentative of his work, which by the time it was released – only four months after he recorded it – it was.

The album was recorded in a mere two days, Dylan recording some twenty songs over both sessions. Though often popping the mike and occasionally over-zealous in a vocal performance, managing to record an album in two days suggests remarkable discipline on Dylan's part, even if both Hammond and Dylan were later unhappy with the results.

Evidence of how fast Dylan was moving was provided a month to the day after his final session for the first album. Having selected some thirteen songs for his recorded debut, he proceeded to perform twice as many at Bonnie Beecher's apartment in Minneapolis on 22 December. Tony Glover recorded them on a reel-to-reel tape recorder. The legendary so-called Minneapolis Hotel Tape was a far more diverse selection of songs, and illustrated

Dylan's harmonica and guitar work to much greater effect, than the bulk of his debut album.

As an illustration of how quickly he outgrew the hastily assembled material chosen for his commercial debut, there are only four songs from his month-old album on the Hotel Tape. Dylan also premiered for his friends two new songs he had written during the previous month, 'I Was Young When I Left Home' and 'Hard Times in New York Town'. 'Hard Times in New York Town' was based on the traditional 'Down on Penney's Farm' and was really no more than 'Talkin' New York' revisited. 'I Was Young When I Left Home', though, was a superb adaptation of 'Nine Hundred Miles'. Its portrayal of a young man who, having made his home 'out in the wind', is needed back home but feels he 'can't go home this way' remains one of Dylan's rare attempts to write a song that sounds authentically traditional, yet bears the stamp of his personality. It also proved that Von Schmidt's assessment back in June that Dylan 'wasn't at that time quite able to handle material that related to the blues' no longer applied. Tony Glover was certainly impressed.

Tony Glover: By the time he came back . . . he'd really grown, from being a run-of-the-mill kind of player and singer he'd turned into this really dynamic picker and performer. He was doing bottleneck blues, he was playing pretty decent harp – he could do a harp solo piece, he'd written a few songs and he had Woody Guthrie down to a T. When he came back he was pretty impressive . . . He was sitting on the bed enjoying it, finishing the bottle of Jim Beam, and he was pretty dynamic – he had a way of playing, a rhythmic style, he mixed a certain amount of rock'n'roll drive into the folk and blues stuff. He had a lot of energy, always tapping his feet . . . That 'Hotel Tape' was done then on one night over two and a half hours, pretty much straight through.

On the Hotel Tape Dylan was interpolating lines into songs that had never previously included them. Thus his 'Wade in the Water' is not the simple spiritual tale that the traditional song told. Rather it was a reworking that resembled more Robert Johnson's hell-hound-on-my-trail form of the blues than a gospel song basking in the promise of eternal salvation. 'Cocaine Blues' blends lines from both 'Cocaine Blues' and 'Cocaine Bill and Morphine Sue' into a cogent whole, in the style of the Reverend Gary Davis. 'Stealin'' lifts verses wholesale from well-known blues tunes, but Dylan delivers the lines with such verve that he carries it off. If only Hammond could have brought a CBS recording machine to

Beecher's apartment that night! Dylan proved he was the master interpreter his friends in New York knew him to be. In the New Year he would prove that he could interpret his own words just as well as those of others.

4

1962–3: I Am My Words

Bob Dylan: I just wanted a song to sing, and there came a certain point where I couldn't sing anything. So I had to write what I wanted to sing 'cause nobody else was writing what I wanted to sing. I couldn't find it anywhere. If I could I probably would have never started writing. [1984]

If, by the end of 1961, Dylan had established himself as a unique and compelling performer, he was not as yet considered a song-writer of note by his Village contemporaries. Only 'Song to Woody' had drawn any plaudits from his peers.

At the beginning of 1962, though, Dylan started writing at a furious rate. In January he was once again recording songs. This time, though, he was recording seven of his own songs. John Hammond, in an attempt to raise some funds for him between the recording and release of his debut album, had arranged a music publishing deal with Leeds Music. The seven originals were to be included in Dylan's first songbook, along with five arrangements of traditional songs recorded for the first album. Though the tape of these demos includes two nondescript blues and three less notable 1961 compositions, there were also two new and important originals.

The more remarkable song was originally called 'Reminiscence Blues' (it would be copyrighted as 'Ballad for a Friend'). It shared its theme with the traditional 'He Was a Friend of Mine', recorded at the sessions for his first album, and showed that Dylan had mastered the blues form with remarkable ease. In six three-line verses he wrote his first song about the North Country, in this case a eulogy to a friend whom he heard later had been left dead 'on a Utah road' by a diesel truck. By no means a conventional blues, the three-line verses are understated and leave appropriate gaps in the story for the listener to use his own imagination – a common Dylan technique, but one rarely used by fellow 'topical' singers, who seemed bent on describing every minute detail.

The lesser song, both in terms of the writing and the performance, was 'Ramblin' Gamblin' Willie'. It was the first in an
extensive catalogue of outlaw songs by Dylan. Willie is the
supreme Robin Hood figure, spreading 'his money far and wide,
to help the sick and poor'. He meets his death when he is gunned
down after being dealt the dead man's hand – aces backed with
eights. The song ends, as did most of Dylan's songs at this time,
with a moralistic verse. In this case he informs us 'the moral of the
story is very plain to see', gamble and you'll end up like Willie –
a strange moral after the earlier portrayals of Willie's glorious
exploits.

What is perhaps surprising and pertinent to observe is that
Dylan had not as yet written about political issues like civil rights,
racism, nuclear holocaust etc. His songs of 'protest' to date, if they
could be considered as such, were about little men in the grip of an
uncaring system – 'Man on the Street', 'Hard Times in New York
Town' – or straightforward tales of man's exploitation of man,
like 'Talkin' Bear Mountain Picnic Massacre Blues'.

This would soon change. At the end of January, Dylan wrote
the first of what for two years would be a steady flow of
contemporary protest songs. Despite her subsequent protestations,
it can be no coincidence that such songs started to flow from
Dylan's pen shortly after he moved into a West 4th Street
apartment with Suze Rotolo. Suze came from a family with a
strong left-wing bias, and at the age of seventeen she was stuffing
envelopes at the headquarters of the Congress of Racial Equality.
On 23 February 1962 Dylan was due to appear as part of a benefit
for CORE. On 1 February he walked into Izzy Young's Folklore Center and told him he had written a song especially for
that benefit. It was called 'The Death of Emmett Till', hardly a
topical song, given that Till was murdered for whistling at a
white woman in 1955, but it was appropriate to the CORE
cause.

Possibly Dylan was not consciously aware at this point of the
profound influence Suze was having on him, though he would
later tell Shelton that Suze 'was into this equality-freedom thing
long before I was. I checked the songs out with her.' After all she
was considerably better read, her sister had access to the most
impressive archive of American folk music anywhere in the
world, and her views on authentic expressions of protest provided him with valuable feedback. Others worried about Suze's influence.

Eve MacKenzie: Suze . . . wanted him to go Pete Seeger's way. She wanted Bobby to be involved in civil rights and all the radical causes Seeger was involved in. Suze was very much with the cause . . . She influenced Bobby considerably that way.

Certainly Dylan was going through a major change. Within four weeks of writing 'Emmett Till', he had written an uproariously funny skit on the anti-Communist John Birch Society, 'Talkin' John Birch Society Blues'; a song about the building of fall-out shelters, 'Let Me Die in My Footsteps', the best of his early protest songs; and a song about a murderer who had never known life outside prison, 'The Ballad of Donald White'. It seemed as if Dylan was now prepared to assume Guthrie's mantle, and he quickly realized that the songs were being well received.

Indeed one of Dylan's early champions was Woody's longstanding friend, Pete Seeger. It was Seeger who that winter, along with Sis Cunningham, instigated the setting-up of a new magazine which would publish nothing but new songs. It was to be called *Broadside*. Not surprisingly the emphasis in the magazine was not just new songs, but topical songs. In the very first issue, Cunningham stated, '*Broadside* may never publish a song that could be called a "folk song". But many of our best folk songs were topical songs at their inception.'

Seeger had heard about Dylan from fellow folksingers but it was a broadsheet of a talkin' blues which Dylan had written for Izzy Young's Folklore Center which first made him take note of Dylan as a songwriter. (The song was almost certainly 'Talkin' John Birch'; 'Talkin' Folklore Center' was not written until March.)

Pete Seeger: He had made up a song called 'Talkin' Folklore Center' . . . I took him up to *Broadside* magazine and introduced him to Sis Cunningham and *Broadside* was the first magazine that published Bob.

At his first meeting with Cunningham, Dylan played her his brand-new talkin' blues about the John Birch Society, and its wry humour and scathing portrayal of the right-wingers made it ideal fodder for *Broadside*. 'Talkin' John Birch' appeared in the very first issue of the magazine late in February 1962. For the remainder of 1962 and through 1963, he would be *Broadside*'s most regular contributor (they would be the first to carry such important Dylan songs as 'Blowin' in the Wind' and 'Masters of War'). It became a further medium for his outpouring of songs, which he seemed to be writing just about any time he was not sleeping or singing.

Bob Dylan: I wrote wherever I happened to be. Sometimes I'd spend a whole day sitting at a corner table in a coffee-house just writing whatever came into my head . . . just anything. I'd look at people for hours and I'd make up things about them, or I'd think, what kind of song would they like to hear and I'd make one up. [1965]

Dylan was happy to feed the rapidly growing myth of his fecundity. There is a famous instance where Pete Seeger asked him about all the songs he was writing during a radio show being recorded for WBAI in May 1962 (it was apparently never broadcast).

Bob Dylan: Sometimes I go for about two weeks without making up a song – well, the songs I sing. I might go for two weeks without writing those songs. I write a lot of stuff, in fact I wrote five songs last night, but I gave all the papers away. It was in a place called the Bitter End . . . But I don't sit around with the newspapers like a lot of people do and pick out something to write a song about. [1962]

To put Dylan's newly discovered skills as a songwriter in context, he was only providing his own words to existing tunes, generally using not only the tune but the same structure as his original source. Often where his tunes seemed to be adaptations rather than straight copies, it was only because Dylan never heard a song the same way everyone else did. He couldn't help but make it sound different. Much has been made of his appropriation of traditional melodies, but in fact this has always been a constant aspect of the folk tradition, Guthrie being perhaps the master at reworking existing tunes for his own purposes; and Dylan was happy to acknowledge his influences. Talking about 'The Ballad of Emmett Till', he admitted to Gil Turner that he 'stole' the tune.

Bob Dylan: When [Len Chandler] plays and sings he uses a lot of chords but he's really good . . . and he's been always trying to tell me to use more chords and sing a couple of songs in minor keys . . . He taught me these chords . . . He was singing a song to these chords and I saw him do the chords and stole it from him. [1962]

Initially, Dylan was reluctant to assume the title of 'protest singer'. He recognized it as limiting, an early attempt to categorize him. In April, at a performance at Gerde's Folk City, Dylan prefaced a new song he had just written by saying, 'This here ain't a protest song or anything like that, 'cause I don't write protest songs . . . I'm just writing it as something to be said for somebody, by somebody.' The song was 'Blowin' in the Wind'.

At this stage the song only had two verses (the first and third –

the inferior second published verse came later), but its impact was fairly spectacular. It was the first song Dylan had written that had such a wide-ranging and intangible theme, and this time he wisely refrained from ending it with a 'the moral of this song' verse. This inventory of unanswerable questions was a far more effective approach.

It would be some months before Dylan would write another protest song of such note. Perhaps he was indeed considering how to reinvent the topical song form to suit his purposes, having already progressed beyond its existing form. This did not mean that Dylan back-pedalled on his new-found political consciousness. When Gil Turner interviewed him for *Sing Out* that summer, Dylan was happy to admit to his credentials as a singer of topical songs.

Bob Dylan: I don't have to be anybody like those guys up on Broadway that're always writin' about 'I'm hot for you and you're hot for me — ooka dooka dicka dee'. There's other things in the world besides love and sex that're important too. People shouldn't turn their backs on 'em just because they ain't pretty to look at. How is the world ever gonna get any better if we're afraid to look at these things? [1962]

Likewise Dylan still seemed happy to talk about his songs. Though a song like 'Blowin' in the Wind' was difficult to describe (with admirable obtuseness he informed one inquirer at the time, 'There ain't too much I can say about this song except that the answer is blowing in the wind'), he was less guarded when discussing more obvious songs like 'Let Me Die in My Footsteps', 'Donald White' and 'Emmett Till'. He talked to journalist Nat Hentoff at great length about the genesis of 'Let Me Die in My Footsteps', one of his great unreleased gems from this period:

Bob Dylan: I was going through some town . . . and they were making this bomb shelter right outside of town, one of these sort of Coliseum-type things and there were construction workers and everything. I was there for about an hour, just looking at them build, and I just wrote the song in my head back then, but I carried it with me for two years until I finally wrote it down. As I watched them building, it struck me sort of funny that they would concentrate so much on digging a hole underground when there were so many other things they should do in life. If nothing else, they could look at the sky, and walk around and live a little bit instead of doing this immoral thing. [1963]

After writing 'Blowin' in the Wind', which was published on the front page of *Broadside* No. 6 in May, Dylan had personal concerns about which he wished to write. Suze was leaving him. She was going to Italy to work on her art – Suze was a talented painter – and would be away for several months. She left on 8 June. Dylan was pining by the 9th.

A month and a day after Suze had 'sailed away in the morning', Dylan was in Columbia's New York studios recording material for his second album. Though the first session for the album had taken place back in April, it was with this session that he began the album in earnest. The original working title for the album was *Bob Dylan's Blues*, and Dylan stuck to this theme – having already recorded four blues 'adaptations' at the April session – for most of this second session, recording versions of 'Corrina, Corrina' and 'Rocks and Gravel', songs which illustrated the increasing inventiveness of his arrangements. In the case of 'Corrina, Corrina' he used very little of the traditional song 'Corrina', abandoning its conventional four-line ballad form in favour of the more suitable six-line blues mode, and liberally borrowing most of the song's imagery from Robert Johnson, the great delta blues singer who had begun to fascinate him in the early months of 1962. Of course a major part of Johnson's appeal was the mystique surrounding his life and early death, at the age of twenty-seven (or twenty-six), poisoned (or was it stabbed?) by a jealous woman (or her husband), having made just twenty-nine of the greatest blues recordings ever. Indeed, in February Dylan had informed Izzy Young he was writing a song called 'The Death of Robert Johnson'.

'Rocks and Gravel' likewise used very little of Brownie McGhee's 'Solid Road', the song it appeared to be based on, and little more of Big Joe Williams's own version of the same song.

Bob Dylan: I learned one verse of ['Rocks and Gravel'] from Big Joe Williams and the rest I put together out of lines that seemed to go with the story. [1963]

Dylan also recorded two of his own blues, both inventive uses of the medium. 'Quit Your Lowdown Ways' castigates a woman in the tone of a righteous preacher seeking the repentance of a fallen woman, though the person the singer is trying to save her for is himself. 'Down the Highway', which did appear on the second album, is a straight-forward blues akin to 'Standing on the Highway', an earlier Leeds Music demo, which itself was based heavily on Robert Johnson's 'Crossroads Blues'. However, Dylan's performance is anything but standard – a real lonesome tone drives this song, which is about his love taking his heart in a suitcase all the way to Italy.

At this session he also recorded 'Blowin' in the Wind' and an adaption of Henry Thomas's 'Honey, Just Allow Me One More Chance', which demonstrated that he could perform exuberant blues tunes as readily as he could the more plaintive. Under John Hammond's guidance, Dylan was clearly determined to show how far he had come since November 1961. If talk at CBS about Hammond's Folly had affected Dylan, it only hardened his determination to succeed. The first album, released in March 1962, had sold poorly – supposedly 5,000 copies in the first year. Hammond's reputation and his commitment to Dylan ensured he would get a second chance. He knew that a third opportunity would be asking too much. So he worked long and hard on album number two, harder than on any other album he would make over the next twenty years. There were sessions in April, July, October, November and December 1962 and finally a last session in April 1963 before he was happy with the results. Not surprisingly *Freewheelin'* comes across as a real *tour de force*, a milestone in Dylan's development as a performer and as a writer.

Throughout September and October Dylan was writing at a furious pace. Now that his pain and sorrow at Suze's departure had eased a little, he turned his pen to each of the genres he knew. Of course, the love songs of a lonely man still predominated. Indeed, only now did he approach his anguish with sufficient perspective to write two of his greatest love songs, 'Tomorrow Is a Long Time' and 'Don't Think Twice It's Alright'. The first of these was a late-night 'tomorrow may never come' song, with the singer unable to face sleeping in an empty bed, preferring to hark back to better days. 'Don't Think Twice' is a different kind of song altogether, and could be considered the first of his 'make me feel better' songs. Though the tone could be considered light, lines that on the surface seem just wry putdowns also suggest a real hurt – 'she wanted my soul', an absurd request if he had not already given his heart.

Dylan was also writing songs about broader concerns. In September, with the Cuban missile crisis imminent and tension-filled talk in all the coffee-houses, he wrote a song which catalogued a world gone mad, full of worried souls, a world where 'black is the colour and none is the number'. According to some, he wrote 'Hard Rain's a-Gonna Fall' as a poem and only later put it to song. However, the fact that it was loosely based on the Child ballad 'Lord Randall' suggests he had a song in mind all along – particularly as the last verse insists, 'I'll know my song well before I start singin'.'

Within a matter of days of 'Hard Rain's' composition, Dylan was part of a hootenanny organized by Pete Seeger at Carnegie Hall. He decided he would premier his new song to the largest audience of his career as part of his twenty-minute set. It would be the first time that Seeger – whose own version of the song became a concert favourite in the following twelve months – heard the song.

Pete Seeger: We had a Carnegie Hall hootenanny. I think it was '61 or '62 . . . Once again they had too many people on the programme and I had to announce to all the singers, 'Folks, you're gonna be limited to three songs. No more. 'Cause we each have ten minutes apiece and no more.' And Bob raised his hand, and said, 'What am I supposed to do? One of my songs is ten minutes long.'

Inevitably the hard rain that Dylan referred to in this song was taken to be nuclear fall-out, but he was at pains to point out that the song had a broader sweep, a wider meaning, one appropriate before, during and after the Cuban missile crisis. This hard rain had more in common with a biblical apocalypse than with bombs falling through the air.

Bob Dylan: It's not atomic rain, it's not fall-out rain . . . I mean some sort of end that's just got to happen. [1963]

Bob Dylan: I wrote it at the time of the Cuban crisis. I was in Bleecker Street in New York. We just hung around at night – people sat around wondering if it was the end, and so did I. Would 10 o'clock the next day ever come? . . . It was a song of desperation. What could we do? Could we control men on the verge of wiping us out? The words came fast – very fast. It was a song of terror. Line after line after line, trying to capture the feeling of nothingness. [1965]

At about the same time Dylan also wrote an anti-war song, the crass 'John Brown' – proving that he was still unable to apply rigid quality control to the songs he was writing – as well as a song about the civil rights struggle down in Mississippi, the jaunty 'Oxford Town', and a grim tale of a father killing his starving family, the 'Ballad of Hollis Brown', introduced by him at a Canadian concert many years later as 'a tragic tale of independence and free will'. By now it seemed as if these types of songs were expected of him. 'John Brown' in particular reads like a song written to form.

In the months after Suze's departure, Dylan seemed more conscious of his commercial goals. Though always motivated to achieve fame via his music, Dylan in 1962 seemed to be approaching his career for the first time in a business-like way. Through 1961 he had lacked the guidance of a truly motivated entrepreneur working on his behalf. It had been sufficient for Terri Thal to arrange a few out-of-town gigs; he could always play the Village clubs. Now Albert Grossman, a well-known entrepreneur on the folk scene, had made moves to assume control of Dylan's career. He immediately extricated Dylan from the Leeds Music contract and signed him to Witmark, a higher-profile publisher, with whom Grossman could do business. In August 1962 Robert Zimmerman legally changed his name to Bob Dylan, and in November 1962 Grossman began his campaign against John Hammond, aiming to remove Dylan from his field of influence. Hammond was, after all, the other music business figure that Dylan placed his trust in. During an experimental session with a studio band Grossman's partner, John Court, was ordered out of the studio by Hammond. His association with Dylan was unlikely to last much longer, and Hammond knew it.

John Hammond: While he was doing his second album for us, he came up to me and asked me about Albert Grossman. He said that Albert Grossman . . . wanted to sign him and what did I think. I said we'd been on the board of the Newport Festival together and I thought I could work with him. I found out later I couldn't . . . Grossman's first idea was to combine Dylan with a Dixieland band and that didn't work very well.

Albert Grossman was a man about whom everyone had a point of view. Dylan's association with Grossman was seen by some as tainting him; others saw it as incontrovertible proof that Dylan's aim all along was *to succeed*. Not surprisingly, it was primarily Dylan's contemporaries who resented Grossman. They knew that Dylan was being groomed for success and both envied and feared him.

Izzy Young: Al Grossman, he was smarter than Bob Dylan was, 'cause he was managing Bob Dylan, then he was managing Peter, Paul and Mary, then he was owning the company that had the copyrights to the songs that Bob Dylan was writing and Peter, Paul and Mary were singing, then he owned a recording company that was recording everybody . . . Everytime there was a move, he was getting a slice out of it. He probably ended up making more money out of Bob Dylan at that point than Bob Dylan.

Though many believe that Grossman was the main reason that

Dylan grew into the national phenomenon he became, Dylan's career had a momentum of its own in this period. Nevertheless Grossman's influence was a stabilizing factor during the increasingly fraught rise to fame.

Peter Yarrow: Albert was a man of unusual tastes and a different kind of insight into music. He was concerned first and foremost with authenticity. Did the music have real substance, value and honesty? But he was also concerned with having impact and influence in the larger world, the heartland. It was a very rare combination ... There never would have been a Peter, Paul and Mary, there never would have been a Bob Dylan who could have survived and made it without Albert Grossman. Personally, artistically and in a business sense, Albert Grossman was the sole reason Bob Dylan made it.

Don Pennebaker: I think Albert was one of the few people that saw Dylan's worth very early on, and played it absolutely without equivocation or any kind of compromise. He refused to let him go on any rinky-dink TV shows, refused to let Columbia do bullshit things with him ... And Dylan in his early stages required that kind of handling – 'cause Dylan himself would go off at spurious tangents.

The 'spurious tangents' Dylan liked to indulge in manifested themselves in November 1962, when he recorded and released his first single. 'Mixed Up Confusion' would later be seen as indubitable evidence of his undiminished love of rock & roll during his folk period. Sounding like an out-take from one of those fabled mid-fifties Sun sessions (he recorded a version of 'That's Alright Mama' at the same session), 'Mixed Up Confusion' sank without trace and was quickly deleted.

Despite such diversions, on 6 December 1962 Dylan completed his second album – or so he believed. An album featuring 'Blowin' in the Wind', 'Hard Rain's a-Gonna Fall', 'Oxford Town' and 'Let Me Die in My Footsteps' seemed destined to be well received by a politically conscious audience. He was already a major figure in the Village, and perhaps considered the most talented of the 'young 'uns'.

In December, Dylan also completed a major part of his not-so-formal education in folk music. He made his first trip to England, home of the folk-ballad tradition. Albert Grossman had somehow managed to convince the BBC to pay his air fare to London simply to play a small part in a BBC drama called *Madhouse on Castle Street*. Why the BBC would pay for someone with no acting experience to fly all the way across the Atlantic to play a minor part in an unexceptional television play has never been adequately explained.

Dylan flew to London Airport in mid–December, a couple of weeks early (filming was scheduled for 30 December), planning to explore London and immerse himself in its folk scene. Grossman and Odetta, another talent on Grossman's roster, were both already in London when Dylan arrived. Ironically, as he headed for Europe, Suze was returning home. She had set sail from Italy on 13 December, arriving home five days later. Dylan meanwhile arrived in London on or around Tuesday, the 18th.

Tuesday nights were Troubadour nights. Perhaps the most renowned English folk club at the time, the Troubadour was an obvious starting point for Dylan's sojourn through the London folk scene that winter. Having abandoned the Mayfair Hotel, into which he had been booked by the BBC, for the Cumberland, a more homely locale near Marble Arch, Dylan headed for Soho, where most of the London folk clubs lay.

Anthea Joseph: The day before he turned up I had been in Collet's record shop ... And I got the latest copy of *Sing Out* that they had, in which was the first Shelton interview [*sic*] with Dylan and I read it and thought this sounds interesting ... The following day, which was the Tuesday, there I was [at the Troubadour] ... So I'm sitting there being bored stiff by the Strawbs [*sic*] and these feet came down the stairs – cowboy boots, which in those days were rather unusual, and jeans, which were also fairly unusual. Then the jacket. Then this face. Then the hat. He had the hat on ... He trundled up to my cubby hole and started shoving money at me and said, I'm looking for Anthea. Can I come in please? And I said, Well I'm An:hea – and the penny dropped – and I said, You're Bob Dylan, aren't you? And he said Yes. I said, Right, well you can have your money back provided you sing for us.

Pete Seeger had suggested Dylan look up Anthea Joseph, who ran the Troubadour on Tuesday nights. Having made his first important contact on the English folk scene, he soon made his second. At some point in the evening Martin Carthy arrived at the Troubadour. Carthy was a talented English singer, about the same age as Dylan, not a member of the old guard, and willing to recognize and accept a new face on the scene. Carthy soon struck up a strong friendship with Dylan, and over the next four weeks he would often crash on Martin and Dorothy Carthy's floor.

Martin Carthy: He was in England for about three months [*sic*] ... We'd see each other at the various clubs there were. There was the King & Queen, there was the Troubadour, there was the Ballads & Blues on a Saturday night, at the Roundhouse pub down on Wardour Street ...

I've read a lot of books about him and not one of them talks in any detail about his time in England. As far as I can hear, by listening to his records, his time in England was actually crucial to his development. If you listen to *Freewheelin'*, most of which was made before he came to England, and you listen to the next album after that, which is *Times They Are a-Changin'*, there's an enormous difference in the way he's singing, in the sort of tunes he's singing, the way he's putting words together . . . Bob Dylan's a piece of blotting paper when it comes to listening to tunes. If he doesn't learn the tune he learns the idea of the tune and he can do something like it. It had a colossal effect on him.

Carthy himself was a strong influence on Dylan and introduced him to traditional English songs that Dylan was unaware of or only knew from Appalachian derivatives. By the end of 1962 Dylan had become something of a walking encyclopedia of American folk music, but his knowledge of English folk music was minimal. Of course there were considerable similarities, and for nearly three years Dylan had been singing English ballads which had been transposed to America. Indeed, recordings from two months prior to this visit have him performing songs like 'Barbara Allen', 'Handsome Molly' and 'The Cuckoo Is a Pretty Bird'.

When Carthy played him songs from his own repertoire, Dylan, ever the sponge, was soon working on his first adaptations of authentic English folksongs. Two of the songs certainly introduced to him by Carthy were 'Scarborough Fair' and 'Lord Franklin'. 'Lord Franklin' was rewritten as 'Bob Dylan's Dream', 'Scarborough Fair' provided him with the basic melody for two of his most beautiful love songs, 'Girl from the North Country' and 'Boots of Spanish Leather', both started during a five-day holiday in Italy at the beginning of January.

Bob Dylan: I ran into some people in England who really knew those [traditional English] songs. Martin Carthy, another guy named Nigel Davenport [*sic*]. Martin Carthy's incredible. I learned a lot of stuff from Martin. 'Girl from the North Country' is based on a song I heard him sing. [1984]

Carthy was not the only English folksinger from whom Dylan learnt something of the English folk tradition. A good friend of Carthy's, Bob Davenport, was considerably more knowledgeable than Carthy at this time, and he also befriended Dylan. Though Davenport's influence is less apparent than Carthy's, Dylan certainly wrote at least half a dozen songs based directly on English folk songs, either during his stay in England or shortly after his return to America. Two of these may well have been based on original versions played by Davenport. 'Masters of War', his scathing attack on warmongers, and 'Only a Hobo', a superior reworking of the earlier 'Man on the Street', took as their respective sources 'Nottamun Town' and 'Poor Miner's Lament'. Both Dylan songs were composed in January or February 1963.

Also written at the time was 'Fare Thee Well' (or 'Farewell', to use its published title), a straightforward reworking of 'The Leaving of Liverpool'. The Clancys claim that Dylan lifted the song directly from their arrangement of the tune, but this appears to be incorrect. All evidence indicates that Dylan learned the song from Scottish folksinger Nigel Denver, another important influence on Dylan at this time. Indeed he would often ask Denver to play the song.

Martin Carthy: He would always ask me to sing 'Scarborough Fair' or 'Lord Franklin'. If Nigel was on, he would ask him for 'Kieshmul's Galley' or 'The Leaving of Liverpool'.

'The Leaving of Liverpool' was not the only song in Denver's repertoire that intrigued Dylan. According to Jim McLean there was one song that Denver sang, Dominic Behan's 'The Patriot Game', which Dylan took a particular interest in. He asked McLean about the song and within three months had adapted the tune and indeed the theme of the song. It became Dylan's most brilliant debunking of the God and Country ethos, 'With God on Our Side'.

Jim McLean: [Dylan asked me], 'What does it mean, Patriot Game?' . . . I explained – probably lectured him – about Dr Johnson, who's one of Dominic [Behan]'s favourite writers, and that's where Dominic picked up [the] saying: 'Patriotism is the last refuge of a scoundrel.' I explained the song to Dylan at the time.

However, unlike Carthy and Davenport, Denver and Dylan never became friends. Indeed, after an incident in late December they became rather estranged.

Anthea Joseph: They had a row. It was [over] the fact he considered Bob couldn't sing his way out of a paper bag, couldn't play a guitar and couldn't play a harp, and that Nigel was infinitely better.

Needless to say Dylan did not appreciate Denver's opinions, and on New Year's Day 1963 he proceeded to show what he thought of Mr Denver at the King & Queen pub, a venue where, according to Carthy, Dylan had previously met with an extremely good reception.

Ron Gould: The featured guest that night was a Scottish singer called Nigel Denver – a Scottish Nationalist, fiercely patriotic. He was singing an unaccompanied Scottish ballad, nice and quiet, when Dylan came in and stood at the back of the audience. Straight away he began to create a disturbance, talking very, very loudly, saying 'What's all this fuckin' shit?' or something of that nature, really nasty. 'What's going on? Where's the drinks? How do you get a drink here?' And this went on all through the song, with people in the audience telling him to be quiet. Nobody knew who he was. Then Nigel said, 'I don't know if you realize it but we allow the performers to perform, during which time the audience keeps quiet.' And Dylan looked up and said, 'I don't fuckin' have to keep quiet. I'm Bob Dylan.' Which really enamoured him with the audience!

According to Anthea Joseph, who was present, Dylan had good reason to heckle Denver that night.

Anthea Joseph: He was drunk . . . And so was Nigel – again . . . And he was awfully bad that night.

In London Dylan himself generally seemed to be consuming more than enough drink. In the final week of his stay, he was providing some harmonica accompaniment for an album Richard Farina and Eric Von Schmidt were recording at Dobell's. Farina and Von Schmidt had hooked up with Dylan at the beginning of January, and again after his return from Rome, where he had gone for five days with Odetta.* Farina and Von Schmidt proved serious drinking companions. The first day at Dobell's Dylan arrived with a carrier bag full of beer. A loose session was on the cards. Offered a bottle of Guinness, he took a swig, exclaimed, 'My God, what's this?!', and emptied the remainder of the bottle on the floor. By the evening Dylan, Von Schmidt and Farina were well juiced. Having completed the session, they headed down to the Troubadour one last time (Dylan and Von Schmidt were going home in two days).

Anthea Joseph: They all turned up about eleven o'clock absolutely out of their gourds except for Ethan Signer, the fiddle player. Ethan was straight as a die and very embarrassed by this collection of bozos that he

---

* Scaduto's story that he went to Italy to find Suze is wholly apocryphal, Dylan being fully aware that she was back in New York.

was looking after . . . The Troubadour has – you can't call it a stage – a platform. [It's] less than a foot. [Dylan] was falling off it. And finally I supplied him with a stool and said, You'd better sing sitting down 'cause otherwise you're gonna hurt yourself.

In the middle of Dylan's impromptu set Nigel Denver arrived at the club, fully expecting to sing with Judy Silvers, the scheduled act that night, who had already performed her first (and as it turned out last) set. Denver began heckling Dylan from the floor, but Dylan was too stoned to care, and no matter how much Denver taunted Dylan, he refused to admit to Denver's existence. Denver finally stormed out of the club. As Von Schmidt later commented, 'Dylan [just] wouldn't let him exist.'

Perhaps Dylan's most legendary performance in London, though, had been shortly before Christmas, when he went to the Singers' Club with Anthea Joseph. Part of Denver's fierce resentment of Dylan was that he wrote his own songs, and Denver had the purist's view that all folk performances must be exclusively traditional. Carthy and Davenport were prepared to accept Dylan as a valid troubadour who utilized but was not mired in the folk tradition. Of course the Village had its fair share of purists. But in London there were the purest of the pure, those for whom even Appalachian ballads were a trifle sullied, and their home was the Singers' Club, run by Ewan MacColl and Peggy Seeger.

Anthea Joseph: I took him to the Singers' Club. Bert Lloyd was there and I walked into the bar with Bob, clutching guitar, and we went up to the bar, bought a drink and Bert knew about Dylan and I introduced them. So Bert then introduced him to Ewan and Ewan sort of looked at the guitar and we all trailed upstairs. The first half of the Singers' Club was deadly serious – no floor singers in the first half, not ever – and the audience by this time had begun to recognize him. Not because of any publicity but because the word had got out. So the muttering was Bob Dylan's here, Bob Dylan's here. They kept on sort of looking at him and Bob was getting the giggles . . . And we went downstairs at half time, had another jar, went back upstairs and it was getting people off the floor, and there was no way they could say no. He had to be got up! . . . [of course] he wasn't trad. And it was distinctly traditional . . . He did 'Masters of War' [sic] and 'Ballad of Hollis Brown', which goes on forever with the chorus and [there were] many extra verses. When you got up off the floor your maximum was five minutes really. [Dylan did] twenty! And he did it on purpose. I'm sure of it. Absolutely sure of it. And brought the house down.

MacColl never forgave this young Yankee upstart and would

later write several vitriolic articles dismissing Dylan's work, but by then Dylan had long progressed beyond the limits of the tunnel vision of the MacColls of this world.* His English visit gave a new dimension to his writing. He returned to New York at last prepared to concentrate on reworking the traditional forms, rather than perpetuating them. From now on it would be exclusively Bob Dylan songs that his audiences would hear, even if some of those melodies he put his chains of flashing images to still sounded mighty familiar.

---

* Ironically, early in his career Dylan was a considerable fan of MacColl, frequently performing his 'Go Down You Murderers'.

5

1963: From Town Hall to Carnegie Hall

If the change in him after his trip to London may not have been as dramatic as on his return from Denver in 1960, his friends noticed a new dynamism in Dylan. Part of this was the gradually increasing influence of Al Grossman. But Dylan no longer seemed content just to write songs and sing them. He required a reason.

In 1965, when he was the king of folk-rock and required to be dismissive of his past, he would repeatedly insist that he had jumped into a scene he saw happening when he began writing protest songs. Many commentators have dismissed this as the rewriting of history by Dylan, arguing that the sincerity evident in songs like 'Only a Pawn in Their Game' and 'Masters of War' belies his later claims. Such commentators mistake sincerity for zeal. The 'finger-pointin'' songs Dylan had written in 1962 and would write in 1963 were unquestionably sincere expressions of frustration and anger at neophobes who attempted to subvert the process of change. However, they represented only one facet of his songwriting skills. It was a conscious decision on his part to suppress the other genres he had mastered in order to emphasize the finger-pointin' aspect of his songwriting.

He made that decision on returning from England in the winter of 1962–3. Part of the reason for his choice was that the times were indeed a-changin', and Dylan was shrewd enough to recognize the first signs. The starting point, though, for the emergence of the Protest Singer goes back to the fall of 1962. He had gradually become more active in making contributions to *Broadside*, Sis Cunningham's mimeographed publication of topical songs. In November 1962, he recorded the first of several sessions for *Broadside*, intended to provide material for the magazine. The first session included three songs in the finger-pointin' vein, of which 'Oxford Town' was the best of the bunch. The other two were 'Ye Playboys and Playgirls', an innocuous little ditty about the sort of people who shouldn't run this world, and 'Paths of Victory', the second of Dylan's 'exhortation' songs. The first such song in his repertoire, 'Ain't Gonna Grieve', had been published by *Broadside* the previous August, his first contribution since 'Blowin' in the Wind'.

Though inconsequential songs in themselves, 'Ain't Gonna Grieve' and 'Paths of Victory' were the direct antecedents of 'The Times They Are a-Changin'' and 'When the Ship Comes In', Dylan's two most famous 'exhortation' songs. They were simple reworkings of the hand-clappin', foot-stompin' form of gospel song, but the promise was of an egalitarian emancipation rather than of some postlapsarian Eden. Indeed, 'Ain't Gonna Grieve' was a straight rewrite of the traditional spiritual 'Ain't Gonna Grieve My Lord No More'.

In the final two months of 1962 *Broadside* published three of Dylan's finger-pointin' songs – two resulting from this session (the other being 'Death of Emmett Till'). Returning to New York in January, Dylan worked up perhaps his most vengeful song of this kind, 'Masters of War'. Delighted with the result, he made a rare appearance at a Gerde's hootenanny the Monday after his return and premiered the song to the by now usual plaudits from his friends, who recognized how quickly he was outstripping their own efforts. Within a couple of days he was recording the song for *Broadside*. In attendance at that session were Sis Cunningham, Happy Traum, Suze Rotolo and Phil Ochs. Ochs, the new kid on the block, was in awe of Dylan's mastery of the protest genre yet was soon attempting to emulate his efforts, the first of a tidal wave of Dylan copyists.

Dylan's new direction that winter led him to reconsider the songs he had already selected for *Freewheelin'*. There is a common belief that Dylan was forced by CBS to replace 'Talkin' John Birch Society Blues' as one of four songs scheduled for his second album but which were finally deemed unsuitable. The chronology of the events surrounding the album's release, though, tends to contradict this assumption. The story presupposes that such an instruction followed Dylan's aborted appearance on the Ed Sullivan Show on 12 May 1963. However, the four replacement songs were recorded at the end of April (the 24th). According to official files, *Freewheelin'* was released on 27 May 1963. This would hardly allow time to recut an album, reprint the sleeve notes and issue the new version, all within two weeks of the Ed Sullivan débâcle.

The decision to replace four of the songs on *Freewheelin'* must have come before the Ed Sullivan Show, it was probably Dylan who made the decision, and the purpose of the 24 April session was specifically to record replacement songs for 'Let Me Die in My Footsteps', 'Ramblin' Gamblin' Willie', 'Rocks and Gravel' and 'Talkin' John Birch Society Blues', all songs written (or in the case of 'Rocks and Gravel' adapted) in the first three months of 1962. Dylan simply felt he had outgrown these songs. The four new songs included two new finger-pointin' songs, 'Masters of War' and his last and wittiest talkin' blues, 'Talkin' World War III Blues'. Dylan himself told a friend in April 1963, the month of this session, that he was unhappy with *Freewheelin'* as it then stood.

Bob Dylan: There's too many old-fashioned songs in there, stuff I tried to write like Woody. I'm goin' through changes. Need some more finger-pointin' songs in it, 'cause that's where my head's at right now. [1963]

Dylan was outgrowing his old songs. He also seemed to be outgrowing a few old friends. In April, John Hammond was finally ousted as his producer due to pressure from Al Grossman, still nursing a grudge against him for ordering his partner John Court out of a Columbia studio. For his April session, Dylan had a new young black producer at the console, Tom Wilson. Wilson had a superb ear for the innovative, though he had no knowledge of folk music. He quickly recognized that Dylan was not 'merely folk'.

Tom Wilson: I was introduced to Dylan by David Kapralik at a time when I was not properly working for Columbia. I was being used by them shall we say. He said, 'Why don't you guys stick around and do a coupla things?' I said, 'What do you mean? I don't even work for Columbia.' What's more, I didn't even particularly like folk music. I'd been recording Sun Ra and Coltrane and I thought folk music was for the dumb guys. This guy played like the dumb guys, but then these words came out. I was flabbergasted.

If the April session tilted the balance on *Freewheelin'* in favour of Dylan's more recent work (only two songs would date from sessions prior to October 1962), he had already presented an even more updated Dylan model to an appreciative audience at New York Town Hall, on 12 April. That Dylan could play the Town Hall, even though he failed to sell out the 900-seat venue (according to Tom Paxton 'there were entire rows that were empty' though it was in fact three quarters full), was a remarkable achievement. His ground-breaking second album had yet to be released, his first album had 'bombed', and less than eighteen months earlier he could hardly find fifty people who would turn up at the Carnegie Recital Hall to hear him perform. It was a notable performance and when the show was enthusiastically reviewed by both *Billboard* and the *New York Times*, executives at CBS were beaming.

Never one to give the audience what they expected, Dylan played no songs from his one and only released album, and for the first time he played a set wholly composed of 'original' compositions. His perversity was such that he did not include 'Blowin' in the Wind', at this point his best-known song. Indeed he played only three songs which would appear on his forthcoming album, and two of those he had yet to record.

The remainder of the set consisted of what can only be described as a wave of new songs from his finger-pointin' pen. Wisely mixing the lightweight with the topical, Dylan combined rag tunes like 'New Orleans Rag' and 'All Over You' with the social commentaries he was becoming known for. Along with earlier songs like 'John Brown', 'Ballad of Hollis Brown' and 'Hard Rain's a-Gonna Fall', he included four brand new finger-pointin' songs, 'Masters of War', 'Walls of Redwing', 'Who Killed Davey Moore' (boxer Davey Moore had died only eighteen days earlier from wounds sustained in a title fight) and the impressive 'With God on Our Side'. Dylan even had the remarkable self-assurance to encore by reading an eight-minute poem he had written, entitled 'Last Thoughts on Woody Guthrie'. CBS recorded the show, ever mindful of the advantages of some live material in the vaults should they require 'product' during a fallow period from one of their artists.

With the emphasis on jocularity or social commentary, by far the most moving moment came midway through the show, when Dylan performed an achingly lovely rendition of the song he had written for Suze during her absence in Italy, 'Tomorrow Is a Long Time'. Dylan and Suze had in fact had a terrible row before the show, which could not have helped to steady his nerves. 'Tomorrow Is a Long Time' sounds like the most beautiful apology possible.

Suze and Dylan had become reconciled on his return from England in January. Despite Suze's soon rekindled expressions of doubt about the nature of their relationship, Dylan himself seemed happy enough to be back with her. He even convinced her to move back into his 4th Street apartment within days of his return, despite her original intention to keep the relationship on a more manageable basis than before her departure. Whatever, Dylan's spurt of songs about love and loneliness temporarily dried up with Suze's return, and the flood of finger-pointin' songs he wrote that spring and early summer seemed a replacement for his songs of sorrow.

Meanwhile Grossman was working on building Dylan's career on a solid bedrock of mystery. Thus he encouraged him to stop playing New York club gigs, despite his inability as yet to progress to larger venues. He also encouraged Dylan to play fewer gigs altogether. Obscure local radio appearances, such as he had made in 1962 on the shows of Cynthia Gooding, Billy Faier and Henrietta Yurchenco, were strictly out. TV was the medium on which to get Dylan across, preferably national TV.

Late in April, Dylan did play an important club date but many miles from New York, appearing at a place in Chicago called the Bear. He was booked to play this small gig because Grossman had a part-interest in the club, and because while in Chicago he was scheduled to appear on Studs Terkel's radio show. Terkel was a renowned social commentator and his show attracted healthy listening figures; and in the mid-West Dylan needed the exposure appearing on Terkel's popular show would provide. While playing the Bear, Dylan also met up with a talented local guitarist called Michael Bloomfield, with whom he jammed, though Bloomfield's original intention in turning up had been somewhat different.

Michael Bloomfield: I had heard the first Bob Dylan album. I thought it was just terrible. I couldn't believe that this guy was so well touted. So I went down [to the Bear in Chicago] to see him y'know, to meet him, to get up there and blow him off the stage. But to my surprise he was enchanting. He couldn't really sing y'know, but he could get it over . . . better than any guy I've met.

Through the spring and summer of 1963 Grossman ensured that Dylan's profile was kept at an optimum and that the phrase 'spokesman for a generation' accompany each report. In May Grossman arranged for Dylan to make his first national TV appearance on the Ed Sullivan Show, but during rehearsals Dylan was informed by the man in charge of 'program practices' that his talkin' blues about the John Birch Society would upset these upstanding American citizens.

Bob Dylan: After they told me I couldn't sing 'Talkin' John Birch Society Blues' I walked out. I could have sung a substitute song, something like 'East Virginia Blues', but I just couldn't do it after coming so close to the 'Talkin' John Birch' thing. [1963]

Ironically the uproar about this blatant act of censorship did Dylan considerably more good, by portraying him as a rebel and counter-culture hero, than if he had appeared on the show and performed a couple of his tunes to an uncaring national TV audience. As it was, the *New York Times* and *Village Voice* both ran major stories on the furore, and *Time* and *Playboy* mentioned the incident in articles on the folk-music revival, both emphasizing Dylan as the most promising of all the up-and-coming folksingers. Nat Hentoff's profile in *Playboy* even included the story of Dylan's original audition for the Ed Sullivan Show at the time of the release of his first album. His friends then told him that they would eventually call and Dylan replied, 'Well, they won't tell me what to sing.'

After the Sullivan débâcle, he did appear on two local TV folk-music specials broadcast that summer, performing two and three songs on WBC-TV and WNEW-TV respectively. More importantly, in July Peter, Paul and Mary released their own version of 'Blowin' in the Wind', and within two weeks it was number two in the national charts. Thus when Dylan played the Newport Folk Festival in the last week in July he was the rising member of the folk pantheon. As if recognized as the heir apparent, that weekend he would perform with both the current King and Queen of Folk, Pete Seeger and Joan Baez, as well as playing his own set. On the Sunday evening he received the ultimate endorsement when the ensemble finale sang not just the traditional 'We Shall Overcome' but also his 'Blowin' in the Wind'.

He had already sung with Joan Baez prior to Newport. She had joined him to duet on the recently written 'With God on Our Side' during his set at the Monterey Folk Festival in May. Baez had first met Dylan when he was playing at Gerde's Folk City in 1961, but had been unimpressed by the urchin look. At a later meeting, Dylan was too busy trying to impress her attractive younger sister Mimi to take undue notice of Joan. According to Von Schmidt she first took note of his music when her manager Manny Greenhill gave her an acetate of his songs (probably a test-pressing of the original *Freewheelin'*). At this point she apparently 'began to realize the power of the lyric content'.

Their next meeting was in Cambridge in April 1963 when, after a show at the Café Yana one Saturday, he appeared at the Club 47 Sunday 'hoot'. Baez was at the Club 47 and when everyone adjourned to Sally Schoenfeld's apartment after the 'hoot', Baez managed to spend some time with him. Presumably she also got to hear 'With God on Our Side', which he had only premiered nine days earlier. When they met at Monterey three weeks later, they picked up where they had left off and Dylan ended up spending several days after Monterey at Baez's home in Carmel. Their 'romance' had begun.

When Dylan turned up at Newport with Suze, Baez showed a slightly bitchy side to her nature by introducing her version of 'Don't Think Twice' as a song about a love affair that has lasted too long. Suze, who suspected Dylan of having an affair with Baez, was furious, and her demeanour did not improve when Dylan informed her that he was going on a brief tour with Baez that August. Suze, tired of Dylan's infidelities and his possessiveness, moved in with her sister Carla. This only resulted in Dylan becoming a virtual resident at Carla's apartment, where ensued a series of rows between Dylan and Carla about Suze, her needs and how each knew what was really in her best interests.

Respite came only when Dylan chose to play out-of-town shows. In August he played half a dozen shows as Baez's guest, singing a couple of songs on his own and then duetting with her on three or four more of his own tunes. The mini-tour culminated in a show at Forest Hills Stadium in front of twelve thousand fans, and gave him much-needed exposure.

Joan Baez: I was getting audiences of up to ten thousand at that point, and dragging my little vagabond out onto the stage was a grand experiment . . . The people who had not heard of Bob were often infuriated and sometimes even booed him.

Because of the self-evident commercial gains Dylan stood to make through his intimate relationship with Baez, some have doubted the sincerity of his feelings for her at this point. Certainly his cavalier attitude towards her throughout most of 1964 and 1965 suggests that he felt none of the soaring heights and gaping depths of emotion that his relationship with Suze engendered. He did not seem unduly perturbed to be away from Baez for long periods of time. After September 1963, they had only limited opportunities to spend time together. In 1964 they managed to spend days rather than hours in each other's company only in February, late July/August and November.

However, in the summer of 1963 they spent a great deal of time together, and Dylan was perhaps at his most susceptible to Baez's undoubted charm. After their August tour, Dylan spent a little time in New York trying to repair relations with Suze before he headed for Carmel for a couple of weeks' 'holiday', and some necessary solitude in order that he could get on with writing songs for his third album. In early October Dylan joined Baez at a prestigious gig at the Hollywood Bowl in Los Angeles, though the Californians were unable to accept Dylan and responded by heckling and booing him, and complaining about the interruption to pure Baez.

Dylan finally returned to New York to complete his third album and play a crucial gig at the 3,000-seat Carnegie Hall, an acid test of whether he had 'arrived' as a performer. It would be four months of disquiet and personal doubt before he saw Baez again.

If Dylan had been avoiding playing headlining gigs throughout the summer, presumably in accordance with Grossman's master plan, he did make a major solo appearance in addition to his sets at Newport, and it was an important one. The location was the Hotel Americana in San Juan, Puerto Rico, not an obvious locale for an important gig. But it was the CBS sales convention he was singing at and, as ever uncompromising in his art if not in his private life, Dylan took the opportunity to remind the reps that here was the man censored by the CBS TV network and he was still singing a few home truths.

Tom Wilson: In the first Columbia convention, in '63, I had two acts, Dylan and Terry Thornton. I'd just joined the company. I was brand new. Dylan had just written that song about Emmett Till and another one called 'With God on Our Side' . . . he sang it and half the cats in the convention got up and split. All the Columbia guys just started to walk out: they didn't want to hear this. Those were his two strongest songs at the time and he didn't spare them.

It was the Southern reps who betrayed their distaste for him, but Dylan was now recognized as an up-and-coming artist on the roster. Less than two months later, *Freewheelin'* finally cracked the *Billboard* album charts, where it would remain for some thirty-two weeks. The song that Dylan sang which so offended the Southern reps was almost certainly not 'Emmett Till' (or indeed 'Oxford Town', another 1962 composition, as Spitz claims), which he had dropped from his set twelve months earlier, but another song about the unjust murder of a black man, Medgar Evers. The song was called 'Only a Pawn in Their Game', and he had premiered it less than two weeks earlier at a registration rally in Greenwood, Mississippi, where he had flown to provide some moral support to those fighting the civil rights battle at the sharp end, and to sing a few of his own finger-pointin' songs. Medgar Evers had been the Mississippi leader of the NAACP (National Association for the Advancement of Colored People). Dylan's song portrayed the murderer as just a poor dumb white bigot manipulated by powerful racist forces.

A month later Dylan was motivated to write another song about the death of a black person at the hands of a white man. 'The Lonesome Death of Hattie Carroll' was written in Carmel during his September idyll there. The finger-pointin' songs seemed to be pouring out of him, despite the troubled relationship with Suze. That summer he wrote not just 'Only a Pawn in Their Game' and 'The Lonesome Death of Hattie Carroll', but also his clarion calls 'The Times They Are a-Changin'' and 'When the Ship Comes In', and two songs which portrayed evil judges, one who used his position to seduce a poor girl trying to save her father from the gallows ('Seven Curses'), the other refusing to reprieve a man unjustly imprisoned for life ('Percy's Song').

These latter two songs would not be included on Dylan's third album, though both were recorded at the sessions. Both showed a new sophistication in Dylan's handling of traditional ballad forms. In an open letter to Tony Glover that July, he had written that he could no longer sing 'Red Apple Juice', he had to sing 'Masters of War', he could not sing 'Little Maggie', he 'gotta sing "Seven Curses"'. Yet he made it clear what a debt he owed to the traditional songs that taught him how to express himself: 'The folk songs showed me . . . that songs can say somethin human.'

In the case of 'Seven Curses' and 'Percy's Song' he seemed to be attempting to write new songs which were self-consciously traditional in form, style and imagery. The melodies of course were authentically traditional (in this case based on 'Anathea' and 'The Wind and the Rain' respectively). It was as if he wished to prove he could write in the traditional ballad forms and yet make them 'say somethin human', a reminder that injustice was an eternal theme and not simply apposite to the sixties. Dylan would later return to such an approach to songwriting for much of the *John Wesley Harding* album.

Of these half-a-dozen topical songs perhaps the two anthems – 'The Times They Are a-Changin'' and 'When the Ship Comes In' – would prove to be the most important. 'The Times They Are a-Changin'', next to 'Blowin' in the Wind', remains the best known of Dylan's songs from his 'folk' period. Yet it seems a far more conscious effort than the half-realized 'Blowin' in the Wind'. Indeed, according to Tony Glover, Dylan's sidekick from his Minneapolis days and the man to whom he wrote the open letter, it was not only a conscious communication of a feeling, it was a deliberate attempt to write a song which would fuse the anthemic nature of 'Blowin' in the Wind' with the apocalyptic conceit of 'Hard Rain's a-Gonna Fall'.

Tony Glover: Later that year, fall of that year, me and Koerner got signed to Elektra, and they flew us out to New York – my first time on an airplane – and I went to see Bob. He was still living on 4th Street. I remember there was some typed pages, song lyrics and shit, lying on the table. I picked one up and it said, 'Come senators, congressmen, please heed the call'. And I said, What is this shit, man? And the guy shrugged and said, Well, you know, it seems to be what the people like to hear.

Glover, along with most of his fellow Minneapolis folkies, was reluctant to see Dylan adopting the mantle of prophet of the civil rights movement. As early as 1962, when they reviewed his first album, the *Little Sandy Review* editors Paul Nelson and Jon Pankake were exhorting Dylan to avoid the topical song vein: 'We sincerely hope that Dylan will steer clear of the Protesty people, continue to write songs near the traditional manner, and continue to develop his mastery of his difficult, delicate, highly personal style.'

When Dylan returned to Minneapolis in late June 1963, Dylan and Nelson got into a friendly but heated discussion at Glover's apartment about the role of politics in folk music. Nelson once again attempted to convince Dylan to abandon the topical song genre, which subverted the music to The Cause. Dylan insisted that 'politics' – in the widest sense – were a binding force for his songs' lyrics, and that social issues 'were more important than music'.

'The Times They Are a-Changin'' was rapidly adopted by wider causes than the civil rights activists. The rebellious young considered it a song as much about the generation gap as about that between the liberal and conservative forces in the country. Dylan would once again be forced to emphasize its wider meaning.

Bob Dylan: It happened that maybe those were the only words I could find to separate aliveness from deadness. It had nothing to do with age. [1964]

Bob Dylan: I can't really say that adults don't understand young people any more than you can say big fishes don't understand little fishes. I didn't mean it as a statement . . . It's a feeling. [1965]

'When the Ship Comes In' was a landmark composition for different reasons. The song itself is a vengefully joyous paean to an apocalypse that will sweep away the fools the author does not suffer gladly: the neophobes, the masters of war, the playboys who run his world. It was written that August in a fit of pique in a hotel room, after he had been refused admission by an impertinent hotel clerk until his companion, Joan Baez, vouched for his good character.

The song, like most of Dylan's at the time, was based on another, older song. However, this time it was not a traditional folksong that he was creating from. 'When the Ship Comes In' is based on the song 'Pirate Jenny' from Brecht and Weill's *Threepenny Opera*, an equally vengeful song in which Jenny dreams of the destruction of all her enemies by a mysterious ship. It was Suze who first introduced Dylan to Brecht.

Suze Rotolo: My interest in Brecht was certainly an influence on him. I was working for the Circle in the Square Theater and he came to listen all the time. He was very affected by the song that Lotte Lenya's known for, 'Pirate Jenny'.

The influence of Brecht was the first indication that Dylan was applying a new sophistication to the sources he was drawing inspiration from. With Suze's encouragement and hints from Van Ronk, both avaricious readers, Dylan was expanding his intellectual frontiers. While in Britain at the beginning of the year he had been reading Robert Graves's *The White Goddess*, a 'historical grammar of poetic myth'. He also began reading the French symbolists, Rimbaud, Baudelaire and Verlaine, as well as Villon and Apollinaire.

'The Times They Are a-Changin'' and 'When the Ship Comes In' also showed a considerable knowledge of the Bible. Allusions to the apocalyptic tracts of the Old Testament abound in both songs, but perhaps the most overt allusion in 'The Times They Are a-Changin'' is to the New Testament Gospel According to Matthew, in which Jesus says of the Last Judgement, 'But many that are first will be last, and the last first.' As the symbolism in Dylan's songs became more sophisticated, the restrictions of the finger-pointin' genre he had been committing himself to throughout 1963 became apparent. In September he composed the most hymnal of his acoustic songs, 'Lay Down Your Weary Tune'. With this song he proved that he was capable of dealing with songs outside the my-baby-left-me and/or topical song fields, and that he could handle more abstract themes and feelings with considerable skill.

If he needed warning about the image he was developing as a civil rights activist, an interview published in the left-wing *National Guardian* (conducted by editor Jack Smith) provided it. The Dylan that comes across in the interview seems wholly committed to 'the Cause'. Yet apparently he was very unhappy with the way he was portrayed in the article. He seemed to misunderstand the workings of the press, not realizing that if he talked for twenty minutes about his youth and twenty minutes about the civil rights struggle, an activist paper like the *National Guardian* would concentrate heavily on pronouncements like:

Bob Dylan: I don't think when I write. I just react and put it down on paper. I'm serious about everything I write. For instance, I get mad when I see friends of mine sitting in Southern jails, getting their heads beat in. What comes out in my music is a call to action. [1963]

Dylan's mishandling of the press did not cause just such relatively minor difficulties as the *National Guardian* article. In October he reluctantly agreed to be interviewed by a *Newsweek* reporter, Andrea Svedburg, after she had dug up something of his Minnesota past and threatened to use the material if he did not agree to an interview. However, their conversation apparently soon deteriorated into a slanging match and Svedburg went ahead and published a vicious hatchet-job on Dylan. Though the unveiling of his Hibbing past was nothing but a minor inconvenience, Svedburg brought up the old story of a high school graduate called Lorre Wyatt writing 'Blowin' in the Wind' and selling it to Dylan for a thousand dollars and, while carefully avoiding saying Wyatt *had* written the song, she managed to sow a large seed of doubt by implication.

Coming hard on the heels of the completion of his third album and a triumphant concert at Carnegie Hall, the Svedburg story brought Dylan down to earth with a resounding thud. As it was on the streets by 29 October, he barely had time to savour his

Carnegie Hall success three nights earlier. As with his Town Hall concert in April, he had used his Carnegie Hall show to present a new Dylan. This time he did perform 'Blowin' in the Wind'. More importantly he performed eight of the songs scheduled for his third album, and four songs recorded for but not eventually chosen to be on *The Times They Are a-Changin'*. The fans who attended the show must have been very disappointed when the *Times They Are a-Changin'* album appeared without 'Lay Down Your Weary Tune', 'Percy's Song' and 'Seven Curses', all of which he performed superbly that night. They made for a more rounded portrait than the album would offer on its release in January. He even had his parents fly in from Hibbing to see his triumph.

Beattie Zimmerman: We knew he was gifted when we went to Carnegie Hall . . . We flew in for the concert and we stayed for a few days and we knew that he was really enjoying what he was doing and that was important to us.

Recording for the third album had gone far more smoothly than for *Freewheelin'*, which was now riding high in the *Billboard* chart. In fact the *Times They Are a-Changin'* album was recorded in just three August sessions and three October sessions. The emphasis though was very different from that of *Freewheelin'*. Though *The Times They Are a-Changin'* is a far more intense album, it is less richly diverse. There is an unrelentedness to the tales of hard times and moral outrages. An album containing 'Ballad of Hollis Brown', 'North Country Blues', 'Only a Pawn in their Game', 'With God on Our Side' and 'The Lonesome Death of Hattie Carroll' could hardly be said to paint an overwhelmingly optimistic view of the world.

Dylan even seemed to emphasize the unrelenting nature of the material with the droning melodies he utilized and the monotony of his vocal delivery. Though he recorded the beautiful 'Lay Down Your Weary Tune' and 'Eternal Circle' at the later sessions he refrained from including them, presumably because he felt they would break the mood of the album. The stark black and white cover also reinforced its monochrome feel. Only the two 'love' songs seek to break the mood and both 'Boots of Spanish Leather' and 'One Too Many Mornings' tell heartbreaking tales of love gone wrong.

Although *The Times They Are a-Changin'* was well received by Dylan's politically conscious audience, it is an album which has not worn well. Despite containing a couple of songs of incandescent beauty, the manner of delivery and the length of some of the more turgid finger-pointin' songs make it a gruelling listening experience. However, it was what Dylan fans had wanted – the last album for a very long time about which that could be said. The next album would show another side altogether. Meanwhile Dylan had one more song to record to complete the album, and he recorded it two days after Svedburg's story hit the stands.

6

1963: Troubled and I Don't Know Why

The *Newsweek* story had an immediate consequence. Though he had seemingly finished his third album at the two sessions before the Carnegie Hall show, Dylan returned to Columbia's New York studios on the final day in October to record the concluding song, one he had written in response to the 'dust of rumours' that Svedburg had conjured up in her *Newsweek* article. The song was based on a traditional 'bid-you-adieu' tune called 'The Parting Glass', and was called 'Restless Farewell'. What it was a restless farewell to remained as yet unclear. However, it gave fair warning that he was not content to remain the Woody Guthrie of his generation.

Possibly Dylan envisaged a restless farewell to song. In the next three months, he would write a profusion of poems, but the only 'new' song that he appears to have recorded during this period was a publishers' demo (which he may have written earlier), the ironic 'Guess I'm Doing Fine'. It seems he was temporarily uncertain of his direction. The occasional live performances he gave were presentations of his *The Times They Are a-Changin'* persona, an identity he seemed increasingly uncomfortable with.

Dylan's move away from protest, though it would not be discernible for some months, is generally credited to two events that occurred in the fall of 1963 – the assassination of President John F. Kennedy and the Emergency Civil Liberties Committee award ceremony. Certainly both events affected him considerably. But while they – along with the *Newsweek* story – precipitated his next change in direction, he had in fact already tired of his newly assumed mantle.

Two of the songs left off his third album celebrated the nature of song itself – 'Lay Down Your Weary Tune' and 'Eternal Circle' – but Dylan seemed temporarily reluctant to follow the direction his muse was steering him in. Instead he withdrew from public gaze for three weeks at the end of October, hanging out with Terri and Dave Van Ronk and Barry Kornfeld, writing a lot of poetry. It seemed at this point as if he could best express his own thoughts and feelings without the restrictions that song imposed.

Part of Dylan's problem was that his 'new' songs were becoming increasingly difficult to fit into the rigid patterns of the long-established folk melodies he had been using. Thus, though 'Lay Down Your Weary Tune' was based on a traditional Scottish melody, it required a particularly inventive reworking to allow the words to flow freely within their new context. Yet the songs on *The Times They Are a-Changin'* in most cases still had ascertainable antecedents – 'Hollis Brown' was loosely based on 'Pretty Polly', 'With God on Our Side' on 'The Patriot's Game', 'Boots of Spanish Leather' on 'Scarborough Fair', 'When the Ship Comes In' on 'Pirate Jenny', 'Lonesome Death of Hattie Carroll' on 'Mary Hamilton' and 'Restless Farewell' on 'The Parting Glass'.

On the day he recorded his next album, he discussed the constrictions songs imposed with Nat Hentoff:

Bob Dylan: It's hard being free in a song – getting it all in. Songs are so confining. Woody Guthrie told me once that songs don't have to do anything like that. But it's not true. A song has to have some kind of form to fit into the music. You can bend the words and the metre, but it still has to fit somehow. I've been getting freer in the songs I write, but I still feel confined. That's why I write a lot of poetry, if that's the word. Poetry can make its own form. [1964]

The apex of Dylan's poetry writing would be in these last two months of 1963, though throughout 1963 and the first part of 1964 he regularly turned to free-verse forms to expound his thoughts. In April he had presented two of his first free-verse poems to the audience at his Town Hall show. One, the bio-poem 'My Life in a Stolen Moment', was included in the concert programme. The second, called 'Last Thoughts on Woody Guthrie', was performed as an encore at the show, the only known example of Dylan actually reading his poetry aloud.

'My Life in a Stolen Moment' would later be regularly reprinted in concert programmes and bookleg productions, until it finally formed part of the *Writings and Drawings* anthology. It is a surprisingly straightforward account of his past. Though embroidered to include the myth of running away as a child and the typically anti-intellectual stance of attending university 'on a phoney scholarship that I never had', most of the poem rings true,

save for the outrageous travelogue where Dylan, between Minneapolis and New York, manages to take in Texas, California,
Oregon, Washington, New Mexico and Louisiana. He refers to
learning to play guitar, to sing and to write – 'but I never ever did
take the time to find out why'. Again Dylan refuses to admit to
being anything but the unconsciously inspired troubadour, a
persona that Guthrie, a well-read and informed man himself,
adopted long before him.

'My Life in a Stolen Moment' was the start of a year-long flirtation with free verse, before Dylan's non-lyric writings coalesced
into the prose-poem form adopted for his first book, *Tarantula*.
In that time Dylan contributed to concert programmes, album
sleeves – whether his own or friends' – and to magazines published
by friends.

Bob Dylan: I used to get scared that I wouldn't be around much longer,
so I'd write my poems down on anything I could find – the backs of my
albums, the backs of Joan's albums, anywhere I could find. [1965]

He also wrote a number of unpublished works which hint at a
couple of long-term projects – to write a play and to work on
some form of biography. The biography initially seems to have
been intended to take the form of a series of bio-poems like 'My
Life in a Stolen Moment'. In a famous statement to Studs Terkel
on a Chicago radio show in late April 1963, Dylan suggested that
he had begun work on such a biography:

Bob Dylan: It's about my first week in New York . . . It's about
somebody who has come to the end of one road, knows there's another
road there but doesn't exactly know where it is, and knows he can't go
back on this one road . . . It's got all kinds of . . . thoughts in my head, all
about teachers in school, all about hitch-hikers around the country . . .
I'd never been to New York before, and I'm still carrying these memories
with me so I decided to write it all down. [1963]

In a recently emerged set of manuscripts, the so-called Margolis
& Moss manuscripts, dating from the end of 1963, there is what
appears to be a two-page excerpt from a Dylan 'autobiography'.
The 120-line typescript takes the form of college recollections.
More specifically it is about spending the 1959 Christmas vacation,
wishing he were with Judy Rubin, his girlfriend at that time. It is
a surprisingly frank account of remembered feelings:

I love Judy. Judy says she loves me but she also says she's busy. I told her I love her ... I hate her cause I sence [*sic*] she don't love me ... I wish I didn't love her I wish she'd invite me for christmas for christ's sake.

The poem ends with Dylan phoning Judy, losing his cool, insulting her, and having her hang up on him: 'girls have hung up on me an have hung me up as far back as I remember ... each one promises t be the last.' As a coda to his musings upon that Christmas, he rejects what he experienced of university lifestyle with one of his many anti-intellectual tirades:

what I saw connected with the fraternity house summed up the whole established world ... underpants ... cats standin in underpants being inspected by others with serious looks in their eyes ... jive wide smiles in hairy sweaters ... what the fuck thats got t do with learnin I never will know ... never hope to either.

This remarkable 'excerpt' is part of a sheaf of papers which all appear to date from the week/s following President Kennedy's assassination in Dallas, Texas, on 22 November 1963. Indeed, on the other side of the second sheet featuring his Minneapolis recollections is a poem about Dylan's own response to the assassination, along with a brief six-line poem with a somewhat familiar ring to it:

the colors of friday were dull/as cathedral bells were gently burnin/strikin for the gentle/strikin for the kind/strikin for the crippled ones/an strikin for the blind.

The seed of Dylan's new form of song – the chains of flashing images which would, when bound together, form 'Chimes of Freedom' (and later 'Mr Tambourine Man', 'Gates of Eden' and 'It's Alright Ma') – were being sown while he worked through his inner turmoil. If the *Newsweek* story, his continued doubts about his relationships with Suze Rotolo and Joan Baez, and a general fear of the steadily increasing fame his name was assuming all contributed to this turmoil, it would be unwise to underestimate the effect of Kennedy's assassination on Dylan.

Dylan later told Anthony Scaduto that when he played a show in upstate New York the day after the assassination he began, as always, with 'Times They Are a-Changin''. At this point he felt 'that song was just too much for the day after the assassination ... I couldn't understand ... why I wrote that song, even'. Perhaps Dylan realized that, with the song not even commercially released, it was already redundant. Events had overtaken him and that would always be the way if he continued to write so-called topical songs. It would take Dylan eighteen months wholly to disavow that song and its sentiments.

The Margolis & Moss manuscripts include several unfinished poems about the assassination, clearly written as immediate responses to the events in Dallas. In one he admits, it is useless 't recall the day once more'. In another he uses an image he would later re-use to dismiss the validity of party politics, though this time he uses it to rail against the bullet and assassin/s: 'there is no right or left there is only up an down'.

At the same time as Dylan was struggling to find ways of expressing his anger, frustration and sorrow, he was working on eleven poems which would later form the sleeve notes to his third album. These *Eleven Outlined Epitaphs* would require an insert with the album, such was the stream of free-form poems flowing from his pen at this point.

In Epitaph Two, Dylan again recalls his youth in Hibbing, which was clearly something he was coming to terms with in the wake of *Newsweek* uncovering his background for the benefit of 'unknowin eyes'. In Epitaph Four he questions Jim (presumably Jim Forman) about the validity of party politics. Quite possibly this was written after the ECLC dinner. In Epitaph Six he ponders how and why Woody Guthrie was his last idol. In Epitaph Eight he makes his famous confession of plagiarism – 'Yes, I am a thief of thoughts/not, I pray, a stealer of souls'. Epitaph Nine is a further attack upon Svedburg and her ilk, refuting the notion that these hacks could somehow expose him. After all he exposed himself 'every time I step out on stage'.

The final two epitaphs seem more conciliatory, as if they were continuations of 'Restless Farewell', expositions indeed on that song. For here as there he seeks to recall the wrongs he may have done, the causes he may have fought, and the battles he may have lost. Three albums into his career, Dylan was already trying to live down his past. In the tenth epitaph he muses on whether the cockroaches 'still crawl' around Dave and Terri Van Ronk's apartment. But his autobiographical musings at this time were not restricted to his *Outlined Epitaphs* or his unpublished bio-poem/s. Sleeve notes which he wrote for Peter, Paul and Mary's second album were recollections of his first New York winter – once again reminding one of that remark to Studs Terkel: 'Snow was piled up the stairs an onto the street that/first winter when i laid around New York City/it was a different street then.'

Earlier in the fall, he had composed the most ambitious of his bio-poems, quite probably written in September, when he was staying with Joan Baez in Carmel. The poem appeared in October on the sleeve of Baez's second *In Concert* album. The poem starts in Hibbing, with a young Dylan crouching on the grass watching the trains roll by. Passing through the time when he adopted idols as role models – choosing his idols 't be my voice an tell my tale' – he finally rejects them ('I learned that they were only men/ An had reasons for their deeds'). Then he begins to define his own terms, like beauty – 'the only beauty's ugly man' – finally learning to recognize beauty in the voice of a lady singer he knows.

Dylan's 'Poem to Joannie' proved that his free-form poems could retain their own structure and move to their own rhythm. It almost certainly gave him new confidence to work harder and more exclusively at his free-verse poetry that fall. He also enjoyed utilizing even freer forms adopted in prose-poem letters to friends.

Interestingly enough, though the bio-poem approach is not really represented in his book *Tarantula*, Baez has suggested that much of the material he wrote for it at her house but never reclaimed was more akin to the bio-poems than to the sort of material eventually used in the book.

Joan Baez: He wrote some beautiful things about running up to his own house and trying to get in. He had to pee, something about his mother behind the screen door and he was jumping up and down – he had to pee . . . He never edited anything. He couldn't bear to take anything out of the sentence he'd written.

The prose-poem letters would prove the most readable part of *Tarantula*. It was a form he adopted fairly early on, both in private and public correspondence. The first such letter published was one to Dave 'Tony' Glover, which Dylan allowed to be included in the programme for the 1963 Newport Folk Festival. The letter starts with him admitting he hasn't written lately and that Glover has hinted 'in a quiet way if I changed my ways so hard that I don remember old friends'. The remainder of the letter deals with all the reasons why he has not written. Among his musings he hints that he is trying to learn to do unconsciously what he used to do consciously: 'now I really aint thinkin/about what I'm doing no more'.

The poem concludes by saying 'I don know why I aint written t yuh/Maybe cause I never write letters t m'self'. The other two 'open letters' from this period are considerably more troubled affairs. Both were written in December 1963, some six months after his contribution to the Newport programme. The first was written within days of attending a dinner at the Hotel Americana in New York, at which he received the annual Tom Paine award for his contribution to the civil rights struggle given by the Emergency Civil Liberties Committee.

The dinner was a complete fiasco. Dylan was a poor choice for such an award, unschooled as he was in the art of public speaking, and a chronically nervous performer at the best of times. In an environment peopled by middle-aged liberals beneficently donating money for their chosen cause, he was immediately uptight and began drinking heavily. According to Edith Tiger, when it came his turn to speak, she found him vomiting in the men's toilet. Led to the high table, he announced, 'I haven't got any guitar – I can talk though.' His subsequent speech proved that this was not the case. In a speech wholly devoid of diplomacy and finesse, he informed all bald and ageing people they should be on the beach soaking up the sun, not fighting causes in this 'young man's world'. He then revealed that he saw something of Lee Harvey Oswald, Kennedy's alleged assassin, in himself. Not for the first or last time in his life he was subject to a volley of boos. Since the dinner was primarily an excuse for raising funds for the ECLC, his ill-considered speech cost the committee a considerable sum of money.

Afterwards he penned 'A Message to the ECLC', an open letter, which sets out with the intention of apologizing for his actions, but ends up recalcitrant. Forced to speak publicly, he wrote the ECLC, 'I tore everything lose from my mind/an said "just be honest, dylan, just be honest".' He defended his comments about Oswald, insisting he was 'speaking of the times'. Eventually he stated that he was no speaker and that he should remember to stay what he was:

> I am a writer an a singer of the words I write/I am no speaker nor any politician/an my songs speak for me because I write them/in the confinement of my own mind an have t cope/with no one except my own self.

This is an open admission that he does not wish to be a spokesman, but will stay true to his songs. Finally he offers to make up the shortfall in donations, a generous offer but one which he did not in fact fulfil.

In an open letter to *Broadside* magazine, to whom he was providing fewer and fewer songs, published within four weeks of the ECLC débâcle, he still showed a troubled mind. He admits 'I am now famous' and the notion clearly scares him. People ask him 'why do I write the way I do' and it infuriates him.

Dylan also made references to both his novel and his play in the *Broadside* letter. The novel was frustrating him. 'it dont even tell a story/it's about a million scenes long/an takes place on a billion scraps/of paper.' Before it would be finished it would frustrate him considerably more. The play that Dylan was writing, though, he now seemed fully committed to:

an I'm up to my belly button in it./quite involved yes/I've discovered the power of playwritin means/as opposed t song writing means/altho both are equal, I'm wrapped in playwritin/for the minute.

Dylan's ambitions as a poet and prosewriter, rather than song-writer, may have been further fed at the end of December when he met renowned beat poet Allen Ginsberg. Dylan had first been introduced to Ginsberg's writings back in Minneapolis and, along with the French symbolists, the Beats were a primary influence on his development as a songwriter in 1964.

Bob Dylan: I didn't start writing poetry until I was out of high school. I was eighteen or so when I discovered Ginsberg, Gary Snyder, Phillip Whalen, Frank O'Hara and those guys. Then I went back and started reading the French guys, Rimbaud and François Villon. [1985]

The play that occupied Dylan at this point was presumably the untitled, unfinished fifteen-page play that recently emerged as part of the Margolis & Moss manuscripts. If so, the play, which concerns a number of characters with names like John B. Pimp, Mrs Agnas McBroad and Eeny Weeny, who meet in a combination church/barroom/hotel because they have been told they must do so or they will die, shows that he was no playwright. The dialogue is forced and unconvincing, plot development minimal and pacing non-existent. Possibly this was one of several attempted plays at this time: in May 1964 he informed Max Jones he was working on two plays. Fortunately such projects came to naught.

At the end of January and beginning of February 1964, he was in Canada filming a half-hour TV special for the Canadian Broad-casting Company. While there he talked to two Canadian jour-nalists about his work. He informed both that he was working on a novel and a play, and told the journalist from *Gargoyle* magazine that the play would be finished before the novel and that he wanted to see it performed. He also made his most unequivocal statement about his abandonment of topical song, even though at this point he seemed unclear what form of songwriting would replace the genre he had made his own.

Bob Dylan: I used to write songs, like I'd say, 'Yeah, what's bad, pick out something bad, like segregation, OK here we go' and I'd pick one of the thousand million little points I can pick and explode it, some of them which I didn't know about. I wrote a song about 'Emmett Till', which in all honesty was a bullshit song . . . I realize now that my reasons and motives behind it were phoney. I didn't have to write it. [1964]

In the true tradition of the Beats, he had decided to go On the Road, to explore America, and find a way to bring out those chains of flashing images. He had been away from song for too long.

7

1964: On the Heels of Rimbaud

Dylan's trip through the Union in February 1964 has been very well documented by Scaduto and Shelton and to a lesser extent Spitz. All have devoted a respectful chunk of pages to the On the Road Revisited trek. In all instances their primary source has been Pete Karman's notes and recollections of the trip, though Karman seemed a strange choice for a touring companion in the first place. He was after all a close friend of Suze's, and a journalist. Thus when Dylan spent the night with a girl student after his Emory University concert, Karman was there to chronicle it. Finally, when they reached San Francisco and Dylan's presumably long-awaited liaison with Baez, Karman was told to pack his bags. Dylan later told Shelton, 'We had to kick Pete out and send him home on a plane.' In fact according to Karman he actually had to pay for his own way back. The other two companions on Dylan's trek were old friends, trustworthy and above all 'cool'. Paul Clayton and Victor Maimudes knew how to play Dylan's moods.

The twenty-day trek to California from New York by station wagon weaved its way through Virginia and North Carolina – where they stopped off to meet Carl Sandburg in Hendersonville, finding him unimpressed by Dylan's hard-sell of his credentials as a poet – South Carolina, Georgia – where he played at Emory University – Mississippi and Louisiana – where they were intent on experiencing the New Orleans Mardi Gras which took place on the 11th. Setting out from New Orleans on the 12th for the second leg of their journey Dylan's trio of companions took it in turns to hammer the pedal to the floor, roaring through Texas, Oklahoma, Kansas, Colorado – where Dylan premiered a new song at a concert at the Denver Civic Auditorium – and finally on through Utah and Nevada to California.

Dylan's own version of the three-week journey through America was typically fanciful. In his version, 'We hit forty-six halls from

Augusta, Ga. to Berkeley, Calif. We talked to people in bars, miners. Talking to people – that's where it's at, man.' In fact on the one occasion he came into direct contact with the 'common people', when he stopped in a record shop in Charlottesville, Virginia, and was recognized by fans, he apparently said, 'Man, there's a lot of people in here. Let's split.' He was better able to deal with his admirers when expecting public attention, as when he stopped at the Denver Folklore Center on the day of his Denver concert. He had to accept that he was now a famous figure and three-week trips in search of the 'common man' were becoming increasingly impracticable.

However, there is another important factor in Dylan's motives for the trip. He hoped that it would be inspirational. Dylan regularly sat in the back of the station wagon tapping away at his typewriter, working on songs and probably poems. The song he spent most of his time working on as they drove down to New Orleans was 'Chimes of Freedom'. The refrain 'strikin for the gentle/strikin for the kind/strikin for the crippled ones/an strikin for the blind', which appeared in one of the December 1963 Margolis & Moss poems, had obviously been haunting him. While his three companions alternated at the wheel – they generally dissuaded Dylan from taking his turn as he was a notoriously bad driver – he completed the song.

In many ways the antecedents of 'Chimes of Freedom' are to be found in the material he recorded for his third album. Its sense of the power of nature – the song is set during a storm as two friends or lovers huddle in a church doorway to see 'the chimes of freedom flashing' – closely mirrors 'Lay Down Your Weary Tune'. It is also unashamedly apocalyptic, as both 'The Times They Are a-Changin'' and 'When the Ship Comes In' were. It is closer to 'When the Ship Comes In'. The difference is in the promise of universal emancipation (or even redemption?). The song is sung 'for every hung-up person in the whole wide universe', rather than for just the chosen few. Ironically, if the final verse of 'When the Ship Comes In' had been dropped, the effect would have been largely the same. After all, the power of nature is a central part of that song too, and only in the final verse are the foes identified.

Where 'Chimes of Freedom' is similar to 'When the Ship Comes In' is in the way that the lyric details a coherent vision perceived by the singer. As his life became more chaotic, he seemed to take upon himself the visionary mantle that Rimbaud required of the true poet.* In February 1964 Dylan told his companions, 'Rimbaud's where it's at. That's the kind of stuff means something. That's the kind of writing I'm gonna do.'

The composition of 'Chimes of Freedom' reflected an important shift in Dylan's perception, a move towards the intensely poetic songs he would write later in the year. Apart from 'Chimes of Freedom', Dylan worked on scraps of other songs in the back of the station wagon. He mentioned to Karman the rather trite line from 'Ballad in Plain D', 'Are birds free from the chains of the skyway?', though it would take a very personal trauma to engender the remainder of the song.

According to Dylan, in his *Biograph* notes, he also began another song while in New Orleans, entitled 'Mr Tambourine Man'. This certainly makes sense logically and historically. 'Mr Tambourine Man' seems stylistically very close to 'Chimes of Freedom', more so than later visionary songs like 'Gates of Eden'. 'Mr Tambourine Man' was definitely completed before the June 1964 CBS session, when he made his first attempt to record it. According to Al Aronowitz, Dylan was working on the song in New York, which would tend to place it in March/April (Dylan being in Europe for most of the four weeks immediately before the CBS session). According to one recollection, Dylan even performed it at the Royal Festival Hall, London, in May. 'Mr Tambourine Man' also seems to tie in with the idea of Mardi Gras. As Mardi Gras stretches through the night and into the early hours of the morning the 'skippin' reels of rhyme' continue to haunt the streets, until the partying souls collapse into sweet dreams. At such times visions would surely come with relative ease. Dylan later said he got some amazing projections after staying up all night.

In 'Mr Tambourine Man' the singer certainly seems to crave that *'dérèglement de tous les sens'* which Rimbaud wrote about. It is this disordering of the senses that will open him up to the unknown and through which he must follow this Rimbaudian seer on to his 'magic swirlin' ship' (or is it really just a drunken boat?). With 'Mr Tambourine Man' he leapt beyond the boundaries of folksong once and for all. Some would follow him, others would not. Dylan had just begun the most prolific two years of his life.

---

* 'The poet makes himself a seer by a long, prodigious and rational disordering of the senses . . . He reaches [for] the unknown and even if, crazed, he ends up by losing the understanding of his visions, at least he has seen them.' – Arthur Rimbaud to Georges Izambard, 13 May 1871.

Of course 'Mr Tambourine Man' is also a celebration of song. The choice of a musician as the seer is no whim. Dylan was looking to advance his music. Having assimilated the traditional modes of expression which envelop folk and blues, perhaps he felt like bringing it all back home. If he did, time had turned his way. In February 1964, America was shaken by a new wave of popular music from the other side of 'the pond', the vanguard led by the Beatles. According to Eric Burdon of the Animals, Dylan's awareness of the possibilities of fusing rock with folk was first realized when he heard 'House of the Rising Sun'.

Eric Burdon: Well, it seems that one day Dylan was drivin' up to San Francisco from New Orleans or somewhere, when our record came over his radio. When it was announced he said to Joan Baez — who was with him at the time — 'This'll be the first time I've heard this version,' although it was at that time number one in the States. So he listened to it, stopped the car, ran round the car five times, banged his head on the bumper and began leapin' about shouting 'It's great! it's great!'

In fact 'House of the Rising Sun' did not chart until August 1964 and it was September before it reached the number one spot. Burdon's evocative description of Dylan getting out of a car having travelled from New Orleans to San Francisco clearly places the event in February 1964, and the record which was number one at the time, indeed throughout the month, was the Beatles' first US number one, 'I Wanna Hold Your Hand'. Though Dylan would later be impressed by 'House of the Rising Sun', it was the Beatles' incursion into American culture which finally redefined rock & roll. If evidence of the sorry state of American pop music at this time is required, the five number one acts before the Beatles were Jimmy Gilmer and the Fireballs, Nino Tempo and April Stevens, Dale and Gracie, the Singing Nun and Bobby Vinton. No wonder the folkies held 'pop' music in such contempt! Dylan was one of the first to realize that everything had changed.

Bob Dylan: All you heard [back in the late fifties] was rock & roll and country & western and rhythm & blues music. Now, at a certain time the whole field got taken over into some milk, you know — into Frankie Avalon, Fabian and this kind of thing . . . So everybody got out of it. And I remember when everybody got out of it. But nobody really lost that whole thing. And then folk music came in as some kind of substitute for a while, but it was only a substitute . . . Now it's different again, because of the English thing . . . What the English thing did was, they proved that you could make money at playing the same old kind of music that you used to play. [1966]

On 22 February, Dylan and his travelling crew reached San Francisco for a sell-out concert at the Berkeley Community Theater. Apart from his appearance at the Monterey Folk Festival the previous May, and his brief guest appearance at Baez's Hollywood Bowl show, he had not played in California, and the level of anticipation for the concert was unnaturally high. As Richard Farina wrote, it was as if the students 'seemed, occasionally, to believe he might not actually come, that some malevolent force or organization would get in the way.' Dylan's performance was a stunning *tour de force* which even convinced respected *San Francisco Chronicle* reviewer Ralph J. Gleason to recant his previous view that Dylan was overrated, and he wrote up the concert with the zeal of a new convert.

Dylan gave his hip West Coast audience a foretaste of his new direction by performing 'Chimes of Freedom' and 'Eternal Circle', the latter his first song to deal with the nature of song itself. Inevitably Baez insisted on lending her dulcet tones to a few duets of old favourites, but Dylan no longer needed her endorsement. Though he dedicated a song to her in Los Angeles, he did not join her on stage at any of her shows that winter. However, he did return to her home in Carmel for a few days after completing his brief West Coast tour at the end of February, and he was still prepared to continue, or perhaps rather unwilling to discontinue, their romance.

Yet if he felt he could return to the increasingly distraught Suze in New York that March he was displaying a surprising naïvety. Suze could not take his double values any more. He was happy to gallivant around the States, living a life of sex, drugs and folk music,* but he was fiercely possessive and jealous whenever she tried to maintain her own independence. The argument that finally ended their stormy relationship was interrupted by Carla Rotolo's return to her apartment, where Suze was now living. As Dylan accused Carla of setting Suze against him, Suze finally 'freaked out'. Carla ordered Dylan out of the apartment and, though he later returned in a desperate attempt to achieve a reconciliation, the romance was over.

---

* Karman relates the profuse amounts of dope consumed by all the passengers in his account.

Barry Kornfeld: [Clayton and I] walked in and there was Carla practically foaming at the mouth, Dylan practically foaming at the mouth, and Suze sitting in bed, literally in shock. Suze had just sort of tuned out. Bob and Carla were still going at it — they were both totally incoherent.

Looking back on their relationship now, Suze is remarkably forgiving of Dylan. She recognizes that the nature of his ever-increasing fame — and his own hunger for mass status — altered their relationship irrevocably, and made it impossible for them to work out their problems by themselves.

Suze Rotolo: We were young and vulnerable. A lot of crazy things happened. It is strange to think that so much is made of us together in those years. It could have run its course naturally, but it was shaded and formed by all these outside influences, because of his growing fame . . . He began snubbing his old friends. But it was all so understandable in an odd way. He could see these things happening to him and he wanted to make sure they would happen, so at the same time he didn't have time to just hang out anymore. He was working on his image and his career . . . There was a period when I was part of his possessions. I don't think he wanted me to do anything separate from him. He wanted me to be completely one hundred per cent a part of what he was. He was tied up with his own development, and it was just his world that became concentrated in just music.

Dylan was distraught. However badly he had behaved towards her, he still loved Suze and found it hard to accept her loss. In late March, he went back on the road playing a series of dates on the East Coast, up from New York. He was continuing his On the Road Revisited phase, travelling with Maimudes and enjoying wine, women and song. He needed something to keep his mind off the grief he was feeling.

John Cooke: '64 was the year of the greatest Dylan concerts. It was just Bob and Victor Maimudes in a blue Ford station wagon with perpetual bottles of Beaujolais.

As previously, when Suze had run off to Italy for six months, he found himself writing 'makin' me feel better' songs. The first one he performed that spring was 'It Ain't Me Babe'. It seemed a blunt disavowal of whatever roles his ex-lover had tried to foist upon him. In perhaps a fantasy of wish-fulfilment he refuses to take her back, and tells her bluntly that he's 'not alone'. However, 'It Ain't Me Babe' was much more than a neat update of 'Don't Think Twice, It's Alright'. It is difficult not to see the song as directed at the false expectations of certain sections of his audience as well as the hopes of a disappointed lover. When he informs 'her', 'I will only let you down', he was recognizing that he could never live up to the myth, whether imposed by a lover or an audience.

In May 1964 he returned to England. Grossman had arranged a show at the 3,000-seat Royal Festival Hall. Dylan was in demand. The week of his arrival, *Freewheelin'* finally cracked the UK Top Twenty, and his show was a sell-out. It was a very different situation from sixteen months earlier, when he could wander anonymously around London. After his two-hour performance on a sunny Sunday afternoon, he went to make his exit from the hall.

Anthea Joseph: We were walking out of the stage door – now this tells you that nobody realized what a star he was – we were going out to get a taxi to go to an Indian restaurant for supper. I mean CBS hadn't laid on anything. I don't think there was anyone from CBS there even. And Bob was going out in front of me, and I was walking along with Albert, and Bob disappeared under this wave of humanity who were sort of grabbing at his clothes and his hair. He was terrified! And Albert and I dived in and hoisted him out, the two of us being the tallest and the largest people about, and got him back inside ... It wasn't something you expected. I mean that happened to pop stars. You knew it happened to pop stars – but not singer-songwriters.

Clearly Beatlemania had other consequences besides revolutionizing American pop music. One of these consequences was increased media interest in 'pop' stars for interviews, radio and TV appearances. Since Dylan was playing only one show in London, in order to extract maximum mileage out of his visit he had to be accessible to the media. After all it had taken a year to get *Freewheelin'* into the charts. Grossman intended to keep it there.

Thus he was ferried up to Manchester to record three songs for a Sunday TV entertainment programme called *Halleluiah*. He also recorded a song for BBC's *Tonight* programme, though an appearance on the popular *Saturday Club* radio show was cancelled because of a two-day delay in his arrival. He was interviewed by several journalists, including Max Jones from *Melody Maker*, whom Dylan responded to very well, having met him on his previous trip. Other interviewers he treated far more cavalierly, in particular Maureen Cleave from the London *Evening Standard*. Dylan did not take to the uninterested and ill-informed Cleave, while she was not used to such an uncooperative subject.

Anthea Joseph: He didn't like her but he flirted with her unmercifully. That's when he started [the games], having this posey young woman coming up and asking stupid questions and really beginning to get the hang of how to handle these idiots.

Dylan was learning to handle the press his way. If the *Newsweek* story had taught him anything, it was to recognize an adversary in the media. Cleave would later suggest that Dylan rocked back and forwards in the motion of masturbating himself while she talked to him, though the published article did not show her displeasure at this bohemian urchin. However, Dylan remained determined to ridicule the 'straight' press at every opportunity.

Four days after his triumphant Festival Hall concert – the reviews of which were ecstatic, *The Times*'s reviewer comparing Dylan with Segovia – he flew to Paris with Ben Carruthers, another regular sidekick. While in Paris he looked up Hugues Aufray, who had translated some of his songs into French. Initially staying with Aufray, Dylan was soon introduced by Carruthers to an intriguing *chanteuse* called Nico. After going to Nico's studio flat for a meal, Dylan ended up staying over with her, playing her his newly composed 'It Ain't Me Babe' and writing a new song for her, 'I'll Keep It with Mine'. Leaving Paris a week later, Dylan looked up Aufray's cousin, married to Mason Hoffenburg, in Berlin. After a couple of days in Berlin, he finally set out for Vernilya, a small village just outside Athens, where he stayed for a week, writing the bulk of the songs for his fourth album, which he was due to record on his return to New York.

Among the songs presumably composed in Vernilya was 'Ballad in Plain D'. Based upon an old English folksong, 'Once I Had a Sweetheart' (aka 'The False Bride'), the song graphically details the night of his break-up with Suze. His portrayal of Carla as the 'parasite sister' remains a cruel and inaccurate portrait of a woman who had started out as one of his biggest fans and who changed as she saw the emotional blackmail he continually wrought upon her younger sister. A critic once described the song as like reading somebody else's mail, and certainly it still sounds that way today. Asked in 1985 whether there were any songs he regretted writing, 'Ballad in Plain D' was the one song Dylan singled out.

Bob Dylan: That one I look back at and say, 'I must have been a real schmuck to write that.' I look back at that particular one and say . . . maybe I could have left that alone. [1985]

Other songs that he worked on in Greece were more sympathetic studies of a broken relationship, though pain and sorrow sometimes clouded his artistic vision. 'To Ramona' was a particularly beautiful portrait of a woman whose friends betray her with their words of advice. It is probably the reason why 'I'll Keep It with Mine', an equally moving song, did not make the album, dealing as it does with a similar idea. Though Baez would later claim 'Mama You Bin on My Mind' for herself, if it was 'about' anybody, it was surely 'about' Suze. It too failed to make the album. The songs he wrote that week were a catharsis for him, designed to expunge all his feelings of sorrow, remorse, loneliness and desire.

Suze Rotolo: People have asked how I felt about those songs that were bitter, like 'Ballad in Plain D', since I inspired some of those, too, yet I never felt hurt by them. I understood what he was doing. It was the end of something and we both were hurt and bitter. His art was his outlet, his exorcism. It was healthy. That was the way he wrote out his life . . . the loving songs, the cynical songs, the political songs.

Now that his records were selling – *The Times They Are a-Changin'* had made it to the Top Twenty – CBS were pressing him to keep up the flow of albums. After all, this was an era when the Beatles and the Rolling Stones regularly issued two (or, once their respective American labels had bastardized the UK albums, three) albums a year. By the time Dylan returned to New York at the beginning of June it had been more than eight months since he had been in a Columbia studio, and the powers that be wanted a new album in time for the fall sales convention. Dylan allowed himself to record his new album quickly and without due consideration. Indeed, when he arrived at the New York studios on 9 June he informed Nat Hentoff, who was writing a profile on him for *New Yorker* magazine, that he would be trying to record the entire album in that one night. He also informed Hentoff that he was attempting to record an album very different from his previous efforts.

Bob Dylan: There aren't any finger-pointin' songs in here . . . Those records I've made, I'll stand behind them, but some of that was jumping into the scene to be heard and a lot of it was because I didn't see anybody else doing that kind of thing . . . You know – pointing to all the things that are wrong. Me, I don't want to write for people anymore. You know – be a spokesman . . . From now on, I want to write from inside me, and to do that I'm going to have to get back to writing like I used to when I was ten – having everything come out naturally. The way I like to write is for it to come out the way I walk or talk. [1964]

While putting away a bottle or two of Beaujolais, Dylan did indeed record his fourth album, plus half a dozen out-takes, in one night. By the time he recorded the official take of 'My Back Pages' at one-thirty in the morning, the album was finished. The *Another Side of Bob Dylan* session was a prodigious effort even for a man used to recording quickly and with a minimum of fuss. It also turned out to be his last entirely acoustic session. Perhaps he had so mastered recording solo he felt he had nowhere to go to but to record with a studio band. It seems more likely that songs like 'Black Crow Blues' – his first piano-backed song on record – signified a leaning towards his former rhythm & blues roots.

The album was not well received even in his established market, though its flaws were not the reasons why it came in for such flak from former supporters. It did not lack social comment as they said, but when it dealt with large issues, as on 'My Back Pages', it was embarrassingly self-conscious. When it dealt with the break-up with Suze literally, as on 'Ballad in Plain D', it was just plain embarrassing. When it attempted humorous romps like 'All I Really Wanna Do', 'I Shall Be Free #10' and 'Motorpsycho Nitemare', the results sounded forced and unconvincing. Only the familiar terrain of cynical love songs like 'I Don't Believe You' and 'It Ain't Me Babe' proved he could be as incisive as ever and 'Chimes of Freedom' was bound to be the standout track on the album. 'Mr Tambourine Man' was attempted at the session but was left off the album, Dylan later claiming he felt too close to it.

The inconsistency in the material on *Another Side* was precisely the result of being too close to the experiences he was drawing upon. He was also still experimenting with the style of language found on 'Chimes of Freedom' and 'Mr Tambourine Man'. 'My Back Pages' was the least successful, with its bizarre images of 'corpse evangelists' and 'confusion boats'. If it had been written two months later, it would have been a superior song. The album was recorded less than two weeks after most of the songs were written, and little editing seems to have taken place. Inevitably Dylan was forced to defend the album on its release.

Bob Dylan: The songs are insanely honest, not meanin t twist any heads an written only for the reason that i myself me alone wanted and needed t write them. i've conceded the fact there is no understanding of anything. at best, just winks of the eye an that is all i'm lookin for now i guess. [1964]

Matters were not helped by the title of the album, which

seemed a declaration of intent. Dylan clearly wanted to present a different side of himself from the dogmatic tones of the third album, but the title seemed to invite resistance even before the results were heard. It seemed as if he did not wish to let his listeners down gently.

Bob Dylan: I didn't want them to call [my fourth album] *Another Side of Bob Dylan* . . . because I thought it was just too corny . . . I just felt trouble coming when they titled it that. I figured if they could have titled it something else, I wouldn't have had the resistance to it. [1978]

Another Side fared considerably worse than Dylan's previous two albums, failing to make even the Top Forty, indicating that his existing audience was no longer listening and that he was not attracting new fans in sufficient numbers. If he was reluctant to admit that *Another Side* was a mistake at the time, within a year he would recognize its evident faults. He would then tell a university student that the 1964 songs were lacking in substance.

Bob Dylan: The big difference is that the songs I was writing last year, songs like 'Ballad in Plain D', they were what I call one-dimensional songs, but my new songs I'm trying to make more three-dimensional, you know. There's more symbolism, they're written on more than one level. [1965]

By the fall of 1964, with the album barely out, Dylan had already excised songs like 'Ballad in Plain D' and 'My Back Pages' from his repertoire. He was more interested in performing the songs he had been writing in upstate New York that summer. By November 1964 he was performing just 'To Ramona', 'I Don't Believe You' and 'All I Really Wanna Do' (plus 'It Ain't Me Babe' if Baez emerged from the wings) in his regular set. Even 'Chimes of Freedom' had been excluded so that his more recent visions could take centre stage.

8

1964–5: The Ghost of Electricity

On 24 July 1964 Dylan 'premiered'* his new songs at the Newport Folk Festival, scene of his greatest triumph twelve months earlier and of his greatest controversy twelve months later. Surrounded by these two pillars of Dylan iconography, his 1964 appearance has been largely ignored. In fact it was very important, his two sets generating their fair share of controversy. *Another Side* had yet to be released and it had been nine months since his triumphant show at Carnegie Hall.

Dylan's first appearance that weekend, at a Friday topical-song workshop, was brief. In an ironic gesture, lost on the crowd, he opened with 'It Ain't Me Babe'. He then performed 'Mr Tambourine Man', and the crowd responded enthusiastically to the instantly memorable song with its lilting refrain. Indeed, the crowd stood to acclaim another work of genius from their authentic troubadour. This response to 'Mr Tambourine Man' presumably encouraged Dylan to include it in his Sunday set, along with three previews of *Another Side*. Though 'All I Really Wanna Do' was a poor opener to the set, 'To Ramona' and 'Chimes of Freedom' were probably the two most impressive songs on his forthcoming album and had 'the audience frantically calling for more when [he] at last had to leave', according to the *Providence Journal*. He returned to perform a duet with Baez, the inevitable 'With God on Our Side'.

If the audience enjoyed the performance, his previous supporters in the media did not. Robert Shelton felt that he was stoned and that the performance had suffered accordingly. Irwin Sibler wrote an open letter to Dylan in the next edition of *Sing Out*, accusing him of writing maudlin songs and generally letting down his old friends, concluding that the old Dylan 'never wasted our precious time'. In *Broadside* he was also subject to criticism. Paul Wolfe

* He had in fact already played a couple of warm-up shows in Michigan.

recognized that his performance represented 'the renunciation of topical music by its major prophet', an astute enough observation undermined by his then-stated opinion that the new songs 'degenerated into confusion and innocuousness'. Of course, having heard the best of Dylan's new songs – and hated them – the old guard had a field day when they finally heard the entire fourth album.

If the criticism had an effect on Dylan he did not let it show (though he would provide a scathing rebuttal to his critics in the programme notes to his October New York concert, 'Advice to Geraldine on Her Miscellaneous Birthday'). Instead he retired to Woodstock to spend a quiet August in the company of Joan Baez, her sister Mimi and his old buddy (and Mimi's new husband) Richard Farina.

Joan Baez: Bobby invited me, Mimi, and her husband Dick Farina to house-sit Albert Grossman's, in Woodstock, New York . . . Bob had a 350 Triumph motorcycle which I rode around in the woods and on the back roads, sometimes with him on the back. Most of the month or so we were there, Bob stood at the typewriter in the corner of his room, drinking red wine and smoking and tapping away relentlessly for hours. And in the dead of night, he would wake up, grunt, grab a cigarette, and stumble over to the typewriter again. He was turning out songs like ticker tape, and I was stealing them as fast as he wrote them.

Woodstock, two hours from Manhattan, in upstate New York, had become a regular haven for Dylan since the previous summer, when he had spent a happy month at Peter Yarrow's cabin with Suze. Grossman gave him free rein of his house, and in 1964–5 he spent nearly as much time there as he did in New York. Another incentive to visit was a dark-haired beauty by the name of Sara Lowndes, a regular guest at the Grossmans' and one of Sally Grossman's oldest friends. Baez later discovered that, having outlasted Suze, she was not immune from a little two-timing herself.

Joan Baez: [In 1975] When I finally met and became friends with Sara, we talked for hours about those days when the Original Vagabond was two-timing us. I told Sara that I'd never found Bob to be much at giving gifts, but that he had once bought me a green corduroy coat, and had told me to keep a lovely blue nightgown from the Woodstock house. 'Oh!' said Sara, 'that's where it went!'

In fact, despite Baez's recollections of Dylan 'turning out songs like ticker tape' it is not clear what songs he was working on that August. Only two songs seem to date from this lull, and 'If You Gotta Go, Go Now', though amusing enough, would hardly have taxed him for long. Clearly most of the time he was working on his book, which lay somewhere between *Walk Down Crooked Highway* and *Tarantula*. The other new song he would premiere in September was called 'It's Alright Ma (It's Life and Life Only)'. He was probably also working on 'Gates of Eden', premiered in October.

Though introduced later, 'Gates of Eden' seems more closely related to 'Chimes of Freedom' and 'Mr Tambourine Man' than to 'It's Alright Ma'. Like these, it is a visionary song, once again constructed in the form of a dream, though he makes it deliberately unclear whether it is his dream or his lover's who comes to him at dawn 'and tells me of her dreams'. The turns of phrase he was searching for on 'My Back Pages' are now in place. Lines like 'motorcycle black madonna two-wheeled gypsy queen' no longer sound forced, but are powerful and suggestive.

'It's Alright Ma' is an epic that dwarfs even 'Gates of Eden'. If, as seems likely, he wrote it that August in Woodstock, he must have worked long and hard on the structure of the song. Its fifteen verses and five slightly different refrains provide an impressive catalogue of social ills. For 'It's Alright Ma' was far more of a finger-pointin' song than anything on *The Times They Are a-Changin'*. Adopting the apocalyptic tradition he so skilfully used on 'The Times They Are a-Changin'' and 'Hard Rain's a-Gonna Fall', he produced a damning roster of American society's malaises, including perhaps more memorable aphorisms than any other popular song – 'Money doesn't talk it swears'; 'He not busy being born is busy dying' etc. If fans felt that Dylan had abandoned the realms of social relevance, 'It's Alright Ma' reminded them that the topical song was only one way of writing about contemporary America, and that his new, more surreal approach might be a more appropriate way of dealing with the kaleidoscopic nature of the mid-sixties.

Throughout the fall of 1964 Dylan toured extensively, playing far more one-night stands than he had ever attempted before. After Pennsylvania, Michigan, Minnesota, New York, Connecticut and Ontario, the tour culminated in California, where Baez was again waiting for the return of her wandering minstrel. However, he appeared to be tiring of his old songs. The set had become rigid and predictable, as had the audiences' response. Dylan was now screening himself from friends and fans with an entourage of hipsters like Bobby Neuwirth and Victor Maimudes, who would provide both verbal and physical intimidation where necessary.

One interviewer who talked to him that December in Santa Barbara wrote to *Sing Out* berating him for his newly found isolation:

Bob Blackamar: I met and talked with Bob Dylan a few weeks ago. He really has lost contact with his audiences and much of reality . . . I met part of Mr Dylan's clique as well, and it is true that Bob is only interested in singing for their enjoyment as well as his.

Evidently he no longer entertained notions of meeting the 'common people'. He restricted his companions to those who could withstand his word games, the verbal numbers he ran on the unhip simply for the mutual gratification and entertainment of the Hip. Ironically Baez, with whom Dylan continued to involve himself on a sporadic basis, was one of the butts for his verbal jousting; as was any journalist – except those who had received honorary membership of the inner circle during his rise to fame. Thus Robert Shelton, Nat Hentoff, Al Aronowitz, Ralph J. Gleason and J. R. Goddard may have been immune from most of his games, but any new interviewer was tested by the talons of his verbal wit. In February 1965 he appeared on Les Crane's popular TV show, and duly demolished Crane on air. Seemingly content to refer to his host as Less, he neatly ducked each and every question. When, predictably, asked what his main message might be, he replied, 'Eat.' Asked what a movie he was planning to make would be about, he informed Crane it would be a horror cowboy movie. Asked if he played the horror cowboy, he said, 'No. I play my mother.'

His baiting of the press even extended that winter of 1965 to concocting a script for a Dylan press conference with J. R. Goddard of the *Village Voice*, who had reviewed his first album back in 1962. Published in the *Voice* in March 1965 the article, entitled 'Dylan Meets the Press', was the supposed result of a press conference in Woodstock, where 'Dylan had consented to answer all those deep, meaningful, searching questions he's been bombarded with by reporters and TV interviewers through the years'. When asked who he thought could save the world, he replied Al Aronowitz. It was his first flirtation with such parody. It would not be his last.

In rapid succession he also conducted a one-page interview wholly about wearing a tie when writing his songs (for the men's magazine *Cavalier*); and a brief absurdist interview with a relatively hip West Coast journalist called Paul Jay Robbins from the

underground paper *Los Angeles Free Press*. He would have ample
opportunity to sharpen his verbal barbs on the UK press when he
toured England in May.

Meanwhile he had an album to make. He had finally decided
that the time had come to record with a band. After the end of his
West Coast tour he had three or four weeks in Woodstock to
write enough songs to fill out his fifth album. In a fertile burst of
creativity he came up with a dozen new songs.

The eighteen 'new' songs he brought to the first session included
the four songs he had been playing on the road, 'It's Alright Ma',
'Mr Tambourine Man', 'Gates of Eden' and 'If You Gotta Go, Go
Now' plus 'I'll Keep It with Mine', which he had yet to record for
CBS. If none of these songs, save 'If You Gotta Go, Go Now',
seemed to lend themselves to an 'electric' arrangement, the new
songs he had written clearly did. One song in particular, 'Subterranean Homesick Blues', seemed inconceivable without some suitable backing. As Dylan described the problem later that year:

Bob Dylan: I had this thing called 'Subterranean Homesick Blues'. It
just didn't sound right by myself . . . But it fit right in with the band.
[1965]

He had written another three songs, 'Maggie's Farm', 'On the
Road Again' and 'Outlaw Blues', which all lent themselves to
some good ol' rhythm & blues. The major problem was whom to
recruit to play them.

Daniel Kramer: Tom Wilson, his recording producer, started a search
for musicians who could work with him. It was crucial to use musicians
who could really play, who could really accommodate Dylan's needs . . .
[they] would have to adjust to his unorthodox style and method of
delivery.

Dylan insisted on picking the guitarist. His choice was Bruce
Langhorne, whom he had worked with back in 1962 during the
Freewheelin' electric sessions and who had provided second guitar
on a couple of acoustic recordings at that time. The remainder of
the musicians were chosen by Tom Wilson. They were an experienced bunch of session men, including John Sebastian, soon to
form Lovin' Spoonful, on bass, and Bobby Gregg, who would
tour with Dylan later in the year, on drums. John Hammond
Junior, son of Dylan's old producer, provided some acoustic guitar
accompaniment.

The sessions progressed remarkably smoothly. Working through the day and into the night, Dylan completed the album in three sessions over a period of two days. It was astonishing progress considering that he had no real experience of working with bands in the studio. He also showed that he relied heavily on instinct when working up the best version of a song. This aspect of Dylan's work on *Bringing It All Back Home* would remain a consistent feature of his studio recordings. Multiple takes he used as excuses to try different arrangements, different approaches, different tempos, often improvising lyrics on the spot. He did not attempt to perfect an existing version that had not come out quite right. The air of spontaneity was suggested at the beginning of 'Bob Dylan's 115th Dream' when he started the song and the band failed to come in on time. Dylan and Wilson fall about laughing and Wilson's voice can be heard saying, 'Start again,' and sure enough Dylan and the band tumble in – right on time – on what sounds like a first complete take.

Daniel Kramer: It was obvious from the very beginning that something exciting was happening, and much of it happened spontaneously. When the playback of 'Maggie's Farm' was heard over the studio speakers, we were all elated. There was no question about it – it swung, it was happy, it was good music, and, most of all, it was Dylan. The musicians were enthusiastic. They conferred with one another to work out the problems as they arose. Dylan bounced around from one man to another, explaining what he wanted, often showing them on the piano what was needed until, like a giant puzzle, the pieces would fit and the picture emerged whole. Dylan worked like a painter covering a huge canvas with the colours that the different musicians could supply him, adding depth and dimension to the total work. All in all, most of the songs went down easily and needed only three or four takes before they were accepted. In some cases, the first take sounded entirely different from the final one because the material was played at a different tempo, perhaps, or a different chord was chosen, or solos may have been re-arranged . . . His method of working, the certainty of what he wanted kept things moving. He would listen to the playbacks in the control booth, discuss what was happening with Tom Wilson, and move on to the next number. If he tried something that didn't go well, he would put it off for another session. In this way, he never bogged down – he just kept on going.

In fact Dylan did not intend to issue a wholly 'electric' album. Since the songs he had been performing at his acoustic shows did not self-evidently lend themselves to electric arrangements, he chose to record an acoustic side to the album to counterbalance the side of electric music. Langhorne accompanied Dylan on 'Mr

Tambourine Man' and bassist William E. Lee on a new song called
'It's All Over Now, Baby Blue', but these were the solitary
embellishments on side two of the album. 'It's All Over Now,
Baby Blue' was another of his 'go out in the real world' songs, like
'To Ramona', though less conciliatory – the tone is crueller and
more demanding. The three songs which he had already been
performing live and which would make up the bulk of the
acoustic side of the album he had the audacity to record in one go,
with barely a pause between each take.

The completion of *Bringing It All Back Home* in a mere three
sessions must have surprised even Dylan. That the album is one of
his most enduring (he plays more songs from this album in 1990
than from any subsequent album) says a lot for the quality of the
songwriting. Though the folkies would not agree, it was Dylan's
most rounded album to date. The whimsical romps like '115th
Dream' and 'Outlaw Blues' counterbalanced the beautiful 'Love
Minus Zero'/'No Limit' and 'She Belongs to Me', while social
commentaries like 'Subterranean Homesick Blues' and 'Maggie's
Farm' were now set to amphetamine riffs, and the visionary poems
made up a cogent second side.

While CBS set about releasing Dylan's first 'folk-rock' album
and his second 'folk-rock' single ('Subterranean Homesick Blues')
– some two and a half years on from 'Mixed Up Confusion' – he
made his American farewell to acoustic shows with a brief tour
with Joan Baez. A joint tour had been discussed previously and
now that Dylan's commercial stock was as great as Baez's it
seemed practicable. Of course the difference was that Dylan's star
was in the ascendant and Baez's was not. Grossman made sure that
his client's interests were protected.

Bobby Neuwirth: The feeling around that [Dylan/Baez] tour was
pretty good. The only one who was in a sweat about it was Manny
[Greenhill]. As far as Bob was concerned, Albert was the guy who took
care of all that shit ... Albert would ask him if he wanted to do
something, and he'd say yes or no. There was never any of the evil shit
that a lot of people imagined.

Despite the seeming camaraderie on the tour, Dylan was tiring
of his relationship with Baez. It seems strangely bizarre yet oddly
typical that he should play such a tour with her and even stay with
her in Carmel when playing a few solo shows on the West Coast
at the beginning of April, yet treat her so harshly a month later.
However, there remains serious doubts about how committed

Dylan had been to their relationship in the previous six months. Though flattered by her, and despite their 'romance' having lasted nearly two years, six months on from his break-up with Suze, Dylan never seems to have sought to deepen their relationship, and their assignations every couple of months remained set to suit his convenience. Meanwhile he was spending more and more time with Sara Lowndes.

Dylan was increasingly at odds with Baez's commitment to the causes of civil rights and non-violence and her 'Holier Than Thou' attitude. Songs like 'Maggie's Farm' and 'It's All Over Now, Baby Blue' were individualistic expressions of rebellion, without any of the sense of community that was important to Baez. Whatever the reasons for their drifting apart, it seems clear he did not want her to come with him to England. Yet, when she was unable to take the hint, he was unable actually to say no, she could not come. It was to make his first English tour an extremely fraught affair.

9

1965: Over Your Shoulder

If the brief Dylan/Baez East Coast tour is something of a black hole in the record of Dylan's career, the equally brief English tour he undertook at the beginning of May 1965 is generally well documented and fondly remembered. The main reason is Don Pennebaker's primitive *cinéma vérité* study *Don't Look Back*, a ninety-minute monochrome documentary of the tour. The portrait of Dylan which he composed in that movie has become fixed in people's minds as Dylan 1965. Certainly the film is a remarkable study of the pressures of fame as they affected a self-assured and talented young singer. Dylan, though, has never been entirely comfortable with the portrait Pennebaker presented. Indeed, when Pennebaker completed the movie and showed it to him he said they would have to make a lot of changes. Yet having stated that he would detail these changes at a subsequent screening, at this second preview the Gemini Dylan decided to let the film stand.

Bob Dylan: *Don't Look Back* was . . . somebody else's movie . . . I don't think it was accurate at all in terms of showing my formative years. It showed only one side. He made it seem like I wasn't doing anything but living in hotel rooms, playing the typewriter and holding press conferences for journalists. All that is true, you know. Throwing some bottles, there's something about it in the movie. Joan Baez is in it. But it's one-sided. [1978]

Dylan's original intentions in making the film remain unclear. Clearly his hiring of Pennebaker suggested that he had a documentary movie in mind. Sara Lowndes had recommended him. When Dylan, accompanied by Bobby Neuwirth, met Pennebaker at the Cedar Tavern in New York he tested his suitability in the usual way by playing a few verbal games, the test of coolness being to avoid reacting to them. Pennebaker wisely played along.

D. A. Pennebaker: [Grossman] and Dylan had approached us because Sara had worked with us at *Life*. She was working there for about a year and a half, so I knew Sara quite well. Then I came back, and Albert said, 'My client's going to England. Would you like to make a film about it?' I said, 'Sure' ... I think that Dylan had a very parochial sense about his operation. He was going to do things totally differently from the way they'd been done; he was gonna revamp network schedules; he was gonna revamp movies; he was gonna make everything in a new way — without being quite sure how he'd do it.

Pennebaker was taking something of a risk, and with his money as well. He did not really know Dylan's work, nor indeed what filming him would be like, though his meeting with Dylan and Neuwirth gave him something of a foretaste, and Grossman's deal with Pennebaker was that Leacock–Pennebaker Inc. put up the costs of making the film and any profits would be divided equally. So Pennebaker was taking a lot on faith. Yet, as soon as he arrived in London on 26 April, he could see that some fascinating process was taking place.

D. A. Pennebaker: There was the problem of sticking with Dylan who was under a number of pressures, including those from Joan Baez (personal) and the concerts (public). I had to take it on faith the film would not be a series of press conferences and getting in and out of concert halls ... It became clear that Dylan was going through some kind of change, and I knew that if I could stick with him I'd see something of it.

The first indication of the pressures that Dylan faced came the minute he landed at London Airport. How aware he was of the scale of his popularity in England we do not know. Clearly Grossman would have been kept fully informed, and Dylan would have known his records were selling in England. But the commercial snowball that had been rolling since he appeared at the Festival Hall in May 1964 had reached critical mass that April. At the beginning of the month his first UK single had entered the charts. It was, rather incongruously, 'The Times They Are a-Changin'', a song he had spent eighteen months running away from. Two weeks later the steady-selling *Freewheelin'* finally made it to number one on the album charts, having been a regular feature on the charts for nearly a year. This achievement needs to be placed in context. Since 9 March 1963, when the album *Please Please Me* first made it to number one, only albums by the Beatles and the Rolling Stones had been at the top spot. This, after all, was the era that marked the hegemony of English pop.

Not only did *Freewheelin'* create the first fissure in the Beatles/Stones edifice, but Dylan's entire catalogue – *Bringing It All Back Home* was just about to be released – had gone Top Twenty in the last six months, and *The Times They Are a-Changin'* and *Another Side* were in the Top Ten. So Dylan was not merely some well-known folksinger, he was a *star*. Since England had a well-established, tabloid-dominated national press, events that in America might have warranted a mention in the *New York Post* were national news in England.

Dylan almost certainly did not appreciate how famous he now was in England. However, he knew the press would be awaiting his arrival, and he entered his first (genuine) press conference, held in the VIP lounge of London Airport, carrying a large industrial lightbulb. Knowing that he would inevitably be asked what his main message was – after all, no American journalist had resisted asking the question in the last two years – he responded with what seemed a remarkably quick-witted reply, 'Keep a good head and always carry a lightbulb.' If his stunt with the lightbulb was an in-joke at the press's expense (Dylan would repeat his use of props in later press conferences, bringing a doll to his Paris '66 conference, which he christened Finian), he actually seemed happy to talk and surprisingly cooperative.

A further press conference the following day at the Savoy Hotel found him less cooperative and, as the round of interviews filled up the three days before his first concert in Sheffield, he grew tired of the endless questions, always obvious, often demeaning of his work (witness Cleave's question in *Don't Look Back*: Do your fans understand a word you sing?). Subsequent interviews with the 'straight' press would be scathing affairs, with Dylan mercilessly putting on his interviewers. Yet when in the company of the hipper members of the music press, like Ray Coleman of *Melody Maker* or the amateur student journalists occasionally encountered along the way, he played few games and gave straight answers to honest questions. Interviewed in Sheffield for the university paper, Dylan gave a surprisingly frank response as to why he played his games with the 'straight' press.

Bob Dylan: They ask the wrong questions, like, What did you have for breakfast, What's your favourite colour, stuff like that. Newspaper reporters, man, they're just hung-up writers, frustrated novelists, they don't hurt me none by putting fancy labels on me. They got all these preconceived ideas about me, so I just play up to them. [1965]

The most famous of Dylan's verbal batterings must be the interview by the *Time* reporter Horace Judson. In *Don't Look Back* the editing of the interview is such that Dylan is already working on Judson when the scene starts and it cuts away when Dylan informs Judson he can sing as well as Caruso 'and I can hold my breath three times as long'. According to Anthea Joseph, who can sometimes be seen in the background during *Don't Look Back*, Judson did not just crawl away meekly after Dylan's verbal onslaught.

Anthea Joseph: The man was such a prat. And Bob was being absolutely appalling, but so brilliant. By this time I'd learnt that he could pull strips of skin off people, verbally . . . [Judson] was quite abusive as well. He was extremely upset, he really was; and in a way I suppose it was not really his fault, not properly briefed, treating Bob as some sort of curiosity, not as a serious artist.

But Judson was just one of a series of victims fed to Dylan by uncomprehending editors. Not all were as offended as Judson. Laurie Henshaw of *Disc and Music Echo* encountered a Dylan if anything even ruder than he was to Judson. However, his stream of put-ons delighted Henshaw, who published the interview as it was, claiming he had secured Dylan's most outrageous interview to date. And indeed he probably had. Terry Ellis also survived the verbal battering given him as a naïve science student backstage at Newcastle City Hall, going on to found Chrysalis Records and manage Jethro Tull.

Terry Ellis: I remember he had a wicked glint in his eye – I couldn't tell you if that was chemically induced. In retrospect, I don't think he was actually being cruel to me, he was being quite pleasant – but in his own caustic way.

If Dylan's toying with the press makes up a major part of *Don't Look Back*, the film certainly features an 'on' Dylan all the time. He seems always on stage, meeting fans, entertaining friends and hangers-on or putting the press on. Even the hotel jam with Baez is a performance, albeit for a chosen few: Neuwirth, Baez, Grossman and Pennebaker. Even when he is having a party in his room, Donovan asks him to play. The portrait that Pennebaker paints is deliberately one of the public Dylan. In private he was a very different man, able to revert to the self he had shown more easily on his previous trips to England – but only when he was comfortable in the company he was in. And this was becoming increasingly rare.

Anthea Joseph: I think he was being over-peopled . . . It was quite extraordinary the difference . . . when it was just us he was perfectly comfortable, perfectly relaxed and perfectly easy. But once the place was full of people there was a little gear-change in a way and he became the public person. But every now and then he'd go and disappear and start bashing away at the typewriter which was on the desk.

The need to be permanently 'on' was draining Dylan. During a day-off before two shows at the Royal Albert Hall, he was enjoying hanging out with assorted friends in Soho when he heard that his whereabouts had become known to some of his fans and they were heading for the club. For the first time he was having to come to terms with being a teenybopper idol. When he hot-footed it to the Savoy he found he was expected to party.

Anthea Joseph: There was Donovan, the Pretty Things, assorted other odds and sods . . . We take over a table downstairs [at Les Cousins] . . . Baez wasn't there. She was still in the hotel in a sulk . . . And then we got word – a friend of mine came into the pub – and said, Did you know they've heard that Dylan's in here and they're beginning to come up the road. So I said to him we leave. So Dorothy [Carthy] and me hoiked him out and this taxi came round the corner into Wardour Street with his light on. I stopped him and got in and there was this blonde person in it and we do not know where she came from. However she paid the fare. We were halfway to the Savoy and realized that none of us had enough money for the fare . . . [Having managed to reach the Savoy], the three of us [were] planning to just have a really nice chat and Bob invited this girl to come up. She didn't say no. And so we were sort of milling around talking about old times and that sort of nonsense and the phone rang. It was the porter, saying there's an awful lot of people downstairs saying you're having a party. I said, Are you having a party? He said, No. I said, Well they seem to think you're having a party. He said, Well I suppose we ought to have a party. So I said, Okay you get onto room service and order the booze. I'm not taking responsibility for this and they all turned up . . . There's this perfectly good party going on. All sorts of people turned up. Allen [Ginsberg] was there. I mean everybody was there. And I was going around dishing out the drinks. And then this row broke out . . . These two bozos had locked themselves in the bathroom, where it had beautiful glass shelves. Those wonderful sort of thirties bathrooms! Vast marble bath. They were just chucking them out . . . Daryll Adams was trying to smooth everybody down, as I was. And Bob was sort of jumping [up and down]. I'd never seen him lose his temper before. It was really quite frightening. He went up like a little torch and rightfully so, too.

The culmination of this fraught evening is captured in *Don't Look Back* as Dylan explodes − WHO THREW THAT FUCKING GLASS?!?

The evening described by Joseph was not an isolated example. The suite at the Savoy was constantly overrun with people. If it was not cocktail parties arranged by Grossman, it was journalists wanting one-to-one interviews; if not journalists, it was Allen Ginsberg and his beat friends; if not them it would be assorted members of England's thriving beat-group scene come to pay their respects.

The Beatles were in regular attendance. An article in *Melody Maker* announcing that 'The Beatles Dig Dylan', published that January, had been a major fillip to his commercial standing in the UK. He had met them the previous August in New York, when he was introduced to them by Al Aronowitz, and they spent two nights talking at the Delmonico Hotel. Dylan and Aronowitz apparently suggested they all unwind with a little grass. The Beatles had not previously indulged. Yet when Dylan met up with them again in May 1965 he found their experiments with mind-expanding chemicals had progressed somewhat.

John Lennon: I just remember . . . that we were both in shades and both on fucking junk and all these freaks around us and Ginsberg and all those people. I was anxious as shit.

Despite their own status, the Beatles were very much in awe of Dylan. Lennon had already begun to be heavily influenced by him, though their songs had only just begun to explore themes beyond the well-worn 'young love' idiom. The Rolling Stones also regularly attended Dylan's Savoy Hotel suite, though it was Brian Jones who was most taken by Dylan.

Dana Gillespie: Every night the Stones and the Beatles used to come to the Savoy Hotel and they would play each other their latest recordings and you could see them vying for the top spot as the top British band, but . . . [Dylan] was the one person that both the Stones and the Beatles had great admiration for, so when he held court in one of the hotel rooms, everyone sat and listened.

In *Don't Look Back* there is an indication of the constant mayhem that filled the suite when Neuwirth, Dylan and Baez were finally left alone (save for Pennebaker, 'the eye') in Dylan's room, and Neuwirth says, 'Welcome home. It's the first time that this room hasn't been full of a bunch of insane lunatics, man, that I can remember . . . It's the first time it's been cool around here.' However, Baez's presence was hardly conducive to Dylan relaxing at this point. Indeed, in this scene in the film Neuwirth seems to be picking on Baez, telling her, 'Sister, you fagged out long ago,' while Dylan looks on impassively. In fact, according to Baez, Neuwirth was one of the reasons she kept relatively sane during all the games that were being played around her on that tour.

Joan Baez: One night I went to Neuwirth's room crying. He put his arms around me and mopped a pint of tears off my cheeks and chin, and begged me to pack up my bags and leave the tour. 'But Bob asked me to come. He asked me,' I protested. 'I know, but he don't know what's happening anymore, can't you see? He's just out there spinnin' and he wants to do it by himself.'

Whatever Baez's expectations about the tour, Dylan clearly had no intention of introducing her at his concerts. Baez was planning to play her own concerts in England that summer, but she was considerably less well known here than in America and performing with Dylan would have been a considerable endorsement. The implied rejection hurt, but it was in fact only the beginning of Dylan's somewhat ruthless deflating of Baez's considerable ego. Marianne Faithfull, talking at the time, provided a journalist with an example of the way he would demean her in the company of friends.

Marianne Faithfull: [Baez] insisted on singing her high vibrato version of 'Here Comes the Night' and 'Go Now', which Dylan complained about. He hates her voice and tells her so. At one point he held up a bottle as she sang a high note, and drawled, 'Break that!' She just laughed.

Dylan was also happy to seduce other women during his English tour, seemingly unaffected by the heartbreak such activities must have caused Baez, who was by this point overwhelmingly in love with him. Thus when he met up with the amply endowed Dana Gillespie at an official welcoming party on the first day of his visit, Baez discovered at first hand the sort of philandering which had tortured Suze before her.

Dana Gillespie: Dylan and I started talking almost as soon as I walked in. I guess he fancied me. He was fairly blatant about it and made some remark about my 44-inch bust.

If Baez could dismiss Dylan's relationship with Gillespie as purely sexual, she found it harder to deal with the presence of Sara Lowndes, a mysterious dark-haired American beauty who appeared in his company after a brief holiday in Portugal. After the English tour, Lowndes had joined him in Paris and they had then travelled together to Portugal and back to London. Lowndes answered the door of Dylan's hotel suite when Baez called to see if Dylan was okay after a bout of food poisoning. At this point Baez realized it was indeed over, and headed for France herself. They would not sing together again for a further ten years, though Baez would continue to address Dylan in song, and continue to believe that he addressed her in song.

D. A. Pennebaker: Well you've got to understand a peculiar situation around royal entourages, palaces, courts in general, politics, and that is that you can be number four or five, but if you're used to being number one or two it's a big jolt – and that's kind of what that was about. There were other people in Dylan's life – there was Sara – and Baez kind of knew it.

In fact most viewers of *Don't Look Back* don't realize how short the time span covered by the film is. Dylan spent longer in England, France and Portugal after the end of his tour than he did on it. *Don't Look Back* covers only two weeks in his life, and during that time he played only eight concerts, hardly the most rigorous schedule ever devised. The concerts themselves were well received, though Dylan's performances were beginning to sound a little stale. Indeed Pennebaker has said that he didn't feel that playing live was the most important part of what was happening to Dylan in 1965, but that it was in 1966. The tapes bear this opinion out. Though the performances are not exactly lack-lustre, a certain vibrancy is lacking.

Of course part of the problem with the tour was that in England Dylan was still seen as the man who had made *Freewheelin'* and three other acoustic albums. Only at the end of the tour did *Bringing It All Back Home* get released, and 'Subterranean Home-sick Blues' begin to climb the charts. In fact *Bringing It All Back Home* would make number one on the album charts at the end of May, signalling considerable commercial acceptance for his new sound. Irrespective of the sales reaction to his new sound, he was no longer comfortable in his acoustic guise. In *Don't Look Back* he can be seen talking to a band who play electric versions of his songs, and he is keen to hear how they sound. When a fan

tells him she does not like his new single, he mutters, 'Oh you're
one of those. I understand now.' Two days after the conclusion of
his brief tour, Dylan went into the studio with perhaps the finest
of the British rhythm & blues bands, John Mayall's Bluesbreakers.
Tom Wilson had flown over from New York to produce the
session.

Eric Clapton: He was interested in John Mayall. John had recorded a
song called 'Life Is Like a Slow Train Going up a Hill' and that interested
Bob. Bob came in, looked for John Mayall. I was just the guitar player
on the session. He had a friend called Bobby Neuwirth who was a
fantastic player. Bobby Neuwirth was his kind of court jester at the time.
[He] kept coming up to me and saying, You're playing too much blues,
man. He needs to be more country!

Hughie Flint: Dylan wanted to try something out with a British r&b
band, which was the vogue at the time. It could've been anyone . . . but
we were available . . . We thought we were going to accompany Dylan
because we all knew that he was a guitar player and so John Mayall was
going to play keyboards and we were going to play along with whatever
he did. But when he came in, Dylan immediately sat down at the piano
and started playing.

Evidently Dylan at this stage was looking to record some
material for his next album, and this time it would be an all-out
rhythm & blues sound.

Whatever Neuwirth's suggestions, the session was a disaster,
primarily because both Dylan and Wilson were consuming vast
quantities of wine and, as he became the worse for drink, Dylan
started taking an inordinate interest in Nadia Catouse, a singer
who was attending the session. Soon he and Wilson departed arm
in arm, presumably intending to search out further wine and
entertainment.

Hughie Flint: All through the session it was just messing around. I don't
think we played a complete number. It was a real mess. There was a lot
of booze there, crates and crates of wine – I'd never seen so much wine,
and everybody got very pissed, very quickly, no one more so than
Dylan.

On 1 June 1965 Dylan recorded two thirty-five-minute TV
specials for the BBC. He had been due to record them the
previous week but had been laid up in bed in the Savoy, and later
in St Mary's Hospital in Paddington, suffering from a severe bout
of food poisoning contracted in Portugal. The BBC Broadcasts, as

they became known, would be Dylan's last entirely acoustic performance for many years and briefly threatened to be his final performance ever. He had decided to quit.

10

1964–5: A Book of Words

Dylan's most talked-about project during his rise to fame was a book he was supposedly writing. He had referred to it first in April 1963; then repeatedly in interviews and press conferences during 1964 and 1965 – all the while becoming increasingly imprecise about its contents. By the time of his accident in July 1966 it had still not appeared.* Dylan arrived at the approach adopted in *Tarantula* only after going through several unsuccessful projects.

Though there have been several attempts to evaluate *Tarantula*'s literary merits, the history of the book's composition has never really been fully explored. Dylan himself has always given the impression that he was cajoled into producing a book after the success of John Lennon's two collections of whimsical prose and verse.

Bob Dylan: I was doing interviews before and after concerts, and reporters would say things like 'What else do you write?' And I would say, 'Well I don't write much of anything else.' And they would say, 'Oh, come on. You must write other things. Tell us something else. Do you write books?' And I'd say, 'Sure, I write books.' After the publishers saw that I wrote books, they began to send me contracts . . . we took the biggest one, and then owed them a book. [1969]

The reality is that he freely confessed that he was writing at least one book, and somewhere between one and two plays, in several interviews in 1964 – by which point he was already signed up with Macmillan. According to Macmillan's editor Bob Markel, who supervised the publication of *Tarantula*, it was not a hard and fast commitment Dylan had made, and he was as uncertain as Dylan as to what Macmillan might eventually get.

* It would be 1970 before *Tarantula* saw the light of day, at least officially, though booklegs of the 1966 galleys circulated within months of his accident.

Bob Markel: I met Albert Grossman before I met Bob Dylan ... Bob was just beginning to make an impression as a singer and writer. Albert explained to me that he thought Dylan was a very hot property who might want to do a book one day, and that if I were interested, we might be able to work out a contract for a book ... We gave him an advance for an untitled book of writings ... The publisher was taking a risk on a young, untested potential phenomenon. In time we'd figure out a book, but it was worth having a contract. He was uncertain what the book would be.

Uncertainty about the exact nature of the book would last some time. Dylan had first suggested he was working on a book back in April 1963, when he mentioned it to Studs Terkel. The book he discussed then, though, was no surreal voyage through language. It was supposed to be loosely historical, at least in the way that 'My Life in a Stolen Moment' and 'Last Thoughts on Woody Guthrie', two contemporary bio-poems, were 'historical'. That is, it looked back upon the genesis of Bob Dylan, New York folksinger.

Bob Dylan: I'm writing a book now ... It's about my first week in New York ... It's just about somebody who's come to the end of one road and knows it's the end of one road and knows there's another road there but doesn't know exactly where it is and knows you can't go back on this one road ... it's got thoughts in my head all about teachers and school and all about hitch-hikers around the country ... college kids going to college it's got and these are all people that I knew every one of them's sort of a symbol for all kinds of people. [1963]

In the fall of 1963, Dylan met poet Lawrence Ferlinghetti and discussed the possibility of producing a book for his firm City Lights, publishers of the beat poets, and therefore an excellent choice in terms of Dylan's credibility. However, by April 1964 he still had not forwarded any manuscript, and wrote to Ferlinghetti that he kept changing his approach to the project:

I do got things of songs an stories for you. my hangup is tho that I know there will be more. I want t send the more more then I want t send the got. yes I guess that's it. [1964]

By the time that Macmillan expressed an interest in spring 1964, the project was still undefined. According to Markel, the original contract drawn up by Macmillan was for a book of photographs on Hollywood. The photos were to be by Barry Feinstein, husband of Mary Travers and the man responsible for the stark portrait of

Dylan that graced the cover of the *The Times They Are a-Changin'*
album. Text would be provided by Dylan. Dylan discussed this
book with *Melody Maker*'s Max Jones when talking to him in
London in May 1964.

Bob Dylan: It's just pictures and the words I'm going to write that
[not so much] coincide with the photographer's, but somehow fall into
the same direction or mood. All the pictures were shot in Hollywood:
shots of everything, a whole picture of Hollywood from the beautiful
sign on the hill to Marlon Brando speaking while someone holds up a
sign saying Nigger-Lover . . . I dig this photographer, and I dig taking
pictures myself. [1964]

Dylan also informed Max Jones that he had at least one more
book in mind, and that he was working on a play or two as well –
indeed three months earlier he had told a Canadian reporter that
the play 'is going to be done sooner than the novel'. Meanwhile he
was still working on the free-verse form of poetry he had developed in *Eleven Outlined Epitaphs*. As he completed his fourth
album, *Another Side*, in June 1964, he once again wished to include
his own notes on the album sleeve. The problem – as with *The
Times They Are a-Changin'* – was that he had too many poems to
fit on a single album sleeve. As a result the *Another Side* poems –
which were ironically entitled *Some Other Kinds of Songs*, an
admission that despite his best endeavours these free-form poems
were something different from his recorded words – were
crammed onto the album sleeve in microscopic type. Despite this,
only five of these 'kinds of songs' could be included on the back
cover. Six further examples were eventually published as a surprise
bonus in Dylan's 1973 omnibus, *Writings and Drawings*.
    Some Other Kinds of Songs are a step on from *Eleven Outlined
Epitaphs* and the other poems he had been writing in the fall of
1963. The principal difference occurs in the line breaks. In his
Outlined Epitaphs the lines seem to puncture the text at points
where one thought ends and another begins. In *Some Other Kinds
of Songs* it seems as if any kind of line-form is an encumbrance.
They now either directly anticipate the amphetamine jolts of
rhythm later adopted on songs like 'Subterranean Homesick Blues',
or seem random intrusions into free-rolling prose-poems. And
indeed such prose-poems seemed to be the form that Dylan was
now steering towards.
    Macmillan's Bob Markel met Dylan shortly after writing *Some
Other Kinds of Songs*, and clearly Dylan's concept of the book had

already moved towards a *Tarantula*-esque form. The initial working title was apparently *Side One*.

Bob Markel: Our first meeting took place in the great big marvellous
old downtown Macmillan offices. It was probably the winter of 1964 [*sic*].
When I spoke to Bob on the telephone he asked that the meeting take
place after dark as he felt he couldn't travel in broad daylight. He was
driving a motorcycle around New York in those days . . . There was no
book at the time . . . The first title I ever saw on it was *Side One* . . . The
material at that point was hazy, sketchy. The poetry editor called it
'inaccessible'. The symbolism was not easily understood, but on the other
hand it was earthy, filled with obscure but marvellous imagery . . . I felt
it had a lot of value and was very different from Dylan's output till then.
It was not a book.

The best evidence of Dylan's increasingly surreal approach to his
prose-poems comes in four remarkable letters he wrote to Tami
Dean, a student at Oklahoma State University, through 1964. The
letters – not published until 1984, sixteen years after Dean's death
in a car accident – detail a clear development in his style. The first
letter, from early March 1964 going by his reference to visiting
Dallas three weeks earlier, shows a style of writing similar to the
free-verse letters to Tony Glover, Sis Cunningham and the Emergency Civil Liberties Committee from the previous year, albeit in
straight prose form: 'I'll see you sometime. on a strange nite. when
the leaves 're blowin. an it's close t shiverin. when the headlights
pass above the bluff yes I'll meet you by the crossing. on the edge
of town. in the brown dust.' The second letter, which probably
dates from spring 1964, continues in the same style – though it
includes perhaps an oblique reference to 'Chimes of Freedom': 'i
gaze out of cathedral windows when I can. at other times I gaze up
at them from the rainy street.'
Letters three and four though are a world apart from these
chains of thought. Apparently dating from the late summer or
more likely the fall of 1964, both are more explicitly surreal; they
slip easily into a stream-of-consciousness style that piles the incongruous upon the absurd. Neither directly addresses Tami Dean – save
for a momentary incursion in letter three when doctor zen says hi –
but are rather expositions of Dylan's state of mind. The third letter
is the more coherent, and is a hilarious parody of the 'dear ma,
everyone's fine' letter, which he had previously ridiculed in a letter
to Baez's mother from August 1964 (the letter is reproduced in
Baez's autobiography *And a Voice to Sing With*). The character of
doctor zen is in exactly the same tradition as syd dangerous, Silly

Eyes and herold the professor in *Tarantula*; or the family of
lunatics portrayed in 'On the Road Again':

nothin new is happenin. doctor zen says hello. i told him you were off
in oklahoma. he says no she's not. i say ok i dig. there is no oklahoma. he
says you asshole there is no she. i say ok ok he says say hi to her. doc gets
wierd sometimes. he stuffs lsd in his turban most everyday.

The fourth letter has even fewer stylistic antecedents in his
previous poetry. A direct precursor of *Tarantula*'s mixture of
prose-poems and free-verse 'epistles', the letter reads like a Dadaist
chronicle. It opens with 'so there i was. riding on this umbrella'
and progresses through a travelogue which closely parallels the
insane world of songs like 'Bob Dylan's 115th Dream'.

watch for cave ins an dont be too good t nobody. they might get wrong
idea. sneer at graveyard. make patty cake thank you mam good gawd
son is 'at london bridge about t go? i mix up crazy phantoms. exchange
their eyes bust into plate glass predictions. get in two timed position. try
to make it with the manacans.

The letter concludes with twenty-nine lines of free-verse. The
advisory tone in lines like 'watch for cave ins an dont be too
good t nobody', can be found more fully flowered in 'It's Alright
Ma' and in what can perhaps be seen as the first of his fully fledged
prose-poems, which was published at the end of October 1964. In
the programme for his first New York concert in a year, the
famous Halloween '64 show, he included a piece called 'Advice for
Geraldine on Her Miscellaneous Birthday'. In a hilarious romp
about staying in line and conformity in general, he advises the
mysterious Geraldine never to create anything as 'it will be mis-
interpreted' and will haunt you the remainder of your life.
Though more extended than any of the 'letters' in *Tarantula*, the
way in which it directly addresses some abstract friend/critic/
member of his audience – and attempts to undermine some of the
critical flak he had started to pick up since the fall of 1963 – ties it
thematically and stylistically to the letters of the butter sculptor
and herold the professor (both in *Tarantula*).

In the first few months of 1965, Dylan's published writings
began wholly to adopt the prose style found in *Tarantula*. Indeed,
two prose-poems published in the winter of 1964–5 were credited
as being from his forthcoming book. The first such 'excerpt' was
included as an introduction for 'All I Really Wanna Do' in *Sing
Out*. The excerpt was apparently 'condensed from *Walk Down*

Crooked Highway', clearly a working title for *Tarantula*, and its stream-of-consciousness prose makes it likely that at one time it was indeed intended for inclusion in *Tarantula*, given lines like 'laura speaks of God almighty dragon up avenue B cut throat lyer in long pants'.

The next 'excerpt' from his, on this occasion untitled, forthcoming book, was published in the Chicago-based magazine *Pageant*, along with a photographic portfolio by Daniel Kramer. Brief 'commentaries' – like 'i would like to do something worthwhile/ like perhaps plant some daisies on the desert/but i'm just a guitar player' – were printed alongside each photo and had in fact been created in a spare couple of hours in Woodstock at Kramer's request, though they could just as easily have been part of the book. The final prose-poem published by Dylan in the winter of 1965 was in the form of sleeve notes for his forthcoming album, *Bringing It All Back Home*. In fact this prose-poem was his most unorthodox to date – and was perhaps the closest he ever came to using Burroughs' cut-up technique in his writings. When talking about his forthcoming book to Paul Jay Robbins in early April, he suggested that cut-ups had some part to play in the way the book – now supposedly called *Off the Record* – would be constructed.

Bob Dylan: [The working title is] tentatively, *Bob Dylan off the Record*. But they tell me there's already books out with that 'off the record' title. The book can't really be titled, that's the kind of book it is. I'm also going to write the reviews for it . . . I've written some songs which are kind of far out, a long continuation of verses, stuff like that . . . I haven't really gotten into writing a completely free song. You dig something like cut-ups? . . . I wrote the book because there's a lot of stuff in there I can't possibly sing . . . Something that has no rhyme, all cut up, no nothing except something happening which is words. [1965]

It would appear that he was here describing a finished form for the book. The vast bulk of *Tarantula* was written in the last weeks of 1964 and the first few months of 1965. Dylan seemed to be working flat out on the book, despite not having found a title he was happy with. Staying with Baez in Carmel, as winter turned to spring he wrote and wrote. According to Baez he left a huge wad of drafts for the book at her house and never reclaimed them.

By the time he arrived in England at the end of April, he had nearly completed what would become *Tarantula*. He had also finally come up with a title, which he revealed to Michael Hellicar of the *Daily Sketch* before embarking on his English tour. The choice of *Tarantula* as the title has rarely been convincingly

explained. Like the name Dylan, only he knows the real reason for
the choice. However, there can be little doubt that he had by now
read a particular chapter from a classic of nineteenth-century
philosophy, entitled 'On Tarantulas':

> Behold, this is the hole of the tarantula. Do you want to see the
> tarantula itself? Here hangs its web; touch it, that it tremble! There it
> comes willingly; welcome tarantula! Your triangle and symbol sits black
> on your back; and I know also what sits in your soul. Revenge sits in
> your soul: whenever you bite, black scabs grow. Your poison makes the
> soul whirl with revenge . . . therefore I tear at your webs that your rage
> may lure you out of your lie-holes and your revenge may leap out from
> behind your word justice. For that man be delivered from revenge, that
> is for me the bridge to the highest hope, and a rainbow after long
> storms.

Thus spoke Nietzsche, via Zarathustra. Nietzsche would get a
name-check in the sleeve-notes to the *Highway 61 Revisited* album;
and though the style of *Thus Spoke Zarathustra* bears little similarity
to that of *Tarantula*, as a book of prose-poems portraying the
visions of a travelling seer it may well have provided some kind of
model. Another book of prose-poems, again with little stylistic
similarity, but the visions of a seer whose memory served him
well, was probably also inspirational – Rimbaud's *A Season in
Hell*.

Yet, whatever *Tarantula*'s antecedents – and there is clearly a
healthy dose of the beats there, in amongst its Symbolist overtones
– its symbolism is uniquely Dylan. So uniquely his that he soon
began to believe that his book of private jokes would be lost on his
fans and those literary critics who were waiting for an excuse to
denigrate the so-called bard of the airwaves. In his own words, he
realized that 'the folks back home just aren't going to understand
this at all'. He was right of course. Perhaps only *Finnegans Wake*
among works of modern literature is as sustainedly unreadable as
the prose sections of *Tarantula*.

His problem now was that everyone expected a book called
Tarantula. Journalists wanted him to talk about the book. Dylan
accordingly developed a potpourri of descriptions for it: vague,
obtuse, generic hints of some hidden theme. Thus 'it's about
spiders . . . It's an insect book . . . My next book is a collection of
epitaphs'; alternatively it was 'a book of confusion, tiny little
sayings. It's like a splash on the wall'; or more honestly, 'I can't
really say what it's about. It's not a narrative or anything like that.'

He began to doubt the worth of what he had written. He carried the galleys with him from show to show, from state to state, all the while reading it to friends and other strangers, seeking their honest opinions. In October 1965 he hinted to Allen Stone that he had very real doubts about the book's merits.

Bob Dylan: I have a lot of words written for it but I can't use anything I've written . . . before a year ago . . . I can't really use the ideas. They're so deformed and just not really right ideas. Stuff which has been expressed a million times in the past . . . I don't write now unless it just happens. [1965]

Later that fall when speaking to Nat Hentoff, he was even more upfront about his serious doubts concerning the book's merits. Though he delivers almost a parable to Hentoff about a novel he was working on 'one time', it seems self-evident he is really talking about *Tarantula*:

Bob Dylan: One time I wanted to write a novel; and so I was putting a lot of time in. It must have been about six months, off and on . . . and finally I just came to the conclusion . . . Is this gonna be THE novel, THE statement? Is this my message? My thing? And no matter how many pages – I had about five hundred pages of it – I said, 'No, of course not.' That's bullshit. This is nothing. If I finish this novel, it's not gonna come out until at least a year and a half to two years from now. It's gonna be a completely different thing by the time it does come out . . . Meantime, I'm not even gonna be there any more . . . It won't even be me that wrote that novel. And from then on I have to live up to that novel . . . People are gonna ask me what I'm doing . . . I'm gonna HAVE to say I'm writing another novel! [1965]

Yet, by the beginning of 1966, he had seemingly committed himself to the book's publication. In January 1966 he assured a bookseller, 'It will be out within two months . . . I've just got to go over it one more time, through the galleys.' Sure enough, the galleys joined him on the world tour. The publicity machine was geared up for a major fall 1966 campaign on its release. It was not to be. He had enough expectations he was unwilling to live up to without adding one more.

Tarantula was the culmination of Dylan's desire to step outside the confines of song. After 'Like a Rolling Stone', he realized he could fit everything he wanted to say into song, even if he had to redefine song in the process. His last prose-poems (save for his 1974 sleeve notes to *Planet Waves*) would be included on the rear sleeve of *Highway 61 Revisited* and in the programme for the

Newport Folk Festival of 1965. The events of that fateful weekend would lead him towards a new direction home. And there would be no spiders tempted to tarantella after him.

Bob Dylan: All my writing goes into the songs now. Other forms don't interest me anymore. [1966]

11

1965: I Accept Chaos

Bob Dylan: If you're talking about what [the] breakthrough [was] for me, I would have to say . . . 'Like a Rolling Stone' because I wrote that after I'd quit, I'd literally quit singing and playing, and I found myself writing this song, this story, this long piece of vomit about twenty pages long, and out of it I took 'Like a Rolling Stone' and made it as a single . . . After writing that, I wasn't interested in writing a novel, or a play. [1966]

Bob Dylan: Everything is changed now from before. Last spring, I guess I was going to quit singing. I was very drained. I was playing a lot of songs I didn't want to play. I was singing words I didn't really want to sing. But 'Like a Rolling Stone' changed it all. It was something that I myself could dig. It's very tiring having other people tell you how much they dig you if you yourself don't dig you. [1965]

As Dylan left London Airport the day after his session for the BBC, he found that not only had he just flown away from a storm of publicity but he was now flying back to one in America. He had been away just over a month, but in that time he had secured his first US Top Forty single with 'Subterranean Homesick Blues', and *Bringing It All Back Home* was making its way towards the Top Ten. Meanwhile another CBS act, the Byrds, were heading for the number one spot with their instantly memorable version of 'Mr Tambourine Man'.

His final days in London had been troubled ones. A week in bed had given him a lot of time to think. In that time it seems that he had made up his mind that he could go no further with his music and he should quit. He would later talk at length about this briefly maintained decision to journalists who interviewed him on his 1965–6 tour with the Hawks.

His decision to quit, however brief a time it lasted, was no frivolous whim. He had previously considered abandoning music back in the fall of 1963. With the chart information that was presumably being relayed from the States, he realized that the media mayhem he had just been subjected to in the UK could be duplicated on the other side of the pond. For most acts in pop music the process of impending fame happens so rapidly there is little time to perceive the phenomenon. The process in Dylan's case had taken three years, since 'Blowin' in the Wind' had been a huge hit for Peter, Paul and Mary. At the end of May he had the choice. He could commit himself to his boyhood dreams and become a rock & roll star, or he could walk away from it all. It would be unwise to underestimate how seriously he considered the latter option. He would later tell Nat Hentoff, 'People have one great blessing – obscurity.'

One of the reasons for his dilemma was simply artistic restlessness. In the fall of 1963 he had considered moving away from song into plays and poems. In the spring of 1965 he was hard at work on his first book. Such diversions were part of a thirst for something more than the acoustic music he was making. If *Bringing It All Back Home* found him back on terra firma, it also seemed to Dylan at the time to represent the limits of where he could see himself going. And his attempts to record with an authentic rhythm & blues band in England had been a disaster.

'Like a Rolling Stone' provided him with the new approach he was seeking. Though he had been impressed by the sound that the Beatles, the Animals and the Byrds had succeeded in getting, he wanted something that was more soulful, that truly brought it all back home – a rhythm & blues sound but with a folk sensibility. When 'Like a Rolling Stone' introduced it to the world it would be called folk-rock, though Dylan always justifiably hated that expression.

Bob Dylan: I was doing fine, you know, singing and playing my guitar. It was a sure thing . . . I was getting very bored with that. I couldn't go out and play like that. I was thinking of quitting. Out front it was a sure thing. I knew what the audience was going to do, how they would react. It was very automatic . . . What I'm doing now, it's a whole other thing. We're not playing rock music. It's not a hard sound. These people call it folk-rock – if they want to call it that, something that simple, it's good for selling the records. As far as it being what it is, I don't know what it is. I can't call it folk-rock. It's a whole way of doing things. [1965]

Though the birth of folk-rock has been attributed by some to the Byrds and their cover of 'Mr Tambourine Man', the sound was too twee and hid the meaning of the song. Dylan required a harder sound that lent meaning to the words. The song which he wrote on his return to America – indeed according to him it was started on the airplane home – had such a sound. Originally, 'Like a Rolling Stone' was an ill-formed mass of words whose purpose and direction were uncertain, a long screed directing all the anger inside him at some abstract point.

Bob Dylan: [When] it was ten pages long, it wasn't called anything, just a rhythm thing on paper all about my steady hatred directed at some point that was honest. [1966]

But he condensed it down and down and down until what was left was the essence, which formed perhaps his most memorable song. Writing 'Like a Rolling Stone' removed all desire to experiment with his 'other' writings, which had distracted him throughout the last two years of his so-called 'folk' period. It was the death knell for *Tarantula*, though he would not yet admit it.

All the evidence suggests that the vast bulk of the published *Tarantula* was finished by this point, though small tinkerings and a few additions would occupy a further twelve months of indecision. But it documented a period of uncertainty for Dylan. If there seems little connection between 'aretha/crystal jukebox queen of hymn and him diffused in drunk transfusion' and 'Once upon a time you dressed so fine', it is surely feasible to envisage 'Like a Rolling Stone' emerging out of ten pages of such 'vomitific' prose.

Of course by writing 'Like a Rolling Stone', he did not 'invent' or even produce the synthesis labelled folk-rock. The nature of recorded song required that he perform it in order to complete it. At times in his career he has shown an almost deliberate lack of discipline when approaching this final process in the production of his works. His desire for spontaneity and improvisation has not always been fruitful. In June 1965 he needed to consider *how* he wanted to record 'Like a Rolling Stone'.

As with the songs on *Bringing It All Back Home*, the first step in his equation was the guitar sound. Then it had been Bruce Langhorne who had provided the solution. This time he remembered Michael Bloomfield, the great white blues guitarist he had jammed with in Chicago back in April 1963. He had run into Bloomfield again at an after-gig party when he was playing Chicago's Orchestra Hall in December 1963. Though they talked, he had his mind on other matters:

Michael Bloomfield: He was trying to get pussy and, believe me, he got a lot of pussy, [but] we hung out at that party and we talked.

However, it was probably reports coming from Chicago in the winter of 1965 that Bloomfield was whipping up a storm in a foot-to-the-floor howl of rhythm & blues called the Paul Butterfield Blues Band that reminded Dylan to renew contact. After all, Butterfield's Blues Band was as close to England's Bluesbreakers as America could provide in 1965, though Dylan was looking for something more soulful. So Bloomfield was summoned to Woodstock in the second week in June.

Michael Bloomfield: I didn't even have a guitar case. I just had my Telecaster. And Bob picked me up at the bus station and took me to this house where he lived . . . and Sara was there . . . and she made very strange food, tuna fish salad with peanuts in it, toasted, and he taught me these songs, 'Like a Rolling Stone', and all those songs from that album and he said, 'I don't want you to play any of that B. B. King shit, none of that fucking blues, I want you to play something else,' so we fooled around and finally played something he liked, it was very weird, he was playing in weird keys which he always does, all on the black keys of the piano . . . We fucked around there for a few days and then we went to New York to cut the record and I started seeing that this guy Dylan was really a famous guy.

The session at CBS Studios in New York on 15 June 1965 is one which has now passed into pop lore. The main source of the lore is Al Kooper's version of events in his autobiography, *Backstage Passes*. Kooper had secured an invitation to the session from Tom Wilson, the producer, harbouring hopes of convincing Dylan to let him play guitar. When Dylan arrived he was accompanied by Bloomfield, who, Kooper soon realized, was out of Kooper's own league as a guitar player. When Dylan started recording his new song, though, he decided he wanted both piano and organ and Kooper volunteered his services at the organ. As Kooper tells it, he felt his 'way through the changes like a little kid fumbling in the dark for a light switch'. Dylan, though, liked the sound and halfway through the playback asked Wilson to turn the organ up. Thus was born that unique mixture of organ and guitar which identified Dylan's 1965–6 sound.

The fluke which resulted in Kooper's unique style of organ-playing making its mark on 'Like a Rolling Stone' was, according to most witnesses, one of many accidents occurring at these sessions, not all of them so serendipitous. The first two sessions for what would become the *Highway 61 Revisited* album took up 15 and 16 June. According to Kooper, versions of 'Tombstone Blues' and 'Queen Jane Approximately' were attempted on the 16th. If so, they ended up unused. Certainly no further songs seem to have resulted from the 15th, and the two released songs that seem most likely to date from the 16th — 'Jet Pilot' and the original version of 'From a Buick Six' (which remains to this day the take available on the Japanese version of *Highway 61 Revisited*) — sound like half-formed ideas looking for a sound. Dylan certainly spent much of these sessions improvising, as evidenced by these two songs, as if the process of reproducing the sound of 'Like a Rolling Stone' was temporarily eluding him. According to Bloomfield a large part of the problem was the producer.

Michael Bloomfield: They had a great bass player named Russ Savakus, a terrific guy. It was his first date playing electric bass. He was scared about that. And they had the best studio drummer. But no one understood nothing. The producer was a non-producer . . . I think it was a black guy named Tom Wilson. He didn't know what was happening man! . . . We did twenty alternate takes of every song, and it got ridiculous because they were long songs . . . It was never like: Here's one of the tunes, we're gonna learn it, work out the arrangement, that just wasn't done. The thing just sort of fell together in this haphazard, half-assed way . . . It was just like a jam session, it really was.

Though Savakus played on the June sessions, he would be replaced after the first of the post-Newport sessions, when his nerves got the better of him and he 'freaked out a bit' during a take of 'Tombstone Blues'. Kooper assured Dylan that he knew a suitable replacement, and secured the gig for his friend Harvey Brooks. Dylan clearly loved Brooks's bass playing as he would ask him to play in his first live band, while Bloomfield would later recruit him for Electric Flag. However, if Kooper and Brooks were relative rookies, Dylan also utilized Bobby Gregg and Paul Griffin at the sessions; both had contributed so much on *Bringing It All Back Home*, and Bloomfield was at the peak of his playing powers. When he returned to the studio after Newport all these musicians would be recalled. Tom Wilson, though, would not be.

Why Wilson was replaced still remains something of a mystery. Despite the assessments of Bloomfield and of Paul Rothschild, who sat in on several of Dylan's acoustic sessions and considered that Wilson was wont to try to move sessions along at the expense of good takes, the results that Wilson produced testify to some empathy with Dylan.

Wilson himself would have been the first to admit that he had never previously recorded folk music and was ill suited to produce acoustic artists. However, once Dylan made the move to electric sounds, Wilson was in his element. It was he who chose most of the band who recorded *Bringing It All Back Home* and, as is well known, had the idea of utilizing the same musicians to overdub some electric accompaniment for an acoustic duo called Simon and Garfunkel. He would also go on the following year to produce the first Mothers of Invention album and the bulk of the first two Velvet Underground albums, all for MGM, three of the most important and innovative albums of the sixties. Al Kooper certainly did not share Bloomfield and Rothschild's assessment.

Al Kooper: I don't think it was a good idea [replacing Wilson] because I think Tom Wilson was more 'something' than Bob Johnston . . . more soulful. Plus he was a real experimenter.

Dylan and Wilson had seemed to be on rather good terms when they departed arm in arm from the May London session, a session which seemed to suggest the esteem which Dylan held Wilson in as he flew over to London to produce it. When specifically asked by Jann Wenner in 1969, Dylan avoided saying why Wilson was replaced after producing the masterful 'Like a Rolling Stone'. Wilson also remained oblique about the reason/s for his removal, though he did make it clear in a later interview with Chris Charlesworth of *Melody Maker* that he and Dylan had had a major disagreement, and Dylan had said to him, 'Maybe we should try Phil Spector.' Of course, Spector's obsession with perfection via endless takes was completely anathema to Dylan's own way of working.

If Wilson was replaced because Dylan was unhappy with his work, Bob Johnston, who produced the subsequent sessions for the album, was hardly an inspired choice.

Al Kooper: Bob Johnston I would say is the kinda guy that just pats you on the back and says you're fantastic and just keeps you going.

As Johnston would later comment, his 'attitude was if Dylan wanted to record under a palm tree in Hawaii with a ukulele, I'd be there with a tape machine.' Hardly an inspired, creative partnership! While Dylan's instinctive genius was working overtime, Johnston's lack of creative input was not a major issue. As Bloomfield later observed, it was really Dylan who was responsible for selecting the mix on *Highway 61 Revisited* and 'it was astutely mixed . . . He knew he had a sound in mind.'

Before he could start work in earnest on *Highway 61 Revisited* Dylan had some songs to write. If he had written several songs in the interim between completing *Bringing It All Back Home* and writing 'Like a Rolling Stone' – in an interview with Max Jones in March he said he had 'about four or five songs' ready for the next album – his new approach probably resulted in them remaining unused. New songs that suited his new sound were required. Thus began a month of intense writing in Woodstock, where he had just bought a house of his own near Grossman's in Byrdcliffe. It seems that his relationship with Sara had been intensifying in the last couple of months, and this may have been a motive for purchasing his own property. Before resuming work on his third album in a year, he had a major commitment to undertake.

He was due to appear at the Newport Folk Festival the weekend of 24 and 25 July. Dylan's set at the 1965 Newport Festival may well be the most written-about performance in the history of rock & roll. Even at the time it was recognized as the point when Dylan went one way and the purists in the folk field went another. There are as many opinions about the events of that weekend as there were witnesses. Most of the major protagonists have axes to grind, particularly in hindsight, having seen that Dylan was right to go his own way, and generally feel obliged to defend their initial resistance to change.

Dylan himself, talking about those events twenty years on, remarked, 'I had a hit record out so I don't know how people expected me to do anything different.' It is important to recall that not only had he already released *Bringing It All Back Home* with its electric side, but he had had a hit single with 'Subterranean Homesick Blues', which – utilizing as it did Chuck Berry's 'Too Much Monkey Business' riff – should have convinced anybody with two ears that Dylan had been a latent rocker all along. More importantly, 'Like a Rolling Stone' was issued the week before Newport – a mere month after it was recorded – as Dylan and his label attempted to capitalize upon the new interest in his work. Within four days of its release the single was in the charts and on the radio, just in time to remind the 15,000 fans who made it to Freebody Park of the direction he was heading in. It is thus pertinent to recall the level of expectation that July weekend.

Joe Boyd: There was a tremendous anticipation at Newport about Dylan – 'Is he here yet? Has he arrived?' – and instead of this blue-jeaned, work-shirted guy who'd arrived in 1964 to be the Pied Piper, he arrived rather secretively; he was staying in a luxurious hotel just on the outside of town and he arrived with Bob Neuwirth and Al Kooper – that was the entourage, Neuwirth, Kooper and Dylan. And they were all wearing puff-sleeved duelling shirts – one of them was polka dot – and they were not wearing blue jeans . . . They wore sunglasses. The whole image was very, very different. They were very clannish, very secretive.

What Dylan's intentions were on arriving at Newport has never been adequately resolved. He surely had no intention of performing a wholly acoustic set after his thoughts on retirement two months earlier. Yet nobody there seemed aware of any arrangement regarding a backing band, and on the Saturday afternoon he was scheduled to appear at a songwriters' workshop, akin to the topical song workshop the previous year where he had premiered 'Mr Tambourine Man'. He would certainly have to play acoustic on this occasion. The workshop, which was on one of the side-stages set up for such events, was in fact absolute bedlam and Dylan's set had to be abbreviated because of the chaos his presence was causing. The tension was mounting and inevitably the resultant fury was directed at Dylan and his high-and-mighty manager Albert Grossman.

Joe Boyd: The crowd around the Songwriters' Workshop was so immense that it was swamping the other workshops. People were complaining: 'Turn up the Dylan one because we're getting bleed from the Banjo one on the other side!' This was very much against the spirit of what the Festival was supposed to be about . . . Grossman became a focus of hostility for a lot of [the officials]. He'd never been popular amongst these people. He'd always been seen as one of the money changers at the gate of the temple and not a priest, y'know. And Grossman was arrogant, particularly with Dylan now being so big. Grossman was being very cool, but Grossman's way of being cool got up people's noses.

The tide of resentment did not spill over until later that afternoon, during another workshop. It is often forgotten that the Newport Folk Festival was intended to be – and was billed as – a folk and blues festival. Anyone watching *Festival*, the Howard Alk documentary film, can gain an idea of the mixture of folk and blues that really made up the Newport festivals. There was to be a blues workshop that afternoon but it was not just folk that was getting an electric shock that weekend. Scheduled to play at the blues workshop were Paul Butterfield's Blues Band, with Bloomfield on lead guitar, and they had added two words in front – 'rhythm and'. The band's appearance on the bill had already been a source of some contention when respected musicologist Alan Lomax stepped up to introduce them.

Joe Boyd: There had been a lot of pressure from Peter Yarrow on adding the Paul Butterfield Band to the line-up of the Festival – he really put a lot of pressure on the other members of the board to get the invitation, and Lomax was really against it. Against Butterfield. Against white boys doing the blues really ... Lomax was forced to introduce the Butterfield Band at the Blues Workshop, and he gave them an introduction which was very condescending ... As the group started to take the stage Lomax came off stage to be confronted by Grossman who, basically, said unkind words about the introduction that Lomax had just given ... Next thing you know is these two men, both rather over-sized, were rolling around in the dirt throwing punches. They had to be pulled apart. Lomax then called an emergency meeting of the board of the Festival that night ... the board actually voted in favour of banning Grossman from the grounds of the Festival. George Wein, who was a non-voting advisor to the board, had to step in and say, 'Look, I don't have a vote, it's up to you, but I can tell you right now that if you do bar Grossman you have to prepare yourselves for the walk-out of Bob Dylan, Peter, Paul and Mary, and Buffy St Marie!' ... So the board reconsidered and dropped the action against Grossman, but there was obviously a tremendous simmering of feeling.

An important point to consider here is that acts who appeared at Newport were not paid anything more than nominal fees, certainly not the sort of fees people like Dylan, Peter, Paul and Mary and Baez now commanded. They appeared for the exposure and for the sense of community. The threat of a walk-out by Grossman's acts was no exaggeration; it was a likelihood.

At this point the chronicling becomes a little unclear. The primary issue is whether Dylan arrived at Newport with any specific intention of playing with a band, particularly the Paul Butterfield Blues Band. According to Al Kooper, he did not meet up with Dylan until he arrived and Grossman informed him that Dylan had been looking for him. According to Eric Von Schmidt, Dylan 'heard Butterfield in the blues workshop a couple of days earlier [sic] and realized they were a great blues band, and he said, "Wanna do 'Maggie's Farm'?"'

In fact this reliance on serendipity sounds a shade unconvincing, not to say implausible. First of all it assumes that Dylan was unaware of the Paul Butterfield Blues Band up to this point. This does not seem likely. Paul Rothschild, a good friend of both Dylan's and Neuwirth's who regularly attended Dylan studio sessions, had 'discovered' the Butterfield band early in January 1965 and signed them to his label, Elektra. He had also suggested the recruitment of Mike Bloomfield to the band. Bloomfield was then playing in another blues outfit on the same Chicago scene. The band was brought to New York, where they made several attempts to record a debut album. In the meantime, Rothschild had phoned up Grossman and asked him if he would be interested in managing the band. Grossman, a Chicago native, came and saw them play at the Café A Go-Go and apparently told Rothschild, 'I'll see them at Newport.'

Meanwhile, Dylan had recruited Bloomfield for his studio sessions that June, at least partly because of what he had heard about his playing with Butterfield, and on completing the 'Like a Rolling Stone' single had invited Rothschild over to his apartment in New York to play him the results. This all suggests an awareness of each other's activities which makes it unlikely that Dylan had not already considered using the Butterfield Blues Band for his brief appearance at the Festival. The fact that, on meeting Kooper at Newport, he told him he had been phoning him trying to get hold of him, clearly suggests that he wanted Kooper to play with him at Newport *before* the event. Indeed, Joe Boyd recalls that, 'We had known that Dylan was going to do something with more than just himself.'

Whatever the truth, Grossman apparently told the Butterfield band that Saturday that he wanted to manage them; and Bloomfield, possibly as a result of that decision, told Dylan that he could not go on the road with him. Clearly at this stage Dylan wanted Bloomfield and Kooper to tour with him as integral elements in his new sound (even though he did not tour with Dylan, Kooper was later called up for the *Blonde on Blonde* sessions).

Dylan, along with Bloomfield, Sam Lay and Jerome Arnold – all from Butterfield's band – plus Al Kooper and, at Bloomfield's suggestion, Barry Goldberg, rehearsed through the night at a big house near the Festival site for what threatened to be a stormy Sunday, in all senses of the word.

According to Nick Gravenites, a friend of Bloomfield, this ensemble was selected only after several auditions. If Gravenites' memory is reliable, which is open to doubt, the 'auditions' must have involved very few musicians, as Dylan's options were extremely limited. According to Kooper, 'We rehearsed until dawn.' According to Bloomfield, the rehearsals did not go that well, with Arnold constantly throwing the rest of the musicians out.

Michael Bloomfield: We were all at Newport, Kooper, me, Barry [Goldberg], and this schwartze Jerome from the Butterfield Band playing

bass, . . . and he's fucking up everything, and we're practising there in a
room and Odetta's staring at us and Mary Travers is there and we're
playing and it's sounding horrible and finally it's time for the gig and
Barry and me are throwing up in these outhouses.

They worked up only three songs, two of which were fairly
standard blues tunes – 'Maggie's Farm' and the equally up-tempo
'Phantom Engineer' (which later evolved into 'It Takes a Lot to
Laugh, It Takes a Train to Cry') – but Dylan was happy enough
by dawn to proceed with the unveiling. Both recent biographers,
Robert Shelton and Bob Spitz, have claimed that there was no
soundcheck for Dylan and the band. Spitz does this despite including a photo from the soundcheck in his biography. There is no
question that they did soundcheck. Indeed, filmed footage from
the soundcheck that afternoon is included in Alk's Festival documentary, and Joe Boyd, perhaps the most reliable of the eye-
witnesses to events both backstage and onstage that weekend,
recalls the soundcheck in considerable detail.

Joe Boyd: By the time the concert had finished that [Sunday] afternoon,
and before the start of the Butterfield set that evening, we had two hours
. . . so the whole area was cleared and we got to do our soundchecks.
Now we had known that Dylan was going to do something, with more
than just himself, and that he was going to need a soundcheck . . . We
had taken the precaution of doing soundchecks on almost all the other
performers for Sunday night earlier that morning . . . We hadn't heard
Dylan, but we had kept this time clear . . . Anyway, so on came Dylan with
the Butterfield Band and Al Kooper on keyboards. We set up the stage the
way they wanted it set up. It was set up anyway for Butterfield in the first set.
They started playing. Obviously this was great. We all knew that this was
significant . . . I said, 'How many songs are you going to do?' And they –
Butterfield, Bloomfield and Dylan – looked at each other and said, 'Well,
we only know three, so that's what we're going to do.'

The soundcheck provided the organizers with their first intimation of what Dylan had in mind for Sunday evening, and it was
evidently a cause for concern.

Pete Seeger: It wasn't a real soundcheck. They were tinkering around
with it and all they knew was, 'Turn the sound up! Turn the sound up!'
They wanted to get volume.

Throughout the remainder of the afternoon and early evening,
Dylan stayed backstage. During the first half of the evening
concert the Paul Butterfield Blues Band played their own set.

Then, after a short break, the penultimate act in the first half was Dylan. When he came on stage he was dressed all in black.

Liam Clancy: I was actually filming at the Newport Festival that year. I was up a twelve-foot platform, filming with a telephoto lens, so I could zoom in close. And Dylan came out, and it was obvious that he was stoned, bobbing around the stage, very Chaplinesque actually.

There have been a lot of accounts of the twenty-five minutes that Dylan was on stage that evening. According to the account in Spitz's biography, Pete Seeger was attempting to wrest the mixing board from Paul Rothschild throughout Dylan's set. There have also been several suggestions that the sound was bad and that fans were shouting because Dylan was inaudible. The mix on the soundboard tape certainly does not lend credence to this theory. Of all the accounts of the Festival by those intimately involved with the organization of the event, Joe Boyd's account – from an interview conducted for the *Telegraph* – rings truest.

Joe Boyd: Dylan wasn't on, even, at the end of the concert, he was on in the middle. He was on one act before the interval, at around 9.15. So out comes Dylan and I'm out there on stage before he comes out, setting up all the amps to exactly the right levels, and Rothschild's got everything cranked up, and when that first note of 'Maggie's Farm' hit, I mean, by today's standards it wasn't very loud, but by those standards of the day it was the loudest thing anybody had ever heard. The volume. That was the thing, the volume. It wasn't just the music, it wasn't just the fact that he came out and played with an electric band . . . Care was taken to get Paul Rothschild to mix the sound. Because you had Paul Rothschild on the sound, you didn't have some square sound guy fumbling with the dials and having the thing creep up to where it should have been. You would have had just badly mixed rock & roll. It wasn't. It was powerfully, ballsy-mixed, expertly done rock & roll . . . As soon as I had gotten the stage set, I ran around to the press enclosure which was the front section, press and friends and people, and stood sort of at the door of the gates, and watched at the side of the stage, and I thought, 'This is great!' I was lapping it all up. Somebody pulled at my elbow and said, 'You'd better go backstage, they want to talk to you.' So I went backstage and there I was confronted by Seeger and Lomax and, I think, Theodore Bikel or somebody, saying, 'It's too loud! You've got to turn it down! It's far too loud! We can't have it like this. It's just unbearably loud!' And they were really upset. Very, very upset. I said, 'Well, I don't control the sound, the sound is out there in the middle of the audience.' And so Lomax said, 'How do you get there? Tell me how to get there, I'll go out there.' I said, 'Well, Alan, you walk right to the back – it's only about half a mile

– and then you walk around to the centre thing, show your badge, and just come down the centre aisle.' And he said, 'There must be a quicker way.' So I said, 'Well, you can climb over the fence.' I was looking at his girth, you know! And he said, 'Now look, you go out there. You can get there, I know you know how to get there. Go out there and tell them that the board orders them to turn the sound down.' I said okay. So I went out – there was a place where anyone could climb on top of a box and get over the fence from backstage. By this time I think it was the beginning of the second number, and there was Grossman and Neuwirth and Yarrow and Rothschild all sitting at the sound desk, grinning, very very pleased with themselves, and meanwhile the audience was going nuts ... There were arguments between people sitting next to each other! Some people were booing, some people were cheering ... I relayed Lomax's message and Peter Yarrow said, 'Tell Alan Lomax,' and extended his middle finger; and I said, 'C'mon Peter, gimme a break!' He said, 'Well, just tell Alan that the board of the festival are adequately represented on the sound console and that we have things fully under control and we think that the sound is at the correct level.' So I went back, climbed over the fence, and by this time all I could see of Pete Seeger was the back of Pete Seeger disappearing down the road past the car park ... I was confronted by Lomax and Bikel again, frothing at the mouth, and I relayed Yarrow's message and they just cursed and gnashed their teeth. By this time the thing was almost over.

Seeger himself admits that he was furious with Dylan, but only because he considered the sound so distorted that nobody could understand the words. Unlike Lomax, he saw nothing fundamentally heretical about playing with electric instruments: 'It's all how you use it.' However, this does not explain why he got so worked up that, in his own words, 'I was ready to chop the microphone cord.' Clearly the raucousness of the performance also upset him.

Al Kooper, up on stage, knew better than anybody else that there were problems with the sound, but it was not related to the mix or volume but to the band's own lack of confidence about what they were doing.

Al Kooper: What happened was in 'Maggie's Farm' the beat got turned around so instead of playing on two and four, [the drummer, Sam Lay,] was playing on one and three. That's an accident that can happen and it happened so it was sort of a disaster ... I got lost myself.

Yet Kooper was unaware of the pandemonium that the performance was generating until they finished the three songs, at which point he finally heard the boos.

Al Kooper: They were definitely booing, but they were booing . . . 'cause he only played three songs . . . These people paid a lot of money . . . And I don't think anybody cared who else was on the show. They came to see Dylan and then he played three songs, when someone like Son House played for forty-five minutes . . . 'Like a Rolling Stone' was number one or very close to it at the time of Newport. So what did they expect to hear – 'Who Killed Davey Moore'? . . . But at the festival there definitely was a dispute about electric people playing so I think they got meshed together in the booing legend.

Kooper's belief that the majority of fans were booing at the brevity of the set – though certainly there must have been some very upset people who began booing only when they realized that that was it – does not explain the reaction during the set itself.

There are accounts which have Dylan leaving the stage tearful and being cajoled into returning with acoustic guitar in hand. The reaction from the audience had certainly been mixed, but as Kooper himself observes a large part of the 1965 audience was composed of 'new' Dylan fans who had been only dimly aware of him up to *Bringing It All Back Home*. They must have wondered what the fuss was all about! Dylan had rehearsed only three songs with the band, but the fans were shouting for more. Eventually Yarrow came out and told them he would be coming back – he was just getting an acoustic guitar. In fact, he must have been composing himself. The reaction had been more vehement than perhaps even he expected.

Bob Dylan: I did this very crazy thing. I didn't know what was going to happen, but they certainly booed, I'll tell you that. You could hear it all over the place. [1965]

According to Bloomfield 'he looked real shook up', but, ever the crowd-pleaser, he obliged with two songs solo. However, the two songs were both from his first electric album, and 'Mr Tambourine Man' and 'It's All Over Now, Baby Blue' could hardly be considered in the topical song genre. After the intermission Seeger and Lomax got their wish and had a set composed of all the things they held dear, but the drama of what had happened could not help but cast a shadow over the remaining proceedings.

Joe Boyd: After the interval for some reason the scheduling misfired and every washed-up, boring, old, folky, left-wing fart you could imagine in a row, leading up to Peter, Paul and Mary in the final thing – Ronnie

Gilbert, Oscar Brand, Josh White, who was very much beyond his powers at that point, Theodore Bikel – they all went on, one after another. It was like an object lesson in what was going on here. Like, you guys are all washed-up. This is all finished. There's something else now that we're dealing with ... You knew, as it was happening, that paths were parting.

Meanwhile, there was the traditional after-Newport party for the organizers, the performers and their guests to attend. Maria Muldaur in *Baby Let Me Follow You Down* implies that Dylan was still badly shaken by the events, perhaps racked with worry about the consequences of what he had done.

Maria Muldaur: Dylan was off in a corner buried, and Farina told me to go over and ask Dylan to dance ... So I went over to him and said, 'Do you want to dance?' and he looked up at me and said, 'I would, but my hands are on fire.'

Bloomfield suggests that the after-effects of Newport wore off rather quickly and that Dylan was soon indulging in his old games:

Michael Bloomfield: When I saw him afterward, he looked real shook up and I didn't know the nature of what made him all shook up but the next night he was at this party and he's sitting next to this girl and her husband and he's got his hand right up her pussy, right next to her husband, and she's letting him do this and her husband's going crazy, so Dylan seemed quite untouched by it the next day.

If this was indeed the following day or days, then Dylan had had enough time to assimilate the press reaction and speak to friends about their responses and those of others around them. Clearly what he heard steeled him for the next stage in his transformation into the 'King of Folk-Rock'.

Bob Dylan: There were a lot of people there who were very pleased that I got booed. I saw them afterward. I do resent somewhat, though, that everybody that booed said they did it because they were old fans. [1966]

He was back in the studio within four days of Newport, and in the interim he had written his own personal message to those who had been so vitriolic in their response, those who 'said they did it because they were old fans'. The song was called 'Positively Fourth Street'. It would make 'Like a Rolling Stone' sound like 'I Wanna Hold Your Hand', and it would be his third hit single of

1965 when issued the first week in September, following 'Like a Rolling Stone' into the Top Ten.

One of the other songs from this first July session illustrates the success of Dylan's approach to recording in 1965. Having performed a new song at Newport, the blasting blues 'Phantom Engineer', he recorded a version for his new album. However, after laying down a satisfactory take, while the group took a lunch break, he reworked the tune alone at the piano and came back with a somewhat slower, more soulful approach to the song. The final result was the beautiful album cut of 'It Takes a Lot to Laugh, It Takes a Train to Cry'.

The remaining sessions seemed to progress smoothly enough. Dylan worked on songs but was careful not to work them into the ground. For the final session Johnston had suggested flying Charlie McCoy, a respected Nashville musician, to New York to accompany Dylan recording an eleven-minute Kafkaesque parade of freaks entitled 'Desolation Row'. The song had been attempted with bass and electric guitar accompaniment (provided by Kooper and Brooks), but Dylan was unhappy with the results and held over attempting a further take until McCoy's arrival, when it was recorded with just two acoustic guitars.

Charlie McCoy: They called me up to New York City to play on Dylan's album . . . They just told me to go out and pick up a guitar and play what I felt like playing. I finished and I went in and asked Dylan if it suited him. And he said yeah, that's fine . . . We just did one song. The only one I played on was eleven minutes long . . . We just did two takes and . . . [I] left.

Of course, Dylan's approach was prone to the occasional disaster, but the spontaneity of the situation seemed adequate compensation for those times when nothing came out right. Thus at least a couple of the sessions produced only minimal results (unlike *Bringing It All Back Home*, when an entire album was recorded in three sessions); and Bob Johnston was hardly an improvement on Tom Wilson, who at least was hip to how rock & roll should sound.

Michael Bloomfield: There were chord charts for these songs but no one had any idea what the music was supposed to sound like . . . It all sort of went around Dylan. I mean he didn't direct the music, he just sang the songs and played piano and guitar and it just sort of went on around him . . . But the sound was a matter of pure chance . . . the producer did not tell people what to play or have a sound in mind, nor did Bob . . . I was there man, I'm telling you it was a result of chuckle-fucking, of people stepping on each other's dicks until it came out right.

Dylan clearly loved just grooving with the band and trying out ideas on the spur of the moment. At the 29 July session, he tried to work up another of his largely improvised blues called 'Sitting on a Barbed Wire Fence'. The two known takes illustrate the way Dylan would rework songs from take to take. The second features some nice vamped organ and bluesy guitar flourishes, indicative of the indefinable chemistry the band was finding. The first was loose and more honky-tonk, with piano and harmonica at the heart of the performance.

However, the notion that everything that happened was purely spontaneous and entirely relied upon serendipity is nonsense. After the first two July sessions, there was a weekend break, sessions resuming on Monday morning. Dylan, Al Kooper, Tony Glover and a lady friend all drove to Woodstock, where Dylan spent most of Saturday writing out chord charts with Kooper. It would be a role Kooper would also adopt for the *Blonde on Blonde* sessions.

The album took five July/August sessions to complete – along with the two June sessions, a week of recording. But taking seven days to produce an album of this quality could hardly be considered to be wrenching the music out of Dylan note by note.

Highway 61 Revisited reinvented rock & roll in a way perhaps only half a dozen albums have done in the forty-year history of the art. Next to *Highway 61 Revisited*, side one of *Bringing It All Back Home* sounds like no more than a demo. No one had ever written lyrics for a rock & roll album like these. But there was no mistaking this was a rock & roll album, from that snare drum kicking everyone in on 'Like a Rolling Stone', or the exuberant guitar playing on 'Highway 61 Revisited', to the stately sound of 'Ballad of a Thin Man' or the expressiveness of Dylan's singing on 'Just Like Tom Thumb's Blues'. Clearly he was tapping the same roots as the first Rolling Stones album or Mayall's Bluesbreakers with Eric Clapton or even the debut album by Bloomfield's new band, the Paul Butterfield Blues Band.

If Bloomfield was committing himself to playing with Butterfield, Dylan was going to have to find a new guitarist if he was going to do justice to these songs live with a band. His chances of finding an adequate replacement seemed slim.

12

1965–6: Just Like a Freeze-Out

Allen Ginsberg: Dylan has sold out to God. That is to say, his command was to spread his beauty as wide as possible. It was an artistic challenge to see if great art can be done on a juke box. And he proved it can. [1966]

Whatever really happened at the Newport Folk Festival, it was immediately written up as Dylan playing his new brand of folk-rock and the folkies roundly booing him for his arrogance. The controversy only heightened media interest in Dylan, who was rapidly turning into the pop music phenomenon of 1965. He was also providing a welcome American antidote to the British invasion.

Having completed his follow-up to *Bringing It All Back Home*, though, he needed to take his new sound out on the road, which meant that he had to form a touring band. The two main ingredients he needed had been provided in the studio by Al Kooper and Michael Bloomfield. Kooper was willing to play a couple of prestigious shows lined up for the end of August, and Harvey Brooks, who had been so outstanding on the album sessions, was prepared to take bass duties, but Dylan needed a replacement for Bloomfield.

It seems remarkable now to consider that not only did Dylan record two albums long recognized as classics and two equally notable non-album singles in 1965, but that he used three different but equally talented guitarists in his 1965 studio activities. Langhorne and Bloomfield, though, did not face the ultimate test of playing live night after night with the man. Robbie Robertson would.

Dylan actually required both a drummer and a guitarist to complete his band. Bobby Gregg, his first choice as a drummer, was too busy with his session work. So the drummer in Robertson's band, the Hawks, Levon Helm, was recruited as well. Robertson and Helm had been playing in the Hawks for five years, mainly in their own home patch around Toronto. The band was known as the Hawks after the man they regularly provided support for, the imposing rock & rollin' hulk of Ronnie Hawkins. Recently, though, Helm, Robertson and organist Garth Hudson had been providing backing on sessions for an album by John Hammond Junior entitled *So Many Roads* and were gigging around New York and New Jersey. As with Butterfield, it was Robertson and Helm's work on an album with an old friend of Dylan's that provided the initial contact.

Robbie Robertson: He'd heard of us somehow, maybe through Ian & Sylvia, maybe through John Hammond [Junior], I'm not really sure . . . we were lolling in the sand when he phoned us and said, 'You wanna play Hollywood Bowl?' So we asked him who else was gonna be on the show. 'Just us,' he said.

In fact the first of two major gigs, one on the East Coast, one on the West, was not the Hollywood Bowl, which was scheduled for 3 September. It was 28 August, when Dylan was due to play the fifteen thousand capacity Forest Hills Stadium in New York, and this time he intended to be prepared. His new four-piece ensemble rehearsed with him at Carroll's Rehearsal Hall for two weeks, working up a forty-five-minute electric set (and two encores).

The day of the Forest Hills show the sky was overcast and black and the wind was cold and rainy, whipping through the open-air stadium, as Dylan ran through the band set one more time during an afternoon soundcheck. Yet when it came time to go onstage that evening fans were delighted to see he was alone, armed with just a harmonica and a guitar. For forty-five minutes he mystified his 'new' fans and delighted his folk-loving audience with a version of the 'old' Dylan. In fact it was no such thing. Only 'To Ramona' was drawn from his pre-1965 albums, and for ten minutes he weaved a spell with a new, and on first hearing incomprehensible, song called 'Desolation Row'. The incongruous images brought titters and occasional laughs from the audience, but aside from such moments the mood was deadly serious among the freezing fans.

Al Kooper: [Of course] anybody else 'cept Bob Dylan would have said, 'Well, I'm gonna take a break and then we're gonna come out and play a few electric songs.'

After a short intermission, Dylan was set to return and it

occurred to the more perceptive members of the audience that he probably had a reason for all those imposing speakers and amps enfolding the stage. The second set was going to be a little noisier than the first. Dylan and the band were fully rehearsed and suspected a rocky ride in store.

Al Kooper: He knew something was gonna happen because he gave us like a pep-talk before the show. He said, 'Now there's gonna be some kinda circus out there. Just ignore whatever happens and play the show.' He knew something was gonna happen.

In a pre-concert telephone interview with Robert Shelton to provide quotes for a write-up in the *New York Times*, Dylan had told him that if his so-called fans 'can't understand green clocks, wet chairs, purple lamps or hostile statues, they're missing something'. There were a lot of uncomprehending individuals out there that night. This time there was no mistaking the reaction. If 'catastrophe and confusion are the basis of my songs', they were also the basis of his concerts throughout the momentous ten months of touring inaugurated by Forest Hills.

Al Kooper: They booed at Forest Hills because they'd read that they were supposed to . . . They booed us when we came out and they never really stopped booing us.

Dylan did not make it easy on his audience by playing the light, skiffling form of electric music found on the first side of *Bringing It All Back Home*. The sound that the band was making that night was intense and immense, rich and rhythmic. Meanwhile he dismissed talk of rock & roll and folk rot, yet refused to define what it was he and the band were playing.

Bob Dylan: It's easy for people to classify it as rock & roll, to put it down. Rock & roll is a straight twelve-bar blues progression. My new songs aren't. I used to play rock & roll a long time ago, before I even started playing old-fashioned folk. [1965]

The forty-five minute electric set at Forest Hills was also largely composed of new songs, songs which would seem initially oblique even in ideal listening conditions with a modern PA. On a chilly night, with a furious wind roaring around the stadium, and a primitive PA system, opening a set with 'The sweet pretty things are in bed now of course . . .' was not conducive to enlightenment. Of the new songs, 'Ballad of a Thin Man' was the only one remotely intelligible that night, and that was performed by Dylan at the piano. A story which has gained much currency has Dylan instructing the band to play the introduction to this song over and over again until the crowd quietened down. In fact, there is no evidence of this on the audience tape of the show, though his desire for a little quiet would be understandable when playing a piano to fifteen thousand fans in an open-air stadium. He may indeed have wanted the so-called fans to hear the immortal refrain: 'Something is happening and you don't know what it is.'

Though the ever-optimistic Dylan had worked up two possible encores with the band, the virulence of the response was enough for him to abandon the stage after 'Like a Rolling Stone'. A week later, in Los Angeles' Hollywood Bowl the response – though still mixed – was more than positive enough to warrant that encore. Perhaps he was beginning to win them over.

If everyone thought he was putting his fans on, by this point he was certainly putting the press on. Throughout the fall of 1965 and into 1966 Dylan would become the *enfant terrible* any journalist feared to interview. His moods were wildly unpredictable. Thus in December two press conferences in San Francisco and Los Angeles, conducted a mere two weeks apart, were worlds apart in mood. In San Francisco his fifty-minute press conference – broadcast on local TV – showed him being witty, sharp, playful. When asked if he wrote some of his songs to show some people the error of their ways, he replied, 'I just want to needle them.' But the way he put it across belied any real sense of hostility. In Los Angeles thirteen days later he looked tired, his answers seemed more than a little tinged with bile, and there was a cynical air to his words.

The day after his September Hollywood Bowl show, Dylan gave his first *bona-fide* American press conference, at the Beverly Hills Hotel. Unlike his second LA press conference three months later, he was in a good mood, though this did not restrain him from playing word games designed to be unrevelatory. When asked how he felt about the power grabbers, Dylan launched into one of his outrageous surreal screeds:

Bob Dylan: They can't hurt me. Sure they can crush you and kill you. They can lay you out on 42nd and Broadway and put the hoses on you and flush you in the sewers and put you on the subway and carry you out to Coney Island and bury you on the Ferris wheel. But I refuse to sit here and worry about dying. [1965]

Whenever questions threatened to delve seriously into his success, Dylan would become flippant (when asked if his songs now had more urban imagery than previously, Dylan replied, 'Well, I watch too much TV I guess'); whenever those he was putting on became antagonistic he would ridicule them ('Hey, well I don't wanna disappoint anybody. I mean, tell me what I should say'). The press conferences gave him the best opportunity for such games, because they did not allow journalists the opportunity to nail him down and say, 'I'm sorry but what exactly did you mean by that?'

Dylan's games were not confined to such ribaldry at the expense of the unhip. As he had constructed a press conference with J. R. Goddard back in March, so in the fall of 1965 he 'rewrote' two major articles about him to provide two of his funniest comedy scripts. The first such piece was published in the *New York Herald Tribune* in December 1965 accompanying a photo-portfolio of Dylan shots by Daniel Kramer. It was called 'A Night with Bob Dylan'. Jointly composed by Al Aronowitz and Dylan himself the article debunked the very notion of prying into his personal life by putting the reader through a surreal journey of New York night clubs and hotel rooms peopled by characters like Soupy Sales and Mr Egg.

His second and more famous rewrite was the legendary *Playboy* interview conducted by Nat Hentoff in the fall of 1965. For years, fans found it hard to believe that even Dylan could be as sustainedly and spontaneously funny as the 1966 *Playboy* interview implied. Scaduto then suggested that Dylan had recomposed the whole interview after having a surprisingly straight interview hacked up by a *Playboy* editor, but that Hentoff was reluctant to discuss it. In fact, Hentoff seemed perfectly happy to discuss the saga when interviewed by Brian Stibal of *Zimmerman Blues* some years later:

Nat Hentoff: There were two [*Playboy*] interviews. The first was really an almost unusually straight interview. As I recall it was a quite sober, almost historical, biographical account, a lot of opinion, a certain amount of his — you know he can't avoid being sardonically funny, but just a straight interview. The galleys were sent to him and I don't recall him making more than two changes of no significance. Then the final set came to him after they messed with it in Chicago. I don't know what they did but I think they put some words in his mouth. They fooled around with it. I got a call and he was furious. I said, 'Look, tell them to go to hell. Tell them you don't want it to run.' And he said, 'No, I got a better idea. I'm gonna make one up.' I said it probably will work if they very much want to have a Dylan interview. We were on the phone and I did not have a tape recorder then. This was all by hand. I'll never forget,

I could hardly move the damn thing for a day. He made up an interview. I helped I must say. Some of the good straight lines in there are mine, but all the really funny stuff . . . is his. It was run as was with absolutely no indication it was a put-on. I remember I saw him two or three times in the month or two after and he'd say, 'Hey, when's it coming out, when's it coming out?' because he thought it was a very funny caper, which it was.

The problem was that Dylan's games did not begin and end with toying with the media. Throughout the summer and fall of 1965 he became increasingly difficult to communicate with. Both his friends and other strangers were repeatedly subjected to verbal put-ons – straight answers became wholly a thing of the past. The small coterie of the Hip that Dylan seemed prepared to associate with became an exclusive club delighting in ridiculing each and every combatant foolish enough to confront them. Even those who genuinely liked Dylan found an unmistakable glee to the cruel games he played.

Michael Bloomfield: He changed . . . I would see him consciously be that cruel, man, I didn't understand the game they played, that constant insane sort of sadistic put-down game. Who's king of the hill? Who's on top? To me it seemed like much ado about nothing but to David Blue and Phil Ochs it was real serious.

Folksinger Phil Ochs in particular was the subject of Dylan's 'bayonet', to use Carla Rotolo's phrase. The increasing pressures of fame seemed to increase his cruelty with each notch up the *Billboard* charts. In one incident that fall Ochs was ordered from Dylan's car after daring to criticize his new single, 'Can You Please Crawl out Your Window?'.

Phil Ochs: I had a fight with Dylan. He used to come around to the Kettle of Fish, and he was . . . super-arrogant then. He used to try to categorize all the other writers, in terms of how good he was. He used to say, well, Eric Anderson you're not really a writer, or he'd say Phil, you're not really a writer you're a journalist, you shouldn't try to write. And he went through this whole fantastic riff of how we shouldn't try to write, and that he was really the writer. Which, on straight aesthetics, I would admit was true. Y'know he was the best writer. Anyway, one day he was being photographed by Jerry Schatzberg and he was playing one of his new singles. And he was asking everybody what they thought. And he asked me what I thought, and I said I didn't like it. And he said, 'What do you mean you don't like it?' I said, 'Well it's not as good as your old stuff, and speaking commercially I don't think it'll sell.' We

were all in a limousine, David Blue was there . . . and Dylan had gotten
furious. He said, 'Get out of the car.' So I got out of the car.

Clearly Dylan was finding it hard to accept opinions which
contradicted the ones he was getting from ingratiating sycophants.
Though he would constantly invite comment, his response to
Ochs suggests that he did not take criticism well. The irony was
that, despite the unmistakable quality of 'Can You Please Crawl
out Your Window?', Ochs was right on both counts. It was not 'as
good' as 'Like a Rolling Stone' and 'Positively Fourth Street'. It
trod the same ground as both singles, with its vengeful put-downs
of the (male) subject; and the chorus was but a marginal rewrite of
ideas more successfully explored in 'To Ramona' and 'It's All
Over Now, Baby Blue'. And after two Top Ten singles, 'Can
You Please Crawl out Your Window?' peaked at a mightily
disappointing fifty-eight. When the more masterful follow-up
single, 'One of Us Must Know', failed to chart at all, it seemed as
if Dylan's commercial credibility was in tatters.

If most of Dylan's games seemed harmless enough to him and
his friends, his so-called truth-attacks were very hurtful and vindic-
tive. As we have seen, Dylan was something of a womanizer. He
seemed capable of bewitching a lot of women into believing they
were more important to him than they were. In the fall of 1965 he
had been skirting the edges of Andy Warhol's coterie, befriended
by Barbara Rubin (who is the lady on the rear sleeve of *Bringing It
All Back Home* seen massaging his hair) and Edie Sedgwick, two
women with strong Warhol associations. Sedgwick, who had
become a minor starlet-in-the-ascendant appearing in Warhol's
films, was looking for new frontiers. She latched onto Dylan and
Neuwirth, who were both patently attracted to her, and set about
extricating herself from Warhol's influence.

Paul Morrisey: The Dylan relationship came up one night when we
saw Edie at the Ginger Man. She told us that she didn't want Andy to
show her films anymore . . . She told us that she had signed a contract
with Bob Dylan's manager Albert Grossman . . . Dylan was calling her
up and inviting her out, telling her not to tell Andy or anyone that she
was seeing him. He invited her up to Woodstock and told her that
Grossman hoped to put her together with him. She could be his leading
lady . . . She signed with Grossman at Dylan's urging . . . She said,
'They're going to make a film and I'm supposed to star in it with
Bobby.' Suddenly it was Bobby this and Bobby that, and we realized
that she had a crush on him . . . So Andy couldn't resist asking, 'Did you

know, Edie, that Bob Dylan had gotten married?' She just went pale. 'What? I don't believe it.'

Edie took the revelation of Dylan's recent, secret marriage badly. It has been suggested that his 'rejection' of Edie was the beginning of her decline into drug dependency. According to Nico, it was Edie who was the subject of 'Leopard-Skin Pill-Box Hat', a rather ironic look at a woman and her affectations.

Gerard Melanga: It was after Edie left Andy and got involved with Dylan and then she started being passed around from hand to hand so to speak, that she got involved with heavy drugs . . . It's probably not true that the Dylan group were responsible for Edie's demise, though they probably helped it along.

Edie Sedgwick was not the only one amazed by the revelation that Dylan had married in November 1965. Sara Lowndes was largely unknown to the habitual attenders of Dylan's nightly gatherings at the Kettle of Fish or other Village hang-outs. Dylan seemed to feel unhindered by his marriage vows when it came to restricting his infidelities, or indeed his whole frenetic pill-poppin' lifestyle.

Since Sara was a friend of Sally Grossman's, she had always been a regular visitor to Grossman's Woodstock residence. Dylan clearly felt especially comfortable in her presence. When Daniel Kramer took some photographs in Woodstock in the spring of 1965 for a possible cover for *Tarantula*, it was the then unknown Sara who was seen peering round doors and holding enigmatic items alongside Dylan. When he took a relaxing holiday at the end of his English tour, it was with Sara that he chose to do it, and when Bloomfield arrived in Woodstock that June, it was Sara who seemed to be his constant companion. Clearly the relationship had progressed steadily, and his increasing attachment to Sara may have been an important motive in the brutal way that Dylan intimidated Baez into realizing that it was over between them.

Part of Sara's appeal to Dylan was that she did not seem after a piece of the legend. Indeed initially she did not even know who he was.

Sally Grossman: I remember the first time Bobby was ever on television. I watched the program with Sara. I probably shouldn't say this, but she thought we were going to watch Bobby Darin!

Yet despite their increasing closeness and her Zen-like detachment from the paraphernalia of fame that surrounded Dylan, his marriage seemed a surprising move, particularly when he was due to spend most of the next six months on the road, away from her. He himself hinted rather obliquely of some underlying motive for his timing in marrying Sara on 22 November 1965, talking shortly after his divorce.

Bob Dylan: I'd rather not tell the world why I got married. Even though my ex-wife and I don't have a relationship now, she is still the mother of my children and I see fit to protect her. [1978]

Given the birth of their first child in the early months of 1966, it is clear that Sara was by now pregnant with Dylan's child. However, if Dylan had persuaded Suze to have an abortion as Spitz contends, he would not necessarily have seen the fact that Sara was pregnant as requiring the ultimate commitment from him. Perhaps he just felt the time had come to put at least some of his life in order.

After all, he was increasingly spinning out of control. The pressures were such that he seemed to need stronger and stronger stimulants to maintain his ability to perform, both on and off stage. Dylan's 'official' position on drugs, as stated in the published *Playboy* interview in 1966, was that grass was fine but hard drugs were not.

Bob Dylan: I wouldn't advise anybody to use drugs – certainly not the hard drugs; drugs are medicine. But opium and hash and pot – now, those things aren't drugs; they just bend your mind a little. I think everybody's mind should be bent once in a while. [1966]

This somewhat contradicts his actual statement to Hentoff during the original interview intended for *Playboy* magazine, conducted back in the fall of 1965.

Bob Dylan: It's fine if they use pot and LSD and heroin and sex and everything. I mean, that's groovy ... To know pot – or to know any drug – is fine; and it's not gonna fuck you up ... I mean, LSD is a medicine. You take it and you know ... you don't really have to keep taking it all the time. [1965]

Dylan would later dismiss the influence of drugs on his songs, saying that they just helped him keep pumping new songs out. He would also later dismiss the psychedelics that came into vogue in the mid-sixties, suggesting that their use made people abandon reality in favour of some surreal dreamscape.

Bob Dylan: Grass was everywhere in the clubs. It was always there in the jazz clubs, and in the folk-music clubs. There was just grass and it was available to musicians ... When psychedelics happened, everything became irrelevant. Because that had nothing to do with making music, or writing poems ... People were deluded into thinking they were something that they weren't: birds, fire hydrants, whatever. [1978]

However, by 1965 he was clearly indulging in a lot more than grass or Beaujolais, his two traditional stimulants from 1960 to 1964. What he would refer to as 'powerful medicine' certainly included the regular use of amphetamines, particularly Methedrine and Benzedrine. He also seemed to be experimenting with harder, more dangerous drugs, including LSD, and quite probably cocaine. The drugs certainly were a major contributory factor in sending his world view askew, spiralling downward into dark paranoia.

As the saying goes: Just 'cause you're paranoid does not mean they are not out to get you! Dylan and his touring band were playing night after night to largely hostile crowds and the wave of critical indignation was not letting up. Izzy Young, Irwin Sibler, Tom Paxton and Ewan MacColl all wrote articles critical of Dylan's new stance in *Sing Out*, the bi-monthly bastion of folkdom (though in MacColl's case he had never been impressed by Dylan, even when his fellow folksingers were).

Ironically, after their mildly successful performance at the Hollywood Bowl, Kooper finally plucked up the courage to tell Dylan he was not looking forward to the prospect of converting the heartland of America to this new music, starting with two dates in Texas. As Kooper observed in *Backstage Passes*, 'Look at what they did to J.F.K. down there, and he was the leading symbol of the establishment.' Not surprisingly the news of Kooper's decision to quit was greeted enthusiastically by Robertson and Helm, who badly wanted to be reunited with their fellow Hawks, and who had been working on Dylan to convince him to dispense with Kooper and Brooks's services and utilize the entire band.

Al Kooper: I think my call was probably like a day before his call would have come to me ... Garth and Richard and them really wanted to get the band back together.

Dylan duly went to Toronto a week before the fall tour was scheduled to start in earnest to rehearse with the newly reconstituted Hawks, who were back in their home town playing a residency at Friars. Though Robertson and Helm had already fully briefed the band, he insisted on two all-night rehearsals before being convinced that here was a band who could play with sufficient invention and flair to be suitable support for America's premier folk-rocker.

Of course he would have been well and truly stuck if the Hawks had not worked out. A week was barely time enough to rehearse other musicians. Fortunately Dylan and the Hawks gelled immediately and there were two warm-up shows in Texas to iron out any problems before playing an important gig at Carnegie Hall on 1 October. The shows in Austin and Dallas proved surprisingly successful, and Dylan and the Hawks managed a few days' rehearsals in Woodstock prior to Carnegie Hall. The New York show was equally well received, with Dylan this time rewarding his fickle New York fans with an encore.

But Dylan was in for a shock if he felt that the tide had irrevocably turned. The out-of-town shows he played most week-ends in October still attracted a fair few hecklers, suggesting he 'Go back to England!' or 'Get rid of the band!' If he was upset by the renewed hostility, he was delighted with his new band. The Hawks were a superb outfit who were determined to make great music, leaving the waxing poetic to Dylan – though his primary opportunity to do so came in the forty-five-minute acoustic set which preceded the set with the Hawks.

Robbie Robertson: We never remarked, 'Oh, that third line in that fourth verse is such a whammy,' I mean nobody cared about the third line in the fourth verse, we cared about how it phrased and connected and slid into that fourth line much more. If it said anything really incredible at the same time, terrific, that was a bonus.

Surprisingly, the first person to want to bail out of the most controversial tour in rock's brief history was not one of the new boys but Levon Helm, who soon tired of the barracking, and felt that perhaps there was a genuine fault with the band which he was unable to hear. By the end of November, just before a two-week tour of the West Coast, Helm left the Hawks. He was replaced for the West Coast leg by Bobby Gregg, who had performed such an outstanding job on both of Dylan's 1965 albums but who normally preferred session work to the rigours of nationwide gigging.

Levon Helm: Back in those days when you played for some of the folk-purist crowds, the electrical portion, which was us, would get all the booing and hissing and stuff. After a while it wasn't a whole lot of fun ... I figured maybe we should practice or something.

Robbie Robertson: I don't think Levon could handle people just booing every night. He said, 'I don't want to do this anymore.' ... To me it was like, 'Yeah, but the experience equals this music in the making. We will find the music. I: will take some time but we will find it and eventually we'll make it something that we need to get out of it.' In the beginning, it was a little too much bashing.

The drummer's stool would actually have two more residents before the conclusion of the world tour in May 1966. When Dylan resumed touring the States in February 1966, Sandy Konikoff took up the sticks. On the world tour, and thus the legendary so-called Royal Albert Hall bootleg, it would be the hefty Mickey Jones.

While *Highway 61 Revisited* entered the charts the day after Carnegie Hall, remaining there until he completed his world tour, Dylan had to give serious thought to recording his follow-up. Once again – despite insisting he had nothing more (or is that Ma?) to live up to – he was the victim of increased expectations. Talking in the fall of 1965, he would tell reporters that he thought *Highway 61 Revisited* represented the best that he could do. In fact he was having serious problems coming up with a successor that would have equal, or even greater, impact. Never one to tread the same old ground, he was again looking for a breakthrough.

There were several attempts to record material for the next album before he actually got anything down for *Highway 61 Revisited*'s successor. The first post-*Highway 61* studio session was in New York on 20 October. The results are unknown, though it would appear that it was at this session that Dylan and the Hawks recorded the single version of 'Can You Please Crawl out Your Window?'. (A version of the song had in fact been recorded during the *Highway 61* sessions.) A few early mispressings of the 'Positively Fourth Street' single contained the *Highway 61* version of 'Can You Please Crawl out Your Window?' by mistake, which presumably explains the haste with which the newly recorded version was released in December, as disc jockeys were playing the mistaken version as if it were his new single.

A further session was scheduled for the beginning of November in Nashville but was cancelled at the last minute. Later that month, Dylan and the Hawks did make it into a Los Angeles studio for an all-night session to work on a major new song that he had just written. The song was called 'Freeze Out'. It would later be slightly rewritten and renamed 'Visions of Johanna'. The November version features a wholly different arrangement, though the words are pretty much all in place. Once again Dylan had achieved a quantum leap for the popular song form. 'Freeze Out' (or 'Visions of Johanna') may well be his most perfect song. The imagery is bone-chillingly precise – conveying an ominous if indefinable sense of apocalypse which surrounds the seemingly omnipresent yet physically absent Johanna – while the Hawks here lend a verve to the performance missing from the *Blonde on Blonde* version (which in its own stately way is perfect as well).

Despite the presence which the Hawks stamped on their studio recordings with Dylan, the sessions in the fall of 1965 did not produce the results he wanted. Dylan persevered with the Hawks in the studio, setting up three whole days of sessions in New York in January 1966. However, the only positive result from the sessions was a new single, 'One of Us Must Know'. Another attempt at 'Freeze Out' still did not satisfy him. A further seven-minute-plus masterpiece, 'She's Your Lover Now', was never completed in any satisfactory way and remains one of his greatest unreleased songs. On Bob Fass's radio show the night after the final session, Dylan admitted 'going [in] to make an album' but coming out with only one song.

By the time he took a break from his US tour in mid-February to make another attempt to record a new album in Nashville, Tennessee, 'One of Us Must Know' was already failing to generate sufficient airplay to suggest a chart contender. If he was serious about establishing himself as a credible competitor to the Beatles/Stones' domination of pop music, he needed to consolidate the earlier successes of 'Like a Rolling Stone', 'Positively Fourth Street' and the *Highway 61 Revisited* album. A five-day respite in his tour schedule meant he had precious little time to achieve this goal, particularly as he had only scraps of songs to take to Nashville with him.

According to his producer Bob Johnston, he had been trying to convince Dylan to try recording in Nashville for some time. The aborted session in November represented months of cajoling. Dylan himself had been greatly impressed by Charlie McCoy's work on the version of 'Desolation Row' on *Highway 61 Revisited*.

Dylan, though, still had very specific ideas about how he wanted to sound and insisted on sticking to the organ-guitar twin-engined sound which had worked so well on *Highway 61*. The change in the equation was Robbie Robertson's guitar sound, which was very different from Bloomfield's. Despite three months of playing live with Garth Hudson, he recalled Al Kooper to provide the organ sound once again. The Roberston/Kooper combination, ably supported by crack Nashville musicians like Charlie McCoy, Kenneth Buttrey and Joe South, was the culmination of that 'wild, mercury sound' Dylan was seeking, the Nashville musicians adding a full, rich warmth only hinted at on the previous album.

Bob Dylan: The closest I ever got to the sound I hear in my mind was on individual bands in the *Blonde on Blonde* album. It's that thin, that wild mercury sound. It's metallic and bright gold, with whatever that conjures up. That's my particular sound. I haven't been able to succeed in getting it all the time. Mostly I've been driving at a combination of guitar, harmonica and organ. [1978]

Al Kooper: They didn't know who [Dylan] was, but everybody gets treated the same way down there, with a lot of respect and a lot of room. They knew he was somebody ... There were some incredible people on those sessions. I was just knocked out to play with Joe South.

However, on day one of the sessions Dylan found that Nashville musicians were not used to someone with his love for spontaneity and improvisation. Whereas Dylan had improvised a lot at the *Highway 61* sessions, he barely had the time and the Nashville musicians the inclination to allow him to lay down a set of half-formed songs in the hope that they would come together in the studio.

Allen Ginsberg: Dylan always did improvise quite a bit ... 'Round '65 he told me that ... he used to go into a studio and chat up the musicians and babble into the microphone then rush into the control room and listen to what he said, and write it down, and then maybe arrange it a little bit, and then maybe rush back out in front and sing it!

Dylan therefore had to spend large chunks of the booked studio time finishing the lyrics to songs he had only partially completed before the sessions. One song in particular seems to have been all but wholly written during the first session, while the baffled Nashville session musicians played cards. Thankfully the twelve-minute 'Sad Eyed Lady of the Lowlands' was then recorded in one take, the musicians falling easily into a groove and Johnston duly setting the tape machine rolling.

Pete Rowan: People weren't going over licks and saying, 'Yeah, we'll use this lick,' and stuff like that . . . Everyone was just sitting around, the drums were going, and pretty soon everyone would fall in with the drums and play.

As with the *Highway 61* sessions, Dylan worked overtime in his hotel room to hone the material he wanted to record. Kooper was present during these hotel writing sessions and learned the songs well enough to be able to run through them later with the Nashville musicians, so in most cases they were not as unprepared as the legends tend to indicate.

Al Kooper: He had a piano in his room at the hotel and during the day I would go up there and he would teach me the song. I would be like a cassette machine. I would play the song over and over on the piano for him. This served a double purpose. One, he could concentrate on writing lyrics and didn't have to mess with playing the piano; two, I could go to the studio early that night and teach it to the band before he even got there so they could be playing the song before he even walked through the door.

As well as 'Sad Eyed Lady of the Lowlands' those four days of sessions resulted in two eight-minute masterpieces: a version of 'Visions of Johanna' which Dylan was finally happy with; and the kaleidoscopic 'Stuck Inside of Mobile'. There were also two more lightweight pieces recorded at these Nashville sessions – 'Leopard-Skin Pill-Box Hat' and 'Fourth Time Around', two of Dylan's wittiest parodies, the latter of which was his second pastiche of the Beatles in six months, the butt of this one being their own piece of whimsy, 'Norwegian Wood' (the other, 'I Wanna Be Your Lover', would not be released until 1985 on *Biograph*).

Along with 'One of Us Must Know', the Nashville songs gave Dylan enough material for an album, including three of his longest and most intense slabs of surrealism. These six songs would certainly have made a remarkable follow-up to *Highway 61 Revisited*, but he still had something left to say and arranged for further sessions in Nashville in three weeks' time, during a further week-long break from the road.

The March sessions would introduce some pop sensibility to the double album he now seemed bent on recording. Among the eight titles recorded at the two March Nashville sessions were three of his most enduring songs: 'Rainy Day Women', 'I Want You' and 'Just Like a Woman', which between them would return him to the status of important singles artist and provide him with three Top Forty singles before the end of 1966. 'Rainy Day Women' in particular would duplicate the success of 'Like a Rolling Stone', reaching number two in the American charts and generating considerable controversy regarding what exactly he meant by the word 'stoned' — as if it were not self-evident. Though 'Rainy Day Women' would open the *Blonde on Blonde* album, it was in fact the last song to be cut.

Charlie McCoy: Dylan said he wanted to get kind of a Salvation Army sound so they asked me if I could find a slide trombone player. I got one named Wayne Butler and after he arrived at the studio we cut 'Rainy Day Women' in about seventeen minutes . . . in one [complete] take.

Dylan later expressed his delight with the results of his two sojourns in Nashville. Indeed it would be 1970 before he would return to New York to record an album.

Bob Dylan: You've more space in Nashville than you do in New York . . . In Nashville people sit around if they want to. If they want to make good records they just sit around and wait all night 'til you're ready. But they won't do that in New York. [1966]

On 7 April 1966, having stayed an extra day in Los Angeles to complete the task of supervising the final mix of *Blonde on Blonde*, Dylan packed four one-sided acetates of his new album with a few belongings he required and flew to Hawaii. He was not flying to Honolulu for a holiday. Honolulu was gig number one on a two-month world tour, his first such trek. It represented two months away from Sara. She had been with him as he completed the final leg of an exhausting winter tour of the States, less than two weeks earlier.

He was once again facing the unknown, playing under unknow-ing eyes in Hawaii, Australia, Sweden, Denmark, Ireland, England, Wales, Scotland, France and then England again. Perhaps at some point he recalled Rimbaud's thoughts about confronting the un-known: '[When] the poet makes himself a seer . . . he reaches [into] the unknown and even if, crazed, he ends up by losing the understanding of his visions, at least he has seen them!' How prophetically Rimbaud's words would read in the light of the events on that famous world tour.

13

1966: A Curious Way to Make a Living

Suze Rotolo: People live with hope for green trees and beautiful flowers, but Dylan seems to lack that sort of simple hope, at least he did from 1964 to 1966. This darkness wasn't new to me. [But] it became stronger as the years passed by.

Dylan's world tour of 1966 seems a very small-scale schedule these days, both in terms of the size of venues which he was playing (virtually without exception these were theatres of three to four thousand capacity) and the breadth of the tour itself, which consisted of one show in Hawaii, seven in Australia, three in mainland Europe and thirteen in Britain and Eire – a mere twenty-four shows. On the face of it hardly a punishing schedule, particularly as the tour lasted from 7 April to 27 May.

However, Dylan's lifestyle and the nature of his new-found fame made these twenty-four dates seem like 124 dates. The first problem was that, ever since Newport, the folk-rock controversy had steadily been casting a shadow over his work. His own moods had become very dark and his temper unstable.

D. A. Pennebaker: I don't know what kind of chemicals he and Robbie were putting down but I'm telling you it made him very irascible and very peculiar. He never slept – and I just couldn't take it after a while.

When Pennebaker suggested that he never slept, this barely qualifies as an exaggeration. Dylan himself has admitted that they were constantly 'on' during this tour, if not playing concerts, then filming, or being interviewed, or giving press conferences (he gave a press conference for every single concert in Australia and mainland Europe, though only one in Britain).

Bob Dylan: We were going all the time, even when we weren't going.

We were always doing something else, which is just as draining as performing. We were looking for Loch Ness monsters, staying up for four days running – and making all those 8 o'clock curtains, besides. [1974]

Required to be 'on' all the time, Dylan became imperious towards outsiders and conspiratorial in relation to members of the inner sanctum. In Melbourne, Australian journalist Adrian Rawlins was temporarily admitted to that inner sanctum, showing Dylan, Robertson and Victor Maimudes around Fitzroy, Melbourne's slum district, and hanging out with him after his Melbourne shows.

Adrian Rawlins: Bob Dylan came into the [hotel] room. His entrances at that time were very choreographed, athletic events. He danced everywhere and couldn't keep still – head moving, feet shuffling . . . He said he and Robbie Robertson had been driving around Melbourne looking for me. 'Where have you been . . . come up and talk.' Then he twirled around and said: 'You, you, you and you can come too.' It was very much a power situation . . . We went up to his suite, ordered cokes and pots of tea and sat there talking from 2 a.m. till about 7.30 the next morning.

The all-night session Rawlins describes was typical of many nights on the world tour. Shelton details a similar session in Denver in March, as does another Australian temporarily befriended by Dylan, an actress called Rosemary Gerrette. He had met Gerrette at his final Australian press conference in Perth, and she 'hung out' with him for the remaining three days in Australia

Rosemary Gerrette: I sat up with the group until dawn . . . They were leaving for Stockholm for concerts. They were trying to get tired so they could sleep through the twenty-seven-hour flight and I was able to listen to a composing session. Countless cups of tea; none of the group drinks. Things happened, and six new songs were born. The poetry seemed already to have been written. Dylan says 'picture one of these cats with a horn, coming over the hill at daybreak. Very Elizabethan, you dig? Wearing garters.' And out of the imagery, he and the lead guitarist work on a tune and Dylan's leg beats time with the rhythm, continuously, even when the rhythm is in his own mind. Six a.m. and he asks me am I tired? Later he plays a melody to us, a very special one. 'I'll never have it published, recorded. I wrote it for this way-out moon chick. We just sat on the floor on these mattresses . . . and like for two hours I spoke to her with my guitar. And she understood . . . of course, this isn't quite like I played it, because it meant something to me at the time, but now it doesn't.'

Gerrette, though, was one who suffered from Dylan's wildly oscillating moods, and he ordered her out of the hotel room later that morning. Like many who came across Dylan on the tour, Gerrette was convinced that he was on some kind of death-trip. Certainly his dark moods, the apocalyptic conceit in his new songs and in his utterances to the press, his copious consumption of chemicals, his refusal to sleep and the intensity of his performances on stage all seemed to support that theory. If Dylan himself never considered he was on a death-trip, he certainly felt the pressures of expectation and they were slowly crushing him. He would later tell Scaduto:

Bob Dylan: The pressures were unbelievable. They were just something you can't imagine unless you go through them yourself. Man, they hurt so much. [1971]

Anthea Joseph: I don't think he was on a death-trip. I just think he was working unbelievably hard. He was constantly working. I mean if he wasn't actually on the stage he was travelling, he was writing. He just never ever stopped . . . You get so wired on adrenalin and you daren't stop 'cause you know if you do you'll be in bed for a week.

The booing had not ceased. In fact it was more intense. By the early months of 1966, when Dylan was touring the States, his fans knew what to expect. But in England his 'old' fans had seen him less than a year ago performing his acoustic, indeed topical, songs like 'Lonesome Death of Hattie Carroll' and 'Talkin' World War III Blues'. Perhaps this partially explains why the reception in the English-speaking countries now was the most hostile, though Dylan seemed oblivious to the booing. He was revelling in the sheer majesty of the sound that he and the Hawks were making.

D. A. Pennebaker: In Ireland, I recall there was a lot of reaction when he did the electric. But in general, he was having so much a better time with the band than he was by himself that you could see right away that the difference was night and day in terms of his performance . . . Dylan was so happy, he was jumping around like a cricket in the middle of the thing . . . Oh there was a lot of weird behaviour on that trip, [but] I don't think it was a death-trip. The pressures were enormous . . . Albert Hall was the wildest . . . people were really shouting at him and he was screaming back. He was very wild at Albert Hall.

If Dylan was relishing the experience, neither did the Hawks seem unduly fazed by the reception they were getting night after night. They had played many an authentic redneck joint with Hawkins. They had paid their dues.

Robbie Robertson: We didn't mind the booing so much. After all, we'd played in joints where they'd thrown beer bottles. Our main thought was that it was a strange way to make a living. You get in this private plane, they fly you to a town, we go to this place, we play our music and people boo us. Then we get back on the plane, we go to another town, we play our music and they boo us.

By this point, though, Dylan and Robertson knew instinctively that what they were doing was right, in every sense of the word. If the Hawks had been a little hesitant in their playing back in the fall of 1965, the sound they were producing now was stately, immense, compelling.

Robbie Roberston: By the time we did the Australia and Europe tours we had discovered whatever this thing was. It was not light, it was not folky. It was very dynamic, very explosive and very violent.

Listening to live recordings of the Rolling Stones and the Beatles from 1966, it is clear just how far behind Dylan both bands were in producing their music onstage. Ironically, according to Robertson the reason that we can compare the live 1966 sound of Dylan with those of his contemporaries is that Dylan and he wanted to analyse why the response was so fierce.

Robbie Robertson: The only reason tapes of those [1966] shows exist today is because we wanted to know, 'Are we crazy?' We'd go back to the hotel room, listen to a tape of the show and think, shit, that's not bad. Why is everybody so upset?

Of course, the reality is that the response was wholly unconnected to the music or its majesty. Indeed, the more powerful the sound, the less authentic Dylan's ex-fans considered his 'new' music to be. Perhaps in the power of his performances Dylan was perversely feeding upon the anger of the audiences, as if determined to hurl back their fury at them.

Robertson's explanation for the preservation of the concerts is partially true. However, the tapes in common circulation among collectors (and there are parts of nearly half of the shows on the world tour) cannot be accounted for simply because the Hawks were curious about how they sounded. In fact, many of the shows were recorded to provide a musical soundtrack for the documentary that Pennebaker was filming of the European leg of the tour. A nightly ritual, which involved Dylan in further late-night sessions, was the process of preliminary selections for the sound-track, which generally took place after each show.

French reporter: The entire group meets in a suite. Five musicians, four film-makers and sound-technicians, one sound-man, Tom – the driver of the Rolls who is also acting as Dylan's bodyguard, Henri – who looks after the guitars, Al Grossman, Bob Neuwirth, Fred Perry (. . . the tour manager), Bob Dylan and myself, plus a few girls picked up at the end of the show . . . They have to listen and choose the recordings made of the concert. It's a daily routine. Sitting on the floor, on cushions, every one listens in silence . . . The music is played very loudly, and apprehensive waiters come and go with trays full of cups of tea and beer. The night will go on for a long time yet. Bob is having a film made of the tour for American television and these recordings have to be synchronized later with the pictures. Gradually people begin to leave; one by one they go to bed. At 6 a.m. there are only three or four people left: Bob, myself and a couple of musicians.

The documentary, which would later become *Eat the Document*, a one-hour TV special only ever broadcast on a local New York TV station once in 1979, had been commissioned by ABC for a series to be called *Stage 66*. Dylan insisted on complete control of the finished product and was duly allowed full artistic rein. Penne-baker was thus enlisted by Dylan not as a film producer/director as in 1965, but simply on a filming assignment, for which he would be paid a flat fee. Yet Dylan seems to have had very few specific ideas about what kind of film it should be. He certainly did not seem intent on adopting a *cinéma vérité* approach akin to the 1965 documentary.

D. A. Pennebaker: He'd put little scenes together. I believe there was one up in my room in the hotel. We were at the George V. There was this huge mirrored clothes cabinet. And he had people going in, closing the doors and coming out. There would be a succession of people – I don't know where they came from . . . There would be strange women and guys and I would just film these little scenes.

Pennebaker felt that Dylan was missing a remarkable op-portunity, failing to exploit the real-life drama taking place every time he stepped on stage. Indeed, he felt that Dylan was deliberately avoiding documenting the events happening onstage, preferring the type of scenes described above. So one night in Glasgow, Pennebaker actually filmed Dylan with the Hawks, right under his nose.

D. A. Pennebaker: When I came back [from Cannes], that's when I shot that thing on stage with him. We didn't tell Dylan I was going to do it or anything – Robbie and I cooked it up. And so when he came out on stage and I was out there with a camera alongside Robbie and everybody else with the band, Dylan really cracked up ... I filmed the whole thing by just walking around on stage with him.

In fact Glasgow was one of the less well-received shows, fans shouting 'Rubbish' and 'Shut up' and slow-handclapping him before 'Leopard-Skin Pill-Box Hat' (a similar occurrence is immortalized on the Albert Hall bootleg). Dylan, though, saved most of his interest for scenes like the one that later appeared in *Eat the Document* where he and Richard Manuel attempted to buy a Swedish boy's girlfriend from him. Pennebaker himself had business at the Cannes Festival that year and missed two or three shows during the British leg, giving his assistant Howard Alk the ideal opportunity to film his type of footage, which more closely accorded with Dylan's own ideas.

D. A. Pennebaker: Making home movies ... simply doesn't interest me very much ... I'm not sure how to ... make other people's home movies for them ... Let them shoot whatever they want. And in a way, we were doing that. Howard [Alk] was doing some of that himself.

Alk did capture some immediate post-concert interviews with disgruntled fans coming out of Dylan's Manchester show on 17 May. Their angry responses are cleverly cut up in *Eat the Document* with parts of a particularly fierce version of 'Ballad of a Thin Man', Dylan's portrayal of Mr C. W. Jones adrift in a world wholly peopled by freaks. It makes a pleasing counterpoint to the fury of the ex-fans. One in particular seems as likely a candidate for the man who shouted Judas as any. In *Eat the Document* the earnest young man spouts, 'Any pop group could produce better rubbish than that. It was a bloody disgrace, it was. He wants shooting. He's a traitor.'

Manchester constituted the most notorious battleground on the tour, and it forms the bulk of the legendary Albert Hall bootleg. Though there are many eye-witnesses who attended the Albert Hall show, Anthea Joseph and D. A. Pennebaker among them, who swear it was there that a fan shouted 'Judas' at Dylan, at Manchester he was slow-handclapped before 'One Too Many Mornings' and burbled nonsense into the microphone until the clapping stopped, at which point he said, 'If only you just wouldn't

clap so hard.' Before the final song of the electric set immortalized
on the bootleg album, a disaffected fan shouted Judas, to which
Dylan retorted, 'I don't believe you, you're a liar.' Then he turned
to the Hawks, as Mickey Jones held his drumsticks aloft, and
instructed them, 'Play FUCKING LOUD!!!'

Dylan had presumably decided that CBS should record the final
shows on his world tour to prove, to posterity at least, that he was
right and the heckling fans wrong. At Manchester, Dylan and the
Hawks rehearsed in the afternoon (filmed by Alk) in preparation
for another stormy evening. Both his seductive and extremely
stoned solo set and the set with the Hawks were recorded. Columbia also recorded the final two shows of the tour, at the Albert
Hall in London.

Before that, though, he was to play his first concert in Rimbaud
country. The hype surrounding his Paris concert was considerable.
L'Olympia had been sold out for weeks, even though the tickets
were set at an unprecedented forty and sixty francs. *France-Soir*
announced Dylan's arrival with typical sourness, calling him Champion of the Singing Beatniks. On the plane, he interrogated the
journalist from *Salut les Copains* who had accompanied the entourage on much of the second part of his English leg, concerned
as to what exactly might be the response of the French fans and
media:

French reporter: [Dylan said] 'Can you tell me what I'm doing in a
country where nobody understands a word I say? Do you think they'll
boo at the Olympia?' As we assured him that this wouldn't happen he
went on: 'What questions are they going to ask at the press conference?'
Nothing important, don't worry — what you think about the war in
Vietnam, why you changed your style, what you think of long hair —
that kind of stuff. 'Good. In that case I'll say the first thing that comes to
mind.'

He certainly said whatever he felt like saying at the press conference, conducted at the deluxe Hôtel George V the day after his
arrival. Carrying an old puppet, which he introduced as Finian, he
informed the press, 'It's a religious symbol.' If not prepared to state
what he *did* believe in, he did deem to provide a clear statement
of what he did not believe in: 'I don't belong to any movement.
I've only got some ideas in my head and I tell them. I don't support
anybody's cause. No revolution ever came about because of
songs.'

The following day, Dylan was twenty-five. In just five years he had transformed popular music beyond recognition, making rock & roll capable of saying a great deal more than just Awopbopaloobop, and had been vilified, glorified, even deified for his trouble. If he never produced another album – or indeed if he died on top of the hill – he could rest assured that he would be considered as one of the most important artists of his era.

The final three shows of the world tour replicated previous hostilities. The Paris show was unique in that Dylan managed to antagonize the audience even before bringing on the band. Having genuine difficulty tuning his guitar, which was one he had been forced to use after his favourite guitar 'got broke' in Australia, his usual forty-five minute acoustic set that night extended to somewhere between sixty and sixty-five minutes. When fans expressed dissatisfaction he told them to read their newspapers or maybe go down a bowling alley until he had finished.

Having not endeared himself to the bemused Parisians, he appeared for the second 'electric' half with a large American flag draped across the rear of the stage – a highly provocative act in the light of America's unpopular involvement in Vietnam – prompting shouts of, 'Get rid of the flag!' and 'US go home!' The Paris headlines were suitably brusque in their assessment of the show. *Paris-Jour* suggested 'Bob Dylan Go Home!', *24 Heures* considered 'Mr Dylan's Reputation Is Too Flattering' and *France Soir* remarked that 'Bob Dylan Disappointed the Most Loyal Audience of the Season'.

The Albert Hall shows were no less traumatic. At the final show, Dylan finally lost his cool and suggested to one fan, 'Come up here and say that!' If he had previously restrained himself from making more than the occasional passing comment about the furore he was creating, the Albert Hall shows saw Dylan finally talking back. In fact he had made a few comments previously. In Liverpool, when someone suggested the (still living) Guthrie would turn in his grave, Dylan informed everyone, 'There's someone down here looking for a saint.'

He told the London audience before 'Visions of Johanna' that this was what the English press would call a 'drurg song'. He then told them he didn't write 'drurg' songs, 'It's just vulgar to think so.' If he was not writing about them, he was certainly using them just to keep going. Mainly he confined himself to popping pills.

Anthea Joseph: I was the only one that drank. They were all dropping pills and eating acid and generally misbehaving . . . Anything that was going to tear my mind to pieces I had no interest in whatsoever. So I was happy smoking dope in a corner while they ate things.

Bob Dylan: We were taking a lot of chemicals which doctors had prescribed for entertainers and athletes. [1978]

One strange aspect of the shows, though, was that Dylan's demeanour on stage during the acoustic sets seemed indicative of someone stoned on dope; yet by the time he returned with the Hawks he had seemingly metamorphosed into a speed-freak. Thus from the slurred diction in his lengthy acoustic renditions of 'Fourth Time Around' or 'Just Like a Woman' in the first half, he emerged for the second half spitting his words like a demon bastard child of Verlaine and Rimbaud. The three songs extant from that final electric set are if anything even more furious than the more famous Manchester recordings. Dylan, though, seemed at breaking point. The *Daily Telegraph* reviewer of that final London show pertinently observed, 'He is beginning to show the signs of a man who does not care whether he communicates or not.'

If Dylan was asking himself: Can this really be the end? it was despite the knowledge that Grossman was already in the throes of organizing a fall tour of the States which would dwarf his previous tours. Perhaps at this point he recalled a pointed warning made in print by Phils Ochs, in an article defending Dylan published in *Broadside* in October 1965, before their falling out. In it Ochs wrote that he could not conceive of Dylan touring even a year hence because of the danger of an attack by a mad assailant.

Phil Ochs: There's something very dangerous, something very frightening about this whole thing now. Dylan is very disturbing. Dylan gets up there and sings great thoughts and great poetry to everybody, and when you say everybody you mean also to neurotics, to immature people, to the lumpen proletariat, to people not in control of themselves. Dylan is forcing everybody to listen to him, the quality of his work is so good and so communicative . . . I wonder what's going to happen. I don't know if Dylan can get on the stage a year from now. I don't think so. I mean the phenomenon of Dylan will be so much that it will be dangerous . . . He's gotten inside so many people's heads – Dylan has become part of so many people's psyches – and there're so many screwed up people in America, and death is such a part of the American scene now.

The difference between Ochs's prophecy and Dylan's actual retirement was that there would be no externalized threat. It would take an altogether different flirtation with death itself to bring him round and make him realize it was his own dark self that he had to come to terms with.

Part Two:
Learning to Do Consciously...

14
1966-7: Evening Things Up

Dylan and Sara went to Spain for a brief holiday after the rigours of the world tour where Dylan must have mused upon the unrelenting pressure of the cauldron he had allowed himself to be placed in. A daunting fall schedule of concerts in America to publicize the imminent release of *Blonde on Blonde* was being finalized.* This tour promised to be even more daunting than his fall '65 schedule. Meanwhile, *Tarantula* was just about ready for publication and an hour-long special on the 1966 tour was also expected for the fall, composed from the footage Pennebaker had shot throughout May.

Dylan's two immediate concerns then were to approve the final galleys of *Tarantula*, and to compose a rough-cut of the documentary which he intended to present to ABC. Having returned to Woodstock in June 1966, he needed time to recuperate from the tour. Above all he had to consider more personal matters now that he had returned from gallivanting around the world. Sara, his bride of seven months, had given him a son, Jesse.

Obviously pleased to escape from the pressures of the outside world, he remained in Woodstock throughout most of July.† When Macmillan's editor Bob Markel needed final approval of the galleys for *Tarantula* before going to press, he had to travel up to

---

* According to official records the album was released on 16 May, but since it did not enter the US charts until the day after his motorcycle accident, in late July, this would appear to be incorrect.

† According to Spitz, Dylan attended a party in the last week of July at the Chelsea Hotel, with both Brian Jones and Mick Jagger also present. However, Jones and Jagger were not in New York at this point, they were in California. If Dylan attended such a party it was on or around the second of July, when the Stones played Forest Hills.

Woodstock, where he found Dylan attempting to unravel the footage Pennebaker had shot in Europe.

Bob Markel: We brought a set of galleys to him so he could take one last good look at it before we printed it and bound it and started to fill all the orders that had come in. Bob took a break from some film-editing he was doing. We talked a little about the book and about Rameau and Rimbaud and Bob promised to finish 'making a few changes' in two weeks. A few days after that, Bob stopped working.

The editing of *Eat the Document* — as the 1966 documentary would later be called — was not initially undertaken by Dylan and Howard Alk, who would end up making the finished movie. Dylan had asked Pennebaker if he and Bobby Neuwirth could put a suggested version together, and he would look at the results. It seemed he was already disenchanted with the footage that Pennebaker had shown him, and did not really want to be involved in producing the film. Yet Pennebaker had never been employed to edit the film — he still had to organize the release of *Don't Look Back*. He had simply been hired to shoot the necessary footage. Pennebaker was clearly as unhappy as Dylan to be placed in the position he now found himself in.

D. A. Pennebaker: He came sometime in July. He drove down and looked at stuff — we spent two or three days looking at stuff in the studio and then he said, 'Well, I want you guys to go ahead and make some sort of a rough edit to get an idea of what you did because ABC is coming after it.' . . . So Neuwirth and I started to edit something together . . . a twenty or thirty minute thing . . . Then Dylan had his accident and Albert got pissed at me 'cause he said I wasn't helping him edit enough and I explained to him that I was never supposed to be editing it.

A cut of that film still exists in Pennebaker's private collection. It is, needless to say, very different from, and far more straightforward than, the film Dylan and Alk would produce.

On 29 July 1966 the whole wheel on which Dylan was bound came crashing down, bringing him with it: he fell off his motorcycle. Dylan himself has been asked about his motorcycle accident on many occasions, part of the attempt to unravel why he 'changed' after the accident; as if there were some cathartic point as he sailed over the handlebars when he realized all is phoney (Ray Lowry, the cartoonist, would later parody such notions with a drawing of Dylan flying over the bike and a lightbulb saying 'Country Rock' coming on over his head). His most extensive answer was given to Sam Shepard in an 'interview' for *Esquire*.

Bob Dylan: It was real early in the morning on top of a hill near Woodstock. I can't even remember how it happened. I was blinded by the sun ... I was drivin' right straight into the sun, and I looked up into it even though I remember someone telling me a long time ago when I was a kid never to look straight at the sun ... I went blind for a second and I kind of panicked or something. I stomped down on the brake and the rear wheel locked up on me and I went flyin' ... [Sara] was followin' me in a car. She picked me up. Spent a week in the hospital, then they moved me to this doctor's house in town. In his attic. Had a bed up there in the attic with a window lookin' out. Sara stayed there with me. [1987]

If a shade metaphorical, Dylan's account here rings reasonably true. He told Shelton that, 'It happened one morning after I'd been up for three days,' clearly suggesting he had not entirely abandoned his punishing lifestyle during his break from the road. The extent of the damage from the accident seems to have been cracked vertebrae and mild concussion. He was taken to hospital, though in little more than a week he was back in Woodstock, where he may have temporarily recuperated at a doctor's house.* He was in a neck brace when Don Pennebaker arrived in Woodstock a few days after the accident, but he was fully functioning.

D. A. Pennebaker: I heard about the accident when I was in California and then I came and I saw him a couple of days later, walking around with a brace. He didn't appear very knocked out by the accident so I never quite knew what happened ... But he was very pissed [off] at everybody and I don't know whether it was because they were putting pressure on him to get the film ready for TV.

Another visitor who called on Dylan was Allen Ginsberg. On 19 August, exactly three weeks after the accident, Ginsberg brought him a pile of books to read while recuperating. According to Ginsberg, contradicting Pennebaker, it would be another two weeks before Dylan was really up and about.

Allen Ginsberg: I brought him a box full of books of all kinds. All the modern poets I knew. Some ancient poets like Sir Thomas Wyatt, Campion, Dickinson, Rimbaud, Lorca, Apollinaire, Blake, Whitman.

---

* According to Spitz, the stay at the doctor's house came some time later, which accords with Pennebaker and Ginsberg.

The motorcycle accident was the axial event round which Dylan's career is still perceived to revolve. This neat fracture in the chronology of his career has been seized on ever since as evidence that Dylan lost 'it' the day he fell off his motorcycle. In recent years there has been considerable speculation whether Dylan ever had an accident at all, though such suggestions have never been based on any sound evidence. However, there is considerable evidence that the accident was nowhere near as serious as Dylan and Grossman made it appear as 1966 wore on and Dylan evidently decided that he was no longer interested in honouring contractual obligations at the expense of his health and sanity.

His full recuperation from the crash was undoubtedly hindered by the poor physical shape he was in. The punishment his body had undergone in the last year was more than enough to tax a healthy man, but the chemicals he had been liberally taking in 1966 cannot have improved his constitution. The stories in the press at the time seemed determined to portray the accident as a near-death trauma. *Time* magazine claimed in its 12 August edition that Dylan was not wearing a crash helmet and had sustained 'severe face and back cuts'. The *Daily News* hinted that Dylan might never perform again, so disfigured had the accident made him. Though the reports were all wildly off the mark, they provided Dylan with an opportunity to avoid fulfilling his obligations. The men from Macmillan, ABC and CBS (to whom he owed one more album under his existing contract) were hardly likely to trek up to Woodstock to remind a badly injured man of his legal duties.

Thus in the latter months of 1966 Dylan had the opportunity to re-evaluate where he had come to at the age of twenty-five. It was not the accident but the breathing space it gave him which afforded him an opportunity to change his lifestyle, and made him realize that he could not carry on living as he had been doing. He quickly realized he no longer had the will to play live. Yet the accident had only compounded the Dylan iconography. With his decision to retire came an awareness of his new responsibilities. He now had a baby boy named Jesse, as well as a wife, to consider. The last people he wanted to think of were the agents and managers who wanted him back out in the marketplace.

Bob Dylan: [When] I had that motorcycle accident . . . I woke up and caught my senses, I realized I was just workin' for all these leeches. And I didn't want to do that. Plus, I had a family, and I just wanted to see my kids. [1984]

Talking about the weeks after the accident as he was returning to the stage in 1974, he recalled one particular night in Woodstock. He hinted at a bitterness, a desire for revenge, a sense that he had been taken in by the 'leeches'.

Bob Dylan: The turning point was back in Woodstock. A little after the accident. Sitting around one night under a full moon, I looked out into the bleak woods and I said, 'Something's gotta change.' There was some business that had to be taken care of. [1974]

He made a similar reference to taking care of some business – his phrase was 'evening things up' – when he was interviewed by Michael Iachetta in May 1967. Iachetta, who had interviewed him back in 1963, tracked him down to his house in Woodstock to obtain his first public pronouncements in a year. Dylan told Iachetta of the self-analysis which his rest had allowed.

Bob Dylan: What I've been doin' mostly is seein' only a few close friends, readin' little 'bout the outside world, porin' over books by people you never heard of, thinkin' about where I'm goin', and why am I runnin', and am I mixed up too much, and what am I knowin', and what am I givin' and what am I takin' . . . Songs are in my head like they always are. And they're not goin' to get written down until some things are evened up. Not until some people come forth and make up for some of the things that happened. [1967]

It seems likely that a part of Dylan's therapy was simply sitting down and viewing again the footage Pennebaker had shot on the 1966 tour. The man he saw, at centre-stage even in the offstage scenes, must have seemed a crazed individual to him. He was also profoundly unimpressed by the quality of the footage that had been shot.

Bob Dylan: They had made another *Don't Look Back*, only this time it was for television. I had nothing better to do than to see the film. All of it, including unused footage. And it was obvious from looking at the film that it was garbage. It was miles and miles of garbage. That was my introduction to film. [1978]

The chance to run through that footage again also made Dylan realize that Pennebaker and Neuwirth's ideas for the film were not

the same as his own, and he decided to set about re-editing an
entirely new movie from the footage, with the help of two
friends, Howard Alk – who had shot much of the footage in both
Don't Look Back and *Eat the Document* and was an old friend of
both Grossman and Dylan – and Robbie Robertson, whom Dylan
now encouraged to come up to Woodstock with the remainder of
the Hawks.

Robbie Robertson: The first reason I went to Woodstock was that he
was working on *Eat the Document* and he asked me to help on the film,
and that's what I did, I went up and lived at his house and worked on the
film for a while, and Bobby Neuwirth was kind of in and out . . . and it
seemed like a nice scene.

At this point in the project Pennebaker was happy to bow out.
He had never considered Alk's ideas about movies to be compatible
with his own, and was clearly annoyed that Dylan was going to
produce a movie which did not really represent what he thought
had happened on the tour, in the way that his *cinéma vérité* study of
the 1965 tour, *Don't Look Back*, would.

D. A. Pennebaker: I've always felt that he made [*Eat the Document*] out
of our outs . . . he set out to make his own film. How much of it is his
film and how much was Howard Alk's film I don't know . . . I think he
was very influenced by Howard's film ideas, which didn't interest me
much . . . I think they tend to be sort of intellectual ideas but they're not
visual ideas.

As his first creative activity since the accident, Dylan wanted
to produce more than just a conventional one-hour TV documentary. The *cinéma vérité* approach did not particularly appeal to
him. Both Alk and Dylan had specific ideas about setting scenes up
and letting people act out certain ideas. A small number of such
scenes do appear to have been filmed in England during a brief
period when Pennebaker was in Cannes and Alk was able to film
footage unsupervised and unhindered. Alk and Dylan were also
keen to use a lot of cuts in the film to achieve a sense of the
amphetamine pace of the tour. With *Eat the Document* they found
'the eye' (Pennebaker) had limited the scope of their more ambitious ideas.*

---

* Their ideas would not be fully realized until nine years later, when they began
work on *Renaldo and Clara*.

Bob Dylan: What we had to work with was not what you would conceive of if you were going shooting a film. What we were trying to do was to make a logical story out of this newsreel-type footage . . . to make a story which consisted of stars and starlets who were taking the roles of other people, just like a normal movie would do. We were trying to do the same thing with this footage. That's not what anyone else had in mind, but that is what myself and Mr Alk had in mind. And we were very limited because the film was not shot by us, but by the eye, and we had come upon this decision to do this only after everything else had failed . . . What we tried to do was to construct a stage and an environment, taking it out and putting it together like a puzzle. And we did, that's the strange part about it. Now if we had the opportunity to re-shoot the camera under this procedure, we could really make a wonderful film. [1968]

Robertson, more than happy with the approach adopted by Dylan and Alk, also contributed his own suggestions.

Robbie Robertson: It's an incredible film. It's very far out. It's very strange. It's not a documentary. It was hard to make it so it wouldn't be a documentary. But it was done and we liked it. Then after the film, we started to make some more music together.

Apart from viewing the footage from the European tour, Dylan once again read through the galleys for *Tarantula*. Though the book had changed little in the previous twelve months, it seemed that before the accident, Dylan had decided it would be too much effort to rework the book and had finally prepared himself for its publication. The accident allowed him to change his mind again and halt publication.

He decided he could not proceed with the book as it stood, and informed Macmillan that he was going to work on a new book. He had always been uncertain about the merits of *Tarantula*. Its lack of any coherent thread had made him feel that the book would not be understood by his fans and would be lambasted by literary critics. In 1968, talking to Happy Traum and John Cohen, he dismissed the book. It would take some time for him to revise that opinion.

Bob Dylan: I just put down all these words and sent them off to my publishers and they'd send back the galleys, and I'd be so embarrassed at the nonsense I'd written I'd change the whole thing. And all the time they had 100,000 orders . . . The trouble with it, it had no story. I'd been reading all these trash books, works suffering from sex and excitement and foolish things. [1968]

While Dylan was hard at working editing *Eat the Document* and preparing to start making music again, Pennebaker had finally arranged for *Don't Look Back* to be released. With Dylan's sudden disappearance from public gaze, Pennebaker's film, premiered in San Francisco on 17 May 1967, allowed fans a rare glimpse of the 'real' Dylan, in turn warm, funny, abusive, gentle, sarcastic, up, down, onstage and backstage, all in ninety grainy minutes of black and white celluloid. The film reinforced a public perception of Dylan that was already outdated.

The first hint that Dylan was preparing to emerge from his self-imposed hiatus in music-making came in an article by an old friend of his, Al Aronowitz, published in *Cheetah* in 1967. Aronowitz visited Dylan in Woodstock in the spring of that year and sat listening to him jam on some new songs with the Hawks (minus Levon Helm, who had yet to return to the ranks).

Al Aronowitz: 'Dylan has been doing nothing, absolutely nothing,' said Jamie Robertson, Dylan's guitarist, to an inquiring reporter . . . But that was just a contribution to the Dylan mystery. Actually, Dylan was writing ten new songs a week, rehearsing them in his living room with Robertson's group, the Hawks, and trying to complete a one-hour film TV special for ABC, which said it couldn't use the programme because it was seven months late.

There seems some doubt about when the sessions which would result in *The Basement Tapes* started. Some credit April as the starting point, but according to the album's sleeve notes it was June. Whatever the case, in the spring of 1967 Dylan was 'hanging out' every day with the Hawks, who had all recently settled in Woodstock at a rented house in West Saugerties, which with its distinctive bright pink exterior was known locally as Big Pink. According to Robertson, their daily sessions would commence early in the afternoon.

Robbie Robertson: We used to get together every day at one o'clock in the basement of Big Pink. And it was just a routine. We would get there and to keep [every] one of us from going crazy, we would play music every day. And he wrote a bunch of songs out of that.

The informal sessions served to unlock Dylan's muse. Once he was writing again, the flood of new songs was if anything even greater than during his days in New York City. In less than six months Dylan and the Hawks recorded at least thirty new Dylan compositions, including some of his best (and best-known) songs, gems of the quality of 'I Shall Be Released', 'This Wheel's on

Fire', 'The Mighty Quinn', 'Million Dollar Bash', 'Tears of Rage' and 'You Ain't Going Nowhere'.

Songs of equal worth were recorded but remain considerably less well known, and in many cases unreleased, even after the 1975 issue of *The Basement Tapes* double album. Several songs of real quality were largely improvised on the spot, notably 'Apple Suckling Tree', 'I'm Not There (1956)' and 'Sign on the Cross'. Of course Dylan had always improvised in the studio. The *Highway 61 Revisited* sessions in particular had seen Dylan and the band often playing purely on intuition.

In 1967 Dylan returned to such an approach, working in the intimate surrounds of the Big Pink basement, often almost extemporizing while the band played round him. He was once again spontaneously experimenting with country and blues forms, mouthing line upon line of oblique but dazzling images. On 'Sign on the Cross' he delivers a lengthy monologue in the style of a fundamentalist preacher which is both inspired and inspirational. On 'I'm Not There (1956)' he seems to be free-forming words around only a rudimentary outline, and indeed a typescript of the song confirms this impression.

Garth Hudson: We were doing seven, eight, ten, sometimes fifteen songs a day. Some were old ballads and traditional songs, some were already written by Bob and Richard, but others Bob would make up as he went along . . . ['Sign on the Cross'] would have been a real good one, but Bob never finished it. We'd play the melody, he'd sing a few words he'd written, and then make up some more, or else just mouth sounds or even syllables as he went along. It's a pretty good way to write songs.

The monologue style used in the bridge of 'Sign on the Cross' was repeated on several of the other recordings Dylan made that spring and summer. 'Clothes Line Saga' was delivered in its entirety in that 'hi, 'm gonna tell y'all a story' voice. One of the takes of 'Nothing Was Delivered' features an animated middle section where Dylan seems to be exhorting a congregation to accept the fact that nothing was indeed delivered. The verses of 'Million Dollar Bash' and 'Lo and Behold' also feature a half-spoken, half-sung, intonation unique to these sessions. The original source of the persona Dylan was adopting here can be found on one of the many 'country' covers they also recorded that summer, '(Be Careful of the) Stones That You Throw', a song about gossip originally written and performed by Hank Williams in his adopted persona of Luke the Drifter, a character who specialized in this type of moralistic monologue. The culmination of this style by Dylan would come on the longest song on *John Wesley Harding*, 'The Ballad of Frankie Lee and Judas Priest', which even parodies the form with its use of a moralistic final verse.

When Dylan was singing his fair share of country and folk standards at these sessions, it was as if he was attempting to tap into some common constituency in American popular music. Thus he recorded Curtis Mayfield's spiritual, 'People Get Ready'; country classics like 'I Don't Hurt Anymore', 'Stones That You Throw', 'Rock Salt and Nails' and 'A Fool Such as I'; and traditional nuggets like 'Young But Daily Growin'', 'Bonnie Ship the Diamond' and 'The Hills of Mexico' (all three of which appear to have been recorded at the same session).

Not everything they ran through was recorded. And there are no recordings of Dylan, Robertson, Danko, Manuel and Hudson working on the new songs they were writing, only attempted finished takes. The procedure was to work up an arrangement of a song, either an original or a cover, and, if they liked it, record it on a basic reel-to-reel using just three microphones.

Robbie Robertson: When we were inspired we'd go down to the basement and put something down on tape. Eventually it became quite a collection of songs that we had there. But it hadn't been recorded professionally, just on a little tape-recorder.

Not all the songs were improvised or covers. The inspiration provided by the daily sessions was encouraging Dylan to work on new songs, and for the first time he seemed to be writing the words first and adding the music later, a technique that would carry over to the *John Wesley Harding* songs that fall. This resulted in two of the best songs from the sessions being co-written with members of the Hawks, 'Tears of Rage' and 'This Wheel's on Fire'. In both cases he presented the typewritten lyrics, to Manuel and Danko respectively, to see if they could come up with some music.

Richard Manuel: He came down to the basement with a piece of typewritten paper . . . it was typed out – in line form – and he just said, 'Have you got any music for this?' I had a couple of musical movements that fit . . . so I just elaborated a bit, because I wasn't sure what the lyrics meant. I couldn't run upstairs and say, 'What's this mean, Bob: "Now the heart is filled with gold as if it was a purse"?'

Rick Danko: We would come together every day and work and Dylan would come over. He gave me the typewritten lyrics to '[This] Wheel's on Fire'. At that time I was teaching myself to play piano. Some music I had written on the piano the day before just seemed to fit with Dylan's lyrics. I worked on the phrasing and the melody. Then Dylan and I wrote the chorus together.

The *Basement Tapes* songs stand as one of Dylan's greatest achievements. Yet he had no idea what he wanted to do with them. He seemed to have no desire to release them himself, and the songs ended up being used as demos by a wealth of other artists, many already with a reputation for covering Dylan songs. In November 1967 Peter, Paul and Mary were the first to chart with a *Basement Tapes* song, having released their version of 'Too Much of Nothing' as a single. They were soon followed up the charts by Manfred Mann (with 'The Mighty Quinn') and in the UK Julie Driscoll and the Brian Auger Trinity (with 'This Wheel's on Fire'), while the Band featured a further three songs on their debut album, *Music from Big Pink*, and the Byrds included versions of 'You Ain't Going Nowhere' (also a hit single) and 'Nothing Was Delivered' on their superb foray into country-rock, *Sweetheart of the Rodeo*.

Bob Dylan: They were written vaguely for other people ... I don't remember anybody specifically those songs were ever written for. They must have been written at that time for the publishing company ... We must have recorded fifty songs at that place. At that time psychedelic rock was overtaking the universe and so we were singing these homespun ballads or whatever they were. [1978]

When, after the release of the long-awaited *John Wesley Harding*, it became apparent that a whole stack of classic Dylan originals had been written and recorded in 1967 but remained unreleased, many fans began to search for a copy of the rumoured tape which featured Dylan's own versions of all these songs appearing on other artists' records. On 22 June 1968 the newly formed *Rolling Stone* magazine printed as their cover story an article on the missing Bob Dylan album, the fourteen-song acetate of these demos, which was now being written up as the missing link between *Blonde on Blonde* and *John Wesley Harding*. The story of rock bootlegging had begun.

15

1968: Drifters, Immigrants, Messengers and Saints

By the time the Band began working on their own debut album in the fall of 1967, it had been eighteen months since the completion of *Blonde on Blonde*. In the meantime the Beatles had recorded *Sgt Pepper's Lonely Hearts Club Band* – a cornucopia of studio gimmicks obscuring a plethora of lightweight tunes – which was a definite retrograde step from the inspired *Revolver*. Nevertheless, its so-called innovations caused a lemming-like rush of West Coast hippies intent on recording psychedelic versions of their most recent acid trip. 1967 became the summer of Love, and the media, always quick to recognize a bandwagon, responded with predictable alacrity.

Dylan, though, knew that one didn't need to tune in and turn on to drop out. Indeed, only by turning off and tuning out had he found his own retreat. If there was much speculation at the time as to how Dylan would attempt to 'top' *Sgt Pepper*, Dylan himself was not interested in performing such an exercise. He was not unduly impressed by what he had heard coming from California or England.

Bob Dylan: I didn't know how to record the way other people were recording, and didn't want to. The Beatles had just released *Sgt Pepper*, which I didn't like at all ... I thought that was a very indulgent album, though the songs on it were real good. I didn't think all that production was necessary, 'cause the Beatles had never done that before. [1978]

If Dylan had returned from the edge a little jaundiced in his world-view, he was still open to outside influences. In 1967 the Bengali Bauls came to the United States at the request of Albert Grossman and stayed on his estate in Woodstock, where they were introduced to Dylan. The Bauls were wandering minstrels who sang songs based on Baul tradition, dating back to the ninth or tenth century. Containing elements of Buddhism and Sufi Islam, their songs had some similarities to Western popular song, using a repetitive refrain after each verse. And the frequent theme of their poems and songs was the right of the individual to develop freely. Two of the Bauls, Purna and Lakhsman Das, are the figures on either side of Dylan on the cover of *John Wesley Harding*, the album he recorded that fall. It was an album which detailed the struggles of individuals to pursue their own destiny, often outside the restrictions of societal restraints. It was an album full of outlaws, drifters, immigrants, messengers and saints.

It was also an album full of religious imagery, its language reminiscent of the King James Bible, its characters seemingly lifted from the Old Testament but adrift in a land akin to some postlapsarian American frontier, on a border between past and present. According to Dylan's mother, Beattie Zimmerman, talking to Toby Thompson in 1968, he was increasingly delving into the Bible.

Beattie Zimmerman: In his house in Woodstock today, there's a huge Bible open on a stand in the middle of his study. Of all the books that crowd his house, overflow from his house, that Bible gets the most attention. He's continuously getting up and going over to refer to something.

On the *John Wesley Harding* album there are allusions to both Old and New Testaments. In his study *The Bible in the Lyrics of Bob Dylan*, Bert Cartwright cites some sixty-one biblical allusions on the album.*

'All Along the Watchtower' features perhaps the most overt allusions to the Bible. The song's setting seems to be largely based on the section of Isaiah which deals with the fall of Babylon. Yet when the thief cries that 'the hour is getting late' it seems apparent that this is the thief in the night foretold in Revelation, that is, Jesus Christ come again, for it is He who says in Revelation: 'I will come on thee as a thief, and thou shalt not know what hour I will come upon thee.'

Dylan would later say of *John Wesley Harding* that he was 'dealing with the devil in a fearful way'. It does seem as if he was not joking when he told Neil Hickey in 1976 that *John Wesley Harding* was 'the first biblical rock album'. None of this received much attention at the time of the album's release. Rather it was

---

* The breakdown for each song is: 'As I Went out One Morning' (1); 'All Along the Watchtower' (5); 'I Dreamed I Saw St Augustine' (3); 'Ballad of Frankie Lee and Judas Priest' (15); 'Drifter's Escape' (4); 'Dear Landlord' (6); 'I Am a Lonesome Hobo' (5); 'I Pity the Poor Immigrant' (16) and 'The Wicked Messenger' (6).

the sound of the album and the directness of the imagery which surprised most commentators and fans.

The surreal imagery of *Blonde on Blonde* had disappeared. Yet if there seemed to be little one could read into a song like 'As I Went out One Morning', it, like most songs on the album, contained a symbolic figure who was not quite what he seemed (in this case Tom Paine). Here the character of Paine, like St Augustine and John Wesley Harding in their songs, is slightly askew of the historical stereotype. Perhaps, as in 'The Ballad of Frankie Lee and Judas Priest', Dylan was deliberately parodying those who looked for hidden meanings in his songs, as he most certainly was in the album's sleeve notes. According to Dylan, he was looking to strip bare his language. He discussed the approach with Ginsberg at the time.

Allen Ginsberg: In '68 he was talking poetics with me, telling me how he was writing shorter lines, with every line meaning something. He wasn't just making up a line to go with a rhyme anymore; each line had to advance the story, bring the song forward. And from that time came some of the stuff he did with the Band – like 'I Shall Be Released', and some of his strong laconic ballads like 'The Ballad of Frankie Lee and Judas Priest'. There was to be no wasted language, no wasted breath. All the imagery was to be functional rather than ornamental.

Bob Dylan: What I'm trying to do now is not use too many words. There's no line that you can stick your finger through, there's no hole in any of the stanzas. There's no blank filler. Each line has something. [1968]

As with many of the *Basement Tapes* songs, Dylan wrote the words to all but two of the *John Wesley Harding* songs first. Presumably the two exceptions were the last two songs, which seem to have none of that 'sense of fear', nor the biblical allusions.

Bob Dylan: There's only two songs on the album which came at the same time as the music. The rest of the songs were written out on paper, and I found the tunes for them later. I didn't do it before, and I haven't done it since. That might account for the specialness of that album. [1978]

The sound of the album was startling primarily because initially it was seen as a regressive step, more folk than rock, and had little in common with the more 'contemporary' sounds being heard on albums by the Beatles, the Rolling Stones, Jefferson Airplane, the Doors or the Velvet Underground. After *Blonde on Blonde*, fans had expected more of the same. In fact Dylan may have originally intended a quite different sound from the one he ended up with on *John Wesley Harding*.

Bob Dylan: I heard the sound that Gordon Lightfoot was getting, with Charlie McCoy and Kenny Buttrey. I'd used Charlie and Kenny both before, and I figured if he could get that sound, I could. But we couldn't get it. [1969]

After the final session for the album, in November 1967, he even considered embellishing the album by getting Robbie Robertson and perhaps Garth Hudson to overdub some guitar and organ over the basic tracks. But Robertson felt that the album sounded fine as it was, and anyway the Hawks, now named the Band, were hard at work on their own album, having recently reunited with Levon Helm.

Robbie Robertson: As I recall it was just on a kind of whim that Bob went down to Nashville. And there, with just a couple of guys, he put those songs down on tape. Then we did talk about doing some overdubbing on it, but I really liked it when I heard it and I couldn't really think right about overdubbing on it. So it ended up coming out the way he brought it back.

The recording and release of *John Wesley Harding* was a relatively painless affair. Having resolved his contractual difficulties with CBS and re-signed to them in August 1967, Dylan was in the studio in October, and the album was completed in three sessions. Before completing the deal with CBS he and Grossman had agreed terms with MGM, dissatisfied with CBS's royalty scale and their failure to give Dylan the support an artist of his stature deserved. However, MGM was involved in a boardroom struggle at the time and Allen Klein in particular was keen to avoid signing Dylan, because of the seven-figure advance and 12 per cent royalty Grossman was demanding.

When Clive Davis, trying to keep Dylan at CBS, kindly furnished Klein with the *real* sales figures for his albums, Klein became even more opposed, and Grossman, realizing MGM were stalling, resumed negotiating with CBS and obtained an unheard of 10 per cent royalty rate, but no advance. Thus MGM managed to lose one of the two most significant American acts in sixties rock music. The other, the Velvet Underground, they would abandon in 1969. Klein failed to appreciate that Dylan's low profile since July 1966 might have actually increased his saleability. His next two albums would in fact generate higher initial sales than any of his previous albums.

The final session for *John Wesley Harding*, at which the bulk of the album was recorded, was on 29 November 1967. Within four weeks the album had been issued in the States, and, despite minimal publicity, shot to number two in the charts, sandwiched between the Beatles and the Rolling Stones.

Bob Dylan: I asked Columbia to release it with no publicity and no hype because this was the season of hype. [1985]

In retrospect, *John Wesley Harding* is one of Dylan's most enduring albums. When *Nashville Skyline* came out eighteen months later, many fans re-examined the earlier album and recognized its real quality. Fans would also note the way he had presaged his movement towards country music with the final two songs on *John Wesley Harding*, both of which featured the distinctive steel guitar of Peter Drake. If the remainder of the album had also been so embellished, perhaps fans would have recognized the country tinges around the edges of the album's sound sooner than they did. As it is the dry, crisp sound remains unique, discernibly different from both the *Basement Tapes* songs, which in most cases were recorded without drums, and the syrupy *Nashville Skyline* material. What it did share with *The Basement Tapes* was its moralistic tone. It was a remarkably prolific burst of creativity to write an entire album within weeks of concluding the *Basement Tapes* sessions, particularly as he used none of the material already worked out.

At the end of 1967 Dylan must have been pleased with his way of life in Woodstock both personally and artistically. Sara gave birth to a daughter that summer, named Anna. He had also signed a lucrative contract with CBS, and recorded and released his first album in two years, which had proved a major addition to his *œuvre*.

In January 1968 he returned to live performance, even though it lasted less than fifteen minutes. In October 1967 Woody Guthrie had finally lost his fight against the hereditary disease which had slowly ravaged his body for over ten years. When he heard about the death, Dylan phoned Harold Leventhal, Guthrie's long-time friend and manager, and said that if there was going to be a memorial show he wanted to be there.

Thus on 20 January 1968 he shared a bill at the Carnegie Hall, with singers like Judy Collins, Tom Paxton and Guthrie's son Arlo, for the first Woody Guthrie Memorial Concert (a second was held on the West Coast in 1970). Dylan asked the Band, billed as the Crackers, to back him. Despite the fact that all acts played sets entirely composed of Guthrie songs, it was Dylan's presence which overshadowed the concert and attracted all the publicity. His first concert appearance in twenty months was more of an event than Guthrie's death, at least as far as the media were concerned. Ever perverse, the three songs he did perform – 'Grand Coulee Dam', 'Dear Mrs Roosevelt' and 'I Ain't Got No Home' – were hardly in the folk style that Guthrie had espoused, and which all the other performers used that night. The sound the Crackers whacked out was more akin to rockabilly, and Dylan's singing was a cross-breeding of his *John Wesley Harding* tone, his 1969 'chewing the cud' voice and his early sixties hollering.

Robbie Robertson: Everybody else was taking a different plane musically, you know it was a very folk-orientated show. But we just played what we were doing at the time. I can't help but think Woody Guthrie would have approved. I mean, if a song is going to live it must live in its contemporary surrounding.

However, if the fans hoped that Dylan's appearance would whet his appetite for live performance again they were to be sorely disappointed. In his June 1968 interview for *Sing Out*, Dylan made it clear that his touring days were over – at least for the moment.

Bob Dylan: When I was touring, it was my line of work, to go out there and deliver those songs. You must accept that in some way. There's very little you can do about it. The only other thing to do is not to do it ... It's pretty straining to do a show like that, plus a lot of really unhealthy situations rise up ... I did it, and I did it enough to know that there must be something else to do. [1968]

The Guthrie Memorial allowed the press their first real opportunity to view the new-look Dylan. Now bearded, he looked like a country squire who had accidentally wandered through a door marked Stage. The new look accorded with his whole new manner. Since the accident he seemed to have mellowed out. Everybody who had contact with him in the two years following his accident commented on his new self. Bob Markel travelled to Woodstock in February 1968 to see if he had made any decision about the publication of *Tarantula*.

Bob Markel: He was far more friendly, far less distracted. He was more grown up and professional, easier to be with. He said he didn't know if he wanted the book published at all. It wasn't something he wanted to improve; it didn't interest him anymore. He'd gone past it. He wasn't sure if he wanted it published as a 'relic' or an unfinished work.

Others who spent time with Dylan in Woodstock in 1968 were less delighted by his demeanour. They thought him uncommunicative and out of touch with what was happening in the outside world. It was as if Dylan had actually absolved himself from a role in the world when recuperating from his accident.

George Harrison visited him in November 1968 and stayed a few days, even co-writing a song with him, 'I'd Have You Anytime', though only after Dylan had requested he show him some chords, as if trying to develop his musical skills while in his self-imposed isolation. Possibly he was just anxious to share his music with somebody, now that the Band were rarely around.

George Harrison: He'd gone through his broken neck period and was being very quiet, and he didn't have much confidence, anyhow – that's the feeling I got with him in Woodstock. He hardly said a word for a couple of days.

Elliott Landy: He doesn't talk very much, he wants to hear. He needs people, to find out what's happening you know? . . . The down side of it is that you can't really get a straight answer out of him sometimes.

In June 1968 Dylan had told Happy Traum, who had moved to Woodstock the previous year, that perhaps he might do an interview for *Sing Out*. *Sing Out* was experiencing considerable financial difficulties, and a Dylan interview would boost sales considerably. It would, after all, be his first major interview since the accident. Traum suggested John Cohen, a local musician and painter, to do the interview, and Dylan readily agreed. However, at the interview his new mellow persona was in full evidence, and he seemed reluctant to express any opinions about the pressing political issues of the day. A second interview went the same way despite Traum's intervention. Traum was extremely unhappy with his lack of commitment. The interview, when it was published, appeared to indicate a man who was unconcerned with anything outside Woodstock.

Happy Traum: He was totally not giving interviews. In fact he was so changed by his accident that he had become religious; he had become a family man; he'd stopped smoking. You know there'd been a total change in his personality . . . Then one day he just said to me, why don't we do an interview, he just said that, let's do an interview for *Sing Out* . . . So I called John [Cohen] and he came up, stayed with me at my house, and we went out and saw Dylan. Through most of the interview I just sat and listened, I didn't say anything. I was letting John do it, because John is a very smart fellow, he has a very specific point of view. He's an artist, he's a photographer, as well as being a musician. Then about three-quarters of the way through the interview – I believe it was two separate sittings – I began to feel that John was being too careful with Bob, he wasn't pushing him on anything . . . He was intimidated by the fact that he was doing an interview with this man. But he was not pushing him, he was just too weak with him. And I felt that in order to be a good interview it needed some life, it needed somebody to stick something in there . . . Now at this time – you've got to remember it was 1968 – there was still a lot of talk about him leaving politics, about him not singing political songs anymore. He was writing only love songs and he had made some statements about how he had finished with politics and he wasn't interested, and all that kind of stuff. So I thought it was important to try to get some answers out of him, something of his ideas about politics, because people wanted to know that . . . At the time the Vietnam War was on and we were upset about that, and I really wanted him to say something about that. I was trying to get Bob to make some definitive statement about where he stood. But he didn't say anything, he was just talking about this stone-mason he knew.

Dylan himself refused to admit that he was retreating from the real world. He told reporter Hubert Saal that winter that he didn't think 'living in the country is a retreat from anything. It's not as if I were getting ready to go out in a bouncing wave or anything like that. You have to be let alone to really accomplish anything.'

Yet he had certainly cut himself off. Clive Davis at CBS was concerned that, without Grossman's input, he might lose contact with CBS, forgetting his commitment to his record label and his public. Contact with him had become sporadic and was only achieved through an intermediary, Dylan's secretary Naomi Saltzman.

Clive Davis: [Dylan and Grossman had] stopped working together. He did not have another manager; I had the feeling that he needed someone to bring him ideas, goad him a bit, make suggestions, offer help if he needed it . . . I had to tread very softly. I began calling him. I could never reach him directly, for he guards his privacy very carefully. The technique was to call his secretary, Naomi, who would call him; then, if he chose to, he would call back.

Dylan's relations with Grossman had certainly cooled somewhat. Though Woodstock had been Grossman's home for far longer than it had been Dylan's, he now kept his contact with Grossman to an absolute minimum. Indeed, speculation was rife that the song, 'Dear Landlord', his plea to some individual not to put a price on a soul, was about Grossman. Though he would later deny it, it certainly seems an appropriate address to a man who had pushed him so hard during that gruelling world tour, and whose contract gave him huge cuts of all of Dylan's earnings until their seven-year contract expired at the beginning of 1969.

Quite possibly Dylan was waiting for his legal commitment to Grossman to expire before entering the recording studio again.* Certainly at the end of 1968 he made moves to gain total control of his music publishing, forming his own company, Big Sky, to deal henceforth with his music. Dwarf Music, set up by Grossman and Dylan at the end of 1965, would no longer receive new compositions. However, all the evidence suggests he actually had very little to record.

Part of the problem for Dylan was Woodstock itself. As an artistic community for a hundred years, it did have a sense of retreat and otherworldliness about it. And, though this was exactly what he had required whenever he had retreated there during his New York days, and even more so as he recovered from his accident and discovered the joys of family life, by 1968 it was stifling his creative spirit.

Elliott Landy: Woodstock is a very womb-like place. It's very special there . . . It's filled with personal spiritual growth opportunity there . . . and people who go to Woodstock are transformed, people who live there that is. And he was going through a transformation, I feel . . . He was learning love and learning to feel love and express it and experience it in the family way. That's what *Nashville Skyline* was about — very introspective, very country-like, very haven-like music.

Landy, a photographer, had moved to Woodstock himself, and befriended all the musicians living in this artists' colony, people like the Band, Dylan and Van Morrison. He was taking photos of all of them, and becoming a regular provider of album covers. Landy visited Dylan on several occasions throughout 1968 and 1969, and he noticed that Dylan was working on a new interest which was perhaps distracting him from the serious business of writing songs. He was trying his hand at painting. Indeed, a

* Marc Elliott in his woefully poor *Rockanomics* book manages to suggest that Dylan held back from writing songs until 1974 in order to avoid giving Grossman a share of his royalties!

typical Dylan painting graced the cover of the Band's debut album, *Music from Big Pink*.

Elliott Landy: His paintings I remember seeing a lot. I've seen the original Big Pink painting and it's incredible. It doesn't look so good on the album cover . . . His painting is really good and his drawings were like Van Gogh. I mean, it's the same hand. He started painting when he was in Byrdcliffe. His neighbour was a painter and taught him how to use the tools of painting. That's what you do in Woodstock . . . It's in the air.

Despite the success of *John Wesley Harding*, which remained on the *Billboard* charts throughout 1968, the year would be the first of Dylan's 'lost' years. Though it seemed he had been in retreat since June 1966, 1967 had in fact been an extraordinarily creative period for him. Though the convenient myth persists that he was never the same after his accident, in no one year up to 1967 could he be said to have written as many masterful songs as he did in that year.

As if operated by a tap, the songwriting stream was turned off in 1968. The only songs Dylan is known to have written in that year were 'I Threw It All Away', 'Lay Lady Lay' – which he wrote for the *Midnight Cowboy* movie but submitted too late – and a bridge in George Harrison's 'I'd Have You Anytime'. Whatever the quality of the former two songs, this was hardly prolific, especially by the standards he had previously maintained!

Bob Dylan: One day I was half-stepping, and the lights went out. And since that point, I more or less had amnesia . . . It took me a long time to get to do consciously what I used to be able to do unconsciously. [1978]

When Dylan later talked about this 'amnesia' – the period when he forgot how to create the way he had always done – he was not referring to the period directly after the accident, but to a period that began in 1968. It was the first time he had been without his muse for more than a few months.

Bob Dylan: I . . . didn't sense the importance of that accident till at least a year after that. I realized [then] that it was a real accident. I mean I thought that I was just gonna get up and go back to doing what I was doing before . . . but I couldn't do it anymore. [1969]

What I survived after that was even harder to survive than the motorcycle crash. That was just a physical crash, but sometimes there are things in life that you cannot see, that are harder to survive than something which you can pin down. [1978]

If he was looking for peace and quiet while he attempted 'to learn to do consciously what I used to do unconsciously', he was not getting a great deal of it in Woodstock. By the end of 1968 too many people had found out about his home in Byrdcliffe. He had after all been living there since before the accident, having purchased it in the summer of 1965 as a retreat from the city. It was a lovely old house built by one of Woodstock's original founding fathers.

Elliott Landy: Everybody had rented beautiful, big, old wooden houses that are typical of Woodstock, or they lived on farms. Dylan's house in Woodstock, for example, had a huge living room with a high wood-panelled ceiling, all a little gloomy and spooky. Upstairs it looked like an old-fashioned hotel – long walkways with wooden floors and a red carpet, numberless children's and guest rooms. It was a so-called Byrdcliffe house, named after the man who built it. Byrdcliffe was a wealthy man who at the turn of the century had tried to found an artists' colony at Woodstock, and with his money had splendid and solid houses built.

At the beginning of 1969, Dylan moved his family to the southern part of Woodstock, purchasing a larger house previously owned by economist Walter Weyl. The Weyl place was considerably more private and far fewer people knew about it. Yet he would not even remain at his new home for the remainder of 1969. By September Dylan's Woodstock period was over.

16

1969: What's the Matter with Me?

In February 1969, Dylan flew to Nashville to record (or begin to record, depending on whom you believe) the follow-up to *John Wesley Harding*. It had been fifteen months since he had recorded that album and he had not ventured into a recording studio or written more than a couple of songs in the interim.

Nashville Skyline confirmed the drought that fifteen months of silence had presaged. Though the album came quickly, this time it was a result more of the simplicity of the lyrics and downright obviousness of the arrangements than of any innate chemistry between Dylan and the musicians. Using Charlie McCoy, Ken Buttrey and Pete Drake again may have helped the recording process, but the new songs hardly tested musicians of their quality.

Bob Dylan: We just take a song; I play it and everyone else just sort of fills in behind it . . . At the same time you're doing that, there's someone in the control booth who's turning all those dials to where the proper sound is coming in . . . [1969]

Norman Blake: He came in and Charlie McCoy was the session leader, Charlie was playing electric bass and he just kind of run them down in front of us with his guitar and harmonica and Charlie would take them down in the number system they use there in Nashville, the number changes, and Charlie would pass out numbered cards with the changes on them to all of us. As I recall, a lot of those tunes . . . seems like we got pretty quick.

According to Dylan, he had not gone to Nashville with the intention of recording an entire album.

Bob Dylan: The first time I went into the studio I had, I think, four songs. I pulled that instrumental one out . . . then Johnny came in and did a song with me. Then I wrote one in the motel . . . pretty soon the whole album started fillin' in together, and we had an album. I mean, we didn't go down with that in mind. [1969]

In fact to call songs like 'Peggy Day' and 'To Be Alone with You' fillers would be a considerable insult to so-called 'fillers' on previous albums like 'On the Road Again' and 'Leopard-Skin Pill-Box Hat'. Despite padding out *Nashville Skyline* with an instrumental jam called 'Nashville Skyline Rag', plus a re-recording of 'Girl from the North Country' taken from two days of studio duets with Johnny Cash, the whole still failed to clock in at half an hour — short measure even if the twenty-seven minutes of music had been full of the inspiration evident on *John Wesley Harding*.

The aspect of the album which drew most comment, though, was Dylan's voice. He had mysteriously developed a 'country' twang, which he put down initially to giving up smoking, though family and friends from his youth soon pointed out that his new voice bore a remarkable similarity to the voice he used to sing in when he played the Ten O'Clock Scholar and the Purple Onion in the winter and spring of 1960.

Bonnie Beecher: Do you know *Nashville Skyline*? . . . well, Dylan's early voice sounded like that. I was startled when I heard him again on *Nashville Skyline*. He got this bronchial cough that lasted almost a year, and he wouldn't take care of it because he thought the rougher his voice sounded, the more [it was] like Woody Guthrie. I thought he had lost . . . that sweet voice altogether.

The two sessions with Johnny Cash took place three days after the *bona-fide* album sessions, and were intended to result in a separate Dylan/Cash album, but the results were pretty disastrous. Never the greatest harmony singer in the world, Dylan's duetting on this occasion was simply inept. The band plodded through the baker's dozen of 'country' standards Dylan and Cash decided to do, collected their paychecks, and hurried home. Perhaps the only notable aspect of the Dylan/Cash sessions was that they signalled an intent on Dylan's part to record an album of country standards to reinforce the change in direction evident on *Nashville Skyline*. Meanwhile, he was called upon to defend his new album to the two members of the press he deigned to talk to, Hubert Saal of *Newsweek* and Jann Wenner of *Rolling Stone*.

Bob Dylan: These are the type of songs that I always felt like writing when I've been alone to do so. The songs reflect more of the inner me than the songs of the past. They're more to my base than, say, *John Wesley Harding*. There I felt everyone expected me to be a poet so that's what I tried to be ... [My old] songs were all written in the New York atmosphere. I'd never have written any of them – or sung them the way I did – if I hadn't been sitting around listening to performers in New York cafés and the talk in all the dingy parlors. [1969]

In fact Dylan was being surprisingly frank when he said the old songs reflected the 'New York atmosphere' he had written them in. By default he seemed to be admitting that *Nashville Skyline* in turn reflected the 'Woodstock atmosphere' – all of which suggested that his critical and creative faculties were rotting in upstate New York. If recuperating in Woodstock had probably saved his life, he was no longer finding the place the creative hive it had been in 1967. A large part of that decline must have been down to his lessening contact with the Band. With them to spark off and work with, he had produced some of his greatest work in 1967.

By the end of 1968, the Band were on their own, hard at work on their masterful self-titled second album. It took Dylan some time to realize that he had overstayed his time in Woodstock, and even then his eventual departure was only dimly connected to a desire to locate his absent muse. He would later disavow *Nashville Skyline*, and on his cross-country tours of America in the seventies and eighties would almost entirely ignore its contents, save for an occasional 'Lay Lady Lay'.

Bob Dylan: On *Nashville Skyline* you had to read between the lines. I was trying to grasp [for] something that would lead me on to where I thought I should be, and it didn't go nowhere – it just went down, down, down. [1978]

Ironically, *Nashville Skyline* proved to be one of Dylan's best-selling albums ever. This was primarily due to the success of the three singles issued from the album – particularly 'Lay Lady Lay', which gave him his first Top Ten single since 'Rainy Day Women'. Both 'I Threw It All Away', the first single from *Nashville Skyline*, and 'Tonight I'll Be Staying Here with You' were also Top Fifty singles. Yet he provided virtually no input when it came to the choice of singles. He had never really been concerned with the singles market save for a brief period in 1965–6 which ended with the commercial failure of 'One of Us Must Know'.

Clive Davis: Our area of greatest difficulty was singles. Bob always said that he would leave the choice up to me – yet he was invariably surprised by my choices, and sometimes balked at them. He didn't think about singles, he said, and he didn't think AM radio was *that* important. None of his friends listened to it.

Whatever his reservations about Davis's selections, he stayed in the spotlight through 1969 mainly thanks to the release of the only three worthwhile songs on the album as singles, and to two important one-off performances which garnered him maximum publicity for minimum effort.

Performance number one was his first national TV appearance in over four years, on the Johnny Cash show. Filmed in May 1969, its broadcast was designed to coincide with the album's climb up the charts. The show was recorded at the Grand Old Opry in Nashville, and Dylan used the trip as an opportunity to spend a few days in a Nashville studio, working on his next project, an album of 'country standards' in the style of the 'new' Dylan, though this time without Cash's contribution.

Dylan's performance on the show was a little stilted. Included was a lightweight new ditty called 'Living the Blues', which was due to be his next single until 'Lay Lady Lay' was chosen instead. What was apparent to most of his long-standing friends was that he was terrified out of his wits. After all this was his first TV appearance since he had achieved real mass success, and was the public unveiling of his *Nashville Skyline* persona. The new Dylan was destined for another stormy reception.

Johnny Cash: I think Bob Dylan was scared ... When he went out to rehearse they had an old shack hanging from wires behind him to try to give it a backwoods look. He came offstage upset. He said, 'I'm gonna be the laughing stock of the business! My fans are gonna laugh in my face over that thing!' I said, 'What would you like?' He said, 'Have 'em get that out of the way. Just put me out there by myself.'

Nashville Skyline's mixed reception had bought Dylan no real breathing-space in which to work on something more ambitious. To many of his fans, *John Wesley Harding* as the solitary worthwhile product in three years seemed poor return for their loyalty. After all in the same period the Beatles had come up with *Sgt Pepper*, *The White Album* and *Abbey Road* (and had recorded their own version of *The Basement Tapes* – *Let It Be*). The Stones, after a stormy 1967, had come up with *Beggars Banquet* and were hard at work on the equally impressive *Let It Bleed*.

If Dylan was considering a way to return to the public arena, an offer suddenly arrived which seemed to provide him with the perfect vehicle to see if the flame still burned. He had played no concerts since his fifteen-minute appearance at the Woody Guthrie Memorial Concert in January 1968. He was reluctant to play in America because he felt there would be too much media attention, and no suitable venues sprung to mind.

Another problem was arising. A large pop festival was being planned for the mid-August weekend in Woodstock, and there was no way he wanted to be around when a hundred thousand children of the sixties started wandering through the brush trying to locate the home of their guru. He had to get out! Thus, when two English promoters suggested to Bert Block, his personal manager, that he play a festival on a small island just off the south coast of England, and that he and his family could travel first class on the *QE2* and have a two-week holiday away from Woodstock, he became seriously interested.

Ray Foulk: One thing I had discussed with Block was the way we could entice Dylan to do it. So we came up with the idea of making it a holiday for him and his family. We obtained a farmhouse in Bembridge which was suitable. It had a swimming pool and a barn that had recently been converted which was suitable for rehearsing in ... We were offering Dylan a fortnight stay there, no expense spared, car with driver. Also we would have him come over on the *QE2*. The fee offered to Block was 50,000 dollars.

The holiday would start on 13 August, two days before half a million people descended on Max Yasgur's farm in Woodstock, with his entire family accompanying him on the *QE2*. Obviously he had to establish whether the Band could accompany him, though, as he had insisted that, as well as his own fifty-thousand-dollar fee, the Band receive a further twenty thousand dollars, they were hardly likely to refuse. Dylan then decided to remind himself what playing to a large crowd was like, and became a surprise guest during the Band's set at the Mississippi River Festival in mid-July. Introduced as Elmer Johnson, he ran through four songs with the Band, to a rapturous reception.

Unfortunately a slight mishap scuppered Dylan's plans. Boarding the *QE2*, his eldest son, Jesse, temporarily lost consciousness after banging his head against a cabin door, and the ship's doctor refused to accept responsibility for the boy's ability to make the voyage. They had to disembark and take Jesse to a doctor in New York. So much for sailing to England!

When Dylan and Sara finally flew into Heathrow Airport twelve days had elapsed and they were minus the children, who stayed at home in New York. Curiously, Sara looked extremely pregnant, though the next Dylan child, Jacob, was not born until 1971. Shots of Sara backstage indicate an equally pregnant lady, so clearly the initial impression at Heathrow was not one of Dylan's little japes at the expense of the press. To confuse the issue further, Scaduto, in his biography, refers to a child of Dylan and Sara called Seth, though this was one of his brother's children.

On Dylan's arrival it became apparent that he had again seriously underestimated the international interest in his return to the stage. The British media were running stories every day about the crowds heading for the Isle of Wight, and began to talk of a British Woodstock. It was clear that he would have to make some concession to the press, and on the Wednesday before the Festival he reluctantly held his first press conference since May 1966. The results were suitably farcical. He affected a country twang, and when asked about drugs responded, 'I think everyone should lead their own lives, you know'; informed the press 'I don't want to protest anymore'; and disavowed his 1966 activities, saying, 'That stuff was all for publicity. I don't do that kind of thing anymore.'

Meanwhile, Dylan and the Band got down to some serious rehearsing in the barn at Forelands Farm. Though they had briefly rehearsed in Woodstock at the end of July, three or four days' rehearsing on the Isle of Wight was required to whip the set into shape. As three of the Beatles arrived by helicopter for a game of tennis and a jam session on the Friday – day one of the Second Isle of Wight Festival – the island began filling up with mainlanders.

By the time Dylan took to the stage on the Sunday night there were an estimated two hundred thousand fans awaiting his appearance. The size of the audience clearly unnerved him. Matters were not improved by a two-hour delay between Ritchie Havens' set and the Band's own set, as the press enclosure over-spilled with a surfeit of journalists and hangers-on. The huge crowd became impatient.

The Band abbreviated their own set but when Dylan finally appeared and launched into 'She Belongs to Me' it was past eleven, and he had been waiting to go on for over two hours. The one-hour set he performed that night was not well received. On the first couple of songs his singing was understandably hesitant, and many fans, fed by tall stories planted in the press of a three-hour performance climaxing with an all-star jam, were bound to be unhappy. Throughout the show, Dylan stuck doggedly to his *Nashville Skyline* voice, and only on a raucous 'Highway 61 Revisited' did some of the old fire return to his singing. His whole appearance drew unfavourable comments, his bearded serenity and white suit making him look like a Hassidic rabbi on an exchange programme.

Levon Helm: I would've liked to have gotten carried away. I was ready, but I don't think everybody else was ... If things were like we hoped they would be, we were prepared to play for another fifteen minutes or so, just our part. And Bob had an extra list of songs with eight or ten different titles with question marks by them, that we would've went ahead and done, had it seemed like the thing to do. But it seemed like everybody was a little bit tired and the festival was three days old by then; and so, if everybody else is ready to go home, let's all go.

Dylan himself seemed to leave the island with undue haste. Departing the following day, he was back in New York on the Tuesday. On his return he informed waiting pressmen that he would not be returning to England: 'They make too much of singers over there. Singers are front page news.' He said his original intention in playing the Festival was to 'get away from it all and give myself a chance to break back in'.

His attempt to 'get away from it all' had not been a great success. Neither had his return to live performance. CBS had recorded the show for a possible live album but, despite bootlegs of the show appearing before the end of the year, the project was shelved, though four 'highlights' were later used on *Self Portrait*. The disappointing performance also seems to have scuppered any plans to resume touring. In late June Dylan had talked freely to Jann Wenner of *Rolling Stone* about going back on the road in the fall. If he had been testing the water at the Isle of Wight, he had clearly decided to stay on the beach.

In fact Dylan had been staying on the beach already. Woodstock was no longer a practical locale for him. Even his new house was becoming known to itinerant hippies on their pilgrimages to Woodstock, and it was no longer a creative environment.

Bob Dylan: Then came the big news about Woodstock, about musicians goin' up there, and it was like a wave of insanity breakin' loose around the house day and night. You'd come in the house and find people there, people comin' through the woods, at all hours of the day and night,

knockin' at your door. It was really dark and depressing. And there was
no way to respond to all this . . . They kept comin'. We *had* to get out of
there. This was just about the time of that Woodstock Festival, which
was the sum total of all this bullshit . . . I couldn't get any space for
myself and my family, and there was no help, nowhere. I got very
resentful about the whole thing, and we got outta there. [1984]

As early as the spring of 1969 he had been looking to move on.
When he was in Tennessee in May 1969 he considered purchasing
a house there.

Bob Johnston: I took him around to see some places, but he was in such
an uncommunicative mood.

Most of the summer, he avoided Woodstock. Apart from his
trip to England, he spent a lot of time on Fire Island, an outpost of
civilization off the New York coastline. It was there that he
seemed to have found a hideaway, and the picture he later painted
of these times in the song 'Sara' suggests an idyll. He even found a
little time for music-making with a musicologist called David
Amram.

David Amram: In the summer of 1969, I was about a quarter of a mile
down the beach from where Bob Dylan and his family were staying, and
I used to go by his place every day, bring my French Horn, and play.

But he knew that Fire Island was impracticable as a new
permanent home. The children were approaching school age.
With the benefit of hindsight, his decision to return to New York
may seem a little baffling, but it was in part intended as a return to
the well-spring of his former creativity; it was also his home patch,
Sara's home patch, and allowed the kids to attend local schools.
The Woodstock Festival had signalled the death knell of the old
Woodstock, the artists' colony, and in September 1969 he was
back in the Village, having purchased a spacious town house on
MacDougal Street.

17

1970: A Restless, Hungry Feeling

Having moved back to New York, Dylan did not take long to regret his decision.

Bob Dylan: Lookin' back, it really was a stupid thing to do. But there was a house available on MacDougal Street, and I always remembered that as a nice place. So I just bought this house, sight unseen. But it wasn't the same when we got back. The Woodstock Nation had overtaken MacDougal Street also. There'd be crowds outside my house. [1984]

The worst times of my life were when I tried to find something in the past. Like when I went back to New York for the second time. I didn't know what to do. Everything had changed. [1989]

Inevitably the return to New York became common knowledge and even those who did not know Dylan's exact address would wander around the Village in the expectation of running into him. The most famous of these wandering devotees was A. J. Weberman, who had been writing a series of articles about him in underground magazines like *East Village Other*. Except that Weberman was not really a fan of Dylan — or at least the new Dylan. Indeed he had convinced himself that it was his duty to make Dylan see the light, revert to his mid-sixties counterculture ways and give up producing capitalist shucks like *Nashville Skyline*.

If *Nashville Skyline* had upset Weberman and his ilk, then they were in for a shock because the album that Dylan was working on throughout the latter part of 1969 and the early months of 1970 was not a return to form, more a descent into parody. *Self Portrait*, a sprawling double album graced with a cover painting by Dylan, presumably a self-portrait, was issued in June 1970. According to Dylan's later pronouncements about the album, the sense that he was parodying himself was absolutely deliberate, a concerted attempt to defuse the mythology that had begun to surround him.

Bob Dylan: That album was put out . . . [because] at that time . . . I
didn't like the attention I was getting. I [had] never been a person that
wanted attention. And at that time I was getting the wrong kind of
attention, for doing things I'd never done. So we released that album to
get people off my back. They would not like me anymore. That's . . .
the reason that album was put out, so people would just at that time stop
buying my records, and they did. [1981]

Bob Dylan: I said, 'Well, fuck it. I wish these people would just forget
about me. I wanna do something they can't possibly like, they can't
relate to' . . . And then I did this portrait for the cover. I mean, there was
no title for that album . . . And I said, 'Well, I'm gonna call this album
Self Portrait.' . . . And to me it was a joke. [1984]

Certainly the album contains considerable hints that Dylan had
such a purpose in mind. The choice of songs from his Isle of
Wight concert seems deliberately perverse. Of the four songs
chosen, only 'Minstrel Boy' seems remotely palatable, and perhaps
that is only because there is no other version to compare it to. The
Isle of Wight version of 'Like a Rolling Stone', his most famous
song, is certainly a joke. He forgets the words, strips the song of
any feeling, and even the Band fails to inject any enthusiasm into
the proceedings. 'The Mighty Quinn' is equally disappointing,
despite being the first official Dylan version of the most successful
of all the *Basement Tapes* 'spin-off' singles (Manfred Mann's version
reaching number one in the UK and number five in the US). 'She
Belongs to Me' sounds as though he is singing with a frog rammed
down his throat, but is perhaps in reality simply the sound of a
very nervous man playing in front of 200,000 people after three
years off the road.

The studio songs that make up the remainder of the album also
seem to contain their fair share of in-jokes. The opening song, a
Dylan original, features no Dylan vocal. Instead a chorus of girl-
singers repeatedly sing, 'How'm I s'ppose to get any ridin' [or is
that 'writing'?] done?' Dylan's version of Paul Simon's 'The Boxer'
features two versions of himself taking Art Garfunkel and Paul
Simon's parts. One version is the 'old' Dylan, who had been
considered by some to be the subject of the song – the whores on
7th Avenue being CBS. In the 'new' smoother, richer tones of his
Nashville Skyline voice, he sings the harmony vocal.

The album even features two versions of two songs, 'Alberta'
and 'Little Sadie', performed in a ludicrously fast rag version and
then as a more sympathetic, not to say sedate, ballad. Even the one
new original Dylan lyric seems a parody, 'Living the Blues' more

than closely resembling Guy Mitchell's 'Singing the Blues'. On top of all these insults, real or imagined, there was the cover versions chosen to make up the bulk of the album. Six of the songs date from his *Nashville Skyline* period and feature the same style of crooning. More disconcertingly these songs included an excruciating version of 'Blue Moon', the syrupy 'Take Me as I Am (or Let Me Go)' (presumably intended as an ironic choice) and 'I Forgot More Than You'll Ever Know'.

According to Charlie McCoy, many of the songs' backing tracks were recorded without Dylan even being in town, so unconcerned was he with obtaining takes he was entirely happy with.

Charlie McCoy: Dylan sent the tape down with instructions that we were to just play over what he'd already recorded on it ... The tape was mostly other people's songs and it sounded like he was experimenting with them. The tempos didn't really hold together real well and he wasn't real steady with his guitar, either ... I assumed ... it was just stuff he'd thrown together for the heck of it.

And yet ... In order for Dylan to release an entire double album which said Fuck You, it would surely have had to consist wholly of instrumental riffs *à la* 'Wigwam' and 'Woogie Boogie'; crooning covers like 'Blue Moon'; butchery of his own masterpieces at the Isle of Wight; and ludicrously unsuitable arrangements of perfectly good songs like 'The Boxer' and 'In Search of Little Sadie'. And *Self Portrait* does not. Parts of it seem simply, and quite acceptably, to be the work of a man who is going through a creative drought and has decided to record some of his favourite covers. Certainly when he discussed the idea for the album with Clive Davis that seemed to be the type of album he had in mind – not that even Dylan would go to the CBS president and say I have this great idea to issue an album which is one big Fuck You to my audience and will hopefully alienate most of them so much they will not bother to buy my records in the future!

Clive Davis: Bob asked my opinion of the album's concept early on. My objections wouldn't necessarily have stopped the album, but I knew he'd been having some difficulty coming up with his own material ... so I encouraged him.

There are a couple of beautiful performances on the album. 'Copper Kettle' in particular is one of the most exquisite recordings in his entire *œuvre*. Other 24-carat nuggets among this mountain of fool's gold include a restrained version of 'It Hurts Me Too' and a lovely tribute to the Everly Brothers, 'Let It Be Me'. Even the two 'Albertas' and his version of Gordon Lightfoot's 'Early Mornin' Rain' have something to commend them. Such performances confused listeners about his real intentions, at the same time engendering hope that when his creative drought was ended he would still be able to produce quality performances.

Not surprisingly, the album was panned on its release. The reviews were almost universally scathing and included an extensive and famous review in *Rolling Stone* by Greil Marcus which began with the question on most people's minds when first hearing the album – What is this shit? (Dylan would later label Marcus's review 'a piece of shit'.) In the sprawling review, Marcus compared the album to the scattered collections which were making up bootlegs like *Great White Wonder* and *Stealin'*. Ultimately, though, he wrote: '*Self Portrait* is a concept album from the cutting room floor. It has been constructed artfully, but as a coverup, not a revelation.' For Marcus it was the construction of the album which made it clear that the album's effect was deliberate; and that made it doubly unpalatable.

Yet, if having produced nothing for what seemed an eternity, and then producing *Self Portrait*, seemed incontrovertible evidence of a creative drought, Dylan had a new album of original songs out within four months of *Self Portrait*'s release. Fans and critics alike concluded that the vituperative response to the double album had prompted him to scurry into the studio and record a 'proper' album to appease them, and to convince the world that he still had something to say. As so often with Dylan, this feeling was primarily an illusion, a conjurer's trick.

Whether Dylan realized it at the time or not, and logic says he would have, it was inevitable that even a halfway respectable collection of original songs was bound to be greeted with undue fanfare, coming so swiftly on the heels of such an extravagant caricature of his former selves. Though he may have quickly realized that whatever his intention/s with *Self Portrait*, it had failed, he had started work on *New Morning* three months before *Self Portrait* was released and, in all likelihood, did not consider *Self Portrait* anything more than a minor diversion from more serious fare. In fact, the *New Morning* album began with the last of the *Self Portrait* sessions, Dylan recording 'Went to See the Gypsy' at the same session as he recorded 'Woogie Boogie' and 'In Search of Little Sadie'.

Bob Dylan: We had a few of the tracks for *New Morning* before that *Self Portrait* LP came out. I didn't say, 'Oh my God, they don't like this, let me do another one.' It wasn't like that. It just happened coincidentally that one came out and then the other one did as soon as it did. The *Self Portrait* LP laid around for I think a year. We were working on *New Morning* when the *Self Portrait* album got put together. Some of that stuff [on *Self Portrait*] was left over from *Nashville Skyline*. [1975]

An important point to consider is that, whatever disadvantages moving back to New York had brought with it, it did mean that Dylan was in close proximity to studios in the Village and to CBS's own studios uptown. Setting up sessions on a whim, at minimal notice, was considerably easier than when he was located in Woodstock. The move also suggests that he was serious about working at his music again. In the three years he had resided permanently in Woodstock he had spent a grand total of between eight and ten days in CBS's studios.

If the final sessions for *Self Portrait* took up most of the winter of 1970, work on *New Morning* started in earnest in May. Two days before May Day, George Harrison phoned Dylan, having arrived in New York the previous day, to arrange to meet that evening and discuss a joint recording session, scheduled for 1 May. On 30 April they jammed informally at Dylan's apartment in preparation for the following day's session. The actual session was largely unproductive, despite using a stripped-down band featuring just Dylan, Harrison, Bob Johnston on keyboards, Charlie Daniels on bass, and probably Billy Mundi on drums. The real problem was the lack of enough strong original songs to record. Most of the session was spent running through old Dylan originals like 'Song to Woody', 'Mama You Bin on My Mind' and 'Just Like Tom Thumb's Blues', almost as if he were still working on *Self Portrait*. Though at least three new originals were recorded – 'If Not for You', 'Working on a Guru' and an unknown song which according to *Rolling Stone* was about a father's wish to leave his son 'air to breathe and water to wash in' – only 'If Not for You' was under serious consideration for *New Morning*.

Nevertheless, Dylan persevered with work on a new album and early in June managed to record a further version of 'If Not for You' (the official take) and another mellow original, 'Time Passes Slowly', at a session featuring two former cohorts on bass and guitar respectively, Harvey Brooks and Al Kooper.

Other sessions were also scheduled for May and June, one with Johnny Cash, one with Ringo Starr and one with the Byrds. The

Byrds session did not take place, the band failing to appear. The session with Starr supposedly did take place but was later described as 'not a success'. With Dylan's return to New York, Bob Johnston's role as producer was discernibly devalued. Never the most technical producer, in New York Dylan ignored Johnston's favoured Nashville musicians and Al Kooper carried out many of the producer's duties, Johnston not attending all the sessions. *New Morning* would be the end of Dylan and Johnston's association.

The problem was not really the recording of the songs, but the writing of them. Dylan was simply not coming up with enough good new songs. In the summer of 1970, he became involved with the production of a new 'musical' with the poet Archibald Mac-Leish. The play was called *Scratch*. According to Dylan in the *Biograph* notes he played MacLeish and the producer three new songs – 'New Morning', 'Time Passes Slowly' and 'Father of Night' – but they 'didn't see eye to eye' on 'Father of Night', 'so I backed out of the production'. In fact, according to a letter MacLeish wrote to his publisher in October of that year, the production was not meant to be a musical, but 'a play with songs by Dylan'. However he 'proved simply incapable of producing new songs, and things looked desperate until [we] decided about a month ago to use old songs of Dylan's'.

Al Kooper: He was writing some songs for a stage play, a musical version of *The Devil and Daniel Webster*, so some of these songs were from there. That was pretty much the fulcrum for that album. 'Well, I have these songs. Let's go in and cut these.' That got him writing a little more. 'Day of the Locusts' came from real life. And 'Went to See the Gypsy'. Same thing. It was just things that were going on in his life. It's like a diary.

Too late for MacLeish, Dylan produced half a dozen songs in the latter part of that summer. In June, he had received an honorary doctorate in music at Princeton University, which seems to have directly inspired 'Day of the Locusts'. As well as 'New Morning' and the truly awful 'Father of Night', he came up with a few of his best songs since his Woodstock heyday of 1967. 'Sign on the Window', 'The Man in Me' and 'Winterlude' suggested a man at last finding a few shards of inspiration.

In August he assembled such notables as Al Kooper, Ron Cornelius, Dave Bromberg and Charlie Daniels for a full week of recording sessions in New York. If the official excuse for his 'new' voice on *Nashville Skyline* was that he had given up cigarettes, the huskiness of his voice on the *New Morning* album would be down to a cold that he nursed throughout the entire week of sessions.

Ron Cornelius: Dylan had a pretty bad cold that week. You can hear it on one song, y'know, that bit about 'Brighton girls are like the moon', where his voice really cracks up. But it sure suits the song. His piano-playing's really weird; you fall over laughing the first time you see it, because his hands start at opposite ends of the keyboard and then sorta collide in the middle. He does that all the time, but the way he plays just knocks me out ... I asked him about 'Went to See the Gypsy', and he told me that it was about going to see Elvis in Las Vegas. I really flashed on that!

In fact the cracks around the edges on his vocals were most audible on two covers later released (as a B-side and on the shameful Dylan album respectively) — a stunningly intense solo piano take of the traditional 'Spanish Is the Loving Tongue' and a heartfelt 'Can't Help Falling in Love'. As with previous sessions, he and the band warmed up with a series of 'standards' like 'Jamaica Farewell', 'Mr Bojangles' and 'Big Yellow Taxi'.

But if Dylan managed to complete the sessions for the album with relative ease, he seemed genuinely unsure of the worth of what he had recorded, and how best to present the songs. His previous sureness deserted him at the production stage. Song selection and mixing became a tortuous affair. Al Kooper, his co-producer in all but name, was driven to distraction by Dylan's vacillating.

Al Kooper: When I finished that album I never wanted to speak to him again ... I was cheesed off at how difficult [the whole thing was] ... He just changed his mind every three seconds so I just ended up doing the work of three albums ... We'd get a side order and we'd go in and master it and he'd say, 'No, no, no. I want to do this.' And then, 'No, let's go in and cut this.' ... When we finished that I was just furious with him ... There was another version of 'Went to See the Gypsy' that was really good ... It was the first time I went in and had an arrangement idea for it and I said, 'Let me go in and cut this track and then you can sing over it.' So I cut this track and it was really good ... it sounded like Cream. And he came in and pretended like he didn't understand where to sing on it, 'Well I can't sing to this track.' But in fact he could have 'cause I took the meter from the original.

When *New Morning* was released in October it met with predictable euphoria. After the profound disappointments of *Nashville Skyline* and *Self Portrait*, it was clearly a step in the right direction. In *Rolling Stone* Ralph Gleason proved most enthusiastic, his rave review headlined 'We've Got Dylan Back Again'. It was perceived as a stamp of approval by a previously disillusioned fan. In retrospect, *New Morning* is defined by the word patchy. There are songs of real beauty, notably 'If Not for You', the title track and 'Sign on the Window'; songs of unfulfilled promise like 'The Man in Me' and 'One More Weekend'; and a not-so-healthy handful of real clunkers. At the time songs like 'Three Angels', 'If Dogs Run Free' and 'Father of Night' were seen as audacious attempts to work in new forms. Hindsight suggests there is little on *Self Portrait* as excruciatingly bad as these three songs.

Nevertheless, Dylan must have been pleased with the reception of *New Morning*, and he was back in the Top Ten with an album of original songs. According to one report, Dylan even considered going back out on the road shortly after the album's release, going as far as rehearsing a small band featuring Al Kooper and Harvey Brooks. Apparently the results were disastrous, and he soon abandoned the idea.

He was still clearly unhappy with his decision to return to New York. As in his final days in Woodstock, this was reflected in him and the family regularly disappearing from New York for a week or two, presumably on vacations of various sorts. In the summer of 1970 Dylan allegedly went to Israel. In June, when he attended a post-concert party at the Fillmore East, he had apparently just returned from one of his little trips.

Joel Bernstein: After the last Crosby, Stills, Nash and Young show at the Fillmore East . . . Bill Graham threw a party for CSNY and the Who, who had just done *Tommy* at Carnegie Hall . . . And Bob was there . . . He said, 'I just flew in from Venice for this.' I didn't know whether he meant Venice, California, or Venice, Italy.

Sadly the pressures, particularly from the absurd Dylan Liberation Front, Weberman's collection of misfits, would become particularly burdensome in the early months of 1971.

18

1971-2: Smooth Like a Rhapsody

In no sense could 1971 be considered a 'lost' year, like 1968. For an artist who would issue only two singles of new material in this twelve-month period, Dylan maintained a surprisingly high profile. The reason for this perhaps goes back to a quote in the 1969 *Rolling Stone* interview about the period after the motorcycle accident: 'I thought that I was just gonna get up and go back to what I was doing before . . . but I couldn't do it anymore.'

Having learnt that he could not just 'get up and go back to doing what I was doing before', Dylan spent 1971 testing the water. Rather than attempting to force the pace, he tried different studios, different line-ups at sessions in March, October and November. He tried another much-heralded 'comeback' performance at a benefit concert in August; and he was the subject of a well-publicized biography published in the fall, written by ex-crime reporter Anthony Scaduto. All these various activities were seized upon by the media as examples of Dylan stirring again. In fact at the end of the year he concluded that the water was still a little too hot for his taste, and returned to lying on a bank of sand and watching the river flow.

In March he booked three days of sessions at a small studio in the Village, Blue Rock Studios, his first ever official sessions not held at a CBS studio. The sessions were to be produced by Leon Russell. It is unclear what the exact purpose of the sessions was. Only two originals were definitely recorded, 'Watching the River Flow' and 'When I Paint My Masterpiece', plus at least half a dozen 'covers', none of which ended up officially released. Clearly an album was not what he had in mind as no further sessions were booked.

However, both original compositions were superior to anything he had recorded in the last three years – and both confronted head-on his continuing dearth of inspiration. 'Watching the River

Flow', a glorious honky-tonkin' three-minute roller-coaster ride, opens with a classic Dylan line, 'What's the matter with me, I don't have much to say'. The remainder of the song has him musing upon whether he wishes to be in the city or stay by this riverbank. The suggestion is that only in the city 'with the one I love so close at hand', could the singer rediscover his muse, but the will seems to be lacking.

'When I Paint My Masterpiece' is an even more overt admission that his muse has deserted him, and for the first time in song he confronts his own doubts whether he will ever paint his masterpiece. The song is set in Rome, a city where two millennia of culture overawe the singer. He wanders the streets, looking for inspiration. Though he longs to return to 'the land of Coca-Cola' (these lines were omitted from the released Dylan version), he heads for Brussels, but he cannot escape from his own notoriety.

Despite the quality of the song, 'When I Paint My Masterpiece' would be first released by the Band, on their *Cahoots* album, and only later included as a 'bonus' track on Dylan's second collection of greatest hits. 'Watching the River Flow' was released as a single in June 1971 but failed to reach the Top Forty, despite being his first non-album single since 'One of Us Must Know'. By the time the single was released, he was abroad, enjoying a holiday in Israel with Sara.

On 24 May 1971 he was photographed by a UPI photographer at the Wailing Wall in Jerusalem. When the photographer realized he had captured Bob Dylan, né Robert Zimmerman, in the homeland of his forefathers on his thirtieth birthday, the photo was widely syndicated around the world. Rumours of him embracing the religion of his father, the religion he had rejected when leaving his fraternity house early in 1960, began to feature regularly in the press.

In fact, there was some basis for such speculation. The children had been brought up as Jews and, with his father Abraham Zimmerman's death in June 1968, Dylan had begun to explore his Jewish heritage.

Harold Leventhal: After his father died, Bob became quite conscious of his Jewishness. He was very excited about Israel when he got back and it was around that time he started talking with Rabbi Meier Kahane who formed the Jewish Defense League.

Dylan himself would later attempt to play down the importance of his May 1971 visit, suggesting that he had just been 'testing the water', as with his musical endeavours in 1971.

Bob Dylan: There was no great significance to that visit. But I'm interested in what and who a Jew is, I'm interested in the fact that Jews are Semites, like Babylonians, Hittites, Arabs, Syrians, Ethiopians. But a Jew is different because a lot of people hate Jews. [1976]

Yet while in Israel he did pursue the possibility of taking his family into a kibbutz for a year and, though he did not carry the project through, he did approach the Kibbutz Givat Haim.

Eve Brandstein: Dylan came to Kibbutz Givat Haim with an interest in bringing himself, Sara and the children to the kibbutz. The only thing was he wanted to get a guest house, have the kids go each day to the kibbutz for the experience, but that he and his wife would not have to work on the kibbutz. Rather, they'd stay in a guest house and pay for the stay and the keep of the children. He wanted to put some time in . . . He was turned down . . . He wanted special privileges and they were afraid that if word got out the kibbutz would be overrun.

Clearly Dylan was still looking for a new home, away from the pressures he was subjected to in New York. If he needed further evidence that life would continue to be difficult as long as he remained in New York, it came while he was in Israel. At the same time as he and Sara were at the Wailing Wall, A. J. Weberman was holding a birthday bash outside his MacDougal Street town house. The birthday bash, like most of A. J.'s stunts, had a polemical purpose, A. J. addressing the small crowd assembled outside about Dylan's CB (Current Bag, Weberman's slang expression referring to the 'bag' Dylan was currently into).

At the beginning of January, Dylan had attempted to establish a dialogue with Weberman in an attempt to find out what the real motives were for his campaign against Dylan in the underground press. After talking to Weberman outside his house, he phoned him the following day and invited him to his Village studio to talk some more. After this informal discussion with Weberman he was disconcerted to discover that A. J. intended to write an article for *East Village Other* about their meeting, and requested the opportunity to see a draft of the intended article.

In a final telephone conversation on 9 January Dylan attempted to persuade Weberman not to publish his article, but without success. It was the last contact he had with Weberman until some time in 1972 when, after Weberman had promised to stop rummaging through Dylan's garbage searching for evidence of his drug habits, he returned to the MacDougal Street town house with a reporter in tow, to hunt once more through the garbage as part of a feature on his new science, garbology. Sara came out of the house while this was going on and freaked at Weberman's reappearance. Later Dylan, having returned home to a presumably distraught Sara, went looking for Weberman.

A. J. Weberman: I was walking around with my head bowed down to my shoes y'know. I was down on Elizabeth Street to get some Coca-Cola from the neighbourhood store, when all of a sudden I felt this arm around my neck. I thought I was being mugged y'know. I said Oh God what's happening here? And I wrenched loose and I turned around and it was Bob Dylan. I said, 'Hey man, let's talk man, what are you doing?' He started punching me, and I said, 'Come on, stop! stop!' I thought, is this really happening to me? Could Bob Dylan be punching me out? My idol, the guy that wrote all that great poetry? And a punch to my head convinced me it was. So then I thought maybe I'd wrestle him down, calm him down a little. But that didn't work out 'cause he had spirit on his side. He got me down on the sidewalk and started banging my head against the pavement. And then some hippies came along and broke it up.

Dylan's reaction was an indication that by the end of 1971 he had had enough of people imposing their own hang-ups on him and his family or attempting to hold him responsible for the failure of the liberal forces in America to get the US out of an increasingly unpopular war. After all, he had not written a protest song in eight years.

At least not until November 1971. On 3 November, having heard of the death of George Jackson, the incarcerated black activist, Dylan wrote a straightforward elegy for Jackson. The following day he hurriedly assembled a small band in Blue Rock Studios to record his new song as a single. He recorded two versions, a simple acoustic version and a 'Big Band' version. Despite also recording another original song at the session, a lightweight 'country' song called 'Wallflower', he decided to put a version of George Jackson on both sides of his new single, presumably to ensure that radio stations could not get away with playing an innocuous B-side as the new Dylan single.

The speculation aroused by this seemingly sincere expression of grief at the death of a man he admired was remarkable. Those keen to take potshots at him questioned his motives for releasing the single, suggesting it was an attempt to get certain sections of his audience off his back. Despite the controversy, the single did not sell discernibly better than 'Watching the River Flow'.

Whatever Dylan's motives behind 'George Jackson', it would appear that the recording of the single was his last attempt to 'test the water'. Perhaps he was disappointed by the sales, perhaps by the way his motives were questioned. Whatever the reason, it would be over a year before he would once again enter a studio to record for CBS.

He did return to a studio only thirteen days later, to work on an entire album on which he provided the majority of the music but which would never be released. The album was an intended collaboration between Allen Ginsberg and Bob Dylan. The idea seems to have originated at a poetry reading given by Ginsberg and Peter Orlovsky at the end of October.

Allen Ginsberg: That fall in NY Peter Orlovsky and I gave a poetry reading at NYU in Greenwich Village, and improvised for an hour on the theme 'Why write poetry down on paper when you have to cut down trees to make poetry books?' . . . Unbeknownst to us Bob Dylan was in the audience, in the rear with old musician fellow-actor companion David Amram.

Dylan was intrigued by the way Orlovsky and Ginsberg had improvised poetry on the spot. He had after all been interested in the results achievable by improvisation since at least 1965, and several of his classic songs from the peak years 1965–7 featured largely improvised sections in their lyrics. Ginsberg had set Dylan thinking. Perhaps he had been working too hard at creating new songs, perhaps he should see what happened if the sounds and the words just flowed naturally. That night he called Ginsberg, excited by this notion.

Allen Ginsberg: He called us up at our apartment in Lower East Side and said he liked the reading – so he came over the same evening and picked up a guitar that was around and began improvising. He started playing the blues and I started making up lyrics, just weird things that made him start giggling at first. Then Dylan said: Why don't we go over to the studio and do this? . . . A week later we got a gang of musicians together, including some of the people who worked with him on his last album, and some musicians I'd worked with in movies, and a Buddhist cellist from San Francisco, and we improvised in the studio – a bunch of lyrics and music . . . [On 'September on] Jessore Road', I provided the chord changes, the mantra is traditional, and Dylan provided the music on everything else. He'd just start strumming – da da da dum, chang chang, and I'd start babbling words.

The sessions, which lasted two days, took place on 17 and 20 November. Ginsberg composed 'September on Jessore Road' between sessions to give Dylan something a little more ambitious to work with.

Happy Traum: It was a very loose happening – as usual when Allen organizes something – we were laughing and falling all over the floor. Corso was running across the studio like a neurotic, accompanied by a Tibetan female singer. The others were in a 'state of transition' and walked around deliriously. Soon, only Allen, Bob and I were left. Then we recorded the music.

If the results were a little loose, Ginsberg and Dylan seemed happy enough with the sessions. Happy Traum omits to mention that his brother, Artie, David Amram and John Sholle all contributed, as did Peter Orlovsky. Pleased at the success of the idea, Ginsberg appeared with assorted 'friends' (including Dylan), a couple of days after the final session, on a local PBS half-hour TV programme called *Freetime*, and performed much of the material they had recorded. Unfortunately, when Ginsberg attempted to get the album he had recorded with Dylan released, he found few interested parties. An entire album of improvised poetry, however distinguished the musical accompanists, was not considered a likely big money spinner. Another major problem was some of the language used on the record, which was thought to lean towards the obscene, particularly 'Jimmy Berman', Ginsberg's homosexual paean to a newsboy. Though John Lennon expressed an interest in releasing the album through Apple Records, as with most projects that involved his label it came to naught and it would be 1983 before even three songs from the sessions were finally officially released on a double-album compilation entitled *First Blues*. Dylan though continued to encourage Ginsberg to develop such musical and lyrical experiments, visiting him in January 1972 to hear several new compositions and volunteering to appear on any further sessions that Ginsberg arranged.

Happy Traum's involvement in the Dylan/Ginsberg sessions was not his first collaboration with Dylan that fall. In October, Dylan had asked him to help re-record a few of his old songs for a greatest hits compilation CBS had planned for that Christmas, lacking as they did any new Dylan product. The songs he had in mind were from *The Basement Tapes*, though he had largely rewritten 'You Ain't Going Nowhere', and in such a way that the new version seemed to be a dig at Roger McGuinn, whose Byrds had had a hit with the song back in 1968. According to Traum, 'Afterwards he told me that he felt stimulated to prove himself again.'

Happy Traum: He knew that they had songs chosen out for this double album and there were some songs that he didn't agree with their choice. He felt there were some songs that he had written that had become hits of sorts for other people that he didn't actually perform himself and he wanted to fit those on the record as well . . . So we just went in one afternoon and did it, it was just the two of us and the engineer and it was very simple. We cut about five songs and chose three on the spot and mixed them on the spot in the space of an afternoon . . . Sometimes I wasn't even sure if it was a final take until we would just finish and Bob would say, 'Okay, let's go and mix it.'

Despite his sporadic studio activities, there can be no doubt what was Dylan's most-publicized activity of 1971 – his first public appearance since the Isle of Wight. On 1 August 1971 George Harrison organized two benefit concerts for Bangladesh, which was threatened by both civil war and drought, at Madison Square Garden. Both Harrison and Ringo Starr were on the scheduled bill along with such luminaries as Eric Clapton and Ravi Shankar. Rumours soon began to circulate that at least one more Beatle would also turn up, and even that Dylan was considering appearing. Nothing was definitely confirmed as 1 August came round, and, though Dylan had turned up for the soundcheck, even Harrison was not sure he would be there when the crunch came.

George Harrison: Right up to the moment he stepped on stage I wasn't sure if he was going to come on. So it was kind of nerve-racking. I had a little list on my guitar and I had a point after 'Here Comes the Sun' – it just said 'Bob', with a question mark. So it got to that point, I turned around to see if Bob was there, to see if he was going to come on. Because the night before when we went to Madison Square Garden [to soundcheck] he freaked out, he saw all these cameras and microphones and this huge place. He was saying, 'Hey man this isn't my scene, I can't make this.' . . . I was just tired of trying to organize the whole thing, and he was saying, 'Got to get back to Long Island, got a lot of business.' So on stage I just looked around to see if there was any indication if Bob was going to come on or not, and he was all ready, he was so nervous, he had his harmonica on and his guitar in his hand and he was walking right on stage, like it was now or never.

The real surprise, though, was not Dylan's appearance but the songs he chose to perform. All the songs were from his early and mid-sixties albums, though he had rehearsed a version of 'If Not for You'. Among the five songs he performed at both afternoon and evening shows were 'Hard Rain's a-Gonna Fall' and 'Blowin' in the Wind'.

Phil Spector: When he broke into 'Blowin' in the Wind', it was a great surprise. We didn't expect him to do it ... [At the first meeting with Harrison] George said to Bob, 'Do you think you could sing ... "Blowin' in the Wind"' – the audience would just love it' ... and Bob looked at him: 'You interested in "Blowin' in the Wind"? ... Are you gonna sing "I Wanna Hold Your Hand"?'

The response to Dylan's set was tumultuous, and even the press responded enthusiastically, particularly delighted that he was singing in his good ol' nasal style, and had abandoned the syrupy *Nashville Skyline* voice. In fact, listening now to Dylan's evening set, which made up side five of the three-album boxed set of the shows, his singing sounds thin and pinched, as if he did indeed have some kind of adenoidal complaint. But the concerts kept him aware of public demand for his return to the stage and he obviously enjoyed the response, commenting later, 'That was a good feeling, being on stage there.'

The two Concerts for Bangladesh were Dylan's only live appearances in 1971, though he appeared after midnight at the Band's New Year's Eve 1971–2 show at the Academy of Music in New York, where he performed four songs with them (three of which were post-accident compositions) as if hinting that 1972 might be the year he resumed regular live appearances.

In fact, as part of Dylan's 1972 activities, his guest appearance with the Band stands in a fairly empty room. 1972 would be the second great lost year of his career. Until the fall of the year, he kept an exceptionally low profile. If he had been looking for the pressures in New York to ease, then Weberman's considerably toned-down activities only partially helped. Dylan was still looking to get out of New York. Indeed, the reason he had such a low public profile in 1972 was partly due to the fact that he spent so little time there.

Between January and June 1972 there is no evidence that he was in New York at all. Comments by Dylan in 1985 indicate that he was far, far away from the East Coast, on the arid plains of Arizona, where he owned a ranch. According to Dylan it was here that he wrote one of his most enduring songs, 'Forever Young', for his youngest son, Jacob, born the previous year. Yet, if he thought he had managed to get away from it all in Arizona he was mistaken, for whenever he turned on the radio he was reminded of his songs, not by any of his own tunes the stations might be playing, but by a song by Neil Young called 'Heart of Gold', which was riding high in the charts that year.

Bob Dylan: I was living in Phoenix, Arizona, and the big song at the time was 'Heart of Gold'. I used to hate it when it came on the radio. I always liked Neil Young, but it bothered me every time I listened to 'Heart of Gold' . . . I'd say, 'Shit, that's me. If it sounds like me, it should as well be me.' There I was, stuck on the desert someplace, having to cool out for a while. New York was a heavy place. Woodstock was worse, people living in trees outside my house, fans trying to batter down my door, cars following me up dark mountain roads. I needed to lay back for a while, forget about things, myself included, and I'd get so far away and turn on the radio and there I am, but it's not me. [1985]

Neil Young's song habitually haunted the airwaves through February, March and April. By May, Dylan was coming up for air, and was sighted in Los Angeles attending a Joe Cocker recording session. He was ready to return to New York, albeit reluctantly. After these months of crashing silence he restricted his 'public' appearances that summer to non-performing activities like attending Mick Jagger's twenty-ninth birthday celebrations and shows by Elvis Presley and the Grateful Dead, and turning up in Toronto in July, for the Mariposa Festival, to enjoy sets by Dave Bromberg, Gordon Lightfoot and Bukka White. He apparently considered performing himself, but the organizers feared that there would be bedlam if he did, and dissuaded him. However, he made a brief guest appearance at the beginning of September, appearing at the Bitter End in New York to see John Prine perform.

John Prine: I gave Dylan one of the first pressings of the [first] record. Two weeks later I played my first gig ever outside of Chicago. I was playing with David Bromberg and Steve Burgh and Goodman, but I needed a harmonica player. I asked if there was anyone around. Now, this is only my second night, and Dylan comes up. He had brought a harmonica and learned the words to all the choruses of my songs. I introduced Dylan and about two people were clapping. No one believed it. They thought Dylan was either dead or on Mount Fuji.

Dylan had already recorded (at the George Jackson session) one of the songs he accompanied Prine on that night, 'Donald and Lydia'. Prine was considered part of that early seventies tribe, New Dylans. Like Loudon Wainwright III, he was foolishly marketed under this banner. The following year a new talent from New Jersey, Bruce Springsteen, would be the last of this breed of New Dylans, and would go on to become as famous as Dylan himself.

During the latter months of 1972, Dylan oversaw the completion of his second book. *Tarantula* had finally been officially sanctioned for release in November 1970, though it drew few favourable reviews. He now planned a collection of all his lyrics and poems in a book to be entitled *Words*. At some stage though he decided to illustrate a few of the songs with his own line drawings, and the title became *Writings and Drawings*. The book appeared in June 1973, though the last songs to be included, with perhaps a hint of irony, were 'Watching the River Flow' and 'When I Paint My Masterpiece'. Dylan's role in the book's production should not be underestimated and, unlike the later *Lyrics, Writings and Drawings*, it shows signs of real care and attention, as publisher Bob Gottlieb observed in 1973

Robert Gottlieb: At the time that this came to me as a publishing project the manuscript was complete. Bob demanded, and had every right to have, complete artistic control over his book. No editorial changes were made in the text . . . Bob was involved in all its aspects and phases . . . I know it wasn't a rushed, overnight piece of hysteria because too many books happen that way and I can recognize the signs. There was nothing sloppy or careless or rushed or hysterical about this. It seemed to me very carefully worked, and I imagine over quite a period of time.

The disconcerting aspect of this beautiful-looking book was the air of finality that hung over it. It almost seemed as if he was saying, 'Well here it is. Don't expect any more.' Perhaps with hindsight he was really saying, 'This is my past. I have dispensed with it, and thus cleared the decks for the future.' Yet at the time of the book's release it had been nearly three years since he had issued his last official studio album, and the imminent release of the soundtrack to *Pat Garrett & Billy the Kid* was not suggestive of a major creative renaissance.

There seemed further evidence of a lack of current inspiration on opening the book, for on the inside of both front and back covers were two pages of what looked like drafts of songs, and they seemed to be contemporary with the final stages of the book's composition. If songs like 'Bowling Alley Blues' and 'Field Mouse from Nebraska' were indeed representative of his current output, it was clear why there had been no Dylan album since *New Morning*. As always, though, there were hints of his playfulness and delight in illusion. At the bottom of the front cover was an interesting piece of advice − 'sing something safe' − and a question. The question was one he needed to come to terms with: 'Is it right to think about what [one] can do or . . . to think about what one has done?'

As a step in the right direction, he made guest appearances on two albums recorded at the end of September and beginning of October at Atlantic's recording studios in New York. The more important of the two was a Doug Sahm album, Dylan sitting in for two weeks of sessions, playing keyboards and guitar, and even providing backing vocals on a version of his own 'Wallflower' and the well-known 'Blues Stay Away from Me'. Though Dylan later denigrated his own contributions to the album, it represented an important opportunity to play music with other quality musicians, something which he had been denying himself recently.

Bob Dylan: I just went to see [Sahm] . . . We went out to Jerry Wexler's house . . . I don't recall why he wanted me on that album . . . I was just playing a Telecaster guitar and he was playing all the fills anyway. [1978]

He also recorded with Steve Goodman and 'popped in' on sessions for Bette Midler's album that month,★ as well as attending one of Loudon Wainwright's shows at Max's Kansas City. Maybe his mind was once again turning to what he could do, rather than what he had done.

★ Both Goodman and Midler were Atlantic acts, as was Doug Sahn. Given Dylan's role in arranging a one-album deal with Atlantic for Barry Goldberg at the beginning of 1973 it seems likely that Dylan was considering signing with Atlantic now that his CBS contract had expired.

19

1972–3: Alias What?

Pat Garrett & Billy the Kid, the Sam Peckinpah film that landed Dylan in Durango for three hellish months at the end of 1972 and into 1973, is generally considered to be a minor episode in his life. In fact, the filming proved to be the necessary jolt to get him writing again and to abandon New York for new pastures.

It has always been something of a mystery how Dylan ended up in a Western by the notoriously eccentric Peckinpah. He had been out of circulation for some time – in terms of popular perception he had never really returned from the accident – and talk about him appearing in movies, prevalent in 1965–6, had long subsided. However, the writer of the screenplay for *Pat Garrett & Billy the Kid*, Rudy Wurlitzer, was not only a novelist in his own right, but a friend of Dylan's. It was Wurlitzer who approached him, originally hoping to persuade him to provide the film's musical soundtrack.

Bob Dylan: Rudy needed a song for the script. I wasn't doing anything. Rudy sent the script, and I read it and liked it and we got together and he needed a title song. And then I saw *The Wild Bunch* and *Straw Dogs* and *Cable Hogue* and liked them. The best one is *Ride the High Country*. Sam's really . . . the last of a dying breed. They don't hire people like that to make movies anymore. So I wrote that song ['Billy'] real quick. [1973]

'Billy' proved once again Dylan's mastery of the ballad form. Though a conventional ballad, it manages to convey a sense of inevitability about Billy's fate, while portraying a certain heroic quality to the figure. Having written 'Billy', Dylan began to consider the possibility of a small role for himself to play in the movie, an idea already mooted to him by Wurlitzer. He was still keen to escape New York. His three-year sojourn there had been unproductive, and several weeks in Durango would allow him to savour at first hand the Mexican culture he professed to love.

Bob Dylan: I'd gotten my family out of New York, that was the important thing, there was a lot of pressure back there. [1985]

At the tail end of November he went down to Durango with his wife to meet the fabled Peckinpah and play him the two songs he had written for the movie. Peckinpah was genuinely unaware of Dylan's status, and required some coaxing from Wurlitzer as well as Kris Kristofferson and James Coburn – who were playing the title roles in the film – even to approach Dylan.

James Coburn: Rudy was a friend of Bob's, and he'd written this song about Billy . . . Sam says, 'Who's Bob Dylan? Oh yeah, the kids used to listen to his stuff. I was kinda thinkin' of that guy Roger whatsisname, King of the Road guy to do it.' And we all said, 'What!! You gotta see Dylan.' . . . He said, 'Okay, bring Dylan down.' And Dylan had been in hiding – meditating or something – since his motorcycle accident and he came down with his tall Indian hat and his little moustache. Very strange cat . . . Wonderful guy. He was like quicksilver. You could never put your finger on Bobby . . . So the night we were over at Sam's house and we were all drinking tequila and carrying on and halfway through 'tween dinner, Sam says, 'Okay kid, let's see what you got. You bring your guitar with you?' They went in this little alcove. Sam had a rocking chair. Bobby sat down on a stool in front of this rocking chair. There was just the two of them in there . . . And Bobby played three or four tunes. And Sam came out with his handkerchief in his eye, 'Goddamn kid! Who the hell is he? Who is that kid? Sign him up!' He was very moved.

If Peckinpah's meeting with Dylan convinced him that here was an ideal choice to write the film's soundtrack, Wurlitzer felt he had a tailor-made role in the film for Dylan to play, one which he could readily expand to create a role worthy of Dylan's stature. The character he had in mind was as enigmatic and elusive as Dylan himself. His name was Alias. Dylan has been responsible over the intervening years for giving the impression that Alias was an invented character who was introduced into this border waste-land simply to provide him with a role in the film.

Bob Dylan: I don't know who I played. I tried to play whoever it was in the story, but I guess it's a known fact that there was nobody in that story that was the character I played. [1974]

In fact, Alias was a real historical character, mentioned by

Garrett himself in his own account of Billy's life; and the character was present right from the beginning of the project, appearing in Wurlitzer's original version of the script. He was not only a member of Billy's gang, he could be considered to be Billy's right-hand man, as hinted by his riding alongside him during the Turkey Chase sequence. If anything Alias's role in the film was reduced in importance after Dylan's adoption of the character. According to Wurlitzer, this was Dylan's own intention. According to Kristofferson, it was because Peckinpah's problems with the film studio meant that Dylan's role remained undefined.

Kris Kristofferson: Unfortunately Sam was going through so much shit with MGM that he was never able to sit down and figure out what Dylan was in the movie . . . Bob kept sayin' to me, 'Well, at least you're in the script.'

Certainly the stuttering character Wurlitzer had created in the original script was soon gone. Not only did the stutter vanish, possibly because it required a degree of acting technique beyond Dylan's range, he only joined Billy's gang after witnessing his escape from Lincoln. Whatever the reasons for the change in the character of Alias, Dylan soon found that instead of the planned respite from troubles in New York, he had placed himself in another very difficult situation – in relation not just to Peckinpah and the film but also to his family, whom he had brought down to Durango with him.

Bob Dylan: My wife got fed up almost immediately. She'd say to me, 'What the hell are we doing here?' [1985]

Peckinpah had been delighted with Dylan's songs for the movie and had offered him a role in the film without really being aware of who he was, and what he was not. He was not an actor. He was a legend. Only as shooting started did Peckinpah become aware of this status, and realize here was a spirit very different from his own.

Rudy Wurlitzer: The really interesting thing [is] what's going on between Peckinpah and Dylan. Sam is really Western, like an outlaw, looking to the wide open spaces, and he didn't know about Dylan before. Dylan . . . brings a different point of view, especially to a western. The part is small, but it's important in a funny sort of way. Do the two of them have any common ground to meet on?

Dylan was by no means Peckinpah's only headache. His whole

relationship with MGM, the studio financing the film, was frag-
menting with every day of shooting. The underlying tension
affected everyone. A major disaster had wiped out two weeks of
filming; and the film's producer, Gordon Carroll, soon became
Peckinpah's adversary as the director fought to retain artistic
control of the film.

James Coburn: Somebody dropped the main camera and for a while we
had focusing problems – the left and right of the screen were fine, but
the bottom wasn't in focus. We needed to reshoot when we finally got
the camera fixed but the studio said 'No.'

According to the studio the focus problems were unimportant
and few viewers would be unhappy with the footage. Peckinpah
wanted to reshoot all of the problem footage. MGM were not
prepared to extend the budget or shooting schedule to accommodate the necessary delay such reshooting would cause.

Gordon Dawson: Sam would tell me to set up a scene. Carroll would
veto it because it wasn't authorized. Then there'd be a race to see if I
could get a wrap before they could rip it out.

The conflict soon affected Peckinpah – considered an eccentric
character at the best of times – and his behaviour became progressively more unstable. Dylan probably felt that the role of Alias
was not high on Peckinpah's list of priorities in such a situation.

Bob Dylan: That was Peckinpah's kingdom – and he was sort of a
madman. He kept saying, 'It's my movie, my movie.' [1986]

Dylan, like his fellow actors, admired Peckinpah and naturally
sided with the creative artist in his struggle with the powers that
be. Peckinpah's problems confirmed in him a long-held suspicion
that artistic concerns were anathema to big business interests, and
helped shape his own jaundiced view of major film studios, an
attitude which would later manifest itself in the way he set about
releasing and distributing *Renaldo and Clara*.

Bob Dylan: I learned by working in *Pat Garrett* that there is no way you
can make a really creative movie in Hollywood . . . You have to have
your own crew and your own people to make a movie your own way.
[1978]

Dylan was cast adrift by Peckinpah's problems, and became
even more diffident than usual when in company. The press, who
had started coming down to Durango to see the elusive Dylan,

found him uncommunicative. It wasn't only to journalists that he was subdued.

Kris Kristofferson: He's writing really dynamite songs but I never know where his head's at. There are times when it can really be upsetting when somebody doesn't talk. Hell, he doesn't even talk to his old lady sometimes for weeks . . . according to her.

Sara was not enjoying her time in Durango any more than her husband was, and during a Christmas break she managed to convince Dylan to fly over to England to spend a week with the Harrisons. Though this break temporarily restored their spirits, there were a further four weeks of filming awaiting him on their return — along with the actual recording of a soundtrack album, Dylan's first studio work in over a year.

Kris Kristofferson: He had a hell of a hard time down there, man. I admire him for sticking it out.

As Superbowl weekend approached, Dylan arranged to fly to Mexico City, where CBS had their own studios, to record the title song 'Billy' and some incidental music. By this point, it was not only he who wanted a respite from Durango. On the plane out of Durango were the film's two stars, its writer and assorted wives and girlfriends.

Rudy Wurlitzer: Sam knows he's losing to Dylan. He's giving a screening of *The Getaway* in town tonight, but everybody wants to go to Mexico City with Dylan. [Sam] also just called a 6.30 rehearsal for Monday morning because he knows we won't be back till after eight. But I don't care, man. I've got to get away.

Unfortunately, when Dylan arrived at the CBS studio in Mexico City, he discovered that for once his chaotic recording techniques were not going to work. His attempts to record a couple of songs with Mexican trumpeters did not meet with success; and his undisciplined approach to recording infuriated the other musicians.

Kris Kristofferson: I flew my band down figuring they would love to pick with Bob Dylan. Because of the Mexican musicians' union they had to have one Mexican musician for every American musician on the session. Bob doesn't speak Spanish so I asked him if he wanted me to talk to the trumpet players. I figured he wanted border trumpets. So I went over to talk to them and he said something real curt like, 'You can do that on your own song!' That really pissed me off, so I left him alone . . .

I didn't understand what he was goin' through. I didn't really understand how he records. My band would come up to me and say he was barely showing them something, they would almost learn it, and he'd move on to the next one. And they were trying to be so perfect for Dylan! But he wanted their first impressions. He's like a certain kind of painter. But I didn't understand that at all. I thought he was just fuckin' with my band.

None of the repeated takes of 'Billy' satisfied Dylan so he began to pare the sound down until, having dispensed with first trumpets, then drums, then organ and electric guitar, he finally cut a take of the song accompanied by just Terry Paul on bass – a sound he would later adopt for much of *Blood on the Tracks*. At four in the morning he finally concluded the session and prepared to go back to the hotel for some sleep. Apart from the final take of 'Billy' (later issued as 'Billy 4') and a brief instrumental called 'Billy Surrenders', thirty seconds of which was utilized in the movie, there were no usable takes from the all-night session. Even the other vocal track, 'Goodbye Holly', ended up on the cutting-room floor. He would have to record most of the soundtrack in California at the end of shooting.

The prospect of even more work on the film cannot have pleased Dylan, though he seems to have responded without vociferous complaint or wild tantrums. However, his delight in the little games he played in his medicine days once again came to the fore.

Kris Kristofferson: This one scene, Sam wanted him to come riding up to me, and as usual, it wasn't in the script. So they put Bobby on a horse and told him what they wanted. Now it's hard for Bobby to hit his marks in a scene with his own feet 'cause he doesn't think like that. But he's supposed to come through these sheep to where I'm standin', and old Sam says, 'Okay, Bobby, you just come straight by the camera here.' Well, Bobby went into a gallop, man, scaring sheep, horses, cameramen, and everybody. And I was laughin' so hard I was in tears. So was Sam. And old Sam says, 'No, Bobby, I really didn't mean that.' The strange thing is, I don't know whether Bobby did that on purpose or not.

The disappointing results from the Mexico City recording session required a rethink regarding the film's musical soundtrack. Perhaps the intuitive nature of Dylan's art required a little professional guidance. So Jerry Fielding, an experienced hand at scoring movies, was brought in to 'supervise' Dylan's music soundtrack. Sadly, Fielding considered him an amateur who had written 'a lot of nonsense which is strictly for teenboppers'; an attitude which –

though probably not expressed directly to Dylan – was readily apparent. Nevertheless, Dylan seems to have done his best to comply with Fielding's recommendations. According to Fielding his idea was to have 'Dylan sing a relevant verse' of the song, 'Billy', 'as it fit the story at roughly nine separate points throughout the picture'.* Dylan's other lyrical contribution to the soundtrack, 'Goodbye Holly', had been dropped, and it was decided another song was required, this time to represent the death not of Holly but of Sheriff Baker. When Fielding heard the song Dylan had promptly provided to replace Holly's lament, he was not impressed.

Jerry Fielding: I set up two dubbing sessions. Dylan had this song ['Billy'] he'd written for which he had a limitless number of verses that he would sing in random order . . . So I had to tape Dylan's song, because he had nothing written down, and have it transcribed. Dylan never understood what I wanted. At the same time I asked that he write at least one other piece of music because you cannot possibly hope to deal with an entire picture on the basis of that one ballad. So finally he brought to the dubbing session another piece of music – 'Knock-knock-knockin' on Heaven's Door'. Everybody loved it. It was shit. That was the end for me.

The egregious Fielding was and is in a very small minority in not recognizing 'Knockin' on Heaven's Door' as one of Dylan's most evocative songs. With its plaintive gospel feel, the song made no attempt to glamorize the bloody tapestry of death that suffuses the film. It provided the film with a theme tune, just as 'Billy' gave it a running narrative to counterpoint the action. It would also give Dylan a much needed hit single.

With shooting finally completed in February, and editing of this complex and at times confused narrative due to commence immediately, Dylan and his family headed for California. His professional concern was the completion of the film soundtrack, further recordings for which were to take place in Hollywood at Burbank Studios; his personal concern was to ensure that one of his children, who had become ill during filming in Durango, received the best treatment. Los Angeles was as good a place as any to obtain the necessary medical supervision – and at least it wasn't New York!

The sessions at Burbank Studios went very well. Dylan was working with experienced session musicians able to adapt easily to

* Though the idea was adopted it was modified so that 'Billy' appeared in partial form at just four points.

his individual approach to recording: drummer Jim Keltner, guitarist Bruce Langhorne, Terry Paul – who was retained from Kristofferson's band – and even Roger McGuinn all lent a hand. If producer Gordon Carroll had not formed the best of working relationships with Peckinpah, he seems to have been able to deal with Dylan's temperament far better. The most complex piece of music – and perhaps the most successful instrumental in *Pat Garrett & Billy the Kid* – was 'Final Theme', a haunting variant on 'Billy', which provided the theme to Billy's death. With recorder, flute, harmonium and cellos, a three-piece ensemble of backing singers, three guitars and a rhythm section, it proved Dylan could indeed master some of the complexities of writing numbers for film scores.

Unfortunately the problems with the film's editing resulted in much of the music Dylan recorded being used inappropriately and ineffectively. The final shooting script provided a story which, though Wurlitzer considered it had been 'reduced to its most simplistic components', was a poignant commentary on the way two old friends confronted the demands of the New West. The film as it was released cut several important scenes, including the opening sequence where Garrett is gunned down by Poe (the film was intended to be a flashback by Garrett at his death). Indeed, Poe's role was drastically cut, altering the whole film. In the shooting script Garrett's reluctance to track down his old friend – he wanders in a convoluted circular route around Fort Sumner knowing all along that Billy is there – eventually requires Poe to inform him where Billy can be found, in order to galvanize Garrett into providing the inevitable sacrifice. Other scenes cut include Poe's brutal beating of two old codgers in order to find out Billy's location; a vignette featuring Garrett and his wife, who informs him that she will leave him if he guns down the Kid; and an extended scene where Peckinpah himself plays an undertaker building a child's coffin at Fort Sumner as Garrett rides in.

With the version cut by MGM, after Peckinpah had produced a working version, these pivotal scenes vanished, the tempo of the film was irrevocably altered and the careful synchronizing of musical soundtrack to the appropriate scenes forgotten. All the leading players in the drama of making *Pat Garrett & Billy the Kid* were bitterly disappointed with the released version.

Bob Dylan: Sam himself just didn't have final control and that was the problem. I saw it in a movie house one cut away from his and I could tell that it had been chopped to pieces. Someone other than Sam had taken a knife to some valuable scenes that were in it. The music seemed to be scattered and used in every other place but the scenes in which we did it for. Except for 'Heaven's Door', I can't say as though I recognized anything I'd done [as] . . . being in the place I'd done it for. [1985]

It was not only Peckinpah who became disillusioned with Hollywood because of MGM's shoddy treatment of him. Dylan now viewed major Hollywood studios as pariahs who would never be allowed to get their hands on his own film, should he ever manage to get his vision onto celluloid. As late as 1986 he expressed his bitterness at what MGM had done to his soundtrack when talking with Richard Marquand, the next film director he would work with.

Richard Marquand: What hurt him was that they took his music and they relaid it, the studio did, behind Peckinpah's back, so that Bob would write a piece of music for a particular sequence, and then the studio afterwards, in post-production, re-edited the whole thing and put that piece of music against another sequence and just completely screwed up what had been Bob's concept of the movie in conjunction, presumably, with the director.

In its edited form, the film was not well received. Dylan's role was considered minor for a star of his renown, and he rarely looked comfortable with his dialogue – though on film he still exuded the same indefinable presence shown in *Don't Look Back*.

Kris Kristofferson: I've seen prints, and he's got a presence on him like Charlie Chaplin. He's like a wild card that none of 'em knew they had. I think they just hired him for the name and all of a sudden you see him on screen and all eyes are on him. There's something about him that's magnetic. He doesn't even have to move. He's a natural.

The soundtrack album was not well received either, and in a particularly scathing review in *Rolling Stone*, Jon Landau – using a variant on Marcus's famous 'What is this shit?' by-line, adopting the headline, 'Merely Awful' – proceeded to accuse Dylan of actually stage-managing his decline into irrelevance. The review incensed Dylan.

Bob Dylan: Landau's . . . got his head up his ass. He wrote that article from a very inexperienced and immature position . . . He wasn't connecting it to the film. He's into rock & roll, man, the way it was in the 50s . . . [but] Landau I had already crossed off as someone who just didn't understand. [1975]

Of course, part of Landau's and others' disappointment was down to unreasonable expectations. Landau seemed angry that it was merely a soundtrack album – as if it should have been anything else. Tuned in to the sort of populist myths which promised the Great Comeback, at which point the artist returned once again as Americana Personified, Landau was angry at an artist who fitted into none of his preconceived role models for rock & roll stars.

If Landau didn't recognize a stirring in Dylan's soul, the public were more perceptive. The obvious single, 'Knockin' on Heaven's Door', gave him his first Top Thirty single since 'Lay Lady Lay', four years earlier. It also helped boost the film's flagging receipts. Yet despite the single's obvious commerciality it almost wasn't released. There were problems with the album which were unrelated to poor reviews. CBS seemed determined to hijack Dylan's mini-renaissance. Through David Braun, Dylan's lawyer, he had been negotiating with Clive Davis at CBS over the terms of a new contract, having also had discussions with Warner Brothers and perhaps Atlantic Records, and was led to believe he had reached an agreement with Davis.

Clive Davis: Early in 1973 I finally did conclude negotiations for a new contract with Bob. Basically, it was limited to a commitment for two more albums, plus the *Billy the Kid* soundtrack album – there was no time period involved . . . the guaranty was about four hundred thousand dollars per album . . . Columbia [then] backed out of the deal after I left. Since the *Billy the Kid* movie had just been released, Braun screamed that the soundtrack album commitment had to be honoured; they couldn't go elsewhere in so short a time. So Columbia released it at the royalty rate agreed upon during my negotiations with Braun . . . When the single broke out of the album, and clearly showed Dylan's continued fertility, Lieberson tried to resume negotiations.

Not surprisingly, Dylan became disgusted with CBS at this point, and the removal of Davis – with whom he had always had a healthy working relationship – cannot have helped convince him to continue his association with the label (Dylan would later be a character witness on Davis's behalf during some of the legal repercussions resulting from his sacking). He decided to look elsewhere. In fact his rejection of CBS was in part a rejection of New York. After a couple of pleasant months in California, he was seriously considering settling on the West Coast, and when he finally resolved upon a recording label for his new album, it would be with a West Coast label he would sign. After a brief season in hell (aka Durango), he could look forward to a Californian summer. Finally Dylan had come to believe that Jim Morrison was right – the West was indeed the Best.

20

1973–4: Into the Flood

In April 1973 Dylan leased a property in Malibu. Back in December 1971 he had bought a modest property on the Malibu coastline from a sports writer. However, despite buying some adjoining land, the original house needed extending if it was to accommodate the entire Dylan clan. His leasing of 21336 Pacific Coast Highway was therefore a temporary measure. He certainly seemed intent on remaining in Malibu, even though he informed a reporter during the January 1974 tour that 'We're just there temporarily. It was cold in New York and we didn't want to go back there after Mexico.'

Dylan was enjoying his summer in Malibu. He was hanging out with old friends like Roger McGuinn and Barry Goldberg, and he was writing songs and making music again.

Roger McGuinn: [I'd] been hanging out a lot with Bob in Malibu, playing basketball and stuff. One day, he was sitting on my couch and we were trying to write a song together and I asked him if he had anything and he said he had one that he started but he was probably gonna use it himself and he started playing 'Never Say Goodbye'. He hadn't written all the verses yet, but he had the tune.

Barry Goldberg: I left a message with his service that if he ever wanted to jam to call me. He called me that same day and said he was coming over. That night he showed up ready to play and we played in my living room for eight or nine hours, everything from 'Pledging My Time', Johnny Ace to 'Watching the River Flow' . . . It was so good he came back the next night.

Dylan was having fun, and his wife was equally pleased to be away from New York. Everybody seemed far more relaxed in California. However, one of the most important factors in his decision to move permanently to Malibu seems to have been Robbie Robertson and the Band's own decision to resettle there.

They too had finally tired of Woodstock. Indeed, like Dylan, Robertson was currently suffering something of a creative drought, and had been since the completion of *Cahoots* in 1971.

Robbie Robertson: For a year or two I was planning on going to Malibu; I was ready to leave Woodstock. When I went out there [Dylan and I] picked up on our talks and at this point it was more advanced, and we were coming out with a more positive attitude.

The talks were about the possibility of Dylan and the Band playing some gigs together – i.e. going back on the road. If Robertson had tired of life in upstate New York, Dylan also seemed to have a restless, hungry feeling again. In June he recorded three songs for a possible album, 'Forever Young', 'Never Say Goodbye' and the still unreleased 'Nobody 'Cept You'. A sense of release seemed to follow on from completing *Pat Garrett & Billy the Kid* and was galvanizing Dylan into seriously considering touring for the first time for nearly eight years. Robertson sounded out the other members of the Band, the only group Dylan could feel comfortable touring with, and they now joined Robertson in Malibu.

Robbie Robertson: We'd been talking about a tour for years. All of a sudden it seemed to really make sense. It was a good idea, a kind of step into the past . . . The other guys in the band came out and we went right to work. We started rehearsing anyway so we thought we'd do the *Planet Waves* album and get back to rehearsing, and that's exactly what we did.

In the summer of 1973, Dylan found himself at the Band's new ranch studio in Malibu, Shangri-La Studios, working up a repertoire of some eighty songs for an as yet undefined series of dates.

Robbie Robertson: We sat down and played for four hours and ran over an incredible number of tunes. Just instantly. We would request tunes. Bob would ask us to play certain tunes of ours, and then we would do the same, then we'd think of some that we would particularly like to do.

The late summer of 1973 was a buzz of activity. Dylan had finally decided to leave CBS and duly signed a one-album deal with David Geffen's fledgling Asylum label, a label which seemed as Californian as the raisins that grew in the West Coast sun.

Bob Dylan: It was long overdue. Just a feeling it was time to go on . . . Suspected [CBS] were doing more talk than action. Just released 'em and that's all. Got a feeling they didn't care whether I stayed there or not. [1974]

If Dylan had tired of CBS, Geffen seemed enthusiastic, supportive of his decision to tour and on good terms with Bill Graham, the ideal promoter to arrange a 'comeback' tour.

If he was to go back on the road again, corporate wisdom said that he needed a new product to promote. This was certainly true in Dylan's case, as he needed to prove that his decision to tour again was part of a creative renaissance, not merely an attempt to cash in on an already burgeoning sixties nostalgia. As it happens he was keen to produce his first album of new songs in three years, and set to work on putting together enough material to record.

Surprisingly, given Dylan's determination to leave New York, and his failure to find it conducive to songwriting since his return from Woodstock, it was to New York he flew in October to compose some new songs for the sessions, scheduled for November. He returned to California two and a half weeks later with half a dozen new songs he was happy with. It was almost like the old days: an album session was imminent, so dash off a few songs to put with those he had written since the last album.

On 2 November, Dylan and the Band assembled in the Village Recorder Studio A in Los Angeles to begin recording the as-yet-untitled *Planet Waves*. It was the first (and last) time that he recorded a studio album with his most famous and regular backing band, though only Helm had not previously recorded with him at the December 1965/January 1966 sessions and/or the 1967 *Basement Tapes* sessions, so everyone else knew exactly what to expect. In fact on day one Levon Helm was not in attendance. They came in that Friday just 'to get set up and to get a feel for the studio', as engineer Rob Fraboni later observed, but still managed to lay down a cut of 'Never Say Goodbye', a song Dylan had introduced the Band to that summer.

The sessions started in earnest on the following Monday, and the bulk of the album came very quickly and with a minimum of fuss in just three days, though 'Wedding Song' was recorded the following Saturday, the first day set aside for mixing the album.

Rob Fraboni: They cut three or four things for the album on Monday . . . Then on Tuesday they cut about four more things, and we used

about three of them. We took two days off. Then they came in Friday
and we cut the balance of the album that day ... Then we were
assembling on Saturday, the next day ... around noon, Bob said, 'I've
got a song I want to record later,' and I said fine. He said, 'I'm not ready
right now. I'll tell you when.' We were doing what we were doing, and
all of a sudden he came up and said, 'Let's record.' So he went out in the
studio, and that was 'Wedding Song' ... Usually he wouldn't sing unless
we were recording. That's the way he was. You couldn't get him to go
out and just sing, unless he was running something down with the Band
... [this time] he asked, 'Is the tape rolling? Why don't you just roll it.'
So I did, and he started singing, and there was no way in the world I
could have stopped him to say, 'Go back to the top.' It was such an
intense performance. If you listen to the record, you can hear noises from
the buttons on his jacket. But he didn't seem to care ... I mentioned
recutting it to eliminate the button sounds, at one point, and Bob said,
'Well, maybe.'

Robertson, for one, was surprised how easily the album came.
'It was over before we realized we'd started.'

How happy Sara Dylan was at her husband's decision to resume
touring we do not know. The new songs clearly suggested that
Dylan was psychologically preparing himself to confront his public
for the first time since she picked up the pieces after the motorcycle
accident. On 'Tough Mama' he again seemed to be cavorting with
his muse, and in the final verse addressing his audience, asking
them not to expect too much, because he would not be 'hauling
any of my lambs through the marketplace anymore'. However,
the song which came in for the most intense speculation, particularly from those seeking to connect Dylan's art with his life,
was 'Wedding Song'.

'Wedding Song' is the final song on Planet Waves. It begins
with the narrator attempting to convince his subject that he loves
her 'more than life itself', after which he talks about her giving
him babies, and saving his life. Suddenly there seems to be a very
direct connection to Dylan's own life and his own wife. This
becomes disconcerting when, in the following verse, he tells her,
'we can't regain what went down in the flood', perhaps a suggestion that they should give up looking for a new Eden. With the
sixth verse we finally come to the crux of the song. The singer is
saying that he does not wish 'to remake the world at large',
because he loves her 'more than all of that'. Yet why does he
protest his good intentions unless there is some doubt – in her
mind at least – whether he intends 'to remake the world'? It is

logical to see the main theme of 'Wedding Song' as an attempt to reconcile his wife with the new Dylan ('I love you more than ever now that the past is gone'), to try to ask her to accept his decision to go out in the world again, because it does not mean in any way that he loves her less or that he will not return to her and the kids very soon.

If Dylan seemed concerned to exorcise 'Wedding Song' on the first take, the most possessed vocal of the album would be reserved for the last song to be recorded – 'Dirge'. He had in fact recorded this song at one of the three sessions from which the bulk of the album came, with a simple acoustic guitar accompaniment. However, while he, Fraboni and Robertson listened to the playbacks, he decided he wanted to re-record the song.

Rob Fraboni: We had mixed about two or three songs ... Bob went out and played the piano while we were mixing. All of a sudden, he came in and said, 'I'd like to try "Dirge" on the piano.' We had recorded a version with only acoustic guitar and vocal a few days earlier ... we put up a tape and he said to Robbie, 'Maybe you could play guitar on this.' They did it once, Bob playing piano and singing, and Robbie playing acoustic guitar. The second time was the take.

The take of 'Dirge' on the album is an astonishing catharsis of years of seething resentment, seemingly directed at an ex-lover but surely one of that small body of songs in his *œuvre* directed as much at his audience as at some disembodied ex-lover (along with 'It Ain't Me Babe', 'What Was It You Wanted' etc.). Though the imagery is not as finely honed as he would later manage on 'Blood on the Tracks', 'Dirge' came in for much praise at the time of the album's release.

The album itself seemed to pass most critics by in the euphoria of the 1974 tour. Indeed it sold disappointingly, despite shooting to number one on the basis of advance orders, Dylan's first number one album in the US. As the tour faded from memory a few critics began to question the worth of *Planet Waves*. Surprisingly, several thought it a disappointment after the 'promise' of *New Morning*, despite *Planet Waves'* patent superiority to that motley collection of half-formed ideas. The sheer quality of the playing by the Band and Dylan's return to a strong melodic line in his songs for the first time since *John Wesley Harding* were barely commented on. The directness of his lyrics again came in for most of the criticism, apparently because again they contained none of the surreal flights of imagination found on *Blonde on Blonde*.

Robbie Robertson: *Planet Waves* was as good as we could make it in the situation . . . he really didn't have a bag of songs there so it was just a last-minute thing . . . Under those circumstances, I thought it was extraordinary . . . But it wasn't an appropriate Bob Dylan album, that's what the problem was, and it wasn't superunusual, so it got a different kind of credit. People put so much weight on the words that it really limited that album, all those songs . . . [were] as simple as he's ever done and people just thought it wasn't a real effort.

The album was slightly delayed by Dylan's decision to change the album title at the last minute from *Ceremonies of the Horsemen* to *Planet Waves*. This meant that instead of being released as the tour began, and benefiting from the full six-week span that Dylan and the Band remained on the road, it did not come out until two weeks into the tour. This could have been a commercial disaster. If his 'comeback' had been a major disappointment the album would have 'stiffed' and Geffen would have caught a serious financial cold. At least a pre-tour release would have enabled a healthy number of units to be shifted on the hype, before any disappointment set in.

It is difficult now to conceive of the degree of risk that Dylan was taking by touring with the Band in 1974. The tour had attracted unparalleled media interest, and demand exceeded even the most optimistic expectations. According to Graham, there were twelve million applicants for the 658,000 tickets, a phenomenal response, particularly for an artist who had not issued an album of new songs in over three years and had never had either a number one single or album in the US.

Bob Dylan: It wasn't a tour where a bunch of buys get together and say, let's go out and play. There was a great demand for that tour and it had been building up, so we went out and did it. You know we were playin' at that point three, four nights at Madison Square Garden and three, four nights at the Boston Garden but what justified that? We hadn't made any records. When we were playin' out there earlier in the era we weren't drawing crowds like that. [1989]

Dylan had committed himself to a forty-date tour in twenty-one cities, playing mostly arenas. This was very different from his original conception of hitting maybe a dozen cities, playing the larger theatres. This was testing the water by jumping in head first. A syndicated article by Lynn Van Matre, voicing the fears of many, was published the week he opened in Chicago:

Dylan will always sell no matter what he does – or doesn't – have to say, or how he says it. The memories are there, and it is the memories and the mystique that spurred millions of ticket requests on this long-awaited tour. What sort of musical [*sic*] Dylan takes to the stage remains to be seen and heard, but the concerts promise to be of as much interest as sociological events as musical ones. There is always something fascinating about watching a performer try to live up to his legend and emerge stronger than his mystique. There is generally something depressing about it as well ... Whether or not the clock of Dylan's creativity has ticked out all this time is the question.

On 3 January 1974 Dylan and the Band opened the tour at Chicago Stadium in front of 18,500 fans. Despite playing well away from the West and East Coasts, every major daily or weekly publication in America and Europe seemed to have sent a representative. Dylan opened the show with an unfamiliar rollicking blues, the 1963 composition 'Hero Blues', which, despite having been especially rewritten for this tour, was dropped after the first two shows. At least its new lyrics announced that the singer was 'walking down the highway just as fast as I can go'.

The two-hour show, which featured two brief sets by the Band, one solo set by Dylan, and an hour of rousing anthems by them together, was rabidly written up by the press, even if there were signs of road rust, and the pacing of the show required a little tightening up. Dylan sounded in good voice, even if he did seem prone to shouting his way through a few songs. The acoustic set in particular was very effective, Dylan being cheered at every stop on the tour when he sang the line 'Even the president of the United States sometimes must have to stand naked', during 'It's Alright Ma'. As the newspapers were daily filled with reports of the Watergate scandal, clearly incriminating the elected president of the United States, Richard Nixon, it seemed that even Dylan's ten-year-old songs were still politically relevant.

Ironically the hysteria and hype surrounding the tour seemed to grow as the quality of the performances diminished. After the first few shows in Chicago, Philadelphia and Toronto, Dylan's penchant for shouting his way though the bulk of the electric sets started to become more and more pronounced. Though the acoustic sets continued to have moments of greatness, they, too, often seemed unduly hurried, as if he just wanted to get the whole thing over with. Songs like 'Just Like a Woman' became stripped of emotion, sounding harsh and unfeeling. It became apparent that he was pushing himself through the tour, almost willing himself on to complete it. In 1978 he admitted he 'hated every moment', and in 1980, when he commented on the 1974 tour, he compared it with Presley's fall from grace when he returned to the stage in 1969.

Bob Dylan: From the first moment I walked on stage at the opening concert, I knew that going through with the tour would be the hardest thing I had ever done . . . The problem was that everyone had his own idea of what the tour was about. Everybody had a piece of the action. The publicity people. The promoters. I had no control over what was going on. [1978]

Bob Dylan: When [Elvis] did 'That's Alright Mama' in 1955, it was sensitivity and power. In 1969, it was just full-out power. There was nothing other than just force behind that. I've fallen into that trap, too. Take the 1974 tour. It's a very fine line you have to walk to stay in touch with something once you've created it . . . Either it holds up for you or it doesn't. [1980]

Of course the demand for the tour was such that it was inevitable that the concerts would be recorded for a possible live album. Even before the tour the decision to release a live album seems to have been taken. In Lynn Van Matre's article she noted, 'The tour concerts are also to be recorded on the label, with a live album slated for release later in 1974.' This was Dylan's first tour since the advent of bootlegging, and, as the reluctant father of the bootleg industry, he could be assured that the bootleggers would be out in force. Sure enough, fourteen bootleg albums, culled from eleven gigs, resulted from this tour. If an official album would not quell the demand from obsessive collectors, it would satiate most fans' desire for a memento.

As such Dylan's first official live album was sure to be a big seller, and involve minimal cost. Unfortunately the shows which all but one of the songs that constitute *Before the Flood* came from were the final three shows at Los Angeles's huge Inglewood Forum. By this point he was singing with 'just full-out power', as if really unable to embrace these old songs himself. At times he seemed to be rolling the words around in his mouth then spitting them out, like a wine connoisseur. This was not a successful approach. Clearly by this point he just wanted to get back to Malibu.

Yet if Dylan 'hated every moment' the Band were clearly enjoying the experience somewhat more than in 1966. Indeed the rich, warm tones of Hudson's keyboards and Robertson's sensitive guitar fills compensated a great deal for Dylan's overly raucous vocals.

Robbie Robertson: We enjoyed playing with him; there was no ego consciousness at all. This was a Dylan/Band tour. We got accepted very well. Ten years ago we were just some musicians working with Bob Dylan, but this time we were more than a backing band.

If Sara was concerned that Dylan would rekindle his taste for the road on this tour, she must have been a mightily relieved wife when she met him in Los Angeles for those final shows. Joining him for a final post-tour party at the Forum Club on the evening of the 14th, she also accompanied him to the Beverly Wilshire Hotel for a more intimate gathering early the next morning with the members of the Band and their families. Dylan had returned to the fold. For a while.

21

1974–5: From Renaissance to Reformation

Dylan remains a master of illusion. Subsequent actions often belie what seems self-evident at the time. Thus Steven Goldberg, in 1970, could write in the *Saturday Review*, 'There will be no more bitterness, no more intellectualization, no more explanation. There will be only Dylan's existence and the joyous songs which flow naturally from it.'

Goldberg mistook, as have many before and after him, Dylan pulling over at the roadside for the 'finishing end', viewing him as an artist in final stasis, not temporarily at rest.

Planet Waves and the 1974 tour seemed to be some kind of return to form. Only with the release of *Blood on the Tracks* – the true unveiling of a masterpiece – would many fans recognize the lesser stature of *New Morning* and *Planet Waves*, and the lack of finesse evidenced by Dylan on the 1974 tour. To those close to him, the conclusion of the 1974 tour must have seemed like the end to a period of frenetic activity. In fact it was only the beginning. If, throughout the remainder of that winter, Dylan seemed content to remain in Malibu, with spring came a reawakening of his search for new artistic frontiers.

While Rob Fraboni and Phil Ramone edited down the tapes accumulated in New York, Seattle, Oakland and Los Angeles into a double album of the tour, and while Geffen attempted to remind Dylan of his moral obligation to release the live album of the tour he had helped set up on his label, Asylum, Dylan headed for New York.

Disappointed by the sales of *Planet Waves*, which had sold something like 600,000 units, a fact he found hard to equate with twelve million ticket applications, Dylan was already looking to move on. Geffen, who had perceived his relationship with Dylan as being a long-standing one, stood to look ridiculous in the press if he failed even to secure the album of the tour. After considering marketing the album himself Dylan did give *Before the Flood* to Asylum, but it now seemed he was ready to resume his association with Columbia.

In the meantime, Dylan returned to school. Having arrived in New York, at the end of April, he was soon seen scouting round the Village again, trying to sense if there was a scene about to happen. After all, even during the 'amnesia' he had maintained a rapacious interest in what was happening in the music scene; he was particularly interested in the singer-songwriters who had emerged from behind his own shadow. The first act he caught that spring was Buffy Sainte-Marie, who was performing at the Bottom Line. A couple of days later he ran into Phil Ochs, who was desperately trying to arrange a benefit for the recently ousted communist forces in Chile at the Felt Forum, but had so far failed to attract the sort of name required to sell out such a large venue. Dylan was the best possible answer to his prayers. After an Ochs hard-sell about the plight of the Chileans, and given his currently open schedule, he agreed to appear at the benefit, scheduled for three days hence.

Unfortunately he arrived for the show well ahead of time, and passed the hours by drinking wine and chatting with old friends like Dave Van Ronk, Pete Seeger and Arlo Guthrie. By the time he took the stage for his brief fifteen-minute set he was virtually legless – literally – and the performance remains probably the most excruciating of all his many guest appearances, challenged only by his equally drunken contribution to Levon Helm and Rick Danko's Lone Star Café appearance in February 1983.

At about the same time as his well-publicized appearance at the Friends of Chile benefit, Dylan looked up an art teacher named Norman Raeben, who had been recommended by some friends in California. Raeben proved to be the man who would teach him to 'do consciously what I used to do unconsciously'.

Bob Dylan: [Some friends] were talking about truth and love and beauty and all these words I had heard for years and they had 'em all defined ... I asked them, 'Where do you come up with all those definitions?' and they told me about this teacher. I made a point to look him up the next time I was in New York, which was in the spring of 1974. And I just dropped [in] to see him one day and I wound up staying there for two months ... Five days a week I used to go up there and I'd just think about it the other two days of the week. I used to be up there from 8 o'clock to four. That's all I did for two months. He was a painter ... He came to this country in 1930 and he made his living boxing. He's a big guy. And then he started making his living painting portraits, but in the thirties in France he roomed with Soutine, the painter. He knew people like Modigliani intimately . . . Anyway he didn't teach you how to paint so much. He didn't teach you how to draw. He didn't teach you any of these things. He taught you [about] putting your head and your mind and your eye together – to make you get down visually something which is actual . . . He looked into you and told you what you were . . . My mind and my hand and my eye were not connected up. I had a lot of fantasy dreams. He doesn't respect fantasy. He respects only imagination . . . In this class there would be people like old ladies – rich old ladies from Florida – standing next to an off-duty policeman standing next to a bus-driver, a lawyer. Just all kinds. Some art student who had been kicked out of every art university. Young girls who worshipped him . . . Needless to say it changed me. I went home after that and my wife never did understand me ever since that day. That's when our marriage started breaking up. She never knew what I was talking about, what I was thinking about and I couldn't possibly explain it. [1978]

Though Norman Raeben had never in fact 'roomed with Soutine' or known artists like Modigliani intimately, he put Dylan in touch with his creative self in a way that had been absent for at least six years. He attended Raeben's classes throughout May, June and at least part of July. Raeben treated him as just another student. As an ex-student of Raeben mentioned, during a WBAI special on Dylan in 1986:

Norman Raeben . . . used to call everybody an idiot because they couldn't see the nose on their face. They couldn't understand that it was a shadow and a light put together . . . He called Dylan an idiot all the time, and Dylan stayed for about six months and took off and never said a word to any of us and just left. But he took a lot from Norman.

Dylan talked at great length about his time with Raeben in 1978, after his divorce from Sara and the failure of *Renaldo and Clara*, a film which used many of the ideas he learnt from Raeben. He recognized his time with Raeben as a turning point in his career.

Bob Dylan: It locked me into the present time more than anything else I ever did . . . I was constantly being intermingled with myself, and all the different selves that were in there, until this one left, then that one left and I finally got down to the one that I was familiar with. [1978]

At this point he began writing the songs which would make up the *Blood on the Tracks* album. Throughout the summer he applied the techniques he had learnt from Raeben, which were techniques primarily intended for use in painting, to write new songs. The results were truly remarkable.

Bob Dylan: [Norman Raeben] taught me how to see . . . in a way that allowed me to do consciously what I unconsciously felt. And I didn't know how to pull it off. I wasn't sure it could be done in songs because I'd never written a song like that. But when I started doing it, the first album I made was *Blood on the Tracks*. Everybody agrees that that was pretty different, and what's different about it is there's a code in the lyrics and also there's no sense of time. [1978]

Dylan has generally avoided discussing his songs, except in essentially abstract terms. Yet the songs he was now writing were so strange, so unlike anything he had done before, that he was required to analyse the process that was taking place. Talking about the songs he released on *Blood on the Tracks*, he has repeatedly referred to the way that he dealt with the nature of time on that album. It seems as if he was trying to encapsulate past, present and future into each audio painting. 'Tangled Up in Blue' in particular would take an entire full-length movie to disentangle visually, and even then the results would be unsatisfactory when compared with the five-minute song.

Bob Dylan: 'Tangled Up in Blue' . . . was another one of those things where I was trying to do something that I didn't think had ever been done before. In terms of trying to tell a story and be a present character in it without it being some kind of fake, sappy attempted tearjerker. I was trying to be somebody in the present time while conjuring up a lot of past images. I was trying to do it in a conscious way. I used to be able to do it in an unconscious way, but I just wasn't into it that way anymore . . . See, what I was trying to do had nothing to do with the characters or what was going on. I was trying to do something that I don't know if I was prepared to do. I wanted to defy time, so that the story took place in the present and the past at the same time. When you look at a painting, you can see any part of it or see all of it together. I wanted that song to be like a painting. [1985]

But the power of the *Blood on the Tracks* songs was not merely the result of the new techniques he had developed under Raeben's tutoring, but of the pain and sorrow, passion and bitterness he was feeling, which he so faithfully communicated in his new lyrics and the performances in the studio.

Dylan's marriage was in trouble and it is this which remains the underlying concern of *Blood on the Tracks*. When *Blood on the Tracks* was finally released in February 1975 Dylan found he was once again the subject of intense speculation, particularly about the state of his marriage. He responded predictably by denying any notion that the songs on the album were *about* him, and any problems he might or might not be having with his wife. Such defensiveness, while wholly understandable, was nothing more than a classic Dylan smoke-screen.

Bob Dylan: A lot of people thought . . . that album, *Blood on the Tracks*, pertained to me . . . [1985]

Bob Dylan: 'You're a Big Girl Now' well, I read that this was supposed to be about my wife . . . I don't write confessional songs. [1985]

But he could not escape such speculation once he committed himself to making such a public declaration of the pain the separation from his wife was causing him. He told Mary Travers in March 1975 that he found it hard to understand how people could enjoy hearing that type of pain.

The overwhelming spectre of his loss hangs over it, however metaphorically or literally he dealt with it in specific songs. On one of the songs which did not make the album, entitled 'Call Letter Blues', the children are crying for their mother and the narrator has to explain that their mother has gone on a trip. This is too close to real life to ignore the biographical connection.

Of course, the sophistication of *Blood on the Tracks* was markedly superior to the juvenile angst he had displayed on *Another Side*, his last 'confessional' album, recorded ten years before. *Blood on the Tracks* is the album of a mature man, coming to terms with his life. It is an album haunted by remembrances, 'ancient footsteps are everywhere'. When he later described 'Tangled Up in Blue' as 'a song it took me ten years to live and two years to write', he is perhaps suggesting that it not only dealt with a quest for a woman, but that it was also an attempt to come to terms with all the water that had passed under the bridge in the sixties. For the first time he was confronting that decade as a survivor, reminiscing about a time when 'revolution was in the air', and yet suggesting that then, as now, his concerns lay elsewhere. And indeed at the end of the song there can be no doubt he is a survivor, 'still on the road', just as at the end of the album, though life may be sad, it may even be 'a bust', 'all ya can do is do what you must'.

The choice of 'Buckets of Rain' as the final track on the album seems to hint of reconciliation, or a desire for reconciliation. If the album had ended with 'Up to Me', though 'Up to Me' may be a superior song, and though it would have been a most poignant conclusion to an album haunted by the past, the tone would have been very different. Dylan clearly did not want the album to end with that final verse followed by his sorrowful harmonica refrain: 'And if we never meet again, baby remember me . . .'

Of course, there is an air of self-delusion about many of the songs on *Blood on the Tracks*. The male narrator on 'Idiot Wind' and 'If You See Her Say Hello' comes across as the wronged party. Hints of conciliation are offered with magnanimity. The central male figures in 'Tangled Up in Blue' and 'Lily, Rosemary and the Jack of Hearts' are of heroic proportions. The Jack of Hearts is a figure who wins hearts readily and whose outlaw lifestyle embodies freedom from responsibility. After Rosemary kills Big Jim to save the Jack of Hearts, he leaves behind the consequences of these events free to rob and roam. The narrator in 'Tangled Up in Blue', though less cavalier, is no less heroic, devoting his life to some form of romantic quest, ever 'keepin' on', ever searching.

The reality is less palatable. Dylan had come to New York in April, without his wife. How long he had originally intended to stay is not known. However, he appears to have stayed for something like three solid months, regularly attending Raeben's classes, all the time being separated from Sara. Inevitably this led to press speculation. A syndicated report in July suggested he had been dating Lorey Sebastian, John Sebastian's ex-wife, though she quickly refuted such allegations. However, he was certainly spending a lot of his time with a lady called Ellen Bernstein, a CBS A&R executive, and according to Joel Bernstein she was the subject matter of at least one song on *Blood on the Tracks*, 'You're Gonna Make Me Lonesome When You Go'. Though Dylan hints at the infidelity and promiscuity of the woman or women who populate the songs on *Blood on the Tracks* (writing in the original version of 'If You See Her, Say Hello', 'If you're making love to her . . .'), it would seem his own personal infidelity was the major source of strife in his relations with his wife at this point.

The plot duly thickened when Dylan returned to the record label Ellen Bernstein worked for, signing again with CBS on 2 August 1974 at the Century Plaza Hotel in Los Angeles. After the commercial success of 'Knockin' on Heaven's Door', the huge demand for the 1974 tour and a number one album in *Planet Waves*, CBS seemed to have belatedly realized their mistake in letting him go. Negotiations had begun again early in spring and at one point it seemed that CBS might even secure the live album of the 1974 tour. Though Geffen finally secured the rights for that album, Dylan had clearly decided that, having increased the demand for his own product, he could now benefit from the sort of commercial muscle only a company the size of CBS could offer.

He may also have been keen to ensure that CBS issued no more product like *Dylan*, their November 1973 'revenge' album, composed wholly of covers recorded by him as warm-ups at the *Self Portrait* and *New Morning* sessions. Ironically they may have decided to release that album rather than more obvious (and aesthetically satisfying) unreleased recordings like the legendary Albert Hall 1966 show, because they felt that a large number of potential punters would already own the bootleg version of the latter. Of more interest now was new product. After all, Dylan was very keen to record his new songs.

Bob Dylan: I had a few weeks in the summer when I wrote the songs for *Blood on the Tracks* and then I recorded them. [1985]

When he returned to Los Angeles in August 1974 he had just come from a holiday in Minnesota with his children, visiting relatives and friends. While in Minneapolis, he played Stephen Stills and Tim Drummond at least half a dozen of his new songs, sounding out their opinions. His jam session at the St Paul Hilton Hotel was the first evidence that he had enough songs to record a new album and, according to Tim Drummond, the new songs were of a very high quality.

Tim Drummond: Dylan's got an album. It's great . . . it's gutsy, bluesy, so authentic. I heard eight or nine new songs and it's the first time I've sat in a room and liked everything I heard.

Though in Los Angeles in August, Dylan was not looking to stay around. He soon returned to New York, making plans to record his second studio album in a year. After three years without really writing songs, they seemed to be pouring out of him again. As he considered whom to enlist to help him record them, Dylan thought of some of the musicians who had helped him construct his mid-sixties masterpieces. His first selection for a possible guitarist was Michael Bloomfield. He had not seen Bloomfield since the Woody Guthrie Memorial Concert in January 1968. However, he decided to go over to Bloomfield's and play him his new songs, just as back in June 1965 he had brought Bloomfield up to Woodstock so he could teach him 'Like a Rolling Stone'. This time the results were less successful. Dylan seemed wound up and overly tense and Bloom-field was made to feel somewhat uncomfortable.

Michael Bloomfield: He came over and there was a whole lot of secrecy involved, there couldn't be anybody in the house. I wanted to tape the songs so I could learn them so I wouldn't fuck 'em up at the sessions . . . and he had this horrible look on his face like I was trying to put out a bootleg album or something . . . He started playing the goddamn songs from *Blood on the Tracks* and I couldn't play, I couldn't follow them . . . There was this frozen guy there. It was very disconcerting . . . He took out his guitar, he tuned to open D tuning and he started playing the songs nonstop! And he just played them all and I just sort of picked along with it . . . He was singing the whole thing and I was saying, 'No man, don't sing the whole thing, just sing one chorus and if it's not gonna change let me write it down so I can play with you.' And he didn't. He just kept on playing. He just did one after another and I got lost. They all began to sound the same to me, they were all in the same key, they were all long. It was one of the strangest experiences of my life . . . He was sort of pissed [off] that I didn't pick it up . . . I just felt this big wall, this enormous barrier that was so tangible that there was no way you could say, 'Hey man how are you? You getting much pussy? Drinking a lot still? How are your kids?'

As usual, Dylan's approach to recording proved disconcerting to many musicians, even those who knew his working practices. He decided not to use Bloomfield, though what alternatives he had in mind remained unclear. He booked CBS's A&R Studios in New York – the old studio where he used to record in the sixties, but which was scorned by most modern recording acts – yet appeared to have no specific backing musicians in mind. Possibly his initial intention was to record acoustically and have some embellishments overdubbed later. Yet he told John Hammond, his old mentor, who popped in on the first day of the sessions to welcome him back to the fold, that this was not the case. More likely is that all along he wanted *Blood on the Tracks* to be an understated album like *John Wesley Harding*, and therefore intended to use minimal backing.

John Hammond: Bob said to me, 'I want to lay down a whole bunch of tracks. I don't want to overdub. I want it easy and natural.' And that's what the whole album's about. Bobby went right back to the way he was in the early days and it works.

When he entered the studio that first September afternoon, he began recording solo while his office attempted to track down Eric Weissberg, the renowned guitar and banjo player whom Dylan wanted to use, perhaps conceiving of getting him to provide the type of accompaniment Happy Traum gave on the October 1971 *More*

Greatest Hits session. Weissberg himself was not informed what instruments to bring along to the studio and arrived there at six in the evening no wiser as to what Dylan might have in mind. When Weissberg asked Dylan whether he wanted him to ask his band to come to the studio, he said, 'Sure, bring the whole band over.'

When recording started, Dylan again proved difficult to follow. Just as Bloomfield had struggled to learn the new songs, so Weissberg, an equally respected musician, found Dylan's way of recording bizarre and unsatisfactory. The most disconcerting thing of all was that he appeared to be playing everything in open tuning, just as he had with Bloomfield, evidently not explaining to Weissberg what key he was tuned to, making it almost impossible to follow him.

Eric Weissberg: It was weird. You couldn't really watch his fingers 'cause he was playing in a tuning arrangement I had never seen before. If it was anybody else I would have walked out. He put us at a real disadvantage. If it hadn't been that we liked the songs and it was Bob, it would have been a drag. His talent overcomes a lot of stuff.

However, Charlie Brown, who played guitar at that first session, seemed delighted with Dylan's approach and revelled in the spontaneity of the session.

Charlie Brown: He seemed to be having a good time. His whole concept of making an album seemed to be go ahead and play it and whichever way it comes out, well that's the way it is. It's what happens at the moment. He didn't want to do a lot of takes, and I don't blame him 'cause some of the songs are so long. We'd just watch his hands and pray we had the right changes.

The only song definitely resulting from the first session was 'Meet Me in the Morning', which featured some blistering blues guitar – one assumes courtesy of Brown. When Dylan later attempted to re-record this song in Minneapolis the results were so patently inferior to the original version that he stuck with this recording, the only song on the album to feature Weissberg's Deliverance.

Despite attempting several other songs with Weissberg and his band, Dylan clearly felt that the session was not a great success. Though Weissberg was an original choice of his, the following day he was phoned and told that neither he nor the band would be required for the remaining sessions. Dylan seemed to have decided to revert to the more subdued sound he had originally intended, and he asked that only Deliverance bassist Tony Brown return for subsequent sessions, on which he was supplemented by just bass, organ (provided by Paul Griffin) and, where appropriate, steel guitar (Buddy Cage).

Cage had been suggested by Ellen Bernstein, who turned up at the sessions. His country-tinged guitar playing on the New Riders of the Purple Sage's version of 'You Angel You' had particularly impressed Dylan. Bernstein was delighted at the restrained sound of the album.

Joel Bernstein: I knew Ellen Bernstein — no relation — who was the Columbia A&R representative, very intelligent, smart woman, and she was thrilled that Bob had recorded the album acoustic . . . She was shocked when she heard that Bob's brother had said he should re-record it all with a band. She thought it was a bad idea, but of course he did re-cut it.

Having completed the album in three September sessions, CBS initially planned to issue *Blood on the Tracks* before Christmas 1974, making it his third album of 1974. However, having heard a test pressing, Dylan decided he wanted to re-record some of the tracks. Returning to Minnesota for Christmas, he played the album to his brother David, who suggested he re-cut some songs in Minneapolis with some local musicians. David had good contacts among the Minneapolis music community and soon assembled a motley ensemble of local talent.

Dylan proceeded to re-cut six of the songs which had been recorded in New York over two sessions, on 27 and 30 December, completing the album for February release. Unfortunately, not only did he re-record the songs, he also rewrote them. The Minneapolis versions of 'Idiot Wind', 'Tangled Up in Blue' and 'If You See Her, Say Hello' all featured different lyrics.

In the case of 'Idiot Wind' only the first verse remained largely intact, and the new version was less personal, more ambiguous. Though the Minneapolis version may have had more sound, it had less passion. The understated delivery of the New York version had seemed actually to add to the venom of the words. 'If You See Her, Say Hello' had only minor rewrites but one change — 'If you're making love to her' becoming 'If you get close to her' — was a step back from the intimacy and hint of real hurt in the original. The worst new version was 'You're a Big Girl Now', though in this case it was not because he rewrote the song, it was just the considerable dilution of the sense of pain the New York version betrayed. The naked sorrow of the original take was now masked in a swirl of sound.

Though the cuts of 'Lily, Rosemary and the Jack of Hearts' and 'Tangled Up in Blue' from Minneapolis probably have the edge on the New York takes, it is difficult not to conclude that Dylan 'copped out' by issuing the new versions of the songs, compromising his art to tone down his previously naked pain; that, three months on from the original sessions, he decided he had laid himself a little too much on the line on the original recordings.

Despite, or maybe because of, his decision to tamper with the original album (which was rapidly bootlegged), *Blood on the Tracks* was greeted by press and fans alike as the album they had been waiting seven years for. Though there were a couple of dissenting voices, the majority of the UK and US music press loved the record. Jonathan Cott in *Rolling Stone* spent two pages on his view of Dylan 'Standing naked'. Michael Gray, in the English monthly *Let It Rock*, wrote a perceptive review which attempted to come to terms with the historic importance of the album:

> I don't know how, but some adjustment in our consciousness must now follow from the fact that it is Bob Dylan who has produced, in *Blood on the Tracks*, the most strikingly intelligent album of the seventies. That seems to me to change everything. It transforms our perception of Dylan – no longer the major artist of the sixties whose decline from the end of that decade froze seminal work like *Blonde on Blonde* into a historic religious object . . . Instead Dylan has legitimized his claim to a creative prowess as vital now as then – a power not, after all, bounded by the one decade he so much affected.

The fans seemed to agree. *Blood on the Tracks* became Dylan's second consecutive studio album to reach number one in the United States. The issue Gray raised in his review would become a central one in the succeeding years – whether *Blood on the Tracks* did indeed legitimize 'his claim to a creative prowess as vital now as then'. *Blood on the Tracks* is the central point of Dylan's career. With this album Dylan moved the posts. Instead of having to stand against *Blonde on Blonde*, as had all the albums from *John Wesley Harding* to *Planet Waves*, his subsequent albums have been up against *Blood on the Tracks*. The renaissance also, of course, allowed critics to talk about a new decline, should he let them down again.

But *Blood on the Tracks* is more than just an affirmation of his genius. For here Dylan had released an album at least the equal of his masterpieces from the mid-sixties. No other artist in white rock & roll can be said to have done that. When individuals or bands hit their stride and begin producing their 'classic' albums, it becomes a self-fulfilling prophecy that they had better exploit the streak of genius while they can because they will never recapture it. The Rolling Stones would never top the four albums, *Beggars Banquet* through *Exile on Main Street*; neither Lennon nor McCartney would come close to the quality of *Revolver*, *The White Album* or *Abbey Road*; David Bowie would never match his early seventies trilogy; Bruce Springsteen would never again reach the heights of *Born to Run* and *Darkness on the Edge of Town*. And so on.

Only Dylan, whose mid-sixties *œuvre* was itself more daunting than any of the above, succeeded in producing an album which stoked up his genius quotient nearly ten years after it was thought to be gone. And he did it by reinventing his whole approach to language. Gone were the surrealistic turns of phrase on *Blonde on Blonde*, gone was the swirl of sound that surrounded those mystical words. In their place was a uniformity of mood, a coherence of sound, and an unmistakable maturity to the voice – as if he had had to make *Nashville Skyline*, *Self Portrait* and *New Morning* just so that he could assimilate those aspects of his voice into a stronger whole. He had never sung better.

Then, hard on the heels of the critical and commercial acceptance of *Blood on the Tracks*, Dylan decided to release *The Basement Tapes*. It was the ideal time to confront those songs from happier times. After *Blood on the Tracks*, no sensible critic could write the review that undoubtedly would have been written six months earlier, that *The Basement Tapes* was a final reminder of Dylan's lost genius. It also provided further proof that he lost none of his creative drive when he fell off that damned bike!

It was in fact Robbie Robertson, rather than Dylan, who was the prime mover in the project. Indeed, there were suggestions in the press that the album was being released to shore up the Band's depleted funds, which had fallen to a low after two years of relative inactivity and their commercial decline following *Cahoots*. It was Robertson who compiled the songs for the double album, which included eight songs the Band had recorded on their own in that famous basement, and which they had originally intended for their first album. All these songs were subsequently replaced by superior material on *Music from Big Pink*, which may explain why, in subsequent conversation, Robertson seemed slightly defensive about the motives for releasing this album.

Robbie Robertson: It wasn't put out to combat anything. All of a sudden it seemed like a good idea . . . It just popped up one day. We thought we'd see what we had. I started going through the stuff and sorting it out, trying to make it stand up for a record that wasn't recorded professionally. I also tried to include some things that people haven't heard before, if possible . . . I just wanted to document a period rather than let them rot away on the shelves somewhere. It was an unusual time which caused all those songs to be written and it was better it be put on disc in some way than be lost in an attic.

In fact, the album that Robertson compiled from these tapes was a poor document of those heady days in Woodstock. Whatever his reasons for conjoining the Band material with the Dylan material, they do not mesh comfortably together. This is hardly surprising, given that the Band songs were recorded after Levon Helm rejoined the Band at the end of the summer, and so were not really the product of the same sessions as the work with Dylan. Secondly, though undoubtedly interesting, the Band material had not been released because the recordings for *Music from Big Pink* were generally superior. The Dylan material was unreleased for different reasons, unrelated to the merits of the songs, many of which stand alongside anything the man has done in thirty years of music-making.

Robertson also betrayed poor judgement in his selections. Though digging up the lovely 'Goin' to Acapulco', never previously bootlegged, he chose to leave off 'Sign on the Cross', 'I'm Not There (1956)', 'I Shall Be Released', 'Quinn the Eskimo' and 'All You Have to Do Is Dream', songs of real inspiration. He also selected inferior versions of 'Tears of Rage' and 'Too Much of Nothing', both songs available in superior form on the widely bootlegged fourteen-song Dwarf Music acetate of *Basement Tapes* recordings. Though it shows commendable modesty on Robertson's part to omit his beautiful solos on 'I Shall Be Released', 'All You Have to Do Is Dream' and the alternative 'Tears of Rage', the results were a real disservice to Dylan. The omissions preclude any real appreciation of the full scale of his songwriting triumphs that summer.

The final stages of the album's release seem to have occurred without Dylan's input. In March 1975, when talking to Mary Travers on her West Coast radio show, he told her that *The Basement Tapes* were going to be released 'in their entirety'. By the time the finished product reached the presses, he was in France.

Though there seems to have been some form of reconciliation between Dylan and Sara that winter, he made the trip to France alone. Sara had been very visibly in his company at a show in San Francisco in March, being photographed with him backstage at the

SNACK (Students Need Athletic And Cultural Kicks) benefit in Golden Gate Park, before his half-hour appearance with Neil Young and assorted members of the Band in a communal performance of personal favourites for a 50,000-plus crowd. The informality of the performance, with Dylan sharing vocal duties with Neil Young, Levon Helm and Rick Danko, and the atmosphere of the event – designed to raise funds to make up a cut in the schools' leisure and sports budget – would be closely mirrored by the later Rolling Thunder Revue.

Despite Sara's public return to Dylan's side all was clearly not well. She had apparently been due to accompany him to France that April, but did not. While in France, he stayed in regular contact with Sara but she refrained from joining him. He evidently experienced a terrible sense of loneliness throughout his stay there. He stayed with painter David Oppenheim, who had painted the mural which graced the rear cover of later copies of *Blood on the Tracks* (the first pressing containing sleeve notes by American journalist Peter Hammill), and seems to have continued to compensate for his loneliness with the occasional lusty liaison.

David Oppenheim: At that time I had just built myself a house in Savoie . . . He arrived at two in the morning. We stayed together for two months [*sic*] . . . Two of us together here alone. To see this bloke completely despairing, isolated, lost – I didn't want to be like him . . . He was having problems with his wife. She was supposed to have come with him but she hadn't arrived. He phoned her every day . . . We lived an adventurous life. No complications. We screwed women, we drank, we ate . . . Pathetic and superb at the same time, Dylan is a bloke who invents everything. He's the most egotistical person I know. That's what makes him an incredible person, his amazing self-confidence . . . When I got him to understand that he was completely mad, he would grow pale in the face, and that made me feel good because I identified with the person that I thought he was in those moments of inner understanding . . . This bloke who talked of nothing but love was very, very much on his own.

The word-portrait Oppenheim paints is a harrowing one. Yet Dylan had recently enjoyed a creative peak, and it was probably this which brought out that occasionally dormant 'amazing self-confidence'. He was not about to abandon his muse again, whatever the cost. The one song he definitely wrote during his six-week stay in France was 'One More Cup of Coffee'. It came about as a result of attending a large Gypsy festival. It was Dylan's thirty-fourth birthday when he turned up at the event. Though 'One More Cup of Coffee' is written from the viewpoint of someone seduced by one of the daughters of the king of the Gypsies, it was the king of the Gypsies himself who seems to have originally fascinated Dylan.

Bob Dylan: I . . . went to see the king of the Gypsies in southern France. This guy had twelve wives and 100 children. He was in the antique business and had a junkyard, but he'd had a heart attack before I'd come to see him. All his wives and children had left . . . After he dies they'll all come back. They smell death and they leave. [1977]

As May turned to June, he realized that the time had come to return home and face his responsibilities as a husband and an artist. As a husband he clearly needed to work at mending some of the damage caused by the events of the previous year. As an artist he needed to get back to performing. If *Blood on the Tracks* proved he could still 'cut it' in the cold isolation of a studio, he had yet to prove that his renaissance extended to the medium he had previously been the consummate artist in – performing live. According to Dylan, when talking to Larry Sloman later in the year, it was an awareness that came upon him while musing in southern France.

Bob Dylan: I was just sitting in a field overlooking some vineyards, the sky was pink, the sun was going down, and the moon was sapphire, and I recall getting a ride into town with a man with a donkey cart and I was sitting on this donkey cart, bouncing around on the road there, and that's when it flashed on me that I was gonna go back to America and get serious and do what it is that I do, because by that time people didn't know what it was that I did . . . Only the people that see our show know what it is that I do, the rest of the people just have to imagine it. [1975]

22

1975: From the Bottom Line to the Bitter End

On 26 June 1975 *The Basement Tapes* album was released, some eight years after the sessions which produced it. Dylan could now afford such a reminder of his so-called heyday. By this point he was back in New York and the word was on the wire.

New York was once again the centre of a happening scene, though the focal point was not in the Village but in a seedy little dive on the Bowery, known as CBGBs. There bands like the Ramones, Blondie and Television had been playing for almost a year, slowly establishing reputations. Television, along with New York poetess Patti Smith, had graduated to more esteemed establishments like Max's Kansas City and the Bottom Line. In their wake followed the likes of Talking Heads, the Heartbreakers, Pere Ubu and Richard Hell & the Voidoids.

If the Village was less a centre for New York's new musical explosion, it still had an active club scene – Gerde's was not the old Gerde's, but Mike Porco was still in charge. The Bitter End was now the Other End, and remained a popular venue for Dylan's contemporaries. The Bottom Line was a showcase venue for promising new acts and established artists who still sought a little contact with their audience. In August it would be the venue for ten of the most famous performances of the seventies, when Bruce Springsteen became 'the main contender' during five nights, two-sets-a-night. There were lines round the block every day.

Having recharged his batteries in France, Dylan knew he had to take advantage of the momentum created by *Blood on the Tracks*. California had never really set his creative juices a-flowin'. It was in New York that he had written all the songs that established his reputation, and it was to New York he had returned to re-establish that reputation with *Blood on the Tracks*. In the summer of 1975 he was on a scouting mission, looking for a new sound. Driving around the Village at the end of June, he ran across an exotic-looking violinist by the name of Scarlett Rivera. He invited her to his rehearsal studio to run through some songs. Perhaps he had a violin sound in mind for the next album.

Rivera spent the afternoon playing her electric violin along to some new songs from Dylan's pen, and he realized fairly promptly that he had found the first piece in his new jigsaw. There was a mantra-like quality to the sound of Rivera's violin-playing, and though she was not technically superb there was an obvious chemistry between her and Dylan.

Scarlett Rivera: [I] played all afternoon with him on songs that I could never have possibly heard before at his studio in the Village. And he played them on guitar. I'm sure [he] consciously didn't play anything that he had recorded before so that I couldn't have a head start on knowing how it sounded or how to play it. There was a little half smile after playing a few songs ... 'One More Cup of Coffee' was one of the first songs we did that afternoon ... [We did] 'Mozambique', 'Isis'. Then he moved to piano and tried some of the same songs in different keys. And so it progressed. Then by late, late afternoon we left there and he said he wanted to take me to a club to see a friend and that turned into his sitting in with Muddy Waters ... After that show was my moment of acceptance fully ... A certain chemistry, a certain recognition, a certain indefinable something was part of it – we went to Victoria Spivey's house that very night. I think it was [in] Queens or Brooklyn. The entire Muddy Waters band went and Bob and I spent many more hours jamming, talking to her, listening to old records. He was really excited by the whole evening.

Dylan had been down to see Muddy Waters perform at the Bottom Line a few days earlier, but his surprise appearance with Scarlet Rivera on 30 June was the start of a hectic two weeks when he would be seen in the Village clubs and bars almost every night, sometimes sitting in with old friends, sometimes just enjoying the show. It was the highest profile he had maintained in years. *Village Voice* and *Rolling Stone* soon ran stories about his re-emergence.

Dylan was looking for other components for the sound he had in mind. Jack Elliott provided the next, a bassist by the name of Rob Stoner, who had his own band, Rockin' Robin and the Rebels. He backed Elliott on occasions, and was in the Village most nights when Dylan was hanging out. Stoner had already met Dylan back in 1971 in San Francisco, while playing for the Greenbriar Boys, and they had hung out together in Los Angeles in 1973. Dylan knew his sound, and respected his knowledge of rockabilly.

Rob Stoner: I already knew him ... He ran into me at that Other End scene in '75 ... he was back in New York and *Blood on the Tracks* was a success at the time, it was a very heady period for him. He was really re-establishing himself there.

Though Stoner did not audition in the way that Rivera had, he would get the call when the time came to go in the studio. Dylan sat in on performances by Bobby Neuwirth and Jack Elliott, and even went to the Bottom Line again – though the Other End was a more regular choice as it had an annex to which he and his retinue could escape if the scene became a little too heavy – to see New York's new New Dylan: Patti Smith.

Smith was on the verge of recording her first album for Arista, perhaps the most remarkable debut album of the seventies, *Horses*. Her uninhibited performances, which combined frenetic rock & roll with long between-song raps and smatterings of her poetry, fascinated Dylan (who subsequently offered Patti a place on the Rolling Thunder Revue, though she refused to tour without her own band). Smith's shows at the Bottom Line were landmark performances – her first shows with a drummer in the band. Dylan was loose enough after seeing Patti perform to allow them to be photographed together.

Patti Smith: He started hanging out more – he liked the fact that he could be in a club and people didn't maul him to death, because there were a lot of things happening at that time. And we were all hanging out there, and it was really great 'cause we'd all get drunk and stuff and be falling around. People just started turning up in the Village. It happened very fast. Jack Elliott was around – everybody was around. Then one night, Bob started going up on stage, jamming with these people. I saw him start getting attracted to certain people – Rob Stoner, Bobby Neuwirth – it was great to see him and Bob back together, because he really brings out the worst in Dylan, which is what we usually love the best. And he was working out this Rolling Thunder thing – he was thinking about improvisation, about extending himself language-wise. In the talks that we had there was something that he admired about me that was difficult to comprehend then, but that's what we were talking about ... when he started getting Rolling Thunder together.

Patti included two major improvisational pieces in her performances at this time – 'Land' and 'Birdland'. She referred to them as fields. 'Land' in particular would develop each night as the feeling took Patti, the story of Johnny never being resolved. Dylan himself was working on a song which, like 'Land', was a surreal travelogue, driven by a slow piano riff. It was called 'Isis'. At this point it was, according to Jacques Levy, 'almost a dirge, slow, unlike anything I'd ever heard before, obviously setting you up for a long story'.

If Dylan had a sound in mind, what he did not yet have was an album's worth of songs. There was 'One More Cup of Coffee' from his days in France; and during his first week of club-hopping he had written a remarkable new song called 'Abandoned Love', which he had premiered at the Other End in a brief guest spot during a Jack Elliott gig. However, 'Abandoned Love' still mined the same vein he had explored on *Blood on the Tracks* and, however brilliant he was in excavating such riches, he was not one to repeat himself. Apart from these two songs all he had were scraps and half-formed ideas.

Fortunately one of the individuals he met at the Other End was Jacques Levy, a songwriter then best known for his collaborations with Roger McGuinn on songs like 'Chestnut Mare', though he had also directed the risqué play *Oh! Calcutta*. Levy lived nearby and, since the subject of a possible songwriting collaboration had come up during their discussions at the Other End, Dylan went up to his loft and played him some of the fragments of songs he was working on. Virtually the first thing Levy heard was the original version of 'Isis'. Levy made some suggestions and suddenly Dylan started finding a thread to tie the song together.

Jacques Levy: We were just sitting, just talking . . . and then he went to the piano, sat down, and he started to play 'Isis'. But it was a very different style of 'Isis' than you hear now . . . So the two of us started working on that together. I started writing words, then he would say, 'Well, no, how about this, what about that?' a totally co-operative venture. It was just extraordinary . . . What happened was that we finished 'Isis' that one night, up all night till the next morning. [It was] not the final version, we redid some stuff, but the basic story was there and I would write this stuff down and then type it up and we would go over the stuff. And we went down to the Other End and Bob read the lyrics to a bunch of people sitting around the bar, just read them, and everybody responded to the thing.

The way that Dylan described their initial collaboration was typically less direct, but indicates the value of Levy in their collaboration.

Bob Dylan: I had bits and pieces of some songs I was working on and I played them for him on the piano, and asked him if they meant anything to him, and he took it someplace else, and then I took it someplace else, then he went further, then I went further, and it wound up that we had this song ['Isis'] which was out there. [1975]

Dylan had discovered a companion to accompany him down a new path. If *Blood on the Tracks* had been the product of him 'learning to do consciously what he used to do unconsciously', then Jacques Levy's very deliberate and conscientious approach seems to have naturally complemented his more inspirational but less disciplined way of working. Since Dylan appeared to want to write story-songs again – but story-songs which, though no less cinematic than 'Tangled Up in Blue', advanced the story more directly and with fewer dramatic lurches in time and space – Levy was an ideal collaborator. Under Levy's influence, he even rewrote 'Simple Twist of Fate' so that it was more linear in the telling of its tale. (He performed this 'new' version on the John Hammond TV tribute in September 1975.) He had never really collaborated before (his co-written songs like 'Ballad of Easy Rider' and 'I'd Have You Anytime' were more the result of him writing a verse or a bridge for someone else). It was a new and exhilarating experience to have such measured but immediate feedback as Levy provided.

Roger McGuinn: Bob had never seen a thesaurus before, nor a rhyming dictionary. Imagine all the songs that Bob has written without a rhyming dictionary. When he saw one it blew him out ... He's going, 'What! Think of all the time I could have saved.' He didn't even know they existed.

Though Dylan and Levy now started seeing if they could repeat the 'Isis' experiment on a daily basis, the next major song that they wrote together was again composed on the spur of the moment, a few days later, after a dinner they both attended given by two friends of ex-New York gangster Joey Gallo. On record the ballad 'Joey' would clock in at eleven minutes.

Bob Dylan: I was leaving town and Jacques says he was going up to some place to have supper and I was invited to come if I felt like it and I was hungry so I went with him and it was up to Marty and Jerry Orbach's place and as soon as I walked in the door, Marty was talking about Joey. She was a good friend of Joey's. They were real tight. I just listened for a few hours, they were talking about this guy, and I remembered Joey. At that time, I wasn't involved in anything that he was involved in, but he left a certain impression on me. I never considered him a gangster. I always thought of him as some kind of hero in some kind of a way. An underdog fighting against the elements. He retained a certain amount of his freedom and he went out the way he had to. But she laid all these facts out and it was like listening to a story about Billy the Kid so we went ahead and wrote that up in one night. [1975]

At this point Gallo was in the news. The paperback edition of Donald Goddard's biography of him had been published in June. Dylan, on the release of 'Desire', would come in for some considerable criticism for his song, which appeared to glorify a vicious hoodlum. Lester Bangs wrote a lengthy and detailed attack upon the historical veracity of the song in *Creem* magazine, under the title 'Dylan's Dalliance with Mafia Chic'. Dylan later defended the song as a valid re-creation of the traditional ballad form, which had often eulogized outlaws of the Old West. And in 1987 he even started performing it in concert. Along with 'One More Cup of Coffee' it is the only song from *Desire* to appear in his shows in recent years.

Bob Dylan: I always grew up admiring those heroes . . . Robin Hood, Jesse James . . . those guys who kicked against oppression and had high moral standards . . . It amazes me I would write a song about Joey Gallo . . . [but] I feel that if I didn't, who would? But that's an old tradition. I think I picked that up from the folk tradition . . . I used to sing a lot of those songs and it just kinda carried over. [1981]

Dylan was getting such a buzz from the new songs, he could not resist going out and performing them. Both 'Isis' and 'Joey' were premiered to a lucky few at the Other End during Bobby Neuwirth's one-week residency there. Neuwirth had been hanging out with Dylan throughout his two weeks of Village club-hopping. The more famous Bobby had even got up on stage and sung a duet with his old sidekick. However, the late nights and drunken revelries were not conducive to the writing of new songs.

Jacques Levy: What was happening was that we were going out and hanging out late at night and we were getting together the next afternoon and there were lots and lots of distractions. So we said, 'Let's get out of here,' and suddenly it became serious that we were really going to do some serious work together, so we went out to a place out in the Hamptons. Nobody was around, and the two of us were just there for like three weeks [*sic*] together, that summer. We had already written a couple of songs so there was a feeling of confidence that we both had that we could really do it.

In the seclusion of East Hampton, they wrote fourteen songs together in less than two weeks, including two complex travelogues, 'Black Diamond Bay' and 'Romance in Durango'. Durango was the more conventional tale: an outlaw and his lover on the run, in an exotic Mexican landscape. 'Black Diamond Bay' related, via a highly convoluted rhyme scheme, the destruction of a tiny island as if observed from a hotel on the island itself, before pulling back to reveal a man watching a news report about an earthquake which left behind just a Panama hat and a pair of shoes.

Also probably completed in East Hampton was the lengthy ballad which opens the *Desire* album. The song 'Hurricane' took eight minutes to detail the unjust imprisonment of boxer Rubin 'Hurricane' Carter back in 1967. Dylan had already visited Carter in Rahway Prison in Trenton, New Jersey, upon returning from France, after reading a copy of Carter's autobiography, *The Sixteenth Round*.

Hurricane Carter: When I wrote the book *The Sixteenth Round*, I sent a copy to Bob Dylan, because of his prior commitment to the [civil rights] struggle. I sent a copy to him hoping that somehow I could influence him to come and see me. So I could talk to him . . . So when he got the book and read it he came. And we sat and talked for many, many hours. And I recognized the fact that here was a brother.

Having met the man, Dylan decided that the same pen which had detailed the fates of Hattie Carroll, Emmett Till, Medgar Evers and George Jackson should turn to Carter's aid. Unfortunately he was not really sure how to put across the story. After all, George Jackson had been a simple gut reaction to the death of a man he respected; and it had been twelve years since he wrote the last of his 'topical' songs.

Bob Dylan: The first time I saw him, I left knowing one thing . . . I realized that the man's philosophy and my philosophy were running on the same road, and you don't meet too many people like that . . . I took notes because I wasn't aware of all the facts, and I thought that maybe sometime I could condense it all down and put it into a song. [1975]

Knowing Dylan's love of movies, Levy wisely suggested a cinematic approach, similar to that used in 'Lily, Rosemary and the Jack of Hearts'.

Jacques Levy: Bob wasn't sure that he could write a song . . . he was just filled with all these feelings about Hurricane. He couldn't make the first step. I think the first step was putting the song in a total story telling mode. I don't remember whose idea it was to do that. But really, the beginning of the song is like stage directions, like what you would read in a script: 'Pistol shots ring out in a bar-room night . . . Here comes the story of the Hurricane.' Boom! Titles. You know, Bob loves movies, and he can write these movies that take place in eight-to-ten minutes yet seem as full or fuller than regular movies.

Writing 'Hurricane' also gave Dylan a cause to champion. After writing his best love songs in years the previous summer, he was now writing his best story songs in nigh on a decade.

When they returned to New York, Dylan immediately set about putting together a set of musicians to record the songs that he and Levy had written. He had already attempted recording a couple of the songs with Dave Mason's band before his departure from New York, but now he determined to start afresh.

After the success of his return to Columbia's New York studios the previous September, Dylan not surprisingly opted for a re-run. He also chose to use an in-house producer, Don Devito, though Devito's role was more akin to engineer than producer. As ever, it was really Dylan who made the decisions at his recording sessions.

The initial concept for the album's sound was a little grandiose. Dylan had enlisted the entire eight-piece English pub-rock band Kokomo, Eric Clapton and Yvonne Elliman, violinist Scarlett Rivera, country singer Emmylou Harris — presumably recruited on the basis of her work with the late Gram Parsons — plus assorted trumpeters, saxophonists and mandolin players. The first couple of sessions were disastrous.

Neil Hubbard: The sessions were all pretty chaotic. There were far too many musicians there — five guitarists including me and Eric Clapton played on the 'Hurricane' set. And there was no one in overall control. No producer or anything.

Eric Clapton was having a hard time figuring out what exactly Dylan had in mind, and soon departed, though not before giving his opinion that some slimming down was in order.

Eric Clapton: He was trying to find a situation, you see, where he could make music with new people. He was just driving around picking musicians up and bringing them back to the sessions. It ended up with like twenty-four musicians in the studio all playing these incredibly incongruous instruments, accordion, violin — and it didn't really work. He was after a large sound, but the songs were so personal that he wasn't comfortable with all the people around. But anyway, we did take[s] on about twelve songs. He even wrote one on the spot all in one night. It was very hard to keep up with him . . . I had to get out in the fresh air, 'cause it was madness in there.

Scarlett Rivera, the lynchpin of the whole sound, was also having a hard time of it. They were her first ever studio sessions and she had expected a somewhat more intimate set-up.

Scarlett Rivera: They were very big sessions. It was a big surprise after having worked so intimately. It was all a very big shock to me . . .

Kokomo in particular were unsuited to the type of approach Dylan usually adopted in the studio – the 'tape it and run' method. They were used to working on songs meticulously for take after take until they got the music just how they liked it. Spontaneity and freshness were not major factors at Kokomo sessions.

Mel Collins: Dylan . . . was pretty out of it. He came into the studio, played the songs through a couple of times and then expected everyone to provide some suitable backing material. I mean, he came up to me and this other guy who was playing trumpet – who I'd never met before – with a few ideas for one song but that was all.

Devito and/or Dylan finally decided they needed a helping hand, a new perspective, in order to get these songs down while they still meant something to Dylan. It was to Rob Stoner, the Village perennial, that they decided to turn.

Rob Stoner: He was trying to get what became the *Desire* album together at CBS Studios on 52nd Street . . . Don Devito took me aside one night when Dylan had come down to hear some band I was backing up. I think it was Ramblin' Jack. He said, 'Bob's been recording uptown. I want you to come up to the session tomorrow night and tell me what you think' . . . So next night I was up there and I was listening to it and they were doing the same songs that him and Levy had co-written, that were gonna be the *Desire* album, but they weren't having any success. They were trying to do a superstar session thing: they had Dave Mason, they had this band Kokomo, Clapton was up there. A lot of people. But it was just too much of a hanging-out scene. In fact they had to empty out an adjacent studio to put [on] a . . . buffet for all these overflow people – everybody was bringing their friends, 'Hey, you wanna see me record with Bob Dylan' . . . And Devito came to me at the end of the night, when all these musicians had gone home, and asked me what I thought of it and I told him that I thought it was not a likely way to get a productive project out of Bob Dylan, that it was too crowded, it was too confusing, it was inefficient. Bob's music really is dependent on catching a moment– they're like snapshots, Polaroids . . . The first take is gonna be better even if it's got some wrong notes or something . . . These guys from Kokomo, I think they were the main culprits, 'cause they were really into this very slick, professional [sound] . . . it became their record because they kept doing takes so they would get their parts together and by that time Bob's bored. Bob doesn't want to do a song more than twice and I don't blame him . . . So Devito asked me what I would suggest. I said, 'Why don't you come in with a tiny band and like nobody, no girlfriends, no wives, no nothing! Just the smallest possible band you can get – bass player, drummer and anybody else you wanna keep around.'

As it happened, Kokomo already had impending commitments, and so did not attend any further sessions. Dylan, keen to adopt Stoner's suggestion, now needed a drummer. After failing to get hold of Kenneth Buttrey, the stalwart of previous Dylan sessions, he took Stoner's advice and asked him to bring his buddy, Howie Wyeth, along to the following night's session. With just Scarlett Rivera, Emmylou Harris, Rob Stoner and Howie Wyeth, Dylan would complete the album.

Bob Dylan: We tried it with a lot of different people in the studio, a lot of different types of sound, and I even had back-up singers on that album for two or three days, a lot of percussion, a lot going on. But as it got down, I got more irritated with all this sound going on and eventually just settled on bass, drums and violin. [1978]

Emmylou Harris had also been having a hard time at the sessions, though not because of the big band set-up, but rather Dylan's idiosyncratic phrasing. Reading off lyric sheets and with no opportunity for rehearsal, Emmylou found the whole experience of recording with Dylan bewildering.

Emmylou Harris: I'd never heard the songs before and we did most of them in one or two takes. There were no tapes, we sang live. His phrasing changes a lot, but Gram did that a lot, too. Gram and I had the same feel for phrasing, but I watched him all the time, so I did just the same thing with Dylan. I just watched his mouth and watched what he was saying. That's where all that humming comes from. You can hear me humming on some of those tracks . . . It does take me a while to work out harmony parts and Dylan works very fast. I'm more of a perfectionist. I would have liked more time. There were times when I didn't even know I was supposed to come in and had to jump fast. But I later realized that you just don't overdub on a Dylan album. He's not that kind of artist. I asked to come and fix my parts and he said sure but I didn't have the time; and I really didn't think he'd use any of it.

By the time they had stripped down to the four-piece line-up, Emmylou had had a few days to come to terms with Dylan's unorthodox recording techniques. It was Howie Wyeth who was in at the deep end when they reconvened at Columbia Studios on 30 July 1975. The session did not start well for him.

Howie Wyeth: Emmylou and Bob had their own little table. It was like they were in a little French restaurant or something . . . the rest of us were all over here. It was like a separate scene. Bob would start a tune. He wouldn't tell us the names of the tunes. The first song we did – this is the gospel truth man, I don't think people believe me – the first song we started to do I had just barely met him. We started the song and I think they were recording it, we played the song and we sort of fumbled the ending. And I asked Bob – y'know he said, 'Okay we're gonna do that again' – and I said, 'Bob, are we gonna end this or is it gonna be a fade?' And he went into such a lengthy explanation, he went on and on, that everybody got so confused, it ended up we didn't even do the song [again]. He said, 'Let's not even do it.' And Stoner said, 'Don't ask him anything. Just play.' He gave such a complicated answer. All I wanted to know was, Are we gonna stop or fade? Nobody knew what the hell he was talkin' about so he just said, We better do something else. And we never played the song again.

If this was an inauspicious start, the remainder of the session was a revelation. Next up, they attempted 'Isis', and straightaway Dylan and the band struck a groove. Not since the days of *Bringing It All Back Home* had he hit such a creative groove and managed to maintain it throughout an entire session.

Rob Stoner: Right away that [first] version of 'Isis' was a take. Because it was a small group, there was no confusion . . . Right after we finished 'Isis', Bob came over to me and said, 'Your drummer's great, it sounds great,' and we all felt great because it was intimate. It had the sound that you can hear on *Desire*, just a bunch of people playing in a room with no overdubs, all live, happening right before your ears, and we could get that first-take spontaneity because we didn't have to keep going over and over things to show them to all these musicians who were faking it . . . So we just listened to that take of 'Isis', we just went back into the studio and started running through tunes, bam, bam, bam, just getting every complete take, every complete tune was a take . . . Just like that. We were so hot we did 'Rita Mae', which wasn't on the record, 'One More Cup of Coffee', 'Joey', 'Mozambique', 'Hurricane', 'Oh Sister', 'Black

Diamond Bay', we did them all that night . . . I think we were still doing takes as late as five and six a.m. that morning, and we hung out listening to the playbacks until we had to go out to the street to move our cars at eight so they wouldn't get towed away.

Howie Wyeth: We had a lot of ESP that night. Even in 'Joey' there was a place where I thought the song was ending and I drop out for a second and it wasn't the end but it worked great.

Though they had been working for less than a week in the studio, the relief was enormous. As they filed out of the session there was almost universal euphoria. Dylan and Devito in particular had seen a great weight lifting from their shoulders as the evening progressed.

Howie Wyeth: I remember they drove me down here afterwards and Bob and Devito each had cars and they were like bumping each other, playing bumper cars, I mean I thought we were gonna die. They dropped me off about eight blocks from here. I walked back in the middle of the street 'cause I thought something was gonna fall on me. I thought those guys were gonna kill each other 'cause as they dropped me off they were stopped at a light and Bob was pushing Devito on through the light. There were no cars around.

Though Stoner was equally pleased with the night's results, Emmylou Harris, from whom he hitched a lift, remained less euphoric. If she had been almost hoping that the sessions might be aborted, it was now clear that Dylan had near-as-damn-it recorded an entire album in one night. If a juggernaut had ploughed into him while he played bumper cars, CBS now had fifty-two minutes of top-notch Dylan for his mourning fans.

Rob Stoner: She was a trooper [but] she was really bummed out at the end of that night. She was saying, Oh I can't believe this. Hope they don't put it out. He was so fucking loose.

The following night euphoria had tempered a little. Dylan had spent the day in court, appearing as a character witness on behalf of ex-CBS president Clive Davis, and was understandably exhausted. Accompanying him to the studio was his wife Sara, which inspired him to attempt a take of a song he had written on his own during his time with Levy at East Hampton earlier in the month. 'Sara' seemed self-evidently an honest and open paean to his wife, portrayed here as his eternal muse. However, there are doubts about the literalness of the song as certain lines seem patently untrue – such as his famous one about writing 'Sad Eyed Lady of the Lowlands' in the Chelsea Hotel (it is fairly well documented that he wrote it in Nashville), having just taken some kind of cure (from what? – it would be another six months before he attempted to rid himself of his drug habits).

Ever perverse, Dylan then went on to record 'Abandoned Love', a song about the rejection of an imperious woman whose ensnaring ways have haunted the singer for too long. Though rewritten and considerably less intense than at its premiere at the Other End earlier in the month, the song was hardly a tactful selection to perform before his recently reconciled spouse. Though a fine if decidedly loose performance, perhaps the lack of any hint of reconciliation in the song meant it was never in serious contention for inclusion on an album on which the outlaws end up imprisoned ('Hurricane'), gunned down ('Durango') or imprisoned and gunned down ('Joey'), but on which songs 'about' women appear conciliatory ('Isis', 'Sara', 'Oh Sister'). Despite the failure of the session on 31 July, 'Sara' completed the album – or at least, it seemed so at the time.

Howie Wyeth: He was so bummed out . . . the night we played 'Sara' and 'Abandoned Love' and a bunch of other stuff. We thought everything sucked at that point and then Bob said, 'Okay the next day we're gonna come in, we're gonna play everything and decide what makes it and what doesn't make it.'

The following day Dylan, Devito and the band all listened to playbacks of the songs recorded both with the stripped-down ensemble and from the big-band sessions. 'Romance in Durango' was the only example of the big band to make it to vinyl. In fact the stripped-down band never recorded it. Apart from 'Sara', the remaining songs on *Desire* were drawn from that one remarkable session on the 30th. *Desire* was now a reality. Dylan had recorded a follow-up, and a strong one, to *Blood on the Tracks* within seven months of concluding the sessions for that album.

With the album completed, Dylan and Sara travelled to their farm in Minnesota for a month's holiday, which they concluded by attending the marriage of his cousin, Linda Goldfine, at the Temple Israel Camp in Minneapolis. Stoner, Rivera and Wyeth had gone back to their regular gigs in the Village, expecting a cheque in the post, but not any phone call from Dylan. Then, less than a week after he returned from Minneapolis, Dylan called them all. He wanted the three of them to accompany him to

Chicago to perform three songs for a tribute to John Hammond which was being filmed by PBS for screening in the New Year.

Scarlett Rivera: We had less than twenty-four hours' notice. It was basically the night before that we got the call to be in Chicago the next day . . . Our rehearsal basically took place in the dressing room, talking over the songs and what key they would be in and just mental refreshers . . . We ran over [the new] 'Simple Twist of Fate' in the dressing room.

At this point it became apparent to the trio that Dylan considered them to be his new band, and perhaps even had in mind touring with them. In fact he had been talking with friends about a low-key tour since those humid July nights at the Other End. At that time a Columbia rep indicated to *Rolling Stone* that Dylan had such an idea already in mind.

Columbia rep: You get the feeling he really digs being back in New York. He's looking into doing a show on Broadway, maybe a play. And he's looking closely at TV, maybe a special. But most of all, after these nights down here at the Other End, he'd like to tour small clubs like this. There has been some talk of getting a van and driving around the country, dropping in, unannounced like tonight, playing a couple of nights and moving on. Nobody would know he was there until he showed up, so there wouldn't be a crowd scene. And nobody would know where he would strike next.

In fact the idea of a touring revue had not started at the Other End. It was an old Dylan dream. He had told Phil Ochs that he would love to play a tour of small clubs 'and give the money away' when they were hanging out together after the Friends of Chile benefit. In 1972, according to Maria Muldaur, Dylan had said to her, 'Wouldn't it be great if we got a train and put a revue together that would travel across the country?' He had even discussed the idea with Robbie Robertson back in the sixties.

Robbie Robertson: This thing has been a thing that Bob's been talking about for years. I'm sure he would have liked to have taken it all the way and done it by train. He's always wanted to have that kind of gypsy caravan situation happening where it was loose and different people could get up and do different things at different times and nothing would be out of place.

After the filming in Chicago, Dylan returned not to New York but to his home in Malibu. But he was back in New York in the middle of October, moving into the Gramercy Park Hotel, while rehearsal time was booked at Studio Instrument Rentals. Ever secretive, only at this point did he assemble a touring band around the nucleus that had completed the *Desire* album (though Emmylou Harris was busy promoting her own album, *Luxury Liner*).

Rob Stoner: [We] start rehearsing up at S.I.R. in mid-town there, 54th Street. We're rehearsing for like a day or two – it's not really so much a rehearsal as like a jam, tryin' to sort it out. Meanwhile all these people who eventually became the Revue started dropping in. Baez was showing up. McGuinn was there. They were all there. We had no idea what the purpose for these jams was except we were being invited to jam. I think the only people who were being paid were the group that was already working for Bob – namely Scarlett, myself and Howie. So we're up there jamming and it turns out what we're really doing is rehearsing.

As the sessions progressed, it became considerably more than the stripped-down band that had recorded the album. Four multi-talented instrumentalists were drafted in from Los Angeles: Luther Rix, Steven Soles, T-Bone Burnett and the angel-faced David Mansfield. Mick Ronson, Bowie's ex-lead guitarist, was also brought in. He seemed an incongruous choice, though Dylan had kept him in mind since hanging out with Ian Hunter and Ronson during the July late-night sessions at the Other End. Of course the idea of a revue format for the shows required other headline acts as well as Dylan. In what was seen as a repaying of some old debts, he recruited Roger McGuinn, Jack Elliott and Bobby Neuwirth, who had all been in on the initial discussions back in July. Neuwirth was an obvious compere for the show. Dylan also asked Joan Baez. Dylan/Baez – a bill with true nostalgia appeal!

Lou Kemp: Bob called Joan up, and invited her, just the week prior to leaving New York for the Cape . . . We'd go out at night and run into people and we'd just invite them to come with us. We started out with a relatively small group of musicians and support people and we ended up with a caravan.

On 22 October Dylan turned up at the Other End to watch David Blue perform. He was with Ronee Blakely, a talented actress who had made such an impression in Robert Altman's three-hour cult classic, *Nashville*. A powerful singer in her non-acting time, Blakely joined Dylan on stage for a few duets at the end of Blue's show. Dylan had found another member for the Revue. Blakely could also be deployed in the film he intended to shoot on the tour.

Meanwhile, though, he was required back in the studio. The version of 'Hurricane' recorded at the *Desire* sessions had become a source of concern to CBS lawyers. It was felt that a couple of the lines could lead to litigation, particularly the reference to Bello and Bradley 'robbing the bodies'. The song would have to be re-recorded.* By now, Dylan was deeply involved with rehearsing for the tour.

Rob Stoner: The first or second day all these suits from CBS come in and they're all talking about this 'Hurricane' controversy, saying, 'Look the band is here. You got these guys sitting here right now. Let's go across town and do another version of it now so at least we got an alternate one.' So that's what it was. They interrupted this rehearsal/jam thing to go across town and just do this quickie thing that they put on the *Desire* album – they just slapped it on to appease the legal problems.

On 24 October, Dylan returned to CBS studios, along with Stoner, Rivera, Wyeth, Luther Rix, Steven Soles and Ronee Blakely, to re-record a song he had got right the first time. Warming up with old nuggets like 'Sitting on Top of the World' and 'That's Alright Mama', he attempted to get the song down quickly. However, the chemistry was not right.

Howie Wyeth: We ended up doing it after we'd been rehearsing for about fourteen hours and they said, 'Okay. Now we're gonna go and record.' Everybody was burnt. It was not the right night to record. Everybody was drinking. Ronee was starting to ad-lib more and more. At first I think she hit an ad-lib that worked. Then of course everyone went Yeah, which we shouldn't have 'cause then she started ad-libbing. I think she was juiced.

Never one to enjoy repeated takes, Dylan was required to attempt eleven of them. He kept stumbling over the rewritten words, and by five in the morning he had had enough.

Larry Sloman: After the tenth take [*sic*] Don says, 'Do you wanna hear it?' and Bob just put his coat on and says, 'Man, I don't know. You mix it. You let me know which one you pick out.'

Dylan just wanted the song out. In the end Devito had to edit two of the takes together. Dylan's mind had not been on recording. The album was a thing of the past. What mattered now was the tour. He was going on the road with a package tour he had put together himself, billed as the Rolling Thunder Revue. First stop

---

* Ironically they were sued anyway, by Patty Valentine, who lost her suit in 1979.

would be Plymouth, Massachusetts, the place where the first Pilgrims landed, an appropriate start to a bicentennial tour. In Plymouth Dylan discussed with Allen Ginsberg, who was the official bard for the Revue, his return to performance.

Bob Dylan: I've been up the mountain and I had a choice. Should I come down? So I came down. God said, 'Okay, you've been up on the mountain, now you go down. You're on your own, free. Check in later, but now you're on your own.' [1975]

He had indeed been in the wilderness. It was now time to go back out in the wind.

23

1975: You Come On to Me Like Rolling Thunder

The New York rehearsals had gone well. To celebrate the beginning of a great adventure Dylan and the Revue turned up at
Gerde's Folk City for a last New York City jam session on 26
October. The following day they headed for Falmouth, Massachusetts, and two days of final rehearsals. The show that had been
put together was not intended to be a standard rock & roll
performance. Dylan asked Jacques Levy, with his theatre experience, to put together a format for the show so that it could be
carefully choreographed for maximum effect. The format, like
Dylan's 1966 shows, was to be rigorously defined, set variations
few.

Jacques Levy: Bob said, 'Can you figure out a way of doing it – a
presentation? What would it be like?' So I sat down and I did something
not unlike the kind of work I had to do in *Oh! Calcutta*: to figure out
what goes first and what follows what – the batting order. I knew we
were talking about a big show – four hours or more. So I wrote up a
thing like that and I left open spots so there could be guests and shifts. It
wasn't really a rigid thing at all, the key point [was] how exactly we'd
get to the point where Bob came on, and when to play the new material.
We rehearsed the show in New York for almost two weeks. Again we
had this enormous pile of material, and it had to be arranged and worked
out and staged. And the idea was that it should not look staged. We
didn't want it to be a flash show, because that didn't fit anybody's style.
The thing was to make it appear like it was a spontaneous evening . . .
like a travelling vaudeville show or a travelling circus . . . There was
almost a hootenanny feel . . . There was [to be] no tuning up between
songs, there were no pauses. Big chunks of the show were the same
every night.

If song selection was intended to remain fairly constant for each
show, actual performances of the songs would vary considerably.
Dylan had always looked to change the way a song could be

performed from night to night, keeping the experience fresh for him and the listener.

Mick Ronson: He used to come on one night and play real fast. Then next night he'd play the same songs real slow. Either he was doing it on purpose or . . . I reckon he had a bad memory . . . 'Cause he was all over the place some nights. He'd just wander off somewhere, expecting us to follow him. Come to think of it, he had problems knowing what key he was playing in. We'd just have to look at him all the time 'cause otherwise he'd have finished one song and be into another. There were nights when – if you weren't looking – you'd find yourself still playing when the song was over . . . He really forced you to look at him, what with him being a bit shaky on his timings, key changes and all, he didn't know what he was doing half the time . . . Plus he never played anything the same way twice.

Though Rob Stoner agrees with Ronson that Dylan would 'never play anything the same way twice', he adamantly disagrees with Ronson's assessment that it was his poor memory and musicianship that caused this. According to Stoner, the changes of key and tempo were absolutely deliberate, and specifically designed to keep the musicians on their toes. Most of the musicians who have worked with Dylan in performance seem to share this view.

Rob Stoner: For instance, 'Isis' – we did a reggae version, we did funk versions, we did the waltzy one, we did the fast metal version. That's one tune that comes to mind but Bob was really into that . . . That's why he does that. He's not doing that to be a prick. He's doing that to keep himself from getting bored . . . anybody who's gonna complain about that shit shouldn't be on his bus! That's the gig!

The Rolling Thunder Revue attracted considerable interest from the media for a variety of reasons, most of them unrelated to the merits of the shows. There was the veil of secrecy that surrounded the location of the Revue at any given point; the advocating of Hurricane Carter's cause; the new material that Dylan was premiering; the fact that he was playing his first tour since *Blood on the Tracks*; the stated intention to play smaller venues, primarily theatres; and the inclusion of Joan Baez on the same bill as Dylan for the first time in ten years. Any of these factors alone would have guaranteed media interest. Together they were a potent brew.

The three days at the Seacrest Motel in Falmouth before the tour acclimatized the crew to being out on the road, and allowed the musicians to begin to feel like a creative unit and to socialize together. This was not viable in New York, where each had his own circle and many had a home to return to after rehearsals.

In Falmouth, Dylan also began to work seriously on the film he intended to make on this tour. Back in 1968 he had told John Cohen that if he and Howard Alk had the opportunity to reshoot the type of footage they composed *Eat the Document* from, then 'we could really make a wonderful film'. They had not given up on the idea. In October 1975, Alk picked up the phone at his home in Montreal to hear a voice say, 'Bob wants to know if you're ready.' Dylan had begun filming some scenes in New York: David Blue telling stories about the early sixties in Greenwich Village while playing pinball; Dylan's surprise appearance at Mike Porco's birthday party at Gerde's; a meeting between Dylan and Walter Yetnikoff, the CBS record division president, to discuss the release of the 'Hurricane' single. But it was in Falmouth that he started filming in earnest.

According to Mel Howard, who was the man in charge of Film Crew A, the film did not in fact start to come together until some way into the tour. The majority of the footage shot early on, he disliked, saying 'the stuff was home movies', the same accusation Pennebaker had made about some of the scenes in *Eat the Document*.

Mel Howard: A lot of the stuff that we were shooting in New York and at the beginning was stuff that was conversational and worse than that . . . To take that opportunity [to film Dylan] and just parade him around as though he were some lame dick and everybody's gonna freak out over him and we can take funny movies of girls giggling, that to me was lame and a drag . . . I thought the stuff was home movies, and I really disliked it.

As well as bringing in Howard Alk as co-editor, Dylan had also recruited Sam Shepard to write some scenes for the movie. At the time Shepard was a promising New York playwright, but he had yet to establish a firm reputation. Possibly Bobby Neuwirth suggested Shepard. They had both been friends of Patti Smith's in the early seventies and knew each other. Or possibly even Smith herself, who co-wrote the play *Cowboy Mouth* with him, mentioned Shepard. Whatever, Shepard was summoned from California to New York, arriving during final rehearsals. His first meeting with Dylan was not auspicious. Dylan's first words to him were, 'We don't have to make any connections. None of this has to connect.'

Shepard soon discovered he meant the scenes in the film. Dylan asked him whether he had seen Marcel Carné's *Les Enfants du Paradis* or Truffaut's *Shoot the Piano Player*, adding that those were the types of films he had in mind. *Shoot the Piano Player* was a rather ironic choice on Dylan's part, being a film about an ambitious girlfriend's attempts to get the anti-hero to resume his once-prominent concert career. This would appear to be the reverse of Dylan's own circumstances. Sara Dylan would join the Revue during November, but she stayed detached from the camaraderie of the musicians and crew.

Shepard in fact soon found his supposed role to be largely redundant. Even before they left Plymouth, it became apparent that the film would be largely, indeed primarily, improvised, and that there was little need for a scriptwriter. As Shepard himself later wrote in his *Rolling Thunder Logbook*, a fragmented chronicle of the Revue, by November they had 'abandoned the idea of developing a polished screenplay or even a scenario-type shooting script, since it's obvious that these musicians are not going to be knocking themselves out memorizing lines in their spare time . . . So we've veered onto the idea of improvised scenes around loose situations.' In the end, Shepard found himself sitting in on scenes in the film, providing him with his only real role in the Revue.

Bob Dylan: *Renaldo and Clara* was originally intended as a more structured film. I hired playwright Sam Shepard to provide dialogue but we didn't use much of his stuff because of a conflict in ideas. [1978]

From Plymouth onwards the film took its own course, not charted by Dylan, but sailing from rock to rock. The amount of direction provided to his actors was minimal. Certainly the other members of the Revue were not at all sure what he had in mind. Joan Baez told Nat Hentoff, covering a story for *Rolling Stone*, that 'The movie needs a director. The sense I get of it so far is that the movie is a giant mess of a home movie.' She would later write a far more damning appraisal of the way the movie was shot in her autobiography, *And a Voice to Sing With*.

Joan Baez: One day I was trudging around in the snow on a farm in Canada with Dylan, doing a 'scene' . . . Naturally, I was playing a Mexican whore – the Rolling Thunder women all played whores. The scene opened with Bob shoving me through the snow toward a shack. In fact there was neither a plot nor a script so the characters 'developed' as we went along . . . It was a cold day, and I wondered what I was doing in this monumentally silly project, and if Dylan was taking it seriously. Sam

Shepard was there, supposedly directing it, or writing it, but it was never written, and barely directed. Bob would stand in back of the camera and chuckle to himself and get everyone to run around and act out his mind movies. The filming happened in gleeful little happenings, enacting whatever dream Dylan had had in the night.

Dylan himself observed at the time of the film's release that some of the members of the Revue had not been particularly keen to enter into the spirit of the movie. When Scarlett Rivera says, 'Nobody's behaviour was monitored or really worked out,' she saw that as a positive aspect of the filming. Others, and this presumably included Baez, despite her major part in the film, considered the lack of structure to be a hindrance.

Bob Dylan: There was a lot of chaos while we were making the film. A lot of good scenes didn't happen because we had already finished improvising them by the time the cameras were ready to film. You can't recapture stuff like that. There was a lot of conflict during filming. We had people who didn't understand what we were doing because we didn't have a script. Some who didn't understand were willing to go along with us anyway. Others weren't and that hurt us, and hurt the film. [1978]

However, some sense of coherence, some themes pertinent to the Rolling Thunder Revue experience, began to emerge as the Revue weaved its way through Massachusetts, Rhode Island, Vermont, New Hampshire, Connecticut, upstate New York, Massachusetts again, Maine, Quebec and Ontario. In particular, certain Revue figures on the fringe of the music were providing real input into the film. Larry Sloman was scouting for potential scenes after nearly every show; Sam Shepard was providing input, though on a wider basis than originally envisaged, and devised several scenes, including one between an alchemist and an emperor which featured Dylan and Ginsberg; and Ginsberg seemed excited by the whole bicentennial idea, seeing the Revue as a reclaiming of American heritage.

Mel Howard: Allen saw Dylan rightly connected to the whole tradition of the Beat generation and through that to the earlier poets, Poe, the whole sense of the American vagabond. So Allen was keen to add that element too.

Gradually, indeed haphazardly, the themes of the movie began to come together. When Howard talked to Larry Sloman on the flight from Montreal to New York at the end of the tour, he felt that the footage necessary to construct a great movie had been filmed, and that the central story which had emerged was one which involved Dylan, Sara and Baez in some kind of *ménage à trois*, though like the critics who later savaged *Renaldo and Clara*, Howard found it difficult to perceive Dylan, Sara and Baez as playing the characters they were assuming, rather than themselves. It was an important distinction. If Dylan had succeeded in shooting enough footage to put his vision onto celluloid, the movie Howard talked to Sloman about would only partially mirror *Renaldo and Clara* in its final form.

Mel Howard: There were all these themes running through it. Ginsberg had the idea of Dylan as an alchemist, rediscovering America, then [there are] the women, Sara is very much into Robert Graves and his notion of the muse . . . that's probably a big part of their relationship . . . So there was this scene in Niagara Falls where Sara played this kind of witch goddess creature and she set tasks for him to fulfil, and nothing was ever good enough and that was the constant prod to keep him going. So we had a whole subplot, all of the women in the film, black magic and white magic, and the different powers of women and men and the focus of all of this was Dylan himself . . . We started to use some of the songs as mythological characters, with horses in Quebec and escape scenes, all sorts of zany hijinks, but the thing that started to evolve as a general theme was Dylan, Sara and Joan. And Sara and Joan as opposing forces, in different mythological guises, Joan as a certain kind of energy, Sara as a different kind of energy, and Dylan in between, being attracted to both . . . I guess in the last two weeks [of the tour] . . . the tour took hold enough so Dylan was sufficiently secure and the film just possessed him and it took him over . . . But I'm afraid how the film is gonna turn out . . . I think it's important to push Dylan in some way to make the film that's there.

Echoing Baez, Sara Dylan's own comment about the film was, 'After all that talk about goddesses, we wound up being whores,' a reference to the bordello scene where Sara and Baez reminisced about past loves and David Mansfield was brought in by Allen Ginsberg for his initiation. Dylan later claimed the scene was meant to represent Diamond Hell.

What the film did give Sara was a function on the tour apart from being Dylan's wife. She was clearly ambivalent about even being on the tour, but presumably felt obliged to support her recently reconciled husband. She informed Revue chronicler Larry Sloman:

Sara Dylan: I really can't take the travelling. And I have no real function here. Back home, I have the kids, and other things, but there's really nothing for me to do here.

It is important to remember that making the film was part of the motivation for Dylan to go back on the road. The type of film he was making during November 1975, whatever its final structure would be, was clearly not the sort of movie for which he could readily raise finance. He used his own money to finance the filming, or perhaps more accurately the money from touring.

Bob Dylan: My lawyer used to tell me there was a future in movies. So I said, 'What kind of future?' He said, 'Well, if you can come up with a script, an outline and get money from a big distributor.' But I knew I couldn't work that way. I can't betray my vision on a little piece of paper in hopes of getting some money from somebody. In the final analysis, it turned out that I had to make the movie all by myself, with people who would work with me, who trusted me. I went on the road in '76 to make money for this movie. [1978]

For this reason, and because of the expense of taking on the road such a large group of talented musicians, often headliners in their own right, it was inevitable that the Revue would have to play some large gigs. This aspect came in for considerable criticism from the media. Shows at the Civic Center in Providence, the Veterans Memorial Coliseum in New Haven and the Maple Leaf Gardens and the Forum in Toronto and Montreal respectively were considered to be against the original spirit of the Revue, as supposedly suggested by Dylan. Dylan was thus being forced to defend a position he had never advocated in the first place. The suggestion that he had said that the Revue would only play small theatres had taken root. Yet he had always known that he would have to play certain larger shows to defray expenses. As he told Larry Sloman during the tour:

Bob Dylan: We're gonna go any place we can. But we also have a lot of expenses to meet. I mean we're not gonna go out and play living rooms, you know. It's not a nightclub show . . . But we are gonna play small theatres and we have played theatres and we're going to continue to play theatres. [1975]

The Rolling Thunder Revue shows themselves were remarkable. They still stand as the most innovative shows of Dylan's career in a musical sense. Mansfield's country steel guitar, Ronson's glam-rock lead guitar and Rivera's electric violin combined to give the ensemble a unique sound, locked in as they were with a tight rhythm section (Wyeth and Stoner) and some occasional percussion (Luther Rix). Dylan was also singing with a precision even he rarely displayed, snapping and stretching words to cajole every nuance of meaning from each line. The new songs in particular seemed to bring out an extra degree of vocal commitment from him. Every night he performed six of the songs which later appeared on *Desire*, 'Romance in Durango' and 'Isis' closing the first half, 'Oh Sister', 'Hurricane', 'One More Cup of Coffee' and 'Sara' making up the bulk of the concluding electric set.

Every night he also sang one, two, then three acoustic songs; and a five or six song set with Joan Baez. Once again the press had an opportunity to ring out the old clichés – The King and Queen of Folk Sing Together Again! Dylan would mercilessly play Baez up, leaning into her face and the microphone when she least expected it, stretching the notes to see who could hold them longest and informing her they were going to do 'Times They Are a-Changin'' and then singing 'I Dreamed I Saw St Augustine'. Through it all Baez managed to retain her usual I'm-going-along-with-this manner and piercing voice; she even appeared in white face at one show to duet with Dylan, and dressed up as Dylan for the final benefit show, while he introduced her as Bob Dylan. According to one Rolling Thunder musician, Baez even managed to score one over Dylan during the tour:

Joan and Bob are doing a duet ... She's really moving. I mean dancing. She starts doing the Charleston and the audience is digging it and we're digging it. Dylan though, he's plunking his guitar, moving his eyes around quick, like he does, looking at Joannie, looking at us, looking at the audience. Like 'What the hell is she doing that's going over so damn big?' It's over, and Joan walks offstage, grinning, sees a friend in the wings, and says to him, 'You won't be hearing that number again from this little old duo on this tour.'

Actually the story does not accord with the usual set pattern, which had Baez remaining on stage at the end of their joint set. Next to singing with Baez again, Dylan drew the most comments for the white face he donned at most shows. At a couple of the shows he even came onstage wearing a plastic mask which he tossed aside when required to play harmonica on the second song, 'It Ain't Me Babe'. No one seemed sure what the reason for the look was, and one person shouted to him at the Lowell show, asking why he appeared so.

Scarlett Rivera: There was a point where a heckler in the audience . . . said like, Why are you wearing the mask? What is it all about? And I think his response was, 'The meaning is in the words' . . . 'Cause it made him angry for that moment. I guess because he wanted to be understood.

In the film of the tour all the footage was drawn from shows where Dylan donned his whiteface, and in talking about *Renaldo and Clara*, he mentioned masks and the search for identity as integral to the film's unique symbolism. It is tempting to see the white face as essentially connected with the making of the film. But perhaps the best clue to his motives behind the mask lies in a comment he made to Sloman during one of their interviews on the 1975 tour.

Bob Dylan: Ever see those Italian troupes that go around in Italy? Those Italian street theatres? *Commedia dell'arte*. Well, this is just an extension of that, only musically. [1975]

In the *commedia dell'arte* the majority of the players wore masks. The nature of the *commedia dell'arte* has been described by novelist Anne Rice thus: 'Each actor had his role for life, and . . . they did not use memorized words, but improvised everything on the stage. You knew your name, your character, and you understood him and made him speak and act as you thought he should. That was the genius of it.'

And that was perhaps the link between the Revue and the movie. The players, both on stage and in the film, were living out their roles to their logical conclusions. The musicians stuck to the same core material, yet every night it was different, spontaneous, and of the moment. The movie tried to capture that sense as well, though less successfully than the music. Every musician speaking of the 1975 tour talks of an atmosphere unique to the Revue, of a sense of freedom to express oneself fully, almost a belief that they could redefine themselves.

Scarlett Rivera: I felt this incredible freedom to express whatever feeling, whatever thought, whatever symbolism and actually carry it out.

The 1975 Rolling Thunder Revue wound to an end with a benefit show for Hurricane Carter at Madison Square Garden in New York. They had played to an unsympathetic, largely black audience at the Clinton Correctional Institute for Women the previous day, intended as part of the publicity drive to free Carter, who was temporarily imprisoned there. At the Garden Dylan and the Revue delivered a steaming four-hour show to an ecstatic audience. Even Nik Cohn, a critic renowned for his antipathy towards Dylan, found positive aspects in the performance. It was a triumphant end to the tour, and in stark contrast to the end of his 1974 tour twenty-two months earlier. Or his 1976 tour six months later.

24

1976: Hard Reign or Last Waltz?

1975 was perhaps the most triumphant year of Dylan's career, both artistically and commercially. The release of *Blood on the Tracks* and the recording of *Desire* proved that his creative genius was in full flow for the first time in eight years. His commercial stock had never been higher. He had concluded perhaps the finest tour of his career, and in the meantime filmed enough footage finally to put his vision on celluloid. It even seemed as if by the end of the year he had succeeded in being reconciled with his recently estranged wife. She had after all been a regular fixture on the latter part of the 1975 Revue.

1976 should have been equally triumphant. His long-awaited follow-up to *Blood on the Tracks*, *Desire*, which had been so prominently featured in the 1975 shows, was released in January. Plans were afoot for a second Rolling Thunder tour, and there was that mass of celluloid waiting to be knitted together into something resembling a coherent film. In the interim NBC were interested in filming the Revue for a one-hour in-concert special.

And yet 1976 came to represent something of a series of lost opportunities. Dylan avoided the recording studio, and so his momentum as a recording artist was lost. By the time he released the follow-up to *Desire*, thirty months had elapsed and his commercial stock was in discernible decline, while the 1976 Revue failed to recapture the previous year's spirit.

The year started promisingly enough. *Desire* was released on 16 January and within three weeks was number one on both sides of the Atlantic – the one and only such occasion in Dylan's career. The Revue also reassembled in Santa Monica to rehearse for a one-off benefit show, a second Night of the Hurricane, originally scheduled to be held at the Louisiana Superdome but soon moved to Houston.

The show proved an absolute disaster. Flying the entire Revue out to Los Angeles to rehearse for just one show was an expensive exercise in itself. The new venue, the Astrodome, was an acoustical nightmare and, at 70,000 capacity, it seemed unlikely that it would be filled by Texas bottoms. Stevie Wonder and Stephen Stills both volunteered to appear at the show — and then both brought their own bands with them.

Howie Wyeth: It was just too much. That show went on forever. And the air — you couldn't breathe. There was just too much. The show was like twenty-four hours long, everybody did too much, everybody did too many songs and there were too many stars there . . . All these guys brought their own bands. They weren't doing it the way we'd been doing it . . . We lost the whole togetherness thing.

Even the Hollywood starlets got in on the act, swelling the size of the Revue, and the band itself sounded under-rehearsed and ramshackle — the sound bounced off the cavernous Dome like a ricocheting bullet in a tin barrel.

Rob Stoner: I was surprised he did it again after that one. Woah, that was nightmarish that one. Could have been Bob Dylan's worst gig of his entire career, that one — but he meant well. That was the hanger-on junket. All these Hollywood people were just tagging along with Bob Dylan. We chartered our own plane.

If the sense of intimacy was gone, so now was any pretence at marital fidelity on Dylan's part. Sally Kirkland, an up-and-coming American actress, was at this point his 'motion of the moment', to use Stoner's descriptive phrase. If Houston did not start 1976's touring activities auspiciously, the trail of concert disasters, sexual infidelities and economic problems would not end there. The financial result of Night of the Hurricane II, which grossed some half a million dollars, was a mere 50,000 dollars net into Carter's defence coffers. Dylan himself returned to Malibu for a rethink, after a few days in Texas hanging out with Doug Sahm and Joni Mitchell.

In March Rubin 'Hurricane' Carter was finally granted a retrial. Dylan had performed his last live version of 'Hurricane' (despite Carter being found guilty on two more occasions before finally being freed in 1985). With arrangements for a spring tour of the Southern States in the formative stages, and with no intentions to record himself, Dylan started turning up at sessions for Eric Clapton's new album, which was being recorded down the road at the Band's Shangri-La Studios. He seemed at ease here. There were no pressures. He did not have to go home; and musicians like Clapton and Ron Wood were always good for a jam or two. Disinclined to save any new songs for himself, he even gave Clapton and Wood a song apiece. 'Sign Language', featuring a Dylan/Clapton duet, appeared on Clapton's *No Reason to Cry*. 'Seven Days', a song about waiting for the singer's true love to return, he donated to Ron Wood. The singer insists he's been good while he's been waiting. Obviously this was not one of his more literal songs.

Ron Wood: One night I was up on Sunset in Hollywood and I happened to ring Shangri-La [Studios] and said, 'Anything happening up there tonight?' And they said, 'Nothing, other than Bob Dylan's here playing.' I went, 'What?!' They said, 'Yeah. Bob's here. Playing bass. On one of your songs.' I said, 'Don't let him leave!' . . . Anyway this session went on for a couple of days solid. There was a point where we stopped the master-tape and just ran a two-track. That's where I got 'Seven Days' from . . . He made this tent up from the clothes on my bed. He made off with my sheets and pillows and everything. At the sessions we very rarely got the chance to have a break and crash . . . one night I went to creep off to my room and there were no bedclothes at all, and the window was wide open, and I looked out and I could see this tent in the distance, right in the middle of this big field. And Bob had made off with this girl, but she was in a plaster cast – her leg and her arms in plaster! That was quite funny. It was like *Invasion of the Zombies*.

Clearly, restlessness was an important factor for Dylan when he arranged to reassemble the Revue at a large Florida hotel at the beginning of April. If he had no desire to return to the studio, and was reluctant to stay at home, a reassembled Revue would hopefully revive the magical spirit created throughout their New England tour the previous fall.

Rob Stoner: It was an attempt to recapture that Rolling Thunder thing. 'Cause what we did . . . the first time was we all holed up in a hotel and rehearsed in the ballroom and it worked that time. But here everybody was too far from home. There was a problem with the water down there, too.

The rehearsals had barely started when word came through that Phil Ochs, in a manic-depressive state, had hung himself in New York. Ochs had desperately wanted to be a part of the Revue, though Dylan knew that he had become too unstable to take along on a lengthy tour. Despite his minimal contact with Ochs in the previous ten years, Dylan took the death badly. Perhaps he recalled how he had learnt of Richard Farina's and Paul Clayton's deaths during that manic 1966 world tour.

Scarlett Rivera: I was sitting at the table, when he got the word about that [suicide]. And he was really upset and angry that he had done that to himself . . . It was a combination of real sadness and anger. A couple of days went by when he was missing. I think he took the news very, very hard . . . Before he came back to the rehearsals he wanted to clear his mind.

Dylan's mood did not substantially improve after his two days of solitude, and the rehearsals became tortured affairs. Dylan, on the occasions when he deigned to turn up, failed to communicate with the band, and his melancholia affected the whole, homesick, Revue: 'A month and a half of this, and the boss won't talk to anyone,' to quote Rob Stoner, who did his best to keep the band in a good groove.

Joel Bernstein: The rehearsals were in the Starlight Room of the Bellevue Biltmore Hotel in Clearwater and they went on for some time before the tour. It was somewhat strange. Bob would show up late for rehearsals, he wouldn't talk to the band, he'd just start a song. I never liked Rob Stoner's playing very much but I have to give him credit. He really understood, could follow Bob by looking at his foot, following his heel, listening for the first note and then he'd get a feel for the key, and the rest of the band took their cue from him. Bob spoke very little – he wasn't talking to me for a while – and it seemed a very strange way to proceed with rehearsals . . . And the rehearsals went on for quite some time. The first rehearsals were in the poolhouse, and that proved to be too small, so after a day or two we moved into the ballroom, which of course they had to pay more money for. Usually rehearsals began around noon and Bob wouldn't show up until two or so and not say anything, just pick up a guitar and play a song. My impressions were that he was either angry about something or that the whole thing was getting old for him. It was just a mood he was in.

Dylan's mood did not discernibly lighten once the tour started. At the first show, in Lakeland, Florida, he introduced a very different set from the one he had performed a mere five months earlier. Opening with two acoustic songs, the choice of material was perhaps indicative of the mood he was in. Gone were the vignettes-in-song found on *Desire*. At the first couple of shows 'Mozambique' was the solitary inclusion from the album which had just spent five weeks at number one. Dylan replaced 'Sara' with 'Idiot Wind', a brutal substitution.

Indeed *Blood on the Tracks* seemed generally restored to favour for this tour. Rather than the solitary acoustic versions of 'Tangled Up in Blue' or 'Simple Twist of Fate' that he performed in 1975, he chose to sing most of the album at some point on the tour. 'Tangled Up in Blue' was given a grinding stop-start arrangement late in the tour. 'Shelter from the Storm' and 'Idiot Wind' became savage denunciations. 'You're Gonna Make Me Lonesome When You Go' was given an easy, almost fatalistic vocal over a wistful country arrangement.

But the most startling inclusion from *Blood on the Tracks* was an acoustic version of 'If You See Her, Say Hello', performed as song number two at the opening show, and wholly rewritten. In the new version, the singer is haunted by the lady, but he hates her power over him, and himself for allowing her such power (almost a continuation of 'Dirge'). His tone starts as dismissive; becomes threatening towards her new lover ('If you make love to her/ Watch it from the rear'). Finally he admits to his own doubts about having the strength to reject her should she return: 'I know that she'll be back some day/Of that there is no doubt/And when that moment comes Dear Lord/give me the strength to keep her out.'

A rewritten 'Going Going Gone' also suggested a man who was getting used to 'sleeping in the dust'. In fact, Dylan now seemed to be spending his time with a lot of unusual women. As so often in his life, his unhappiness seemed to have a direct effect upon his libido. And clearly he was looking as much for guidance as companionship. He later said he had had enough of witchy women, but he was certainly having his fair share of mystics, seers and sages along for the ride through the Southern States that spring.

Howie Wyeth: [There was] the tight-rope walker. The girl from *The Dating Game* . . . She was a circus performer, she walked tightropes and stuff. She sort of seemed like a mystic but then we found out she also wrote a book about *The Dating Game* . . . There was a real tall chick that was also a magician that was with Bob, sort of off and on, and then there was this other chick . . . they were sort of both with Bob off and on. They were on the tour, they had their own room. They didn't do anything else. There was a faith-healer too, though she was real innocent. She was really a nice lady from Vermont, into all sorts of weird foods . . . My old lady at the time was an astrologer and she was on the tour and I know she'd been talking to Bob and there was a guy on the tour that was into pyramid power, a cat from England, and he looked like a pyramid.

If witchy women failed to improve his mood as the tour progressed through Florida and Louisiana, neither did the way the shows were going. There were major problems which had never occurred the previous year. Part of it was just the general mood; part was inexperience on the part of Dylan's management; part was down to the poor choice of the Southern States in the first place.

Rob Stoner: Bob was going through a lot of personal changes. It was just shit, man ... I mean, 'Idiot Wind' is a very angry song and it definitely reflects what must have been going on with him. I mean he was really upset back then ... He was drinking a lot. Ronson was frozen out of the '76 tour. He was on the bus but they never let him play. [Dylan] had leaditis then. I don't know what the fuck came over him ... It was a big void in his life. The marriage was falling apart and this thing which had seemed so exciting and promising – Rolling Thunder – that wasn't [working] and he couldn't figure out why, I don't think ... It was like a mid-life crisis. He was confused and he was searching. He tried a lot of chicks; he tried one chick; he tried [every] kind of chick.

If the show was reasonably well received by fans in Louisiana and Florida, Texas proved a complete wipe-out. Ever since September 1965 when Dylan went to Dallas and Austin with his new rhythm & blues band the Hawks and had been enthusiastically welcomed by the locals, he had been under the illusion that Texas was a good place to play. In fact, the type of music most Texans preferred was a shade less sophisticated than that of Dylan and his band of East Coast folk-rockers.

This was a shame, as the April performances in Florida had been steadily improving. Indeed when the band returned to Clearwater four days into the tour to film a TV special for NBC the band really started to click.

Howie Wyeth: The rehearsals sucked in that place ... it just wasn't happening ... Then we did the [Clearwater] concerts and they were filming it and it happened. That was the first day that the music started feeling right again. Bob did a really hip version of 'Like a Rolling Stone'. He did some tunes that he hadn't done at all.

Unfortunately Dylan took a dislike to both the celluloid results achieved by Bert Sugarman's *Midnight Special* team, and to Sugarman personally, at least according to Wyeth.

Howie Wyeth: Well, Bob got into a fight with [one of] the guys that were doing [the Clearwater special] ... He got into a big argument with the guy over the dinner table one night after we'd already done half of it. And then he said, No! We're not doing it. Fuck it! So he decided that wasn't the way we were going to do it and then they decided to record right at the end [of the tour].

By the time Dylan's own film crew came to shoot the penultimate show of the tour, at the end of May, the Revue had passed through Texas, and the mood was very different from those Clearwater performances. Though the filming of the aborted special is crass and obvious (during the final chorus of 'Just Like a Woman' the camera actually cuts from a woman to a girl in the audience), the second half of the show featured some terrific performances by Dylan and the band, as he produced a seething 'Like a Rolling Stone', a delicate 'Just Like a Woman', and that raucous rewrite of 'Lay Lady Lay' which became the bawdiest moment of each and every one of the 1976 shows. No longer subtly coaxing the lady, Dylan now hollers: 'Let's go upstairs/Let's take a chance/Who really cares?'

After two great sets in New Orleans (during which he performed the one and only live version of 'Rita May', his 'tribute' to lesbian writer Rita Mae Brown), and one in Baton Rouge at the beginning of May, the Revue's first Texan date was back in Houston. It came after a four-day break, the result of a cancelled show at Lake Charles in western Louisiana, on 6 May, scrapped because of poor ticket sales. The cancellation presaged a disastrous sortie through the second largest state of the union. Less than five months after the catastrophe which was Night of the Hurricane II, the Rolling Thunder Revue failed even to sell out Houston's 11,000-seat Hofheinz Pavilion, despite the late addition of Willie Nelson to the bill. The gig was barely three quarters full; and the following day's show was cancelled altogether.

Three days later, the Revue's San Antonio gig was moved from the Hemisfair Arena to the somewhat smaller Municipal Auditorium. The next day two shows at Austin's Municipal Auditorium were combined into one, again because of poor ticket sales (reserved seating also became general admission and 900 fans were excluded from the show). Here was someone who two years ago had generated twelve million applications for tickets for his American tour and who, since then, had secured the only three American number one albums of his career, yet he was failing to sell out small arenas in Texas. Ironically the Austin show turned out to be one of the best dates of the tour.

Howie Wyeth: There was a whole bunch of hassles. The promoter didn't get along with the people out west. He was Jewish. I heard there was a whole bunch of stuff he just didn't know. He said the wrong things to the wrong people and they were prejudiced ... In Austin they booked us the same night as four other concerts and then they made all the kids stay out in the rain all night to get the good tickets and then they decided to make it general admission after these guys had waited to get tickets so they could be in the front row. Oh boy were they pissed [off]. They were ready to kill us ... The papers had been saying, 'These guys are from the East. They came down here just to grab your money. They don't give a fuck about you.' Neuwirth came out [at the start of the show] and said all that ... but then once it was said and done, then it was great. 'Okay, let's have the concert!' And it really worked.

Even a show in Dallas on 15 May was cancelled owing to poor ticket sales, despite Dylan's high opinion of Dallas fans. Instead the Dallas fans had to trundle out to the already arranged show at Fort Worth the following day, which remained on the schedule in preference to the Dallas date since there was a recording crew taping the show for a possible live album. Though the show seemed to go well, and the sound was good, Dylan was clearly unhappy with the results, and only four tracks were subsequently used on the *Hard Rain* album. Finally heading out of Texas, shows in Oklahoma City and Wichita, Kansas, showed him experimenting with the set in an attempt to keep from being bored. In Wichita, he even performed the first ever live version of 'One of Us Must Know', a twisted look at an ended relationship.

After Wichita, the Revue headed into Colorado and friendlier territory. They were there informed that they had a weekend off in a well-appointed cabin-cum-hotel up in the mountains, where they could hang out and prepare for the Fort Collins show, a big show in an open-air stadium, which was being filmed for the NBC TV special and recorded for a live album. But even this seemingly innocent gesture on Dylan's part backfired, as it poured down throughout the weekend.

Howie Wyeth: All of a sudden they said, We got four days off before we do Fort Collins and the record. They said, You're gonna love this. We got you in this dude ranch up in the mountains. And it was raining so you couldn't go riding and it was up in the mountains so you couldn't breathe. There was nothing to do. And we were all stuck up there. So after all this adrenalin it was like detoxing or withdrawal ... for four days we had nothing to do. And it was raining. It was dreary.

Rob Stoner: Bob was really hitting the bottle that weekend. That was a terrible fuckin' weekend. There was a lot of stuff that makes *Hard Rain* an extraordinary snapshot – like a punk record or something. It's got such energy and such anger . . . It was an outdoor stadium and it had rained for days before the gig. We had done this aborted Bert Sugarman special for NBC in Clearwater. I think the deal was that Bob had the right of refusal if he didn't like the video tape, but the terms were that he had to make good on it, at his expense, by doing his own thing to deliver to NBC. Therefore Bob had to hire video, sound crew, twenty-four-track remote truck, all this extra stuff and every day you have these people sitting around and they've all driven this shit from LA – which is the reason we did it in the west. So they could get a crew there from LA, video and audio, which was a lot more expensive then than it is now, relatively speaking . . . We were supposed to do the gig [on] two or three consecutive days – each time the [alternate] 'rain date' was supposed to be the next day – but it was pouring for days and days and meanwhile it's costing Bob a lot of bread. Everybody's holed up in this little hotel up in the mountains in the middle of nowhere, with nothing to do except get drunk . . . Here's the last gig and it's taking forever to do it. The boss is getting in a progressively shittier mood . . . Eventually they just decided to go and do it in the rain anyway. As it turns out the rain cleared up on the last fucking song – it was the first time that the sun had shone in a week.

Dylan's mood was not greatly improved by the surprise arrival of his wife, who had brought his kids and mother along with her, apparently intent on celebrating his thirty-fifth birthday.

Howie Wyeth: She showed up the day of *Hard Rain* . . . But she didn't tell him and he had two of his girlfriends there. It was tense.

According to Baez, Sara just waited outside Dylan's room quietly, but in a seething rage, and eventually he emerged to face his comeuppance.

Joan Baez: Sara showed up late in the tour, wafting in from a plane looking like a madwoman, carrying baskets of wrinkled clothes, her hair wild and dark rings around her eyes . . . Bob was ignoring her, and had picked up a local curly-headed Mopsy who perched on the piano during his rehearsals in a ballroom off the main hotel lobby. Sara appeared airily at the front door dressed in deerskin, wearing her emerald necklace and some oppressively strong and sweet oils. She greeted me with a reserved hello and talked distantly about nothing in particular, all the while eyeing the closed door to the ballroom.

Possibly Sara had arrived with the intention of confronting Dylan. If she had any idea of the lifestyle he had adopted on the tour, she was certainly entitled to confront him. Whatever her reasons, Dylan was not in a mood to listen as, according to both Stoner and Wyeth, Sara censured him in the parking lot, refusing to ignore his adulterous activities. Such personal trauma cannot have improved Dylan's mood as he prepared for the most important gig of 1976.

Finally on the 23rd the Revue performed their penultimate show to a wet but surprisingly appreciative Fort Collins audience. And, perhaps not surprisingly, Dylan and the band responded with one of the best shows of the tour. The sense of desperation and frustration is there on the film and on the record. It may be ragged but there was real fire in the performance.

Rob Stoner: Everybody's soaked, the canopy's leaking, the musicians are getting shocks from the water on the stage. The instruments are going out of tune because of the humidity. It was awful. So everybody is playing and singing for their lives and that is the spirit that you hear on that record.

Scarlett Rivera: There was a lot of pressure on that day to get that filmed [and recorded] . . . This was the last possible moment for this recording to be made and it was under the worst circumstances.

Can it be coincidence that Dylan sang perhaps the most rancorous version of 'Idiot Wind' of the tour the night that Sara was there to watch him? On the final verse when the singer seems finally to accept the fact that he is as much an idiot as the subject of the song, at Fort Collins he rocks his head from side to side on the word sorry, clearly implying that he feels no such remorse. On 'One Too Many Mornings' he had also added a new coda to the end of the song: 'I've no right to be here/And you've no right to stay/Until we're both one too many mornings and a thousand miles away.'

The Dylan singing on *Hard Rain* has never been more attuned to his performance art. The results may be harsh. As Stoner says, the album comes across as almost a punk record. But for sheer vitriol there can be few songs ever performed which stand up alongside 'Idiot Wind' at Fort Collins. 'Shelter from the Storm' also brought a demonic performance from a man seemingly prepared to face the consequences of his own actions. When he says one day he is bound to cross the line, you feel sure he means it.

The final Rolling Thunder show was in Salt Lake City. Playing in a half-empty 17,000-seat Salt Palace, the Revue gave another great performance. They did not want the tour to just fade out. To make the show extra special, Dylan even pulled out 'Gates of Eden' during his acoustic set, and sang 'Lily, Rosemary and the Jack of Hearts' as a duet with Baez.

Joel Bernstein: Salt Lake City was the only show that I recall that Bob and Joan did 'Lily, Rosemary and the Jack of Hearts' together. The song has something like eighteen verses, and Bob wrote the first lines down on the back of his hand, on his cuff, on his sleeve . . . They did a very good version of it, really good. It was a very spirited show, perhaps because it was the last show. People knew that it wouldn't happen again.

If Dylan's public profile had been upfront during the first half of 1976, he seemed to disappear off the face of the earth during the second half. In September NBC screened the one-hour *Hard Rain* TV special to disappointing ratings and unfavourable reviews. The album of the TV special clocked up healthy initial sales but rapidly dropped from the charts. A period of hibernation was approaching. Dylan and his old friend Howard Alk, with whom he co-edited *Hard Rain*, had more pressing editing tasks to undertake.

In November he flew to San Francisco to appear at the Band's farewell concert. After sixteen years on the road (though their touring since 1966 could hardly be described as incessant), the Band had decided to call it quits. The concert was being filmed by Martin Scorsese for a movie of the occasion, and Dylan performed four songs with his old backing band before leading everyone through a communal encore of 'I Shall Be Released'. He looked considerably less wired than at Fort Collins six months earlier. Indeed he looked positively loose. Yet his strident singing contrasted markedly with the beautifully understated power of the Band. Still, he had done his duty. Now he had to return to Malibu to attend to his duties as a husband and father. Or not.

25

1977: Everything Went from Bad to Worse

Sara Dylan: I can't go home without fear for my safety. I was in such fear of him that I locked doors in the home to protect myself from his violent outbursts and temper tantrums ... He has struck me in the face injuring my jaw ... My five children are greatly disturbed by my husband's behaviour and his bizarre lifestyle.

On the face of it 1977 might seem like another of Dylan's 'lost' years. He played no shows and recorded no albums. Yet in fact it was a year of considerable activity, both artistically and personally. Personally it was the year of the divorce, a divorce that would be only a prelude to the primary trauma, a lengthy and bitter custody struggle for the children. Artistically there were also problems in the editing of the film Dylan and Alk worked on throughout 1977, the four-hour *Renaldo and Clara*. At the end of the year, extensive and untogether tour rehearsals proved a further distraction, reflected in Dylan's state of mind during an unparalleled series of press interviews given at the time, designed to promote his new film at minimal expense.

It would appear that Dylan's adulterous behaviour, which had been a constant backdrop to the 1976 Rolling Thunder tour, had not ceased by the beginning of 1977. Rather, it had become more blatant. According to a declaration by Sara Dylan's legal representative, released to the press in March 1977: 'On February 13th of this year, she came down to breakfast and found Dylan, the children, and a woman named Malka at the breakfast table. She said that it was then that Dylan struck her on the face and ordered her to leave.'

If the prospect of a very public and acrimonious divorce had tabloid hacks sharpening their pencils, on the day proceedings commenced in Sara's divorce suit a plea was made for the sealing of the documents relating to the court case. The *Los Angeles Times*

noted: 'Mrs Dylan's attorney, Marvin Mitchelson, concurred in
the request of Dylan's attorney, Marvin Burns, to prevent dis-
closure of the marriage dissolution filed by Mrs Dylan March 1st.
Judge Raffedie additionally sealed other documents stipulating the
assets of the Dylans, and ordered sealing of a response by Dylan
yet to be filed.'

The divorce thus proceeded in relative privacy, without, it
would appear, any particular attempt by Dylan to be reconciled
with Sara, and by June the divorce was final, though the com-
missioner announced he was 'retaining jurisdiction of their communal property for future determination'. The question of the
custody of the children would not be settled for some time.
Initially Sara retained legal custody of the children. The situation
became charged only when Sara decided to go to Hawaii to look
for a new home for herself and the children. While in Hawaii, she
left a woman called Farida McFree in charge of her home. McFree
had originally been employed by Sara to help the children during
the legal wrangles, using a technique called 'art healing', which
involved encouraging children to express themselves through art.

Farida McFree: Rosanna [Taplin] came to me and she said, 'Farida, Sara
is in such a bad way would you please help her with the children. You're
doing art healing and the children really benefit by it' . . . So that's how I
got involved with the children and I did art healing . . . We'd work
together on the same piece [of art].

At some point it became apparent that Sara and Farida were not
getting along. Yet Sara needed someone to look after her house
while she and the children were in Hawaii, and she had little
recourse but to ask McFree.

Farida McFree: I started off with her, and then she really treated me
very badly. I just said, I'm here to help you, I'm not here to be abused. I
don't think you need my services anymore. And she went to Hawaii.
But she said, Do me a favour. Just stay in the house please. Do me this
one favour because I really want someone in the house and I trust you. I
said Okay.

While Sara was in Hawaii, McFree, who had met Dylan in 1975
at the wedding of Rosanna and Jonathan Taplin, awakened from
an intense dream involving Dylan.

Farida McFree: I fell out of bed. I mean it was so intense, this loneliness,
and I didn't understand it. Then that morning the next door neighbour,

[who] was a film-maker, a very big one, called me and said, Did you hear Farida that Bob got a divorce last night from Sara in Santa Monica? And I said, No, Sara's getting the divorce. And he said, Uh-uh, he beat her to it. And then I had this pain again in my heart all day. I said, I can't stand it. I picked up the phone and I said, Bob, this is Farida. I work with Sara and the children. I'm the children's art teacher. Are you okay? And he said, No I'm not okay. So I said I had this strong feeling that I should call you. And he said, Isn't that nice? And then he [asked me], What are you doing right now? I said, Nothing. He said, Why don't you come over? I really, really need to talk to someone. I said, It's late. I don't really want to. 'Cause he was thirteen miles from the house that she had rented at the colony. So he said, Well I really need to talk to someone tonight, and I was a little afraid of him so I said, I don't think so. He said, I really do. So I said, Oh okay . . . Anyhow I go there and I was scared because there are all these bodyguards and it just seemed very scary, all these guys. So they let me in. It just seemed very spooky and then Bob came towards the light and as I was driving slowly, he looked like he was crazed. And I got so scared. I said, Oh my God what am I doing here? But he came to the car and he drove with me to the house and we just never stopped talking . . . We just talked into the night. I don't think we stopped talking until four or five o'clock in the morning. He just poured and poured and poured out his heart and all these grievances that he was feeling, grief and everything else. So he never stopped talking. We talked right around the clock. And that's how [our affair] started.

Dylan's involvement with McFree was bound to make an already complex situation more difficult; and Sara's response was an understandable one. She had had to deal with so many women who had befriended her with the single intent in mind of getting close to Dylan.

Farida McFree: When she came back I was already with him. I had moved into his house. It was fast with us. She was totally freaked out. And I said, Bob I don't know what's happening with us but I feel it's the wrong move. I don't think I should move . . . But he insisted that I move in with him. And I said, I think this is a bad move. She is going to misunderstand all this. So he said, Well is she your mother? I said, No, she's not my mother but I don't want to start any problems. 'Cause she had told me all these stories about all these women that would use her to get to him.

Like Sara, Dylan now wanted to get away from it all and decided to take a temporary rest from editing his film, which he had begun with Howard Alk. He, too, wished to take the children along. He also invited McFree, who had already established a rapport with the children with her art healing. His chosen locale was less exotic than Hawaii and more familiar to the children, his farm in Laredo, Minnesota. At last, in the relative calm of a Minnesota summer, he began to write songs again. It had been two years since the burst of creativity which had produced *Desire*. Now he began writing perhaps the most complex and convoluted lyrics of his life. The new songs like 'Changing of the Guards' read like poems which were later put to music, something he had not attempted since *John Wesley Harding*. These new songs would require a new sophistication in their musical arrangement if the complex words were to rise above the sound that enfolded them.

Farida McFree: He started to write *Street-Legal* when we were together. He would show me some of the songs that he was writing. [It was] practically the entire album . . . It started when we were on the farm . . . He was very down. Don't forget, he was suffering when I met him. He was in a bad way. I brought him back to life. He was practically dead . . . this guy was shot emotionally and he had to get away from all the pressures in Malibu and the farm was really where he got back up on his feet again. But then that custody case was so vile and so treacherous. I mean I kept running away 'cause I couldn't handle it. The kids were on the farm.

If Dylan was starting to get 'back up on his feet again', there was one real moment of sadness for him during his time in Laredo. On 16 August 1977, at 3.30 p.m., Elvis Presley was pronounced dead at the Baptist Memorial Hospital in Memphis, Tennessee. Like the death of Phil Ochs in April 1976, the death of Elvis Presley made him temporarily morose and difficult to communicate with.

Farida McFree: I was with him the night Presley died. It was in August. He really took it very bad. He didn't speak for a couple of days. He was really grieving. He said that if it wasn't for him he would never have gotten started. That he opened the door.

Bob Dylan: I went over my whole life. I went over my whole childhood. I didn't talk to anyone for a week after Elvis died. If it wasn't for Elvis and Hank Williams, I couldn't be doing what I do today. [1978]

Dylan's time with the children had helped him to make an important decision. He decided he was going to contest the custody of the children with Sara. He probably already knew that Sara had been considering the possibility of setting up home in Hawaii with the children, and was understandably reluctant to have them so inaccessible. Possibly he felt that he could set up a home with Farida, who had a good rapport with them. If so, such hopes were decidedly unrealistic. It was inevitable that Marvin Mitchelson, Sara's lawyer, would exploit the relationship with McFree to Sara's advantage.

Farida McFree: That's when he decided that he was going to keep the children. And then the custody case followed that immediately . . . Right after the divorce, that was going to be decided and he felt that he wanted them and the children wanted to be with him, and that's when he decided to go to court and fight for them. And Marvin Mitchelson . . . used everything he could to win the case and Bob's lawyers knew that and warned Bob to get rid of me. They said, Let her go. She shouldn't be around you 'cause you'll lose the case. And he just wouldn't. So I used to go into hiding when they came over. This was both on the farm and in Malibu. They knew I was on the farm and said, Send her away. She's going to ruin the case – your just being with her. Mitchelson will use that. And he did.

Matters came to a head in September. Marvin Mitchelson, on behalf of Sara, asked the court to give her permission to move the children to Hawaii to live there with her. The original settlement had required that the children not be taken out of California without a court order or the other parent's written consent. Within four days Dylan's attorney Robert Kaufman filed papers alleging Sara Dylan had violated the original court order by taking the children with her to Hawaii at the beginning of the summer. Dylan had previously chosen not to press the issue, but changed his mind on hearing of Sara's 2 September petition.

Dylan now asked that the court grant sole custody of the children to him after Sara's 'direct violation of the court's order'. Mitchelson repudiated the charges and insisted that the legal action Dylan had taken was 'precipitous, hysterical and without foundation'. Meanwhile Sara had returned to Hawaii to finalize her attempts to set up home there, leaving the children in California.

At this point, according to press reports of a November custody hearing, Dylan took the opportunity provided by Sara's absence to take physical custody of the children. In a declaration to the court Mitchelson claimed that Dylan and Farida McFree were 'attempting to brainwash the minor children and to deprive them and [Mrs Dylan] of the natural love and companionship of each other'. Dylan refrained from responding to the allegations at the 3 November hearing, though his attorney made it clear that he denied them.

A further hearing was set for 1 December. In the interim Sara Dylan obtained physical custody of the children. In the case of

Jesse, their eldest son, she managed this only after a Santa Monica court ordered Dylan to return him to Sara's custody at an interim hearing. According to Mitchelson, Dylan had employed 'body-guards and armed guards'.

The return of the children to Sara did not resolve the custody battle. Within days of the Santa Monica hearing, Sara was involved in assaulting a teacher at the children's school in Malibu. According to a syndicated report of the incident, Sara had invaded a classroom, 'flanked by three private detectives, chased the Dylan children through the school, frightening other students' and attacked teacher Rex Burke 'when he asked to see the court order'. The children 'apparently resisted going with Mrs Dylan'. Sara was later fined for her assault on the teacher. Quite why Sara acted in this way is unknown, as she already had a court order giving her custody of all five children (including Maria, her daughter from a previous partner). According to Farida McFree the 'raid' could have been a life-threatening affair for her. For once though Farida was not with the children.

Farida McFree: She came in with two detectives, two burly guys, into this schoolhouse . . . I was always with the children and that was the first day that I wasn't and she went into the school system and they took the children by force. I think they didn't get Anna and Jesse. It was really a traumatic experience for them.

Though custody had been temporarily restored to Sara, a legal settlement had yet to be reached. When it was finally made, late in December, the conditions that Sara Dylan and Mitchelson imposed apparently included the complete exclusion of Farida McFree from the children's circle of influence. It would seem that Sara had never forgiven Farida for what she saw as her traitorous actions towards her, and Farida became the necessary sacrifice required to resolve the custody battle.

Farida McFree: The upshot in our relationship was, when I came to New York, Mitchelson made him sign a paper that he would never see me again. It was either me or the children . . . there was a lot of money involved too, and he didn't want that case to go on any longer. It was really painful. I don't know what all the details were but he told me that and I just knew it was the end for us . . . He told me that Mitchelson made him sign a piece of paper that he would never see me again and then the case was settled . . . If your children are at stake and your life is upside down, you're gonna sign that piece of paper . . .

The exact details of the custody settlement are unknown. When Dylan was giving a plethora of interviews in the first two months of 1978, he seemed to consider his relations with Sara had been irrevocably breached. Though they would later be reconciled, at least as parents of their children, he hinted to at least one reporter that the custody battle had taken a considerable toll.

Bob Dylan: No one in my family gets divorced. It's just unheard of, nobody does that. And so when I did get married I never conceived of getting divorced. I figured it would last forever. But it didn't, and now there's a marriage and there's a divorce. And the circumstances in my life have led to the divorce really being a divorce ... most people don't really get divorced. They keep some contact which is great for the kids. But in my case, I first got really married, and then got really divorced. [1978]

The custody battle took place against a backdrop of Dylan assembling his massive, sprawling opus *Renaldo and Clara* with Howard Alk. Inevitably the inclusion of scenes with Sara and Dylan led to speculation that he was washing his dirty laundry in public. He denied all such intentions.

The footage had been filmed during a period of reconciliation for Dylan and Sara, and it was only the editing which took place during the divorce and custody struggle. The editing lasted most of the winter, spring, late summer and early fall of 1977. Dylan and Alk soon realized they had a lot of footage to work with.

Howard Alk: We knew from the beginning that the film was going to be too long ... [Though] our final ratio of what was shot to what's in the final film is the standard documentary ratio of 20 to 1 ... Actual cutting took about six months. We began work on the film [in 1976] ... but we were interrupted by the second leg of the tour and by the television show, so we were actually in the editing room for six months [in 1977].

Bob Dylan: I knew it was not going to be a short hour movie because we couldn't tell that story in an hour. Originally I couldn't see how we could do it under seven or eight hours. But we just subtracted songs and scenes and dialogue until we couldn't subtract any more. [1978]

Dylan realized that the length of the film would scare off just about all major studios. Though he approached at least one major studio before starting editing it was readily apparent that there could be no *rapprochement* between Dylan's ideas about the structure of the movie and its theme and the studio's desire for a movie that had a direct storyline and traditional structure.

Bob Dylan: All the financiers wanted something more definite than an improvisational film with just an outline and based on death and rebirth. [1978]

When the movie was completed he again considered using the major studios to ensure that *Renaldo and Clara* received adequate distribution, despite his understandable aversion to dealing with studio moguls after the shameful way MGM had treated Peckinpah over the filming and editing of *Pat Garrett & Billy the Kid*. With *Renaldo and Clara*, Dylan wanted to present a *fait accompli*.

Bob Dylan: We took the movie to one of the major studios. They treated us like dogs. As far as I can remember they didn't want to see more than fifteen minutes of the film before they bought the picture. We felt it only proper they should see it all. Besides a major studio would never release this as a four-hour movie. They thought it should run for one and a half hours and that it had to be all music. [1978]

The structure, symbolism and sheer length of the film inevitably meant that Dylan had to put up most of the money himself. Though the film would be attacked for its lack of cohesion, it was in fact structured very carefully and with a very specific approach in mind. Dylan talked at length to the press about its oblique symbolism, but it was its structuring which was the most innovative aspect of *Renaldo and Clara*.

Bob Dylan: People were told this, this, this – the rest of it is up to you, what you say in this scene is your business, but at the same time beyond that, the only directions you have are: you're going to die in a year, or see your mother for the first time in twenty years. So far as instructions to actors go, less is more. [1977]

Bob Dylan: This was a movie done without a script. There were ideas from the beginning, but a lot of this film developed as we were doing it. Quite a bit was improvised, but only within certain rules. [1978]

The idea of structuring the film around improvised scenes was obviously preconceived. Only a general framework was provided by Dylan. According to the production notes which accompanied its release there were four types of scene shot for the movie:

(i) Dylan would set up a scene for improvisation, and let the actors work around a given concept. Various people such as Ronee Blakely, Ronnie Hawkins and Mick Ronson had great talent in expanding on a Dylan idea, and they took off from this starting point and embellished with their own contributions.

(ii) Dylan would give the cameramen an assignment to get a certain type of image, then he would let them go about their work.

(iii) After shooting proceeded and cast and crew had picked up on Dylan's *modus operandi*, the director opened the film up for people to create their own types of drama. Characters had taken on lives of their own, and actors were given free rein to extend these lives out to their logical conclusions.

(iv) Documentary coverage had its place in *Renaldo and Clara* – when Dylan visited Jack Kerouac's grave in Lowell, Massachusetts, with Allen Ginsberg, or when he travelled to a New York CBS Records executive meeting, the camera was present to record the activities.

Having accrued this mass of footage, the film was then constructed according to very rigorous criteria. The problems with its reception by the American media could perhaps have been alleviated if Dylan had been given a better chance to explain how it was constructed. As it was few reporters were interested in the way he had spent a year of his life putting the film together. All they wanted to know was why Bob Dylan was played by someone else (Ronnie Hawkins) in the movie, and whether there was not a literal connection between the *ménage à trois* of Renaldo, Clara and the Woman in White in the film and Dylan, Sara and Baez in real life. Allen Ginsberg attempted to explain the way that the film was built up, trying to dissuade people from approaching it as a conventional linear construct.

Allen Ginsberg: It's built in a very interesting way. You'd have to study it like *Finnegans Wake*, or Cézanne, to discern the texture, the composition of the tapestry. He shot about 110 hours of film, or more, and he looked at all the scenes. Then he put all the scenes on index cards, according to some preconceptions he had when he was directing the shooting. Namely, themes: God, rock & roll, art, poetry, marriage, women, sex, Bob Dylan, poets, death – maybe eighteen or twenty thematic preoccupations. Then he also put on index cards all the different characters, as well as scenes. He also marked on index cards the dominant colour – blue or red ... and certain other images that go through the movie, like the rose and the hat, and Indians – American Indians – so that he finally had a cross-file of all that. And then he went through it all again and began composing it, thematically, weaving these specific compositional references in and out. So it's compositional, and the idea was not to have a 'plot', but to have a composition of those themes. So you notice the movie begins with a rose and a hat – masculine and feminine. The rose is like a 'travelling vagina' – those are his words. The hat is masculine – crowns. The rose . . . travels from hand to hand . . . it's a painter's film, and was composed like that. I've seen it about four times, and each time I see it, it becomes more logical – not rational, but logical.

Like Ginsberg, Dylan wanted to talk about the texture of the film. *Renaldo and Clara* to him was a further step in advancing the approach adopted on *Blood on the Tracks*, the one advocated by Norman Raeben, but which Dylan sought to apply not just to painting but to other artistic media.

Bob Dylan: The film is no puzzle, it's A–B–C–D, but the composition's like a game – the red flower, the hat, the red and blue themes. The interest is not in the literal plot but in the associated texture – colours, images, sounds. [1977]

Significantly, when talking about the film Dylan referred more often to painters than to film-makers. To him *Renaldo and Clara* was a moving painting. He refused to admit to any real connection with America's populist film heritage.

Bob Dylan: I'm . . . doing this . . . to put forth a certain vision which I carry around and can't express on any other canvas. [1978]

He perceived his primary influences not as Ford, Houston or Hitchcock but Cézanne, Modigliani and Dali. When talking to one reporter, he claimed, 'In writing songs I've learned as much from Cézanne as I have from Woody Guthrie.' The only film that he referred to as an influence was *Les Enfants du Paradis*, which he had previously mentioned as a signpost to both Sam Shepard and Allen Ginsberg.

Bob Dylan: Regardless of what it's about – Renaldo and Clara, a guy selling a horse, a guy singing on a stage or fighting with a man, whatever it is – we have stopped time in this movie. We've grasped that time. And we are the only ones. I've never seen a film except one other that has stopped time – *Les Enfants du Paradis*. [1977]

As he did when discussing the songs on *Blood on the Tracks*, Dylan talked a great deal about the nature of time in *Renaldo and Clara*. There does indeed seem to be no discernible chronology to the film. Everything happens at once, the history of the characters is given only by their actions and their conversation. Dylan made it clear that the film had to be perceived as a dream. In Renaldo's dream the identity of a given individual represents no more than some form of latent manifestation of his subconscious, symbolic rather than realistic. And this is the case throughout the film.

Bob Dylan: The man on the floor [at the end], who's obviously dreaming, no one asks him anything – but the whole movie was his dream . . . Renaldo has faith in himself and his ability to dream, but the dream is sometimes so powerful it has the ability to wipe him out. Renaldo has no ordinary mind – he might not even have a soul. He may in actuality be Time itself, in his wildest moments. [1977]

The dream nature of the film allows for the distortion of identity. It was this factor that bemused so many critics. Of course, Dylan did not make it easy on them. Even when talking to Allen Ginsberg about the movie, he never resolves the question of whom Bob Dylan plays.

Bob Dylan: Renaldo is everybody . . . Renaldo is you, struggling within yourself, with the knowledge that you're locked within the chains of your own being . . . He's Everyman in the movie, and he survives. He is a man contemplating the future . . . At the opening of the movie he's in a mask you can see through – it's translucent. At the end he's seen putting on face paint. [1977]

Yet when he is seen putting face paint on, this does not necessarily mean he is about to become the man with the white painted face. According to Dylan this white-faced figure has no name, he is 'the Chorus of the movie'. He is the figure that Renaldo aspires to become, in his dreams.

Bob Dylan: The man in whiteface is what Renaldo cannot become at the moment. At the Indian party that isn't Renaldo, that is the man in whiteface. He represents the compelling figure of authority. [1977]

But the presence of Bob Dylan cannot fail to hang over the movie. It is after all billed at the beginning as 'A film by Bob Dylan'. He is referred to throughout the movie, notably when the CBC reporter is waiting 'breathlessly for Bob Dylan'. He even gets Ronnie Hawkins, this rather grotesque figure, to play a character called Bob Dylan. It was this overwhelming presence which was seized upon by critics as evidence of a giant ego at work, and *Renaldo and Clara* was characterized by many as one massive exercise in narcissism. Dylan's conceit in using his own name was certainly deliberate:

Bob Dylan: Bob Dylan is being used here as a famous name, so we don't have to hire Marlon Brando! . . . Let's say that in real life Bob Dylan fixes his name on the public. He can retrieve that name at will. Anything else the public makes of it is its business. [1977]

If Dylan's intention was to require the audience to abandon their preconception of who Bob Dylan was, the ruse did not work. As a symbol, Bob Dylan proved too potent an image. He overshadows the movie. The implication that beneath the whiteface of Bob Dylan-as-Chorus lies Renaldo, the real self behind the mask, was too oblique for the film-going public.

Likewise, the identity of Clara was a further source of (deliberate) confusion. Sara Dylan plays Clara, but she also plays a whore stuck in Diamond Hell, during the so-called bordello scenes. Meanwhile Mrs Dylan is played by the ravishing Ronee Blakely.

If the figure in Diamond Hell is Clara, she appears to be deep in conversation with the Woman in White (dressed in red), if that is whom Joan Baez is playing here. Logic says not. Yet Baez plays the Woman in White in the film. But so does Sara (or is that Clara?). It soon becomes apparent that Clara and the Woman in White are different aspects of the same symbolic figure.

Bob Dylan: Clara is the symbol of Freedom in this movie. She's what attracts Renaldo at the present. Renaldo lives in a tomb, his only way out is to dream . . . You know at the end of the movie he's about to or has broken out of that tomb . . . you feel that even though he may be under strenuous times, he might transcend them . . . He's trying to break out of himself – not only that, he's trying to break out of himself by means of reason . . . He's actually in the process of conquering his own soul . . . [the end of the movie] is in fact the morning of Renaldo's life. He has ceased to be Renaldo. From that moment on he will become what he wishes to become. No more will he answer to Renaldo . . . [The Woman in White] is the ghost of Death – Death's ghost. Renaldo rids himself of death when she leaves, and he goes on, alive, with his greasepaint. He's becoming the hero of his own dream. [1977]

Dylan has never stated that Clara and the Woman in White were intended as aspects of the Triple Goddess, Graves's all-encompassing conception of the muse as Virgin/Lover/Hag, though he admitted to Jonathan Cott that the Death Mother is represented in the movie. However, it is difficult not to see the women in the film in these terms, particularly with the way he uses the primary colours of white/red/black to represent the many women.

Clearly *Renaldo and Clara* remains Dylan's most deliberate exposition of himself as a conscious artist. In the many interviews he gave at the time about the film, of which his conversations with Ginsberg (from which the above quotes are drawn) are the most important, he seemed for the first time prepared to talk about his art in an authentic, expository way.

Bob Dylan: I am a conscious artist . . . I had a teacher who was a conscious artist and he drilled it into me to be a conscious artist, so I became a conscious artist.

Again Dylan is referring to Norman Raeben, the painter who had helped him to learn the conscious approach which resulted in *Blood on the Tracks*. And in many ways *Renaldo and Clara* attempts to duplicate aspects of Dylan's writing on that album. On songs like 'Tangled Up in Blue' and 'Lily, Rosemary and the Jack of Hearts', identity is often unresolved or opaque. In 'Tangled Up in Blue' he seems to meet his lost love in a topless bar, yet he does not recognize her. Later on he 'lives with them on Montague Street', but who are they? Only hints are given. The Rimbaudian figure starts 'dealing with slaves', but is this figure and the narrator one and the same (a common enough interpretation)? In 'Lily, Rosemary and the Jack of Hearts', events are even vaguer. Who pulled the empty gun on whom, when 'a cold revolver clicked'? Who is the man who Lily 'couldn't stand, who hounded her so much'? On celluloid such ambiguities of identity could have been made readily apparent, shoved into the faces of the paying customers. Dylan, though, challenged such notions by constantly asking the viewers to question the identity of those whom they think they see on the screen.

The notion of time in *Blood on the Tracks* could be illusory. In 'Tangled Up in Blue' Dylan used a dream sequence as the basis for the song – 'I was layin' in bed/Wonderin' . . .' Yet the dream itself seems to be a flashback, the narrator reminiscing from 'the side of the road' as he's 'headin' for another joint'. The time scale in the song is in no way linear. Rather the song is like a cut-up of incidents involving the singer and a woman (or is it Woman?). The order is seemingly random, but the effect cumulative. In *Renaldo and Clara*, Dylan applies a very similar technique. The viewer is not sure how scenes relate to the primary struggle of Renaldo. Likewise there is no linear chronology to the events in the movie. The Narrator in the film, played by David Blue, is not narrating the film. Like everyone else in the movie, he is a figment of Renaldo's dream.

Bob Dylan: David seems to know what's going on, but he's only existing in Renaldo's dream. He's the narrator who links the movie to generational history . . . he's a figment of Renaldo's imagination that attempts to reconcile the past that never was. [1977]

As in 'Tangled up in Blue', there is a strong journeying element to the movie. There is a constant procession of people coming and going, and the rose and hat become linking symbols.

Bob Dylan: In the symbol of the rose we see the vagina travelling around. You see it a lot. You could trace it every time it comes up. Go to the movie and pick up all the signs where the rose goes. First on the table in front of the truckdriver, who's almost contemplating it; then Clara in one of her former selves – a manifestation of her as desperation – picks up the rose and then travels with it. It was nobody's rose. Clara picked it up and went off alone to the train station, where she sees and lures Renaldo for the first time. [1977]

Renaldo and Clara took all of Dylan's creative energies through most of 1976 and 1977 to complete. It was the most sustained and conscientious work that he had ever done, or would ever do. If in the recording studio he sought spontaneity, in the editing suite progress was necessarily slow and required an immense amount of discipline from this diehard maverick.

Having completed this monumental work, for the scale of the film is certainly impressive, Dylan undertook some market research. In October, Allen Ginsberg spent a week with him watching and discussing the movie, and Ginsberg, albeit not your average film punter, gave the film a thumbs-up. Ginsberg also recorded at least three interviews with Dylan about *Renaldo and Clara* intending to publish a brief study of the film. Two further major interviews were arranged in the fall of 1977, one with Ron Rosenbaum of *Playboy* magazine, the other with Jonathan Cott of *Rolling Stone*. Both were shown the movie, and Dylan went to great lengths to explain any queries that the film might have raised. Cott in particular seemed positive about the movie, though he did observe 'how easy it is to mistake people in the film for one another'; and how 'some people will obviously think that this film either broke up your marriage or is a kind of incantation to make your marriage come back together.' This was only the beginning.

In early December, Dylan conducted his own preview for *Renaldo and Clara*. Stopping at a restaurant near Goldwyn Studios, where he had been completing the film, he invited some of the customers to a screening of the picture. The mixed response proved a fair barometer of the public's view of the film. Comments varied from, 'An avant-garde piece of work' through 'It's Dylan. That's all that counts' to one disgruntled attendee who moaned, 'I'm a little upset. I missed Carl Perkins on the Johnny Cash Christmas TV special for this.' To such people would he have to sell his movie.

In December 1977 Dylan was required to become adept at juggling time. Embroiled in the last stages of the custody battle, he also began to give his first interviews to promote the release of *Renaldo and Clara*. Meanwhile he summoned Rob Stoner to bring a band to Los Angeles to start rehearsing for a Far East tour which he had now committed himself to.

Rob Stoner: I was really surprised when I got the call to do the '78 gig. Man, I thought the *Hard Rain* thing was the last I'd ever hear from Bob to work ... Then suddenly I get this call – I think Bob called me up personally. He called me up and asked me to bring Howie and a couple of other people to LA to just try some things out ... I brought a guy who used to play with Charlie Bird Parker, Walter Davis Jnr on piano ... and Otis Smith, a great percussionist and singer, friend of Howie's and mine. No girls.

The band, though, seems to have initially taken a back seat, as Dylan dealt with his other distractions. After all, the Far East tour was two months away, and the film was due for its premiere in January. Dylan was largely absent from the initial rehearsals with the musicians Stoner had arrived with. Even when he made it to rehearsals his mind was not on playing, and the musicians were finding him difficult to communicate with.

Rob Stoner: I brought this weird band out with me and Bob kept us sitting around for a week or two. He just never showed up. Meanwhile we have this rehearsal hall right down the street from where we're all staying. We're waiting for the guy to show up. Meanwhile to pass the time and keep everybody together I was doing the surrogate singing – I was just singing the tunes that I thought everybody should know in case Bob does show up. And we keep waiting. And he drops in and he's distracted. Maybe he didn't like the band. He was really fucked up [mentally]. He was always bummed out. He was chain smoking and he was really in a bad mood. He was short with people. It just wasn't working out.

As December turned into January, though, the other distractions became less important. The custody struggle was finally resolved, and the majority of the important interviews for the film were out of the way — reporters from *Rolling Stone, Playboy*, the *New York Times* and the *Los Angeles Times* had all come and gone. Meanwhile he realized he had a month at best to put a band together and get them roadworthy.

Joel Bernstein: I wound up actually living [at Rundown Studios] from about September 1977 until we left for the Japanese tour early the following year. Bob actually had a room too. I turned one of the offices into my bedroom and he had an office that was set up as a bedroom too . . . There were auditions and rehearsals all the time. There were members of the band that he knew that he wanted, like Steven Soles and Rob Stoner, but he was looking for other players.

Dylan certainly had specific musicians in mind — Rob Stoner, Steven Soles, David Mansfield, Howie Wyeth — but he also wanted a saxophone player and some girls. He had decided from the start that it would be a big band that he would take on the road. However, his approach to recruiting the girl singers seems to have been a shade unorthodox, having little to do with the sound of their voices.

Rob Stoner: He starts inviting all these chicks to come down and sing and I felt it was like: Is he doing these things to impress these girlfriends of his. 'Cause they weren't professional singers. I tell you one of 'em was Katie Segal from that show *Married with Children*. She was down there for a couple of days. I mean they were like actress-singers. Not like real singers . . . The first time he shows up to do anything serious it's 'cause he's got these chicks around. Oh God, and we tried rehearsing with them. It was a revolving door. Eventually we settled on the three or four that ended up doing the tour — but they were pros . . . When the chicks start showing up to rehearsals, then Bob starts to get interested in it. Suddenly he's in contact with me every day. He says, Well call Jesse Ed Davis. Have him come down and play. He tried to get Al Kooper, he couldn't make it, he had Barry Goldberg down there — Barry couldn't do it for another reason. We had Mickey Jones, the actor . . . He was calling up people from like twenty years ago. It was like he was gonna have a reunion party and check everybody in LA out. I was having a good time doing this! Every day we were having a jam with people who Bob had called to show up. Some of them he'd say, Call this guy and have him show up, call that guy and get him to show up. And I'd do that. And there would also be people who he showed up with. And things went on like that for a couple of weeks and nothing was getting done, and there were gigs booked.

As Stoner implies, constructing the actual band Dylan finally ended up touring with became something of a rushed affair. Even the basic core of Rolling Thunder musicians were not as certain about doing the tour as Dylan perhaps thought they would be. In May 1977 he had signed to Jerry Weintraub's management company for personal representation, Weintraub effectively becoming his first manager since the days of Albert Grossman. Weintraub was known for his middle-of-the-road acts like Neil Diamond, and for his strictly moral views on sex, drugs and rock & roll. Touring Japan also presented serious problems for anyone who indulged in even a minor drug habit. Paul McCartney had only recently been busted there for something as innocuous as cannabis. Dylan found that Howie Wyeth was reluctant to play a country where even this most mild of drugs could have supply problems.

Howie Wyeth: I went to LA on Christmas Eve. I showed up out there and they weren't ready yet and I tried to rehearse with them and then I heard that Bob had a new manager and that the guy said, We're not gonna even have any grass on this tour. I think they were serious. They were going to Japan. I was thinkin', Man if they're not even gonna have grass I'm really gonna be in trouble, because really on the previous tours there was a guy carrying duffel bags full of coke on the tour and you could buy grams for $25 and just get 'em written off to your *per diem* . . . So I went out there and we tried to play and it didn't feel right and I was tryin' to kick too, 'cause I knew I couldn't get high once we'd left so [with] the combination of all these things I could see the writing on the wall. I realized I was either gonna get busted or I'd end up being tortured to death. So I literally had to just tell Bob one night, Bob I can't do it. That was terrible. He had his own problems. He felt bad that I wasn't gonna do it and he called me up when I got back to New York and said, Are you sure?

Suddenly the axis of the band was undermined. Securing the right girls and horns was not a big deal. But a drummer like Wyeth held the whole sound together. The first replacement for Howie Wyeth was ex-Wings drummer Denny Siewell, but, though he gelled very well with Stoner and the rest of the band, visa problems prohibited him from getting the gig.

Joel Bernstein: He needed a drummer and he auditioned a number of drummers, maybe ten or a dozen. It was an interesting experience for

me, watching all these different musicians trying to play Bob's songs . . .
Bob had settled on Denny Siewell. He was very happy with his playing
but it turned out that he couldn't be used because of the Wings bust in
Sweden – he wouldn't have been allowed into Japan, much to Dylan's
disappointment, and I'm sure his.

The final choice for drummer was detrimental to the sound of
the band. Ian Wallace had played with King Crimson, and so had
a pedigree, but he seemed unable to apply the same crisp dispatch
as Wyeth, and his sense of time was occasionally wayward, speed-
ing songs up unduly. Stoner did not enjoy playing with Wallace,
and this would be a contributory factor in Stoner's premature
departure at the end of the first leg of the world tour.

Rob Stoner: It was tough, everybody had to stop doing drugs. We had
that guy from Wings. I can't remember half the people that showed up
to that . . . We had the guy from Derek and the Dominoes, Jim Gordon,
great drummer. Man, we had all kinds of drummers. But y'see because
we waited so long to make the final cuts in the band the deadline was
pressing and eventually we had to settle on somebody. And Wallace
happened to be it . . . The guy from Wings sounded great, man, but he
had a visa problem 'cause he was with McCartney. Wallace was just
convenient – he was Mr Right for the night. It's just that the night was
too fuckin' long . . . So the band that ended up being that band was
something that I had to do hastily because we had blown our time
having all these jam reunion things. But Bob had no relationship with
that band. He wasn't hanging out . . . I had tried out a lot of people but
because of this casual attitude until the last week, then everyone got
scared. We had to get Steve Douglas who costs a fuckin' fortune. He's
one of the top sax men in Hollywood . . . I was in LA don't forget – I
don't know people in LA, so I'm depending on recommendations from
other people who are not people I really know. I had to come to the
office early every day and be his secretary and then I had to go rehearse
and then I'd finish rehearsing and there'd be like a hundred messages
from musicians.

Stoner had arranged for Billy Cross, a lead guitarist from an old
band of his, to fly in from Sweden to play. Dylan had settled on
Steve Douglas to play sax. With these two final additions the band
was at last a unit – by the last week in January. For the two weeks
before flying to Japan, Dylan and his new ensemble worked on the
repertoire without distraction. *Renaldo and Clara* was finally out
(though not for long), and Dylan was providing some real input
into the arrangements.

According to Stoner, they had been working up arrangements
just to make a song different, and this was how they ended up

with a Douglas/Mansfield penny whistle/violin arrangement on some songs, and even a 'quasi-baroque' version of 'If You See Her, Say Hello' (which actually worked quite well). As Stoner notes, when they put these arrangements to Dylan, 'Sometimes he'd like it and he'd use it and other times he'd say, Forget it.' In an attempt to get the maximum out of the final two weeks of rehearsals, Dylan began having the sessions taped.

Joel Bernstein: The [rehearsal] recording[s] was specifically for him to listen back to, not for him to ever use, but to let the band hear how things were progressing, and for him to hear how arrangements were coming together. He was much more disciplined than ... [on] the 1976 tour. Not only was everything taped but he would have the band stay over after rehearsals finished and he would have me play back particular performances of the best versions of each song that day that either I would pick or he would pick, and spend an hour, hour and a half, listening back to things ... Rehearsals would usually begin about one o'clock ... People would show up and have lunch and then we'd start around one and play until six ... The band got bigger as time went on, and once it was reasonably together he got them to play certain songs in different ways, in one key and then another key and then half-time, then country, then reggae, then rocked up. It was really an experimental thing. And then listening to those songs he would just pick one, say, Yeah! That's the one! And I would inwardly groan and go, Oh no! Not the reggae one! But he had his own idea about what was the best one to do.

The tapes that exist from these final rehearsals suggest that, despite his lackadaisical approach to the earlier rehearsals, the band were sufficiently together to tour. Indeed they were clearly better rehearsed than on some of Dylan's subsequent tours. Comparing a recording of a rehearsal from 30 December 1977 with one from exactly one month later, the sound is a world apart. If the early rehearsal sounds like a jam session from a rather untogether Rolling Thunder band with some girl singers wailing along for good measure, by the end of January the band had its own identity and some of the new arrangements were worthwhile – even if the reggae-style versions of 'Don't Think Twice' and 'Knockin' on Heaven's Door' smacked of different for different's sake. Still, Dylan was going back on the road, away from Malibu, away from legal battles and financial difficulties, and, like a new musical, they were opening well out of town and could work on the show away from the scrutiny of the Western media. CBS–Sony in Japan had other ideas.

26

1978: Someone's Got It In for Me

When Dylan finally flew to Japan on 16 February 1978 he was especially glad to leave behind the American press, who had just given him the most intense critical roasting of his career. On 25 January *Renaldo and Clara* had been premiered simultaneously in Los Angeles and New York. The reviews were almost universally hostile, not to say spiteful. In one astonishing attempt to assassinate the film's credibility, the *Village Voice* sent no less than four reviewers to savage it. Farida McFree, who was staying at Dylan's town house in New York recovering from the trauma of the custody battle and the end of her relationship with Dylan, read the New York reviews to him over the phone. His reaction suggests he had anticipated that the film would not be accepted by the critics, though he seems to have underestimated the amount of bile they would be sending in his general direction.

Farida McFree: I read the reviews to him over the phone and it was horrible, absolutely horrible what they said about him, especially in the *Village Voice*. One guy said they hated him and they wished he'd die. And I said Bob they actually really wish you were dead, and he said It doesn't bother me . . . It just rolled right off of him. And he said, Farida they say all kinds of things about me so I've just learned to live with it . . . My experience being around him [was that] people were so obsequious and therefore how could you trust anybody.

The *New Yorker* utilized Pauline Kael who, fresh from trashing Orson Welles's reputation in her *Citizen Kane Book*, felt that a little more debunking of a certified genius was in order. Her view of Dylan was betrayed by statements like, 'The Bob Dylan [his fans] responded to [in the sixties] was a put-on artist. He was derisive, and even sneering, but in the sixties that was felt to be a way of freaking out those who weren't worthy of being talked to straight . . . In *Renaldo and Clara* his mocking spirit is just bad news.' In fact Kael's sour review was one of the least personalized assaults upon the movie. In most of the reviews, there seemed to be a sense of personal grievance, as if the critics believed now that everything Dylan had produced to date was somehow a con, a put-on as Kael would say. He, not surprisingly, felt a need to defend himself and the movie.

Bob Dylan: Reading the reviews of the movie, I sensed a feeling of them wanting to crush things. Those reviews weren't about the movie. They were just an excuse to get at me for one reason or another . . . I was disappointed that the critics couldn't get beyond the superficial elements. They thought the movie was all about Bob Dylan, Joan Baez and Sara Dylan . . . and [it] wasn't. [1978]

Despite his attempts to defend the movie in the press by committing himself to a further flurry of interviews at the beginning of February, the film sank without trace. It opened in only one more city, Minneapolis, and disappeared from American cinemas within weeks, never to reappear. A consortium later convinced Dylan to edit the movie down to two hours – their two million dollar offer for this edited version helping at least to reduce the film's financial deficit – and re-released it to American cinemas. Dylan, mocking those who had savaged the film so mercilessly, gave the consortium the film all the critics had claimed the four-hour version to be, that is, an inchoate jumble of improvised scenes, edited in a seemingly random order with little evidence of a rationale. He included virtually all the concert footage featured in the original movie, presumably to appease the uncomprehending consortium. It was his final revenge on those responsible for the brutal reception given to *Renaldo and Clara*.

Ironically, when the film received its European premiere at Cannes in May, it was enthusiastically received, and when it made its London debut in July it ran for three months, proving to be a regular favourite at repertory cinemas for the next few years. TV rights were later bought up in England, Germany and Sweden. Though reviews were still mixed, several considered it an audacious work and even those who were unhappy with it showed considerably more restraint than their American counterparts. The more friendly response to the film in Europe would mirror the more favourable reviews there for the 1978 concerts and the *Street-Legal* album, which between them would constitute a year of considerable artistic activity from Dylan.

To describe the reviews of the shows in the Far East and Europe as kinder is something of an understatement. They verged on the ecstatic. The new arrangements of a cross-section of his finest songs were enthusiastically welcomed in Japan and Australia. Despite Stoner's distaste for the sound, which would be shared by American critics, the two-hour-plus shows seemed well thought out, and Dylan genuinely communicative. The early shows were lacking in punch, and some of the more incongruous elements in the band, such as the flute and congas, seemed temporarily in the ascendant. But Cross's guitar playing and the saxophone of Douglas became more dominant as the tour progressed, and Dylan's voice became harder, more insistent. In Japan, though, he was still finding his feet, looking for a way to work this band into a cohesive unit.

Rob Stoner: He had in mind to do something like Elvis Presley, I think. That size band and the uniforms. Also he wasn't very sure about it which is why he opened way out of town. I mean we didn't go anyplace close to Europe or England or America forever, man . . . He was very insecure about it and I don't blame him. I think he knew subconsciously he was making a big mistake.

Unfortunately Dylan once again picked the wrong end of the tour to record a live album. In 1974 and 1976 the earlier shows on the tour were certainly superior. In this case he would have been well-advised to hold back until the European leg before recording an album. As it was, *Bob Dylan at Budokan*, the double album released in November 1978 in Japan, and April 1979 in America and Europe, was intended only as a souvenir for the Japanese of those particular shows, rather than the testament to a 115-date world tour it has become.

Bob Dylan: They twisted my arm to do a live album for Japan. It was the same band I used on *Street-Legal*, and we had just started findin' our way into things on that tour when they recorded it. I never meant for it to be any type of representation of my stuff or my band or my live show. [1984]

The scale of the band and the size of the arenas he was playing precluded Dylan from trying out new songs live, and there were few surprises after the first couple of dates, as the band settled into a standard format for the tour. The major set variation on the first leg of the tour was which of several blues standards he would open each show with. Over the course of the Far East tour fans heard

Dylan's versions of Billy Lee Riley's 'Repossession Blues', a dig at those who sought to dub this the Alimony Tour, Ernest Lewis's 'Lonesome Bedroom Blues', Tampa Red's 'Love Her With a Feeling' and at one show Robert Johnson's 'Steady Rollin' Man'. In Europe and America Tampa Red's 'Love Crazy' and Willie Dixon's 'I'm Ready' vied for inclusion with 'Love Her With a Feeling'.

On the Far East leg Dylan had no new album to promote, indeed his last album was over two years old, so there was a nagging sense that he was playing an oldies show, an effect not helped by the Japanese promoter's insistence that he include certain songs in his set, a demand he would have resisted in previous years. But now his new manager, Jerry Weintraub, was attempting to instil the ethos of the professional entertainer in Dylan. Also his serious financial difficulties, primarily the result of his messy and expensive divorce and the commercial failure of *Renaldo and Clara*, precluded him from aborting what would be a very profitable Far East tour.

Rob Stoner: That guy [Weintraub] accompanied us to Japan and he was like always around. Yeah, suddenly we were the Entertainer and it was a little too stodgy. I'll never forget one day [at rehearsals] a telegram arrived from the Japanese promoter and in it he had a manifest of the songs he expected Bob to do on this tour. In other words he was a jukebox, he was playing requests. We don't want you coming here and doing like your new experimental material or getting up there and jamming. It's not good enough for people to be paying good yen to see Bob Dylan. They want to see Bob Dylan doing 'Blowin' in the Wind' and like on and on − the most predictable greatest hits ten songs you could name ... By then I might as well have been working in Wayne Newton's band or something.

If the press reacted well in the Far East, there was already dissension in the band. Dylan had become very close to one of the backing singers, Helena Springs, and this inevitably caused animosity and envy among some of the other members of the crew. Helena Springs had been recruited during the impressing-women-I-like phase of the rehearsals, and she had no experience of singing in a band on this scale. Her lack of experience was thus frowned upon. However, she was a fresh and vivacious personality and the band benefited from her inclusion. Dylan tried to encourage her in her development as a singer, and even started teaching her to write songs. While in Brisbane in March, they worked up a few songs together.

Helena Springs: We were together in Brisbane one evening and he was playing on the guitar and we were just goofing around, laughing and I said I can't really write . . . He said, 'Well, come on, I'll write something with you. We'll write something together.' And I said, 'Okay.' He said, 'You start singing some stuff and I'll start playing.' So he started strumming his guitar and I started to sing, just making up lyrics. And he'd make up stuff and that was when we got 'If I Don't Be There by Morning' and 'Walk Out in the Rain'.

Dylan and Springs remained close for some time to come. They also wrote many songs together on the 1978 tour. Springs did not leave his employ until the winter of 1980, when ironically she was replaced by Carolyn Dennis, her fellow backing singer on the 1978 tour.

If certain members of the crew were unhappy with Springs' intimacy with Dylan they refrained from comment, in his earshot at least. However, by this time Rob Stoner was very unhappy, and Springs was not the source of his dissatisfaction. He did not feel that the 1978 band suited Dylan's music, and he was bored by the lack of spontaneity. He was also getting, because of his position as band-leader, all the complaints the musicians wanted to direct at Dylan. Even the way his co-player in the rhythm section played was getting to him.

Rob Stoner: Ian Wallace, man, had a beat like a cop . . . The drummer sounds like fuckin' sludge . . . when he was playing with Bob he couldn't swing from a rope . . . I was not happy and Bob knew this and my not being happy meant that I was fucking every chick on the bus and I was getting a little wild myself. Fortunately you can't get drugs in Australia and Japan as easily as you can places that you know [but] . . . I was drinking a lot.

When the Far East tour wound to an end on 1 April at the Sydney Fairgrounds, Stoner told Dylan he wanted out. Dylan, after spending a three-day holiday in New Zealand with Ra Aranga, a New Zealand princess he had met in Auckland earlier on the tour, returned to Los Angeles to find a new bass player and band-leader, and to set about recording his first album in thirty months.

Dylan's choice for Stoner's replacement was not a cheap option. Jerry Scheff, like Steve Douglas, had made his reputation as part of Presley's touring band in the early seventies. With Scheff's recruitment it did seem as if Dylan really was intent on assuming Presley's mantle. Scheff was thrown in at the deep end as, within a week of joining the band, he was required to take part in the sessions for *Street-Legal*.

Dylan had very little time to record his new album. A European tour was scheduled to begin in June, and the members of the band were looking for a brief respite in the interim. Realistically he had something like two weeks to record the album. In order for the sessions to proceed as smoothly as possible, he decided to record with the touring band, who had worked on several of the scheduled songs during soundchecks and rehearsals, and were by now conversant with his idiosyncrasies. He also decided to use his own rehearsal studio, Rundown in Santa Monica, as the venue for the recording sessions, with the help of a mobile studio console. The album was recorded even more quickly than required.

Bob Dylan: It took us a week to make *Street-Legal* – we mixed it the following week and put it out the week after. If we hadn't done it that fast we wouldn't have made an album at all, because we were ready to go back on the road. [1978]

The outcome however was unsatisfactory. Dylan had always recorded 'on the run' and the results were normally perfectly acceptable, if not always the best achievable. But this time he was using a large band, a band which required more than the basic sixteen-track set-up that had been suitable for his purposes in the past. The sophistications of modern studio techniques had overtaken him, and *Street-Legal* would be the first of three albums which would eventually force him totally to re-evaluate his approach to recording. Dylan himself soon admitted to a sense of disappointment with the results, though he would persevere with his time-tested approach for some time yet.

Bob Dylan: There were some problems with the record: I didn't want to do it there; couldn't find the right producer. But it was necessary to do it. So we just brought in the remote truck and cut it, went for a live sound. During that whole period we forgot about the shows. So they were a little stiff. [1978]

The sound on the album is thin yet muddy, a poor representation of a band who on their day could produce a full and rich sound and sophisticated arrangements. Also, Dylan's vocals lacked the crisp clarity that he had achieved on *Blood on the Tracks* and *Desire*. The results, though well received in Europe during the euphoria of his tour there, were savaged in the American press. The critics had gotten their teeth into the impudent runt with his film and they were not going to let go just because he was doing what he did best, writing and recording new songs. Greil Marcus's ill-considered review in *Rolling Stone*, headlined 'Never So Utterly Fake', set the tone for the jaundiced US press, who chose in the late seventies to forget survivors of the sixties like Dylan and Van Morrison, ignore or castigate innovators of the seventies like Patti Smith and Television, preferring instead the regressive 'authenticity' of Bruce Springsteen or the mock artistry of David Bowie. Dylan was in for a hard time in the second half of 1978.

June broke promisingly enough, with seven sold-out shows at Los Angeles' Universal Amphitheater, intended to whip the band into shape for Dylan's first European tour in twelve years. When he arrived in London on 13 June, it was the Isle of Wight mayhem all over again. The English press had hyped his six sell-out dates at London's massive 17,000-seat Earls Court to such an extent that he must have been somewhat nervous about how the English would respond to his new arrangements, particularly in the light of the punk revolution which had transformed the English music scene beyond all recognition in the previous two years.

He need not have worried. One newspaper review, headlined 'The Greatest Concert I Have Ever Seen', set the tone for most UK press reviews. *Melody Maker* included an eight-page pull-out with its next issue, which celebrated the residency with four enthusiastic reviews of the London shows. From London, he headed for Rotterdam, where 55,000 fans were waiting; then Dortmund, Berlin and Nuremberg, where he played to 80,000 in the stadium where Hitler held his rallies. Six shows in Paris were as triumphant as the London residency, as were two shows in Gothenburg. He finally returned to England a month to the day after opening his European tour at Earls Court. This time he was concluding the tour with a massive open-air show at a disused aerodrome in the Surrey countryside, attended by an estimated 200,000 fans.

The Blackbushe show represented the high point of the 1978 world tour. Playing to his most devoted fans — the English — in his largest show since the Isle of Wight, Dylan performed for two and a half hours, singing ten songs not performed at the shows a month earlier, including six from the newly released *Street-Legal*. The fans loved it and accorded Dylan a rapturous reception.

Ironically Dylan was not the only one to 'clean up' on that hot summer day. Bootleggers had rapidly pressed up an album from the last Earls Court show and were selling copies on the site. Later he expressed considerable anger at this new wave of illicit vinyl. Yet his failure to respond to the euphoria of the European tour by releasing an official live album meant inevitably that the bootleggers would create product to meet the demand.

The European tour was extensively bootlegged, twelve of the twenty-seven shows appearing, at least partially, on vinyl. Conversely, only two concerts were bootlegged from his somewhat lengthier sixty-five-date tour of America that fall, an indication of the demand in Europe for the 1978 Dylan and the lack of demand in America. Dylan's fall tour of North America began in Augusta, Maine, on 15 September, after two months off the road. The backdrop to the tour was not promising. Aside from the critical flak he had been subjected to in the US press all year, *Street-Legal* had sold poorly. His three previous studio albums had all reached number one. *Street-Legal* failed even to reach the Top Ten. Meanwhile the first single from the album, 'Baby Stop Crying', which had been a smash hit in Europe, providing Dylan with his first Top Twenty single in the UK since 'Knockin' on Heaven's Door', had failed to even make it onto *Billboard*'s Hot Hundred. If he was to remain a commercial force into the eighties, the 1978 US tour would have to reaffirm his big-league status.

This was his first nationwide tour since that legendary 1974 tour, when twelve million people had scrambled for tickets to a mere forty shows. This time Dylan, though still playing the large arenas, would not even sell every show out, as the US press suggested that the show was an indication of Dylan's desire to end his days playing Las Vegas, his big band belting out those classic tunes from his sixties heyday. He reacted with understandable anger.

Bob Dylan: The writers complain the show's disco or Las Vegas. I don't know how they came up with those theories. We never heard them when we played Australia or Japan or Europe. It's like someone made it up in one town and the writer in the next town read it. [1978]

Determined to disavow the notion that he was copying Presley or even Bruce Springsteen (whose 1978 tour was the biggest commercial and critical success of the year), and refuting the idea that he was deliberately playing the entertainer, he attempted to illustrate how every aspect of this band had been represented in his past work.

Bob Dylan: I don't know how radically different it is from things in the past, considering the elements that I have in this band I've . . . used before. I made an album called *New Morning* and we used singers on just about every track, so I've done that. As far as using the horn sound, I used the horn sound in Nashville on 'Rainy Day Women' . . . there isn't really anything new, just a bunch of pieces put together. [1978]

In fact, there was one discernible similarity between Dylan's fall shows and the concurrent Springsteen tour: it represented the first time Dylan had ever prefaced songs with brief rap-stories, along the lines of Springsteen's reminiscences and tall tales which often served as introductions to his best-known songs. The most peculiar of Dylan's raps was the one before 'Senor'. It may be tempting to read some kind of religious meaning into it in the light of subsequent events, particularly as it appeared in the shows sometime during November:

I was riding on a train one time through Mexico, travelling up north to San Diego; and I must have fell asleep on this train and I woke up and it was about midnight . . . and the train had stopped at a place called Monterrey . . . This bunch of children were getting off the train, this family – there must have been about seventeen children and a mother and father and they were getting off the train. And at the time I was watching it all through the glass; it was dark outside so the whole side of the train was like a mirror. So I was watching it all happen and I saw this old man stumble up onto the train and he gets onto the car; and he was walking down and he took a seat right across the car from me. I felt a vibration in the air. I turned to look at him and I could see he wasn't dressed in anything but a blanket; he was just wearing a blanket. He must have been 150 years old. I turned around to look at him and I could see both his eyes were burning out – they were on fire and there was smoke coming out of his nostrils. I said, 'Well, this is the man I want to talk to.'

The sound Dylan was presenting to the Americans was considerably harsher than that the Europeans had heard and loved. He was giving most songs a raucous, hollering delivery which sometimes stripped the songs of their sensitivity, notably 'Tangled Up in Blue', whose torch-ballad arrangement had come in for such praise in Europe. But some songs really benefited from the treatment, notably the *Street-Legal* songs, which now really came into their own. New arrangements of songs like 'I Threw It All Away', 'The Times They Are a-Changin'' and 'Mr Tambourine Man' were also more inventive than on the previous legs of the world tour.

Yet he was fighting a losing battle. Though the fans who saw the shows were as enthusiastic as ever, it seemed that his over-whelming self-confidence and unerring sense of timing was audibly draining from him with each successive performance. His best performances now seemed to be given to the empty arenas when he was soundchecking, as he would frequently work on new songs like 'I Must Love You Too Much', 'You Treat Me Like a Stepchild' and 'This Way That Way' or run through favourite covers like Lowell Fulson's 'Reconsider Baby', Shel Silverstein's 'Daddy's Little Girl' or Tampa Red's 'But I Forgive You'. The two-hour shows were wearing on his vocal chords, his temper and his spirits. He needed someone to pull back on the reins.

Part Three:
Busy Being Born Again ...

27

1978-9: Pulling Back on the Reins

By mid-November 1978, Dylan was in a poor state of mind. He was forty dates into a tortuous sixty-five-date American tour – his first nationwide tour in four years – which had been lambasted by the US press; and attendances at some of the shows had been disappointing. The cumulative effect upon him of the negative receptions for *Renaldo and Clara*, *Street-Legal* and now the American tour – contrasting starkly with the response for both the album and tour in Europe – can only be surmised. After an impressive show in his home town, Los Angeles, on 15 November, he still had a month to go on the road. His next stop was in San Diego on the 17th, where something remarkable happened.

Bob Dylan: Towards the end of the show someone out in the crowd . . . knew I wasn't feeling too well. I think they could see that. And they threw a silver cross on the stage. Now usually I don't pick things up in front of the stage. Once in a while I do. Sometimes I don't. But I looked down at that cross. I said, I gotta pick that up. So I picked up the cross and I put it in my pocket . . . And I brought it backstage and I brought it with me to the next town, which was out in Arizona . . . I was feeling even worse than I'd felt when I was in San Diego. I said, Well I need something tonight. I didn't know what it was. I was used to all kinds of things. I said, I need something tonight that I didn't have before. And I looked in my pocket and I had this cross. [1979].

Stuck in a Tucson hotel room, Dylan – in his own words – needed something that he did not have before. He later talked about what being 'born again' meant to him. He seems to have experienced a literal vision of Christ, Lord of Lords, King of Kings. The state of mind Dylan was in clearly made him susceptible to such an experience. In the song–lyrics on his next two albums he would refer again and again to a feeling that Jesus entering his life literally saved him from an early grave.

Bob Dylan: There was a presence in the room that couldn't have been anybody but Jesus . . . I truly had a born-again experience, if you want to call it that . . . Jesus put his hand on me. It was a physical thing. I felt it. I felt it all over me. I felt my whole body tremble. The glory of the Lord knocked me down and picked me up. [1980]

Jesus did appear to me as King of Kings, and Lord of Lords . . . I believe every knee shall bow one day, and He did die on the cross for all mankind . . . they call it reborn . . . it changes everything. I mean it's like waking one day and can you imagine being reborn, can you imagine turning into another person? It's pretty scary if you think about it . . . It happens spiritually, it don't happen mentally. [1981]

On the road, 'heading towards the sun', Dylan started to question his own moral values, though he still seemed uncertain how to interpret his vision. The meaning of his born-again experience temporarily eluded him. He turned to those in his band who had discovered peace with Christ, notably Helena Springs, the lady with whom he had been writing songs of betrayal and loneliness, songs like 'If I Don't Be There by Morning' and 'Coming from the Heart'; and who, of all the musicians, was closest to Dylan at this point.

Helena Springs: I think he was having some problems . . . He called me and he asked me, and they were questions that no one could possibly help with. And I just said, Don't you ever pray? . . . And he said, Pray? Like that, you know. And he said, Really? And he asked me more questions . . . He started inquiring . . . He's a very inquisitive person — which is one good thing about searching for truth.

When Springs referred to Dylan 'having some problems', it would appear that his soul-searching was primarily motivated by 'woman trouble'. Since his divorce, he had been involved with several women, notably Farida McFree, Springs herself and a black actress by the name of Mary Alice Artes, who receives a name-check on *Street-Legal*. If the subject-matter of the songs on that album was not related to his divorce from Sara, as Dylan repeatedly insisted it was not, then it clearly indicated that his problems with 'witchy women' remained. In his 1979 composition 'Trouble in Mind', Satan whispers to the singer that when he grows bored of Miss So-and-So he has 'another woman for ya'. If Dylan was on the run from the Triple Goddess, he would need the protection of a strong, patriarchal religion.

Bob Dylan: Beauty can be very, very deceiving and it's not always of

God. Beauty appeals to our eyes ... The beauty of the sunset ...
that's God-given. [But] I spent a lot of time dealing with man-made
Beauty, so that sometimes the beauty of God's world has evaded me.
[1981]

David Mansfield and Steven Soles, who had both been in
Dylan's various touring bands since 1975, were committed 'born-
again' Christians, and both were subjected to his inquiries about
the nature of their faith, as was ex-Rolling Thunder member
T-Bone Burnett. One thing they said, in particular, struck a chord
with Dylan, and reflected the toll the custody battle and his
subsequent enforced separation from his children had taken on
him.

Howie Wyeth: T-Bone [Burnett] read Bob that line in the Bible, that
says if you listen to astrologers and people who are into the black arts ...
your family will be taken from you. And he'd just lost the battle in court
... T-Bone told me that the thing that really nailed it was when he
showed him in the Bible that quote.

Steven Soles: I kept telling him that I was so glad that I didn't have to
place my faith in man any longer.

Dylan gave few clues to the thousands of fans he was playing
to every night in the final four weeks of his year-long world
tour that he was re-evaluating his moral code. A 'small silver
cross', though, clearly represented a new starting point. Six days
after Tucson, Dylan was in Fort Worth playing the Convention
Center. On stage he was wearing a not-so-small metal cross
around his neck. For a man raised a Jew this could not be a
casual gesture. He also began to improvise a new line for the
powerful, stripped-bare version of 'Tangled Up in Blue' he was
performing at the time. Rather than having the mysterious lady
in the topless bar quoting an Italian poet from the fourteenth
century, she was now quoting from the Bible, initially from the
Gospel According to Matthew – the gospel written to convince
Jews that Jesus fulfilled the Old Testament prophecies regarding
their Messiah. Gradually, though, the lines she quoted changed,
until Dylan settled upon a verse from Jeremiah, the very verse he
would quote on the inner sleeve of the *Saved* album: 'Behold, the
days come, saith the Lord, that I will make a new covenant with
the house of Israel, and with the house of Judah' (Jeremiah
31.31).

As he entered the final two weeks of the 115-date world tour,

Dylan began to attack the shows with renewed vigour. The songs he had been writing on the American tour to date had titles like '(You Treat Me Like a) Stepchild' and 'I Must Love You Too Much'. He now began writing songs which addressed some of the more pressing issues that were whirling around in his head. At soundchecks he worked on a new song called 'Slow Train'; for the final show of the tour, in Miami, he introduced another new song. It was called 'Do Right to Me Baby (Do unto Others)', the first song he had ever written wholly around a dictum from the Bible, and a New Testament gospel at that: 'All things, therefore, that you want men to do to you, you also must likewise do to them; this, in fact, is what the Law and the Prophets mean' (Matthew 7.12).

It was not only Dylan's fellow musicians who were steering him in this particular direction. His sometime girlfriend, Mary Alice Artes, had been brought up as a Christian; but her faith had faded. On returning to Malibu, he discovered she too was re-evaluating her religious beliefs. Indeed, according to most reports, Artes had moved out on him after deciding to re-embrace her founding faith. According to Ken Gulliksen, pastor of the Vineyard Fellowship in west Los Angeles, this was not quite the case. Rather Artes attended a Vineyard Fellowship meeting in Tarzana, California.

Ken Gulliksen: At the end of the meeting she came up to me and said that she wanted to rededicate her life to the Lord . . . That morning she did rededicate her life to the Lord. Then she revealed that she was Bob Dylan's girlfriend and asked if a couple of the pastors would come there and then and talk to Bob. And so Larry Myers and Paul Esmond went over to Bob's house and ministered to him. He responded by saying, Yes, he did in fact want Christ in his life. And he prayed that day and received the Lord.

Dylan was duly baptized at the home of Bill Dwyer, one of the pastors from the Vineyard Fellowship.

Before he embraced the uniquely Californian brand of Christianity advocated by the Vineyard Fellowship, Dylan could not be described as a fundamentalist. Indeed, he does not seem to have immediately considered his vision in Tucson to be a 'born-again' experience. Only when the 'born-again' creed was outlined for him did he recognize the nature of his vision – that this change was not merely a shift in his moral values but a total rebirth, an awakening from original sin.

Bob Dylan: Being born again is a hard thing. You ever seen a mother give birth to a child? Well, it's painful. We don't like to lose those old attitudes and hang ups. Conversion takes time because you have to learn to crawl before you can walk. You have to learn to drink milk before you can eat meat. You're reborn, but like a baby. A baby doesn't know anything about this world and that's what it's like when you're reborn. You're a stranger. You have to learn all over again. [1980]

Bob Dylan: What they mean by saying that is that they're born again by the spirit from above. Born once is born with the spirit from below – when you're born, that's the spirit that you're born with. Born again is born with the spirit from above. That's a little different. [1981]

The first stage in having 'to learn all over again' required him to go back to school. Dylan had never been the best of students when it came to formal learning, and when it was suggested that he undertake an intensive course in learning to walk in the spirit of the Lord, he was his usual recalcitrant self. The three-month course at the Vineyard School of Discipleship demanded regular attendance – four days a week – something he had not attempted since his time with Norman Raeben, back in 1974.

Bob Dylan: At first I said, 'There's no way I can devote three months to this [Bible course]. I've got to be back on the road soon.' But I was sleeping one day and I just sat up in bed at seven in the morning and I was compelled to get dressed and drive over to the Bible school . . . I didn't know myself if I could go for three months. But I did begin telling a few people after a couple of months and a lot of them got angry at me. [1980]

If the simple acceptance of Christ as his saviour did not imbue Dylan with righteous fervour, the adoption of the Vineyard Church brand of Christianity transformed him into a Bible-thumping evangelist. The classes at the Vineyard School of Discipleship were held in a back room above a realtor's office in Reseda, California. They lasted from half past eight in the morning until noon, four days a week. The kind of classes they were is best described by an anecdote recounted in *Stairway to Heaven*, a thorough survey of Christian rock music by Davin Seay and Mary Neely.

Seay and Neely: During class breaks, Dylan would often walk into the parking lot in back of the prefab building, dressed against the brisk morning air in a leather jacket and stocking cap, to smoke Marlboro cigarettes and talk with his girlfriend . . . One morning a student stood to report a dream he had the night before. In the dream, the members of the class were gathered in an upper room, a beautiful cedar-panelled loft lit golden by sun pouring through a skylight. One corner of the room, the student said, had been left unfinished, exposing insulation padding, ducts, and a tangle of dangerously frayed electric wiring. The hazardous wiring, it seemed, had to be pulled down before the room could be made safe for habitation. It was a difficult, dangerous job, and the dreamer was frightened, until an unidentified man assured him that only boldness was required. Encouraged, the dreamer thrust his hands into the wiring and pulled. It fell away, and through the hole in the roof, fresh, clean water began to flow. From his seat in the corner of the room, Dylan's eyes were bright. He was nodding and smiling as a moment of unmistakable recognition passed between the student and the star . . . Bob Dylan's interpretation of his classmate's dream of the upper room was the simple one. Old things are passed away, and all things are made new. Old circuits must be stripped for the cleansing water to flow.

According to Ken Gulliksen, the course taught Dylan all about his basic responsibilities as a Christian; about the message of Jesus and about spreading the gospel.

Ken Gulliksen: Bob went through our School of Discipleship . . . for three and a half months. He was faithful there every day, learning the Word, growing in the Lord. That's basically what happened. It was an intensive course studying about the life of Jesus; principles of discipleship; the Sermon on the Mount; what it is to be a believer; how to grow; how to share. It was very practical, but at the same time a good solid Bible study overview type of ministry.

The important phrases here are '[the] principles of discipleship' and 'how to share'. Possibly, the later controversy surrounding Dylan's conversion might have been somewhat more muted, if it were not for the evangelism present in the songs on *Slow Train Coming* and *Saved*. Many fans could probably have tolerated a Dylan who felt that Christ was the saviour. It was less palatable for him to suggest that there was a clear dividing line between the saved and the damned.

Bob Dylan: That [born-again period] was all part of my experience. It had to happen. When I get involved in something, I get totally involved. I don't just play around on the fringes. [1983]

The *Chambers Dictionary* definition of 'evangelical' goes: 'Of the school that insists especially on the total depravity of unregenerate human nature, the justification of the sinner by faith alone, the free offer of the Gospel to all, and the plenary inspiration and exclusive authority of the Bible.' These were exactly the beliefs Dylan was learning. He was taught to conceive of man as born into a state of sin; that the gospels represented not only figurative but also literal truth; and that the Devil was at work every minute of every day, insidiously undermining Man's morals.

Bob Dylan: You would think the enemy is someone you can strike at and that would solve the problem, but the real enemy is the Devil. That's the real enemy, but he tends to shade himself and hide himself and put it into people's minds that he's really not there and he's really not so bad, and that he's got a lot of good things to offer too ... What Jesus does for an ignorant man like myself is to make the qualities and characteristics of God more believable to me, 'cause I can't beat the Devil. Only God can ... Satan's working everywhere. You're faced with him constantly. If you can't see him he's inside you making you feel a certain way. He's feeding you envy and jealousy. [1981]

The message conveyed by the Fellowship was not merely evangelical, it was imminently apocalyptic. Indeed the key word here is 'imminent'. The end of the world was not merely nigh, it was NIGH, with a capital double-underlined N!

Bob Dylan: What I learned in Bible school was just ... an extension of the same thing I believed in all along, but just couldn't verbalize or articulate. Whether you want to believe Jesus Christ is the Messiah is irrelevant, but whether you're aware of the messianic complex, that's all that's important ... People who believe in the coming of the Messiah live their lives right now as if He was here. That's my idea of it, anyway. I know people are going to say to themselves, 'What the fuck is this guy talking about?' but it's all there in black and white, the written and unwritten word. I don't have to defend this. The scriptures back me up. [1985]

If the classes taught Dylan about the infallibility of the gospels, they were also providing a good grounding for the works and teachings of one Hal Lindsey who, according to poet Steve Turner, was once a leading member of the Vineyard Church. Lindsey's book *The Late Great Planet Earth* became Dylan's second Bible and added an apocalyptic edge to his world-view.

If his doomsday poems had always displayed a keen sense of the apocalyptic, he had rarely drawn from a wholly 'black' or cataclysmic apocalyptic tradition (the only examples that spring to mind are 'I'd Hate to Be You on That Dreadful Day', 'All Along the Watchtower' and 'Changing of the Guards'). Rather he had preferred to utilize the red, or revolutionary, tradition (as in 'Ain't Gonna Grieve', 'The Times They Are a-Changin'') or the green or pastoral, tradition (as in 'Chimes of Freedom', 'When the Ship Comes In', 'Gates of Eden').*

The black apocalyptic tradition, to quote Campbell, 'finds expression in the Old Testament prophets – Isaiah, Jeremiah, Ezekiel – and in the New Testament, Revelation of St John the Divine'. It was specifically Relevation on which Hal Lindsey based his entire concept that the events predicted there were taking place in the second half of the twentieth century. Little versed in the historical background required to refute Lindsey's dubious tenets, Dylan was an ideal disciple for Lindsey's rhetoric.

According to Lindsey current world events had been foretold in the Apocalyptic tracts of the Bible. Lindsey's basic premise in *Late Great Planet Earth* is that the events revealed to St John the Divine in Revelation directly parallel twentieth-century history, starting with the re-establishment of the Jews' homeland, Israel, and proceeding by identifying Russia as Magog and Iran as Gog – the confederation responsible for the instigation of the Battle of Armageddon. It seems inconceivable that a man as innately sceptical as Dylan could so wholeheartedly embrace Lindsey's interpretations. Yet there can be no question that in 1979 – and for some time to come – he believed that the end was indeed at hand. A lengthy rap from one of his fall 1979 shows illustrates the unequivocal nature of his beliefs at this time.

Bob Dylan: You know we're living in the end times. I don't think there's anybody . . . who doesn't feel that in their heart. The scriptures say, 'In the last days, perilous times shall be at hand. Men shall become lovers of their own selves. Blasphemous, heavy and highminded.' Now I don't know who you're gonna vote for, but none of those people is gonna straighten out what's happening in the world today. But what's happening in it right now? Take a look at the Middle East. We're heading for a war. That's right. They're heading for a war. There's gonna be a war over there. I'd say maybe five years, maybe ten years, could be fifteen years . . . I told you 'The Times They Are a-Changin'' and they did. I said the answer was 'Blowin' in the Wind' and it was. I'm telling you now Jesus is coming back, and He is! And there is no other way of salvation . . . There's only one way to believe, there's only one way – the Truth and the Life. It took me a long time to

---

* My terminology here is largely derived from Joseph Campbell's important essay, 'Bob Dylan and the Pastoral Apocalypse', in *Journal of Popular Culture*, 1975.

figure that out before it did come to me, and I hope it doesn't take you that long. But Jesus is coming back to set up His kingdom in Jerusalem for a thousand years. [1979]

As well as songs like 'Precious Angel', 'When You Gonna Wake Up' and 'When He Returns' – all subsequently included on *Slow Train Coming*, and all of which drew heavily and directly upon the Book of Revelation – Dylan also wrote at this time a song called 'Ye Shall Be Changed', perhaps the most extreme of all his songs from this period. 'Ye Shall Be Changed' was based upon Chapter 11 of *The Late Great Planet Earth*, in which Lindsey interpreted the passage in 1 Corinthians (15.52) – 'In the twinkling of an eye, at the last trumpet . . . we shall be changed' – to signify that 'when God has the last trumpet blow it means He will move out all Christians – and at this point we shall be changed' into essence. Only at this point will the Battle of Armageddon be fought.

Lindsey takes a classic pre-millennialist position – that Christ will return before the thousand-year rule and defeat Evil. The alternative view – adopted by the post-millennialists – that Christ returns only after the Christians have established a thousand-year rule by 'their own efforts' – is subjected to considerable scorn by Lindsey. The gradual transformation into a truly Christian kingdom on Earth was never likely to appeal to the author of 'The Times They Are a-Changin'' and 'When the Ship Comes In', songs steeped in the apocalyptic fervour rediscovered on *Slow Train Coming*. In the early months of 1979 Dylan was writing his most 'political' album in sixteen years. This time, though, it was the politics of the millennium.

Indeed a positive aspect of Dylan's spiritual quest was that he was once again writing songs at a prolific pace. Just as his classes with Raeben soon resulted in the *Blood on the Tracks* material, the intense tutorship from the Vineyard Fellowship provided the necessary inspiration for a number of remarkable new songs. During the three months of classes at the School of Discipleship, he wrote at least a dozen songs later recorded for *Slow Train Coming*. Of course the Vineyard Fellowship was careful to ensure that such an important public figure was seen to be unequivocally adopting their creed.

Ken Gulliksen: He shared his music with Larry Myers, one of the pastors who had originally ministered to him. I freed Larry to go with Bob as much as possible. Bob asked him to come with the band on the road, so that Larry would be there to lead them in prayer and Bible study, and to minister to him personally. He and Bob became very close and trusted each other. Larry was often the backboard for Bob to share the lyrics.

28

1979: On the Holy Slow Train

When Dylan feels he has something important to say, he seems to approach recording with considerably more discipline than on those occasions when he just feels it is time to record another album. The album he planned to record in the spring of 1979 was bound to be controversial, irrespective of what care he took with it. The more palatable the sound of the album, though, the easier it would be to assimilate the message contained within it.

The essential ingredient in previous successful formulas had been the guitarist. On previous landmark recordings Dylan's selections had been inspired. This time his choice was ingenious. On 29 March 1979 he attended the final show of a successful residency at Los Angeles' Roxy by British outfit Dire Straits. In their homeland they were regarded by the music press as a band who would have sought to join the finishing school for pub-rockers but had arrived too late, and were certainly too twee to pass the New Wave entrance exam.

In America in 1979, when the average journalist's conception of 'punk-rock' was Elvis Costello, the pleasant melodic sensibilities in the Straits' tunes, and their easy assimilation into the uniquely West Coast concept of AOR (Adult Oriented Rock), meant they were embraced with considerable enthusiasm. Guitarist and song-writer Mark Knopfler's distinctive instrumental flourishes defined mellifluous. If Dylan had a bitter pill for his audience to swallow, a spoonful of Knopfler's sugar would help the medicine go down. After the Roxy show, he approached Knopfler about playing on his next album. Knopfler agreed.

Though Dylan had succeeded in recording albums like *Highway 61 Revisited*, *Blonde on Blonde*, *John Wesley Harding* and *Desire* with the producer serving as little more than a well-paid engineer, by 1979 he needed help to get his vision onto vinyl. The complexities of recording a big band sound had eluded him on *Desire* and

Street-Legal. Determined to persevere with girls and even horns, he required an experienced hand at the helm. He already had someone in mind.

Back in December 1977 he had dropped in on an Etta James session at Cherokee Studios. While there he had taken the opportunity to play some new tunes at the piano for James and her producer, Jerry Wexler. One eye-witness to the session later suggested that the songs Dylan had played were in fact 'pieces of his new [1979] songs'.

It was suggested in the press at the time that Wexler would produce Dylan's next album. After all they had worked together – as co-producers – on Barry Goldberg's debut album back in 1973, and Dylan was a great admirer of Wexler's previous work as the prime exponent of the Muscle Shoals sound, a soulful amalgam of horns and a tight rhythm section, originated at Memphis's Muscle Shoals studio and seemingly the exclusive property of Wexler's Atlantic acts in the sixties.

Dylan's next album had of course been *Street-Legal*, which had been recorded with nary a pause, or notice, in one week in April 1978. Yet the idea of working with Wexler remained, and after the commercial failure of *Street-Legal*, using a producer who could provide his own creative input became imperative. Wexler's background in gospel and soul made him an ideal collaborator in producing the most unequivocally Christian album a white rock musician had produced since the times when repentant rock & rollers came out of the fifties, bottle in hand, in search of some solid ground to stand upon.

The sessions duly commenced on 1 May. Wexler had suggested that Barry Beckett play keyboards. Beckett could also provide charts of individual parts for Knopfler and the rhythm section. He would later receive a co-producer's credit for the album. On drums was Pick Withers from Dire Straits, and on bass Tim Drummond, to whom in a St Paul room back in 1974 Dylan had played the songs later included on *Blood on the Tracks*, and who was now a member of Ry Cooder's touring band. The horn section came courtesy of Muscle Shoals studio. Two of the three girl singers, Helena Springs, inevitably, and Carolyn Dennis, were the sole survivors of Dylan's 1978 band.

There were equally few survivors among the songs he had been writing on the European and American tours that summer and fall. The only song recorded at these sessions from those shows was 'Do Right to Me Baby', which had been premiered at the final

1978 show in Miami, 'in the theatre of divine comedy'. Another song he had been working on in December, called 'Slow Train', would provide the 1979 album with its title track, though the lyrics were wholly rewritten during his period at the School of Discipleship.

The songs which were recorded at these historic May sessions fell neatly into two distinct categories: those which testified to Dylan's personal redemption, such as 'I Believe in You', 'Precious Angel', 'Gonna Change My Way of Thinking' and 'Trouble in Mind'; and those which admonished the unrepentant and foretold their imminent damnation if they refused to embrace his message of salvation. The latter formed by far the bulk of the songs recorded, and spanned the full gamut of browbeating, from the gentle cajoling of 'Do Right to Me Baby' to the out-and-out menace of 'When You Gonna Wake Up' and 'Slow Train'.

For non-believers like Pick Withers, Mark Knopfler and Tim Drummond, the unrelentingness of Dylan's evangelism proved initially disorientating. As Withers has observed, 'Things were a little strained the first day we went in the studio.' Knopfler had already been forewarned about the nature of the material when Dylan had played him his new songs before the sessions, just as he had with Bloomfield before *Highway 61 Revisited* and *Blood on the Tracks*.

Mark Knopfler: Bob and I ran down a lot of those songs beforehand. And they might be in a very different form when he's just hittin' the piano and maybe I'd make suggestions about the tempo or whatever. Or I'd say, 'What about a twelve-string?' . . . Each song has its own secret and needs teasing out.

Yet even Knopfler, phoning his manager Ed Bicknell during the sessions, remarked on the Bible-thumping nature of the material, and how it had required some conscious adjustment by him.

Mark Knopfler: The first night was pretty awful – it just didn't happen – but once we got into it, it was good. But all these songs are about God!

Even Wexler himself, who had worked with singers like Aretha Franklin, Otis Redding and Ray Charles, all of whom had been raised within the gospel tradition, was a little taken aback by Dylan's stance – particularly when he decided to work on his producer's 'beliefs' during the sessions.

Jerry Wexler: I had no idea he was on this born-again Christian trip until he started to evangelize me. I said, 'Bob, you're dealing with a sixty-two-year-old confirmed Jewish atheist. I'm hopeless. Let's just make an album.'

According to a later statement by Dylan he had not originally intended to record the *Slow Train Coming* material himself. He realized that the songs were extremely controversial, and knew that the name Bob Dylan would only provide further furore. If the songs on *John Wesley Harding* had dealt with 'the Devil in a fearful way', then *Slow Train Coming* was its bastard son.

Bob Dylan: The songs that I wrote for the *Slow Train* album [frightened me] . . . I didn't plan to write them, but I wrote them anyway. I didn't like writing them, I didn't want to write them . . . But I found myself writing these songs and after I had a certain amount of them I thought I didn't want to sing them, so I had a girl sing them for me . . . A girl I was singing with at the time, Carolyn Dennis . . . I [would give] them all to her and [have] her record them, and not even put my name on them. I wanted the songs out but I didn't want to do it [myself] because I knew that it wouldn't be perceived in that way. It would just mean more pressure. I just did not want that at that time. [1984]

Though Dylan had clearly abandoned the notion of Carolyn Dennis recording the *Slow Train Coming* songs when he approached Knopfler at the conclusion of Dire Straits' US tour, he originally intended to conclude the album with the girl singers performing his most apocalyptic vision to date, 'When He Returns'. When he talked about the new songs frightening him, he must have had 'When He Returns' in mind. He was initially reluctant to give the song his own voice.

He had, at least temporarily, abandoned his usual practice of recording songs without running through them in order that the musicians could pick the basic structure up. Thus the sessions progressed smoothly and the musicians blended together easily. The band's composition had proved perfect.

Jerry Wexler: Whatever we did was live. Bob might run it down on piano or guitar, just singing and playing the background until we had a rough shape in our minds, then the Muscle Shoals band would start to play it. As soon as it sounded right, Bob and the girls would start to sing . . . [On] *Slow Train* [*Coming*], we furnished Bob with a band. It was something that we projected and thought might work.

Yet 'When He Returns' required something different. Dylan

recorded a demo vocal for the song, accompanied – apparently
spontaneously – on the piano by Barry Beckett, in order that the
girls could learn it. However, Beckett's remarkable, sparse accompaniment made him think again and, after practising overnight, he sang a new, impassioned vocal over Beckett's original
piano track, thus endowing the album with perhaps his strongest
vocal since the exquisite 'Visions of Johanna'. He was right in his
original thoughts – concluding the album with this stark, intensely
foreboding song which dealt so unequivocally with The End was a
terrifyingly audacious move, one which was bound to bring its
own fair share of righteous anger down upon him.

With the album barely completed, the news of Dylan's 'conversion' to Christianity began to filter through to the media. On
22 May, he was required to give a pre-trial deposition in Beverly
Hills to answer a defamation of character suit by Patty Valentine,
regarding the song 'Hurricane'. Asked about his wealth, he replied,
'You mean my treasure on earth?' Asked about specifics in the
song he referred to the song's 'fool' as being 'whoever Satan gave
power to' and to 'whoever was blind to the truth and was living
by his own truth'. Five days later the *Washington Post* reported his
pre-trial statements and that Ken Gulliksen had revealed that
Dylan had accepted Christ into his life and joined the Vineyard
Christian Fellowship.

In June, Dylan provided Capital Radio in London with an
acetate of 'Precious Angel' in order that they could premiere the
song on Roger Scott's afternoon show. Despite the unequivocal
nature of the line about either having faith or 'unbelief/And there
ain't no neutral ground', the song failed fully to convince his
British followers of the truth of his conversion. By July, though,
pre-release tapes of *Slow Train Coming* were being freely passed to
the media, the intent presumably being to cushion the blow with a
little forewarning, and were widely reviewed. The British music
press responded with unmistakable glee at the opportunity of
joining the US media in taking potshots at Dylan's new creed.
New Musical Express came up with the most original headline
for their gossipy report on the conversion: 'Dylan & God – It's
Official'.

Dylan presumably did not expect the album to be well received.
Certainly the songs on *Slow Train Coming* contain their fair share
of hints of already received ridicule and vilification at his embracing
of Christianity, notably in 'Precious Angel' and 'I Believe in You',

in which the singer claims 'they' want to drive him from their town because he believes in Him.

When the album was officially released on 18 August, an important endorsement was received from a most surprising and welcome quarter, *Rolling Stone* magazine. *Rolling Stone* had not always been supportive of Dylan's activities in the seventies and as the only major bi-weekly US music journal its opinion carried unwarranted weight with American consumers. Editor Jann Wenner gave *Slow Train Coming* a two-page review in which he affirmed that in his opinion it was Dylan's finest work since *The Basement Tapes*. He concluded the review with words of unstinting praise:

Musically, this is probably Dylan's finest record, a rare coming together of inspiration, desire and talent that completely fuses strength, vision and art. Bob Dylan is the greatest singer of our times. No one is better. No one, in objective fact, is even very close. His versatility and vocal skills are unmatched. His resonance and feeling are beyond those of any of his contemporaries. More than his ability with words, and more than his insight, his voice is God's greatest gift to him.

Dylan found that the care he had taken with the album's sound was reaping rewards. Despite preferring 'Gotta Serve Somebody' to the more instantly palatable 'Precious Angel' as first single release from *Slow Train Coming*, he was back in the singles chart before the album was even released. 'Gotta Serve Somebody' provided him with his first Top Thirty single in six years. Though it did not make number one, *Slow Train Coming* was a surprise commercial success, indeed Dylan's second best-selling album, outselling both *Blood on the Tracks* and *Blonde on Blonde*. Its twenty-six weeks on the chart again proved his remarkable durability when it seemed that his commercial standing had reached an all-time low. Possibly he benefited from a recent spate of newly Christianized rock artists whose own albums had presaged his. Both Van Morrison's *Into the Music* and Patti Smith's *Wave* had preceded *Slow Train Coming*, and though both were less overt testaments to newfound beliefs, they suggested that rock & roll and religion could be appropriate bedfellows.

Meanwhile Dylan was pressing on. By the time *Slow Train Coming* had entered the charts in early September, he had begun rehearsals for a fall tour which would take his new message into the theatres. Even as apologists prepared their texts suggesting that *Slow Train Coming* merely represented another phase in his chameleon career, and would quickly fade, he was hard at work on even more songs of faith and salvation. Wrapping his words in palatable sounds was not meant to obscure the import of the message!

Bob Dylan: I follow God, so if my followers are following me, indirectly they're gonna be following God too, because I don't sing any song which hasn't been given to me by the Lord to sing. [1979]

As Gulliksen has observed, at this stage Dylan was sharing his music with pastor Larry Myers, who 'was often the backboard for Bob to share the lyrics'. What he needed to decide before he went on the road was: Did he intend to perform any of the songs he had written before being born again? Despite Myers assuring him that his old songs were not 'anti-God', and ever delighting in upsetting preconceptions, Dylan decided he had already spent the previous year touting around new versions of his old songs. The time had come to perform something wholly different.

Bob Dylan: In 1979 . . . we started out with a different show. We didn't play any song you'd ever heard before. Played a completely different show, with no song that anybody had ever heard. I thought that was interesting, you know . . . I had never heard of . . . anybody who'd recorded songs for twenty years and then one day just didn't play any of 'em again, just played nothing but new songs . . . I got a kick out of that. [1981]

Having envisaged such a format, he could hardly go out on the road and perform only the songs from *Slow Train Coming* and a couple of out-takes. He needed new material, particularly as at this stage his faith was changing with each passing day. The songs he wrote that summer and early fall were less self-evidently apocalyptic, concentrating more on affirming his own personal sense of gratitude at his redemption. 'What Can I Do for You', 'Covenant Woman', 'Saving Grace That's over Me', 'Saved by the Blood of the Lamb' and 'Pressing On to a Higher Calling' were songs about the joy of salvation, rather than the fear of hellfire which had fuelled *Slow Train Coming*.

Initially, the rehearsals were fairly grandiose affairs. Despite the more stringent economics affecting a theatre tour as opposed to an arena tour, Dylan seemed intent on having as large a band as in 1978. He soon realized the impracticality of this.

Dave Kelly: There was an intensive period of rehearsals before [the Warfield shows]. There was more than the band then . . . They started with a five or four piece horn section as well. Jim Horn, a well-known

horn player, and some of the more famous LA session men. They were
supposed to go with the horns on one side and the girls on the other. He
had percussionists. Russ Baboo, the Jamaican guy ... [David] Lindley
made two solo albums with Baboo, having brought him from Jamaica to
America. He also introduced him to Dylan. He did all sorts of weird
things. Playing saucepan lids and things. He's a real percussionist ...
About a week [sic] before we went on the road ... he said, 'What do
you think, the horns or the girls?' I was totally flabbergasted! He said,
'We can't really have both financially. It's just ridiculous' ... I didn't
know what to say ... the horns were not doing a lot. The next day I
came in and there were no horn players.

The rehearsals acted as a further spur to Dylan's muse. Having
made the decision to perform only new songs, he entered rehearsals with only 'Saving Grace That's over Me' definitely
composed.

Dave Kelly: He did write an awful lot of stuff [during rehearsals] ...
There must have been twenty songs that he pulled from to do that tour,
and they probably had forty. It was like nearly every day he'd come up
with two or three new songs.

Dylan was not pausing to take stock after a successful album, he
was already thinking about his next record. According to Kelly,
his personal assistant at this time, Jerry Wexler was regularly in
attendance at the rehearsals, making suggestions for the new songs'
arrangements. Dylan envisaged again working with Wexler on his
next Christian album, which was likely to be more of a hit-and-
run affair, slotted in during a respite from touring through
the fall of 1979, the winter and spring of 1980 and into the
summer. Any album would have to be recorded much as *Street-
Legal* had been. However, this time the musicians would be fully
conversant with the material, playing the songs night after night
on stage.
    As a final warm-up before the tour, Dylan and his slimmed-
down touring band flew to New York in mid-October to perform
three of the songs from *Slow Train Coming* on the popular late-
night comedy show *Saturday Night Live*. His performance was
rather intense for such light fare, and he seemed at pains not to
crack anything that might pass for a smile. If on his last national
TV appearance, the John Hammond tribute, he had been positively
loose, it seemed he had reverted to his previous demeanour when
performing on this most popular of mediums – out-and-out terror.
At least the performance suggested that no one looking for an

evening of light entertainment need attend his forthcoming shows, scheduled for November and early December in the American West.

29

1979–80: Middle of the Road – East Coast Bondage

On 1 November 1979 Dylan played his first show since his conversion, at an intimate 2,000-seat theatre in one of the seedier parts of San Francisco. He had originally been booked into the Warfield Theater for seven dates, but exceptional demand led to a further seven shows being slotted in. For six months he would tour the US with his new show. And new it was. He had abandoned all the songs he had exhumed the previous year. The message he delivered that first and every subsequent night on his gospel tour was uncompromising.

The evening opened with his three-girl backing singers performing six gospel songs, concluding with the traditional 'This Train (Is Bound for Glory)'. The tone did not change perceptibly when Dylan took to the stage. He launched straight into 'Gotta Serve Somebody', and followed it with six more songs from his new album, without a single spoken comment interspersed. Finally a song was introduced that was not on the new album. 'Covenant Woman' was a beautiful tribute to the woman who had led him to the Lord. It was the first song of the night to be fully convincing, Dylan having seemed tense throughout the first seven songs. After a brief interlude while one of the girls sang another spiritual, he returned and ran through the two songs he had yet to perform from *Slow Train Coming*.

By now it was clear that there would be no concessions to the audience, no memorable anthems. After 'Do Right to Me' the set became distinctly unfamiliar. The remaining five songs of the main set were all new, with titles like 'Hanging On to a Solid Rock Made Before the Foundation of the World' and 'When They Came for Him in the Garden'. There could be no doubting the message being reiterated in each song. Despite some sections of the audience being less than enthusiastic about what they heard, Dylan and the band returned for an encore and after running through the traditional 'Blessed Is the Name', Dylan walked to the piano where, unaccompanied by the band, he began to sing 'Pressing On to the Higher Calling of My Lord'. After one verse he got up from the piano, walked to the front of the stage and, with no guitar between him and the audience, picked up the mike and sang the remainder of the song.

Unfortunately the two most important local reviewers, Philip Elwood of the *Examiner* (Headline: 'Born-Again Dylan Bombs!') and Joel Selvin of the *Chronicle* (Headline: 'Bob Dylan's God-Awful Gospel!'), were obstinately unimpressed by even this touching instance. If Elwood considered the show 'a pretty gruelling experience', it was Selvin's review which was most widely syndicated and which caused the most damage. The conclusion of his syndicated article ran: 'Dylan is no longer asking hard questions and raising an angry fist. Instead, he has opted for the soothing soporific which the simple "truths" of his brand of Christianity provide.'

Yet perhaps the most damaging part of Selvin's review was the statement that 'cat-calls and boos echoed throughout the ornate hall.' These cat-calls and boos remain wholly inaudible on the audience recordings of this, and subsequent, Warfield shows. Other journalists were more fanciful still. Michael Goldberg claimed 'only four or five hundred remained' for the encore, suggesting that the theatre was only a quarter full at the end of the show. In fact the Warfield audiences were generally responsive to the naked intensity of Dylan's performances. The reviews clearly upset Dylan. On the 2nd and the 3rd he bought copies of the *Examiner* and *Chronicle* respectively.

Dave Kelly: Next morning we would go to this little restaurant next to the gig and he'd buy all the papers and we'd read the reviews, and you would not believe that these people were at the show ... I mean yeah, there were some people that walked out, but they were small by comparison with people that were there.

Dylan continued to resent the inaccuracies and untruths in these reviews for some time to come. Talking at the conclusion of his evangelical tour he admitted that the preaching aspect in his new songs had been unrelenting, but was mystified by the attacks on the music and the musicians.

Bob Dylan: All my stuff at that time was influenced or written right off the Gospel but that was no reason to say it wasn't a musical show. [1980]

In fact he had assembled a band which was an imaginative blend of the soulful (Spooner Oldham), the rock-solid (Tim Drummond and Jim Keltner), the melodic (Fred Tackett) and the technically superb (Willie Smith). Of course the American press had been down on him for at least the past two years. The problem would remain throughout a further two years of touring with this band. Dylan gave his view on the recent critical response in a 1984 interview:

Bob Dylan: The reception's always good . . . The problem is media problems. For some reason the media reportage of the shows I've done has never been entirely accurate since 1978 . . . They say it was all gospel or the crowd booed and walked out. This wasn't true. Maybe three or four people walked out. [1984].

Dylan had other problems at these shows, from those around him seeking to ensure that he remained an important example, and enthusiastic advocate, of the Vineyard Fellowship's particular brand of evangelism. Sometimes he felt that he was being hemmed in.

Helena Springs: I remember a lot of people [backstage at the Warfield Theater] were from the Vineyard in Los Angeles . . . I remember a lot of them pressuring him about a lot of things . . . Like if he'd drink some wine . . . They were not allowing him to live. They were just being too much of a headache. And I remember one time he said to me, 'God, it's awfully tight, it's so tight, you know.' And I thought and said, 'Yeah, it seems like you gotta get out from under it a bit.' And I felt a lot of pressure from those people . . . Also he found a lot of hypocrisy from those people . . . They were saying one thing, and doing another. He mentioned that to me too.

Dylan commented, albeit obliquely, on the hypocrisy he came across from professed Christians, during one of the later gospel shows.

Bob Dylan: I know a lot of country and western people do that. They sing, very often, 'You can put your shoes under my bed anytime.' And then they turn around and sing, 'Oh Lord, Just a Closer Walk with Thee'. Well, I can't do that. That's right, you cannot serve two masters. You gotta hate one and love the other one. You can't drink out of two cups. [1980]

This seems a somewhat paradoxical comment in view of Dylan's own continuing relationship with women. He seems to have remained intimate with Helena Springs throughout the first leg of the tour, before a furious row occurred between them.

Dave Kelly: At the end of the first tour [Dylan and Helena] had a big row and he told her to leave. They were pretty close . . . I remember her throwing things around the room and Bob standing there. But it didn't work out.

What exactly had happened to his 'covenant woman', Mary Alice Artes, remains unclear. According to a report in *Rolling Stone*, while in Seattle, Washington, in January 1980 – by which time Springs had left the tour – Dylan purchased a $25,000 engagement ring. Clydie King, with whom he was involved throughout most of the early eighties, did not join his band until a month later, just before the recording of *Saved*. The intended recipient of the ring remains unknown, though before the year was out he would write his masterful 'The Groom's Still Waiting at the Altar'.

If Dylan's performance on 1 November had been somewhat hesitant, a further thirteen dates at the same small theatre gave him plenty of opportunity to work on the new songs and to grow comfortable with playing live again. The show had obviously been rigidly structured, and the set remained constant night after night. However, his demeanour did not. Starting in the second week at the Warfield, he became positively verbose between songs. His between-song raps were really an extension of his *raison d'être* for touring in the first place. If the dictionary definition of 'to evangelize' is 'to make acquainted with the Gospel . . . to preach the Gospel from place to place', that is exactly what he was doing. Talking to the crowd also allowed him to gauge the responses more accurately than just belting through a seventeen-song set. Thus one night he informed the audience:

Satan is called the god of this world. Anyone here who knows that? That's right – he's called the god of this world, and Prince of the Power of the Air. [Someone shouts: 'He sucks.'] That's right! He does! But anyhow, we know he's been defeated at the cross. I'm curious to know how many of you all know that? [1979]

In 1985 Dylan talked about the element of self-righteousness in these shows. He made it clear that evangelizing was the primary motive behind the entire tour.

Bob Dylan: Self-righteousness would be just to repeat what you know has been written down in scripture some place else. It's not like you're trying to convince anybody of anything. You're just saying what the original rule is, and it's just coming through you. But if someone else can get past you saying it and just hear what the message is, well then it's not coming from you but through you. And I don't see anything wrong in that. [1985]

Despite the amount of ridicule he was subjected to, it would appear that Dylan himself does not consider this period as an embarrassing episode in his career. It was something he felt he had to do, almost as if the tour itself answered the question he asked in the penultimate song of the main set, 'What Can I Do for You?'.

Bob Dylan: I was saying stuff I figured people needed to know. I thought I was giving people an idea of what was behind the songs. [1980]

He was certainly willing to give some fairly extreme and eschatologically unsound sermons. Of the Warfield shows, the final one on the 16th, apart from being one of his two or three finest performances, featured his most talkative self to date. As usual it was before 'Slow Train' and 'Hanging On to a Solid Rock' that his sermonizing came. Before 'Slow Train' he gave the bare bones of a rap that would expand to epic proportions as the tour progressed:

Bob Dylan: You know we read in the newspaper every day what a horrible situation this world is in. Now God chooses to do these things in this world to confound the wise. Anyway, we know this world's gonna be destroyed; we know that. Christ will set up His Kingdom in Jerusalem for a thousand years, where the lion will lie down with the lamb. Have you heard that before? I'm just curious to know, how many people believe that? Alright. This is called 'Slow Train Coming'. It's been coming a long time and it's picking up speed. [1979]

If Dylan had gradually won over most of the attending San Franciscans, it seemed those in attendance at his next four shows needed little convincing. Two days on from the Warfield, he returned to Los Angeles for shows at the Santa Monica Civic Auditorium, his first concerts there in nearly fifteen years. The shows were benefits for World Vision, a non-denominational Christian charity. This, plus the fact that this was home territory for the Vineyard Fellowship, had a positive effect upon both Dylan and the band. In fact on the first night, when Dylan asked the audience how many knew that Satan had been defeated at the cross, the response was ecstatic. Dylan was clearly delighted, affirming, 'Awwright! At least we're not alone.' The following three shows were *tours de force*. He was singing with a passion that only a new-born burning conviction could induce. His apocalyptic sermons were becoming more and more imbued with the same fiery fervour. The second night his pre-'Solid Rock' rap was his most lengthy pronouncement to date:

Bob Dylan: You wanna know something, we're not worried at all – even though it is the last of the End times; because we see all these hostages being taken here and drugs being outlawed there. All these sad stories that are floating around. We're not worried about any of that – we don't care about the atom bomb, any of that, 'cause we know this world is going to be destroyed and Christ will set up His kingdom in Jerusalem for a thousand years, where the lion will lie down with the lamb. Y'know the lion will eat straw that day. Also, if a man doesn't live to a hundred years old, he will be called accursed. That's interesting, isn't it? And we don't mind. We know that's coming, and if any man have not the spirit of Christ in him, he is a slave to bondage. I know you're all into bondage, so you need something just a little bit tough to hang on to. This song's called 'Hanging On to a Solid Rock Made Before the Foundation of the World'. And if you don't have that to hang on to, you better look into it. [1979]

The nights in Santa Monica were the culmination of eighteen increasingly impressive shows. The new songs had come into their own, and could be perceived as heartfelt testaments of faith, a development upon the more overtly sermonizing songs on *Slow Train Coming*. However, it would be some time before he would play to such friendly crowds again. As he and the band headed for Arizona, they were unaware of the uproar awaiting them. Dylan was booked for two shows in Tempe, his first shows away from the coast. He would be playing primarily to the students of the local university. The students were not at all tolerant of his new stance.

Dave Kelly: In Arizona he had to talk. I don't think they were walking out but they were definitely heckling. They were insisting on the old songs . . . At the first one I thought he was going to put his guitar down and leave, but he stayed and talked to them.

The first night the audience refused to sit still, shouting between songs until Dylan asked his lighting crew to 'turn the light on them down there'. As the heckling continued he began to sermonize, but this time without the gentle coaxing tone adopted in San Francisco and Santa Monica.

Bob Dylan: In San Francisco, we opened there about a month ago, about three or four people walked out because they didn't get the message. But we're still here. Don't you walk out before you hear the message through. Anyway, 'The lamb of God which taketh away the sins of the world' – I wonder how many of you people understand that? I'm curious to know how many of you understand. [1979]

The response was more shouting, and, as the second half progressed, the heckling started up again. If they found his songs unpalatable, though, they liked what he had to say even less:

Bob Dylan: The world as we know it now is being destroyed. Sorry, but it's the truth. In a short time – I don't know, in three years, maybe five years, could be ten years, I don't know – there's gonna be a war. It's gonna be called the War of Armageddon . . . As sure as you're standing there, it's gonna happen. [1979]

If the first night in Tempe had been an unhappy experience for Dylan, matters only grew worse with the second show, when he met the most hostile audience of this entire tour. Indeed, the barracking 1966 fans pale in comparison to the uniform hostility he met in Tempe. The result was Dylan openly haranguing the crowd. Not waiting until 'Slow Train', he gave his first sermon, which lasted five solid minutes, after song number two. It was delivered against repeated shouts of 'Rock & roll!', until finally he spat words of damnation at the non-believers.

Bob Dylan: Hmmm. Pretty rude bunch tonight, huh? You all know how to be real rude! You know about the spirit of the Anti-Christ? Does anyone here know about that? Ah, the spirit of the Anti-Christ is loose right now. Let me give you an example [begins to tell story about a guru spraying his disciples with a fire extinguisher at which point someone loudly shouts Rock & Roll] . . . If you want rock & roll, you go down and rock & roll. You can go and see Kiss and you can rock & roll all the way down to the pit! . . . [continues story until, responding to further shouts of 'Rock & roll'] You *still* wanna rock & roll? I'll tell you what the two kinds of people are. Don't matter how much money you got, there's only two kinds of people: there's saved people and there's lost people. Yeah. Remember that I told you that. You may never see me again. You may not see me, but sometime down the line you remember you heard it here, that Jesus is Lord. Every knee shall bow!! [1979]

This was not the end of his battle with the Tempe crowd. His pre-'Solid Rock' rap took another five minutes and again emphasized the imminence of the End. It concluded with a direct retelling of Hal Lindsey's Armageddon scenario.

Bob Dylan: Russia will come down and attack in the Middle East. China's got an army of two million people – they're gonna come down in the Middle East. There's gonna be a war called the Battle of Armageddon which is like something you never even dreamed about. And Christ will set up His Kingdom and He'll rule it from Jerusalem. I know far out as that may seem this is what the Bible says. [Somebody shouts, 'Everybody must get stoned!'] . . . I'll tell you about getting stoned – what do you want to know about getting stoned? What you're gonna need is something strong to hang on to. You got drugs to hold on to now. You might have a job to hold on to now. But you're gonna need something very solid to hang on to when these days come. Let me tell you one more thing. When Jesus spoke His parables, He spoke them to people . . . everybody could hear the parables. Some people heard them and understood them, some didn't. He said the same thing to everybody. Do you understand? He didn't try to hide it. He just said it. Those that believed it believed it and understood it. Those that didn't didn't . . . You talk to your teachers about what I said. I'm sure you're paying a lot of money for your education, so you'd better get one. [1979]

The first night in Tempe, he had not played a second encore. Tonight, for the only time on the tour, he refused to play any encore at all. Instead, before the final song, 'In the Garden', he preached one last message.

Bob Dylan: Remember what I said if you ever hear some other time that there is a truth, a life and a way. You may not get it now – it may not be next week or so, not the next year or so – but you remember the next time it happens. [1979]

At a show in Toronto the following April, which he was having filmed for possible release, he talked at length about his sermonizing at the second Tempe show in particular, and at these shows in general. Though the Toronto audience was reasonably tolerant of Dylan's new set, he soon worked himself into another frenzy.

Bob Dylan: Actually I wanna tell you a story. We were playin' about four months ago some place that was a college or a campus. I forget exactly where. Arizona I think it was. Anyway, I read the Bible a lot; it just happens I do. It says things in the Bible that I didn't really learn until recently, and I really mentioned these because there are higher learning people there, preaching their philosophy. So people can study all the different philosophies, of Plato and, uh, who else? Who? Well, I definitely recall reading Nietzsche and those people like that. Anyways, in the Bible it tells a specific thing in the Book of Revelations that just applies to these times . . . [Dylan retells Lindsey's interpretations of Gog and Magog as Russia and Iran.] So anyway, I was telling this story to these people. I shouldn't have been telling it to them. I just got carried away. I mentioned it to them and then I watched, and [I said] Russia was going to come down and attack in the Middle East. It says this in the Bible. And I been reading all kinds of books my whole life: magazines, books, whatever I could lay my hands on anyway, and I never found any truth in any of it, if you wanna know the truth. But I said, This country is gonna come down and attack. And all these people – there must've been 50,000 . . . maybe it wasn't 50,000 – 5,000 maybe . . . they all booed. Everybody just booed; and it was the whole auditorium of people . . . And a month later Russia moved her troops into, I think, Afghanistan. And the whole situation changed, you know. I'm not saying this to tell you they were wrong and I was right, or anything like that. These things that it mentions in the Bible I'm gonna pay mighty close attention to . . . been a lot of previews of what Anti-Christ could be like . . . You need something strong to hang on to. It was manifested in the flesh! Testified in the Spirit! Received by angels! Preached out in the world! [1980]

This was not his only account of the Tempe 'experience'. Even six years later, when talking about the gospel tour to Cameron Crowe for the *Biograph* book, he commented on the college kids, and there can be no doubt which particular shows he was recalling.

Bob Dylan: We'd play the so-called colleges, where my so-called fans were. And all hell would break loose – 'Take off that dress,' 'We want rock & roll,' lots of other things I don't even want to repeat, just really filthy mouth stuff. [1985]

The remaining shows on the first leg of the gospel tour, which concluded with two shows back in Arizona, at Tucson on 8 and 9 December, were less eventful. Still, before his two shows in Tucson, Dylan agreed to a telephone interview on the local KMEX station to respond to a press release from the Tucson chapter of the American Atheists Association, stating that they planned to leaflet his two Tucson concerts. Throughout the brief interview he remained quite restrained, agreeing that religion was 'just another form of bondage', though a necessary one.

Bob Dylan: Religion is another form of bondage which man invents to get himself to God. But that's why Christ came. Christ didn't preach religion. He preached the Truth, the Way and the Life. [1979]

He also made it clear that he believed in the literal truth of the Scriptures, that he considered them to be divinely inspired.

Bob Dylan: My ideology now would be coming out of the Scripture. Y'see, I didn't invent these things – these things have just been shown to me. I'll stand on that faith – that they are true. I believe they're true. I know they're true. [1979]

His 'preaching the gospel from place to place' began again in January with shows in Oregon. The show remained the same, though Helena Springs had departed from the tour. For the month-long winter leg, Dylan restrained himself from preaching much between songs, though occasionally he made brief asides about the reception, at one show sarcastically observing, 'Well, the hits just keep a-comin'' and in Nebraska suggesting that potential hecklers leave right away.

Bob Dylan: Shan't be hearing any old songs tonight, so anyone who wants to leave better leave right now. Might be somebody outside who wants the seat. [1980]

At the final two winter shows, in Charleston, he introduced a new song, which seemed a continuation of his between-song raps. Called 'Are You Ready?' it was a catalogue of questions about what you should be ready for, notably Armageddon.

Within a week of the Charleston shows, Dylan and his touring band were ensconced in Muscle Shoals studio to record the songs they had now been performing for three months. The intention was to get the new songs down on tape quickly, so that the new album could be released in time for the continuation of the gospel tour later that spring. This should have been relatively easy, as everyone knew the songs. Jerry Wexler was again filling the producer's chair.

Jerry Wexler: The arrangements were built-in, because the band had been playing the songs live. Most of the licks are their own licks, which they perfected on the road, as opposed to the Dire Straits confections on the last album, which were all done in the studio. This one was like when Ray Charles used to call me up and say, 'Hey, pardner, I'm coming in in three weeks, let's do a record.'

Certainly the songs came easily enough. The bulk of the album was recorded in a mere four days, with two songs then re-cut the following day. The sessions were over by 19 February.

Jerry Wexler: On the fifth day ... we re-examined everything we'd done and wound up re-cutting 'Covenant Woman' and 'Saved' . . . It was pretty much Bob's instinct to redo them . . . We did a little touching up. In five days it was ready for mixing.

Yet the album was massively flawed. In the cold isolation of the studio, the band seemed to be going through the motions and Dylan's singing lacked the attention to detail he had brought to the live performances. Evidence of lack of care in producing the songs in the studio lies strewn across the album.* 'Solid Rock' is devoid of the insistent tension that its rumbling bass riff had previously given it; in 'What Can I Do for You' the 'I'm sure to make it through' had become 'I sure did make it through', a line totally out of accord with the humility of the remainder of the song; in 'Covenant Woman' he rewrote another line, preferring to commend his precious angel for knowing 'those most secret things of me', rather than the original 'the invisible things of Him'. The most successful song on the album was 'Pressing On', which required a wholly different arrangement on record from that utilized in performance. Dylan attacked the song with considerably more vigour than the other tracks.

Dave Kelly: They were all dissatisfied with the album. He wanted to redo it but there was no time . . . He was contemplating issuing a live record . . . It occurred to him to record the shows, but the record company were not interested. They wouldn't put any money into it.

Ironically, a mere eight days after the final session, Dylan and the band delivered a definitive rendering of another song they had been nightly regurgitating in concert over the last three months. The song was 'Gotta Serve Somebody'. The occasion was the annual Grammy awards ceremony. Nominated for best male rock vocal performance for his single of 'Gotta Serve Somebody', Dylan proceeded to deliver a vocal considerably superior to the official version he had been nominated for, impressing a nationwide prime-time TV audience and collecting the award.

Saved was beyond redemption! Though Dylan seems to have seriously considered issuing the songs in the form of a live album, even recording two shows in Toronto in April at his own expense using a twenty-four-track mobile studio, CBS dissuaded him, thus negating all the good work achieved by the surprise commercial

* For a more extensive commentary on the *Saved* album readers are referred to Paul Williams' *What Happened – One Year Later* pamphlet.

success of *Slow Train Coming.** When Dylan approved a garishly arrogant sleeve, which seemed to suggest that only the chosen few should buy the record, it was inevitable that sales would not repeat those of his previous album. Not released until a month after the conclusion of his spring tour, the album failed to even make the top twenty. Dylan remained philosophical about the failure, though he was not to know that he had seen his last Top Ten album of the eighties (save for the Wilburys) leave the charts a week after accepting his Grammy award.

Bob Dylan: *Slow Train* was a big album. *Saved* didn't have those kinda numbers but to me it was just as big an album. I'm fortunate that I'm in a position to release an album like *Saved* with a major record company so that it will be available to the people who would like to buy it. [1981]

In mid-April he resumed his touring activities in Canada, aiming to spend a month working his way across to and down the East Coast. He had written three new songs for this leg of the tour, none of which suggested any lessening of his evangelistic fervour: 'Ain't Gonna Go to Hell (for Anybody)', the somewhat strange 'Coverdown Breakthrough' and 'I Will Love Him'.

On night one he half-jokingly asked the audience, 'I know you're gonna read in the newspapers tomorrow that everybody walked out, but will you tell them the truth now?' In fact the Canadian journalists were considerably kinder than their West Coast equivalents, and his four shows in Toronto and four in Montreal went well.

If there were now fewer apocalyptic sermons, this did not stop Dylan attempting to evangelize. The main subject matter of the raps at the East Coast shows was the Devil and his demons. The two shows in Hartford, Connecticut, saw a more talkative Dylan than at any show since Tempe. On the first night he seemed to sense a degree of hostility and asked, before the fourth song:

Bob Dylan: Anybody left yet? They tell me everybody leaves at these shows. I don't know – it's kinda hard to see out there. Middle of the road, East Coast bondage. But God's waiting to set you free. I know you don't hear much about God these days. We're gonna talk about Him all night. We're not gonna be talking about no mysticism, no meditation,

---

* Dylan still put together a live album entitled *Solid Rock* to be issued after *Saved*, which was an amalgam of songs from both 'gospel' albums, though again CBS would not release it.

none of them Eastern religions. We're just gonna be talking about Jesus.
Demons don't like that name. I'll tell you right now, if you got demons
inside you they're not gonna like it. [1980]

The following night the crowd was more evenly divided between believers and non-believers, and though Dylan seemed in a
considerably better mood he still preached extensively to the
crowd. Before 'Coverdown Breakthrough' he tried an alternative
version of his demons rap.

Bob Dylan: I know the modern trend. It's not fashionable to think
about heaven and hell. I know that. But God doesn't have to be in
fashion because He's always fashionable. But it's hard not to go to hell,
you know. There's so many distractions, so many influences; you start
walking right 'n' pretty soon there's somebody out there gonna drag you
down. As soon as you get rid of The Enemy outside, The Enemy comes
inside. He got all kinds of ways. The Bible says, 'Resist the Devil and the
Devil will flee.' You got to stand to resist him. How we got to stand?
Anybody know how to stand? How do we stand? Anybody know how?
[muted response] We gotta stay here and play another night. [1980]

The final four shows of what proved to be the final leg of his
gospel tour were away from the East Coast, in Ohio. At both
Akron shows he found a surprisingly friendly crowd, leading him
to observe, in his introduction of girl singer Regina McCreary,
'Seems like I don't have to tell you about Jesus – seems like you
know all about Him.' On both nights the Akron fans were
rewarded with a third encore. In Dayton, the locale of his final
gig, the audience were also suitably appreciative, yet Dylan talked
little between songs. After the show, though, he was extremely
talkative, giving his first major interview of 1980 to young Australian journalist Karen Hughes. Hughes had conducted her first
ever interview back in April 1978 in Sydney, and Dylan was the
subject. Having hooked up with him again at Hartford, she found
him in considerably better shape than he had been in 1978. He
talked about his continuing faith, and exactly what he meant by
Christianity.

Bob Dylan: Christianity is making Christ the Lord of your life. You're
talking about your life now, you're not talking about just part of it,
you're not talking about a certain hour every day. You're talking about
making Christ the Lord and Master of your life, the King of your life.
And you're also talking about Christ, the resurrected Christ; you're not
talking about some dead man who had a bunch of good ideas and was
nailed to a tree. [1980]

30

1980–82: In the Summertime

When Dylan concluded his spring 1980 tour in Dayton, Ohio, he envisaged only a temporary hiatus, fully intending to return to the road that summer after the release of the *Saved* album. A major heatwave sweeping the North American continent pre-empted his plans, leaving him with several months to work on new songs.

The new songs abandoned the evangelism present on *Slow Train Coming* and *Saved*, though the apocalyptic conceits remained. In the summertime he wrote four of his finest songs of the eighties, though only one of these would be included on his next album. The two that had the closest links with the songs on *Saved* were 'Every Grain of Sand' and 'Yonder Comes Sin'. The seven-verse 'Yonder Comes Sin', though not specifically exhorting repentance, provided an extensive catalogue of the 'total depravity of unregenerate human nature', both throughout history and during these End times.

Another song dealing with depravity in the context of the Second Coming was 'Ain't Gonna Go to Hell'. Though performed as a straightforward Bible-thumping brandishment of threats during the spring East Coast tour, Dylan wholly rewrote the song before his brief fall tour. Though the message remained the same, the imagery was more Dylanesque, less evidently biblical. Thus the glorious image of the woman in a cold black dress 'walking away with your legs spread apart' was a typically Delta Blues-drenched line.

The other overtly Christian song that he wrote that summer was his most sublime song from this intensely creative period. 'Every Grain of Sand' was the summation of his attempts to express what the promise of redemption meant to him personally. One of his most intensely personal songs, it also remains one of his most universal. Dealing with 'the time of my confession', the song was perhaps also the real conclusion of his evangelical period as a songwriter. Though several later songs on *Shot of Love* dealt with living dead men and the property of Jesus, they did so in a worldly manner. The ethereal fragility of 'Every Grain of Sand' was not attempted again.

Surprisingly the other songs he wrote that summer, either on his farm in Minneapolis or while sailing around the Caribbean, dealt more with his perennially troubled relations with women than with the higher calling. Two of these songs could be considered soul partners, dealing with if not the same relationship then markedly similar ones, and both are set within a familiar landscape of imminent apocalypse. In 'Caribbean Wind' the story has as its backdrop messengers 'bringing evil reports, of rioting armies and time that is short'. It seems that this time the 'distant ship of Liberty' was not coming in but sailing away, as the singer attempted to resolve whether he should stay with the mysterious lady from Haiti, 'fair brown and intense'. By the time he decided she had left.

Bob Dylan: I started it in St Vincent when I woke up from a strange dream in the hot sun . . . I was thinking about living with somebody for all the wrong reasons. [1985]

'Caribbean Wind' was the first of a number of songs that he wrote while sailing the Caribbean in his newly constructed schooner. A sense of the power of nature returned to his songwriting. Interestingly, 'Jokerman', written two years later in the Caribbean, has the self-same 'distant ships' making a reappearance, on this occasion 'sailing into the mist', possibly never to return.

Bob Dylan: I'm usually either [in New York] or on the West Coast or down in the Caribbean. Me and another guy have a boat down there. 'Jokerman' kinda came to me in the islands. It's very mystical. The shapes there, and shadows, seem to be so ancient. The song was sorta inspired by these spirits they call jumbis. [1984]

Like the other songs written in the summer of 1980, Dylan recorded 'Caribbean Wind' using a mobile studio, presumably located in Minneapolis. However, the original version has never emerged, and when the song was recorded for *Shot of Love* (this take appears on *Biograph*) it was wholly rewritten, losing much of its drama along the way. Asked why he left the song off *Shot of Love*, Dylan later admitted:

Bob Dylan: We left [it] off the album [as it was] quite different to anything I wrote . . . The way the storyline changes from third person to first person and that person becomes you, then these people are there and they're not there. And then the time goes way back and then it's brought up to the present. I thought it was really effective. [1981]

The companion-piece to 'Caribbean Wind' was entitled 'The Groom's Still Waiting at the Altar'. It was also largely rewritten in the spring of 1981, and recorded for but originally omitted from *Shot of Love*.* In the rewritten version Dylan included 'cities on fire', the killing of nuns and 'fighting on the border'. The sense of doom surrounding the original version was less overt but was still a constant undercurrent. Claudette, the lady in this song, seems to be toying with the singer's affections, finally leaving him for parts unknown. She could be on the notorious Fanning Street immortalized by Leadbelly, she could be 'in the mountains or prairies', or even be running a brothel somewhere down in South America. The singer insists with each chorus of the first version that he will forget her, setting his 'affections on things above', letting 'nothing get in the way of that Love'.

'Caribbean Wind' and 'The Groom's Still Waiting at the Altar' are important songs in Dylan's *œuvre*, particularly as their synthesis of apocalyptic conceits and his familiar theme of disaffected love was more familiar terrain to his fans than anything explored on his previous two albums, suggesting that he was at last learning to assimilate rather than ignore his pre-'Born Again' work. That the songs reflected Dylan's own problems with women, given past history, seems extremely likely. Helena Springs had left his employ that winter; and Mary Alice Artes, the black actress supposedly most directly responsible for his conversion, was now on the East Coast, according to pastor Ken Gulliksen.

The two songs presaged a move away from a purely evangelical format in both his recordings and his performances. Both were worked on at October rehearsals at the familiar Rundown Studios, as part of preparations for a nineteen-date tour of the North-West, starting with a further twelve shows at the Warfield Theater in San Francisco. The shows were billed as a retrospective, and radio ads for the shows included rehearsal versions of songs like 'Blowin' in the Wind' and 'Gotta Serve Somebody' in the background. Dylan even gave two radio interviews during the Warfield residency, during which he insisted, 'This is a stage show we're

---

* It was added to the album before reissue on Nice Price vinyl and CD.

doing, it's not a salvation ceremony.' He also hinted that the next album would be something of a departure from *Saved*.

Bob Dylan: You can't record every album and have it be a *Saved* type album because you just don't get that many kinda songs all in a row like that. So I'm sure there'll be a difference. [1980]

Yet on the first night at the Warfield, a year and a week on from his 1979 debut there, the show opened with an identical six-song set from the girl singers, and Dylan then appeared on stage singing 'Gotta Serve Somebody' and 'I Believe in You'. Indeed only five songs – 'Like a Rolling Stone', 'Girl from the North Country', 'Just Like a Woman', 'Senor' and 'Blowin' in the Wind' – were performed from his pre-born-again albums, though he did duet with Clydie King on the old Dion classic 'Abraham, Martin and John'. Still, with only one encore and a show that lasted well under ninety minutes, he had some very dissatisfied customers that first night.

Dylan's exact intentions in embarking on this brief tour were not clear. It promoted no product, and did not precede a major US or a European tour. Presumably he intended to work up a new set as the tour progressed, rather than present the finished article as in 1979. Predictably the first night was lambasted by the same syndicated columnists who had attacked the previous year's shows with such relish. Dylan himself commented on these critics when thanking Bill Graham, the promoter, at the final 1980 Warfield show: 'Last year we came in here with the show and the newspapers they distorted it and slandered it and lied about it, whatever they did that's enough for most promoters in the business just to cancel out the rest of the shows.' Graham in 1980, as in 1979, kept faith with Dylan and was duly rewarded.

After that first night the late 1980 tour became Dylan's most consistently inventive tour. The shows got better and better with every performance. The arrangements of old chestnuts like 'To Ramona', 'Senor' and 'Girl from the North Country' were inspirational. The introduction of new songs like 'The Groom's Still Waiting at the Altar', 'Caribbean Wind', 'City of Gold' and 'Let's Keep It Between Us' provided a rare opportunity for fans to hear songs Dylan had not even recorded for CBS, affirming the 'new Dylan' on display at these shows. Dylan even sang rewritten versions of 'Ain't Gonna Go to Hell' and 'Simple Twist of Fate', the latter now featuring the glorious lines: 'With the neon burning dim/He looked at her and she looked at him/With that look that can manipulate/Brought on by a simple twist of fate.'

He also introduced some superb and surprising covers into the set: a contemporary Christian ballad called 'Rise Again', Shel Silverstein's 'Couple More Years', Dave Mason's 'We Just Disagree', the traditional 'Mary from the Wild Moor' and an absolute knock-'em-dead version of Little Willie John's 'Fever'. As if such delights were not enough, night after night he brought on special guests to help out on a few songs. Carlos Santana helped out on the 13th; on the 15th Michael Bloomfield reproduced the ringing guitar riffs he had immortalized on the original 'Like a Rolling Stone' (sadly his last live performance); and even Jerry Garcia seemed comfortable playing along on the 16th. Maria Muldaur contributed a song on the 19th; and finally, at the concluding Warfield show on the 22nd, Roger McGuinn joined Dylan for two songs they could both feel familiar with, 'Mr Tambourine Man' (complete with a Byrds-like intro) and 'Knockin' on Heaven's Door'. While Dylan's singing was as impassioned as during the previous year's shows, the band seemed more comfortable with the material, guitarist Fred Tackett in particular coming into his own.

As the shows progressed, Dylan grew positively talkative, though he resisted the temptation to preach. On the 16th he prefaced 'Just Like a Woman' with a story about a beautiful transvestite approaching him as a woman and then an hour later as a man; on the 18th he told a lengthy and bizarre story about being stranded in a underwater cave during one of his stays with Joan Baez in Carmel; on the 22nd he told the audience improbably about his first experience of live rhythm & blues at the age of twelve in a bingo parlour in Detroit; on the 26th he told a story about a couple of newly-weds accidentally stumbling onto his hotel balcony the previous night; and on 3 December he dedicated 'Senor' to a lady in the audience called Victoria, whom he had met in 1972 in Durango. Some raps became regular nightly occurrences, such as introducing 'Mary from the Wild Moor' with, 'People always talk about old songs, this is a *real* old song.' He also couldn't resist making a few digs at the press, correcting one reviewer who claimed he performed 'Maggie's Farm' the previous night, and dedicating one song to Greil Marcus, 'one of the top rock & roll critics of the era – whatever that is!' He made a subtle point about the way the media had portrayed him in the past year, during his introduction to the one and only live version of 'Caribbean Wind':

Bob Dylan: The first person I ever heard of play[ing] a twelve-string guitar was named Leadbelly . . . He was a prisoner in Texas State Prison . . . and he was recorded by a man named Alan Lomax . . . Anyway he got Leadbelly out and brought him up to New York and he made a lot of records there. At first he was just doing prison-songs and stuff like that . . . until he'd been out of prison some time and decided to do children's songs. People said, 'Oh, what, has Leadbelly changed?' Some people liked the older ones, others liked the newer ones. But he didn't change – he was the same man. [1980]

Reacting to the failure of *Saved*, he refrained from taking his band into the studio to record his next album straight after the tour. Rather he took a three month 'breather' in the winter of 1981 to work on further songs. The sad result of this 'breather' was that the bulk of the songs written in the summer of 1980 were excluded from his 1981 album, *Shot of Love*, which instead featured its share of inferior, lightweight tunes presumably dating from the winter.

'Caribbean Wind' and 'Groom's Still Waiting' were both recorded for *Shot of Love* but ended up excluded. Another classic Dylan composition recorded at the sessions was about a witchy woman manipulating the singer, against a backdrop of marching men 'trying to take heaven by force'. This time the woman's name was Angelina, though she was clearly a close relative of Claudette and the lady from Haiti. The exclusion of three songs of real quality might suggest that Dylan had written even finer material that winter, but this was not the case. Though 'Shot of Love', 'Dead Man Dead Man', 'Property of Jesus' and 'In the Summertime' warranted inclusion alongside such works, his ill-considered tribute to Lenny Bruce, the lightweight 'Heart of Mine' and the energetic if unexciting 'Trouble' were several notches down from them.

After a couple of days in late March trying to produce results at Muscle Shoals, the sessions were moved to Clover Studios in Los Angeles, where the bulk of the album was completed (save for 'Shot of Love', which was the result of a preliminary session/s at Rundown Studios). Though he relied primarily on his touring band, Dylan did draft in guitarists Steve Ripley and Danny Kortchmar, organist Benmont Tench of Tom Petty's Heartbreakers, and Steve Douglas from his 1978 band to provide saxophone on a few songs. For Tench, who had no experience of Dylan in the studio, it proved a disorienting experience.

Benmont Tench: The first day I worked with him, he didn't say a word the whole session, and I didn't know anybody at the session. [But] at the end of the day, when I was leaving, he said, 'Can you come back to-morrow?'

Aside from these musicians, Dylan continued to embellish just about every song with a wailing chorus of girl singers, his fourth consecutive album to feature such a distraction. On this occasion they were his touring singers, and still featured Carolyn Dennis, the only survivor from 1978, plus Clydie King, a large, effusive lady with a pair of lungs that could put out a forest fire. King had joined Dylan's band before the *Saved* album sessions, replacing Helena Springs. She also appears to have quickly replaced Springs in his affections. When Dylan indulged in a hotel jam session with Mark Knopfler during Dire Straits' October 1980 tour, it was King who remained on his arm throughout the night. When Ron Wood arrived at the final session/s for the *Shot of Love* album, which featured a different line-up of musicians including Ringo Starr and Donald 'Duck' Dunn, he found Dylan and King on the best of terms.

Ron Wood: Bob was with Clydie King then. He used to go to her for solace all the time. She was great with him, but they were like chalk and cheese. Two [more] different people you couldn't hope to meet – her a black, outrageous, hamburger-eating soul-singer, and Bob all quiet and white, nibbling off the side of her hamburger. I always remember him trying to share her hamburger, and she was bossing him around and stuff. He needed it at the time.

In 1982 Dylan and King spent much of their time together and even recorded an album of duets, though it remains unreleased and unheard, Dylan later claiming this was because 'it doesn't fall into any category that the record company knows how to deal with'. Clearly he was having major problems with CBS after two commercially unsuccessful albums. The Dylan–King relationship lasted into 1983, when King duetted on a couple of the songs recorded at the *Infidels* sessions, though they appear to have parted company shortly after the completion of that album.

Shot of Love was completed by the middle of May, though there was no prospect of it being released in time for his summer '81 European tour. Dylan himself has always had something of a soft spot for his 1981 album, describing it in 1983 as his personal favourite. As late as 1989 he was still performing 'Dead Man Dead

Man', 'Trouble', 'Heart of Mine', 'Lenny Bruce' and 'Every Grain of Sand' in his concert sets, when his other eighties albums received scant attention indeed. However, the album was considered by the public the third in his 'religious' trilogy, and, though relatively successful in Europe in the wake of his tour there, was his first studio album since *Another Side* to fail to make *Billboard*'s Top Thirty.

Bob Dylan: The record had some thing that could have been made in the 40s or maybe the 50s . . . there was a cross element of songs on it . . . the critics . . . all they talked about was Jesus this and Jesus that, like it was some kind of Methodist record. [1985]

Dylan was still committed to the road and undertook two tours in 1981, both twenty-seven shows, one in Europe in the summer, the other in the States in the fall. They were markedly different affairs. The European shows, prefaced by four warm-up gigs in the mid-West and Maryland, were almost universally impressive and included eight shows in England, where he had been so well received in 1978. The American shows were lacklustre affairs, the sound a mush of drums and guitars and Dylan's singing lacking any real variety, each song delivered in the same high-pitched whine.

The contrast escaped the media, and the European shows were not well received, critics viewing even the modified show that was now being presented as overly religious in content, preferring to ignore the extra commitment Dylan seemed to bring to his gospel material. The American press on the other hand, after reports of gruelling evangelist sets the previous year, were relieved at how much pre-gospel material he was playing. He also seemed to be deliberately avoiding the areas where he had met most media resistance in the recent past: the West Coast, Arizona and Texas (save for one show in Texas).

Part of the reaction in the European media was down to the contrast between the new shows and his 1978 'experiment', which had been so well received there. The new shows, as orthodox rock concerts, were attacked for lacking audacity and originality. Dylan was also a victim of The Bruce Springsteen Effect. Springsteen had delayed his first major European tour that spring, and ended up leaving England less than three weeks before the Dylan shows, thus making his much-hyped 1981 tour a fresh experience to contrast with Dylan's considerably more demanding show. Springsteen benefited from European critics having no benchmark to compare his 1981 shows against. (It had been six years since a somewhat less famous Springsteen played four European shows.) Thus an endless procession of critics lived out a new version of the Emperor's New Clothes, none prepared to admit to being anything other than overwhelmed by his performances.

Dylan sprang surprises with every line he sang, twisting words and phrases, wringing meaning from each tapestry of song he wove. Though his new, highly mannered vocal delivery was initially disorienting, repeated performances suggested he had found a voice which, in *NME* editor Neil Spencer's own words, 'was quite astonishing, clearly superior to all his many past styles; from all of which he borrows for the present'. Though not required to defend his new show to Spencer, Dylan had this to say:

Bob Dylan: I feel very strongly about this show. I feel it has something to offer. No one else does this show, not Bruce Springsteen or anyone. [1981]

Sadly, it seemed that Dylan had stretched even the most flexible vocal chords in rock & roll too far. At two shows in Birmingham, two days on from his six-night residency at London's cavernous Earls Court, he sounded in physical pain on stage and on the first night cut short his set. Though a respite before playing mainland Europe repaired some of the damage, allowing Dylan to impress throughout the few remaining European shows, when he returned to the American stage three months later he sounded as if he was unwilling or unable to provide any of the legendary vocal gymnastics of yore.

He had also added a second drummer on this US tour, a baffling decision, coming after the addition of an equally unnecessary second guitarist, Steve Ripley, on the European tour. If any drummer in modern rock music does not require assistance it is Jim Keltner. For the first part of the tour the second drummer was in fact a roadie, Arthur Rosato. Though the more impressive Bruce Gary was brought in as a replacement for the last ten shows, the rationale behind two drummers was still not readily apparent.

Also lost was the sympathetic Willie Smith on keyboards, whose departure seems to have been something of a surprise. His replacement, the versatile Al Kooper, was given only a matter of days notice and then on the tour was largely restricted to providing his trademark organ sound. Inevitably the recruitment of Kooper was seen as a concession to 'greatest hits'-loving fans and indeed 'I Want You' received its first live outing in three years, while both 'Hard Rain's a-Gonna Fall' and 'Senor' were also restored to favour.

Al Kooper: I was asking him to do that because we were together so why not play the songs that we used to play because we were together and it wasn't a common occurrence . . . So I'd say, 'Let's play "I Want You".' . . . 'Cause I think when it started it was almost totally Christian and when it was over it was almost totally greatest hits . . . The shows were long. We did like two and a half three-hour shows. It was brutal. One of the first nights we played 'Like a Rolling Stone' so slow it must have taken him twenty minutes to go through the whole song. So after the show I put my arm around him and said 'You can't play "Like a Rolling Stone" that slow or if you do let's do it really slower and then we won't have to do any more songs.' . . . By the end of the tour the old Bob was back.

But the band's chemistry had been inextricably altered. They had played so majestically on every tour since November 1979. Now they sounded as though they were going through the motions. The twenty-seven American shows, which spanned the latter part of October and most of November, concluded in America's favourite resort state, Florida. It was time for Dylan to take a vacation. After all, he had been on the road for the last four years. It would be two and a half years before his next tour.

1982 was Dylan's third 'lost' year since 1961. As in 1968 and 1972, he made no officially released recordings, nor did he play any shows save for a single ten-minute guest appearance (joining Joan Baez during the Peace Sunday benefit show at Pasadena in June).

After spending much of the summer of 1982 attending gigs with his eldest son, Jesse, in Minneapolis, taking in shows by the Clash, Elvis Costello and the Attractions, X, the Stray Cats and Squeeze, all new-wave bands that were idols of young Jesse, Dylan's thoughts finally turned to the question of a new album. In December 1982 he approached Frank Zappa with a view to him producing it. Though Zappa considered the idea interesting, nothing came of their discussions. By January 1983 other 'name' producers were being considered, including Elvis Costello and David Bowie.

Yet unlike the two previous 'lost' years, 1982 was not without its recording activity. He made several recordings with Clydie King at Gold Star Studios in Los Angeles, and at least four songs were copyrighted in the spring, though only a rewritten version of 'You Changed My Life'* suggested any real merit. The lyrics also

---

* An unequivocal version recorded at the Shot of Love sessions in April 1981 is included on 'The Bootleg Series' vols. 1–3.

suggested a worrying degree of self-doubt about his constancy to his newly found faith, Dylan asking in the final verse for his Lord to make his faith stronger.

Indeed, at the same time as Dylan was recording songs of doubt the media began to speculate about an element of backsliding in his much-vaunted Christian beliefs. In March 1982 a syndicated article was published which alleged that 'a source close to' Dylan was quoted as suggesting that he had reverted to the religion of his forefathers, and that, 'In a sense, he never left his Judaism. My interpretation is that the New Testament and Jesus were a message he thought he got, but that he was still testing.' Who the source was remains unknown, but Dylan typically remained silent in response to such speculation, though voices refuting such stories attempted to be heard.

The speculation became more acute as Dylan was photographed at the bar-mitzvah of one of his sons in Jerusalem in September wearing a yarmulke. The photos were widely published. Then, early in 1983, came reports that he had been spending considerable time with a Jewish Hassidic sect called the Lubavitchers, and it was even said that he had recorded an album of Hassidic songs. While fans speculated upon what Dylan's new album may have in store, the Vineyard Fellowship and the Lubavitchers set about attempting to interpret Dylan's actions in diametrically opposed manners.

Paul Esmond: I don't think he ever left his Jewish roots. I think he is one of those fortunate ones who realized that Judaism and Christianity can work very well together, because Christ is just [Jesus the Messiah]. And so he doesn't have any problems about putting on a yarmulke and going to a bar-mitzvah, because he can respect that.

Rabbi Kasriel Kastel: He's been going in and out of a lot of things, trying to find himself. And we've just been making ourselves available. As far as we're concerned, he was a confused Jew. We feel he's coming back.

The release of *Infidels* would not abate the speculation. Indeed the lack of overtly evangelistic lyrics only fuelled the sceptics who doubted the strength of Dylan's beliefs, despite the fact that, as Bert Cartwright has written, 'There is no song without direct allusion to the Bible.' However, only two songs draw heavily upon New Testament works, 'Jokerman' and 'Man of Peace', songs which both seemed to enmesh the narrator in a battle with false prophets who assume attributes of Christ with evil intent. Thus 'Man of Peace' was based upon the dictum: 'Even Satan disguises himself as an angel of Light' (2 Corinthians 11.14).

Both songs contain allusions to the Book of Revelation, suggesting an abiding belief in the imminent apocalypse. In an interview published in July of 1983, conducted at the mixing sessions for *Infidels*, Dylan clearly seemed to be suggesting that, after years of being acclaimed a prophet, he was finally prophesying, only to be misunderstood:

Bob Dylan: Roots, man — we're talking about Jewish roots, you want to know more? Check on Elijah the prophet. He could make rain. Isaiah the prophet, even Jeremiah, see if their brethren didn't want to bust their brains for telling it right like it is, yeah — these are my roots I suppose. Am I looking for them? . . . I ain't looking for them in synagogues with six-pointed Egyptian stars shining down from every window, I can tell you that much.

Despite that final sentence, the extensive references to Old Testament prophets in his interview with Martin Keller and the preponderance of allusions to Old Testament works on *Infidels*, were cited as evidence of Dylan's reversion to Judaism. Despite all the evidence to the contrary on the album and Dylan's unequivocal statement in a *Rolling Stone* interview in March 1984 that he believed in the Book of Revelation, in which Christ returns to judge humanity, the media painted *Infidels* as an album from a lamb returned to the fold.

Then on the 1984 European tour Dylan seemed to make no effort to reaffirm his beliefs. Only one song from *Slow Train Coming* and *Saved* was performed — 'When You Gonna Wake Up' — and though the song was wholly rewritten, the new words were so garbled it was impossible to discern them. Likewise *Shot of Love*'s only contributions to the tour set were 'Every Grain of Sand', with its almost pantheistic tones, and the un-religious 'Heart of Mine'. It seems likely that Dylan was genuinely concerned that an overly religious tone to the shows would have disastrous commercial consequences on his first-ever stadium tour. Yet in interview after interview on the tour he referred to his abiding faith in the prophecies foretold in Revelation.

Towards the end of 1984 two Christian writers published books attempting to prove that Dylan's spiritual journey was still on that slow train, and that it was picking up speed. Bert Cartwright's important *The Bible in the Lyrics of Bob Dylan* attempted to evaluate Dylan's use of biblical references in all his work to date but received minimal distribution. Don Williams published a book which received much wider dissemination and was considerably more polemical, entitled *The Man, the Music, the Message*. However, it was clear that, despite his enduring beliefs, Dylan had spent much of 1982 re-evaluating his values and that with the release of *Infidels* his evangelical phase was over. From now on, fellow believers would have to read between the lines.

31

1983: Songs of Experience

1983 could, and should, have been the beginning of Dylan's second major creative renaissance. The songs he recorded for the album that year were the strongest since *Blood on the Tracks*, nine years earlier. The fact that Dylan issued a bastardized version of the album and then failed to promote the record with a tour or even a spate of interviews, but preferred to spend his time jamming with local musicians in the privacy of his Malibu residence, meant he reversed neither his commercial nor his critical decline.

When Dylan entered Power Station Studios, New York, on 11 April, to begin recording his follow-up to *Shot of Love*, he knew the importance of these sessions. It had been two years since *Shot of Love*, which – like *Saved* – had been disastrous commercially. Since *Shot of Love* MTV had come to prominence, a cable station which supplied a perennial diet of promotional videos, brief 'newsy' items on today's pop stars, and the occasional half-hour 'in-concert' special. No longer were the kids listening to their radios for the latest 'fave rave', they wanted an image *and* the music, all wrapped into one.

Two years on from *Shot of Love*, there were abundant stories in the press that Dylan had abandoned Christianity. A Dylan returned to secular values or even the faith of his father was certainly news. After all, it implied that Dylan had seen the error of his ways in having advocated a born-again creed.

It is easy to say that Dylan ploughs his own furrow and if the world catches up all well and good. But he has always thrown in a sweetener to make each dramatic change more palatable. On *Bringing It All Back Home* the second side gave the folkies some solace, on *Slow Train Coming* he used Knopfler's sinewy sounds and Wexler's superlative production to give fans his best-sounding album in years.

For his 1983 album Dylan again turned to Knopfler. Since the recording of *Slow Train Coming*, Dire Straits had become one of the most successful acts of the early eighties. Using Mark Knopfler would in itself attract sales and press coverage, though Dylan's main motive for recruiting Knopfler was his need for a co-producer. He wanted to produce the album himself, but technology had passed him by. He needed an artist that felt at home in the modern recording studio. Hence the approaches to names like David Bowie and Frank Zappa.

Knopfler was the best choice he could have made. They had worked together. Knopfler knew it was better to coax Dylan than command him and his own ego was likely to be considerably less of a problem than some of the names previously considered. Knopfler was also a highly distinctive guitarist.

Bob Dylan: Mark ... encouraged me to go to the studio when I didn't feel like it, when I'd rather have been someplace else ... [and] As far as guitar playing goes he never steps all over with fancy licks. [1983]

Dylan had had no touring band for eighteen months, and was required to start from scratch. Mark Knopfler's syrupy tones required a harder, bluesier second guitarist to compensate and provide the cutting edge needed on the record. Dylan's choice was Mick Taylor, who had worked his apprenticeship with John Mayall's Bluesbreakers in the sixties before spending six years with the Rolling Stones.

Dylan's choice of rhythm section was also inspired. His most successful recordings and performances had always been founded on a dynamite rhythm section 'grounding' the sound while he extemporized, whether it was Ken Buttrey and Charlie McCoy, Howie Wyeth and Rob Stoner or Jim Keltner and Tim Drummond. Sly Dunbar and Robbie Shakespeare were already well established in their own field, and they were able to provide Dylan with a sound that was contemporary without adopting the whomp-synth-whomp approach so prevalent among the synthetic forms of music then assailing the airwaves. The final member of the band was Knopfler's suggestion, his fellow Dire Straits member Alan Clark, who would provide keyboards.

Mark Knopfler: Bob decided on the whole band, although I did suggest that Alan [Clark] be there ... And I suggested the engineer, Neil Dorfsman ... We were like a three-man team at that point. Sly Dunbar and Robbie Shakespeare were Bob's ideas, as well as Mick Taylor. I suggested Billy Gibbons, but I don't think Bob had heard of ZZ Top.

Predictably, recording with digital technology at a top modern studio was not going to dissuade Dylan from recording live with the band, nor from avoiding multiple takes. As throughout his career, he winged it and the band was required to wing it too.

Alan Clark: He doesn't play anything more than once. If you can get him to play it twice, you're doing well. Three times is *really* pushing it. We used to just sit at our instruments . . . and Bob would wander in, sit down, put his headphones on and struggle with his guitar strap for a couple of minutes, light a cigarette and then stub the cigarette out, take his guitar off, take his headphones off and walk across to the organ where I was sitting and write down about . . . half a dozen lines of the next tune in tiny, meticulous hand-writing. It was quite interesting! And he'd sort of wander back over, maybe forget to put the headphones on, and start playing the track. Just like that! If you weren't sitting there – if you had to go to the bog or something – he just started, y'know. It was amazing. And that's the way the album went.

The advantage now was that if anyone did blow an otherwise fine take, the technology enabled that particular part to be overdubbed without in any way impairing the rest of the performance. This meant that the songs could be 'got down' relatively easily, leaving Dylan time to experiment with the words or the arrangement.

Mark Knopfler: I remember some things worked really well. If you get the chance to get the band sorted out you can get it really fast. I remember 'License to Kill' was first take for instance.

A remarkable recording exists of Dylan and the band working on 'Sweetheart Like You', which gives the best idea of what working with him in the studio is really like. As the tape starts Dylan and the band are running through a verse of the song. It is clear that the arrangement is pretty much in place, but he has only a skeleton of the words. As in so many sessions before, he chooses to work on the song in the studio, filling in loose lines and gaps while he can hear the song taking shape. Thus as a second take starts up he cuts it dead after one line – '"The boss ain't here, he gone north, he gone north" . . . No, wait a sec. That ain't right. [Sings to himself.] "Well the boss ain't here." Oh shit. [Strums guitar while tapping his foot to the rhythm of the song.] Okay. [Count in.] "Well the boss ain't here/he gone north/I can't remember where/he caught the Redeye/it left on time/he's starting a graveyard up there."' After the take Dylan says, 'Let's try it again. I think it's getting closer. The bass part is getting right. It's got that feel, y'know.' It is obvious as the tape runs out that Dylan is becoming bored and disenchanted with the way the song is developing and they will have to return to the song again, by which time he will have rewritten large chunks of it.

This process became a major factor during both the recording sessions and the subsequent mixing sessions. Whole verses were rewritten, dropped, resurrected in new form. The original version of 'Union Sundown' featured a final verse which was a thinly veiled attack upon a masked man in the White House who if 'he understands the shape of things to come' will be allowed to remain there until he dies. Another verse was also wholly rewritten. 'Jokerman' and 'Sweeheart Like You' were substantially altered during the mixing sessions. A fine verse on the original 'Jokerman', about women sitting in a shack and sowing a shirt for the jokerman because he cannot afford a store-bought shirt, was lost. In the case of the marvellous 'Someone's Got a Hold of My Heart', the rewriting process did not finish until 1985, when it was recorded for *Empire Burlesque* as 'Tight Connection to My Heart'.

If a song like 'Sweetheart Like You' had a fairly straightforward arrangement, other songs at the sessions went through various forms before Dylan was happy. 'Blind Willie McTell', perhaps the strongest song recorded at these sessions, was attempted *à la* 'Dirge', with just acoustic guitar and piano, as well as with the full band, Dylan's powerful vocal embellished with some gorgeous slide guitar. 'Foot of Pride' was attempted bossa nova style, with backing singers, and eventually laid down as a grungy riff-driven slab of primeval rock & roll.

The sessions did not always progress smoothly. It was widely reported in the press that Knopfler walked out of one session in disgust for reasons unknown. Thankfully he did return and the sessions were completed by the beginning of May, in time for Knopfler and Clark to resume touring Germany with Dire Straits. Before leaving, though, Knopfler and Dylan compiled and mixed a rough version of the album they intended to release.

Mark Knopfler: I had to go on tour in Germany . . . I had a bag at the studio and went to the airport from the studio having just finished recording pretty much the album. But then Bob went on and overdubbed certain things.

The album they put together was Dylan's finest album in eight years. Though it contained two meritless tracks – 'Neighbourhood Bully' and 'License to Kill' – the remaining seven songs were all of a high calibre, and included four of Dylan's finest works of recent years, 'I and I', 'Jokerman', 'Blind Willie McTell' and 'Foot of Pride'. It was an album that was bound to re-establish both his commercial standing and his critical credibility. Even with the omission of the superb 'Someone's Got a Hold of My Heart' it was the album all Dylan fans were hoping for.

Sadly it was not the album that Dylan chose to release. In the past he had always trusted his first instincts as the truest. On the only previous occasion he had re-recorded part of an album, *Blood on the Tracks*, he had produced mixed results. If the recording of the *Infidels* material had been a collaboration between Dylan and Knopfler, Dylan's decision to 're-work' the album allowed no input from his collaborator. Not surprisingly, Knopfler later disowned the album as released.

Mark Knopfler: Some of [*Infidels*] is like listening to roughs. Maybe Bob thought I'd rushed things because I was in a hurry to leave, but I offered to finish it after our tour. Instead he got the engineer to do the final mix and I must say that listening to it makes me wish I'd done it myself.

After a couple of weeks away from the material, Dylan had returned to Power Station studios to complete the mixing of the album. At this point he seems to have decided to reconstruct the album, even going as far as re-recording the vocal track for three of the songs.

Bob Dylan: Somehow, I figured I could always get away with just playing the songs live in the studio and leaving. It got to the point where I felt people expected that from me. But I decided [on *Infidels*] to take my time like other people do. [1983]

Though he had used overdubs in the past, there is no evidence that Dylan had ever re-dubbed a new vocal track over an existing backing track before. He had always preferred to retain the chemistry of a live take. With *Infidels*, he began to reconsider his view of recording technology. The opportunity to re-record vocal tracks was too great a temptation and, as with 'Idiot Wind', 'Tangled Up in Blue' and 'If You See Her, Say Hello' on the released version of *Blood on the Tracks*, he rewrote parts of both 'Jokerman' and 'Sweetheart Like You'. Ironically, though the 'Jokerman' rewrites were an improvement, the vocal was not. The original vocal performance was a *tour de force*. The new 'Jokerman' was less arresting, the vocals unsuccessfully vying with the band for attention.

Bob Dylan: We didn't really approach [*Infidels*] any differently than any other record. We put the tracks down and sang most of the stuff live. Only later when we had so much stuff, we recorded it over [again] . . . I wanted to fill it up more, I've never wanted to do that with any other record . . . Did you ever listen to an Eagles record? . . . their songs are good, but every note is predictable, you know exactly what's gonna be before it's even there. And I started to sense some of that on *Infidels*, and I didn't like it, so we decided to redo some of the vocals . . . [But] that record's not an overly produced record. [1984]

The prime disaster though was Dylan's decision to restructure the entire album. If the album had been released as it was – even with the new vocals – it would have been well received. However, he decided to delete 'Blind Willie McTell' and 'Foot of Pride' from the album and replace them with a reworked version of 'Union Sundown'. It was as if he had taken 'Visions of Johanna' and 'Stuck Inside of Mobile' off *Blonde on Blonde* and replaced them with 'If You Gotta Go, Go Now!'. The album tilted off its axis. It had previously been able to support 'Neighbourhood Bully' and 'License to Kill'. The change made *Infidels* a pale reflection of its former self. Few would ever hear the out-takes which proved that his muse had been working overtime, even if his critical faculties were not.

The remixing also meant that the album was not released until November, a full six months after the sessions, when Dylan's mind had long passed on to his next project. Yet if his perspective on his own songs had never been poorer, there was no doubt that he was writing songs of true quality, as indeed he had been back in 1979–80, when *Saved* and *Shot of Love* provided equally minimal evidence of a creative renaissance. *Infidels* seemed to reinforce the false impression of Dylan's well having run dry.

Larry Sloman: When he was finishing up *Infidels*, one night we were leaving the studio, he was talking about the next album. This one was barely even mixed, and already he was talking about getting in the studio to do another album . . . that means his creative juices are cooking!

If Dylan didn't actually hot-foot it back into the studio after completing *Infidels*, he seemed to be compensating for his lack of touring by jamming with as many people as he could. In February he had turned up at the Lone Star Café to jam with Levon Helm and Rick Danko, though the results were a little loose; he was even rumoured to have recorded an album of Hassidic songs (taken as further evidence of his reversion from Christianity to orthodox Judaism); and in the fall he recorded a series of demos at informal sessions at his house in Malibu. It is not known what songs resulted from these sessions. But they clearly followed well-established patterns, with Dylan requiring the musicians to respond as best they could, refusing to provide guidance himself. Two of those who played on these sessions were Charlie Sexton and Charlie Quintana.

Charlie Quintana: I got word that maybe I could come over and jam once in a while. Bob was really cool about it. Either he'd call or some-body else would, and they'd say, Come over! Or, bring another guitar player! So I would take other musicians down there . . . I'd just go down there, sit and wait, and he'd just come in and we'd start playing. He'd start tinkering, then I'd jump in, the other guitar player, and we'd go on for five minutes, or for forty-five minutes, and then he'd stop . . . I took a lot of local musicians from Los Angeles . . . My impression of what was going down there is that he was trying to get back into playing, that he just wanted some guys, low-key, to jam. And that's what we did. We didn't sit around and talk a lot. He came in, we played, we had some cof-fee, we played again. He'd say, Alright, that's it, and he'd split, walk out.

Charlie Sexton: He'd just pick up his guitar and start singing and playing without any introduction or explanation – no keys, no chords, nothing! And my job was to figure out all the charts and produce it on the spot. We must have cut about nine or ten songs. I'd keep asking him, 'Is this one yours?' and he'd just mumble in that gravelly voice, 'Nah, it's from the Civil War.'

Dylan was still reluctant to return to touring, and he was not granting interviews, save for one with Robert Hilburn of the *Los Angeles Times*, in which he barely mentioned the new album. Yet the release of *Infidels* required some promotion. 'Sweetheart Like You' had been released as a single before the album and become his first Top Sixty single since 'Gotta Serve Somebody'. It was the logical choice for a video. But he was reluctant to involve himself with the medium without having specific ideas in mind. Three songs had been filmed in the studio during the *Infidels* sessions for possible use as promo videos, but the footage was never used. Dylan himself wanted to produce a video of 'Neighbourhood Bully', but it was a poor choice for a single – particularly with its Zionist slant – and his own ideas for the video were typically vague.

Bob Dylan: I'm not quite sure I know what a video is except that the market for video is new, but the form has always been there. Yeah, [they view] 'Subterranean Homesick Blues' as a video. I don't know if it was a

video. We didn't think of it as a video at the time, we just needed a piece
of film to go at the beginning of a movie ... We wanted to do
'Neighbourhood Bully' but [it's difficult] tryin' to explain to somebody
what you see and drawin' up storyboards; I haven't really found anybody
that really thinks a certain way that needs to be [done], like the German
film-makers, the English film-makers. In the States there aren't people
like that. They just don't exist ... I visualized 'Neighbourhood Bully'
... there were certain segments which I just wrote down one night
which I thought would look great on film and it would be like a
Fassbinder movie. [1984]

Despite Dylan's disavowal, 'Subterranean Homesick Blues' had
been adopted as an early example of the promo video, and was
considered an inspired example of the genre. Perhaps not surprisingly he was expected to produce something other than a standard
promotional video. Yet, with the rejection of his idea for 'Neighbourhood Bully', he was uncooperative, and unwilling to provide
any creative input into one for 'Sweetheart Like You'. Mark
Robinson, the video director, seemed equally short of ideas.

Mark Robinson: We were ... about to do a simple club scene where
one woman's face was every woman's face, and we had thirty extras ...
lined up ready to shoot. But while we were setting up the club with
upturned chairs on table tops, there was someone sweeping up the
cigarette butts ... I went to Bob and suggested we take an old lady and
have her sweeping up, with it all coming from her point of view.

The 'Sweetheart Like You' video may have got Dylan onto
MTV but it did nothing to persuade younger music fans to
investigate this guy who looked like a rabbi and evidently one
whose barber had a sense of humour. Nevertheless, *Infidels*, having
garnered good reviews on its release in November, was a consistent
seller in the run-up to Christmas, and proved to be Dylan's only
top twenty album of the eighties (excluding the *Traveling
Wilburys*), and stayed on the charts through to April 1984. As a
result CBS were keen on him producing a second video to
promote the album and February single release of 'Jokerman', a
strange choice for a single given its oblique content and six-minute
length.

Dylan recruited two old friends from his Rolling Thunder days
to co-direct the video, Larry Sloman and George Lois. However,
when he turned up at their initial meeting he still had his heart set
on making the 'Neighbourhood Bully' video, and again he lacked
enthusiasm for the 'Jokerman' project.

Larry Sloman: Dylan walked into that [video] meeting with the
intention of doing a video for 'Neighbourhood Bully' . . . But Lois had
each lyric from 'Jokerman' blown up and tacked to the wall in the
conference room and underneath each line was the corresponding visual
image we had selected. Now the big pitch . . . Lois began his lecture.
'Now when you say "You were born with a snake in both of your fists",
that's the Minoan Snake Goddess from Crete, *circa* 1500 BC. Case closed.
That's what you meant, right Bob?' Dylan managed something between
a shrug and a nod.

Sloman and Lois's video of 'Jokerman' was based upon a remarkable idea – combining Dylan's lyrics, which were featured at the
bottom of the screen, with visual images which complemented
them. It meant they only needed to film Dylan for the refrain,
though even this proved difficult enough, Dylan being reluctant to
be filmed close up, and perpetually squinting at the camera lights.
The results, though still failing to impress Dylan, were able to
convey a sense of the song's significance.

Whatever his reservations, Dylan clearly recognized the growing
value of this new medium. The promo video was not going to
reduce in importance, particularly for an artist with only a marginal
profile on AM radio in America. Throughout 1984 and 1985 he
harangued journalists about the insidious influence of the video. It
remains a medium he has never really mastered, despite having
one of the most cinematic imaginations of any songwriter today.
Indeed, in 1975 he intended to make a film of 'Lily, Rosemary and
the Jack of Hearts' with Jonathan Taplin. In 1986 a film could have
been made of the epic 'Brownsville Girl'. The essential problem is
that the scale of Dylan's story-telling songs is such that they can
never be contained in three minutes of celluloid and Dylan has
preferred to refrain from solidifying images intended to be left to
each listener's imagination. However, in March 1984, the same
month that Lois and Sloman finished the 'Jokerman' video, Dylan
went on national TV and proved once again that, filmed in
performance, there was still no one who could exude the same
swaggering authority and charismatic fury. He also reminded
himself that he could trust his performing instincts considerably
more than his recording instincts.

32

1984: Still Life and Real Live

By spring 1984 Dylan had been off the road for thirty months, by far his longest break since he resumed touring in 1974. In the interim, he had produced his strongest and most commercial album since *Slow Train Coming*, though *Infidels* was already old hat to Dylan, even if the album was still selling healthily and CBS were still keen on promoting it.

David Letterman had been trying to get Dylan to appear on his popular *Late Night with David Letterman* programme for some time. In March 1984 he finally said yes, though he would not be interviewed and he would supply his own band (it was usual to perform with Letterman's in-house band). He then asked Charlie Quintana to put a band together, though the purpose was not made immediately apparent.

Charlie Quintana: Originally it was all very vague. There was talk of going to Hawaii and doing a show there for his label or something, and then it fell through. And then the Letterman show came out of nowhere really. I think it was about a week's notice ... It didn't really matter whether it was a week or a month because we didn't know what we were going to play until about a minute before we went on the air!

The band Quintana recruited consisted of two fellow members of LA's burgeoning post-punk scene, Justin Jesting on guitar and Tony Marisco on bass. This was Dylan's first real dalliance with third generation American rock & rollers. If his inexperienced new cohorts expected guidance from the man, they did not know Dylan. Flying to New York, they rehearsed for what they now knew to be a major national TV appearance the day before Letterman's show. The rehearsals followed the familiar Dylan pattern.

Charlie Quintana: We rehearsed at the TV soundcheck and we'd rehearsed the night before, but the night before we went through fifty fuckin' songs we didn't know! At the soundcheck they sealed off the studio and all the NBC brass was there 'cause it's Bob, and we'd never start 1–2–3. He'd just start strumming and we'd just jump in and follow it. And it would end up the same way – he'd just stop playing. There was none of this Da-da-da-da, Boom Boom! to end a song, none of that! And it was five minutes before we were supposed to go on and I'm asking Bill Graham, saying, 'Jesus Christ, we're shitting bricks over here! Can you please go in and ask Bob what songs we're gonna do?' And he'd come back and say, 'He's not sure yet.' And we're going, 'Oh shit! We only learned 150 songs!'

In fact the TV soundcheck formed the basis for their three-song performance, Dylan and the band having run through two tunes from *Infidels* – 'License to Kill' and 'Jokerman' – and a version of Roy Head's 'Treat Her Right'. The difference in performance between soundcheck and TV appearance, though, was night and day. At the last minute he decided that instead of 'Treat Her Right' he would open with a cover of Sonny Boy Williamson's 'Don't Start Me Talking', a song which Quintana does not think was even rehearsed. Fortunately a band of post-punk LA musicians could hardly fail to know a somewhat different version of the song, recorded in the early seventies by punk's godfathers, the New York Dolls. Dylan's vocal may have been a nod to Williamson, but the band played pure Dolls! And it worked. Dylan blew an impressive harp solo and the whole thing sounded the freshest and most intense performance he had ever given on national TV. 'License to Kill' was equally astonishing, with Dylan wailing away on harmonica again and revelling in the sledgehammer sound of that Marisco–Quintana rhythm section. 'Jokerman', the final song, was abbreviated to three verses but still raged with an incandescent passion, until he picked up his harp for one final blow and realized it was in the wrong key. While technicians fumbled around looking for the correct harmonica the band played on. And on.

Charlie Quintana: Maybe if we had rehearsed a song from beginning to end, it would have fallen apart. But because we were used to not knowing what was happening, when he was fumbling around for the harmonica I was just able to keep on tapping it out – a couple of verses, a chorus. It seemed like ten years! The cameraman got so bored he actually did a close-up of me.

Dylan finally blew in with a terrific harp solo and finished to a rousing reception from the stunned studio audience. Letterman asked if perhaps they could make it every Thursday and Dylan finally cracked a grin. But he knew that he had delivered a definitive TV performance. Indeed, any viewers who raced out to buy *Infidels* on the strength of this set must have been mighty disappointed when they heard the leaden, soul-less version of 'License to Kill' which was included on the album.

The appearance seems to have stirred Dylan's desire to perform again, and he was soon framing plans with Bill Graham for a South American tour with an as yet unspecified band. He had never played South America, and had had a hankering to play there for some time. With no recording sessions scheduled his thoughts turned to recruiting a new touring band. His previous touring bands had been relatively extravagant affairs. This time he wanted to stick to a fairly basic set-up – organ, guitar, bass, drums.

Given the success of his brief association with Quintana's ensemble, they would have seemed a logical starting point. However, it seems that only Quintana was ever a serious candidate for the gig. Indeed, after playing regularly at Malibu, where Dylan conducted his informal auditions for the band, Quintana was not notified until the last minute that he would not be on the summer tour. Colin Allen had been preferred.

Charlie Quintana: I remember it was about a week before the tour started, and I was calling two or three times a day, asking whether or not I was going. They'd say, 'We're not sure yet. Call back in an hour.' This happened for a fucking week. I didn't sleep for a week. I really wanted to do it.

Perhaps the essence of any great band Dylan has ever played with has been the rhythm section. He has certainly been extremely fortunate to have played with combinations like Rick Danko and Mickey Jones (or Levon Helm), Rob Stoner and Howie Wyeth, and Tim Drummond and Jim Keltner. Indeed Sly and Robbie, who had done such a sterling job on *Infidels*, had expressed an interest in touring with Dylan.

His selections in 1984 showed none of his previous unerring judgement when it came to musicians. Perhaps, as in 1978, when Ian Wallace played the sticks, there was just not enough time to work at finding a worthwhile rhythm section. Which still does not explain Dylan's baffling decision to prefer the wholly unknown and unimpressive Colin Allen to the supremely rhythmic Quintana.

The likely explanation is that Dylan once again left a great deal of the decision-making to his appointed band-leader, in this case Mick Taylor. Colin Allen was a friend of Taylor's, they had worked together in the past, and he was auditioned at Taylor's suggestion. If it was Taylor who convinced Dylan to prefer Allen to Quintana, he did him a great disservice. Aside from the profound difference in rhythmic sense, Quintana was used to Dylan's idiosyncrasies, Allen was not, and had barely a week of serious rehearsing to learn them.

Allen was not the only unfortunate choice, though the other selections — if not ideal — were more than competent. Having decided not to utilize Marisco it was somewhat surprising that Dylan and/or Taylor should then select an equally inexperienced (if promising) LA bassist by the name of Greg Sutton.

Greg Sutton: Mick Taylor liked the way I played, so [Dylan] told me about a week before the tour began that I had the gig! He was very mysterious about it . . . The same was true with Ian McLagen. He told Ian McLagen about three days before the tour.

Dylan had initially wanted Benmont Tench of the Heartbreakers to play keyboards on the tour. Tench would have been an excellent choice. He had worked on the *Shot of Love* album and, as he later proved in 1987, had a natural sense of dynamics in his playing and was not afraid to wing it with Dylan. Unfortunately he could not spare the time to play the tour.

Colin Allen: Benmont couldn't do it — he would've been perfect, the best choice — 'cause he was involved with Petty and they were going to do some recordings . . . So I said, What about Nicky Hopkins? . . . And so he came up. But he was really . . . a piano player. He was saying to me on the phone, Get Bob to get a grand piano in to rehearse on . . . So he came up with this manager guy, and maybe it was all a bit too much for Bob. But anyway, then we got Ian McLagen . . . Ian finally got the word only a couple of days before we actually left Bob's estate and went to the Beverly Theater in Beverly Hills to rehearse in a theatre situation for about five days.

Ian McLagen had a good pedigree, notably from his time in the Faces, though again he was a Mick Taylor selection rather than a Dylan one. As Sutton and Allen have indicated, McLagen did not get the call until a week before the tour, of which the location had now changed dramatically: South America had fallen through, so, since Dylan had put a band together, Europe was the only feasible location for a tour at such short notice.

Bob Dylan: I wanted to do a South American tour. It was just not feasible at this time so I took this tour . . . There's no particular reason for it . . . I specifically wanted to do a South American tour . . . At the last moment I had sort of set my mind mentally to do something so I did this 'cause the other one didn't come off. [1984]

Serious rehearsals started at the Beverly Theater in Los Angeles barely a week before the first show was booked for Verona, Italy. The rehearsals were frankly awful. The band sounded as though they were playing underneath half a hundredweight of porridge, and Dylan's singing sounded devoid of passion. The choice of material they rehearsed was also predictable. Never before had Dylan toured without an album in the can, or new material to premiere. Yet *Infidels* was a year old as far as he was concerned. Only some four songs from his 'new' album were even rehearsed. Likewise his seventies *œuvre* was largely ignored as Dylan constructed his first Oldies show. Even 1978 had featured a cross-section of his career, and the songs had been spruced up with new arrangements. In 1984 Dylan had a much more basic sound to work with, and a rhythm section best utilized by sticking to basics.

Four or five days' rehearsals was clearly nowhere near enough time to get the band into shape, particularly as Dylan was wont to get the band to work on a few new songs he had written, which had titles like 'Angel of Rain', 'Dirty Lie' and 'Enough Is Enough', or old slices of MOR like 'Always on My Mind', rather than work on arranging his older songs, the songs his fans would be expecting.

Flying into Italy, Dylan knew he would have to rehearse further with the band. A rehearsal on the 27th, the day before his first Italian concert, saw him continue to treat the rehearsals as an extended jam session. On the afternoon of 28 May he ran through the basic set with his band before the opening of the ancient portals of the Arena di Verona to his eager Italian fans, about to get their first glimpse of Bob Dylan in concert. The evening's show started disastrously. Dylan seemed reluctant to give the band any guidance about when to end songs, and without any obvious direction from Taylor either, the songs spluttered to their conclusions. The first half was as ramshackle as any performance he had ever given.

Though the band sounded a little more together during their second set, Dylan must have been seriously worried about it. Taylor was a poor choice for leader, and seemed determined to prove his undoubted pedigree as a guitarist by playing extended

and indulgent solos during songs which did not require such embel-
lishment.

Surprisingly, though, within a week of the tour beginning, the
band began to shape up. Part of this was down to Dylan, who
seems to have realized that he had better stamp his authority on
the proceedings before everything collapsed around his ears. By
the time they reached Rotterdam, seven days on from that first
Verona show, he was at last singing with a little of the old fire and
was brimming with ideas, to the extent that he set about rewriting
two of his greatest songs, 'Tangled Up in Blue' and 'Simple Twist
of Fate'.

Bob Dylan: There's a version [of 'Tangled Up in Blue'] we used to do
on stage with just electric guitar and a saxophone – keeping the same
lyrics, thinking that maybe if I did that to it it would bring it out in an
emotional way. But it didn't hold up very well that way. So I changed
the lyrics, to bring it up to date. But I didn't change it 'cause I was
singing it one night and thought, 'Oh, I'm bored with the old words.'
The old ones were never quite filled in. I rewrote it in a hotel room
somewhere. I think it was in Amsterdam . . . When I sang it the next
night I knew it was right. [1985]

'Tangled Up in Blue' rapidly became a nightly highlight for the
fans. At the first few performances you could feel the crowd
hanging on every word, waiting to see where the story led. The
end of the song was an audacious inversion of the original narrator's
intent. In 1974, the singer was 'still on the road, heading for
another joint', for that is where he felt the subject of his quest lay.
In 1984, the singer was 'still walking towards the sun, trying to
stay out of the joints'. The joints are now distractions along the
way and he must avoid them as he heads towards the light of
Knowledge. It also seemed a subtle admission that he was still
walking in the spirit of the Son.

'Simple Twist of Fate', unlike 'Tangled Up in Blue', was a full
band performance and McLagen started to come into his own
with some effective organ playing. The new version was an
imaginative reworking, a little more surreal than the original. As
the first set settled into a rigid seven-song pattern nightly, the band
started to sound a lot more comfortable, and both Sutton and
Allen started to play with something approaching competency.
Sutton soon realized Dylan enjoyed his little game of changing
keys.

Greg Sutton: Bob was saying, 'What key are we in now?' 'Cause he started 'Maggie's Farm' wrong and he asked me, 'What key are we in?' I said, 'Bob we're in G, the key you started it in.' And he says, 'Well, can you go back to the right key?' I said, 'Whatever you say, Bob.'

Allen also began to understand the boss a little better in Rome when he asked him about those song endings, which earlier had been so disastrous and even by mid-tour were on occasions shaky. Dylan was his usual helpful self.

Colin Allen: One day we were sitting in this hotel in Rome, the Lord Byron Hotel . . . We were sitting outside, and Bob was there, and I said, Hey Bob, you know when you look at me at the end of a song, what's the story? Do you want me to end the song[s] immediately, as soon as possible, or wait 'til the sequence goes? He said, Well, I just figure we've done enough with the songs and that we should finish them when we felt comfortable.

The 1984 tour established a fairly standard pattern for subsequent Dylan tours. It was his first nostalgia tour, and subsequent tours would all rely heavily on his more famous sixties material, generally at the expense of his no less impressive seventies and eighties *œuvre*. Subsequent tours also generally discounted contemporary product, with only a small sampling from the previous album, generally a year old by the time he hit the road. From this point on he favoured a basic guitar/organ/bass/drums or even guitar/bass/drums set-up. Though the girls would make a temporary comeback in 1986–7, Dylan has mainly relied on his own vocals to get him through the later eighties. The voice has meantime deteriorated. In 1984 Dylan rarely chose to go for the notes he was attempting on his last European tour, but at least when he did he could still hit them. By his next European visit, in the fall of 1987, he knew there was little point in trying to hit some of those notes – even if he could still hold his breath three times as long as Caruso.

This decision by Dylan to adopt a more nostalgic, perhaps to be fair a more conciliatory, approach – since most of the crowds did genuinely seem to want to hear tired retreads of 'All Along the Watchtower' – inevitably and justifiably led to some critical flak during the 1984 tour. The size of venues – large arenas or stadiums – required that Dylan adopt some kind of profile to the press simply in order to sell tickets. After all his 'special guests', the wearisome Santana, were hardly major crowd-pullers in 1984. In France he actually agreed to his first televised interview in nineteen years to help sell tickets for the Paris, Grenoble and Nantes shows. All along he was constantly queried: Are your songs relevant today? Have you any longer a role to play in modern music? At press conferences in Verona and Hamburg he was surly, uncommunicative, indeed downright rude. As the tour progressed, and he felt more confident about the worth of what he was peddling this time round, he became more talkative, more prepared to defend himself.

Bob Dylan: For me, none of the songs I've written has really dated. They capture something I've never been able to improve on, whatever their statement is . . . People say they're 'nostalgia', but I don't know what that means really. *A Tale of Two Cities* was written 100 years ago; is that nostalgic? This term 'nostalgic', it's just another way people have of dealing with you and putting you some place they think they understand. It's just another label. [1984]

A month to the day after that disastrous first Verona show, Dylan arrived in Barcelona for his second ever Spanish show (the first had been in Madrid two days earlier). His performance in Barcelona proved that he was still the consummate performer. The band, if lacking invention, had at least become tight and professional; and Dylan sang like a bird, albeit one with a touch of laryngitis. The final song of a two and a half hour set, 'Blowin' in the Wind', found Dylan actually cajoling the huge stadium crowd into chorus after chorus of the song – 'Once more'; 'Just once more' – before delivering an impassioned last verse which expressed more sense of the song's meaning than had any version he had sung in the last twenty-two years.

Playing to stadium crowds of between thirty and a hundred thousand, Dylan then weaved his way through Nantes, Paris, Grenoble, Newcastle, London and finally Dublin. Though the last two shows – which constitute the bulk of the disappointing live album, *Real Live* – were a little slick and lacking in passion, they were well received and Dylan had, by 8 July, completed his one and only stadium tour without in any way diminishing his reputation as a charismatic performer. Considering the huge, roofless barns he was playing, the wasted rehearsals and the disappointing choice of rhythm section, this was certainly far more than any unfortunate member of the Verona crowd six weeks earlier would have expected.

33

1984–5: Burlesques and Benefits

Perhaps the buzz of being 'on the road again' was what was necessary to get Dylan writing once more. He had two or three nearly finished songs which he had tried out at the rehearsals in May, though only 'Enough Is Enough' became a feature of the tour, and his writing on the tour had not been confined to rewriting earlier classics. Within two weeks of the tour's end he was back in the studio working on a new album.

It had been fourteen months since the *Infidels* sessions, and a strong album might indicate a mid-eighties revival to parallel his mid-seventies surge of creativity. The summer sessions were not confined to one studio or one burst of activity. Over July and August, Dylan worked at Intergalactic Studios, Delta Studios and even returned to the Record Plant. Rather than forming a nucleus of musicians to record a new album with, he tried out different combinations, in search of a new sound. This time he had decided to produce the sessions himself.

A session at Intergalactic was unsuccessful, even though Dylan had brought old friend Ron Wood along to help out and provide moral support. He had temporarily recruited Al Green's usual band of shit-hot Memphis musicians. Unfortunately they were not used to the idiosyncratic approach Dylan took, particularly when he not only refused to sing any song the same way twice but kept changing the keys on them.

Ron Wood: [There was one session], it was at Intergalactic, the old Hit Factory, in New York, with the Al Green band. All these guys from Memphis couldn't understand Bob's chord sequences. Every time he started off a new song, he'd start in a new key, or if we were doing the same song over and over, every time would be in a different key. Now I can go along with that with Bob, but the band were totally confused, and one by one they left the studio.

Apart from recording a straightforward shot of rhythm & blues called 'Honey Wait', and a run-through of the old chestnut 'Mountain of Love', the session seems to have been without result. Sessions at Delta Sound studios were more successful, with Ron Wood again providing a helping hand, along with Anton Fig and John Paris as the rhythm section. 'Clean Cut Kid', originally an out-take from *Infidels*, was successfully recorded, as were two new songs, the funky 'Driftin' Too Far from Shore', which later ended up on *Knocked Out Loaded*, and an insidious blues number called 'Who Loves You More'. However, Dylan still seemed uncomfortable with the technology available to him in digital thirty-two track studios. Talking at the end of July in a radio interview, he revealed he was still a Luddite at heart.

Bob Dylan: We were recording something the other night and we were gonna put some handclaps on it. And the guy sitting behind the board, he was saying, 'Well do you guys wanna go out there and actually clap? I got a machine right here that can do that.' . . . We went out and clapped instead . . . But that's just a small example of how everything is just machine orientated. [1984]

Unfortunately, once again Dylan's lack of discipline in failing to stamp his personal artistic authority on his songs let him down. At the end of the sessions at Delta, which had proved the most productive of the summer, Ron Wood looked on with astonishment as he allowed the engineer/s to mix the material without his own input. In the case of 'Driftin' Too Far from Shore' this meant that, when he came to use the song for *Knocked Out Loaded*, they had to re-record the entire drum track.

Ron Wood: When we'd go in at . . . Delta for a playback, every time he'd have the same attitude. The weak side of him would come out. They'd say, 'Hey Bob, we don't need this,' and he'd say, 'Oh. OK.' And they'd make a mix to their ears, and he'd just stand outside and let them do it. And I'd be saying, 'Hey! You can't let these guys . . . Look!! They've left off the background vocals!' or 'What about the drums?!' But there would be something going on in the back of his head which didn't allow him to interfere. And yet if he'd have gone into the control room with the dominance that he had while we were cutting the stuff, it could have been mind-bending.

Still, the burst of new songs suggested that the new album could be a major work, despite Dylan's failure to capitalize on the quality of his songwriting on his last three albums. Meanwhile, he was keeping tabs on a buoyant American post-punk scene, which was producing quality cow-punk bands like Lone Justice, Jason and the Scorchers and Green on Red, along with more sixties-sounding bands like REM and Rain Parade. Indeed his current girlfriend Carole Childs, an executive for Geffen Records, who seemed to have replaced Clydie King in his affections, had been responsible for signing up the most exciting of all the new bands, Lone Justice, and convinced Dylan to give them one of his new songs, a fairly lightweight number called 'Go 'Way Little Boy'. Since Lone Justice were also recording in New York that summer – toiling over their long-awaited debut album with producer Jimmy Iovine – Dylan turned up at the sessions to give them the song in person, accompanied again by Ron Wood.

Maria McKee: Carole Childs . . . was the woman who originally signed me to Geffen Records. She's very close to Dylan – very, very close – and she brought him to a gig or something . . . She said, 'Why don't you write Maria a song?' He said, 'OK.' . . . He came down to the studio when we were recording our first album and taught us the song. And he stayed around. He brought Ron Wood with him and they played on it . . . We ended up working on it a very long time because he didn't like the way I sang it . . . until I sang it like him! It got to the point where finally I just did my best Bob Dylan imitation – and he said, 'Ah, now you're doin' some REAL SINGING!'

Like most of the material recorded by Dylan himself in New York during July, 'Go 'Way Little Boy' did not end up included on the album it was intended for (it was later issued as a bonus track on a Lone Justice twelve-inch single).

By November 1984 Dylan's new album still required a cogent identity. Despite numerous recording sessions, enough normally to produce an entire album, Dylan had very little that he was happy with. New sessions in Los Angeles he again decided to produce himself, relying on house engineers to get the actual recordings down. However, he now had some further important compositions to add to 'When the Night Comes Falling from the Sky'.

One of the first songs recorded was 'Something's Burning, Baby', an ominous tune set to a slow march beat, seemingly an outlandish tangent to his 'Ain't Gonna Go to Hell for Anybody' theme. Dylan reworked the lyrics several times before settling on the final released version. The constantly changing words and his idiosyncratic singing certainly proved difficult for second vocalist, Madelyn Quebec, who was expected to sing live with him.

Ira Ingber: ['Something's Burning'] is a very weird song. And Maddy did not know the words when they did the vocal, 'cause I watched her trying to follow him. She was trying to sing harmonies with him live, which is tough because Bob doesn't necessarily know where he's going.

Even more impressive was a song that Dylan had co-written that fall with Sam Shepard, the playwright originally recruited in 1975 to work on *Renaldo and Clara*. The song was a twelve-minute epic based on a Gregory Peck film *The Gunfighter*, and was called 'New Danville Girl' (after a Woody Guthrie song, 'Danville Girl'). The idea started with Dylan and Shepard deciding to write a song along the lines of Lou Reed's 'Doin' the Things That We Want To', which was about attending one of Shepard's plays. In 'New Danville Girl', the singer seems to identify with the murderer of Peck's gunfighter character. The cinematic sweep of the singer's narrative about his travels through Texas, with and without his Danville Girl, makes the song Dylan's most epic since the comparable 'Lily, Rosemary and the Jack of Hearts'. Like the earlier song, it lent itself naturally to being visualized on celluloid. Indeed, according to Shepard the song was written with such an intention in mind.

Sam Shepard: It has to do with a guy standing on line and waiting to see an old Gregory Peck movie that he can't quite remember – only pieces of it, and then this whole memory thing happens, unfolding before his very eyes. He starts speaking internally to a woman . . . reliving the whole journey they'd gone on . . . We spent two days writing the lyrics – Bob had previously composed the melody line which was already down on tape . . . At one point he talked about making a video out of it.

The sessions at Cherokee Studios, where 'New Danville Girl' and 'Something's Burning, Baby' were recorded, featured some young LA musicians who had been rehearsing with Dylan at his Malibu home. Among them were Ira Ingber and Vince Melamed, who had been in a local band together, and Don Heffington, the then drummer with Lone Justice. According to Ingber, it was Heffington who made 'New Danville Girl' a much less daunting listening experience with his inspired timing and sense of the drama of the song.

Ira Ingber: Don [Heffington] really wrote 'Brownsville Girl's music, because as the drummer he played it with such dynamics that he actually created a song, because it's the same four chords that go over and over again, but the way Don played the drums would accentuate the choruses and come down for the verses.

Yet 'New Danville Girl' did not make it onto *Empire Burlesque*. Like the equally impressive 'Van Zandt' version of 'When the Night Comes Falling from the Sky', it was passed over to allow such fluff as 'Never Gonna Be the Same Again' and 'Emotionally Yours' to fill up the grooves. The inexplicable omission of 'New Danville Girl', like the removal of 'Blind Willie McTell' and 'Foot of Pride' from *Infidels*, gravely impaired the quality of an album which should have been a welcome continuation of the promise even the released *Infidels* managed to display. There seemed to be a deliberate perversity to Dylan's decision. The song's eventual inclusion, under the new title 'Brownsville Girl', on *Knocked Out Loaded*, meant that the song's quality went largely ignored, surrounded by the transparent 'filler' that constituted the remainder of that album.

Ira Ingber: When we first recorded ['Danville Girl'], we ... made a cassette. And he took it out and started playing it. He came back the next day we were working and said, 'Yeah, a lot of people like this thing.' And then he didn't do anything with it. It's like he was doing it to spite people who were all liking it and he just held on to it. He should have put it on *Empire Burlesque*, but he reworked it.

Thus, at the end of 1984, after six months of earnest work on the follow-up to *Infidels*, Dylan had recorded only two tracks which would eventually appear on *Empire Burlesque*. It seemed as if this new approach to recording was providing him with too many choices, too much opportunity to work on more and more material at his leisure.

When *Empire Burlesque* was finally released in June 1985, Dylan talked at length about his new approach to recording. With *Infidels*, he had spent three solid months working on an album. With *Empire Burlesque* the work-load was more evenly spread but it still represented an unprecedented expenditure of time on his part.

Bob Dylan: When I'm making a record I'll need some songs, and I'll start digging through my pockets and drawers trying to find these songs. Then I'll bring one out and I've never sung it before, sometimes I can't even remember the melody to it, and I'll get it in. Sometimes great things happen, sometimes not-so-great things happen. But regardless of what happens, when I do it in the studio it's the first time I've ever done it. I'm pretty much unfamiliar with it. In the past what's come out is what I've usually stuck with, whether it really knocked me out or not. For no apparent reason I've stuck with it, just from lack of commitment to taking the trouble to really get it right. I didn't want to record that way anymore. Now I'm recording more than I used to record. About two years ago I decided to get serious about it and just record . . . What I do now is just record all the time. Sometimes nothing comes out and other times I get a lot of stuff that I keep. I recorded [Empire Burlesque] for a long time. I just put down the songs that I felt as I wanted to put them down. Then I'd listen and decide if I liked them. And if I didn't like them I'd either re-record them or change something about them. [1985]

Further sessions at Cherokee Studios in Los Angeles and Power Station Studios in New York through the winter of 1985 provided most of the *Empire Burlesque* album. One session at the Power Station featured 'Miami' Steve Van Zandt, Springsteen's ex-guitarist, a noted producer in his own right. The only known result from this session with Van Zandt was a stunning new composition called 'When the Night Comes Falling from the Sky', a seven-minute apocalyptic vision which first simmers, then kicks in with an unrestrained Dylan vocal, ably supported by some fine keyboards from Roy Brittan and exemplary guitar work from Van Zandt. This recording would not be used on *Empire Burlesque*. When he chose to 're-record [songs] or change something about them', the results were fairly disastrous. One of the songs re-recorded after achieving a scintillating take was 'When the Night Comes Falling from the Sky', which acquired a whomping synthesizer/horns track which only served to obscure a less than impressive new Dylan vocal.

Also in New York that winter, he chose to rework an *Infidels* out-take, 'Someone's Got a Hold of My Heart'. The many new lines in every single case were inferior to the original and the dreadful overuse of his backing singers, the Queens of Rhythm, produced a disco-funk feel that destroyed the essence of a once-great song. The result, which would open *Empire Burlesque* as 'Tight Connection to My Heart', proved a taste of things to come.

The remainder of the winter 1984–5 cuts were largely mawkish ballads which would not have been out of place on *Nashville Skyline*, and suggested that any creative renaissance was receding fast. 'Seeing the Real You at Last' seems like a cut-up of half-remembered lines from Hollywood B-movies, and indeed contains many allusions to Humphrey Bogart movies, *Shane*, Clint Eastwood's *Bronco Billy* and even a *Star Trek* episode.

The final song for the album was recorded acoustically during preliminary mixing, as 'Wedding Song' had been on *Planet Waves*. 'Dark Eyes', though, is a hollow shell compared with 'Wedding Song'. Dylan sounds as if he were the worse for drink when he recorded the track. When trying to perform his one and only live version of the song, in Sydney in February 1986, he could no longer play the ridiculous, droning melody and wisely abandoned the attempt. Yet, with 'Dark Eyes', he felt that he had completed the album and that he could now turn it over to someone else for mixing.

Bob Dylan: I'm the final judge of what goes on and off my records. This last record I just did, *Empire Burlesque*, there were nine songs I knew belonged on it, and I needed a tenth. I had about four songs, and one of those was going to be the tenth song. I finally figured out that the tenth song needed to be acoustic, so I just wrote it. I wrote it because none of the other songs fit that spot, that certain place. [1985]

By the beginning of March Dylan had accumulated an innocuous enough collection of new songs – only 'Something's Burning, Baby' and 'When the Night Comes Falling from the Sky' having any real substance to them – to put together a pleasant if plain new album, an adequate holding exercise until he could weld his critical faculties to his wanton creative spirit. But having produced the sessions himself he decided he needed a helping hand to mix the album and hired first one producer who proved too meticulous for his tastes before settling on the inappropriate Arthur Baker.

Bob Dylan: [The other producer] listened to the songs too much. I could see him thinking too much, y'know; and then I saw him once and when he was mixing he would have rolls of paper writing notes. I didn't want that. So Arthur just listened to the stuff and said, 'Yeah.' And he fixed it up a lot. I listened to the sound of the previous record I made and the last one and it does sound better. [1985]

Though Dylan has proved skilful at presenting the illusion that he is concerned only with satisfying himself artistically, in 1985, as in 1983 or 1979 or 1970, he wanted his new album to be commercial and contemporary. Baker was the in-vogue producer whose work with Bruce Springsteen, New Order and assorted funk-exponents had given him some kind of pedigree. Unfortunately his idea of remixing was to place several extraneous layers of noise over perfectly acceptable basic tracks, cluttering up the sound and hiding what was in fact a conventional rock album behind the façade of eighties-style whomping drums and glistening synths. Though Baker gave the songs a unity of sound, it was not Dylan's sound. It seemed as if Dylan himself lacked the will to complete the album and passed it to an unsympathetic soul just to get it out.

Bob Dylan: I'm not too experienced at having records sound good. I don't know how to go about doing that, though I thought I got pretty close last time with Arthur Baker ... I just went out and recorded a bunch of stuff all over the place and then when it was time to put this record together I brought it all to him and he made it sound like a record. [1985]

Ron Wood referred to Dylan's inability or unwillingness to impose his authority when mixing the July 1984 material. A similar syndrome now entirely neutered what had started out as a promising follow-up to *Infidels*. Though *Empire Burlesque* was greeted reasonably favourably by the music press, its shallowness could not disguise for long a man treading water. Yet it would be four years before he again summoned up the effort to put in the requisite discipline to record another album of wholly original material.

Empire Burlesque was the end of Dylan's grand experiment in the modern studios of North America, which had all but kept him off the road for four years. Surprisingly Dylan agreed to promote this album – unlike *Infidels* – with a flurry of interviews, promotional videos and TV appearances, as if feeling the need to reverse his commercial decline but unwilling to readopt the punishing lifestyle of the road.

Returning to the States from a brief trip to Russia in early August, where he had been invited to perform at a Moscow poetry festival by Russian poet Yevtushenko and had travelled on to Odessa to visit the homeland of his ancestors, Dylan began an unprecedented bout of interviews intended to promote the new album, though *Empire Burlesque* was already descending the charts after a disappointing peak at number thirty-three, making the publicity a little belated.

Dylan was already beyond any real interest in his last album, and the August and September interviews became more an attempt to confront his own past. With a five-album boxed retrospective set and a revised edition of *Writings and Drawings* (covering up to *Empire Burlesque*) both planned for the fall, it seemed now was a time for summarizing and appraising the past. By far the best of these interviews was a remarkably in-depth series by Scott Cohen intended for a front-cover story in *Rolling Stone*'s new rival publication, *Spin*. Cohen managed to convince Dylan to answer his first questionnaire in twenty years. The categories included Three Authors I'd Read Anything By (Tacitus, Chekhov and Tolstoy) and Questions You Can't Answer. In the latter category Dylan came up with:

How does it feel to be a legend? How does it feel to have influenced a bunch of people? What did you change your name to? Are you somebody? Where's your music taking you? Did you write that song for me? Did you know Nixon?

In August, Dylan also completed two promotional videos for *Empire Burlesque*, a further belated attempt to promote the album. The first attempt to film a promo video for *Empire Burlesque* had been something of a failure. Having selected 'Tight Connection to My Heart' as the first single, Dylan asked for Paul Schrader to film the video of the song. Schrader, a noted film director, had just completed his Japanese epic *Mishima*, which had greatly impressed Dylan. Though Schrader agreed to the assignment, he required the video to be filmed in Japan. Thus in April, Dylan travelled to Tokyo to spend two days filming. The results were most disappointing, a story-video of no fixed abode. Both Schrader and Dylan would dismiss the video, Schrader claiming that it 'was a little piece of eye-candy I shot in Tokyo ... It means as little as it looks like it means.' Dylan was equally disappointed, apportioning a large part of the blame to Schrader. At a press conference in Sydney the following February, he observed:

Bob Dylan: I thought that I might be able to make a video with the man who made the movies and pull it off, but I was wrong. [1986]

Schrader had previously said that Dylan remained uncommunicative throughout the pre-shoot meeting and the two days' shooting, offering few ideas of his own. Nevertheless, Dylan did not abandon his idea of shooting a video which had something of the look of *Mishima*. Unfortunately his reason for wanting to shoot two videos in August in black and white was never relayed from 'executive producer' Dave Stewart, in whom Dylan confided, to the actual video directors Markus Innocenti and Eddie Arno.

Markus Innocenti and Eddie Arno: We were simply told by Dave that black and white was required. We weren't told why. In fact, we wished that Dylan had talked directly to us earlier, because we learned that Dylan wanted it to look like an old Japanese movie, and we could have filmed it differently. When we saw Paul Schrader's *Mishima* we understood why Dylan wanted it. If you ever watch that movie look out for the black and white sequences. It would be interesting to put Dylan's music over the images – there would be something extraordinary, quite beyond what a music video can do. We could really understand why Dylan wanted Schrader for 'Tight Connection to My Heart', but once the project had not lived up to his expectations it is reasonable to think that he wanted to try again [to] get the wonderful beauty and stillness that black and white can achieve.

The two videos to be shot on 22 and 23 August in Los Angeles were the A and B sides of the second *Empire Burlesque* single, 'When the Night Comes Falling from the Sky' and 'Emotionally Yours'. Dylan wanted this time to revert to the performance-type video used on 'Sweetheart Like You', and a little-used church on Sunset Boulevard was the locale suggested. Dylan actually had a tenuous thread in mind to link the two videos, which involved the idea of an ex-girlfriend in the audience during the performance of 'When the Night Comes Falling from the Sky' whom he would later reminisce about in 'Emotionally Yours'.

Markus Innocenti and Eddie Arno: Dylan is having an affair with a new girl. Dressed in buckskin she goes with him to the gig where the band play 'When the Night Comes Falling'. Unknown to Dylan, a former lover – also an attractive brunette dressed in buckskin – has seen Dylan on the way to the gig. She comes to watch the performance but the memories are too much and she has to leave, close to tears. She wanders off down Hollywood Boulevard without approaching him again. This is where 'When the Night Comes Falling' ends and 'Emotionally Yours' begins. But Dylan has carried a torch for this buckskin-clad, dark-eyed beauty – why else would his new girlfriend be such a replica of the first? After the gig Dylan is left alone in the hall. Playing an acoustic guitar, his memories go back to his original Buckskin Girl. With regret, he remembers the moment when he told her the relationship was over.

Another element that Dylan wanted in the videos was having the band look as if it was one of his 'band of gypsies' revues that he still liked.

Markus Innocenti and Eddie Arno: Dylan and Dave wanted . . . a 'band of gypsies' atmosphere. For example, on the bus there was Dylan's Buckskin Girl, Dave's girlfriend Clare playing a journalist, a host of celebrated musicians and one of the waiters from the Talesai restaurant in the role of 'Dylan's Manager'. It was very loose and chaotic. Dylan also wanted a Juggler at the concert. The Juggler was another chaotic/symbolic element who was to be standing in the wings as the band played. We decided to edit him out – it looked too contrived for our taste.

Unfortunately the results were once more disappointing, suggesting again that Dylan could still not come to terms with the video medium. The film–video conversion was poorly executed and the black and white film when broadcast looked washy; it had none of the clarity and stillness Dylan was looking for. At Stewart's behest, several negative flashes intended to resemble the white light of nuclear blasts were inserted into 'When the Night Comes Falling from the Sky' which gave a false ring to the video and detracted from the sketchy storyline. Also the broadcast of the videos separately and several weeks apart meant that any continuity between the two was lost on a jaundiced MTV audience. One positive result, though, came through Dylan's insistence that all the instruments used in the shoot be real, so that the participants could jam between takes, to alleviate the inevitable boredom.

Markus Innocenti and Eddie Arno: He jammed extensively with the band, mostly twelve-bar blues, though he didn't sing. He was more interested in riffing or taking solos on guitar.

Playing to the handful of extras who had responded to a local radio ad wanting help in filming a Dylan video – no one believed the request was genuine until Dave Stewart went on the air himself – Dylan seemed again to be enjoying the idea of playing live, even if they were only jamming. He later told Mikal Gilmore of the *Los Angeles Herald-Examiner*:

Bob Dylan: [Dave Stewart] put together a great band for this lip-sync video and set us up with equipment on this little stage in a church somewhere in West LA. So between all the time they took setting up camera shots and lights and all that stuff, we could just play live for this little crowd that had gathered there. I can't even express how good that felt – in fact, I was trying to remember the last time I'd felt that kind of direct connection. [1985]

Ironically, despite *Empire Burlesque*'s many flaws, the failure of the promo videos to incite any real interest and Dylan's disinclination to return to the road, 1985 was a year in which his public profile was at its highest since 1979. Largely this was because it was the year that American pop music decided to develop a conscience. The 'We Are the World' single, recorded in January 1985, and the huge Live Aid benefit shows in London and Philadelphia in July – both designed to provide funds to aid starving Ethiopians – inevitably involved Dylan, whose profile as the conscience of pop music was perhaps somewhat more long-standing than those of Simple Minds and U2. Though he remained unconvinced of the merits of 'We Are the World', he recognized a worthy cause. And the author of a song about grain elevators bursting while people were starving could hardly refuse to participate.*

Bob Dylan: People buying a song and the money going to starving people in Africa . . . is a worthwhile idea but I wasn't so convinced about the message of the song. To tell you the truth I don't think people can save themselves. [1985]

'We Are the World' reminded the American public that Dylan was still alive and kicking, but Live Aid quickly undid a lot of the good publicity. Though many of the reasons behind his disastrous appearance at Live Aid, in front of an estimated two billion viewers, lay outside his control, it was perceived at the time as evidence that Dylan could not even sing his old songs with any conviction, let alone write new songs of quality and perform them.

Though what happened on stage was largely out of Dylan's hands, his decision not to play solo, nor with Tom Petty's Heart-breakers, as had been suggested, but to perform accompanied by Ron Wood and Keith Richards, was certainly his. And it proved an unfortunate one. Matters started propitiously enough. Dylan was unsure what to do at Live Aid and mentioned his predicament when round at Ron Wood's New York apartment.

Ron Wood: Bob says, 'I'm playing in Philadelphia the day after tomorrow.' I didn't even know about Live Aid. He says, 'It's a big charity thing.' He says, 'Bill Graham's got a band for me and I have to go along with it.' Then he says, 'Do you think that maybe you and me could play together sometime?' I said, 'Sure. Let's do the gig on Saturday.' He said, 'Really?' I said, 'Yeah. You don't necessarily have to go along with Bill Graham.' And I said, 'Keith would love to do it too.' So I rang Keith up and I said, 'Get over here because Bob wants us to do Live Aid with him.' He said, 'You'd better not be lying, Woody.' . . . Some of the rehearsal tapes from my basement in New York are incredible. We were playing in there for a couple of days. We were playing in the upstairs dining room just before we left for Philadelphia and it was brilliant. When we got to the stadium he was saying, 'I wonder what Bill Graham wants me to do?' We were going, 'Do what you want to do, Bob!' But he was saying, 'Bill might make me do this.' Very odd. He wanted to be bossed around again. Even going up the ramps – we'd decided what songs we were going to play and he turns and says, 'Hey! Maybe I

---

* The song was 'Slow Train'.

should do "All I Really Want To Do"!' We were going, 'Aargh! Oh my God!'

When Dylan went onstage he discovered that he could not hear a thing. The stage monitors had been switched off and there were assorted would-be singers practising their grand moment, singing the 'We Are the World' finale behind the curtain at the back of him.

Bob Dylan: They screwed around with us. We didn't even have any monitors out there. When they threw in the grand finale at the last moment they took all the settings off and set the stage up for the thirty people who were standing behind the curtain. We couldn't even hear our own voices, and when you can't hear, you can't play; you don't have any timing. It's like proceeding on radar. [1985]

Also Keith Richards seemed to be on some other planet, which was not as yet receiving this global broadcast. Dylan started with 'Hollis Brown', but was having genuine problems pitching his voice without monitors and with the racket coming from behind. By 'When the Ship Comes In' his voice was all over the place, and 'Blowin' in the Wind' was sung hurriedly and without meaning. Dylan just wanted to get off stage, and Ron Wood seemed anxious to join him!

Ron Wood: We came off looking like real idiots.

Live Aid did have one silver lining. After 'Ballad of Hollis Brown' Dylan asked the millions watching to remember those in their own country who were starving and struggling because of economic events that were beyond their control. In particular he asked that we remember the plight of the American farmers. Though his comments struck an oddly inappropriate, not to say discordant, note among all the self-congratulatory back-patting that had gone on all day, Willie Nelson took it as his cue to organize a further event in September to publicize the plight of American farmers. Farm Aid would signal Dylan's return to peak performing powers.

34

1985–6: Junco and His Partners in Crime

It was inevitable that Dylan would appear at Farm Aid. Having been responsible for the genesis of the idea with his comments at Live Aid, he could hardly refuse Willie Nelson when the call came. Since the conclusion of the benefit was scheduled to be broadcast on national prime-time TV live that Saturday, 22 September, it also gave him an opportunity to reaffirm his credibility as a live performer after the Live Aid débâcle.

This time he decided to follow Bill Graham's original suggestion for Live Aid, and ask Tom Petty and the Heartbreakers if they would like to provide him with the necessary backing. He had already utilized the bulk of the Heartbreakers on *Shot of Love* and *Empire Burlesque*, the latter of which featured organist Benmont Tench, guitarist Mike Campbell and bassist Howie Epstein. The Heartbreakers were scheduled to perform their own set at the benefit, so it was unlikely to be an imposition to back Dylan as well.

Tom Petty: He just phoned up after Live Aid – it was for the Farm Aid thing – he didn't want to try an acoustic set with no soundcheck again. And I said 'come on down and we'll try it out'. And he did, and we had a marvellous time. We played for hours, all week long.

Dylan and the band began rehearsing a week before Farm Aid, on a soundstage at Universal Studios in Hollywood. The Heartbreakers seemed prepared to play just about any kind of song. Dylan was in his element. They tried every genre from Hank Williams through Spector, Motown, blues and Tin Pan Alley. Very little time was spent working on Dylan's own songs. Yet there was clearly a chemistry between him and the Heartbreakers, and everyone seemed to be revelling in the experience of playing whatever they felt like playing.

Benmont Tench: He knows a million songs, old delta blues songs and stuff like that. Well, they sound like they may be delta blues songs. Sometimes I'm not sure if they're blues songs or a new arrangement of 'It's Alright Ma'.

On the final day of rehearsals a film crew arrived to film a brief excerpt for a profile of Dylan scheduled to be broadcast on the 20/20 TV programme. He looked comfortable, chatting between takes with the girl singers he had brought in to augment the Heartbreakers, and even improvising a version of 'Forever Young' for the TV cameras.

On the night before Farm Aid, Dylan and the band ran through a half-hour soundcheck, determined to avoid a repeat of Live Aid. Even here they sounded tight and revved up to play. The performance the following day was a revelation. Though Dylan had given some impressive performances on the 1984 European tour, it had been four years since his triumphant 1981 European tour, and after the disappointing American tour of that year and the only sporadically impressive '84 tour, little was expected from him.

Yet, at Farm Aid, from the first song Dylan was magnificent. The band also played with a fire lacking at recent Heartbreakers shows. Having ripped through 'Clean Cut Kid' and a semi-original reworking of an old blues tune, 'Shake', Dylan quietened things down with a surprisingly effective 'I'll Remember You', during which he duetted with poor Madelyn Quebec, who bravely wrestled with his vocal idiosyncrasies. 'Trust Yourself' had him punching the air with the exhilaration of it all; then a heartbreaking rendition of 'That Lucky Old Sun' led into the appropriate 'Maggie's Farm', Dylan's timing and intonation never more impressive.

Though only three and a half of the six songs were broadcast on national TV, the sheer verve of the performance and the joy of a man back on stage with a great band were evident for all to see. Farm Aid proved the perfect antidote to Live Aid. It also represented the culmination of a period when Dylan was rarely out of the news. With three videos receiving regular rotation on MTV; two live broadcasts in just over two months on national TV; a fifteen-minute profile on the popular 20/20 TV show; and interviews syndicated that fall by the *Los Angeles Times* and the *Los Angeles Herald-Examiner*, plus the *Spin* front-cover on their December issue and further interviews with *Rolling Stone* and *Time*, he had never had such a high media profile.

In November a five-album boxed set retrospective, featuring a
dozen rare cuts to entice the collectors, provided a bewildering
summary of the most important *œuvre* in rock music. Dylan
himself was not unduly impressed by the project, which had been
compiled by Jeff Rosen, an employee of his music publishing
company, Special Rider. The set was entitled *Biograph*.

Bob Dylan: There's some stuff that hasn't been heard before, but most
of my stuff has already been bootlegged, so to anybody in the know,
there's nothing on it they haven't heard before . . . All it is, really, is
repackaging, and it'll just cost a lot of money. About the only thing that
makes it special is Cameron's book. [1985]

'Cameron's book' was a lavish thirty-two page album-size
résumé of Dylan's career, freely composed from a series of anecdotes provided by Dylan to Cameron Crowe. Allowed the opportunity to comment on his own history, he talked effusively
about matters which he most delighted in, or which had most
upset or angered him. Also, following in the tradition of Neil
Young's *Decade*, he provided brief (and some not so brief) commentaries on the songs chosen for the five-album set, which
proved occasionally illuminating.

The combination of Dylan's high profile, the impressive look of
the set, and its motley assortment of favourites and unreleased
gems proved surprisingly popular in America, where *Biograph*
became only the second ever such boxed set to receive a gold disc
(the other being the posthumous eight-album *Elvis Aaron Presley*
collection), and the first to reach the heights of thirty-three in the
Billboard charts. *Biograph* would spawn a plethora of imitations. In
the age of eighty-minute CDs, record companies now realize the
potential of such retrospectives, and, with rock music well into its
fourth decade, many sixties artists warrant such collections.

Biograph was not the only résumé of his career Dylan provided
at this time. As well as the interviews he was freely giving, and in
which he seemed happy to talk about all aspects of his career,
November also saw the publication of *Lyrics*, which provided the
lyrics to all of Dylan's published songs up to and including *Empire
Burlesque*. Though *Lyrics* was something of a disappointment, in
that Dylan refrained from including many of the songs he had left
off his post-*Desire* albums – songs of the quality of 'Blind Willie
McTell', 'New Danville Girl' and 'Angelina' – the book was well
produced and sold well.

Also in November, Dylan began rehearsing with the Heartbreakers and working on his follow-up to *Empire Burlesque*. Clearly Farm Aid had been a necessary fillip to getting him active again. The studio sessions which he undertook in November were in fact conducted in London, his first English sessions in twenty years. At the behest of Dave Stewart of the Eurythmics, he travelled there to record for four days at Stewart's own studio in Crouch End. However, he had few new lyrics, and the sessions were primarily used to provide backing tracks, of which supposedly some twenty were recorded, two of which were excerpted on the BBC's *Whistle Test* programme. Only one of the tracks from these sessions was later included on *Knocked Out Loaded*.

Preliminary rehearsals in early November confirmed Dylan and the Heartbreakers' interest in continuing their association. Now that he had the itch to perform again, plans were made for a Far East tour in the winter of 1985–6, his first Far East tour in eight years, and, if these gigs went well, a summer US tour was on the cards. Rehearsals for the tour were quite extensive, taking up most of December and January. The precedent set by the Farm Aid rehearsals was upheld, as Dylan and the band again worked up reams of 'covers', including several songs more associated with crooners than with the croaky chords of Dylan: 'This Was My Love' (made famous by Sinatra), 'We Three' (an old Inkspots chestnut) and 'All My Tomorrows' (another Sinatra song).

Though this helped maintain Dylan's interest in the extensive pre-tour rehearsals, these diversions were again leading him away from the matter at hand – to work up a professional set of primarily Dylan originals which would constitute a two-hour show for the Japanese and Australasians. When Dylan and the band arrived in Auckland, New Zealand, on 3 February 1986 a further rehearsal was in order and, the night before opening at the open-air Wellington Athletic Park, they ran through a three-and-a-quarter-hour soundcheck-cum-rehearsal. The volume of the sound-check and the open-air stadium's proximity to local residences led to many complaints to the police, and the opening concert was under serious threat of cancellation.

Ironically, after probably more rehearsals than for any previous tour, the first shows in Wellington and Auckland were both scrappy affairs, with little evidence of two months' rehearsing. Petty was quoted as saying, 'What we've done is take the rehearsals on the stage.' If not the literal truth, Petty's comments were not far off. Apart from including such obscure 'covers' as Ricky

Nelson's 'Lonesome Town', Warren Smith's 'Uranium Rock', Hank Snow's 'I'm Movin' On' and John Hiatt and Ry Cooder's 'Across the Borderline', each Australasian show featured an opening blues jam and a Dylan/Petty duet on the country nugget 'I Forgot More (Than You'll Ever Know)'. Throughout the tour Dylan continued to pull his usual set of surprises on the band, though the Heartbreakers were more adept than most at dealing with them.

Mike Campbell: There's a lot of room for free playing in his songs, which makes everything pretty spontaneous. It's just never the same – that's the only way I can describe it. During one show in Australia we were supposed to do 'When the Night Comes Falling from the Sky', and he didn't feel like doing it. He turned around to me and said, 'You know the chords for "All Along the Watchtower", don't you?' And we'd never rehearsed it. I said, 'There's only three, right?' And he said, 'Yeah, let's go!' You never know what's coming. There'll be different songs, or we'll do the same thing in different keys. It reminds me of a highschool dance band. It's more polished maybe, but it has that looseness, that freshness, that chaos.

Perhaps Stan Lynch, the Heartbreakers' drummer, came closest to unravelling the rationale behind Dylan's approach, an approach which has remained consistent throughout twenty-five years of playing live with bands.

Stan Lynch: There's nothing tentative about Dylan onstage. I've seen gigs where the songs have ended in all the wrong places, where it's fallen apart, and it's almost as if, in some perverse way, he gets energy from that chaos.

The results, though, were considerably more hit-and-miss than Farm Aid had been. After the first show, Dylan seemed to have decided the pacing of the second half needed tightening up. The sad result was that three of his recent songs were dropped from the set – 'Shot of Love', 'Heart of Mine' and 'Gotta Serve Somebody' – making the shows considerably more weighted towards his older material, as in 1984. Dylan also was considerably less fired up than at Farm Aid, possibly burnt out by the rehearsals. The Far East shows still had their moments, and throughout Dylan was surprisingly talkative, regularly quoting Tennessee Williams in a prologue to 'Lenny Bruce':

Bob Dylan: Here's a song about recognition, or lack of recognition. Tennessee Williams, it was he who said: 'I don't ask for your pity, just your understanding. Not even that, but just your recognition of me in you, and Time, the enemy in us all.' Tennessee Williams led a pretty drastic life. He died all by himself in a New York hotel room without a friend in the world. Another man died like that . . . —

He regularly prefaced 'Ballad of a Thin Man' with a story about how he refused to answer questions at a press conference in England in 1965, insisting that a man's life speaks for itself; concluded 'Rainy Day Women' by admitting it was a song that could be taken a couple of ways, as could a lot of his songs; and one night in Sydney introduced a one-off performance of 'License to Kill' by stating that it was 'a song about the space-programme', before dedicating the song to the seven people who had tragically been killed in an American rocket days earlier. If he seemed to be supporting the space programme, he then added, 'They had no business being up there in the first place . . . as if we haven't got enough problems down here on earth.' Though the Sydney crowd roared their approval, it suggested he was considerably out of step with American public opinion. His most unequivocal statement, though, came before the final song of the main set, 'In the Garden'. The 1986 shows suggested he had successfully assimilated the religious songs into his repertoire, after the 1984 tour, when the religious songs were virtually ignored, and he obviously wished to make it clear that his beliefs remained intact.

Bob Dylan: This last song now is all about my hero. Everybody's got a hero. Where I come from there's a lot of heroes. Plenty of them. John Wayne, Clark Gable, Richard Nixon, Ronald Reagan, Michael Jackson, Bruce Springsteen. They're all heroes to some people. Anyway, I don't care nothing about those people. I have my own hero. I'm going to sing about him right now . . . When they came for him in the garden . . .

Dylan reinforced the message by using a version of this rap to open an hour-long cable TV special filmed at Sydney and broadcast on American TV in June. His talkativeness and the length of the shows suggest he remained in good humour throughout the month-long tour, as does a TV interview he gave in Sydney and a well-publicized press conference, also in Sydney. He enjoyed the company of two special guests at different Sydney shows, Mark Knopfler and Stevie Nicks, and returned the favour for Knopfler by joining Dire Straits for four songs in Melbourne. The final four shows in Japan also suggested that Dylan and the Heartbreakers were increasingly comfortable with each other and that a US tour would make sense.

With a three-month gap in Dylan's schedule, CBS succeeded in convincing him of the importance of having 'product' available for such a major tour – his first US tour in five years and with the Heartbreakers, a popular outfit in their own right. As such early in April he set about recording a new album at a small studio in the beautiful Topanga Canyon, conveniently located between Malibu and LA. His initial intention was to get an album down quickly and with a minimum of fuss, as in the old days. Gone was the will to toil over the finished product evidenced on his previous two albums.

Ira Ingber: He did some stuff with Petty that was done somewhere else in the Valley, but we did pretty much a month-long run. He said, 'Can we do it in a week?' I said, 'I don't think we can do it in a week.' He just wanted a band to play and to sing, but then we got into the recording world, which is a different mentality. He realized he was into this thing a little deeper than he initially thought.

The various ensembles that came and went during his month-long stint at Skyline Studios would take an entire book to catalogue as Dylan looked to produce the necessary chemistry with assorted West Coast musicians. Charlie Quintana was invited one day with two guitarists he knew, but the results were unimpressive.

Charlie Quintana: There was . . . a studio session, proper full-blown recording studio at Skyline in Topanga Canyon. I took these two guys, one an incredible bass player and an incredible guitar player, both extremely good technically. I said, When we get there and start playing, just follow me. Just follow me. Rule number one . . . I'd already played with Bob for three months, so I knew more or less the way the routine was. But when we got to the session, these guys both wanted to get the gig so desperately bad and they were just so in awe of Bob that they rushed the whole fucking thing . . . In the middle of it all I took 'em to the bathroom and said, 'What the fuck are you guys doing? I told you, watch me!' But it went over their heads.

Ira Ingber, who had done sterling work on 'Something's Burning' and 'New Danville Girl', was asked to work out an arrangement of an old Ray Charles song, but when it came to recording the song, Dylan seemed unable or unwilling to stick with it.

Ira Ingber: He wanted me to do an arrangement for him of 'Come Rain or Come Shine'. It's a beautiful song and he gave me the record. We took down the chords, brought in the band and tried playing it. It's a fairly complicated song and he wanted me to show him how to play it

... I showed him, but there's some really weird chords because it's an orchestra arrangement, not piano or guitar. The chords more or less reflect the complexity, and Bob couldn't play those chords too well because they're not even guitar-player chords, they're orchestral chords, and he got kinda discouraged by that.

According to Mikal Gilmore, who attended several of the sessions for a cover-story for *Rolling Stone*, the early sessions also featured the Tex-Mex band Los Lobos, T-Bone Burnett, Al Kooper and Steve Douglas, though only Douglas would make a major contribution on the finished album. Kooper became rapidly disenchanted with the whole ambience of the sessions and Dylan's approach to the recording and, after doing his best to provide input, gave it up as a bad lot. He insists, however, that there was much of worth recorded at these early sessions.

Al Kooper: I didn't care for the drive, I didn't care for the engineer or the studio too much either. There was enough stuff cut on *Knocked Out Loaded* to have put out a great album. There was some really wonderful things cut at those sessions, but I don't think we'll ever hear 'em ... I was really frustrated because then I was involved in a way that I get involved and I made suggestions and all that and then I just sort of fucked off. And then I heard that record, and the only thing was 'Brownsville Girl'. There was more stuff as exciting as that was.

According to Gilmore, Dylan recorded some twenty songs of 'r&b, Chicago-steeped blues, rambunctious gospel and raw-toned hillbilly forms'. Yet *Knocked Out Loaded* provides precious little evidence of these recordings, only the opening track, 'Junior' Parker's 'You Wanna Ramble', falling into any of the above categories.

Though Kooper suggests there was quality original material recorded, the inescapable problem was simply Dylan proving to be incapable of writing new songs of sufficient quality to merit release. Generally in the past the prospect of imminent recording commitments proved a fillip to his writing, but this time little of worth came about. Taking a brief respite to work with the Heartbreakers at a nearby studio in Van Nuys, he attempted to produce some new songs with them.

Tom Petty: I had booked some time at Sound City for something Dylan wanted to do – he was makin' a record. Then it turned out he wasn't gonna be ready at that time.

Petty and the band got on with recording their own album,

managing just one track with Dylan, 'Got My Mind Made Up', though Dylan also contributed to a Petty song called 'Jammin' Me'. Clearly even working with a band whom he felt comfortable with was not producing results. The final evidence of his writer's block came when he returned to Topanga Canyon and decided to abandon most of his previous work and to produce a pot-pourri collection of half-finished songs and out-takes from earlier sessions.

Mikal Gilmore: Somewhere along the line he has decided to put aside most of the rock & roll tracks he had been working on in Topanga . . . [instead] assembling the album from various sessions that have accrued over the last year. 'It's all sort of stuff,' he says. 'It doesn't really have a theme or a purpose.'

Whatever the flaws evident on his albums of the previous decade, all had maintained a certain integrity. *Knocked Out Loaded* sounds like Dylan's first 'bootleg' album since *Self Portrait*, another album with an identity crisis. Of the eight basic tracks, one came from the session/s with the Heartbreakers at Sound City, one from the November 1985 London sessions, three from the *Empire Burlesque* sessions and the remaining three from the Topanga Canyon sessions — all of which were covers. The final few sessions at Skyline were taken up with reworking the 1984–5 out-takes. 'Maybe Someday' was given new words, as was 'Driftin' Too Far from Shore' and 'Under My Spell'. More importantly, Dylan decided to rework 'New Danville Girl', now retitled 'Brownsville Girl'. Utilizing the basic backing track from November 1984, he changed several lines, added an over-zealous wailing girls' chorus (courtesy of the omnipresent Queens of Rhythm), a trumpet and Steve Douglas's saxophone plus an impressive new Dylan vocal.

Dave Garfield: ['Brownsville Girl'] was one of the ones he would stop in the middle of things, sit down for fifteen minutes or so right here in the lounge and start penning some new lyrics.

'Brownsville Girl' saved *Knocked Out Loaded* from total disposability, but it also highlighted the dearth of comparable material now coming from Dylan's pen. Despite a lovely seductive sound to the album, lapses of taste in the use of children and steel drums on 'They Killed Him' and 'Precious Memories', a total running time of thirty-five minutes and perhaps the most gaudy of all his album covers quickly destined the record for the cut-out bins.

Knocked Out Loaded continued the steady commercial decline since *Infidels*, failing even to make the Top Fifty, despite its release at a time when Dylan was making a very successful tour of the US. The punters preferred to spend their money on concert tickets. Dylan himself seemed equally unconvinced of the album's merits, refusing to play any songs from it throughout a two-month long tour, save for 'Got My Mind Made Up' on the opening night and a chorus of 'Brownsville Girl' at the final show.

On 6 June Dylan and the Heartbreakers warmed up for their US jaunt with a three-song set at Inglewood Forum, part of an Amnesty International benefit. Dylan chose the appropriate 'License to Kill' and his new single 'Band of the Hand', recorded with the Heartbreakers back in February but omitted from *Knocked Out Loaded*. Both songs' portrayals of a world run by the mad and the corrupt were apposite to the cause of political prisoners. The concluding 'Shake a Hand' was less relevant, though it featured an outrageously loose Dylan vocal. All in all the Amnesty show was a very positive omen for the forthcoming tour.

Sadly the 1986 US tour acted out in reverse the progress of the 1984 tour, starting with impressive shows on the West Coast but rapidly running out of steam and spluttering to a conclusion two months later back at Inglewood Forum. Dylan seemed to be coasting through most of the songs and there were few highlights. Dylan also adopted his 'arena voice', more shouting than singing, so in evidence in 1974, 1978 and 1984. The torpor seemed to affect even the Heartbreakers, who, on their home patch, were given a larger part of the show but whose eight songs defined the meaning of the phrase 'going through the motions'.

At the age of forty-five, Dylan was clearly not able to give his all throughout two-hour shows, but seemed determined to defy time by pushing himself through them rather than performing a briefer more cogent set. The tour was well received, though more for the selection of old favourites performed than the way they were actually sung. The summer US tour was a disappointing conclusion to twelve months of considerable activity, which had failed to produce much of enduring worth save for the single performance at Farm Aid. Yet, when compared with the next twelve months, the period from September 1985 through to August 1986 would later seem like an oasis of creative genius.

1986-7: Down Among the Deadheads

Typically, Dylan reserved his best performance in six months for a soundcheck. In early August, singing with verve and commitment and backed by the Heartbreakers, he ran through Hank Williams' 'Thank God', for a Lubavitchers' telethon intended to raise funds for an anti-drug programme. It was not broadcast until September, by which time he was in England.

He had decided it was time to make his return to celluloid. He had talked to Dave Stewart about wanting to make his own film when shooting the two *Empire Burlesque* videos in August 1985, and when interviewed during filming in England in September 1986, he admitted to an abiding interest in making his own film.

Bob Dylan: I do have plans to make a movie ... It's a complicated story about a piano player who gets into trouble because of a good buddy of his, and then he winds up doing some book work for a woman whose husband has disappeared, marries her, then falls in love with his daughter. And the other guy finally shows up again and the movie comes to a screeching halt. [1986]

This did not exactly accord with the elemental film he had discussed with Stewart, but clearly *Renaldo and Clara* had not satisfied his filmic impulses. As part of the process of feeling his way back into movie-making he had agreed, before the summer tour, to star in a movie to be directed by *Jagged Edge* director Richard Marquand. It was called *Hearts of Fire*.

Richard Marquand: I discovered that he's always been interested in film – I mean not only the Peckinpah film but his own film; that it's always something that has intrigued him, and now at this stage of his life, forty-six, forty-seven, he's thinking, 'Well, let's really try it out, let's see if I'm any good.'

The storyline of the script he was given featured him as Billy

Parker, a disillusioned ex-rock & roll star who takes an aspiring singer with him to England. There she meets James Colt a contemporary rock star played by Rupert Everett, who shares with Parker a mystifying lust for the distinctly asexual leading lady, played by Fiona Flanagan.

Portraying Dylan as an ageing and somewhat cynical rock & roll star who threw his hand in at the height of his fame and retired to the backwoods to raise chickens was playing on popular perceptions of him. However, the element in the screenplay which gave his character an added dimension by having him play some Jesse James–type outlaw figure who enjoyed robbing toll booths, Burger Kings and even concert halls was cut from the final film.

The rather predictable shooting script required that the Fiona character exude enough charisma and sensuality to ensnare two very jaundiced rock & rollers, while also impressing a modern rock audience. In fact Flanagan exuded the sensuality of Kleenex and the charisma of a parrot, and inevitably the film was a commercial and critical disaster. Ironically Dylan, despite insisting that there were 'a hundred guys I know who could have played this role', was one of the few highlights of the movie. Though still unable to mime to a pre-recorded track, and struggling to memorize his words, on screen he did exude a kind of stiff charisma, as the film's line producer observed:

Iain Smith: In *Hearts of Fire* I think he's arguably the best thing in the film. It's not because he's a great actor, it's because Richard has worked very hard to bring out, by cutting and editing Bob's material, what is in the man, which is his natural charisma ... He's funny and quirky and strange and you watch him on the screen and you think, Well he's not acting ... but, and it's a bit odd, he's very very watchable. You just want to watch him. And it's a totally undefinable quality.

A premonition of the likely reception for the movie came at a hastily arranged press conference on Dylan's arrival in England before the start of filming. Despite his insistence that he was only interested in making the movie, the journalists expressed no interest in his co-stars or director, and doggedly pursued him to answer the one question that burned in all their minds: What the hell was a poet and songwriter like Dylan doing in tripe like this?

The one revealing reply from Dylan came when he was asked about the half-a-dozen songs he had supposedly written for the movie. Admitting that he had not yet written them, he stated he would be writing them during filming. In fact the soundtrack sessions were due to commence in just ten days. However, his writer's block had not let up. Ten days later all he had come up with was two execrable efforts, 'Had a Dream about You Baby' and 'Night after Night'. At least two further songs were required, so he drew from other writers, singing John Hiatt's 'The Usual', with some panache, as well as a pleasant enough acoustic version of Shel Silverstein's 'Couple More Years', a song which summed up the theme of the movie far more concisely and artistically than the ninety minutes of squandered celluloid that made up *Hearts of Fire*. When in 'Couple More Years', he sang: 'It ain't that I'm wiser/It's just that I spent more time with my back to the wall' it perhaps defined the experience of making the movie.

Ironically Dylan did make one of his more notable film appearances while on the *Hearts of Fire* set. The highly respected BBC Omnibus team was intent on making a fifty-minute documentary about him, entitled *Getting to Dylan*. Marquand, as a former Omnibus director himself, provided what help he could, but as Dylan flew out of England for Ontario at the beginning of October, they had so far failed to ensnare their prey.

Richard Marquand: They didn't know quite what they were going to do, but they knew that this was a chance to maybe find some sort of framework to do a film on Bob – the framework of the making of the movie. Bob, in the end, opened up to them quite a lot.

It took a further two weeks of filming in Hamilton, Ontario, before Dylan finally consented to a filmed interview with Omnibus director Christopher Sykes. When he did, the twenty-five minute interview, which was the centre-piece of the *Getting to Dylan* documentary, proved to be a remarkable exchange. It may not have been Sykes's intention to produce a fifty-minute update on *Don't Look Back*, yet that is the way *Getting to Dylan* comes across. It was as if Sykes had been intent on saying, 'Well, let us see what happened to that man.'

In 1986 Dylan was twenty-one years on from *Don't Look Back*, the film of the 1965 English tour which perpetually froze him in monochrome hipness. In the first flush of fame he had parried every question with lightning wit. The very prototype of super-cool. The lines, whether scourging self-analysis – 'You're gonna die . . . You do your work in the face of that' – or half-whispered dismissals – 'Oh, you're one of those. I understand now' – defined a Dylan persona for, if not all time, some considerable time.

In 1986 Dylan was again in England to make a movie, though this time there was no tour to punctuate the nights. In *Getting to*

Dylan, we see him pursued by BBC cameras, a mystified *Hearts of Fire* film crew, and of course his fans. The one-to-one interview in *Getting to Dylan*, like Horace Judson's in *Don't Look Back*, represents the climactic point of the film. Are we finally going to see a glimpse of the private Dylan? Can the public image be reconciled with the private man? There is not the brutal intensity of the earlier interview. He insists at the outset that if the interviewer is looking for revelation 'it just ain't gonna come'. Yet he proceeds to show a man with few secrets to conceal.

Bob Dylan: Fame, everybody just kind of copes with it a different way. But nobody seems to think it's really what they were after . . . It's like, say you're passing a little pub or an inn, and you look through the window and you see all the people eating and talking and carrying on, you can watch outside the window and you can see them all be very real with each other. As real as they're gonna be, because when you walk into the room it's over. You won't see them being real anymore.

In 1965 Dylan's screening system had been brutal arrogance – the best form of defence is attack – and there were precious few instances of chinks in the armour. In 1986 the armour had become more of a burden than those it was designed to safeguard against. His response to his iconography now suggested a dramatic isolation from the outside world. By his own admission, he saw only rare glimpses outside the walls he had constructed back in the mid-sixties to safeguard his privacy.

Bob Dylan: I don't know what people think of me. I only know about what record companies say . . . and managers and people like that. People who want you to do things . . . I only hear about that stuff.

Getting to Dylan remains the essential filmed portrait of Dylan in the eighties, an important adjunct to *Don't Look Back*, *Eat the Document* and *Renaldo and Clara*, the three previous films to deal with the Dylan myth.

Hearts of Fire took a year to be released in England, after which it lasted barely three weeks on general release before disappearing from the cinemas; within eighteen months it was released on video, to universal apathy. The film's financiers, Lorimar Pictures, decided to cut their losses and abandoned a US cinema release, which would have required considerable publicity and attendant costs. The film had to wait until the spring of 1990 for commercial video release in the US. It seemed that Dylan was not destined to be a successful actor.

With a new film career still-born, Dylan reverted back to the album/tour-soon-to-come lifestyle that had dominated his life in the late seventies and early eighties, and which had recommenced at Farm Aid.

Perhaps surprisingly, given the dearth of new songs from his pen, Dylan was back in the studio in April 1987 recording his follow-up to *Knocked Out Loaded*. If *Knocked Out Loaded* had been the most disappointing album of (mostly) original Dylan material since *Nashville Skyline*, it seems that Dylan had decided further to reinforce that sense of history being replayed by recording his second version of *Self Portrait*. He had mentioned the idea of recording an album essentially composed of covers several times during his extensive bout of interviews at the time of *Biograph*, and had specifically suggested to one journalist that he was intent on doing 'an album of standards', which he would try to record with the producer Richard Perry. Though nothing came of this, he continued to reiterate his interest in the project when talking to Cameron Crowe for the notes accompanying *Biograph*.

Bob Dylan: I'd like to do a concept album . . . or an album of cover songs but I don't know if the people would let me get away with that . . . 'A Million Miles from Nowhere', 'I Who Have Nothing', 'All My Tomorrows', 'I'm in the Mood for Love', 'More Than You Know', 'It's a Sin to Tell a Lie' . . .

When Dave Alvin of the Blasters was asked to appear at a recording session for the new album, he was told that Dylan was working on *Self Portrait* Volume Two. There was nothing artistically unsound about Dylan attempting an album of covers. He had made the occasional cover a regular feature of his shows since 1975, and they had often been highlights. Indeed, the more Tin Pan Alley form of song had held an increasing fascination for Dylan throughout the mid-eighties. This perhaps explains his own attempts at replicating the genre with the likes of 'I'll Remember You' and 'Emotionally Yours'. In his interview with Mikal Gilmore in late September 1985 he had expressed his admiration for the crooners of the forties and fifties:

Bob Dylan: Sinatra, Peggy Lee, yeah, I love all these people, but I tell you who I've really been listening to a lot lately – in fact, I'm thinking about recording one of his earlier songs – is Bing Crosby. I don't think you can find better phrasing anywhere.

During the *Infidels* sessions he had recorded Sinatra's 'This Was My Love'; in rehearsals for the 1984 tour he had tried out versions of the perennial standards 'Always on My Mind' and 'To Each His Own'; in rehearsals for the 1986 tour he performed Sinatra's 'This

Was My Love' again, as well as 'All My Tomorrows' and the Inkspots' 'We Three'. And a month before the start of his spring 1987 recording sessions, he performed an acoustic version of 'Soon', a George Gershwin composition best known for Ella Fitzgerald's version, at a New York gala to commemorate the fiftieth anniversary of Gershwin's death.

Yet, when the time came to start work on the new album, Dylan produced another collection of songs which lacked any sense of purpose. The songs recorded for the album varied from mawkish ballads like 'When Did You Leave Heaven' and 'Important Words', through the sort of stomping blues favoured in the 1978 shows ('Let's Stick Together', 'Sally Sue Brown', 'Got Love If You Want It'), and, more successfully, traditional country standards 'Rank Strangers to Me' and 'Ninety Miles an Hour', and the traditional folk of 'Shenandoah'.

As if this pot-pourri were not incoherent enough, Dylan insisted on recording two songs he had co-written with Grateful Dead lyricist Robert Hunter, and which even the Dead had refrained from using themselves. Dylan was prepared to defend his decision to record an album of unoriginal material, but was not called upon to explain the sheer lack of thematic coherence in the collection.*

Bob Dylan: There's no rule that claims that anyone must write their own songs. And I do. I write a lot of songs. But so what, you know? You could take another song somebody else has written and you can make it yours. I'm not saying I made a definitive version of anything with this last record, but I liked the songs. Every so often you've gotta sing songs that're out there ... Writing is such an isolated thing. You're in such an isolated frame of mind. You have to get into or be in that place. In the old days, I could get to it real quick. I can't get to it like that no more. [1988]

That final sentence – 'I can't get to it like that no more' – made it clear the trouble he was having. Of course, part of the problem was his constant desire to reinvent himself. However well he could conjure up his many past selfs in concert, he knew that presenting a counterfeit 'new Dylan' (that is, deliberately trying to sound like a previous self) on vinyl had been unsuccessful on the two occasions he had seemed to flirt with such a notion, *New Morning* and *Street-Legal*. When working with the somewhat less talented Bono, at

* Van Morrison was also in the midst of recording an entire album of covers at this time – *Irish Heartbeat* – but the coherence of his collection of Irish 'folk' songs actually garnered his best reviews and sales in years.

the time of the *Down in the Groove* sessions, he made a half-hearted attempt at jointly composing some songs with him.

Bono: He's very hung up on actually being Bob Dylan. He feels he's trapped in his past and, in a way, he is. I mean, no one asks Smokey Robinson to write a new 'Tracks of My Tears' every album, y'know. But, like, we were trading lines and verses off the top of our heads and Dylan comes out with this absolute classic: 'I was listenin' to the Neville Brothers, it was a quarter of eight/I had an appointment with destiny, but I knew she'd come late/She tricked me, she addicted me, she turned me on the head/Now I can't sleep with these secrets, that leave me cold and alone in my bed.' Then he goes 'Nah, cancel that.' Can you believe it? He thought it was too close to what people expect of Bob Dylan.

If Dylan was looking for talented individuals to spark ideas off as he had with Robbie Robertson in 1966, Jacques Levy in 1975 and Sam Shepard in 1984, then turning to Carole Bayer Sager (with whom he wrote 'Under My Spell' from *Knocked Out Loaded*), Robert Hunter and Bono suggested an element of desperation. Originality was hardly a by-word with Bono, one of rock music's more prolific magpies.

It was 1988 before the album Dylan recorded that spring was released. As with his previous eighties albums, he could not resist tampering with it at the last minute, to its detriment. Even when *Down in the Groove* was barely thirty-two minutes long and featured only two songs even co-written by Dylan, it had some sort of sound of its own despite its disparate sources, the up-tempo songs maintaining a momentum right up until the penultimate song.

Originally intended to feature his impressive version of John Hiatt's 'The Usual', the one redeeming tune from the *Hearts of Fire* soundtrack, and his pleasant if workmanlike reworking of 'Got Love If You Want It', at the last minute Dylan decided to cut these two tracks, restructure the running order, and replace them with a turgid out-take from *Infidels*, 'Death Is Not the End', perhaps the only song from those sessions that had *nothing* to recommend it, and a remixed but still abysmal 'Had a Dream about You Baby'. Any charm his *Self Portrait II* had was lost with the changes, which postdated CBS's release of promotional cassettes of the new album. If *Self Portrait* had not been a wholly successful Fuck You to his audience, Dylan's standing was now at such a low ebb that *Down in the Groove* drew none of the controversy *Self Portrait* had generated. It was simply ignored. The maverick was in a land of rank strangers.

Between recording and releasing his worst album, Dylan conducted the most profoundly dull tour of his career. Fortunately this joint tour with the Grateful Dead spanned a mere six shows. Even when his previous tours had been disappointing, moments of real fire had occurred: he occasionally spat his words with real venom or caressed his more lilting melodies. The Grateful Dead, though, played at one tempo, and that was dead slow.

Dylan's association with the Dead went back to July 1972, when he attended a show in New Jersey and was rumoured to be considering recording with them (indeed a finished Dylan/Dead album was a popular rumour for many years). In 1980, Jerry Garcia had joined Dylan at one of his ground-breaking November Warfield shows and provided some suitable guitar embellishments.

Then in early July 1986 Dylan and the Heartbreakers doubled up with the Dead for three stadium shows, and he joined the Dead for a couple of songs during two of their sets. The desecration of the previously sacrosanct 'Desolation Row' and 'It's All Over Now, Baby Blue' by the band's crude insensitivity should have provided Dylan with ample warning to steer clear of future associations. Yet the idea of a brief Dylan/Dead tour was resurrected later in the year.

Jerry Garcia: When he was playing with Tom Petty, we did a few shows with him and Tom Petty and us and when we were doing it we said, 'Hey, Bob, you wanna sing a song or two with us?' He said, 'Yeah, sure. That'd be fun.' So he agreed and did it a couple of times. And it was fun. We always loved his music – we still do. It was one of those things we'd always thought, 'Wow, that'd be far out.' Bob Dylan and the Grateful Dead. So we hit on him later in the year and we talked about it and he said Yeah. And he came around for two or three weeks and we rehearsed stuff, and tried stuff out, and played through things and goofed around and hung around a lot; and we ended up doing it.

Dylan first admitted to a serious interest in the idea when popping in on the Dead as they rehearsed and recorded at San Rafael in January 1987. By March the tour was being finalized, and he was forced to consider rehearsing with his third touring band in three years. The rehearsals in San Rafael did not go well.

Bob Weir: He was difficult to work with in as much as he wouldn't want to rehearse a song more than two times, three at the most. And so we rehearsed maybe a hundred songs two or three times . . . This is sorta a standard critique of the way he works.

Though Dylan had long delighted in using rehearsals as extended jamming sessions, and could be sure that the Dead were conversant with many of his songs from their own performances, at these rehearsals he seemed barely interested in working up a song, and did not trouble even to sing from a songbook to ensure he got the words right. Songs fizzled out rather than ended. Despite the unfamiliarity of working with the Dead, he refused to restrict himself to a set of a couple of dozen songs, from which he could perm fourteen or fifteen each night. Instead, as Weir says, they gave cursory run-throughs to at least fifty songs, including such off-the-wall selections as the 1963 unreleased composition 'Walkin' Down the Line', Ian and Sylvia's 'The French Girl' and even Paul Simon's 'The Boy in the Bubble'. Dylan seemed most comfortable when jamming on traditional standards like 'John Hardy' and 'Roll in My Sweet Baby's Arms', rather than working up new arrangements of his own best-known songs.

The actual shows were all held in July 1987, in baking hot stadiums spanning both coasts and to crowds primarily composed of Deadheads, the Dead's own super-avid army of obsessives in search of their own or someone else's lost youth. Responding to the self-evident and the superficial, they rousingly applauded anthems like 'Rainy Day Women' and 'Knockin' on Heaven's Door', while Dylan's more audacious works passed them by. For whatever the dubious merits of the actual performances, he was introducing some astonishing songs into his repertoire for the first time ever. Songs like 'Queen Jane Approximately', 'Ballad of Frankie Lee and Judas Priest' and 'The Wicked Messenger' all received first-ever live outings, though they received little recognition from the audiences.

Dylan seemed to have forgotten this brief but embarrassing mini-tour when, in the winter of 1989, nearly two years after the shows, he decided to approve the release of a live album from this absolute nadir of his career as a performing artist. Even the members of the Dead seemed surprised at the notion of releasing such a memento as *Dylan and the Dead*, though they also countenanced its release.

Jerry Garcia: We had this funny experience when we were working on [the *Dylan and the Dead* album]. We went over to his house in Malibu which is . . . out in the country somewhere . . . and he has these huge dogs which are like mastiffs, about seven of 'em. And so we drive up and these dogs surround the car and Dylan's kinda rattling around in the house, this rambling structure, and he takes us into this room that's kinda baronial – y'know, big fireplace and wooden panelling and steep roof.

And on the table is about a $39 ghetto blaster and he's got the cassette and he sticks it in there and he says, Don't you think the voice is mixed a little loud in that one? So we just sat and listened to it on this funky little thing and he'd say I think there ought to be a little more bass.

Mickey Hart: We were trying to back up a singer on songs that no one knew. It was not our finest hour, nor his. I don't know why it was even made into a record.

Happily, by the time the *Dylan and the Dead* album was released, Dylan himself had once again proved he was a consummate live performer, even in his late forties, and had released his most successful recording project of the eighties (with a little help from his friends). The renaissance began within six weeks of the Dylan/Dead débâcle.

36

1987–8: Temples in Flames – Wilburys on the Run

Bruce Springsteen: Dylan was a revolutionary. Bob freed your mind the way Elvis freed your body. He showed us that just because the music was innately physical did not mean it was anti-intellectual. He had the vision and the talent to make a pop song that contained the whole world. He invented a new way a pop singer could sound, broke through the limitations of what a recording artist could achieve and changed the face of rock & roll for ever. Without Bob, the Beatles wouldn't have made *Sgt Pepper*, the Beach Boys wouldn't have made *Pet Sounds*, the Sex Pistols wouldn't have made 'God Save the Queen', U2 wouldn't have done 'Pride in the Name of Love', Marvin Gaye wouldn't have done *What's Goin' On?*, the Count Five would not have done 'Psychotic Reaction', Grandmaster Flash might not have done *The Message*, and there never would have been a group named the Electric Prunes. To this day, wherever great rock music is being made, there is the shadow of Bob Dylan. Bob's own modern work has gone unjustly under-appreciated because it's had to stand in that shadow. If there was a young guy out there writing the *Empire Burlesque* album, writing 'Every Grain of Sand', they'd be calling him the new Bob Dylan . . . So I'm just here tonight to say thanks, to say that I wouldn't be here without you, to say that there isn't a soul in this room who does not owe you his thanks.

Thus did Bruce Springsteen induct Bob Dylan into the Rock & Roll Hall of Fame on 20 January 1988. If the eighties had brought Dylan precious little recognition for his current work, it seemed he could not escape receiving awards for his past achievements. In March 1982 he had been inducted into the Songwriters Hall of Fame. In November 1985 he was the subject of a tribute at Whitney Museum in New York, attended by many of those who owed him their thanks: names like Bowie, Neil Young, Pete Townshend as well as those who had derived less benefit from his work, like Billy Joel and Dave Stewart. In March 1986 he received a Founders Award from ASCAP (the American Society of Composers, Authors and Publishers). And now the Rock & Roll Hall of Fame. Dylan himself seemed surprisingly impressed by the honour.

Bob Dylan: It was a great honour to be included, but more important was the recognition of Leadbelly and Woody, seeing them get the respect they deserve. [1988]

But though Springsteen recognized some quality in his more recent work, *Empire Burlesque*, *Knocked Out Loaded* and the not-yet-released *Down in the Groove* hardly represented works of genius, and his last three American tours, in 1981, 1986 and 1987, had been progressively more disappointing. Ironically in the same period Dylan had conducted three European tours which, though erratic, had all contained flashes of the old consummate performer.

His last European tour, three months earlier, was just thirty dates, and had not received a good press. In the US the only report came from his opening show in Tel Aviv, his first show ever in Israel, where the circumstances – two shows commuted into one at the last minute and attracting a Saturday night crowd of young Israeli drunks who heckled the support acts – obscured what was in fact an audacious opening show. He was backed again by the Heartbreakers, who were at last given their own set, and who welcomed the opportunity to play a major tour in Europe, where their work was considerably less well known than in the States.

This renewed association with the Heartbreakers was much more successful than the previous year's tours, primarily because Dylan approached the shows differently himself. Gone were the relatively uniform sets of the 1986 US tour; as were uniform arrangements. The sets were astonishingly varied and thankfully abbreviated. Playing between seventy and seventy-five minutes most nights, Dylan actually was on the first encore of his third show before he repeated a single song from the two previous shows.

The brevity of the sets and the tour itself meant that Dylan's voice remained in good shape throughout, and the lack of an acoustic set enabled the shows to be paced more consistently. When Petty talked about taking the rehearsals on stage, this tour was what he might have had in mind. Both set list and track order changed every night, and Dylan sometimes decided to lead into a song himself with a harmonica break. Sometimes it would be left to Benmont Tench or Mike Campbell. Likewise endings were extended or abbreviated as the whim took him, and the Heartbreakers, at last put through their paces, responded magnificently, Campbell proving as inventive and sympathetic guitarist as had ever augmented Dylan. If the girl singers were still a trifle overbearing, and the sheer variety of numbers performed meant Dylan stumbled over a few lines, it was clear that he was conducting his finest tour in six years.

Benmont Tench: He's been great to play with. Great fun as well, mostly because you can never let your mind drift. He'll give the most familiar song an odd twist; a change of rhythm or a peculiar delivery. Playing with Bob Dylan certainly gives you a good kick up the arse . . . One night he'll do something like he'll say – onstage – 'Right, we'll begin with "Forever Young",' and the Heartbreakers have maybe played the song once before. Then he'll say, 'And Benmont, you start it off.'

The English and European press did not agree. While in 1978 they had been so supportive when Dylan was at his most audacious, in 1987 they seemed solely concerned with how he looked (old), and how brief his set was. Presumably they would have preferred tired retreads of 'Masters of War', 'Ballad of a Thin Man' and 'Just Like a Woman' night after night, as long as the set clocked in at an extra thirty minutes! What really seems to have upset the press was his new-found taciturnity. Throughout the tour he refrained from commenting between songs and granted no interviews apart from two in Israel to American journalists.

Even if the European press did not recognize the change, the tour signalled the first sign that Dylan was emerging from a period when even his performance art was seemingly in terminal decline. The next matter was to record some new songs to reaffirm his status as a songwriter. Yet CBS had still not released the excruciating *Down in the Groove*. Its 1988 release confirmed the media's view of Dylan's poor standing.

If by the winter of 1987–8 Dylan had recognized the futility of trying to force himself to write new songs, some old friends provided him with the necessary impetus to return to writing. With another summer US tour scheduled to start in June, he was called up one day early in April by George Harrison, who required a studio at short notice to record a bonus track for a European twelve-inch single, and wondered if he could use Dylan's garage studio in Malibu.

George Harrison: Warners needed a third song to put on a twelve-inch single. I didn't have another song, I didn't have an extended version, so I just said to Jeff [Lynne] – I was in Los Angeles and he was producing Roy Orbison . . . I'm just going to have to write a song tomorrow and just do it. I was kind of thinking of 'Instant Karma' – that way. And I said, Where can we get a studio? And he said, Well, maybe Bob, 'cause he's got this little studio in his garage . . . we just went back to his house, phoned up Bob; he said, Sure, come on over. Tom Petty had my guitar and I went to pick it up; he said, Oh, I was wondering what I was going to do tomorrow! And Roy Orbison said, Give us a call tomorrow if you're going to do anything – I'd love to come along.

Thus did Tom Petty, George Harrison, Jeff Lynne and Roy Orbison assemble at Dylan's Malibu home to record a hastily written Harrison song called 'Handle with Care'. With no engineers or extraneous studio personnel present, the session turned into a spontaneous songwriting session.

Tom Petty: We were a very self-contained group. We had one roadie and five Wilburys, and that was it. The funniest thing was I remember the first track we did – out in Bob Dylan's garage – and we didn't have a roadie . . . And you could see us all digging through boxes to find a cable and a cord. 'Well, there used to be one over there. Goddamn, I need new batteries for this.' . . . It was refreshing.

Roy Orbison: We were at Bob's house working on 'Handle with Care' and we needed a couple of lines and Bob and Tom wandered in and just threw in the lines we needed.

The participants realized that a good time was being had by all and, with a gap in all five schedules, their thoughts turned to the notion of perhaps recording more material, having christened themselves the Traveling Wilburys, reflecting the good humour and refreshing lack of ego-massaging in the partnership. When Warner Brothers recognized the quality of 'Handle with Care', a *Traveling Wilburys* album became inevitable.

Roy Orbison: George took the record to his record company and they said, This is much too good for a B-side. We're not sure what to do with this. And then we had the idea of putting together the album. We had all enjoyed it so much; it was so relaxed, there was no ego involved, and there was some sort of chemistry. So we'd go to Bob's house and we'd just sit outside and there'd be a barbecue and we'd all just bring guitars and everyone would be throwing something in here and something in there, and then we'd just go to the garage, the studio, and put it down. Some days we'd finish just one song, sometimes two or three. We put down all the tracks, writing and singing and everything, in about ten or twelve days.

The actual sessions for the album, as opposed to 'Handle with Care', took place in early May, a month after the initial session.

They wrote songs and then immediately recorded them, just as Dylan and the Band had in 1967. The informality and camaraderie was bound to appeal to Dylan, the one Wilbury who had pressing commitments that spring.

George Harrison: It was just a question of timing, 'cause Bob had to go on the road at the end of May, and this is like early April when we did 'Handle with Care', so he said, Well, I got a bit of time at the beginning of May, so we just said OK, we'll meet on – I think it was the 7th of May or something, and we had nine or ten days that we knew we could get Bob for, and everybody else was relatively free, so we just said, Let's do it! We said, We'll write a tune a day and do it that way.

The lack of time was in fact a major advantage. It meant that Dylan's fellow Wilburys had to rely on the precepts which surrounded all his best studio work – spontaneity and first instincts.

Jeff Lynne: That's why the songs are so good and fresh – because they hadn't been second-guessed and dissected and replaced. It's so tempting to add stuff to a song when you've got unlimited time.

The songs came with remarkable ease. Though each song had one or two major composers, each member contributed ideas about the melody, the words or the arrangements. The first song they recorded at the bona-fide Wilburys sessions was 'Dirty World', a typical Dylan pastiche in the tradition of 'Leopard-Skin Pill-Box Hat' and 'Rita Mae'.

George Harrison: Bob's very funny – I mean, a lot of people take him seriously and yet if you know Dylan and his songs, he's such a joker really. And Jeff just sat down and said, OK, what are we gonna do? And Bob said, Let's do one like Prince! . . . And he just started banging away – 'Love your sexy body' . . .

Though 'Dirty World' needed a little rewriting after the initial take, it never seemed the most faithful Prince pastiche. What it did reflect was the joyful ease involved in these collaborations.

Bob Dylan: It wasn't that difficult to make that record. There weren't really a lot of heavy decisions that went into it. Cooperation is great on something like that because you never get stuck. [1989]

Dylan was the main author of two more songs on the album, though the whole album was intended to be a cooperative venture and, if Harrison and Dylan were the main songwriters, the royalties were divided equally. Of his other two lead vocals, 'Tweeter and the Monkey Man' came in for most comment. With its repeated allusions to Springsteen song titles and its New Jersey setting he seemed to be showing he could lampoon Springsteen at least as successfully as Bruce himself. 'Tweeter and the Monkey Man' was the highlight of the album, and was the first suggestion that Dylan's unique turn of phrase could still be put to good use in the late eighties.

George Harrison: 'Tweeter and the Monkey Man' was Tom Petty and Bob sitting in the kitchen, Jeff and I were there too, but they were talking about all this stuff which didn't make sense to me – Americana kind of stuff. And we got a tape cassette and put it on and transcribed everything they were saying and wrote it down. And then Bob sort of changed it . . . He had one take warming himself up and then he did it for real on take two; the rest of us had more time but Bob had to go on the road and we knew he couldn't do any more vocals again, so we had to get his vocals immediately. On take two he sang that 'Tweeter and the Monkey Man' right through.

By the time the Wilburys' album was released in October, Dylan had completed a five-month-long tour of the Union, his most impressive and well-received American tour since the heyday of the Rolling Thunder Revue. The press loved the unrelenting pace and stripped-down sound of Dylan's new three-piece combo. The media seemed to be turning in his favour once again. The Wilburys' album, with its superstar session tag, was expected to sell well, but exceeded all expectations, staying in the American album charts for over forty weeks. It was Dylan's first platinum album of the eighties, his only double-platinum album ever, and one of the great commercial successes of 1989. Though in part a considerable testament to George Harrison's and Roy Orbison's enduring appeal, it confirmed that Dylan himself could still be a highly commercial artist. The good-time feel of the sessions comes over on vinyl, the eclecticism of the musicians makes it a delightfully varied listening experience and, though there is precious little soul-searching going on, the album features some of Harrison and Dylan's best songs in years.

There was however plenty of soul-searching on Dylan's next album. Promoting the Wilburys album with assorted radio interviews, Harrison informed the world that the experience of recording the album had given Dylan the bug to write again, and that his new songs were very strong. If the eighties had been largely disappointing from the viewpoint of Dylan's official vinyl output, a strong album in 1989 would hopefully confirm Dylan's own enduring appeal. Paul Simon's shallow *Graceland* had proved that a contemporary-sounding album with a strong melodic sense and the right promotion could provide renewed commercial status.

Dylan's first problem in preparing the groundwork for a return to form was his choice of producer. The last producer he had worked with had been the in-vogue man of the moment, Arthur Baker, and the 'contemporary' sound he gave him sounded utterly fake. Baker's successor as producer of the moment, Mitchell Froom, had provided some keyboards during the remixing of the atrocious 'Had a Dream about You Baby' at the beginning of 1988, though thankfully Dylan decided to steer clear of a man who on the evidence of his albums with Richard Thompson and Maria KcKee believes bass to be some form of fish.

On the face of it, his final selection was no more inspiring. Daniel Lanois had been responsible for recent works by U2, as well as both Peter Gabriel's and Robbie Robertson's long-awaited 1986 and 1987 solo albums. Both Robertson's and Gabriel's albums were major disappointments, from artists responsible for several of the seventies' finest albums. In both cases the sound of the albums was ultra-contemporary, but inappropriate.

Dylan first met Lanois when he decided to call in on sessions for a Neville Brothers album which Lanois was producing in New Orleans. The meeting occurred at the time of Dylan's September 1988 show there — the final show of his summer US tour. The Neville Brothers were intending to include two songs from the *Times They Are a-Changin'* album, 'Hollis Brown' and 'With God on Our Side', for which they had added an extra verse about Vietnam. Dylan liked the informality of recording with a porta-studio in an old colonial house in Louisiana, and the sound Lanois was getting on what would become the *Yellow Moon* album. Indeed, he was so impressed by the 'new' version of 'With God on Our Side' that he added the new verse in later live performances.

Daniel Lanois: He just sat there and thought that 'God on Our Side' was one of the best records he'd ever heard ... He just kept saying, 'That's a great record.' Kept repeating it over and over again. From Bob that's a big compliment.

Bob Dylan: Bono had heard a few of [my new] songs and suggested that Daniel could really record them right. Daniel came to see me when we were playing in New Orleans last year and ... we hit it off. He had an understanding of what my music was all about. It's very hard to find a producer that can play ... It was thrilling to run into Daniel because he's a competent musician and he knows how to record with modern facilities. For me, that was lacking in the past. [1989]

The songs that Dylan brought to New Orleans six months later were very different from the Wilburys' material. Though some songs trod familiar Dylan territory with their portrayals of a world on the brink of doom, only outlaws and saints remaining true to themselves, there were also songs of scourging self-analysis, notably 'What Good Am I?', a surprisingly frank look at his own moral worth.

Bob Dylan: Most of [the songs on *Oh Mercy*] are stream-of-consciousness songs, the kind that come to you in the middle of the night, when you just want to go back to bed. [1989]

Talking about *Oh Mercy* at the time of the album's release, Dylan admitted that before writing the songs he had had to make a conscious decision to try to put together an album of original material, recognizing that the will might no longer be there.

Bob Dylan: Some people quit making records. They just don't care about it anymore. As long as they have their live stage show together, they don't need records. It was getting to that point for me. It was either come up with a bunch of songs that were original and pay attention to them or get some other real good songwriters to write me some songs ... Everybody works in the shadow of what they've previously done. But you have to overcome that. [1989]

In his own case 'that shadow of what [he'd] previously done' was considerably more daunting than for any contemporary. The sessions began in New Orleans in late March and took up most of April, lasting some six weeks. Lanois had rented a large house on Soniat Street, where he set up his portable Studio on the Move, deciding to create a mood conducive to the subterranean feel Dylan was looking for on the album.

Daniel Lanois: We found an empty turn of the century apartment building – a five-storey building, a fantastic place ... it had a bordello-ish overtone. We essentially turned the control room into a swamp ... we had moss all over the place and stuffed animals and alligator heads.

Despite spending six weeks recording and making preliminary mixes, and with only fourteen or fifteen songs he wanted to try to record, Dylan was still determined to record the songs in the usual fashion – with a minimum of fuss.

Daniel Lanois: Bob likes to get something quickly if possible in the name of spontaneity. On this record . . . some things came quick and we grabbed them that way. And then we spent a lot of time on detail. Some of the vocals we worked on quite a bit and the lyrics were changed and we chipped away at them.

Inevitably it was the process of reworking and recutting alternate versions of the songs which used up much of the time. The vocal tracks in particular were given considerable attention. Dylan seemed intent on a smoky, rumbling resonance – almost a cross between Leonard Cohen and Tom Waits.

Daniel Lanois: We put in a lot of care with the vocals and the sounds. On the Dylan record there's not really the obvious presence of syn-thesizers, just straight ahead drums and bass and guitars, yet there's this blazing strangeness around it.

The bulk of the album was recorded with the same basic collection of local New Orleans musicians who had worked on the Neville Brothers' album. Lanois himself contributed musically to all but one of the album's songs, providing dobro, lap steel, guitar and even omnichord. Engineer Malcolm Burn was also required to turn his hand to tambourine, keyboards and bass in order to capture moments of inspiration from Dylan. Local musicians Willie Green and Tony Hall provided a reliable rhythm section. The ease with which such talented players could be called up delighted Dylan, who had grown tired of the notice that LA musicians required.

Bob Dylan: Daniel just allowed the record to take place any old time, day or night. You don't have to walk through secretaries, pinball machines and managers and hangers-on in the lobby and parking lots and elevators and arctic temperatures. You need help to make a record, in all the directions that go into making a record. Some people expect me to bring in a Bob Dylan song, sing it and then they record it. Other people don't work that way – there's more feedback. [1989]

Though Dylan showed remarkable discipline throughout the weeks of work, as the sessions progressed Lanois's role became more and more that of keeping him motivated and committed to producing a great album, not half a great album. With Dylan's low boredom threshold, this required Lanois to develop skills as a taskmaster and diplomat.

Daniel Lanois: With all records there comes a time when people get a little bit lazy, because it's a tiring and unnatural process. At that lull it's very important to take command and turn that ... valley into a mountain; whatever it takes to reach that mountain is what you have to do at that point to turn the record into a great record. There came a time with Bob Dylan when I felt he fell into old habits – 'Get somebody else to play on it,' he'd say, or 'just hire somebody', when really he should have been playing the parts. And I made it clear to him that we weren't going to fly anybody in and we weren't going to have session players play these parts. The parts would be played by the people in the room – by himself, by myself, by the engineer Malcolm Burn, by the neighbourhood guys that we'd chosen to be on the record. It was not going to be a studio record. He was going to play the parts and if they were a little sloppy they would be accepted that way.

Though most of the press comments about *Oh Mercy* on its release in September 1989 were about the sound of the album, it was evident that rock music's foremost lyric writer had rediscovered his previous flair with words. Though his usual inability to be critical of his own lyrics meant that the album featured two weak songs, in 'Disease of Conceit' and 'Where Teardrops Fall', the ominous 'Man in the Long Black Coat', the resigned 'Most of the Time' and the simply beautiful 'Shooting Star' revealed lyric writing as incisive, audacious and acutely human as the best of his previous work.

Daniel Lanois: Bob Dylan is a very committed lyricist. He would walk into the studio and put his head into the pages of words that he had and not let up until it was done. It was quite fascinating to see the transformation that some of the songs made. They would begin as one story and at the end of the night they would be something else. One of my favourites is 'Man in a Long Black Coat'. Which was written in the studio and recorded in one take.

The release of *Oh Mercy* capped a year when several of the previous decade's survivors had come back with their best work of the eighties: Neil Young with *Freedom*, Pere Ubu with *Cloudland* and Lou Reed with *New York* were the other outstanding examples. Though *Oh Mercy* failed to make the Top Twenty, even after enthusiastic reviews, inclusion in *Rolling Stone*'s Hundred Best Albums of the Eighties, two years of successful touring and the massive commercial success of the Wilburys, it as least proved to be his most consistent seller since *Infidels*, the album that both inspirationally and thematically it seemed to be most closely linked to.

Sharing *Infidels'* sense of imminent apocalypse, and its patchy but occasionally dazzling brilliance, *Oh Mercy* suggested there was considerably more life in this sixties survivor than in the trio of fellow sixties renegades, the Stones, the Who and Paul McCartney, who all made the circuit of American arenas and stadiums that summer, playing to huge numbers of fans, old and new, all in search of a past.

Within a month of the release of *Oh Mercy*, Dylan played a 2,700-seat theatre in New York, while on the same night on the outskirts of the city the Rolling Stones played to 70,000 worshipping fans. The difference was, here was an artist trying to confront his past glories, not merely to regurgitate them.

37

1989–90: Lord Have Mercy!

Bob Dylan: People can learn everything about me through my songs, if they know where to look. They can juxtapose them with certain other songs and draw a clear picture. [1990]

In the eighties, as throughout most of his career, it has been Dylan's songs which have best illustrated his state of mind. The albums since *Saved* certainly confirm the impression that Dylan's troubled relationships with his lady loves has become less important as his apocalyptic conceit has wholly coloured his work. Yet his most successful work in the last decade has generally been a result of fusing that 'black' conceit with his love-ballad strain. Thus 'Shot of Love', 'The Groom's Still Waiting at the Altar', 'Caribbean Wind' and 'Angelina' all tap into this combined theme.

At the time of writing those songs, in 1980–81, Dylan was emerging out of his evangelist phase and the end of intense relationships with Mary Alice Artes and Helena Springs, and it seemed a natural enough process to fuse the two. Since the *Infidels* album, recorded at a time when his three-year relationship with Clydie King was coming to an end, he has been less willing to unite the two forms, though 'Sweetheart Like You' on *Infidels*, 'When the Night Comes Falling from the Sky' and 'Something's Burning, Baby' on *Empire Burlesque* and 'Shooting Star' on *Oh Mercy* have broached both concerns.

However, Dylan's overriding concern has remained 'the end times'. Whereas there seemed to be a refreshing strain of universal redemption creeping into his work with songs like 'Every Grain of Sand' and 'In the Summertime' (with its 'flood that set everybody free') on the *Shot of Love* album, Dylan has steadfastly stuck to the black apocalyptic tradition in his post-*Shot of Love* work. Songs like 'Jokerman', 'When the Night Comes Falling from the Sky', 'Band of the Hand' and 'Ring Them Bells' are littered with allusions

to the finishing end. Some of his bleakest work has gone unreleased
or ignored. The sublime 'Blind Willie McTell' is a valedictory to a
world teetering on the brink. 'Something's Burning, Baby', is a
song overcome by the fumes of hell.

Though Dylan's three pre-*Oh Mercy* works all concluded with
songs which seemed to detail a personal desperation ('Dark Eyes',
'Under My Spell' and 'Rank Strangers to Me'), his two most
recent works combine such personal despair with a more macro-
cosmic disintegration. The bleakness of *Oh Mercy* has not in
any way dissipated on Dylan's most recent album, *Under the Red
Sky*, despite its raunchy sound. On 'God Knows' Dylan reminds
us that the next flood will not be water but fire, and the finale,
'Cat's in the Well', concludes with a prayer for safekeeping of the
near and dear in the troubled times that will be imminently upon
us all. May the Lord indeed have mercy on us all!

Dylan's two most recent albums seem the logical culmination of
a world-view adopted first on *Slow Train Coming*. Since 1979,
Dylan has pursued a solitary path. In the seventies his primary
artistic struggle was 'to learn to do consciously what I used to do
unconsciously', its thematic quandary – the power of Woman:

> Dylan has always believed, not unreasonably, in the power of Woman.
> When he finally lost faith in the ability of women to save him (and he
> seems to have explored the matter very thoroughly, in and out of
> marriage, in the years 1974 through '78), his need for an alternative grew
> very great indeed, and he found what people in our culture most often
> find in the same circumstances: the uncritical hospitality of Jesus Christ.

So wrote Paul Williams, perhaps the most perceptive of all
'Dylan-commentators', in his contemporary study of Dylan's conversion, *What Happened?*. If Williams is correct then Dylan's conversion was – largely if not wholly – an attempt at immunizing
himself against the power of Woman, an admission that he had
indeed 'lost faith in the ability of women to save him'. If so, then it
seems likely that Dylan's failure to maintain a permanent relationship throughout the last decade is as much down to that 'loss of
faith' as an inability to find 'the right woman'.

There are many clues that support this supposition. In 1984
Dylan rewrote what may well be his most perfect love song,
'Tangled Up in Blue'. In the new version, though, the singer is no
longer searching relentlessly for the object of his desires but paints
the woman/women in the song as distractions who have waylaid
him in his 'real' quest, walking towards the sun/Son.

In January 1990, during his mammoth four-hour show in New Haven, Dylan introduced 'Lay Lady Lay' as a song from his romantic period, further noting that romance used to be important to him but not any more. Of course there is a tongue firmly in his cheek here, yet the truth is he could never write such a straightforward song of desire any more.

Since *Shot of Love* Dylan's lovesongs have tended to be the more wistful kind, almost remembrances of things past. Though 'In the Summertime', 'I and I', 'I'll Remember You', 'Shooting Star' and 'Born in Time' all cover familiar terrain, the listener cannot ascertain whether events in the songs date from the recent or the not-so-recent past. All have a dream-like quality to them.

As Dylan has removed himself from the power of Woman so he has reinforced the more judgemental and patriarchal aspects of his faith. In 1985 Allen Ginsberg talked about Dylan's faith in these terms.

Allen Ginsberg: It might have been expected that he'd evolve out of [the Born Again creed] as something closer to his natural Judaism, which he has ... He hasn't been a Born Again Christian for a long time now. People still think he is and five years ago he changed. In the conversation we had a couple of weeks ago there was a great deal of judgemental Jehovaic ... a figure of judgemental hyper-rationality. There's this judgemental Jehovaic theism in his recent work, and he said: 'Allen, do you have a quarrel with God?' And I said: 'I've never met the man.' And he said: 'Then you have a quarrel with God.' And I said: 'Well, I didn't start anything!' So he still has a fixed notion of divinity.

Though Dylan's apocalyptic conceit has driven most of his finest post-conversion songs, his millennial fervour now seems out of step with his audience's view of world affairs. In the sixties the process of change was so imbued with the overthrow of existing structures that Dylan's anthems of doom were freely adopted. In the eighties there has been a sense of a man out of time in all of Dylan's work, compounded initially by his unpopular evangelism and lately by his reactionary distaste for such products of Man's 'progress' as the space programme, television, videos and synthetic music. His songs seem imbued with a sense of isolation.

The isolation also seems to have been personal. In his post-accident career there have only been three periods when Dylan has combined frequent studio activity with prodigious bouts of touring: November 1973 to December 1975, February 1978 to November 1981 and May 1988 to the present. All have coincided with periods of turmoil in Dylan's personal life, almost as if the

road became an easy escape from issues he must face head-on in
life away from the road. During his recent burst of activity Dylan
has recorded two albums with the Wilburys and two original
albums, *Oh Mercy* and *Under the Red Sky*, and played nearly three
hundred shows on his Never-Ending Tour.

If there had been a considerable gap between his previous album
of original material and *Oh Mercy*, the successor followed with
unexpected, and perhaps undue, haste. As in 1989, the early
months of 1990 were primarily taken up with writing and recording a new album. Unlike 1989, Dylan actually sandwiched shows
between sessions, though the follow-up to *Oh Mercy* took up
considerably less studio time than its predecessor. The album was
composed from just five sessions. There was a session in January
and four sessions in early April, featuring such luminaries as
NRBQ – with whom Dylan recorded three songs, none of which
ended up on *Under the Red Sky* – Bruce Hornsby, Elton John,
George Harrison and Slash from Guns'n'Roses.

There was much speculation about Dylan's motives for using
such 'names' to play on his new album. Several writers later
implied it was a ruse to encourage the consumers to buy it. In fact,
the deal that Dylan had struck with his producers, Don and David
Was, was that he would not show Don and Dave his new songs
until they recorded them, and they would select the musicians:

Don Was: The personnel for the first session was Stevie Ray and Jimmy
Vaughan, David Lindley, our keyboard player from Was (Not Was),
Jaimie Muhoberac, Kenny Aronoff. I played bass and Bob was set up at
the piano. And he walked in and Stevie walked up to him. I don't think
they'd ever met before and he said, 'Hi, Stevie Ray Vaughan.' But Stevie
didn't have his hat on and Bob [was] just like, 'Yeah, sure,' and kept
going. He didn't believe it, he thought it was like an assistant engineer
and then he saw Jimmy and he flipped ... And then he saw Lindley.
Then he realized it was Stevie Ray and he went back and he was like
very warm and very excited about having Stevie Ray on the record.

Dylan's choice for producer/s boded well for the album. Don
and David Was may have achieved notoriety primarily for their
work with black artists, but their Detroit background made them
as prone to the influences of the MC5 and the Stooges as more
soulful sounds. As with Lanois, both Don and David Was were
musicians in their own right (indeed Don would contribute bass
guitar on six of the tracks on *Under the Red Sky*).

It was the first session, on or around 6 January 1990, that really
made *Under the Red Sky*. Dylan had played Was a demo of one
song which he had tried at the *Oh Mercy* sessions, but which he

could not get quite right. 'God Knows' could have sat quite nicely in the middle of side two of *Oh Mercy*, with its sense of the inherent fragility of man's tenure here on earth. It still proved to be mighty problematic.

Don Was: We rehearsed it a few times before [we recorded it but] that was one that we had difficulty with. The other ones we cut that day were 'Handy Dandy', 'Cat's in the Well' and one other one. It was originally called 'Hat Pin' – '10,000 Men' . . . They went much smoother than 'God Knows'.

The first session resulted in all but one of the five tracks on side two of *Under the Red Sky*. At this point Dylan seems to have realized another album of real quality was within his grasp. He had nearly half the album already in the can in just one session, and all the songs had an intriguing feel, even if the words on '10,000 Men' seemed a little half-formed. Dylan could always redub a vocal track for that one! He also had another of his wistful ballads already written and 'Born in Time' would be a perfect respite from the tales of the end times already recorded for the album.

The first public intimation of what the new album would actually sound like came from a most unexpected quarter, a promotional CD release of 'Most of the Time'. In late March, Dylan recorded a live version of the *Oh Mercy* song in a rehearsal studio in Culver City, with David Lindley, Randy Jackson and Kenny Aronoff. The intention was to produce a video to promote *Oh Mercy* further. The video was shot by Dylan's eldest son, Jesse, who had attended film school in New York. The best take was included as a bonus track on the promo CD, credited as produced by Don Was. Dylan's voice was very hoarse, but the track had a thudding resonance the more sedate original lacked. It was a promising preview to the new album.

Indeed the video shoot was a dry run for the pukka sessions booked to commence directly afterwards, Dylan intending to complete the album using a basic line-up of Lindley on guitar, Aronoff on drums and either Don Was or Randy Jackson on bass. One session involved them all and resulted in 'Two by Two' and 'Wiggle Wiggle'. A further session with Jackson and Aronoff, supplemented by Bruce Hornsby and Robben Ford, produced 'Born in Time' and 'TV Talkin' Song'. The last of the sessions, featuring just Aronoff, Was on bass and Al Kooper, making his first studio recordings with Dylan since the dispiriting *Knocked Out Loaded* débâcle, provided the last two tracks required. In three sessions the basic tracks for the six remaining songs which would make up *Under the Red Sky* had been completed. The songs recorded with NRBQ at a separate session remained on the cutting room floor.

If the laying-down of basic tracks had been achieved in a mere five sessions, Al Kooper has intimated that a lot of studio time was spent overdubbing (Kooper himself overdubbed on three songs, only one of which appears on *Under the Red Sky*, 'Handy Dandy') and mixing. As with *Oh Mercy*, Dylan spent considerable time working on his vocals.

Al Kooper: On some records I think he learned what the pros were [of overdubbing] and now, Don tells me, he works for hours on vocals getting it just the way he wants it . . . I think that's positive, not negative.

The completed *Under the Red Sky* was in CBS's hands before Dylan began his 1990 summer tour in Montreal on 29 May. It was an album which had a unity of sound and a sense of purpose. The rough edges had not been honed down but rather preserved and the suitably raunchy backing evoked memories of side three of *Blonde on Blonde*, crossed with the sound Dylan had been trying to achieve on *Down in the Groove*.

Yet *Under the Red Sky* was destined for a bumpy ride on its release. The reality is that Dylan did not really have the songs to make up a second half of the album to match the five songs he had ready in January ('Born in Time' was already written though not actually recorded until April). The remaining songs included two badly in need of tunes, 'Unbelievable' and 'TV Talkin' Song', one that was 'written by numbers' (2 × 2), one which was an all-too-brief adaption of an old rock & roll song, 'Wiggle Wiggle', and finally the title track, 'Under the Red Sky', which came in for the most scathing criticism of all. Attacked as trite and nonsensical, the song's use of the nursery-song form to tell a Grimm parable seemed to pass most reviewers by. It was the one song that Dylan discussed with Was:

Don Was: That's the only time I really ever asked him about a lyric and he told me about it. He said, 'It's about my hometown.' . . . It's such a great little fable. These people who have all this opportunity and everything and they choose to be led around by a blind horse and they squander it. It's beautiful and it was so simple and he just sang it one time through and it was perfect.

Though the majority of the songs were attacked for being superficial fodder after the murky magnificence of *Oh Mercy*, the new lyrics only seem to reaffirm Dylan's view of a world gone badly awry. Indeed, *Under the Red Sky* further develops the bleak world-view which has been in evidence on every album from *Slow Train Coming* to the present release. Despite the levity of 'Wiggle Wiggle', the remainder of the album is a typical catalogue of heroes and villains from the end times.

Through the mid-eighties, as he wrestled with his own creativity and indeed his performance art, Dylan seemed to make little attempt to seek a *rapprochement* with his audience. The previous chapters of this book have detailed that struggle to come to terms with modern technology, with the new limits age has imposed on his singing voice and with his second great creative drought. With *Oh Mercy* he banished the doubts and wrapped the songs in an alluringly subterranean sound which garnered good reviews and sales. If the Dylan on *Under the Red Sky* once again offended his critics, he showed he still had the ability to conjure up profoundly disturbing images and wrap them up in a cogent sound spanning the entire era of rock & roll. The album's stripped-down, guitars-blazing sound also tips its hat to the sound Dylan and his band have been touting around the world these last three years. On the road again, Dylan had attempted to span the years and rebuild the bridge between his audience and his art.

38

1988–90: The Never-Ending Tour

Since 1975 the primary arena for Dylan's art has been the stage, not the studio. After his half-hearted return to the stage in 1974, the Rolling Thunder Revue was a triumphant return to form. It affirmed, not only to the press and the punters, but to Dylan himself that he could still cut it, up there where it mattered.

1975 was also the year when Dylan seems to have realized that technology had passed him by. No longer did he feel comfortable in the studio. No one it seemed — at least among his contemporaries — went into the studio and recorded an album in three days. No one except Dylan, who recorded the bulk of *Planet Waves* at three sessions, *Blood on the Tracks* at three (plus a further two when he re-recorded half the album) and all but two tracks on *Desire* in a single session.

From there on, Dylan has increasingly struggled to get his vision onto vinyl. The results have only been sporadically satisfying, though anyone but Dylan would be proud of a post-*Blood* legacy which includes *Desire*, *Slow Train Coming*, *Infidels* and *Oh Mercy*. Most of the time he has committed his artistic energies to something far more instant.

Bob Dylan: What I do is more of an immediate thing: you stand up on stage and sing — you get it back immediately. It's not like writing a book or even making a record ... What I do is so immediate it changes the nature, the concept, of art to me. [1981]

Since 1978 he has talked repeatedly about the nature of live performance, but journalists have continued to judge him by his official output. The maverick, though, has denigrated videos as synthetic and producers as exponents of the artificial; and dismissed musicians who cannot reproduce their work in concert as charlatans. Dylan has cast himself in the mould of the ol' blues musician. Like Cisco Houston he can see himself on the road until the doctor finally says his time is up – only then will he head for that California sun one last time.

If the struggle to reconcile the desire to perform with the inspiration to write has not been an easy one, it would appear that after *Infidels* and *Empire Burlesque* Dylan gave up attempting to come to terms with technology. Since February 1986 he has re-committed himself to the road – as he did from 1978 through to 1981. Two major tours in 1986 and two tours in 1987 confirmed he had the bug to perform again.

The Heartbreakers, though, could never commit themselves to the type of relentless touring Dylan had in mind. A touring band remained an intractable problem for him. In 1975 he had assembled the first of his rolling revues – a tour that would never end, a free-rolling express through the heartland of America. The idea of the Rolling Thunder Revue went back many years, according to close friends like Robbie Robertson and Bobby Neuwirth; and it didn't die in 1976. In 1979 Dylan embarked on another kind of medicine show. Preaching the gospel from place to place, only months after completing an 115-date world tour, he again committed himself to the road, this time the one that 'leads to Calvary'. When that spurt of fervour had died down and his three-year-long touring group disbanded, Dylan seemed, for the first time in six years, weary of the road and reluctant to live that life. A brief twenty-seven-date tour of Europe in summer 1984 proved the only break in his abandonment of the stage, up until February 1986 and the first of three tours with the Heartbreakers in two years.

On 7 June 1988, Dylan embarked on his second major tour of the States in two years. However, it was a very different tour from the True Confessions tour of 1986. Bob Dylan and the Heartbreakers were no more. An arena tour on the scale of 1986 was thus out of the question. Dylan's commercial stock was at an all-time low. *Down in the Groove*, coming hard on the heels of *Knocked Out Loaded*, was his worst-received album since *Self Portrait*. The tour itself did not start auspiciously. His sixty-five minute opening show was not well received. Far worse was the second show, two days later, in Sacramento, when after twelve songs and less than an hour on stage, he departed refusing even an encore. Most fans assumed that it was simply the end of the first half of the show and had to be told that the show had ended. The scathing reception in the Californian press the following day made Dylan realize he could not get away with such stunts and still hope to have an audience into the nineties. Thankfully the band soon kicked into gear and Dylan began to enjoy himself.

The band Dylan toured with in 1988 was as stripped down as stripped down can be. On lead guitar was *Saturday Night Live* band leader, G. E. Smith. The rhythm section was composed of two relatively unknown New York musicians, Christopher Parker on drums and Kenny Aaronson on bass. The considerably better known Marshall Crenshaw had been enlisted as the original bassist but was finally deemed unsuitable.

Kenny Aaronson: They had him playing six-string bass. Six-string bass and Marshall Crenshaw means to me he was probably playing one of those old DanElectro six-string basses that they used to double the upright with in Nashville for more distinction. The six-string bassist would play with a pick . . . Now that's not really the kind of a bass that's gonna give you real low end. It's more of a mid-range instrument . . . Apparently he wasn't really playing as a bass player, more like he was just like floating . . . They would try different amps to get him to be louder but it's just his touch and this particular instrument so I think they just figured it wasn't working out.

The rehearsals in May were even more basic than previous affairs. With no keyboards or girls to work into the arrangements, Dylan was free to go where it pleased him. Even before the tour had started, Dylan and the band had worked up a huge repertoire of something like seventy songs, though 'worked up' is probably something of a euphemism.

Certainly for Aaronson, thrown in at the deep end, it was a daunting experience. Like others before him he was given less than a week to master an entire repertoire, and Dylan would never work a song to death in rehearsal. Indeed, he gave some songs only the most cursory of run-throughs.

Bob Dylan: Rehearsing for me and my band might, in order to rehearse a song, only consist of knowing the title and what key to play it in. If we can do that, that's rehearsing. [1989]

Kenny Aaronson: I got this call from someone who represented him saying, Can you come down to rehearsal tomorrow? He wants you there tomorrow . . . Bob didn't show up that day. I just played with the band . . . So I came down a second day and Bob showed up for that day and then we started playing. They didn't even tell me if I had the gig. They just had me playing for days and I was learning fifteen to twenty tunes a day. Next thing I know a couple of days before the tour starts they finally say, Oh yeah you got the gig . . . I rehearsed for five days and I left for the West Coast . . . I learned sixty tunes in five days.

This was not the end of Aaronson's, or drummer Parker's,

education in Dylan's repertoire. Throughout the tour he added to the repertoire as the fancy took him. In some cases when he introduced a song into the set partway through the tour the song worked so well that it remained in the set, with something else going at its expense. Most, though, did not reappear except on rare occasions.

Kenny Aaronson: On the road every so often . . . before the show G.E. [Smith] would come back and go, Fellows, Bob wants us to do this tune and here's how it goes. And G.E. would show it to me and Chris Parker right before the show.

If Dylan had rehearsed loosely before, if he had introduced one-off songs into the set before, and if he had varied the set from night to night before, never had he done it on the scale he did in 1988. Playing sets on average fourteen or fifteen songs long, he compiled a staggering repertoire of over ninety songs in the space of three months on the road. The pace of the shows was unrelenting, save for a three- or four-song acoustic set at the mid-point of the seventy-minute shows.

Ironically, given his commercial status by 1988 and the complaints made in Europe the previous year about the short sets, the vast majority of reviewers loved the shows. They said that Dylan had not shown such energy and verve in many a moon, and that his stripped-down trio of rockers were breathing fresh air into his music. Certainly the variety of songs in the repertoire was remarkable, Dylan playing more songs on the 1988 tour's seventy-one shows than on the entire 115-date world tour of 1978, when he was playing shows of virtually twice the length.

Every show opened with a shocking blast from the past, the amphetamine rush of 'Subterranean Homesick Blues'; this was the first time the song had ever been performed in concert. The opening volley indicated the shape of things to come, as Dylan stuck fairly doggedly to his sixties repertoire. His work in the seventies and eighties was almost totally ignored save for a regular workout on one-permed-from-three from *Blood on the Tracks* – 'Shelter from the Storm', 'Tangled Up in Blue' or 'You're a Big Girl Now'; a fairly consistent 'In the Garden' and the soon-statutory 'Silvio'. Other gems from Dylan's more recent work, such as 'Forever Young', 'One More Cup of Coffee', 'Gotta Serve Somebody', 'Every Grain of Sand' or 'I'll Remember You', were rare events indeed.

Ironically Dylan reserved his best vocal performances each night for the one or two covers he was including. In most cases these covers formed part of the acoustic set, Dylan showing his roots with gorgeous renderings of folk songs like 'Barbara Allen', 'Trail of the Buffalo', 'Wagoner's Lad', 'Lakes of Pontchartrain', 'The Two Brothers', 'Eileen Aroon' and 'Man of Constant Sorrow', or country standards like 'Rank Strangers to Me' and 'Give My Love to Rose'. Some surprising one-off covers did occasionally crop up in the electric sets, sometimes in home towns of the song's writer: 'Nadine' in Chuck Berry's St Louis and 'Halleluiah' in Leonard Cohen's Montreal.

The tour criss-crossed the North American continent twice, starting in California in June, working across the mid-West to the East Coast, then across Canada, back down to California, up through the North-West States, then back down the East Coast to Florida and Louisiana in late September. As if this were not enough, after a three-week break Dylan played two shows in Philadelphia, then four at New York's Radio City Music Hall. It was a remarkable stint of touring for a forty-seven-year-old man. He was committing himself totally to his performance art again, and the 1988 tour was just the beginning of what Dylan himself later christened the Never-Ending Tour.

Bob Dylan: It's all the same tour. The Never-Ending Tour . . . It works out better for me that way. You can pick and choose better when you're just out there all the time and your show is already set up. You know, you just don't have to start it up and end it. It's better just to keep it out there with breaks . . . extended breaks. [1989]

Within seven months of completing his 1988 tour, Dylan was back on the road with the same band and a tour schedule designed to surpass even that marathon. Starting in May '89, the tour began in Europe with twenty-one shows scheduled through June. A further fifty-one in the States took in July, August and the beginning of September. He then embarked on a further twenty-seven shows in the US in October and November, making it ninety-nine in 1989. Along with the winter 1990 shows, he totalled 114 shows in less than nine months, an even more arduous itinerary than in 1978, when Dylan was eleven years younger.

The differences between the 1988 and 1989 shows though were night and day. Two more contrasting tours featuring such a stripped-down line-up would be difficult to imagine. Though the first couple of shows of each tour were fairly disastrous, in 1988 the quality of the performances peaked in mid-tour and tailed off dramatically after a mid-August eleven-day break. In contrast the 1989 shows were increasingly impressive as Dylan seemed to draw renewed strength from each performance, though he sorely needed his mid-September break to recharge his batteries.

The quality of Dylan's singing varied considerably between these tours. Since his 1981 European tour, a fairly steady decline in the quality of his singing in live performance, checked only by his 1987 shows with the Heartbreakers, had been readily discernible. This is not perhaps surprising given the punishment he inflicted on his singing voice through the seventies and the eighties, and the lack of care he has taken of it. Though some undiscerning critics have dismissed Dylan's singing, or worse still apologized for it, explaining that he does not need a great voice to get what he is saying across, throughout most of his career he has been the master of inflection, the overseer of the most flexible vocal chords in contemporary popular music. In the eighties, and Dylan's forties, the punishment has taken its toll. Without allowing himself reasonable time to repair the damage inflicted with each successive tour, Dylan's voice is no longer the flexible tool it once was.

In 1988 Dylan, seemingly unwilling to accept the passage of time, refused to adapt his voice to bring out the best it was still capable of, and roared through songs, trying to bend and twist the words in that age-old way and going for notes that used to bring gasps of astonishment but now only brought sighs of disappointment. However, his innate sense of timing still existed, and a growling rumble had developed in his voice which was at times most effective. In 1988, though, it was generally used only during the acoustic sets, when he was not raging against the roaring glory around him. The electric sets tended to be brutal affairs. On the bitter-sweet *Blood on the Tracks* songs the snappy delivery and some ill-considered wailing often detracted from the power of the words. Only on 'You're a Big Girl Now', when Dylan adopted a clipped reggaefied inflection, could the new style of singing be considered successful.

In 1988 the acoustic sets were the highlights of the shows night in, night out. Despite a tendency to indulge in unnecessary instrumental doodling with G. E. Smith, who played second guitar on these sets throughout the tour, and his decision not to use his harmonica to add variety to the sound, his singing was often marvellously expressive, his choice of covers adventurous, and the performances full of conviction.

So to 1989 and the Never-Ending Tour Mk2. The rehearsals for the tour suggested that this would be very different. Dylan seemed confident playing with the band, having broken them in in 1988, and began to experiment with a lot of unusual covers during rehearsals — though, surprisingly, they worked on none of the songs he had just recorded in New Orleans.

Christopher Parker: Among the stranger things we did [at rehearsals] were 'I Can See for Miles', the Who tune, 'You Keep Me Hangin' On', the Vanilla Fudge song, slow version, 'Where or When' by Rodgers and Hart, we've done that a lot of times now . . . 'Mystery Train' — that's Junior Parker, something called '12 Volt Waltz' — that was pretty neat, 'Sweet Dreams of You' — Patsy Cline, 'Walking after Midnight', 'Little Queen of Spades', I think that's Robert Johnson, 'Poison Ivy', 'The Blue Ridge Mountains', 'High School Hop' [sic] — Jerry Lee Lewis, 'Mountain of Love' — Johnny Rivers, 'Ring of Fire', 'Give My Love to Rose', 'Love's Made a Fool of You' — Buddy Holly, 'God Only Knows' — the Beach Boys, we do that every set, so that's probably gonna be in there . . . Sometimes G.E. and I request something, like 'Tears of Rage'. I requested 'When I Paint My Masterpiece', and he got out the lyric book and sang the lyrics, and to watch him singing, it was like rediscovering the songs for himself.

In 1988, most of the covers had come during the acoustic sets (only seven of the twenty-three covers performed were with the band). Though the fans did not get to hear all the songs listed above, Dylan performed something like forty covers on his massive 1989 stint, the vast majority with the band. At least one member of the band, bassist Kenny Aaronson, found it a little hard going.

Kenny Aaronson: The second time around this past year when I was rehearsing for the European tour . . . he was pulling out tunes that I'd never heard, and I was having a hard time there for a while. I mean I was like making notes constantly and writing out charts and going home with tapes that the soundman would give me.

Aware that he would be treading familiar terrain for much of the 1989 tour, Dylan even considered ways of making the sound a little different from the previous year's shows. According to Aaronson, he thought of touring with some of the local New Orleans musicians he had worked with in March and April. Having decided to stick with the tried and tested, he brought in an extra musician to add some variety to the sound. Sadly, she did not last out the rehearsals.

Kenny Aaronson: He even had at one point this girl called Mindy – I forget her last name but she's the girl in Billy Joel's new band – playing guitar and she plays fiddle and I guess G.E. knew her so Bob was looking for something possibly to add to the band, so for a few days we were rehearsing with her. And he would just pull out all these songs she could just play fiddle on.

However, there was another change, less welcome, that also threatened to make the 1989 tour very different from the previous one – Dylan's mood. In 1988 he seemed delighted to be playing with a tight, kick-ass band and after the first two shows seemed totally into the performance each night. The musicians found him reasonably outgoing, at least for a man as intensely private as Dylan can be, and there was a definite camaraderie evident at the shows.

If the songs he had recorded in New Orleans in spring 1989 were anything to go by, in 1989 he was a different person. Gone was the light whimsy of the songs on the Wilburys' album. Every song on *Oh Mercy* suggested a mightily troubled man. His songs about personal relationships were sad and resigned, hinting of the irreconcilable ('Most of the Time', 'What Good Am I?', 'What Was It You Wanted'); his songs on wider themes were suffused once again with the apocalyptic ('Ring Them Bells', 'Everything Is Broken'). Each side of the album ends with the narrator stuck in a holocaust of terrifying proportions – 'the water is high', 'tree trunks uprooted', 'the last firetruck from hell goes rollin' by'. The mood seemed to carry over into rehearsals.

Kenny Aaronson: I found during rehearsals the second time around that he was a lot more distant . . . He seemed a bit more distracted. I'm sure that's one of the many moods of Bob Dylan . . . I found rehearsals with him the second time around in 1989 very, very vague . . . Like he'll just play something and you kinda don't know what he wants you to do; and then you mess around and he'll never really tell you much. I mean in rehearsals he hardly said a word or even hardly looked at me at all for [the] two, three weeks I rehearsed with him in '89.

Dylan's mood did not improve when he was informed just before flying to Europe that Aaronson would be unable to complete the European leg of the tour as he had been diagnosed as having skin cancer. An immediate operation would probably be successful but it meant he would have to leave the tour within a week of its start.

Two shows in Sweden opened Dylan's 1989 sortie through

Europe, where just twenty-one shows were planned, scarcely touching base with many centres of support. As in 1988, the opening shows were more than a little disappointing. Opening in Stockholm with 'Subterranean Homesick Blues', he performed just one song new to hardcore fans, an old Eddy Arnold tune 'You Don't Know Me'. Worse still he seemed bored – a rare occurrence at the first gig of a tour – and he performed the entire show with an anorak hood over his head, obscuring all but part of his face. Throughout the first week, during shows in Malmö, Stockholm and Helsinki and the first night in Dublin, Dylan continued to perform with hood up, a peaked hat peeking (*sic*) out underneath, and with the lights very dim. It was not a promising start.

However, at the fourth show, the first of two consecutive gigs in Dublin, though he still remained hooded, he at least started to suggest he was approaching his songs with some commitment. A lengthy show by Never-Ending Tour standards, it crept over the ninety-minute mark. It also featured a seemingly impromptu electric version of 'The Water Is Wide', a beautiful traditional song he had last performed with Joan Baez on the first Rolling Thunder tour.

The tide had turned. The following night the hood was gone, and Dylan brought out U2's Bono for a rabble-rousing encore. On to Scotland and England, where the shows were full of pugnacious energy and Dylan's voice seemed to be in good shape for the first time on the tour. The London show was Kenny Aaronson's final show. A 'sub' called Tony Garnier had flown into Dublin the previous weekend, and rehearsed with the band that Saturday, playing the first Dublin gig, at which Dylan started to unwind, typically providing the most interesting and perverse set of the tour to date while a new man fumbled through the changes.

Unperturbed by Garnier's lack of rehearsal, Dylan began to pepper show after show with previously unperformed covers, from Hank Williams' 'House of Gold', through Sonny Knight's 'Confidential to Me' and Townes Van Zandt's 'Pancho and Lefty' to Thomas A. Dorsey's '(There'll Be) Peace in the Valley', a song perhaps most associated with Elvis Presley. If Garnier felt he was in at the deep end in Europe, matters became no easier back in the United States. At the first three shows, Dylan drew out Van Morrison's 'One Irish Rover', Glen Glenn's 'Everybody's Moving', Gordon Lightfoot's 'Early Morning Rain', and from his own back catalogue 'I Believe in You', 'Gotta Serve Somebody', 'Pledging My Time', 'Driftin' Too Far from Shore', 'I Dreamed I Saw St Augustine' and 'Just Like Tom Thumb's Blues'.

The most encouraging aspect of these shows was that Dylan was singing once again with his previously keen precision, his delivery rarely forced or hurried. He seemed more willing to caress the words he had written, as he had been doing the previous year during the acoustic sets. The covers he was playing were often spectacular. On the summer jaunt through the States, he sang two superb versions of Van Morrison songs, 'And It Stoned Me' and 'One Irish Rover', the former of which Dylan had largely rewritten.* Equally impressive and surprising were versions of Don Gibson's 'I'd Be a Legend in My Time', Steve Earle's 'Nothing But You' and Jimmy Cliff's 'The Harder They Come'.

The 1989 tour also proved a delight because of Dylan's decision to bring the harmonica back to centre-stage. Even today, his picking up the mouth-harp brings whoops of excitement from his fans, and in 1989, though occasionally wayward and even sometimes in the wrong key, most often Dylan's harmonica-playing gave a new dimension to the band's sound.

The one disappointing event that summer was Dylan's decision not to bring the now fully fit and ready for action Kenny Aaronson back into the band. Though Garnier had performed perfectly adequately, his bass playing lacked the rib-thudding resonance of Aaronson, and Aaronson was a more colourful contributor to the band. According to Aaronson there had never been any question that Garnier was anything but a 'sub' while he was treated. He thus headed to Jones Beach in upstate New York on 23 July, three weeks into Dylan's nine-week trek through the USA, to say hi to him and inform him he was ready to return. However, Dylan had clearly decided he would be able to get along without him.

Kenny Aaronson: That was a weird day for me, man ... I got there and every guy in the crew came up to me and hugged me and in my ear whispered, When you comin' back, man? We miss you. And I said, Well I came to talk to Bob. About half an hour, forty minutes before the show Bob's manager came up to me and said, Bob wants to know if you wanna come up and play some tunes. I said sure. Then about five minutes before the show Bob called me into the dressing room just to

---

* Morrison and Dylan had spent some time together on the European tour, culminating, in Athens, with Morrison coming out during Dylan's encore to perform 'Crazy Love' and 'And It Stoned Me', and the pair singing together on the hill overlooking the Acropolis for an Arena documentary on Morrison.

have a chat. He just wanted to talk I guess, and see how I was doing. I was all focused on wanting to come back to work. So we talked for a little while and then I said, Well, do I look like I'm a sick guy? I'm ready to come back to work. And he started giving me this beating around the bush kinda thing. 'Well, I wanna get out of this area and get up back out there and think about it and I'm not sure if I wanna change the band right now.' Just gave me all this shit. Basically I got the vibe y'know . . . He actually said to me, I don't give a shit who plays bass.

Inevitably, as the tour progressed through the Southern States in late August, three months on from Sweden, the shows began to become workmanlike. Dylan had never toured this long without a break, and in previous instances, during the late seventies and eighties, his voice had begun to show signs of real wear if he played more than thirty shows without a break. Though he was still managing to put real enthusiasm into his shows in early August, the voice was already badly tattered, and the band sounded a little burnt out.

Dylan did his best to make these shows sound fresh, introducing new slow, taunting arrangements of some of his 1965 classics – 'Positively Fourth Street', 'Queen Jane Approximately' and 'It Takes a Lot to Laugh' all appearing in the August shows. He also began to embellish more and more songs with the piping whine of his harmonica. The shows were now stretching beyond ninety minutes night after night, though the number of songs generally remained around the sixteen to seventeen mark established at the later European shows. However, by the time he arrived in California the shows were not impressive. The two Greek Theater shows concluded three months' solid touring, and the choice of material was unadventurous save for a spirited if unsuccessful opener for the first night, an electric 'Visions of Johanna'. Three days before, in San Diego, Dylan had seemed to confirm worst predictions by performing an entire show of songs recorded between 1961 and 1967.

Perhaps the Never-Ending Tour, after many glorious moments, had finally run its course. After all the Rolling Thunder band lasted two tours; the 1978 band 115 shows; the evangelist-trilogy band from November '79 to November '81; the Heartbreakers a Far East, an American and a European tour. Though tickets had gone on sale for further shows in October, starting with a four-day residency at the wonderfully intimate 2,700-seat Beacon Theater in New York, perhaps this would be the finale for the Never-Ending Tour. After all, Dylan had generally only previously performed when he had something original to say. If the

Never-Ending Tour was to continue he needed to find that something new.

On 10 October 1989 Dylan was back on the road. A month's respite was all that separated his seventy-one-date summer 1989 tour from his month-long fall tour. In the interim, though, CBS had finally released his last album of the eighties, and his first album of wholly original compositions in four years – *Oh Mercy*. It turned out to be his most critically acclaimed album of the eighties, even warranting inclusion in *Rolling Stone*'s year-end selection of Albums of the Eighties (Dylan's only other inclusion being the Wilburys' album).

The 10th was opening night in a four-date residency at the Beacon Theater. Despite playing seventy-one shows since recording *Oh Mercy*, the summer tour had been singularly bereft of new Dylan songs. He had also paid scant attention to his eighties work, to the extent that he had dropped 'Silvio' and 'Driftin' Too Far from Shore' – the only two 'regulars' in the 1988 sets that were drawn from his previous two studio albums. Despite the undoubted energy and commitment he had displayed through the tour, there was an unfailing sense that Dylan was trucking around with an oldies show.

With the release of *Oh Mercy*, Dylan could now re-evaluate what exactly he wanted to say at his concerts. The fall shows needed to combine the best aspects of the Never-Ending Tour to date – a tight band, interesting sets, inventive singing and harp-playing from Dylan – with a more contemporary song selection, designed to illustrate the fact that here was a still vital artist.

The indications were that Dylan was aware of this. Despite the fact that the band now sounded as smooth as a well-oiled engine, he booked three days of rehearsals in New York before the Beacon shows, suggesting he intended to work some *Oh Mercy* songs into the set. The opening charge at the Beacon was a decent blast from the recent past, 'Seeing the Real You at Last', seguing into a heartfelt 'What Good Am I?' and a rambling 'Dead Man Dead Man'. An opening trio of eighties cuts seemed an invigorating statement of intent, particularly as this pattern remained for all the Beacon shows. The third night even saw the welcome introduction of 'Man of Peace' from *Infidels* into the first set. With two cuts from *Oh Mercy* saved for the second half of the show – 'Most of the Time' and 'Everything Is Broken' – it seemed the most satisfying cross-section of Dylan songs in concert for eight years.

The eighties songs were not the only surprises at the Beacon shows. If Dylan's voice on the summer 1989 shows represented a quantum leap over the 1988 vocals, the fall voice was a further leap back to former glories. It actually seemed as if, after a wasted decade, he had heeded the obvious and obtained some vocal training to teach him how best to use his forty-eight-year-old vocal chords. The version of 'Queen Jane Approximately' at the third Beacon show proved even such hallowed territory as a *Highway 61 Revisited* cut could be redefined and surpassed. The electric 'My Back Pages' was treated to the vocal it had deserved back in 1988. 'Positively Fourth Street' was tinged with an underlying sorrow beneath the vehemence, as he tightly wound the words round a beautiful, brooding arrangement. The harmonica playing remained erratic but also occasionally dazzlingly brilliant.

Ironically, given the remarkable stamina and consistency maintained throughout most of the summer, the fall tour peaked early and declined rapidly into 'more of the same'. Within ten days of the first Beacon show the best dates were over and gone. A show in Poughkeepsie provided the early peak, Dylan performing two songs standing up at the piano, one of which was a unique live 'Ring Them Bells', part of an exhausting hundred-minute set of sustained peaks. Subsequently the *Oh Mercy* songs were all shunted together in an overlong second band set and the more sensitive material became overly strident. The other eighties songs, so welcome at the Beacon, soon disappeared from view.

Yet Dylan himself seemed unaware of any loss of momentum. Within two months of concluding his fall tour in Miami, he was playing his first show of 1990. On 12 January, as a warm-up for two stadium shows in Brazil and ten shows in Paris and London, he played his first headline club show in over twenty-five years, at the 700-capacity Toad's Place in New Haven. This in itself would have been remarkable. That this forty-eight-year-old man then stayed on stage longer than any concert Springsteen, the king of marathon performances, has ever given makes his Toad's performance the definitive testament to his enduring love for performing.

Starting at a quarter to nine, with a cover of Joe South's 'Walk a Mile in My Shoes', Dylan finally left the Toad's stage at twenty minutes past two in the morning, after playing four sets, interspersed by three breaks of just twenty-five minutes each, having played some fifty songs in total, only eight of which were derived from his supposed halcyon days of 1963–6. The majority of the songs were either rare outings for seventies cuts like 'One More

Cup of Coffee' and 'Joey' or previously unaired eighties cuts like
'Tight Connection to My Heart', 'Political World' and 'What Was
It You Wanted'; plus a total of no less than eighteen covers,
including such off-the-wall choices as Springsteen's 'Dancing in
the Dark', Kristofferson's 'Help Me Make It Through the Night'
and the fifties-style 'Wiggle Wiggle'. He was even relatively
talkative, jokingly referring to 'Man of Peace' as from his religious
period, and 'Lay Lady Lay' as from his romantic period, and
responding to requests. He even played 'Joey' after initially insisting
it was too long and reminding the requester this was the fifth such
request he was playing for him.

Two further warm-up shows at colleges on the East Coast,
though somewhat shorter, continued to feature a Dylan experimenting with the format of his shows. At Penn State, he wholly
abandoned his acoustic set and played a hundred-minute set with the
band. Though at Princeton the acoustic set was restored to favour it
came after just one electric number. The reports of these shows
suggested that Dylan was back to his Beacon best in time for his ten
dates in Paris and London, and sure enough the spirit of adventure
prevailed at these shows too. In a mere ten shows, he performed
some seventy-eight songs! From *Oh Mercy*, only 'Shooting Star' and
'Ring Them Bells' remained unperformed that winter, while
lovers of the traditional were treated to acoustic versions of 'Barbara
Allen', 'Man of Constant Sorrow' and 'Dark as a Dungeon', and
electrifying reworkings of 'Pretty Peggy-O' and 'Hang Me O Hang
Me', a song which, prior to Toad's, he had last performed back in
1963 for the BBC production of *Madhouse on Castle Street*. Though
the European fans still welcomed the inevitable greatest hits, the
greatest cheers seemed to be reserved for the *Oh Mercy* songs. The
English press for once sensed the fervour that greeted his revival, and
responded with their best concert reviews for Dylan in twelve years.

If the European shows seemed the logical culmination of the
Never-Ending Tour, Dylan refused to see it that way. Once again
summer shows were scheduled in North America and Europe,
though the schedule was considerably less hectic than in 1988 and
1989 – a mere sixteen dates in Canada and the mid-West, nine
dates in Europe and a further twenty-two dates in the States
represented the sum total of his spring and summer activities. The
early shows, though, affirmed that as Dylan's grasp of his own
inimitable performing abilities was gradually being restored to
him, his perspective on his own career was rapidly deteriorating.

Dylan's motives for this brief summer jaunt remain unclear. The early shows featured some unique moments and several encouraging signs. His singing remained impressive and his harmonica-playing was consistent and often spellbinding. In mid-concert the acoustic slot had given way to a semi-acoustic set, Dylan and Smith remaining on acoustic guitars, Garnier reverting to stand-up bass and Parker playing with brushes or keeping a simple beat on high-hat and bass drum.

The most welcome change, though, was in Dylan's demeanour. At the final Beacon show in October 1989 he had astonished fans by diving into the audience during the last encore. In Miami, at the penultimate fall show, he was seen grinning his way through an acoustic 'Tangled Up in Blue' while a lady from the audience climbed onto the stage and began stripping. At the Hammersmith shows he actually mumbled the occasional one-liner to the audience, informing them that 'Watching the River Flow' was a new arrangement of 'Subterranean Homesick Blues' and so forth. By the fourth of his North American shows in early June, he was being positively gregarious and seemed to be genuinely enjoying his time up on stage, even responding to requests. On one occasion he was in the middle of the introduction to 'It's All Over Now, Baby Blue', when a request for 'Tomorrow Is a Long Time' caused him to stop and observe, 'It sure is. Awfully long,' before switching to the requested tune.

Yet the summer shows were a disappointment after the fall 1989 and winter 1990 shows. They suggested that Dylan had returned to perceiving himself as an oldies act again. The preponderance of sixties 'hits' was overwhelming. Two or three songs from *Oh Mercy* was all fans could expect at each show, and the songs on such remarkable albums as *Planet Waves, Desire, Street-Legal, Shot of Love* and *Infidels* were all wholly ignored.

So why has Dylan so little faith in his own later material and his ability to put these songs across? His feelings about his greatest hits have always been ambiguous. There is a common story that Paul Simon once complained to Dylan that his fans always seemed to want to hear him perform 'Homeward Bound', 'Sound of Silence' etc. Dylan supposedly replied that if he went to a Paul Simon concert those would be the songs he would like to hear. Yet Dylan himself has not always seen fit to 'dish out' his own hits. In 1975 the Rolling Thunder set concentrated on the as-yet-unreleased *Desire* songs. In 1976 the choice of 'old songs' seemed deliberately perverse. In 1979/80 the 'old songs' were wholly excluded, and even when reintroduced in late 1980 were outnumbered by covers and as-yet-unreleased songs. In 1981 the old songs were often tossed away with never a thought, Dylan reserving an extra vocal commitment for his newer material. Yet still the fans bayed for the 'oldies'.

Since 1984 Dylan has not been quite so tenacious in his resistance to the audience's preconceptions. Though on all of his mid-eighties tours (1984, 1986, 1987) he began each time with reasonably audacious sets, within two or three shows he had revised the sets to the detriment of the more recent songs. In 1984 the shambolic first show in Verona featured versions of 'When You Gonna Wake Up', 'Heart of Mine' and 'Man of Peace', all of which were rare events indeed at later shows. In 1986 a similarly ramshackle opening show in Wellington featured 'Gotta Serve Somebody', 'Shot of Love' and 'Heart of Mine', all of which were quickly dropped.

The 1987 European tour featured a more adventurous Dylan, for which he was widely castigated. At the first show in Tel Aviv he played a lovely cross-section of his work with five of the seventeen songs from the seventies, four songs from the eighties and one traditional cover. The response was such that Dylan was required to defend himself in print, insisting to Robert Hilburn, of the *Los Angeles Times*, before his show in Jerusalem:

Bob Dylan: You don't want to just get up there and start guessing with the people what they want. For one thing, no one agrees on that. The songs a few people want to hear may not mean anything to a whole lot of others, and you can't let the audience start controlling the show or you're going to end up on a sinking ship. You've got to stay in control, or you might as well go hole up in Las Vegas somewhere because you're not being true to the music anymore . . . you're being true to something else that doesn't really mean anything except some applause.

Nevertheless the show in Jerusalem saw restored to favour the irksome likes of 'Times They Are a-Changin'', 'Like a Rolling Stone', 'Rainy Day Women' and 'Ballad of a Thin Man'. At the final seven shows of the European tour, in England, he seemed deliberately to parody himself by opening with a 'Times'/'Blowin'' – 'Maggie's Farm' – 'Like a Rolling Stone' trilogy in which he methodically stripped each song of every ounce of meaning. If such disrespect worried new Dylan concert-goers, he then turned up the heat with sets of remarkable intensity. The press were too busy emphasizing Dylan's 'death mask' look and his between-song taciturnity to notice the gesture.

When the Never-Ending Tour started, Dylan seemed more willing to reach a *rapprochement* with those fans there to hear 'the hits'. Yet after 'I'll Remember You' at the fourth show, he retorted, 'I don't think that's an obscure song. Do you think that's an obscure song? I don't think so,' incensed by a review of the previous show, where again he had been attacked for his bold song selections.

Since the mid-seventies Dylan has constantly had to balance the wishes of the members of the audiences there for a night out, who know him mainly by reputation and inferior cover versions and perhaps the odd compilation album once left behind at an all-night party, with his own artistic integrity. With his low commercial stock and the sheer need to fill seats in three years of summer gigs with the same trio, Dylan no longer seems sure of his instincts. Outside the presumably hip havens of the West and East Coast, London and Paris, he seems unwilling to take risks on the mid-West picnic circuit. This is reflected in his unwillingness to perform new, as yet unreleased songs in his sets.

Now that the summer 1990 shows have reverted to the 1988 pattern, Dylan is again perceived as an artist trading on his past, no matter how convincingly he may interpret his sixties material. This seems somewhat incongruous given that in the fall of 1989 and the winter of 1990 he had so convincingly championed his recent work, notably from the impressive *Oh Mercy*. He did this at a time when the survivors of perhaps the three most important British bands of the sixties – the Who, the Rolling Stones and, from the Beatles, Paul McCartney and Ringo Starr – were all touting their wares around the world with shows sold on the back of a nascent nostalgia. Dylan's performances remained a refreshing alternative.

The way that Dylan approaches his *œuvre* has generally belied nostalgia. At his best, when the songs are transformed in arrangement and/or delivery, the songs resonate with new meaning. Yet the simple gesture of playing 'Like a Rolling Stone' or 'I Shall Be Released' remains an all-too-easy option to incite the crowd and reduce his performances to rock & roll spectacles, no more valid and considerably less profitable than the 1989 Stones extravaganza.

That Dylan was still capable of his best in 1990 had been proved in Paris and London, at the earlier of the summer shows in Canada, and at the five shows at the Beacon Theater in October. Despite such welcome exceptions, by October not only had Dylan's commitment to performance dimmed somewhat, but so had the patience of his right-hand man through the entire Never-Ending Tour. The October shows in New York were G. E. Smith's final stand, despite a further twenty G.E.-less dates having already been slotted into the fall 1990 itinerary.

At the August/September shows guitarists had been auditioning for G.E.'s place in the band on stage, playing alongside G.E. as Dylan churned out predictable 'greatest hits' sets. None of the four aspiring incumbents seemed adequate to the task of compensating for the loss of a man that Dylan seems to have considered no more than a hired hand – and whom Dylan has repeatedly ignored when making studio recordings – but who every witness to the shows they played together realizes was the mainspring of the band, a flexible, responsive band-leader who had saved Dylan from many a scrape in mid-concert. G.E.'s gradual disillusionment with the tour after the euphoria of the London shows is probably a major factor in the decline evident in recent months. Without G.E. the band have become rudderless, adrift night after night, and presumably with little faith in Captain Bob's ability to steer them through.

Dylan's treatment of Smith, though G.E. is less evidently bitter than Kenny Aaronson, closely mirrors his treatment of the ex-bassist. Taken together with stories of Dylan's reasons for rejecting the two most suitable candidates for G.E.'s place in the band, Miles Joseph and Steve Bruton, on the grounds that Joseph asked him for an autograph and Bruton had too many hardware guitar effects, hardly inspires confidence in Dylan's ability to command loyalty and respect from the next ensemble he seeks to create.

Gone are the days when the musicians played with Dylan for the experience of playing with the great man. Playing with Dylan has become just another gig. After all, since 1987 Dylan has not reserved his gruff, taciturn exterior for just the fans and media. Band members rarely see the man except on stage and most signals to the band have been relayed though G.E.

The worry that Dylan is showing signs of real paranoia has for many coloured an appreciation of the achievements of the Never-Ending Tour. It would be no exaggeration to say that Dylan and G. E. Smith have literally redefined the meaning of the live rock & roll performance in an era when the pomp of the spectacle has all too often drawn attention away from the essence of the rock & roll experience – live music played and sung with a commitment to the genre. Yet Dylan's increasingly bizarre demeanour as the Never-Ending Tour has progressed suggests that perhaps he is only playing lip-service to the audience he seemed so keen to seek a *rapprochement* with back in 1988.

39

1990: The Finishing End?

In 1973 Dylan insisted, in the song 'Dirge', that he was not one of those that worshipped loneliness. Yet neither *Oh Mercy* nor *Under the Red Sky* sound like the works of a man revelling in the joys of human companionship. Since breaking up with Clydie King in 1983 only two women have definitely been contenders for any kind of serious relationship with Dylan. Undoubtedly the most enduring of his post-divorce girlfriends has been Carol Childs. A respected A&R executive at Geffen Records, Childs has been a recurring factor in Dylan's life since 1984. She has been portrayed as 'long-suffering and intense', Dylan evidently taking a great deal of notice of Childs' opinions, offering her protégés Lone Justice, one of his unreleased songs back in 1984, and even heeding her advice on who to use to produce his 1990 album.

Don Was: She'd played our stuff for him and made him aware of it, talked about us . . . and then six months later I got a call from Carol saying, 'Bob would like to know if you're interested in doing a track [with him].' And that was 'God Knows'.

Far more blatant in advertising her relationship with Dylan has been American actress Sally Kirkland, who since 1989 has rarely given a TV or newspaper interview without detailing at length her 'long-standing' love affair with Dylan. She has implied on American TV that Dylan is a voracious lover. Inevitably she has also suggested that he has written some of his recent songs with her in mind.

Sally Kirkland: He is often away on the road and I am away working, but we keep in touch through his songs and my poems. In . . . 'Everything Is Broken', he wrote the lines for me 'Every time you leave/and go off some place/things go to pieces in my face.'

Kirkland had originally been involved with Dylan at the time of the second Carter benefit in January 1976. Their affair was short-lived (though she was photographed on his arm in March 1977 at the time Sara was filing for divorce). They renewed their friendship in the late eighties. Yet Kirkland is no constant companion. Like Childs, their relationship seems to be bound by occasional mutual gaps in their schedules.

Nor are Childs and Kirkland the only women to have flitted in and out of his life in the last few years. Apart from his many women friends who are indeed friends – and Dylan has always seemed more able to maintain an ongoing dialogue with women than men – he has continued to indulge his love for women on a random basis. As someone recently put it in an article on Dylan's recent lifestyle, 'There are a lot of different women he sees, from all different walks of life. But they all tend to have one thing in common. They're invariably all very weird or very intense.' Which closely accords with descriptions of the women that Revue members recall surrounding him on that 1976 caravan through the Southern States.

What none of these relationships has succeeded in doing is keeping Dylan at home to enjoy the delights of the hearth, rather than playing the perpetual troubadour moving on from town to town. Save possibly for Clydie King, none of his post-divorce girlfriends seems to have managed to sublimate his restless, hungry feelings, and despite regular contact with his children and ex-wife – there was even speculation in the press in 1983 that he and Sara were on the verge of marrying again – Dylan remains a solitary figure.

Of course he has never had a problem being by himself. For much of his youth in Hibbing he kept himself to himself, and he has rarely revealed his inner thoughts and feelings except in song, even to friends and lovers. Now that he has closed himself off from much of the real world – perhaps the only feasible solution to the incursions and impositions made upon him by outsiders – only his close relationships with friends and lovers allow him to maintain contact with a degree of normality.

Indeed several friends have confirmed that in a one-to-one situation or as part of a small group of confidants Dylan remains the same person he has been throughout his creative years, a painfully shy but wry and witty man who genuinely craves sincere input and expression. Certainly Dylan values the long-standing friendships he has managed to maintain in the goldfish bowl-like existence he has been forced to lead for most of his life. Friends and fellow musicians all speak of Dylan's desire to maintain at least sporadic contact with those he has known along the way.

However Dylan has become increasingly wary of strangers, and new faces are very rarely allowed a peek inside the inner circle. His notorious unpredictability also instils a fear in many of the people that work for him. This is perhaps exemplified by the fact that his own musicians and road crew are afraid to ask for something as mundane as a dub of a soundboard tape of a show – Dylan's paranoia about bootlegging being long-standing – preferring to ask the perennial audience tapers who remorselessly pursue the man for dubs of their recordings.

A friend of Dylan's recently insisted that he is not 'a control freak', constantly seeking to control the dissemination of his output, yet in the notes for *Biograph* he described bootleggers as 'outrageous . . . you're just sitting and strumming in a motel . . . the phone is tapped . . . and then it appears on a bootleg record. With a cover that's got a picture of you that was taken from underneath your bed.' When asked by a fan who had been caught videoing a show for an autograph he replied he did not give autographs to thieves. The more meticulously thorough his fans who seek to document his performances become, the more Dylan seems to resent their enterprise rather than embrace them as the Grateful Dead have, even though in the Walkman era efforts to restrict such attempts remain utterly futile.

If Dylan's reputation as a live performer and recording artist has once again been in the ascendant since 1988 – harsh reviews for *Under the Red Sky* notwithstanding – stories of his eccentricities have become more and more prevalent. Even in 1986 he still seemed able to confront his detractors with razor wit while maintaining a refreshingly down-to-earth approach to his own fame. From 1987, though, he has adopted a bizarre Howard Hughes of rock & roll persona, at variance with his less eccentric contemporaries like McCartney and Jagger.

It may seem curious to consider Dylan to again be a Hughes-like figure given the amount of touring, and therefore very public appearances, he has undertaken in the last five years. Yet even in concert his recalcitrance has led to bizarre rituals on stage. Since 1987, when the European press delighted in reproducing photos of Dylan's 'death mask' look on his European tour, he has consistently refused to allow photo passes at concerts and has hounded any illicit photographers. Indeed, at a show in Toronto in June 1990 he requested that anyone in the audience who saw someone next to him taking photos should restrain the offender. When Kenny Aaronson asked for a photo of the 1988 band in rehearsal, he had to swear he would allow no one to take copies. Dylan recently commented in an interview:

Bob Dylan: It rubs me the wrong way, a camera. It doesn't matter who it is, someone in my own family could be pointing a camera around. It's a frightening feeling . . . Cameras make ghosts out of people. [1990]

Dylan has always remained ambivalent about photos of himself. He has previously enjoyed photo sessions where he could provide his own creative input. Yet they are rare events indeed these days. Recently he has made photographing him in concert extra difficult by shrouding himself in darkness for most of the shows. During two shows in Greece in 1989 he insisted that the lights were turned down for the conclusion of his main sets, even barking out a command during mid-song, and the encores were played out in virtually total darkness. Earlier on that European tour he had appeared on stage for the first four shows wearing a hood over his head and a cap underneath, and retained this ludicrous attire throughout the entire show. Though the 1990 shows have been considerably better lit than the two previous summers' shows, Dylan's own features still remain largely shadowed by overhead and back-lighting, particularly with the hats he now generally wears on stage.

His Hooded Man persona would be outlandish enough if adopted solely on stage; but now he seems to have made the cape/cap look his 'public image', complete with a pair of shades to shut himself off wholly from those around him. This look could hardly have been chosen for reasons of inconspicuousness. Sitting in a deserted New York bar on a humid October evening with one's hood up is not the sort of appearance which discourages a second glance. As if this were not strange enough, he apparently turned up at sessions for *Under the Red Sky* and the second Wilburys album similarly attired, sitting in the recording studio with his hood up and cap on. Quite what he fears friends like George Harrison and Tom Petty might see, one can only guess.

Slash: Even when he was talking to me [at the *Under the Red Sky* sessions], all I could see behind all those fuckin' hoods and the shades was his nose and, like, his upper lip.

The recall of Victor Maimudes as his personal assistant through-out the Never-Ending Tour, after a major disagreement with his long-time assistant Gary Shafner during the previous European tour, confirms an unwillingness to allow new faces into the Dylan camp. Members of the crew, indeed members of the band, now rarely see him except on stage. He travels on his own bus, separate from the band, often staying at different hotels. He rarely appears at soundchecks, is often absent at rehearsals and even avoids studio sessions when overdubs or mixing are the major activities. He out-and-out refuses requests for autographs from fans who run across him on his travels and in one instance before a recent show in New York, he was seen running the couple of yards from his limo to the stage-door to avoid no more than two bemused middle-aged English fans standing five yards back from his car.

It should be no surprise that Dylan betrays the occasional sign of paranoia. After all he has been subjected to an incalculable degree of vicarious adulation from fans who have been 'bothered' – to use Dylan's own word – by the lyrics to his songs. An indication of these pressures and Dylan's intense concern about them can be found in a declaration to the courts by his lawyer, David Braun, in March 1977, requesting that the records of his divorce case be sealed:

David Braun: When people know where he is, his garbage is sifted and examined regularly; groups appear in front of his house on his birthday. Fans constantly try to reach him to talk to him, to touch him and to see him. Recently, the Sheriff had to be called to remove a girl from the driveway of his home; afterwards she sprayed black paint all over his windows. A disturbed person has been trying to reach Mr Dylan through me and is threatening to harm himself if he is unsuccessful. As a result of this and much, much more, Mr Dylan has been required to engage twenty-four-hour guards about his property to prevent trespassers and protect the privacy of himself and his family . . . In my twenty-two years' experience of representing famous personages no other personality has attracted such attention, nor created such a demand for information about his personal affairs.

The irony is that whatever commercial success Dylan has enjoyed (and certainly his sales do not start to compare with his fellow sixties 'icons', the Beatles and the Rolling Stones), and whatever degree of adulation has been expended on other rock & roll stars, it is perhaps only Dylan who has been perceived as a seer, even a figure of messianic proportions. That Dylan should thus shirk from the expectations of his audience is perhaps not surprising. Indeed it almost represents a *modus operandi* for much of his work.

It is understandable that thirty years of dealing with the media have made him reluctant to grant interviews. Yet when promoting *Oh Mercy* he was so tight-lipped during an interview for a two-hour syndicated radio special that the producers had to piece together enough material by using chunks of a 1981 interview with Dave Herman and interviewing people who had worked with him. An equally taciturn Dylan was the subject of a major feature in *Q*, yet repeatedly stalled from giving the interview necessary for the feature and finally gave a string of one-line replies to the questions asked. In order to promote *Oh Mercy* with the statutory video, CBS were required to produce their own composite video for 'Everything Is Broken' from existing footage, without any input from Dylan at all. When he finally got around to producing a video himself, of 'Most of the Time', Dylan recorded a live version of the song wholly different in sound and performance from the album version. Produced by Don Was, the new version of 'Most of the Time' seemed more a foretaste of the new album than a promotional item for *Oh Mercy*.

Of course, Dylan's whole career has been driven by acts of perversity. The only thing predictable about Dylan is that he will be unpredictable. Still, his recent eccentricities must give cause for concern. The triumph of his career has been the way he has constantly inverted, desecrated or just downright stomped upon audience expectations, and yet his artistry has survived each chameleon twist.

But perversity in his art does not presuppose a man careering out of control. His recent eccentricities do. Such peculiar practices have inevitably led to rumours of a resumption of drug-taking by Dylan, though save for his abiding penchant for alcohol no concrete evidence has ever been provided of a drug habit in the eighties. John Bauldie commented in the *Telegraph*, in response to such speculation, that 'occasional rantings from the stage in 1986 were possibly the products of his medicinal consumption of rather rough American whisky-like cough linctus. Snufflings on the "Hearts of Fire" set we can put down to the inclement British weather, and the stumblings around on stage in 1987 surely were evidence of a most uncomfortable back problem.' Certainly Dylan's wildly varying demeanour on stage from concert to concert suggests that his drinking habits are not always under tight rein.

About the future for Dylan the artist, a degree of optimism seems warranted. Many great artists have produced their finest works when no longer sprightly youths, and there is no reason to assume that he is no longer capable of producing work as remarkable as *Blood on the Tracks* or *Blonde on Blonde*. As he observed in an interview for *USA Today* at the time of the release of *Oh Mercy*:

Bob Dylan: An easy way out would be to say, 'Yeah, it's all behind me, that's it and there's no more.' But you want to say there might be a small chance that something up there will surpass whatever you did. Everybody works in the shadow of what they've previously done. But you have to overcome that. [1989]

Certainly his latter work will not have the impact his sixties work had on that generation. The work must now stand alone. Yet the fact that Dylan remains a frequently inspirational artist thirty years on from his Minneapolis apprenticeship – only he could have written 'God Knows' or 'Man in a Long Black Coat' – suggests that the flame still burns. He seems to have emerged from his second great creative drought which engulfed him between 1985 and 1988, a trough as daunting as the more famous drought between 1968 and 1972. That he has already completed a new – if only sporadically impressive – album less than nine months after the release of *Oh Mercy* suggests that the faucet is flowing again. Already Dylan has sustained his creativity far longer and with more impressive peaks than any of his sixties contemporaries. I doubt that we have heard the last great Bob Dylan song.

For the man born Robert Zimmerman, who is only Bob Dylan when he has to be, the future seems less rosy. Though *Oh Mercy* suggests that he continues to draw solace from his enduring beliefs, the oppressiveness of the lyrics and his current off-stage demeanour remind me of that sad quote from Suze Rotolo about the twenty-five-year-old Dylan:

Suze Rotolo: People live with hope for green trees and beautiful flowers, but Dylan seems to lack that sort of simple hope, at least he did from 1964 to 1966. This darkness wasn't new to me. It became stronger as the years passed by.

Sara seemed temporarily to rescue him from that darkness and then his faith initially seemed to provide renewed light, but as the eighties progressed his faith seemed only to reinforce him in his view of a world gone mad. Whether the darkness will continue to grow, and how the artist in him will deal with it if it does, is perhaps the most pressing question as Dylan approaches fifty. His work and life will continue to fascinate and intrigue, and like an artistic Rorschach test he will continue to mean different things to each and every fan. And though the worn lines and scruffy beard suggest he is unlikely to stay forever young, long may he endeavour to paint his masterpiece.

Notes

1. 1941–59: In My Younger Days

The Dylan quotes in this chapter are derived from his December 1963 Message to the Emergency Civil Liberties Committee, two raps he gave at concerts at the Warfield Theater, San Francisco, on 22/11/80 and interviews conducted by Philippe Adler (*L'Expresse*, 3/7/78); Chris Welles (*Life*, 10/4/64); Barbara Kerr (*Toronto Sun*, 26–29/3/78); Scott Cohen (*Spin*, December 1985); Les Crane (on his TV show, 17/2/65); Martin Bronstein (Canadian Broadcasting Company, 20/2/66); Sam Shepard (*Esquire*, July 1987); Bert Kleinman and Artie Mogull (Westwood One broadcast, 25/11/84); Bob Aschenmacher (*Duluth News Tribune and Herald*, 29/6/86); Paul J. Robbins (*Los Angeles Free Press*, 17 and 24/9/65); and Nat Hentoff (his October 1965 interview, transcribed as the *Whaaat!* booklet).

Quotes from Bill Marinac, Val Petersen, Georgie Haben, Steve Friedman and Bobby Vee were all derived from a major profile on Dylan's youth in the *Duluth News Tribune and Herald*, published on 29/6/86. Further comments by Bobby Vee were taken from a BBC radio interview broadcast on 4/6/76. Beattie Zimmerman's observation was derived from Larry Sloman's *On the Road with Bob Dylan* (Bantam Books, 1978). Echo Helstrom's comments are drawn largely from *Positively Main Street* by Toby Thompson (Coward-McCann, 1971), and from Anthony Scaduto's Dylan biography (Grosset & Dunlap, 1971). Bonnie Beecher's comments come from an interview by Marcus Whitman, published in *Telegraph* 36.

Dylan's youth has been dealt with in detail by Robert Shelton in his Dylan biography, *No Direction Home*. Anthony Scaduto and Bob Spitz also have useful sections on his Hibbing youth. Also worthy of investigation are Dylan's own free-form poems which provide impressionistic recollections of his youth, notably *My Life in a Stolen Moment*, his notes to *Joan Baez In Concert* Part 2 and *the second of the Eleven Outlined Epitaphs*. All of these are readily available in Dylan's *Lyrics* (Knopf, 1985).

2. 1960: Sammy Bound for Glory

The Dylan quotes in this chapter are derived from a poem which forms part of the Margolis & Moss manuscripts, published in *Telegraph* 35, and interviews conducted by Bob Coburn (*Rockline* radio show, 17/6/85); Barbara Kerr (*Toronto Sun*, 26–29/3/78); Ron Rosenbaum (*Playboy*, January 1978); Cameron Crowe (*Biograph*); John Cohen and Happy Traum (*Sing Out*, October 1968); and Izzy Young (*Other Scenes*, December 1968).

The quotes from Bonnie Beecher are derived from an interview conducted by Markus Wittman published in *Telegraph* 36. Comments by Dave Whitaker are derived from an interview by Stephen Pickering, published in *Telegraph* 26. Terri Wallace's comments are derived from an interview conducted by her sister Karen Moynihan and transcribed by Chris Cooper for *Freewheelin'* fanzine. Ellen Baker's and Maurice Zimmerman's observations have been drawn from Toby Thompson's *Positively Main Street* (Coward-McCann, 1971). Judy Rubin and Stanley Gottlieb's quotes are from Bob Spitz's biography (McGraw-Hill, 1988). Harvey Abrams' quote is from Robert Shelton's *No Direction Home* (Hodder & Stoughton, 1986). Kevin Krown's quote is from Anthony Scaduto's biography (Grosset & Dunlap, 1971). Bill Marinac's comment is from the *Duluth News Tribune and Herald*, 29/6/86. Marshall Brickman's comment is from Robbie Woliver's *Bringing It All Back Home* (Pantheon, 1986).

Also highly useful in helping formulate my ideas about this crucial period of Dylan's development was the second chapter of Paul Williams's *Performing Artist* (Underwood-Miller, 1990).

3. 1961: Hard Times in New York Town

The Dylan quotes in this chapter are derived from a transcript of his acceptance speech for the Rock & Roll Hall of Fame on 20/1/88, and interviews conducted by Billy James (a transcript of the November 1961 interview); Martha Quinn (for MTV, 7/7/84); Bert Kleinman and Artie Mogull (Westwood One broadcast, 25/11/84); Pete Oppel (*Dallas Morning News*, 18–23/11/78); Dan

Meer (*Close Up* radio show, 30/10/89); and Gil Turner (*Sing Out*, October 1962).

Quotes by Izzy Young are derived from an interview by Jorgen Lindstrom. Liam Clancy's comments are from an interview by Patrick Humphries published in *Telegraph* 18. Tony Glover's comment is from an interview by Marcus Whitman. Happy Traum's comment is from an interview by Jacques Van Son. Pete Seeger's is from an interview conducted by myself. J. R. Goddard's observation is from the *Village Voice*, 26/4/62. Paul Davies's and Mark Spoelstra's comments are from Bob Spitz's biography (McGraw-Hill, 1988). Pete Stampfel's is from *Zigzag* 26. Jack Nissenson's is from the *Montreal Saturday Gazette*, 12/1/74. Terri Thal's is from Robbie Woliver's *Bringing It All Back Home* (Pantheon, 1986). Eric Von Schmidt's are from his own *Baby Let Me Follow You Down* (Anchor Books, 1979) and Anthony Scaduto's biography (Grosset & Dunlap, 1971). Robert Shelton's comment is from a May 1966 issue of *Record Mirror*. Carolyn Hester's is from an interview in *Goldmine*, 26/1/90. John Hammond's comments derive from an interview in *Fusion*, 31/10/69.

Of general use in putting this chapter together have been Robbie Woliver's *Bringing It All Back Home* and Eric Von Schmidt and Jim Rooney's *Baby Let Me Follow You Down*. But by far the most detailed study of Dylan's early months in New York is John Bauldie's two-part essay in *Telegraph* 24 and 25, entitled 'Hard Times in New York Town'.

4. 1962–3: I Am My Words

The Dylan quotes in this chapter are derived from interviews conducted by Bert Kleinman and Artie Mogull (Westwood One broadcast, 25/11/84); Henrietta Yurchenco (*Sound and Fury*, April 1966); Pete Seeger (transcript of May 1962 WBAI radio show); Gil Turner (*Sing Out*, October 1962); Nat Hentoff (the original *Freewheelin'* galleys published in *Telegraph* 8); Studs Terkel (*Wax Museum* radio show, 26/4/63); and Kurt Loeder (*Rolling Stone*, 26/6/84).

Quotes by Anthea Joseph and Pete Seeger are derived from interviews conducted by myself. Izzy Young's comments are from an interview by Jorgen Lindstrom. D. A. Pennebaker's are from an interview by John Bauldie (*Telegraph* 26). Martin Carthy's are from an interview on Radio Merseyside, 18/6/83. Ron Gould's and Jim McLean's comments are from interviews by Brian Wells and Val Lawlan respectively. John Hammond's quotes are from an interview in *Fusion*, 31/10/69. Peter Yarrow's are from the July 1987 edition of *Musician* magazine. Eve MacKenzie's observation is drawn from Scaduto's biography (Grosset & Dunlap, 1971).

Of general use in constructing the difficult chronology of Dylan's first trip to London has been the Lawlans' essay on this visit in their *Steppin' Out* pamphlet. For a detailed discussion of Dylan's involvement with *Broadside*, readers are referred to the essay by David Pichaske and myself in *Telegraph* 20.

5. *1963: From Town Hall to Carnegie Hall*

Dylan's quotes in this chapter are derived from a prose-poem published in the 1963 Newport Festival programme, entitled 'To Dave Glover', a statement he gave to the *Village Voice*, published on 16/5/63, and interviews conducted by Anthony Scaduto for his biography in 1971; by Mary Merryfield (*Chicago Tribune*, 21/11/65); by Jack Smith (*National Guardian*, 22/8/63); and by an unknown interviewer for the *New York Post* (12/1/65).

The quote by Tony Glover is drawn from an interview by Markus Wittman. Suze Rotolo's comments come from Robbie Woliver's *Bringing It All Back Home* (Pantheon, 1986). Tom Wilson's observations are from interviews in *Melody Maker* (31/1/76) and *Fusion* (31/10/69). Michael Bloomfield's are from a radio interview given in 1979 (transcribed in the *Friends and Other Strangers* bookleg). Joan Baez's are from her autobiography *And a Voice to Sing With* (Summit Books, 1987). Beattie Zimmerman's are from Larry Sloman's *On the Road with Bob Dylan* (Bantam Books, 1978).

6. *1963: Troubled and I Don't Know Why*

Dylan's prose-poems quoted in this chapter are derived from excerpts from the Margolis & Moss manuscripts published in *Telegraph* 35 and *Isis* 30/31, his sleeve notes to Peter, Paul and Mary's *In the Wind* album, his programme notes for the 1963 Newport Festival, entitled 'To Dave Glover', his December 1963 Message to the Emergency Civil Liberties Committee and his open letter to *Broadside* magazine, published in the 14/1/64 issue. The

quotes by Dylan have been derived from interviews conducted by
Nat Hentoff (*New Yorker*, 24/10/64); Jenny De Yong and Peter
Roche (*Darts*, May 1965); Studs Terkel (*Wax Museum* radio show,
26/4/63); Scott Cohen (*Spin*, December 1985); and an unknown
interviewer for *Gargoyle* magazine (February 1964).

Joan Baez's quote is derived from Anthony Scaduto's biography
(Grosset & Dunlap, 1971). For full details of those prose-poems
omitted from *Lyrics*, readers should refer to my article 'Lyrics: A
Version Short of the Definitive' in the *All Across the Telegraph*
anthology (Sidgwick & Jackson, 1987).

7. 1964: On the Heels of Rimbaud

Dylan's quotes in this chapter are from excerpts of a letter he
wrote to Ralph J. Gleason, reproduced in *This Week* magazine,
22/11/64, and from interviews conducted by Klas Burling (Swedish
public radio, 29/4/66); Bill Flannagan (*Written in My Soul*, Contemporary, 1986); Nat Hentoff (*New Yorker*, 24/10/64); Pete Oppel
(*Dallas Morning News*, 18–23/11/78); and Jenny De Yong and Peter
Roche (*Darts*, May 1965).

Quotes by Anthea Joseph are derived from an interview conducted by myself. Suze Rotolo's comments have been drawn from
Rock Wives by Victoria Balfour (Beech Tree, 1986). Eric Burdon's
comments are derived from an uncredited article reproduced in
Endless Road 5. Barry Kornfeld's quote comes from Bob Spitz's
biography (McGraw-Hill, 1988). John Cooke's is from *Baby Let
Me Follow You Down* (Anchor Books, 1979).

Both Scaduto and Shelton have dealt with the February 1964
trek around America at considerable length, though Shelton's
chronology is for once the more accurate, while Bob Spitz deals
with Dylan's break-up with Suze Rotolo in graphic detail.

8. 1964–5: The Ghost of Electricity

Dylan's quote in this chapter is derived from a transcript of the
September 1965 Beverly Hills Hotel press conference. Joan Baez's
comments are derived from her autobiography *And a Voice to Sing
With* (Summit Books, 1987). Daniel Kramer's are from his photobook on Dylan (Castle Books, 1967). Bob Blackamar's comment is
from a letter to *Sing Out* magazine published in their March 1965

issue. Bobby Neuwirth's is from Eric Von Schmidt and Jim Rooney's *Baby Let Me Follow You Down* (Anchor Books, 1979).

Kramer's brief text in his photobook provides useful background for this period of Dylan's growth. For a detailed study of Dylan's performance at the 1964 Newport Festival and the response thereto readers are referred to Bill Allison's essay on the subject in *Telegraph* 9.

9. *1965: Over Your Shoulder*

Dylan's quotes in this chapter are derived from interviews conducted by Ron Rosenbaum (*Playboy*, January 1978) and Jenny De Yong and Peter Roche (*Darts*, May 1965).

Quotes by D. A. Pennebaker are derived from an interview by John Bauldie, published in *Telegraph* 26. Comments by Anthea Joseph are from an interview conducted by myself. Eric Clapton's are from an interview by Roger Gibbons, published in *Telegraph* 29. Hughie Flint's are from *Telegraph* 36. Terry Ellis's are from an interview by Adrian Deevoy published in *Telegraph* 31. Dana Gillespie's comments are from her story in *News of the World*, 31/8/80, and an interview by Spencer Leigh published in the *British Blues Review*, February 1990. John Lennon's comment has been taken from *Playboy: The Interviews*. Marianne Faithfull's are derived from a May 1965 edition of *Record Mirror*.

The most useful sources for Dylan's 1965 English tour are the film *Don't Look Back*, which is commercially available as a home video, and the private pamphlet *The Circus Is in Town*, written by Chris Cooper and Keith Marsh.

10. *1964–5: A Book of Words*

Dylan's quotes in this chapter are derived from four letters written to Tami Dean in 1964 and published in *Telegraph* 16, a letter written to Lawrence Ferlinghetti in April 1964 and published in *Telegraph* 36, and interviews conducted by Jann Wenner (*Rolling Stone*, 29/11/69); Studs Terkel (*Wax Museum* radio show, 26/4/63); Max Jones (*Melody Maker*, 23/5/64); Paul J. Robbins (*Los Angeles Free Press*, 17 and 24/9/65); Allen Stone (WDTM radio, 24/10/65); and the interviews conducted by Nat Hentoff for *Playboy* magazine (March 1966).

Bob Markel's quotes are derived from Michael Gross's *An Illustrated History* (Elm Tree, 1978). Though there is little of worth that has been written about *Tarantula*, Gabrielle Goodchild's 'A Web Untangled' in the *Conclusions on the Wall* anthology (Thin Man, 1980) is perhaps the best of a bad bunch.

11. 1965: I Accept Chaos

Dylan's quotes in this chapter are derived from a transcript of the December 1965 San Francisco Press Conference and from interviews conducted by Martin Bronstein (Canadian Broadcasting Company radio, 20/2/66); Nat Hentoff (his October 1965 interview, transcribed as the *Whaaat!* booklet, and the *Playboy* interview, published in the March 1966 issue); Nora Ephron and Susan Edmiston (*A Retrospective* by Craig McGregor, William Morrow, 1972); and Jules Siegel (*Saturday Evening Post*, 30/7/66).

Quotes by Joe Boyd are derived from an interview by Jonathan Morley, published in *Telegraph* 31. Comments by Al Kooper and Pete Seeger are from interviews conducted by myself, the former published in *Telegraph* 37. Michael Bloomfield's comments are primarily drawn from Larry Sloman's *On the Road with Bob Dylan* (Bantam Books, 1978), as well as a 1979 radio interview. Maria Muldaur's comments are from Eric Von Schmidt's and Jim Rooney's *Baby Let Me Follow You Down* (Anchor Books, 1979). Charlie McCoy's are from an interview in the October 1966 issue of *Hit Parader*.

The Newport 1965 Festival is probably the most written-about concert in rock's brief history. Bob Spitz devotes a considerable number of pages relating one of the most inaccurate accounts of the events that weekend. Considerably more useful are the sections in *Baby Let Me Follow You Down* and Al Kooper's *Backstage Passes* (Stein & Day, 1971), which also includes a lot of background to the *Highway 61 Revisited* sessions. Details about these sessions were also provided by Tony Glover for Glen Dundas's privately published *Tangled Up in Tapes Revisited*.

12. 1965-6. Just Like a Freeze-Out

Dylan's quotes in this chapter are derived from transcripts of press conferences in Beverly Hills, Los Angeles, and Adelaide, Australia, in September and December 1965 and April 1966, and from interviews conducted by Margaret Steen (*Toronto Weekly*, 29/1/66); Barbara Kerr (*Toronto Sun*, 26–29/3/78); Nat Hentoff (his October 1965 interview, transcribed as the *Whaaat!* booklet, and the *Playboy* interview, published in the March 1966 issue); and Ron Rosenbaum (*Playboy*, January 1978).

Quotes by Al Kooper are derived from an interview conducted by myself, published in *Telegraph* 37. Gerard Malanga's comments are from an interview by John Bauldie, published in *Telegraph* 35. Robbie Robertson's comments are derived from an interview in the January 1967 *Hit Parader*, Larry Sloman's interview in *On the Road with Bob Dylan* (Bantam Books, 1978) and Rob Bowman's notes for the *To Kingdom Come* double-CD set. Allen Ginsberg's comments come from Ralph Gleason's essay 'Children's Crusade' in the March 1966 edition of *Ramparts* and an interview in *Melody Maker*, 18/3/72. Nat Hentoff's come from an interview by Brian Stibal in *Zimmerman Blues* 6. Michael Bloomfield's are from Larry Sloman's *On the Road with Bob Dylan* (Bantam Books, 1978). Phil Ochs's is from his 1968 *Broadside Interview* album. Paul Morrisey's is from Jean Stein's *Edie* (Knopf, 1982). Sally Grossman's is from the July 1987 edition of *Musician* magazine. Levon Helm's is from the August 1984 edition of *Modern Drummer*. Pete Rowan's is from a July 1966 edition of the *Journal of Country Music*. Charlie McCoy's is from *Hit Parader*, October 1966.

13. *1966: A Curious Way to Make a Living*

Dylan's quotes in this chapter are derived from interviews conducted by John Rockwell (*New York Times*, 7/1/74); Anthony Scaduto (Grosset & Dunlap, 1971); and Craig McGregor (*Sydney Morning Herald*, 18/3/78).

Quotes by D. A. Pennebaker are from an interview by Shelly Livson, published in *Telegraph* 16. Comments by Anthea Joseph are derived from an interview by myself. Robbie Robertson's comments are from an interview in *New Musical Express*, 17/6/78, and the notes accompanying the *Biograph* and *To Kingdom Come* sets. The French reporter's are from an article in *Salut les Copains* in June 1966. Rosemary Gerrette's are from a similar piece in the *Canberra Times*, 7/5/66, and Adrian Rawlins's comments are drawn from the relevant chapter of John Bauldie's study of the 1966 world tour, *Ghost of Electricity*. Suze Rotolo's comment is from

Shelton's biography, *No Direction Home* (Hodder & Stoughton, 1986). Phil Ochs's comments are from an interview in *Broadside* magazine in October 1965.

The best general source for the 1966 tour remains John Bauldie's privately published *Ghost of Electricity*. For a detailed study of the recordings available from this historic tour readers may wish to consult my article in *Telegraph* 25.

14. 1966–7: Evening Things Up

Dylan's quotes in this chapter are derived from interviews conducted by Sam Shepard (*Esquire*, July 1987); Barbara Kerr (*Toronto Sun*, 26–29/3/78); Kurt Loeder (*Rolling Stone*, 26/6/84); Ben Fong-Torres (*Knockin' on Dylan's Door*, Straight Arrow, 1974); Michael Iachetta (*New York Daily News*, 8/5/87); Ron Rosenbaum (*Playboy*, January 1978); John Cohen and Happy Traum (*Sing Out*, October 1968); and Pete Oppel (*Dallas Morning News*, 18–23/11/78).

Quotes by D. A. Pennebaker are derived from an interview by Shelly Livson, published in *Telegraph* 16. Robbie Robertson's comments are from Larry Sloman's *On the Road with Bob Dylan* (Bantam Books, 1978), a 1970 Dutch radio interview on VPRO and a 1978 Australian radio interview on Radio 2JJ. Richard Manuel's and Rick Danko's comments are drawn from a March 1985 edition of the *Woodstock Times*. Garth Hudson's were derived from the July 1987 *Musician*. Al Aronowitz's are from his article 'A Family Album', published in volume one of *The Age of Rock* (Vintage Books, 1969). Bob Markel's are from his introduction to the American edition of *Tarantula* (Macmillan, 1970). Allen Ginsberg's are from Miles's biography of Ginsberg (Simon & Schuster, 1989).

The most comprehensive account of Dylan's Woodstock retreat is John Bauldie's in *Telegraph* 20, a highly edited version of which appears in the *All Across the Telegraph* anthology (Sidgwick & Jackson, 1988). For full details of the machinations surrounding Dylan's signing with MGM and his return to CBS readers should seek out Clive Davis's autobiography, *Clive: Inside the Record Business* (William Morrow, 1974).

15. 1968: Drifters, Immigrants, Messengers and Saints

Dylan's quotes in this chapter are derived from Miles's biography of Allen Ginsberg (Simon & Schuster, 1989) and from interviews conducted by Marc Rowland (US radio, 23/9/78); Jann Wenner (*Rolling Stone*, 29/11/69); Cameron Crowe (*Biograph*); John Cohen and Happy Traum (*Sing Out*, October 1968); Jonathan Cott (*Rolling Stone*, 16/11/78); and Matt Damsker (*Circus Weekly*, 19/12/78).

Quotes by Elliott Landy are from an interview conducted by Paul Williams, published in *Telegraph* 30. Happy Traum's comments come from an interview by Jacques Van Son, published in *Changin'* 10. Robbie Robertson's are from a 1978 Australian radio interview on Radio 2JJ. Beattie Zimmerman's is from Toby Thompson's *Positively Main Street* (Coward-McCann, 1971). Allen Ginsberg's is from *Rolling Stone*, 15/1/76. Bob Markel's comment is from Michael Gross's *An Illustrated History* (Elm Tree, 1978). George Harrison's is from his book of songs and anecdotes *I Me Mine*. Clive Davis's is from his autobiography, *Clive: Inside the Record Business* (William Morrow, 1974).

Bert Cartwright's book *The Bible in the Lyrics of Bob Dylan*, published as part of the Wanted Man Study Series, remains an invaluable guide to Dylan's increasing use of biblical imagery in his work.

16. 1969: What's the Matter with Me?

Dylan's quotes in this chapter are derived from interviews conducted by Jann Wenner (*Rolling Stone*, 29/11/69); Hubert Saal (*Newsweek*, 4/4/69); Jonathan Cott (*Rolling Stone*, 16/11/78); and Kurt Loeder (*Rolling Stone*, 26/6/84).

Quotes by Ray Foulk are derived from an interview by Chris Hockenhull, published in *4th Time Around* #3. Norman Blake's comment comes from an interview by Pete Tesoro in *Look Back* #12. David Amram's is from *Rolling Stone* magazine. Levon Helm's is from a September 1969 BBC radio interview. Johnny Cash's is from the May 1988 edition of *Musician* magazine. Bob Johnston's comment is from Spitz's biography (McGraw-Hill, 1988). Clive Davis's is from his autobiography *Clive: Inside the Record Business* (William Morrow, 1974).

The third issue of Dylan fanzine *4th Time Around* was entirely devoted to the Isle of Wight Festival and covers the background to the festival in considerable detail.

17. 1970: A Restless, Hungry Feeling

Dylan's quotes in this chapter are derived from a transcript of the Travemunde press conference on 13/2/81 and interviews conducted by Kurt Loeder (*Rolling Stone*, 26/6/84); Larry Sloman (*On the Road with Bob Dylan*, Bantam Books, 1978); and an unknown interviewer (*El Diario Vasco*, 18/6/89).

Quotes by Al Kooper are from an interview conducted by myself, published in *Telegraph* 37. Joel Bernstein's comments are from an interview by John Bauldie, published in *Telegraph* 35. Ron Cornelius's are from a 1971 edition of *Melody Maker*. Clive Davis's are from his autobiography *Clive: Inside the Record Business* (William Morrow, 1974). Charlie McCoy's comment is from Spitz's biography (McGraw-Hill, 1988).

18. 1971–2: Smooth Like a Rhapsody

Dylan's quotes in this chapter are derived from interviews conducted by Neil Hickey (*TV Guide*, 11/9/76); Scott Cohen (*Spin*, December 1985); and Pete Oppel (*Dallas Morning News*, 18–23/11/78).

Quotes by Happy Traum are derived from an interview by Jacques Van Son (*Changin'* 10) and from *Melody Maker*, 29/7/72. Allen Ginsberg's comments are from his own introduction to *First Blues* (Full Court Press, 1975) and from an interview in *Melody Maker*, 18/3/72. Harold Leventhal's comment is from Miles's *Bob Dylan* (Big O, 1978). Eve Brandstein's is from Michael Gross's *An Illustrated History* (Elm Tree, 1978). A. J. Weberman's is from the Alex Bennet radio show, 28/1/74. George Harrison's is from a BBC Radio One interview in 1976. Phil Spector's is from *Rolling Stone*, 2/3/72. John Prine's is from the *Illinois Entertainer*, November 1981. Bob Gottlieb's is from *Crawdaddy*, September 1973.

19. 1972–3: Alias What?

Dylan's quotes in this chapter are derived from interviews conducted by Chet Flippo (*Rolling Stone*, 15/3/73); Cameron Crowe (*Biograph*); Ben Fong-Torres (*Knockin' on Dylan's Door*, Straight Arrow, 1974); Donald Chase (*San Francisco Chronicle*, 23/11/86); an unknown interviewer (*Photoplay*, September 1978); and Larry Sloman (*On the Road with Bob Dylan*, Bantam Books, 1978).

Quotes by Kris Kristofferson are derived from *Written in My Soul* (Contemporary, 1986), the 15/3/73 and 23/2/78 editions of *Rolling Stone*, and *Peckinpah: A Portrait in Montage* by Garner Simmons. James Coburn's comments come from an interview on an LA cable TV station in 1988 and the London *Evening Standard*, 31/9/89. Rudy Wurlitzer's comments are from *Melody Maker*, 3/2/78, and *Rolling Stone*, 15/3/73. Gordon Dawson's is from the London *Evening Standard*, 31/9/89. Clive Davis's is from his autobiography *Clive: Inside the Record Business* (William Morrow, 1974).

20. 1973–4: Into the Flood

Dylan's quotes in this chapter are derived from interviews conducted by Ben Fong-Torres (*Knockin' on Dylan's Door*, Straight Arrow, 1974); Dan Meer (*Close Up* radio show, 30/10/89); Robert Hilburn (*Los Angeles Times*, 23/11/80); and Barbara Kerr (*Toronto Sun*, 26–29/3/78).

Quotes by Robbie Robertson are derived from *Knockin' on Dylan's Door*, *Crawdaddy*, March 1976, and Larry Sloman's *On the Road with Bob Dylan* (Bantam Books, 1978). Rob Fraboni's comments come from *Recording Engineer-Producer*, March/April 1974. Barry Goldberg's is from *Crawdaddy*, July 1974. Roger McGuinn's is from *On the Road with Bob Dylan*.

Rolling Stone's *Knockin' on Dylan's Door* collects together all the magazine's coverage of the 1974 tour along with other press reports and is well worth seeking out. Stephen Pickering's *Approximately* (McKay, 1975) also covers the entire tour and is beautifully illustrated, though the text is largely unreadable.

21. 1974–5: From Renaissance to Reformation

Dylan's quotes in this chapter are derived from interviews conducted by Pete Oppel (*Dallas Morning News*, 18–23/11/78); Karen Hughes (*Rock Express* No. 1); Jonathan Cott (*Rolling Stone*, 26/1/78 and 16/11/78); Bill Flannagan (*Written in My Soul*, Contemporary, 1986); Cameron Crowe (*Biograph*); and Larry Sloman (*On the Road with Bob Dylan*, Bantam Books, 1978).

Quotes by John Hammond, Eric Weissberg and Charlie Brown are derived from *Rolling Stone*'s feature on the recording of *Blood on the Tracks* in their 21/11/74 edition. The student of Norman

Raeben's comment is from a WBAI radio special on Dylan on 23/5/86. Tim Drummond's is from *Rolling Stone*, 29/8/74. Michael Bloomfield's is from Larry Sloman's *On the Road with Bob Dylan*. Joel Bernstein's is from an interview by John Bauldie in *Telegraph* 35. Robbie Robertson's is from *Crawdaddy*, March 1976. David Oppenheim's is from an English translation of his 'I Could Have Kidnapped Bob Dylan' article, published in *4th Time Around* #1.

As is presumably evident I have lent heavily on Bert Cartwright's ground-breaking articles in *Telegraph* 23 and 26, in which he dealt at length with Dylan's time in Norman Raeben's class and its effect upon him.

22. *1975: From End to End*

Dylan's quotes in this chapter are derived from Miles's biography of Allen Ginsberg (Simon & Schuster, 1989) and from interviews conducted by Larry Sloman (*On the Road with Bob Dylan*, Bantam Books, 1978); Dave Herman (transcribed from *The London Interview* promotional album); and Lynne Allen (*Trouser Press*, June 1979).

Quotes by Scarlet Rivera, Howie Wyeth and Rob Stoner are derived from interviews by myself, save for one quote by Stoner which has come from Larry Sloman's *On the Road with Bob Dylan*. Comments by Jacques Levy and Robbie Robertson are also derived from *On the Road with Bob Dylan*. Patti Smith's comments are from an interview by Miles, published in *Telegraph* 32. Quotes by Rubin Carter and Lou Kemp have come from the 1976 *Rock Around the World* radio show. Comments by Neil Hubbard and Mel Collins are from a 1975 issue of *Liquorice* magazine. Roger McGuinn's comment is from a 1976 TV interview. Eric Clapton's is from *Rolling Stone*, 20/11/75. Emmylou Harris's comments have been taken from a composite feature on the *Desire* sessions in *Occasionally* #5. The CBS rep's quote comes from a feature in *Rolling Stone*, 28/9/75. Larry Sloman's is from an interview in *4th Time Around* #2.

23. *1975: You Come On to Me Like Rolling Thunder*

Dylan's quotes in this chapter are derived from interviews conducted by an unknown interviewer (*Photoplay*, 1978); Ron Rosenbaum (*Playboy*, January 1978); and Larry Sloman (*On the Road with Bob Dylan*, Bantam Books, 1978).

Quotes by Mel Howard and Sara Dylan are derived from Larry Sloman's *On the Road with Bob Dylan*. Comments by Rob Stoner and Scarlet Rivera are from interviews conducted by myself. Joan Baez's comments are from her autobiography *And a Voice to Sing With* (Summit Books, 1987). Jacques Levy's are from *Rolling Stone*, 7/4/77. Mick Ronson's are from *New Musical Express*, 15/12/79. The uncredited tour musician's observation comes from a feature in *Rolling Stone*, 15/1/76.

As a chronicle of the 1975 Rolling Thunder Revue Larry Sloman's *On the Road with Bob Dylan* cannot be commended highly enough, though copies are extremely hard to locate. Also useful is Sam Shepard's *Rolling Thunder Logbook* (Penguin, 1978).

24. 1976: Hard Reign or Last Waltz?

Quotes by Rob Stoner, Howie Wyeth and Scarlet Rivera are from interviews conducted by myself. Quotes by Ron Wood and Joel Bernstein are from interviews conducted by John Bauldie, published in *Telegraph* 33 and 35 respectively. Joan Baez's comments are from her autobiography, *And a Voice to Sing With* (Summit Books, 1987).

25. 1977: Everything Went from Bad to Worse

Dylan's quotes in this chapter are derived from interviews by Robert Shelton (*Melody Maker*, 24/6/78); Barbara Kerr (*Toronto Sun*, 26–29/3/78); Mary Campbell (*Houston Post*, 12/2/78); John Austin (source unknown); interviewer unknown (*Photoplay*, September 1978); John Rockwell (*New York Times*, 8/1/78); and Allen Ginsberg (*Telegraph* 33).

Quotes by Sara Dylan are taken from a press release based on her declaration to the court in March 1977. Quotes by Farida McFree, Rob Stoner and Howie Wyeth are from interviews conducted by myself. Howard Alk's is from an interview in *Take One* magazine in March 1978. Allen Ginsberg's comments are derived from a transcript by John Hinchey of a discussion with students at Swarthmore College, Pennsylvania, in November 1978. Joel Bernstein's are from an interview by John Bauldie published in *Telegraph* 35.

Putting together the story of the divorce and custody battle in this chapter has been possible thanks to the detailed coverage provided in the *Los Angeles Times*.

26. 1978: Someone's Got It In for Me

Dylan's quotes in this chapter are derived from a concert rap given at a show in Nashville on 2/12/78 and from interviews conducted by Robert Hilburn (*Los Angeles Times*, 28/5/78 and 12/11/78); Kurt Loeder (*Rolling Stone*, 26/6/84); Jonathan Cott (*Rolling Stone*, 16/11/78); John Mankiewicz (*Sound*, 12/11/78); and Marc Rowland (US radio, 23/9/78).

Quotes by Rob Stoner and Farida McFree are derived from interviews by myself. Comments by Helena Springs are from an interview by Chris Cooper, published in *Endless Road* #7.

27. 1978–9: Pulling Back on the Reins

Dylan's quotes in this chapter are derived from raps given in concert at the Golden Hall, San Diego, 27/11/79, and the Convention Center, Albuquerque, 5/12/79, a transcript of the Travemunde press conference on 13 July 1981 and interviews conducted by Robert Hilburn (*Los Angeles Times*, 23/11/80 and 30/10/83); Dave Herman (transcribed from *The London Interview* promotional album); Karen Hughes (*Dominion*, 2/8/80); Neil Spencer (*New Musical Express*, 15/8/81); and Scott Cohen (*Spin*, December 1985).

Quotes by Ken Gulliksen are derived from an interview in the November 1980 issue of *Buzz*. Howie Wyeth's comments are from an interview by myself. Helena Springs' are from an interview by Chris Cooper published in *Endless Road* #7. Steven Soles' are from *New Musical Express*, 8/9/79. Also quoted is an excerpt from Davin Seay and Mary Neely's *Stairway to Heaven* (Ballantine Books, 1986).

Worthy of further reading are Bert Cartwright's commendable *The Bible in the Lyrics of Bob Dylan* in the Wanted Man Study Series, Hal Lindsey's *Late Great Planet Earth* and Joseph Campbell's 'Bob Dylan and the Pastoral Apocalypse' in *Journal of Popular Culture*, 1975, where I have purloined much of my terminology from. Also essential to an understanding of this crucial period is Paul Williams's excellent *What Happened?* (and/Entwistle Books, 1980).

28. 1979: On the Holy Slow Train

Dylan's quotes in this chapter are derived from a transcript of the Travemunde press conference and from interviews conducted by Bono (*Hot Press*, 24/8/84) and Bruce Heiman (KMGX radio, 7/12/79).

Quotes by Dave Kelly are derived from an interview by Chris Cooper published in the *Freewheelin'* magazine. Jerry Wexler's comments are from *Rolling Stone*, 27/11/80. Mark Knopfler's comments have been drawn from the 'What About a Farfisa?' article in the Lawlans' *Steppin' Out* pamphlet.

29. 1979–80: Middle of the Road – East Coast Bondage

Dylan's quotes in this chapter are derived from raps given in concert at the Stanley Theater, Pittsburg, 15/5/80, the Civic Auditorium, Santa Monica, 19/11/79, the Warfield Theater, San Francisco, 16/11/79, the Gammage Theater, Tempe, on 25 and 26/11/79, the Massey Hall, Toronto, 20/4/80, the Orpheum Theater, Omaha, 25/1/80 and the Bushnell Memorial Center, Hartford, on 7 and 8/5/80 – as well as interviews conducted by Paul Vincent (*Endless Road* No. 2); Martha Quinn (for MTV, 7/7/84); Scott Cohen (*Spin*, December 1985); Robert Hilburn (*Los Angeles Times*, 23/11/80); Cameron Crowe (*Biograph*); Bruce Heiman (KMGX, 7/12/79); Dave Herman (transcript from *The London Interview* promotional album); and Karen Hughes (*Dominion*, 2/8/80).

Quotes by Helena Springs and Dave Kelly are from interviews conducted by Chris Cooper, published in *Endless Road* and *Freewheelin'* respectively. Jerry Wexler's comments are from *Rolling Stone*, 27/11/80.

The bulk of this chapter has been condensed down from my considerably more detailed survey of Dylan's gospel tour, published as the three-part 'Saved!' feature in *Telegraph* 28 to 30. The complete transcribed raps from those articles have also been published in the US by Handyman Books in their pocket book series.

30. 1980–82: In the Summertime

Dylan's quotes in this chapter are derived from a rap given in concert at the Warfield Theater, San Francisco, on 12 November

1980 and interviews conducted by Cameron Crowe (*Biograph*);
Kurt Loeder (*Rolling Stone*, 26/6/84); Neil Spencer (*New Musical
Express*, 15/8/81); Paul Vincent (*Endless Road* No. 2) and Martin
Keller (*New Musical Express*, 6/8/83).

Quotes by Ron Wood are derived from an interview by John
Bauldie, published in *Telegraph* 33. Al Kooper's comments are
from an interview conducted by myself, published in *Telegraph* 37.
Benmont Tench's comments are from the *Chicago Sun-Times*,
26/1/86. Paul Esmond and Rabbi Kasriel Kastel's comments are
from *Christianity Today* in 1983.

Readers are again referred to Bert Cartwright's *The Bible in the
Lyrics of Bob Dylan*. Paul Williams' *One Year Later* pamphlet
provides a thorough overview of the 1980 Warfield residency.

31. 1983: Songs of Experience

Dylan's quotes in this chapter are derived from interviews con-
ducted by Martin Keller (*New Musical Express*, 6/8/83); Robert
Hilburn (*Los Angeles Times*, 30/10/83); and Martha Quinn (for
MTV, 7/7/84).

Quotes by Mark Knopfler and Alan Clark are drawn from the
article 'What About a Farfisa?' in the Lawlans' *Steppin' Out*
pamphlet. Larry Sloman's comments are from an interview in *4th
Time Around* #2 and from a 1984 edition of *Music Video*. Mark
Robinson's comments are from an article on Dylan's early videos
in *Telegraph* 16. Charlie Sexton's are derived from *The Wicked
Messenger* newsletter. Charlie Quintana's are from an interview by
John Bauldie in *Telegraph* 37.

32. 1984: Still Life and Real Live

Dylan's quotes in this chapter are derived from interviews conducted by Martha Quinn (for MTV, 7/7/84); Bill Flannagan (*Written in My Soul*, Contemporary, 1986); and Mick Brown (*Sunday
Times*, 1/7/84).

Quotes by Charlie Quintana are taken from an interview by
John Bauldie in *Telegraph* 37. Comments by Greg Sutton are from
an interview by Thomas Lasarzik published in *Telegraph* 27. Colin
Allen's are from an interview by Jorgen Lindstrom published in
Telegraph 28.

33. 1984–5: Burlesques and Benefits

Dylan's quotes in this chapter are derived from a transcript of the Sydney press conference, 10/2/86, and interviews conducted by Bert Kleinman and Artie Mogull (Westwood One radio broadcast, 25/11/84); Bill Flannagan (*Written in My Soul*, Contemporary, 1986); Denise Worrell (*Icons*, Atlantic Monthly Press, 1989); Toby Creswell (*Australian Rolling Stone*, 16/1/86); Scott Cohen (*Interviews*, February 1986); Mikal Gilmore (*Los Angeles Herald-Examiner*, 13/10/85); Bob Brown (*20/20* TV show, 20/10/85); and Robert Hilburn (*Los Angeles Times*, 17/11/85).

Quotes by Markus Innocenti and Eddie Arno, and by Ira Ingber, are from interviews conducted by myself, published in *Telegraph* 34 and 27 respectively. Comments by Ron Wood are from an interview by John Bauldie published in *Telegraph* 33. Maria McKee's are from an interview by Thomas Lasarzik published in *Telegraph* 27. Sam Shepard's are from a December 1985 issue of *Rolling Stone*.

34. 1985–6: Junco and His Partners in Crime

Dylan's quotes in this chapter are derived from raps given in concert at the Gymnasium, Nagoya, 8/3/86, and from an interview conducted by Mikal Gilmore (*Los Angeles Herald-Examiner*, 13/10/85).

Quotes by Ira Ingber, Dave Garfield and Al Kooper are from interviews conducted by myself, published in *Telegraph* 27 and 37. Charlie Quintana's comments are from an interview by John Bauldie in *Telegraph* 37. Mikal Gilmore's comments are from his feature in *Rolling Stone*, 17 and 31/7/86. Comments by Mike Campbell and Stan Lynch are taken from *Telegraph* 25, with additional comments by Tom Petty from a 1988 edition of *The Leeds*.

35. 1986–7: Down Among the Deadheads

Dylan's quotes in this chapter are derived from interviews conducted by Christopher Sykes (*Telegraph* 30 and a transcript of *Getting to Dylan*, 18/9/87); Cameron Crowe (*Biograph*); Mikal Gilmore (*Los Angeles Herald-Examiner*, 13/10/85); and Kathryn Baker (*Stars and Stripes*, 7/9/88).

Quotes by Iain Smith and Richard Marquand are from interviews conducted by John Bauldie and published in *Telegraph* 28. Bono's comments are from *New Musical Express*, 19 and 26/12/87. Jerry Garcia's comments are from the *Close Up* radio show, 30/10/89, and *Melody Maker*, 13/5/89. Bob Weir's are from the same radio show. Mickey Hart's are from the same issue of *Melody Maker*.

36. 1987–8: Temples in Flames – Wilburys on the Run

Dylan's quotes in this chapter are derived from interviews conducted by Dan Meer (*Close Up* radio show, 30/10/89) and Edna Gundersen (*USA Today*, 21/9/89).

Bruce Springsteen's quote is a partial transcription of the speech he gave at the Rock & Roll Hall of Fame on 20/1/88. Daniel Lanois's quotes are derived from *New Musical Express*, 7/10/89, the *Close Up* radio show, 30/10/89, *Request*, October 1989, *Stereo Sequence* radio show, September 1989, and in interview with Mark Cooper (published in *Telegraph* 34).

There are two publications which dealt exclusively with the 1987 European tour, one a photo-documentary by Georg Stein simply entitled *Temples in Flames* and the other a pamphlet by John Lindley on the seven English shows, entitled *Seven Days*, which sought to provide an antidote to the uncomprehending media reviews.

37. 1989–90: Lord Have Mercy!

Dylan's comment in this chapter is derived from an interview by Edna Gundersen (*USA Today*, 14/9/90). Don Was's quotes are from an interview by Reid Kopel and Al Kooper's are from an interview by myself, both first published in *Telegraph* 37. Allen Ginsberg's comments are from an interview by Wes Stace published in *Telegraph* 20.

38. 1988–90: The Never-Ending Tour

Dylan's quotes in this chapter are derived from interviews by Neil Spencer (*New Musical Express*, 15/8/81); Dan Meer (*Close Up* radio show, 30/10/89); Adrian Deevoy (*Q*, December 1989) and Robert Hilburn (*Los Angeles Times*, 7/9/87).

Quotes by Kenny Aaronson are derived from an interview by myself published in *Telegraph* 36. Christopher Parker's comments are taken from *Telegraph* 33.

39. 1990: The Finishing End?

Dylan's quotes in this chapter are derived from interviews by Edna Gundersen for *USA Today* (21/9/89 and 14/9/90). The quote from Suze Rotolo derives from *No Direction Home* by Robert Shelton (Hodder & Stoughton, 1986). The quote from Slash comes from an article in *Vox* #1. The Sally Kirkland quote is from the *Daily Mail*, 13/11/89. David Braun's declaration is drawn from a deposition to the courts, dated 1/3/1977.

Dramatis Personae

This dramatis personae provides a brief checklist of the individuals who are quoted in the main text of *Behind the Shades*, and a short summary of their involvement with Dylan. The aim is to provide an easy source of reference as to their credentials as authorities on aspects of Dylan's career. It does not aim to provide any résumé of the individual's own pedigree, however distinguished it may be, as this lies outside the scope of this book.

KENNY AARONSON: Bassist on the entire 1988 tour and six of the first seven 1989 shows, he was then replaced by Tony Garnier.

HARVEY ABRAMS: Fellow student at the University of Minneapolis in 1960, as well as regular drinking companion and fellow folksinger.

HOWARD ALK: Co-owner of Chicago club, the Bear; cameraman on both the 1965 and 1966 English tours; and co-editor (with Dylan) of *Eat the Document* and *Renaldo and Clara*. Alk also filmed several concerts on the 1981 tour. He died in January 1982.

COLIN ALLEN: Drummer on the 1984 European tour.

DAVID AMRAM: French horn player and ethno-musicologist who became friendly with Dylan while staying on Fire Island in the summer of 1969.

EDDIE ARNO: *See* Markus Innocenti.

AL ARONOWITZ: New York journalist and supporter of Dylan; he introduced him to the Beatles in 1964, co-authored an article with him in 1965, and remained in contact throughout his Woodstock period.

JOAN BAEZ: Self-appointed Queen of Folk in the early sixties, she began a sporadic affair with Dylan in spring 1963, which lasted until his May 1965 English tour. They were reunited on the 1975–6 Rolling Thunder Revue and have sung together subsequently in 1982 and 1984.

ELLEN BAKER: A girlfriend in Minneapolis in 1960, whose father's impressive folk music collection provided Dylan with a regular source of reference.

BONNIE BEECHER: Purportedly the 'real' Girl from the North Country, she first met Dylan in 1959 and they remained close throughout his days in

Minneapolis. After he left for New York in December 1960 they remained in regular touch throughout Dylan's rise to fame.

JOEL BERNSTEIN: Guitar technician on the 1976 Rolling Thunder tour and during the rehearsals for the 1978 tour.

BOB BLACKAMAR: Interviewed Dylan before a show in San Diego in December 1964.

NORMAN BLAKE: Guitarist on the sessions for *Nashville Skyline* and the Nashville sessions for *Self Portrait*.

MICHAEL BLOOMFIELD: First met Dylan in Chicago in April 1963. The lead guitarist on the *Highway 61 Revisited* album and at the 1965 Newport Festival appearance, he subsequently jammed with Dylan prior to the *Blood on the Tracks* sessions and made a guest appearance at a November 1980 show, his final live performance. He died in February 1981.

BONO: Lead singer of the Irish stadium-rock combo U2, he interviewed Dylan in 1984 and they subsequently collaborated on a couple of songs, one of which appeared on U2's *Rattle and Hum* collection.

JOE BOYD: One of the behind-the-scene principals responsible for organizing the 1965 Newport Folk Festival; later established himself as a highly acclaimed record producer.

EVE BRANDSTEIN: Member of the Kibbutz Givat Haim in May 1971, when Dylan was looking into the possibility of joining the kibbutz with his family.

DAVID BRAUN: Dylan's lawyer.

MARSHALL BRICKMAN: Was at school in Madison, Wisconsin, rooming with Eric Weissberg, when Dylan passed through on his way to New York in January 1961.

CHARLIE BROWN: Member of Eric Weissberg's Deliverance, he played on the first couple of sessions for *Blood on the Tracks* in New York.

ERIC BURDON: Lead singer of the Animals, the English rhythm & blues outfit responsible for 'rocking up' 'House of the Rising Sun'. He met Dylan in the winter of 1965 in New York.

MIKE CAMPBELL: Lead guitarist of Tom Petty and the Heartbreakers. As well as touring with Dylan through 1986–7, he recorded with him on *Empire Burlesque* and *Knocked Out Loaded*.

RUBIN 'HURRICANE' CARTER: Unjustly imprisoned negro middleweight boxer whose cause Dylan championed in his 1975 single 'Hurricane', though he was not set free until 1986.

MARTIN CARTHY: Respected English folksinger who befriended Dylan on his first visit to London in December 1962.

JOHNNY CASH: Important champion of Dylan's cause during his early days at CBS, Cash duetted with Dylan on his *Nashville Skyline* album, part of an entire unreleased album of Dylan/Cash duets. Dylan subsequently guested on Cash's TV show in May 1969.

LIAM CLANCY: Member of the esteemed Clancy Brothers, who were one of the most popular bands on the early sixties Greenwich Village scene.

ERIC CLAPTON: Originally recorded with Dylan at an unproductive session in London in May 1965. He subsequently worked in the studio with him in 1975 (for 'Desire'), 1976 (for 'No Reason to Cry') and 1986 (for 'Hearts of Fire'), and guested at Dylan shows in 1978 and 1984.

ALAN CLARK: Dire Straits' keyboardist who worked on the *Infidels* album and one song on *Empire Burlesque*.

JAMES COBURN: Actor who portrayed Pat Garrett in Sam Peckinpah's *Pat Garrett & Billy the Kid*.

MEL COLLINS: Saxophonist for British pub-rock combo Kokomo, who played on the first couple of sessions for the *Desire* album.

JOHN COOKE: Photo-chronicler of the early sixties Boston folk scene.

RON CORNELIUS: Guitarist at the *New Morning* sessions.

RICK DANKO: Bass player with the Hawks, aka the Band, recording with Dylan in December 1965, January 1966, 1967 and November 1973 and touring with him in 1965-6 and 1974. He also played one-off concerts with Dylan in 1968, 1969 (twice), 1972 and 1976 (all with the Band) and in 1983 (with Levon Helm).

PAUL DAVIES: A Minneapolis student during Dylan's time there.

CLIVE DAVIS: President of the CBS record division throughout the late sixties and early seventies, and Dylan's most regular contact with Columbia until his sacking in May 1973.

GORDON DAWSON: Associate producer of *Pat Garrett & Billy the Kid*.

TIM DRUMMOND: Bassist in Dylan's touring band from 1979 through to 1981, he also played with him on the SNACK benefit in 1975 and was on the sessions for *Saved* and *Shot of Love*.

SARA DYLAN: Née Shirley Noznisky, first met Dylan through their mutual friend Sally Grossman in 1964. They were married in November 1965 and divorced in 1977, though they have remained in regular contact since.

TERRY ELLIS: The legendary 'science student' who is given such a hard time in *Don't Look Back*, he went on to co-found Chrysalis Records.

PAUL ESMOND: One of the pastors of the Vineyard Fellowship who attended Dylan at the time of his conversion to the born-again creed in 1979. They remained in contact into the early eighties.

MARIANNE FAITHFULL: English *chanteuse* who was one of the habitual attenders at Dylan's Savoy Hotel suite during his May 1965 English tour.

JERRY FIELDING: Brought in to supervise the scoring of the music for *Pat Garrett & Billy the Kid*.

HUGHIE FLINT: The drummer for John Mayall's Bluesbreakers in 1965, when he played at a recording session with Dylan. He subsequently co-founded McGuinness-Flint, who recorded an entire album of (then) unreleased Bob Dylan songs, *Lo & Behold*.

RAY FOULK: Co-organizer of the 1969 Isle of Wight Festival.

ROB FRABONI: Recording engineer on the *Planet Waves* sessions, he also co-supervised the mixing of the *Before the Flood* live set.

STEVE FRIEDMAN: Fellow member of Camp Herzl and a teenage travelling companion of Robert Zimmerman's.

JERRY GARCIA: Guitarist in the Grateful Dead, he played with Dylan in 1980, 1986, 1987 and 1989.

DAVE GARFIELD: Assistant engineer on the *Knocked Out Loaded* sessions.

ROSEMARY GERRETTE: Australian actress cum journalist who spent some time with Dylan at the end of his April 1966 Australian tour.

DANA GILLESPIE: English model/singer whom Dylan 'befriended' on his 1965 English tour.

MIKAL GILMORE: Los Angeles journalist who interviewed Dylan in the fall of 1985 and subsequently attended many of the sessions for the *Knocked Out Loaded* album.

ALLEN GINSBERG: Perhaps the most noted American poet of the 'beat' generation, he first met Dylan in December 1963 and they have remained friends ever since, recording together in 1971 and 1982. He was also a member of the 1975–6 Rolling Thunder Revue.

DAVE 'TONY' GLOVER: Respected folk musician on the 1960 Minneapolis scene, who was an important influence on Dylan in his later months there. They remained in regular contact through Dylan's days in Greenwich Village and he conducted an unpublished interview in 1971.

J. R. GODDARD: Writer for the *Village Voice* who reviewed Dylan's first album and with whom Dylan concocted a 'fake' press conference in 1965.

BARRY GOLDBERG: As a friend of Michael Bloomfield, he was recruited to play piano at the notorious 1965 Newport Festival performance. Dylan subsequently co-produced his first solo album in 1973.

ROBERT GOTTLIEB: Chief editor at Alfred Knopf, responsible for overseeing publication of Dylan's collection, *Writings and Drawings*.

RON GOULD: English folksinger who was an habitué of the London folk scene during Dylan's time there in December 1962/January 1963.

SALLY GROSSMAN: Wife of Albert Grossman and long-standing friend of Sara Dylan. She is the lady languorously stretched out on the cover of *Bringing It All Back Home*.

KEN GULLIKSEN: A pastor at the Vineyard Fellowship whose born-again creed was introduced to Dylan in 1979.

GEORGE HABEN: Classmate of the young Robert Zimmerman at Hibbing High School.

JOHN HAMMOND: Legendary producer who signed Dylan to CBS and produced his first two albums before being ousted at Grossman's behest. He died in July 1987.

EMMYLOU HARRIS: After her sterling work with Gram Parsons, she was recruited to sing harmony with Dylan on the *Desire* album, which proved a fortuitous break in her own career.

GEORGE HARRISON: The Beatle who has maintained the most regular and lasting contact with Dylan; they worked together in 1970 and co-founded the Traveling Wilburys in 1988.

MICKEY HART: Drummer/percussionist in the Grateful Dead.

LEVON HELM: Member of Dylan's first 'electric' band, with whom he played at Forest Hills and Hollywood Bowl; then, reunited with the Hawks, toured through to November 1965. Helm then left the Hawks, only rejoining them after the 1967 *Basement Tapes* sessions. Subsequently gigged with Dylan in 1968, 1969, 1972, 1974 and 1983 and worked on the 1973 *Planet Waves* sessions.

ECHO HELSTROM: Robert Zimmerman's girlfriend from the fall of 1957 to the fall of 1958 who subsequently suggested she was the subject of 'Girl from the North Country'.

NAT HENTOFF: Jazz and folk critic who was an important champion of Dylan's music in the early sixties and who conducted several important interviews with him between 1963 and 1966, including the legendary *Playboy* interview.

CAROLYN HESTER: Richard Farina's first wife, who befriended Dylan in August 1961 and invited him to play on her debut album for CBS, the occasion of his first meeting with John Hammond.

LEROY HOIKKALA: Drummer in Robert Zimmerman's Hibbing combo, the Golden Chords.

MEL HOWARD: Associate producer of *Renaldo and Clara*.

NEIL HUBBARD: Guitarist for British pub-rock combo Kokomo, who played on the first couple of sessions for the *Desire* album.

GARTH HUDSON: Organist in the Hawks, aka the Band, with whom Dylan toured in 1965–6 and 1974; also performing together in 1968, 1969, 1972 and 1976, and recording *The Basement Tapes* and *Planet Waves* in 1967 and 1973 respectively.

IRA INGBER: Guitarist on several Los Angeles sessions for both *Empire Burlesque* and *Knocked Out Loaded*.

MARKUS INNOCENTI: Co-director with Eddie Arno of the promotional videos for 'When the Night Comes Falling' and 'Emotionally Yours'.

BOB JOHNSTON: Producer of *Highway 61 Revisited*, *Blonde on Blonde*, *John Wesley Harding*, *Nashville Skyline* and *Self Portrait* and co-producer of *New Morning*.

ANTHEA JOSEPH: As co-organizer of London's Troubadour folk club, she befriended Dylan on his first visit in December 1962 and they have regularly renewed their friendship on his subsequent visits to the UK.

RABBI KASRIEL KASTEL: A member of the Lubavitchers, a Hassidic sect, and organizer of the Brooklyn Lubavitch centre where Dylan apparently 'studied' in 1983.

DAVE KELLY: Dylan's personal assistant from the summer of 1979 through to the winter of 1980 and a talented musician in his own right.

LOU KEMP: Fellow member of Camp Herzl between 1956 and 1958; subsequently organized the two Rolling Thunder tours of 1975 and 1976.

SALLY KIRKLAND: American actress first involved with Dylan in 1976, who has very publicly renewed her association in the last couple of years.

MARK KNOPFLER: Guitarist on the 1979 *Slow Train Coming* sessions and guitarist/co-producer on the 1983 *Infidels* album. He made a guest appearance at a Dylan show in Sydney in 1986.

AL KOOPER: Organist/guitarist who worked on *Highway 61 Revisited*, *Blonde on Blonde*, *New Morning*, *Empire Burlesque*, *Knocked Out Loaded* and *Under the Red Sky*. He also played with Dylan at Newport, Forest Hills and the Hollywood Bowl in 1965 and toured with him in 1981.

BARRY KORNFELD: Folksinger on the early sixties Greenwich Village scene.

DANIEL KRAMER: Could be considered Dylan's 'official' photographer between the fall of 1964 and August 1965. He attended the *Bringing It All Back Home* sessions and took the photos used on the album sleeve. He subsequently published a book of his photos of Dylan.

ARTHUR KRETCHMER: A member of the Greenwich Village scene and magazine editor.

KRIS KRISTOFFERSON: Actor/singer-songwriter who played the role of Billy the Kid in Sam Peckinpah's *Pat Garrett & Billy the Kid*.

KEVIN KROWN: First met Dylan when an itinerant folksinger in Denver in the summer of 1960. He subsequently provided him with accommodation in Chicago in December of that year when Dylan was on his way to New York.

ELLIOTT LANDY: Woodstock resident and noted photographer who photographed Dylan on several occasions during his Woodstock residency in the late sixties, including the cover for *Nashville Skyline*.

DANIEL LANOIS: Achieved a reputation as the producer in vogue by producing Peter Gabriel, U2, Robbie Robertson and the Neville Brothers before working on Dylan's *Oh Mercy* album in March/April 1989.

JOHN LENNON: Spent some time with Dylan during both of his mid-sixties UK tours, as well as during the Beatles' own American tours in 1964-5. He was assassinated in December 1980.

HAROLD LEVENTHAL: Manager of both Woody Guthrie and Pete Seeger, and organizer of the first Guthrie Memorial Concert in January 1968.

JACQUES LEVY: Dylan's collaborator on the lyrics for the *Desire* album. He also contributed to the genesis and structure of the 1975 Rolling Thunder Revue.

STAN LYNCH: Drummer in Tom Petty and the Heartbreakers, with whom he backed Dylan in concert from September 1985 through to October 1987.

JEFF LYNNE: Co-founder and co-producer of the Traveling Wilburys.

CHARLIE MCCOY: After playing guitar on 'Desolation Row' in New York, he subsequently worked with Dylan on *Blonde on Blonde*, *John Wesley Harding*, *Nashville Skyline* and *Self Portrait*, playing both bass and lead guitar.

FARIDA MCFREE: Having been the art-teacher for Dylan's children she had an intense affair with Dylan against the backdrop of his custody battle for the children.

ROGER MCGUINN: Despite his leadership of seminal folk-rockers the Byrds, he did not record with Dylan until the fall of 1972. Subsequently played on the *Pat Garrett & Billy the Kid* soundtrack album, was a member of the Rolling Thunder Revue in 1975-6 and guested with Dylan in 1980, 1987 and 1990.

MARIA MCKEE: Immensely talented but wayward leader of the now defunct Lone Justice, with whom she recorded one of Dylan's own compositions, donated by the man himself.

EVE MACKENZIE: Wife of Mac, they both befriended Dylan on his arrival in New York in 1961 and provided him with an occasional bed when required.

JIM MCLEAN: Folksinger on the London scene in the winter of 1962/3, during which Dylan made the rounds of the London folk clubs.

GERARD MELANGA: Photographer/film-maker who made a brief celluloid study of Dylan at Andy Warhol's Factory in 1965.

BILL MARINAC: Member of Robert Zimmerman's Hibbing combo, the Shadow Blasters, he also jammed with the young Robert on occasions after the band disbanded.

BOB MARKEL: Editor at Macmillan who supervised the eventual publication of *Tarantula* in all its stages from 1964 to 1970.

RICHARD MARQUAND: Director of *Hearts of Fire* who died shortly after the film's release in 1987.

MARVIN MITCHELSON: Sara Dylan's lawyer during the divorce and custody battle of 1977, who subsequently achieved notoriety as the 'palimony king'.

PAUL MORRISEY: Film-maker and noted member of Andy Warhol's mid-sixties Factory coterie.

MARIA MULDAUR: Grew up in Greenwich Village and was a popular figure on the Village scene in the early sixties, when she played in two jug bands and as part of a duo with husband Geoff.

BOBBY NEUWIRTH: First met Dylan at the Indian Neck Festival in May 1961. He subsequently became Dylan's regular sidekick on his mid-sixties tours. They were reunited on the Rolling Thunder Revues of 1975/6.

JACK NISSENSON: Early admirer of Dylan who had the foresight to record his performance at the Finjan Club, Montreal, in July 1962.

PHIL OCHS: Prolific topical songwriter on the Village scene in 1963/4, he was viewed as a natural heir when Dylan abandoned the genre, but never achieved any substantial commercial success. He had a falling-out with Dylan in November 1965 but later managed to cajole him into appearing at the Friends of Chile benefit in May 1974. He committed suicide in April 1976.

DAVID OPPENHEIM: After he had painted the mural utilized on the rear sleeve of *Blood on the Tracks*, Dylan stayed with him in the south of France for six weeks in spring 1975.

ROY ORBISON: Contributed his trademark vocal chords to the 1988 Traveling Wilburys album. He died shortly after the album's release in 1989.

CHRISTOPHER PARKER: Drummer in Dylan's touring band from 1988 through to 1990.

DON PENNEBAKER: Director of the classic *cinéma vérité* study of Dylan on his 1965 English tour, *Don't Look Back*, he was also utilized to shoot the footage required for a scheduled one-hour documentary on Dylan's 1966 European tour, later shown as *Eat the Document*.

VAL PETERSEN: Robert Zimmerman's music teacher at Hibbing High School.

TOM PETTY: Leader of the Heartbreakers, with whom he accompanied Dylan at Farm Aid in 1985, on Far East and US tours in 1986 and a European tour in 1987. In 1988 he co-founded the massively successful Traveling Wilburys.

JOHN PRINE: American singer-songwriter whose 1971 debut attracted the 'new Dylan' tag, and who in September 1972 had Dylan guest at one of his shows in New York.

CHARLIE QUINTANA: Los Angeles drummer who originally appeared in Dylan's 'Sweetheart Like You' video before jamming with him at his home in Malibu and putting together a band for his appearance on David Letterman's show in March 1984.

ADRIAN RAWLINS: Australian journalist who was temporarily welcomed into Dylan's inner coterie during his April 1966 visit to Australia.

SCARLETT RIVERA: Previously unknown violinist discovered by Dylan on the streets of Greenwich Village in June 1975, whose sound made such a contribution on the *Desire* album and Rolling Thunder tours of 1975/6.

ROBBIE ROBERTSON: Played on all but two of Dylan's live performances between Forest Hills in August 1965 and the final show of the 1974 Dylan/Band tour. He also made sterling contributions as a guitarist on *Blonde on Blonde*, *The Basement Tapes* and *Planet Waves*. They last played together at *The Last Waltz* in November 1976.

MARK ROBINSON: Director of the promotional video for 'Sweetheart Like You'.

MICK RONSON: A surprise inclusion as lead guitarist on the two Rolling Thunder tours in 1975/6, considering his background as David Bowie's right-hand man and bandleader during the heights of glam-rock.

SUZE ROTOLO: Dylan's 'steady' girlfriend from July 1961 through to March 1964. Her six-month sojourn in Italy in 1962 and their eventual break-up in 1964 produced some of Dylan's most beautiful lovesongs.

PETE ROWAN: Was in attendance at the *Blonde on Blonde* sessions in March 1966. He later founded Earth Opera.

JUDY RUBIN: Early girlfriend of Dylan's, first meeting him at summer camp, and later a fellow student at the University of Minnesota.

PETE SEEGER: Highly esteemed folksinger who first befriended Dylan in the early months of 1962 and continued to champion him as a songwriter of note until 1965, when his performance at the Newport Festival annoyed him.

CHARLIE SEXTON: Respected musician in his own right, he recorded a series of demos with Dylan in the fall of 1983.

ROBERT SHELTON: As the *New York Times* folk critic, he came across Dylan in the summer of 1961. His glowing review that September gave Dylan his first major break, and they remained in sporadic contact through the years. In 1986 he published his own biography of the man, which concentrated largely on the Greenwich Village years.

SAM SHEPARD: Playwright commissioned by Dylan to write a screenplay for a film to be shot on the 1975 Rolling Thunder Revue. Though the script idea was later dropped, Shepard contributed his ideas and acting to the film *Renaldo and Clara* and documented the tour in his *Rolling Thunder Logbook*. He subsequently collaborated with Dylan on the 1984 song 'New Danville Girl' and on a June 1987 feature for *Esquire* magazine.

SLASH: Guitarist in American hard-rock merchants, Guns'n' Roses, who played guitar on the opening track of Dylan's 1990 album, *Under the Red Sky*.

LARRY SLOMAN: Unofficial chronicler of the 1975 Rolling Thunder Revue, the results published as the magnificent *On the Road with Bob Dylan*. In 1984 he co-produced the promotional video of Dylan's 'Jokerman'.

IAIN SMITH: Line producer of the *Hearts of Fire* film.

PATTI SMITH: Seventies New York poet and self-proclaimed rock & roll star, considered by some a young 'female' Dylan, she 'hung out' with Dylan during the summer of 1975 and was invited to join the Rolling Thunder Revue.

STEVEN SOLES: Multi-faceted West Coast musician originally recruited for the Rolling Thunder Revues; subsequently played on the 1978 world tour. A devout Christian, he proved supportive of Dylan's own religious rethink in 1979.

PHIL SPECTOR: Notoriously eccentric producer whose only work involving Dylan has been the 1971 Concert for Bangladesh project and Leonard Cohen's 1977 album, *Death of a Ladies Man*.

MARK SPOELSTRA: Fellow folksinger and regular sidekick of Dylan's during his early days in Greenwich Village.

HELENA SPRINGS: Remained very close to Dylan throughout her time as a backing singer in his touring bands in 1978 and 1979, co-writing several songs with him during their time together.

BRUCE SPRINGSTEEN: Last of the New Dylans, so touted in 1973, he finally met Dylan in 1975 and inducted him into the Rock & Roll Hall of Fame in 1988. They finally played together at a Tom Petty and the Heartbreakers gig in March 1990.

PETE STAMPFEL: Arrived in Greenwich Village at about the same time as Dylan and after playing around the Village as a solo artist co-founded the Holy Modal Rounders in 1963.

ROB STONER: Bassist and unofficial band-leader on both Rolling Thunder tours, Stoner was also largely responsible for putting together the 1978 tour band, though he quit after the Far East leg of the world tour.

GREG SUTTON: Bassist on the 1984 European tour.

BENMONT TENCH: Keyboardist in Tom Petty and the Heartbreakers, Tench first worked with Dylan on the 1981 *Shot of Love* album and subsequently on the 1985 sessions for *Empire Burlesque* before touring with him through 1986 and 1987.

TERRI THAL: In 1961 was Dylan's part-time manager and enthusiastic supporter, as was her boyfriend and later husband, Dave Van Ronk.

HAPPY TRAUM: Member of the early sixties Village folk scene. He recorded with Dylan in 1963, 1970 and 1971, and arranged and co-conducted the 1968 *Sing Out* interview.

BOBBY VEE: Rock & roll singer from Fargo, North Dakota, with whom a young Robert Zimmerman played two shows as pianist before Vee dropped him.

ERIC VON SCHMIDT: Cambridge folksinger who first met and befriended Dylan in Boston in June 1961. They renewed their friendship when both in London in January 1963.

TERRI WALLACE: Early fan of Dylan in his Minneapolis days, whose sister Karen (married name: Moynihan) made the first extant recording of Dylan at her apartment.

DON WAS: The co-producer (with his brother Dave) of Dylan's 1990 album, *Under the Red Sky*.

A. J. WEBERMAN: In the late sixties and early seventies was the self-proclaimed world's leading Dylanologist who, after three years of self-publicity, finally met Dylan in January 1971.

BOB WEIR: Guitarist/vocalist in the Grateful Dead.

ERIC WEISSBERG: Banjo player and guitarist who first met Dylan in Madison in January 1961 and later played on the initial New York session for the *Blood on the Tracks* album.

JERRY WEXLER: Producer who defined the Atlantic sound in the sixties, co-produced Barry Goldberg's debut album in 1973 with Dylan, and produced Dylan's own 1979/80 albums, *Slow Train Coming* and *Saved*.

DAVE WHITAKER: Dylan's mentor during his Minneapolis days, versing him in both traditional music and contemporary literature.

TOM WILSON: Dylan's record producer from April 1963 to June 1965, his final session producing the 'Like a Rolling Stone' single. He died in 1980.

RON WOOD: First worked with Dylan in 1976 on Clapton's *No Reason to Cry* album. They subsequently worked together during the summer of 1984 on the early sessions for the *Empire Burlesque* album; and on the 1986 *Hearts of Fire* recordings. He also guested at Dylan shows in 1985, 1986 and 1987.

RUDY WURLITZER: Author of the *Pat Garrett & Billy the Kid* screenplay whose friendship with Dylan was a major factor in Dylan's involvement with the film.

HOWIE WYETH: The drummer (and occasional pianist) on both Rolling Thunder tours and the *Desire* album. He rehearsed for, but withdrew before, the 1978 tour.

PETER YARROW: One third of Grossman's other major act in the early sixties, Peter, Paul and Mary. It was his cabin in Woodstock to which Dylan sometimes retired in 1963/4.

IZZY YOUNG: Owner of the Folklore Center in New York, a regular hang-out for all the Village regulars in the early sixties. Young also arranged Dylan's first concert, at Carnegie Recital Hall, in November 1961.

BEATTIE ZIMMERMAN: The mother of Bob Dylan *né* Robert Allen Zimmerman.

MAURICE ZIMMERMAN: Bob Dylan's uncle.

A Selected Bibliography

This is a bibliography of the sources which have been most useful in the composition of this book. For a more complete bibliography readers are referred to my *Stolen Moments* (Wanted Man/Music Sales, 1988) (a revised edition, *Dylan Day By Day*, is due for publication in December 1991).

Baez, Joan, *And a Voice to Sing With* (Summit Books, 1987).

Balfour, Victoria, *Rock Wives* (Beech Tree, 1986).

Bauldie, John, *The Ghost of Electricity* (privately published).

Bauldie, John, and Gray, Michael (ed.), *All Across the Telegraph* (Sidgwick & Jackson, 1987).

Bauldie, John (ed.), *Wanted Man: In Search of Bob Dylan* (Black Spring Press, 1990).

Cartwright, Bert, *The Bible in the Lyrics of Bob Dylan* (Wanted Man Study Series, 1985).

Cooper, Chris, and Marsh, Keith, *The Circus Is in Town* (privately published).

Davis, Clive, *Clive: Inside the Record Business* (William Morrow, 1974).

Dylan, Bob, *Tarantula* (Macmillan, 1970).

Dylan, Bob, *Lyrics* (Alfred Knopf, 1985).

Flannagan, Bill, *Written in My Soul* (Contemporary, 1986).

Fong-Torres, Ben, *Knockin' on Dylan's Door* (Straight Arrow, 1974).

Ginsberg, Allen, *First Blues* (Full Court Press, 1975).

Gross, Michael, *Bob Dylan: An Illustrated History* (Elm Tree, 1978).

Kooper, Al, *Backstage Passes* (Stein & Day, 1971).

Kramer, Daniel, *Bob Dylan* (Castle Books, 1967).

Lawlan, *Steppin' Out* (privately published).

Lindley, John, *Seven Days* (privately published).

Lindsey, Hal, *The Late Great Planet Earth* (Zondervan, 1970).

McGregor, Craig (ed.), *Bob dylan: A retrospective* (William Morrow, 1972). An excellent anthology recently republished in the USA as *Early Years: A Retrospective* (De Capo, 1990).

Miles, *Ginsberg: A Biography* (Simon & Schuster, 1989).

Rooney, Jim, and Von Schmidt, Eric, *Baby Let Me Follow You Down* (Anchor Books, 1979).

Scaduto, Anthony, *Bob Dylan* (Grosset & Dunlap, 1971).

Seay, Davin, and Neely, Mary, *Stairway to Heaven* (Ballantine, 1986).
Shelton, Robert, *No Direction Home* (Hodder & Stoughton, 1986).
Shepard, Sam, *Rolling Thunder Logbook* (Penguin, 1978).
Simmons, Garner, *Peckinpah: A Portrait in Montage* (University of Texas Press, 1982).
Sloman, Larry, *On the Road with Bob Dylan* (Bantam Books, 1978).
Spitz, Bob, *Dylan: A Biography* (McGraw-Hill, 1988).
Thompson, Toby, *Positively Main Street* (Coward-McCann, 1971).
Webster, Patrick, *Friends & Other Strangers* (private publication).
Williams, Paul, *Dylan: What Happened?* (and/Entwistle Books, 1980).
Williams, Paul, *What Happened?: One Year Later* (Hobo Press, 1981).
Williams, Paul, *Performing Artist* (Underwood-Miller, 1990).
Woliver, Robbie, *Bringing It All Back Home* (Pantheon, 1986).
Worrell, Denise, *Icons* (Atlantic Monthly Press, 1989).

Reference sources:
Bauldie, John (ed.), *Telegraph* #1-37.
Dundas, Glen, *Tangled Up in Tapes* (privately published, 1990).
Heylin, Clinton, *Stolen Moments* (Wanted Man/Music Sales, 1988).
Krogsgaard, Michael, *Master of the Tracks* (SSRR, 1988).

Interviews with Bob Dylan utilized in *Behind the Shades*:
Adler, Philippe, *L'Expresse* 3/7/78.
Allen, Lynne, *Trouser Press* June 1979.
Aschenmacher, Bob, *Duluth News Tribune and Herald* 29/6/86.
Austin, John, source unknown.
Baker, Kathryn, *The Stars and Stripes* 7/9/88.
Bronstein, Martin, Canadian Broadcasting Company 20/2/66.
Brown, Bob, *20/20* TV show 20/10/85.
Brown, Mick, *Sunday Times* 1/7/84.
Burling, Klas, Swedish public radio 29/4/66.
Campbell, Mary, *Houston Post* 12/2/78.
Chase, Donald, *San Francisco Chronicle* 23/11/86.
Coburn, Bob, *Rockline* radio show 17/6/85.
Cohen, John, and Traum, Happy, *Sing Out* October 1968.
Cohen, Scott, *Spin* December 1985.
Cohen, Scott, *Interviews* February 1986.
Cott, Jonathan, *Rolling Stone* 26/1/78.
Cott, Jonathan, *Rolling Stone* 16/11/78.
Crane, Les, transcript of his TV show on 17/2/65.
Creswell, Toby, *Australian Rolling Stone* 16/1/86.
Crowe, Cameron, *Biograph*.
Damsker, Matt, *Circus Weekly* 19/12/78.
Deevoy, Adrian, *Q* December 1989.
De Yong, Jenny, and Roche, Peter, *Darts* May 1965.
Ephron, Nora, and Edmiston, Susan, *A Retrospective*, ed. McGregor (see above).
Flannagan, Bill, *Written in My Soul* (see above).

Flippo, Chet, *Rolling Stone* 15/3/73.

Fong-Torres, Ben, *Knockin' on Dylan's Door* (see above).

Gilmore, Mikal, *Los Angeles Herald-Examiner* 13/10/85.

Ginsberg, Allen, *Telegraph* #33.

Gundersen, Edna, *USA Today* 21/9/89.

Gundersen, Edna, *USA Today* 14/9/90.

Heiman, Bruce, KMEX radio 7/12/79.

Hentoff, Nat, the original *Freewheelin'* galleys published in *Telegraph* #8.

Hentoff, Nat, *New Yorker* 24/10/64.

Hentoff, Nat, his extensive October 1965 interview published as the booklet *Whaaat!*.

Hentoff, Nat, *Playboy* March 1966.

Herman, Dave, the *London Interview* promo album – transcript.

Hickey, Neil, *TV Guide* 11/9/76.

Hilburn, Robert, *Los Angeles Times* 28/5/78.

Hilburn, Robert, *Los Angeles Times* 12/11/78.

Hilburn, Robert, *Los Angeles Times* 23/11/80.

Hilburn, Robert, *Los Angeles Times* 30/10/83.

Hilburn, Robert, *Los Angeles Times* 17/11/85.

Hilburn, Robert, *Los Angeles Times* 7/9/87.

Hughes, Karen, *Rock Express* #1.

Hughes, Karen, *Dominion* 2/8/80.

Iachetta, Michael, *New York Daily News* 8/5/67.

James, Billy, a transcript of the November 1961 interview.

Jones, Max, *Melody Maker* 23/5/64.

Keller, Martin, *New Musical Express* 6/8/83.

Kerr, Barbara, *Toronto Sun* 26–29/3/78.

Kleinman, Bert, and Mogull, Artie, Westwood One broadcast 25/11/84.

Loeder, Kurt, *Rolling Stone* 26/6/84.

McGregor, Craig, *Sydney Morning Herald* 18/3/78.

Mankiewicz, John, *Sound* 12/11/78.

Meer, Dan, *Close Up* radio show 30/10/89.

Merryfield, Mary, *Chicago Tribune* 21/11/65.

Oppel, Pete, *Dallas Morning News* 18–23/11/78.

Quinn, Martha, MTV 7/7/84.

Robbins, Paul J., *Los Angeles Free Press* 17 and 24/9/65.

Rockwell, John, *New York Times* 8/1/78.

Rosenbaum, Ron, *Playboy* January 1978.

Rowland, Marc, US radio 23/9/78.

Saal, Hubert, *Newsweek* 4/4/69.

Scaduto, Anthony, *Bob Dylan* (see above).

Seeger, Pete, transcript of unbroadcast May 1962 WBAI radio show.

Shelton, Robert, *Melody Maker* 24/6/78.

Shepard, Sam, *Esquire* July 1987.

Siegel, Jules, *Saturday Evening Post* 30/7/66.

Sloman, Larry, *On the Road with Bob Dylan* (see above).

Smith, Jack, *National Guardian* 22/8/63.

Spencer, Neil, *New Musical Express* 15/8/81.

Steen, Margaret, *Toronto Weekly* 29/1/66.

Stone, Allen, WDTM radio 24/10/65.

Sykes, Christopher, *Getting to Dylan* 18/9/87.

Sykes, Christopher, Tour programme 1989.

Terkel, Studs, *Wax Museum* radio show 26/4/63.

Turner, Gil, *Sing Out* October 1962.

Vincent, Paul, *Endless Road* #2.

Vox, Bono, *Hot Press* 24/8/84.

Welles, Chris, *Life* 10/4/64.

Wenner, Jann, *Rolling Stone* 29/11/69.

Worrell, Denise, *Icons* (see above).

Young, Izzy, *Other Scenes* December 1968.

Yurchenco, Henrietta, *Sound and Fury* April 1966.

unknown interviewer for *Gargoyle* magazine, February 1964.

unknown interviewer for the *New York Post*, 12/1/65.

unknown interviewer for *Photoplay*, 1978.

unknown interviewer for *El Diario Vasco*, 18/6/89.

Transcripts of Dylan press conferences utilized in text:

Beverly Hills Hotel press conference 4/9/65.

San Francisco press conference 3/12/65.

Adelaide press conference 21/4/66.

Travemunde press conference 13/7/81.

Sydney press conference 10/2/86.

A Bob Dylan Sessionography 1961–90

This sessionography aims to detail the products of Dylan's official studio sessions. It is not intended to include his appearances as a guest musician. Only singles which featured previously unavailable material are included in the discography, and all singles are US releases unless so indicated. Compilation albums, which CBS seem inordinately fond of, are also featured only when they contain material new to vinyl.

Where multiple takes are known, a square bracket [ ] indicates the number for each take. For the sixties material, Columbia reference numbers (bracketed with the prefix CO) are noted where known. If the track is available on single only, the reference number for the single (e.g. CBS 2921) is given in place of an album title. References to Mk. 1 versions of albums indicate that this song/take was included on the original test pressing but not on the final, released version. References in square brackets to edits or backing tracks indicate that the released version either omits parts of the complete take or that a new vocal was added at a subsequent date. Asterisked items are instrumentals.

For a more detailed chronology of Dylan's studio activities readers are referred to my chronology of his career, *Stolen Moments* (Wanted Man/Music Sales, 1988). Finally, please note there is a degree of speculation involved in the compilation of this discography. Generally reliable it is. Gospel it is not.

1. 'Bob Dylan' Sessions, Columbia Studios, New York.

20 November 1961

1. Song To Woody [t1] (CO68731)
2. Song To Woody [t2]   *Bob Dylan*
3. Baby Let Me Follow You Down
   (CO68732)   *Bob Dylan*
4. Man Of Constant Sorrow

 5. In My Time of Dyin'
    (CO68733)   *Bob Dylan*
 6. He Was A Friend Of Mine   *Bootleg Series*
 7. Connecticut Cowboy (intro.
    to . . .)
 8. You're No Good   *Bob Dylan*
 9. Talkin' New York   *Bob Dylan*
10. Fixin' To Die   *Bob Dylan*
11. House Of The Risin' Sun   *Bob Dylan*
12. House Carpenter   *Bootleg Series*

22 November 1961
 1. Man On The Street [t1]
    (CO68743)
 2. Man On The Street [t2]   *Bootleg Series*
 3. Man On The Street [t3]
 4. Man On The Street [t4]
 5. Man On The Street [t5]
 6. Ramblin' Blues [t1] (CO68744)
 7. Ramblin' Blues [t2]
 8. Man Of Constant Sorrow [t1]
    (CO68745)
 9. Man Of Constant Sorrow [t2]
10. Man Of Constant Sorrow [t3]   *Bob Dylan*
11. Pretty Peggy-O [t1] (CO68746)   *Bob Dylan*
12. Highway 51   *Bob Dylan*
13. Gospel Plow   *Bob Dylan*
14. Freight Train Blues   *Bob Dylan*
15. See That My Grave Is Kept
    Clean   *Bob Dylan*

2. 'Leeds Music Demos', Duchess Music, New York.

January 1962
 1. Man On The Street [t1]
 2. Hard Times In New York
    Town
 3. Poor Boy Blues
 4. Ballad For A Friend
 5. Ramblin', Gamblin' Willie
 6. Man On The Street [t2]
 7. Talkin' Bear Mountain Picnic
    Massacre Blues
 8. Standing On The Highway

3. 'The Freewheelin' ' Sessions, Columbia Studios, New York.

24–25 April 1962

1. Ramblin', Gamblin' Willie	*Freewheelin' Mk. 1/Bootleg Series*
2. Talkin' Hava Negeliah Blues	*Bootleg Series*
3. Talkin' Bear Mountain Picnic Massacre Blues	*Bootleg Series*
4. Baby, Please Don't Go	
5. Let Me Die In My Footsteps	*Freewheelin' Mk.1/Bootleg Series*
6. The Death Of Emmett Till	
7. Sally Gal [t1] (CO70086)	
8. Sally Gal [t2]	
9. Sally Gal [t3]	
10. Sally Gal [t4]	
11. Going To New Orleans	
12. (I Heard That) Lonesome Whistle	
13. Talkin' John Birch Society Blues	*Freewheelin' Mk. 1*
14. Milk Cow Blues [t1] (CO70100)	
15. Milk Cow Blues [t2]	
16. Milk Cow Blues [t3]	
17. Milk Cow Blues [t4]	
18. Wichita [t1] (CO70101)	
19. Wichita [t2]	

9 July 1962

1. Blowin' In The Wind	*Freewheelin'*
2. Down The Highway	*Freewheelin'*
3. Honey, Just Allow Me One More Chance	*Freewheelin'*
4. Quit Your Lowdown Ways	*Bootleg Series*
5. Worried Blues	*Bootleg Series*
6. Babe, I'm In The Mood For You [t1]	
7. Babe, I'm In The Mood For You [t2]	*Biograph*
8. Corrina, Corrina	
9. Rocks and Gravel	

26 October 1962
1. Corrina, Corrina   *Freewheelin'*

13 November 1962
1. Rocks And Gravel   *Freewheelin' Mk. 1*

14 November 1962
1. That's Alright Mama [t1]
   (CO76983)
2. That's Alright Mama [t2]
3. Corrina, Corrina   *4-42656*
4. Mixed Up Confusion [t1]
5. Mixed Up Confusion [t2]
6. Mixed Up Confusion [t3]   *4-42656*
7. Mixed Up Confusion [t4]   *Biograph*
8. Kingsport Town   *Bootleg Series*
9. Whatcha Gonna Do?
10. Ballad Of Hollis Brown
11. Don't Think Twice, It's All
    Right   *Freewheelin'*

15 November 1962
1. Mixed Up Confusion [t1]

6 December 1962
1. Hero Blues [t1] (CO77020)
2. Hero Blues [t2]
3. Hero Blues [t3]
4. Hero Blues [t4]
5. Whatcha Gonna Do?
   (CO77021)
6. Oxford Town (CO77022)   *Freewheelin'*
7. I Shall Be Free [t1] (CO77023)
8. I Shall Be Free [t2]   *Freewheelin'*
9. I Shall Be Free [t3]
10. I Shall Be Free [t4]
11. I Shall Be Free [t5]
12. Hard Rain's A Gonna Fall
    (CO77024)   *Freewheelin'*
13. Bob Dylan's Blues (CO77025)   *Freewheelin'*

24 April 1963
1. Girl From The North Country   *Freewheelin'*
2. Masters Of War   *Freewheelin'*
3. Bob Dylan's Dream   *Freewheelin'*

| 4. Talkin' World War III Blues | *Freewheelin'* |
| 5. Walls Of Redwing | *Bootleg Series* |

4. 'The Witmark Demos', New York.

June 1962
1. Blowin' In The Wind
2. Long Ago, Far Away   *7-arts demo LP*

December 1962
1. Tomorrow Is A Long Time
2. Ballad Of Hollis Brown
3. The Death Of Emmett Till   *7-arts demo LP*
4. Hard Rain's A Gonna Fall
5. Let Me Die In My Footsteps
6. Quit Your Lowdown Ways
7. Babe, I'm In The Mood For You

Early 1963
1. Talkin' John Birch Paranoid Blues
2. All Over You
3. Bound To Lose, Bound To Win
4. I'd Hate To Be You On That Dreadful Day   *7-arts demo LP*

March 1963
1. Long Time Gone   *7-arts demo LP*
2. Don't Think Twice, It's All Right
3. Oxford Town
4. Masters Of War
5. Walkin' Down The Line   *Bootleg Series*

April 1963
1. I Shall Be Free   *7-arts demo LP*
2. Bob Dylan's Dreams
3. Bob Dylan's Blues
4. Boots Of Spanish Leather

May 1963
1. Girl From The North Country
2. Seven Curses
3. Hero Blues

August 1963
1. Gypsy Lou
2. Whatcha Gonna Do
3. Ain't Gonna Grieve   *7-arts demo LP*
4. Only A Hobo   *7-arts demo LP*
5. John Brown   *7-arts demo LP*

September 1963
1. When The Ship Comes In   *Bootleg Series*

September 1963
1. The Times They Are a–
   Changin'   *Bootleg Series*

December 1963
1. Paths of Victory
2. Farewell

January 1964
1. Baby Let Me Follow You
   Down
2. Guess I'm Doing Fine

June 1964
1. Mr. Tambourine Man
2. Mama, You Been On My Mind
3. I'll Keep It With Mine   *7-arts demo LP*

5. 'The Broadside Sessions', Broadside Offices, New York.

November 1962
1. I'd Hate To Be You On That
   Dreadful Day   *Broadside Reunion*
2. Oxford Town
3. Paths Of Victory
4. Walkin' Down The Line

November 1962
1. Ye Playboys & Playgirls

19 January 1963
1. Talkin' Devil   *Broadside Ballads*
2. Farewell

24 January 1963
1. Masters Of War
2. Let Me Die In My Footsteps   *Broadside Ballads*

February 1963
1. Only A Hobo	*Broadside Ballads*
2. John Brown	*Broadside Ballads*

March 1963
1. I Shall Be Free	
2. Train a-Travelin'	*Broadside Reunion*
3. Cuban Missile Crisis	

6. 'Times They Are a-Changin' Sessions', Columbia Studios, New York.

6 August 1963
1. North Country Blues	*Times They Are Changin'*
2. Seven Curses	*Bootleg Series*

7 August 1963
1. Ballad Of Hollis Brown	*Times They Are Changin'*
2. With God On Our Side	*Times They Are Changin'*
3. Boots Of Spanish Leather	*Times They Are Changin'*
4. Only A Pawn In Their Game	*Times They Are Changin'*

12 August 1963
1. One Too Many Mornings	*Times They Are Changin'*
2. Only A Hobo	*Bootleg Series*
3. Paths Of Victory	*Bootleg Series*
4. Moonshine Blues	*Bootleg Series*
5. Percy's Song	

23 October 1963
1. When The Ship Comes In	*Times They Are Changin'*
2. The Lonesome Death Of Hattie Carroll	*Times They Are Changin'*
3. Percy's Song	*Biograph*

24 October 1963
1. The Times They Are a-Changin'	*Times They Are Changin'*
2. Lay Down Your Weary Tune	*Biograph*
3. Eternal Circle [t1]	
4. Eternal Circle [t2]	
5. Eternal Circle [t3]	*Bootleg Series*
6. Suzy (The Cough Song) *	*Bootleg Series*

31 October 1963

1. Restless Farewell   *Times They Are Changin'*

7. 'Another Side Of' Session, Columbia Studios, New York.

9 June 1964

1. Bob Dylan's New Orleans Rag
   [t1]
2. Bob Dylan's New Orleans Rag
   [t2]
3. Denise, Denise
4. That's Alright Mama
5. Mr. Tambourine Man
6. Farewell
7. East Laredo (CO79683) ★
8. Mama, You Been On My Mind   *Bootleg Series*
9. All I Really Wanna Do   *Another Side*
10. Black Crow Blues   *Another Side*
11. Spanish Harlem Incident   *Another Side*
12. Chimes Of Freedom   *Another Side*
13. I Shall Be Free No. 10 [t1]
14. I Shall Be Free No. 10 [t2]
15. I Shall Be Free No. 10 [t3]   *Another Side*
16. To Ramona   *Another Side*
17. Motorpsycho Nitemare   *Another Side*
18. I Don't Believe You   *Another Side*
19. Ballad In Plain D   *Another Side*
20. It Ain't Me Babe   *Another Side*
21. My Back Pages   *Another Side*

8. 'Bringing It All Back Home' Sessions, Columbia Studios, New York.

13 January 1965

1. Love Minus Zero/No Limit [t1]
   (CO85270)
2. Love Minus Zero/No Limit [t2]
3. I'll Keep It With Mine
   (CO85271)   *Biograph*
4. It's All Over Now Baby Blue
   (CO85272)
5. She Belongs To Me (CO85274)

6. Subterranean Homesick Blues
   (CO85275)   *Bootleg Series*
7. California (CO85276)
8. On The Road Again
   (CO85277)
9. Farewell Angelina (CO85278)   *Bootleg Series*
10. If You Gotta Go, Go Now [t1]
    (CO85279)
11. If You Gotta Go, Go Now [t2]
12. You Don't Have To Do That
    (CO85280)
13. Bob Dylan's 115th Dream [t1]
    (CO85273)
14. Bob Dylan's 115th Dream [t2]

14 January 1965
1. Mr. Tambourine Man
2. Keep It With Mine ★
3. Maggie's Farm   *Bringing It All Back Home*
4. On The Road Again   *Bringing It All Back Home*

15 January 1965
1. Subterranean Homesick Blues   *Bringing It All Back Home*
2. She Belongs To Me   *Bringing It All Back Home*
3. Love Minus Zero/No Limit   *Bringing It All Back Home*
4. Outlaw Blues   *Bringing It All Back Home*
5. Bob Dylan's 115th Dream   *Bringing It All Back Home*
6. It's All Over Now, Baby Blue   *Bringing It All Back Home*
7. Mr. Tambourine Man   *Bringing It All Back Home*
8. Gates Of Eden   *Bringing It All Back Home*
9. It's Alright Ma (I'm Only
   Bleeding)   *Bringing It All Back Home*
10. If You Gotta Go, Go Now [t1]   CBS 2921
11. If You Gotta Go, Go Now [t2]   *Bootleg Series*

9. 'Highway 61 Revisited' Sessions, Columbia
Studios, New York.

15 June 1965
1. Sitting On A Barbed Wire Fence
   [t1] (CO86444)
2. Sitting On A Barbed Wire Fence
   [t2]

3. Sitting On A Barbed Wire Fence
   [t3]
4. Phantom Engineer (It Takes A
   Lot To Laugh) (CO86445)   *Bootleg Series*
5. Sitting On A Barbed Wire Fence
   [t4]
6. Sitting On a Barbed Wire Fence
   [t5]
7. Sitting On A Barbed Wire Fence
   [t6]   *Bootleg Series*
8. Like A Rolling Stone [t1]   *Bootleg Series*
9. Like A Rolling Stone [t2]
10. Like A Rolling Stone [t3]
11. Like A Rolling Stone [t4]
12. Like A Rolling Stone [t5]   *Highway 61 Revisited*

16 June 1965
1. Can You Please Crawl Out
   Your Window? [t1]
2. Can You Please Crawl Out
   Your Window? [t2]   4-43389 [mispress]
3. Jet Pilot   *Biograph*

29 July 1965
1. Tombstone Blues [t1]
2. Tombstone Blues [t2]   *Highway 61 Revisited*
3. It Takes A Lot To Laugh, It
   Takes A Train To Cry [t1]
4. It Takes A Lot To Laugh [t2]   *Highway 61 Revisited*
5. Positively Fourth Street [t1]
6. Positively Fourth Street [t2]   *Greatest Hits/Biograph*

30 July 1965
1. From A Buick Six [t1]   *Highway 61 Revisited*
                                          [mispress]
2. From A Buick Six [t2]   *Highway 61 Revisited*
3. Desolation Row

2 August 1965
1. Ballad Of A Thin Man   *Highway 61 Revisited*
2. Queen Jane Approximately   *Highway 61 Revisited*
3. Highway 61 Revisited   *Highway 61 Revisited*

4 August 1965
1. Just Like Tom Thumb's Blues   *Highway 61 Revisited*
2. Desolation Row   *Highway 61 Revisited*

3. Highway 61 Revisited

10. 'Blonde On Blonde' Sessions, Columbia Studios, New York, Los Angeles and Nashville.

20 October 1965 (New York)
1. Can You Please Crawl Out
   Your Window? (CO87184)   *Biograph*
2. I Wanna Be Your Lover [t1]
3. I Wanna Be Your Lover [t2]   *Biograph*

30 November/1 December 1965 (Los Angeles)
1. Can You Please Crawl Out
   Your Window?
2. Number One ★
3. Medicine Sunday
4. Visions Of Johanna (Freeze Out)
   (CO88581)

21/24/25 January 1966 (New York)
1. She's Your Lover Now [t1]
   (CO89210)
2. She's Your Lover Now [t2]   *Bootleg Series*
3. I'll Keep It With Mine   *Bootleg Series*
4. One Of Us Must Know [t1]
5. One Of Us Must Know [t2]
6. One Of Us Must Know [t3]
7. One Of Us Must Know [t4]
8. One Of Us Must Know [t5]   *Blonde on Blonde*
9. Visions Of Johanna (Freeze Out)

14–17 February 1966 (Nashville)
1. Visions Of Johanna   *Blonde on Blonde*
2. Stuck Inside Of Mobile   *Blonde on Blonde*
3. Sad Eyed Lady Of The
   Lowlands   *Blonde on Blonde*
4. Leopard Skin Pill Box Hat [t1]
5. Leopard Skin Pill Box Hat [t2]   *Blonde on Blonde*
6. Fourth Time Around   *Blonde on Blonde*

8 March 1966 (Nashville)
1. Pledging My Time   *Blonde on Blonde*
2. Just Like A Woman   *Blonde on Blonde*
3. Absolutely Sweet Marie   *Blonde on Blonde*

9 March 1966 (Nashville)

1. I Want You   *Blonde on Blonde*
2. Temporary Like Achilles   *Blonde on Blonde*
3. Obviously Five Believers   *Blonde on Blonde*
4. Most Likely You Go Your Way
   [t1]
5. Most Likely You Go Your Way
   [t2]
6. Most Likely You Go Your Way
   [t3]   *Blonde on Blonde*
7. Rainy Day Women Nos. 12 &
   35 [t1]
8. Rainy Day Women Nos. 12 &
   35 [t2]
9. Rainy Day Women Nos. 12 &
   35 [t3]   *Blonde on Blonde*

11. 'The Basement Tapes', West Saugerties, Woodstock, N.Y.

June–October 1967

1. Down In The Flood [t1]
2. Down In The Flood [t2]   *The Basement Tapes*
3. I Shall Be Released   *Bootleg Series*
4. Lo And Behold [t1]
5. Lo And Behold [t2]   *The Basement Tapes*
6. Million Dollar Bash [t1]
7. Million Dollar Bash [t2]   *The Basement Tapes*
8. Please Mrs Henry   *The Basement Tapes*
9. This Wheel's On Fire   *The Basement Tapes*
10. Tiny Montgomery   *The Basement Tapes*
11. Yea Heavy And A Bottle Of
    Bread [t1]
12. Yea Heavy And A Bottle Of
    Bread [t2]   *The Basement Tapes*
13. You Ain't Going Nowhere [t1]
14. You Ain't Going Nowhere [t2]   *The Basement Tapes*
15. Going To Acapulco   *The Basement Tapes*
16. Too Much Of Nothing [t1]   *The Basement Tapes*
17. Too Much Of Nothing [t2]
18. Tears Of Rage [t1]   *The Basement Tapes*
19. Tears Of Rage [t2]
20. Tears Of Rage [t3]

21. Quinn The Eskimo [t1]   *Biograph*
22. Quinn The Eskimo [t2]
23. Nothing Was Delivered [t1]
24. Nothing Was Delivered [t2]   *The Basement Tapes*
25. Nothing Was Delivered [t3]
26. Open The Door Homer [t1]
27. Open The Door Homer [t2]
28. Open The Door Homer [t3]   *The Basement Tapes*
29. Get Your Rocks Off
30. I'm Not There (1956)
31. Clothesline Saga   *The Basement Tapes*
32. Odds And Ends [t1]
33. Odds And Ends [t2]   *The Basement Tapes*
34. Apple Suckling Tree [t1]   *The Basement Tapes*
35. Apple Suckling Tree [t2]
36. Silent Weekend
37. Bourbon Street
38. Wild Wolf
39. All American Boy
40. Santa Fe   *Bootleg Series*
41. Sign On The Cross
42. Don't Ya Tell Henry
43. Lock Your Door
44. Baby, Won't You Be My Baby
45. Try Me Little Girl
46. I Can't Make It Alone
47. Don't You Try Me Now
48. Young But Daily Growin'
49. Bonnie Ship The Diamond
50. The Hills Of Mexico
51. Down On Me
52. One For The Road
53. I'm Alright
54. One Single River
55. People Get Ready
56. I Don't Hurt Anymore
57. Stones That You Throw
58. One Man's Loss
59. All You Have To Do Is Dream
    [t1]
60. All You Have To Do Is Dream
    [t2]
61. Baby, Ain't That Fine

62. Rock, Salt And Nails
63. A Fool Such As I
64. Gonna Get You Now
65. Wild Wood Flower
66. See That My Grave Is Kept
    Clean
67. Comin' Round The Mountain
68. Flight Of The Bumble Bee
69. Confidential To Me
70. I'm A Fool For You [t1]
71. I'm A Fool For You [t2]
72. Next Time On The Highway
73. The Big Flood
74. Don't Know Why They Kick
    My Dog
75. See You Later, Allen Ginsberg
76. The Spanish Song [t1]
77. The Spanish Song [t2]
78. I Am A Teenage Prayer
79. Four Strong Winds
80. The French Girl [t1]
81. The French Girl [t2]
82. Joshua Gone Barbados
83. I'm In The Mood
84. Belchezaar [t1]
85. Belchezaar [t2]
86. I Forgot To Remember To
    Forget
87. You Win Again
88. Still In Town
89. Waltzing With Sin
90. Big River
91. Folsom Prison Blues
92. Bells Of Rhymney
93. Banana Boat Song
94. Nine Hundred Miles
95. No Shoes On My Feet
96. Spanish Is The Loving Tongue
97. On A Rainy Afternoon
98. I Can't Come In With A
    Broken Heart
99. Under Control
100. Ol' Roison The Beau

101. I'm Guilty Of Loving You
102. Johnny Todd
103. Cool Water
104. Banks Of The Royal Canal
105. Po' Lazarus
106. Bring It On Home
107. The King Of France
108. It's Just Another Tomato In
       The Glass

12. 'John Wesley Harding' Sessions, Columbia Studios, Nashville.

17 October, 6 November, 29 November 1967

1. John Wesley Harding	*John Wesley Harding*
2. As I Went Out One Morning	*John Wesley Harding*
3. I Dreamed I Saw Saint Augustine	*John Wesley Harding*
4. Ballad Of Frankie Lee And Judas Priest	*John Wesley Harding*
5. All Along The Watchtower	*John Wesley Harding*
6. Drifter's Escape	*John Wesley Harding*
7. Dear Landlord	*John Wesley Harding*
8. I Pity The Poor Immigrant	*John Wesley Harding*
9. The Wicked Messenger	*John Wesley Harding*
10. I Am A Lonesome Hobo	*John Wesley Harding*
11. Down Along The Cove	*John Wesley Harding*
12. I'll Be Your Baby Tonight	*John Wesley Harding*

13. 'Nashville Skyline' Sessions, Columbia Studios, Nashville.

13–14 February 1969

1. Nashville Skyline Rag ★	*Nashville Skyline*
2. To Be Alone With You	*Nashville Skyline*
3. I Threw It All Away	*Nashville Skyline*
4. Peggy Day	*Nashville Skyline*
5. Lay, Lady, Lay	*Nashville Skyline*
6. One More Night	*Nashville Skyline*
7. Tell Me That It Isn't True	*Nashville Skyline*
8. Country Pie	*Nashville Skyline*
9. Tonight I'll Be Staying Here With You	*Nashville Skyline*

17 February 1969, with Johnny Cash
1. One Too Many Mornings
2. Girl From The North Country *Nashville Skyline*

18 February 1969, with Johnny Cash
1. One Too Many Mornings
2. Good Ol' Mountain Dew
3. I Still Miss Someone
4. Careless Love
5. Matchbox
6. That's Alright Mama
7. Big River
8. I Walk The Line
9. You Are My Sunshine
10. Guess Things Happen That Way
11. Just A Closer Walk With Thee
12. Blues Yodel No. 1
13. Blues Yodel No. 5
14. Understand Your Man
15. Wanted Man

14. 'Self Portrait' Sessions, Columbia Studies, Nashville and New York.

May–June 1969 (Nashville)
1. Blue Moon *Self Portrait*
2. Let It Be Me *Self Portrait*
3. Living The Blues *Self Portrait*
4. Take A Message To Mary *Self Portrait*
5. I Forgot More (Than You'll
 Ever Know) *Self Portrait*
6. Take Me As I Am *Self Portrait*
7. A Fool Such As I *Dylan*
8. Spanish Is A Loving Tongue *Dylan*
9. Folsom Prison Blues
10. Ring of Fire
11. Ghost Riders In The Sky
12. Cupid
13. All I Have To Do Is Dream
14. Gates Of Eden
15. I Threw It All Away
16. I Don't Believe You
17. Matchbox
18. True Love, Your Love

19. When's My Swamp Gonna
    Catch Fire
20. Fishin' Blues
21. Honey, Just Allow Me One
    More Chance
22. Rainy Day Women Nos. 12 &
    35

Winter 1969–70 (New York)

 1. The Boxer   *Self Portrait*
 2. It Hurts Me Too   *Self Portrait*
 3. Thirsty Boots
 4. Alberta No. 1   *Self Portrait*
 5. Alberta No. 2   *Self Portrait*
 6. Gotta Travel On   *Self Portrait*
 7. Early Morning Rain   *Self Portrait*
 8. Days Of '49   *Self Portrait*
 9. Little Sadie   *Self Portrait*
10. Lily Of The West   *Dylan*

Late February 1970 (New York)

 1. All The Tired Horses   *Self Portrait*
 2. Wigwam   *Self Portrait*
 3. Copper Kettle   *Self Portrait*
 4. Belle Isle   *Self Portrait*

3 March 1970

 1. Rock A Bye My Saro Jane   *Dylan*
 2. In Search Of Little Sadie   *Self Portrait*
 3. Sittin' On The Dock Of The
    Bay
 4. Went To See The Gypsy   *New Morning*
 5. Universal Soldier
 6. (When A Man's) Out Of A Job
 7. These Working Hands
 8. Spanish Eyes
 9. Woogie Boogie ★   *Self Portrait*

15. 'New Morning' Sessions, Columbia Studios, New York.

1 May 1970

 1. Song To Woody
 2. Mama, You Been On My Mind
 3. Don't Think Twice, It's All
    Right

4. Yesterday
5. Just Like Tom Thumb's Blues
6. Da Doo Ron Ron
7. One Too Many Mornings [t1] *
8. One Too Many Mornings [t2]
9. Working On A Guru
10. If Not For You   *Bootleg Series*

May 1970
  1. If Not For You   *New Morning*
  2. Time Passes Slowly   *New Morning*
  3. Ballad Of Ira Hayes   *Dylan*

August 1970
  1. Day Of The Locusts   *New Morning*
  2. Winterlude   *New Morning*
  3. If Dogs Run Free   *New Morning*
  4. New Morning   *New Morning*
  5. Sign On The Window   *New Morning*
  6. One More Weekend   *New Morning*
  7. The Man In Me   *New Morning*
  8. Three Angels   *New Morning*
  9. Father Of Night   *New Morning*
 10. Can't Help Falling In Love   *Dylan*
 11. Mr. Bojangles   *Dylan*
 12. Mary Ann   *Dylan*
 13. Big Yellow Taxi   *Dylan*
 14. Jamaica Farewell
 15. Spanish Is The Loving Tongue   4-45409
 16. Tomorrow Is A Long Time
 17. Went To See The Gypsy
 18. Running
 19. Alligator Man

16. Blue Rock Studios, New York

16–18 March 1971
  1. When I Paint My Masterpiece   *More Greatest Hits*
  2. Watching The River Flow   *More Greatest Hits*
  3. Spanish Harlem
  4. That Lucky Ol' Sun
  5. Alabama Bound
  6. Blood Red River
  7. Rock Of Ages

17. Columbia Studios, New York.

October 1971, with Happy Traum
1. You Ain't Going Nowhere [t1]
2. You Ain't Going Nowhere [t2]   *More Greatest Hits*
3. I Shall Be Released   *More Greatest Hits*
4. Down In The Flood   *More Greatest Hits*
5. Only A Hobo

18. Columbia Studios, New York.

4 November 1971
1. George Jackson [t1]   4-45516
2. George Jackson [t2]   4-45516
3. Wallflower   *Bootleg Series*

19. 'Pat Garrett and Billy The Kid'. Sessions, Columbia Studios, Mexico City and Burbank Studios, Burbank.

20 January 1973 (Mexico City)
1. Billy [t1]
2. Billy [t2]
3. Billy [t3]
4. Turkey [t1]★
5. Turkey [t2]★
6. Billy Surrenders [t1]★
7. And Then He Killed Me Too [t1]★
8. And Then He Killed Me Too [t2]★
9. Goodbye Holly
10. Peco's Blues [t1]★
11. Peco's Blues [t2]★
12. Billy [t4]
13. Billy 4   *Pat Garrett and Billy the Kid*

February 1973 (Burbank)
1. Billy Surrenders★
2. Knockin' On Heaven's Door★ [t1]
3. Amarillo
4. Knockin' On Heaven's Door [t2]

5. Knockin' On Heaven's Door
   [t3]
6. Knockin' On Heaven's Door   *Pat Garrett and Billy the*
   [t4]   *Kid*
7. Final Theme [t1]
8. Final Theme [t2]   *Pat Garrett and Billy the*
                                    Kid

9. Rock Me Mama
10. Billy 7 [t1]
11. Billy 7 [t2]
12. Billy 7 [t3]   *Pat Garrett and Billy the*
                                    Kid

13. Billy Ride
14. Bunkhouse Theme★   *Pat Garrett and Billy the*
                                    Kid

February 1973 (Burbank)
1. Main Theme (Billy)★   *Pat Garrett and Billy the*
                                    Kid
2. Cantina Theme [t1]★   *Pat Garrett and Billy the*
                                    Kid
3. Cantina Theme [t2]★
4. Billy 1★   *Pat Garrett and Billy the*
                                    Kid
5. Billy [t1]
6. Billy [t2]
7. River Theme★   *Pat Garrett and Billy the*
                                    Kid
8. Turkey Chase★   *Pat Garrett and Billy the*
                                    Kid

20. Ram's Horn Office, New York.

June 1973
1. Forever Young   *Biograph*
2. Nobody 'Cept You
3. Never Say Goodbye

21. 'Planet Waves' Sessions, Village Recorder Studios, Los Angeles.

2 November 1973
1. Never Say Goodbye   *Planet Waves*
2. Nobody 'Cept You   *Bootleg Series*
3. House Of The Rising Sun

5/6 November 1973
1. Forever Young [t1]
2. Forever Young [t2]
3. Forever Young [t3]   *Planet Waves*
4. Forever Young [t4]   *Planet Waves*
5. Hazel   *Planet Waves*
6. Tough Mama   *Planet Waves*

9 November 1973
1. On A Night Like This   *Planet Waves*
2. Going Going Gone   *Planet Waves*
3. Something There Is About You *Planet Waves*
4. You Angel You   *Planet Waves*
5. Crosswind Jamboree ★
6. Dirge

10 November 1973
1. Wedding Song   *Planet Waves*

11 November 1973
1. Dirge [t1]
2. Dirge [t2]   *Planet Waves*

22. 'Blood on the Tracks' Sessions, Columbia Studios, New York, & Sound 80, Minneapolis.

16 September 1974 (New York)
1. Call Letter Blues   *Bootleg Series*
2. Tangled Up In Blue [t1]   *Blood On The Tracks Mk.1*
3. Tangled Up In Blue [t2]   *Bootleg Series*
4. If You See Her, Say Hello [t1] *Blood On The Tracks Mk.1*
5. If You See Her, Say Hello [t2] *Bootleg Series*

17–19 September 1974 (New York)
1. Lily, Rosemary & The Jack Of
   Hearts   *Blood On The Tracks Mk.1*
2. Idiot Wind [t1]   *Bootleg Series*
3. Idiot Wind [t2]   *Blood On The Tracks Mk.1*
4. Buckets Of Rain   *Blood On The Tracks*
5. You're Gonna Make Me
   Lonesome [t1]
6. You're Gonna Make Me
   Lonesome [t2]   *Blood On The Tracks*

23–25 September 1974 (New York)

1. Simple Twist Of Fate	*Blood On The Tracks*
2. Shelter From The Storm	*Blood On The Tracks*
3. Meet Me In The Morning	*Blood On The Tracks*
4. Up To Me	*Biograph*
5. You're A Big Girl Now	*Biograph*

27 December 1974 (Minneapolis)

1. Idiot Wind [t1]	
2. Idiot Wind [t2]	
3. Idiot Wind [t3]	
4. Idiot Wind [t4]	*Blood On The Tracks*
5. You're A Big Girl Now	*Blood On The Tracks*

30 December 1974 (Minneapolis)

1. Tangled Up In Blue	*Blood On The Tracks*
2. Lily, Rosemary & The Jack Of Hearts	*Blood On The Tracks*
3. If You See Her, Say Hello	*Blood On The Tracks*

23. 'Desire' Sessions, Columbia Studios, New York.

28 July 1975

1. Romance In Durango	*Desire*
2. Oh Sister	
3. Mozambique	
4. Hurricane	
5. Wiretappin'	
6. Money Blues	
7. Catfish	*Bootleg Series*

29 July 1975

1. Isis	
2. One More Cup Of Coffee	
3. Black Diamond Bay	
4. Joey	
5. Rita Mae	

30 July 1975

1. Isis	*Desire*
2. Rita Mae	3-10454
3. One More Cup Of Coffee	*Desire*
4. Joey	*Desire*
5. Mozambique	*Desire*
6. Hurricane	

7. Golden Loom	*Bootleg Series*
8. Oh Sister	*Desire*
9. Black Diamond Bay	*Desire*

31 July 1975

1. Abandoned Love	*Biograph*
2. Sara	*Desire*

24 October 1975

1. Jimmy Brown The Newsboy	
2. Sitting On Top Of The World	
3. That's Alright Mama	
4. Ride 'Em Jewboy	
5. Hurricane [t1]	
6. Hurricane [t2]	
7. I Still Miss Someone	
8. Hurricane [t3]	
9. Hurricane [t4]	
10. Hurricane [t5]	
11. Hurricane [t6]	*Desire* [edit]
12. Simple Twist Of Fate	
13. Hurricane [t7]	*Desire* [edit]
14. Hurricane [t8]	
15. Hurricane [t9]	
16. Hurricane [t10]	
17. Hurricane [t11]	

24. 'Street-Legal' Sessions, Rundown Studios, Santa Monica.

10–24 April 1978

1. Changing Of The Guards	*Street-Legal*
2. New Pony	*Street-Legal* [edit]
3. No Time To Think	*Street-Legal*
4. Baby, Stop Crying	*Street-Legal*
5. Is Your Love In Vain?	*Street-Legal*
6. Senor (Tales Of Yankee Power)	*Street-Legal*
7. True Love Tends To Forget	*Street-Legal*
8. We'd Better Talk This Over	*Street-Legal*
9. Where Are You Tonight	*Street-Legal*

25. 'Slow Train Coming' Sessions, Muscle Shoals Studios, Sheffield, Alabama.

1–11 May 1979

1. Gotta Serve Somebody	*Slow Train Coming*
2. I Believe In You	*Slow Train Coming*
3. Precious Angel	*Slow Train Coming*
4. Slow Train	*Slow Train Coming*
5. Gonna Change My Way Of Thinking	*Slow Train Coming*
6. Do Right To Me, Baby (Do Unto Others)	*Slow Train Coming*
7. When You Gonna Wake Up	*Slow Train Coming*
8. Man Gave Names To All The Animals	*Slow Train Coming*
9. When He Returns [t1]	
10. When He Returns [t2]	*Slow Train Coming*
11. No Man Righteous (No Not One)	
12. Ye Shall Be Changed	*Bootleg Series*
13. Trouble In Mind	1–11072

26. 'Saved' Sessions, Muscle Shoals Studios, Sheffield, Alabama.

15–19 February 1980

1. Satisfied Mind	*Saved*
2. Saved [t1]	
3. Saved [t2]	*Saved*
4. Covenant Woman [t1]	
5. Covenant Woman [t2]	*Saved*
6. What Can I Do For You?	*Saved*
7. Solid Rock	*Saved*
8. Pressing On	*Saved*
9. In The Garden	*Saved*
10. Saving Grace	*Saved*
11. Are You Ready?	*Saved*

27. Minnesota Home Studio.

23 September 1980

1. Every Grain Of Sand	*Bootleg Series*

28. Rundown Studios, Santa Monica.

October 1980
1. Caribbean Wind
2. The Groom's Still Waiting
3. Let's Keep It Between Us
4. Yonder Comes Sin

29. 'Shot Of Love' Sessions, Clover Studios and Rundown Studios, Los Angeles.

Early to Mid April 1981 (Rundown)
1. Shot Of Love   *Shot of Love*
2. Caribbean Wind   *Biograph*
3. Is It Worth It?
4. High Away
5. Hallelujah
6. It's Magic
7. You're A Child To Me [t1]
8. You're A Child To Me [t2] ★
9. (Wind Blowing) On The Water
10. All The Way Down
11. On Borrowed Time
12. I Want You To Know I Love You
13. On A Rocking Boat
14. Movin'
15. Say That
16. My Oriental Home ★
17. It's Dangerous To Me ★
18. More To This Than Meets The Eye ★
19. Straw Hat ★
20. Gonna Love Her Anyway ★
21. Walking On Eggs ★
22. Well Water ★
23. All The Way ★
24. Almost Persuaded

Late April–12 May 1981 (Clover)
1. Groom's Still Waiting At The Altar   *Shot of Love Mk. 2/*
2. Angelina   *Biograph*
3. Need A Woman [t1]   *Bootleg Series*

4. Need A Woman [t2]	*Bootleg Series*
5. You Changed My Life	*Bootleg Series*
6. Fur Slippers	
7. Don't Ever Take Yourself Away	
8. Mystery Train	
9. Let It Be Me	A-1406
10. Hear Of Mine [t1]	*Shot of Love Mk. 1*
11. Heart Of Mine [t2]	*Shot of Love*
12. Property Of Jesus	*Shot of Love*
13. Lenny Bruce	*Shot of Love*
14. Watered Down Love	*Shot of Love* [edit]
15. Dead Man, Dead Man	*Shot of Love*
16. In The Summertime	*Shot of Love*
17. Trouble	*Shot of Love*
18. Every Grain Of Sand	*Shot of Love*

30. 'Infidels' Sessions, Power Station Studios, New York.

11 April–8 May 1983

1. Lord Protect My Child [t1]	
2. Lord Protect My Child [t2]	
3. Lord Protect My Child [t3]	
4. Lord Protect My Child [t4]	*Bootleg Series*
5. Tell Me [t1]	
6. Tell Me [t2]	*Bootleg Series*
7. Someone's Got A Hold Of My Heart [t1]	
8. Someone's Got A Hold Of My Heart [t2]	*Bootleg Series*
9. Death Is Not The End	*Down in the Groove*
10. Clean Cut Kid	
11. Julius And Ethel	
12. Blind Willie McTell [t1]	
13. Blind Willie McTell [t2]	*Bootleg Series*
14. Foot Of Pride [t1]	
15. Foot Of Pride [t2]	
16. Foot Of Pride [t3]	*Bootleg Series*
17. Angel Flying Too Close To The Ground	A-3916
18. Green, Green Grass Of Home	
19. This Was My Love [t1]	
20. This Was My Love [t2]	
21. Sultans Of Swing	

22. Dark Groove ★
23. Don't Fly Unless It's Safe ★
24. Sweetheart Like You [t1]
25. Sweetheart Like You [t2]
26. Sweetheart Like You [t3]
27. Sweetheart Like You [t4]
28. Sweetheart Like You [t5]
29. Sweetheart Like You [t6]
30. Sweetheart Like You [t7]
31. Sweetheart Like You [t8]
32. Sweetheart Like You [t9]
33. Sweetheart Like You [t10]
34. Sweetheart Like You [t11]   *Infidels* [backing track]
35. Jokerman
36. Don't Fall Apart On Me
    Tonight
37. Union Sundown
38. I And I   *Infidels*
39. Man Of Peace   *Infidels*
40. License To Kill   *Infidels*
41. Neighbourhood Bully   *Infidels*
42. Jokerman   *Infidels* [backing track]
43. Don't Fall Apart On Me
    Tonight   *Infidels* [backing track]

Early June–5 July 1983
1. Union Sundown   *Infidels*
2. Jokerman   *Infidels* [new vocal]
3. Don't Fall Apart On Me
   Tonight   *Infidels* [new vocal]
4. Sweetheart Like You   *Infidels* [new vocal]

31. 'Empire Burlesque' Sessions, Delta, Intergalactic and Power Station Studios, New York. Cherokee and Oceanway Studios, Los Angeles.

July 1984 (Intergalactic)
1. Mountain Of Love
2. Honey Wait

July 1984 (Delta)
1. Wolf ★
2. Groovin' At Delta ★
3. Clean Cut Kid [t1]   *Empire Burlesque*

4. Driftin' Too Far From Shore
[t1]
5. Clean Cut Kid [t2]
6. Driftin' Too Far [t2]   *Knocked Out Loaded*
                                     [backing track]

7. Go 'Way Little Boy
8. Who Loves You More

November 1984 (Oceanway)
1. In The Summertime [t1]
2. In The Summertime [t2]
3. In The Summertime [t3]
4. In The Summertime [t4]
5. Freedom For The Stallion [t1]
6. Freedom For The Stallion [t2]
7. Freedom For The Stallion [t3]
8. Instrumental I ★
9. Instrumental II ★
10. Instrumental III ★
11. Instrumental IV ★
12. Instrumental V ★
13. Instrumental VI ★

November–December 1984 (Cherokee)
1. New Danville Girl   *Knocked Out Loaded*
                                     [backing track]

2. Something's Burning, Baby [t1]
3. Something's Burning, Baby [t2]   *Empire Burlesque*

January 1985 (Cherokee)
1. I'll Remember You   *Empire Burlesque*
2. Emotionally Yours   *Empire Burlesque*
3. Trust Yourself   *Empire Burlesque*
4. Seeing The Real You At Last
[t1]
5. Seeing The Real You At Last
[t2]   *Empire Burlesque*
6. Maybe Someday   *Knocked Out Loaded*
                                     [backing track]

February–March 1985 (Power Station)
1. When The Night Comes Falling
[t1]   *Bootleg Series*
2. When The Night Comes Falling
[t2]   *Empire Burlesque*

3. Never Gonna Be The Same
   Again   *Empire Burlesque*
4. Tight Connection To My Heart   *Empire Burlesque*
5. Waiting To Get Beat
6. The Very Thought Of You
7. Straight A's In Love
8. Dark Eyes   *Empire Burlesque*

32. 'Knocked Out Loaded' Sessions, The Church Studios, London. Festival Recording Studio, Sydney. Skyline Studios, Topanga Canyon and Sound City Studios, Van Nuys.

19–22 November 1985 (London)
1. Instrumental I★
2. Instrumental II★
3. Under Your Spell [backing
   track]   *Knocked Out Loaded*

8–9 February 1986 (Sydney)
1. Band Of The Hand (It's
   Helltime Man)   MCA 52811

April–May 1986 (Topanga)
1. You Wanna Ramble   *Knocked Out Loaded*
2. They Killed Him   *Knocked Out Loaded*
3. Precious Memories   *Knocked Out Loaded*
4. Come Rain Or Come Shine

May 1986 (Van Nuys)
1. Got My Mind Made Up   *Knocked Out Loaded*

May 1986 (Topanga)
1. They Killed Him   *Knocked Out Loaded*
                                     [overdubs]
2. Under Your Spell   *Knocked Out Loaded*
                                     [overdubs]
3. Maybe Someday   *Knocked Out Loaded*
                                     [overdubs]
4. Driftin' Too Far From Shore   *Knocked Out Loaded*
                                     [overdubs]
5. Brownsville Girl   *Knocked Out Loaded*
                                     [overdubs]

33. 'Hearts of Fire' Sessions, Townhouse Studio, London.

27–28 August 1986

1. The Usual [t1]		
2. The Usual [t2]		
3. The Usual [t3]		
4. The Usual [t4]		*Hearts of Fire*
5. Ride This Train		
6. Had A Dream About You Baby [t1]		
7. Had A Dream About You Baby [t2]		
8. Had A Dream About You Baby [t3]		
9. Had A Dream About You Baby [t4]		
10. Had A Dream About You Baby [t5]		
11. Five And Dimer [t1]		
12. Five And Dimer [t2]		
13. Five And Dimer [t3]		
14. Had A Dream About You Baby [t6]		
15. Had A Dream About You Baby [t7]		
16. To Fall In Love With You		
17. Had A Dream About You Baby [t8]		
18. Had A Dream About You Baby [t9]		*Hearts of Fire*
19. Night After Night		*Hearts of Fire*
20. A Couple More Years		

34. 'Down In The Groove' Sessions, Sunset Sound Studios, Hollywood.

April–May 1987

1. Pretty Boy Floyd	*A Vision Shared*
2. Let's Stick Together	*Down In The Groove*
3. When Did You Leave Heaven?	*Down In The Groove*
4. Sally Sue Brown	*Down In The Groove*
5. Ugliest Girl In The World	*Down In The Groove*
6. Silvio	*Down In The Groove*
7. Ninety Miles An Hour	*Down In The Groove*

8. Shenandoah	*Down In The Groove*
9. Rank Strangers To Me	*Down In The Groove*
10. I Got Love If You Want It	*Down In The Groove Mk. 1*
11. Important Words	

35. 'Traveling Wilburys' Sessions, Garage Studio, Malibu.

Early April 1988

1. Handle With Care	*Volume One*

7–16 May 1988

1. Dirty World [t1]	
2. Dirty World [t2]	*Volume One*
3. Rattled	*Volume One*
4. Last Night	*Volume One*
5. Not Alone Anymore	*Volume One*
6. Congratulations	*Volume One*
7. Heading For The Light	*Volume One*
8. Margarita	*Volume One*
9. Tweeter & The Monkey Man [t1]	
10. Tweeter & The Monkey Man [t2]	*Volume One*
11. End Of The Line	*Volume One*

36. 'Oh Mercy' Sessions, Studio On The Move, New Orleans.

March–April 1989

1. Series Of Dreams [t1]	
2. Series Of Dreams [t2]	*Bootleg Series* [edit]
3. Series Of Dreams [t3]	*Bootleg Series* [edit]
4. Political World [t1]	
5. Political World [t2]	*Oh Mercy*
6. Where Teardrops Fall	*Oh Mercy*
7. Broken	
8. Everything Is Broken	*Oh Mercy*
9. Ring Them Bells	*Oh Mercy*
10. Man In The Long Black Coat	*Oh Mercy*
11. Most Of The Time [t1]	
12. Most Of The Time [t2]	*Oh Mercy*
13. What Good Am I? [t1]	*Oh Mercy*
14. What Good Am I? [t2]	
15. Disease Of Conceit [t1]	
16. Disease Of Conceit [t2]	*Oh Mercy*

17. What Was It You Wanted? [t1]
18. What Was It You Wanted? [t2]   *Oh Mercy*
19. Shooting Star [t1]
20. Shooting Star [t2]   *Oh Mercy*
21. Dignity
22. Born In Time
23. God Knows

37. Bellmont Mall Studio, Indiana.

20 November 1989
  1. People Get Ready   *Flashback – The Soundtrack*

38. 'Under The Red Sky' Sessions, Culver City, Oceanway, Record Plant and The Complex Studios, L.A. Sorcerer Sound, New York.

6 January 1990
  1. 10,000 Men   *Under The Red Sky*
  2. God Knows   *Under The Red Sky*
  3. Handy Dandy   *Under The Red Sky*
  4. Cat's In The Well   *Under The Red Sky*

March 1990
  1. Most Of The Time [t1]
  2. Most Of The Time [t2]
  3. Most Of The Time [t3]
  4. Most Of The Time [t4]
  5. Most Of The Time [t5]
  6. Most Of The Time [t6]
  7. Most Of The Time [t7]   CSK 73326
  8. TV Talkin' Song [t1]
  9. TV Talkin' Song [t2]
  10. TV Talkin' Song [t3]   *Under The Red Sky*
  11. Two By Two [t1]
  12. Two By Two [t2]
  13. Two By Two [t3]   *Under The Red Sky*
  14. Under The Red Sky   *Under The Red Sky*
  15. Wiggle Wiggle   *Under The Red Sky*
  16. Born In Time   *Under The Red Sky*
  17. Unbelievable   *Under The Red Sky*
  18. Shirley Temple Don't Live Here Anymore
  19. Some Enchanted Evening

39. 'Traveling Wilburys Vol. 3' Sessions, Mobile Studio, Los Angeles.

April 1990

1. Like A Ship	
2. Wilbury Twist	*Volume Three*
3. Seven Deadly Sins	*Volume Three*
4. New Blue Moon [t1]	*Volume Three*
5. Cool Dry Place	*Volume Three*
6. Runaway	W9523
7. Maxine	
8. Inside Out	*Volume Three* [edit]
9. Where Were You Last Night?	*Volume Three* [edit]
10. You Took My Breath Away	*Volume Three*
11. If You Belonged To Me	*Volume Three* [edit]
12. Poor House	*Volume Three*
13. She's My Baby	*Volume Three* [edit]
14. Devil's Been Busy	*Volume Three* [edit]
15. Nobody's Child	W9501
16. New Blue Moon [t2]★	

Index

Aaronson, Kenny, 442–3, 446–7, 448, 449–50, 457, 461
ABC, 164, 173, 174, 176, 180
Abrams, Harvey, 17, 19, 22, 28, 31
Alk, Howard, 134, 137, 165, 166, 174, 178–9, 276, 294, 295, 297, 301
Allen, Colin, 383–4, 386–7
Altman, Robert, 271
Alvin, Dave, 416
American Atheists Association, 354
American Society of Composers, Authors and Publishers (ASCAP), 422
Amnesty International, 411
Amram, David, 202, 215–16
Animals, The, 92, 128
Another Side of Bob Dylan, 98–9, 100, 110, 120, 246
Apollinaire, Guillaume, 76
Apple Records, 216
Aranga, Ra, 318
Arista label, 259
Arno, Eddie, 397–9
Arnold, Eddy, 448
Arnold, Jerome, 136–7

Aronoff, Kenny, 436, 437
Aronowitz, Al, 91, 103, 113, 148, 180
Artes, Mary Alice, 328, 330, 349, 361, 433
Asch, Moe, 44
Astrodome, Houston, 285
Asylum label, 234–5, 242–3
Atlantic Records, 221, 231
Aufray, Hugues, 96
Auger, Brian, 183
Augustine, St, 186

Baboo, Russ, 344
Baez, Joan, 40, 45, 76, 92, 99, 101, 102, 123, 292, 363, 368; relationship with Dylan, 71–3, 83, 89, 93, 97, 103, 106–7, 114–15, 151; In Concert, 85; at Newport Folk Festival, 100; tours with Dylan, 106, 108–14; And a Voice to Sing With, 121, 277; Rolling Thunder Revue, 271, 275, 281, 294, 448; in Renaldo and Clara, 277–9, 303, 306
Baez, Mimi (Mimi Farina), 101

Baker, Arthur, 395–6, 428
Baker, Ellen, 18–19, 23, 28
Band, The, 187, 192, 218; Guthrie Memorial Concert, 189; Music from Big Pink, 193, 253–4; The Band, 197; Isle of Wight Festival, 199; Cahoots, 212, 234, 253; settles in California, 233–4; 1974 tour, 235–41; The Basement Tapes, 253–4; farewell concert, 294; see also Hawks, The
Bangladesh, Concerts for, 217–18
Bangs, Lester, 262
Basement Tapes, The, 180–83, 186, 188, 198, 204, 216, 235, 253–4, 257, 342
Bastille, The St Paul, 28
Baudelaire, Charles, 76
Bauldie, John, 463
BBC, 59–60, 95, 116–17, 127, 405, 414–15, 449, 453
Beach Boys, The, 422, 446
Beacon Theater, 451–2, 454, 456
Bear, Chicago, 70
Beatles, The, 92, 95, 97, 109–10, 113, 128, 156,

Beatles, The – *contd*
158, 163, 184, 186,
188, 198, 200, 422
Beats, 87, 88, 278
Beckett, Barry, 338, 341
Beecher, Bonnie
(married name: Jahara
Romney), 12, 16, 17–
18, 19, 22, 27, 29–30,
31, 47–8, 196
Before the Flood, 240, 243
Behan, Dominic, 62
Bengali Bauls, 184–5
Berkeley Community
Theater, San
Francisco, 93
Bernstein, Ellen, 247, 251
Bernstein, Joel, 210, 247,
287, 310, 311–12, 313
Berry, Chuck, 10, 133,
444
Bible, The, 76–7, 185,
329–30, 333, 334, 353–
4, 358, 369
Bicknell, Ed, 339
Big Sky, 192
Bikel, Theodore, 138,
139, 141
Billboard, 69, 73, 78, 149,
193, 321, 404
Biograph, 91, 158, 360,
404, 416, 460
Blackamar, Bob, 103
Blake, Norman, 195
Blakely, Ronee, 271–2,
302–3, 306
Block, Bert, 199
Blonde on Blonde, 136,
143, 156, 157–9, 173,
183, 186, 237, 252,
253, 337, 342, 438
Blondie, 257
Blood on the Tracks, 227,
242, 244–53, 255, 256,
257, 260, 261, 269,
284, 288, 304, 307,
319, 335, 342, 372,
376, 440, 443, 445
Bloomfield, Michael, 70,
129–31, 132, 134, 135–
7, 140, 141, 142–3,
144, 149, 151, 157,
248–9, 250, 363

Blue, David, 149, 150,
271, 276, 308
Blue Rock Studios, New
York, 211, 214
Bob Dylan, 47–8
Bob Dylan at Budokan,
316
Bob Dylan's Blues, 55–6
Bogart, Humphrey, 395
Bono, 417–18, 428, 448
Born in Time, 438
Bottom Line, The, New
York, 257, 259
Bowie, David, 253, 320,
368, 373, 422
Boyd, Joe, 133–4, 135,
136, 137–8, 140–41
Brand, Oscar, 44
Brando, Marlon, 10, 120
Brandstein, Eve, 213
Braun, David, 231, 462
Brecht, Bertolt, 76
Brickman, Marshall, 32
*Bringing It All Back
Home*, 105–6, 110, 115,
123, 127, 128, 129,
131–2, 133, 140, 142,
143, 146, 150, 267,
372
Broadside, 52, 54, 66–7,
86–7, 100–101, 168
Bromberg, Dave, 208,
219
Brooks, Harvey, 131,
142, 144, 153, 207,
210
Broonzy, Big Bill, 38
Brown, Charlie, 250
Brown, Hugh, 22, 28
Brown, Rita Mae, 290
Brown, Tony, 250
Bruce, Lenny, 364
Bruton, Steve, 457
Bucklen, John, 12
Burbank Studios,
Burbank, 228–9
Burdon, Eric, 92
Burgh, Steve, 219
Burke, Rex, 300
Burn, Malcolm, 430, 431
Burnett, T-Bone, 271,
329, 409
Burns, Marvin, 296

Burroughs, William, 123
Butler, Wayne, 159
Butterfield, Paul, 130,
134–7, 143
Buttrey, Kenneth, 157,
187, 195, 266, 373
Byrdcliffe, 193, 194
Byrds, The, 127, 128,
183, 207–8, 216–17

Cable, Paul, 45
Café Lena, Saratoga
Springs, 40
Café Wha, New York,
33, 34–5
Cage, Budd, 251
Cahn, Rolf, 29
Campbell, Joseph, 334
Campbell, Mike, 402,
406, 423–4
Canadian Broadcasting
Corporation, 87
Capital Radio, London,
341
Carné, Marcel, 277
Carnegie Hall, New
York, 57, 73, 77–8, 80,
100, 154, 188
Carnegie Recital Hall,
New York, 44–5, 69
Carroll, Gordon, 225,
229
Carroll, Hattie, 263
Carruthers, Ben, 96
Carter, Rubin
'Hurricane', 263–4,
275, 282, 285
Carthy, Martin, 60–61,
62–3, 64
Cartwright, Bert, 185,
369, 370
Cash, Johnny, 196, 198,
207
Catouse, Nadia, 116
Cavalier, 103
CBGBs, New York,
257
CBS, 49, 59, 68–9, 91,
127, 201, 204, 207,
215, 216, 303, 356,
365, 408; contract with
Dylan, 30, 36, 37, 40,
46–7; *Freewheelin'*, 55–

6, 67; sales convention, 73; Dylan's rise to fame, 95, 97; *Bringing It All Back Home*, 106; *Highway 61 Revisited*, 130; and *Eat the Document*, 166; and Dylan's motorcycle accident, 176; *John Wesley Harding*, 187–8; Grossman leaves Dylan, 191; Mexico City studios, 226; tries to negotiate new contract with Dylan, 231–2; Dylan leaves, 234–5; Dylan returns to, 247–8; *Blood on the Tracks*, 251; 'Hurricane' controversy, 271–2; videos, 379; release *Oh Mercy*, 451, 462

CBS-Sony, 313
Cézanne, Paul, 304
Chandler, Len, 53
Chaplin, Charlie, 230
Charles, Ray, 339, 355, 408
Charlesworth, Chris, 132
Cheetah, 180
Cherokee Studios, Los Angeles, 393, 394
Childs, Carole, 391, 458, 459
City Lights, 119
Clancy, Liam, 42, 43, 45, 62, 138
Clapton, Eric, 116, 143, 217, 264–5, 285–6
Clark, Alan, 373–4, 375
Clash, The, 368
Clayton, Paul, 89, 287
Cleave, Maureen, 95–6, 110
Cliff, Jimmy, 449
Cline, Patsy, 446
Clove Studios, Los Angeles, 364
Club 47, Cambridge, 37, 40, 72
Coburn, James, 223, 225
Cocker, Joe, 219

Cohen, John, 179, 190–91, 276
Cohen, Leonard, 430, 444
Cohen, Scott, 297
Cohn, Nik, 283
Coleman, Ray, 110
Collins, Judy, 25, 188
Collins, Mel, 265
Columbia *see* CBS
Congress of Racial Equality (CORE), 51
Conley, Walt, 24, 25, 26
Connors, Tony, 8
Cooder, Ry, 338, 406
Cooke, John, 94
Cornelius, Ron, 208, 209
Costello, Elvis, 337, 368
Cott, Jonathan, 252, 306, 308
Count Five, 422
Court, John, 58, 68
Crackers, The, 189
Crane, Les, 5, 103
Crawford, Don, 26
Creem magazine, 262
Crenshaw, Marshall, 442
Crosby, Bing, 416
Cross, Billy, 312, 316
Crowe, Cameron, 354, 404, 416
Cunningham, Sis, 52, 66, 67, 121

Daily News, 176
Daily Sketch, 123
Daily Telegraph, 138, 168, 462–3
Dali, Salvador, 304
Dandy, Jim, 12
Daniels, Charlie, 207, 208
Danko, Rick, 182–3, 243, 255, 377, 383
Das, Lakhsman, 185
Das, Purna, 185
Davenport, Bob, 61–2, 64
Davies, Paul, 37
Davis, Clive, 187, 191, 197–8, 205, 231–2, 268
Davis, Reverend Gary, 48

Davis, Walter Jnr, 309
Dawson, Gordon, 225
Dean, James, 6–7
Dean, Tami, 121–2
Delta Studios, New York, 389, 390
Dennis, Carolyn, 318, 338, 340, 365
Denver, Nigel, 62–3, 64
Desire, 262, 263–9, 271–2, 281, 284, 287, 298, 319, 337, 440, 454
Devil and Daniel Webster, The, 208
Devito, Don, 264–6, 268, 269, 272
Diamond, Neil, 311
Dire Straits, 337, 355, 365, 373, 375, 407
Disc and Music Echo, 111
Dixon, Willie, 317
Domino, Fats, 10
Donovan, 111, 112
Don't Look Back, 108–16, 174, 177–8, 180, 230, 414–15
Doors, The, 186
Dorfsman, Neil, 373
Dorsey, Thomas A., 448
Douglas, Steve, 312–13, 316, 318, 364, 409, 410
Down in the Groove, 418–19, 423, 424, 438, 441
Drake, Peter, 188, 195
Driscoll, Julie, 183
Drummond, Tim, 248, 338, 339, 348, 373, 383
Dunbar, Sly, 373
Dunn, Donald 'Duck', 365
Dwarf Music, 192, 254
Dwyer, Bill, 330
Dylan, 248
Dylan, Anna (Dylan's daughter), 188, 300
Dylan, Bob: early life, 3–13; names, 9–10, 16, 58; in Minneapolis, 16–23, 26–31; early recordings, 24, 27–8,

Dylan, Bob – *contd*
30, 37, 39, 40, 47–9;
harmonica playing, 26,
28–9, 35–6; first visit
to New York, 30–32,
33–47; CBS contract,
36, 37, 46–7;
monologues, 39, 41;
song-writing, 40–42,
50–57, 66–8, 80, 87–8;
relationship with Suze
Rotolo, 42, 43, 51–2,
69–70, 72–3, 83, 93–5,
96–7, 98; first visit to
England, 59–65;
relationship with Joan
Baez, 71–3, 83, 89, 93,
97, 103, 106–7, 114–
15, 151; as civil rights
activist, 74–7; poetry,
81–5, 120–24; planned
biography, 82–3; play-
writing, 87, 120; On
the Road Revisited
trek, 88, 89–94; meets
Sara, 101, 133; English
tour, 108–17; decides
to quit, 127–8; at
Newport Folk
Festival, 133–41, 144;
1965–6 tour, 144–7,
153–5; games, 147–50;
marriage, 151–2, 159;
children, 152, 176–7,
188, 200, 202, 218;
drug-taking, 152–3,
167–8; 1966 world
tour, 159, 160–69, 173;
motorcycle accident,
174–7, 193; religious
beliefs, 185–6;
personality change
after the accident,
189–91; paintings,
192–3; 'lost years',
193–4, 218–21, 368;
Isle of Wight Festival,
199–201; returns to
New York, 202, 203;
Weberman's campaign
against, 203, 210, 213–
14; honorary doctorate
from Princeton, 208;

in Israel, 210, 212–13;
Concerts for
Bangladesh, 217–18; in
*Pat Garrett & Billy the
Kid*, 222–31; moves to
California, 232, 233–4;
1974 tour, 234–41,
242; leaves CBS, 234–
5; Norman Raeben's
influence, 243–4;
separation from Sara,
244, 246, 254–5;
returns to CBS, 247–
8; in France, 254, 255–
6; Rolling Thunder
Revue, 259, 270–73,
274–83, 284–5, 286–94,
295; divorce, 295–7,
301, 328; *Renaldo and
Clara*, 277–80, 295,
301–9, 314–15; seeks
custody of children,
295, 296, 298–301,
310, 329; and Farida
McFree, 296–300;
Japanese tour, 311–13,
314, 316–18; financial
problems, 317; and
Helena Springs, 317–
18, 348–9; 1978
European tour, 320–
21; conversion to
Christianity, 327–36,
339–43, 434, 435;
1979–80 gospel tour,
342–4, 346–55, 357–8,
359; evangelizing,
346–58, 359–60; sails
in Caribbean, 360; late
1980 tour, 361–4; and
Clydie King, 365;
1981 tours, 366–8;
return to Judaism,
368–70; videos, 378–
80, 397–9, 437, 440,
462; 1984 tour, 383–8;
Farm Aid, 401, 402–3,
405; Far East tour,
405–7; writer's block,
409–10, 414; 1986 US
tour, 411; *Hearts of
Fire*, 412–15; Grateful
Dead tour, 419–21;

awards and honours,
422–3, 427; 1987
European tour, 423–4;
and the Traveling
Wilburys, 425–7;
millennialism, 433–4,
435; lovesongs, 434–5;
1988 tour, 442–5;
Never-Ending Tour,
444–54, 456–7;
relationships with
women, 458–9; desire
for privacy, 459–63;
*see also individual
albums and books*

Dylan, Jacob (Dylan's
son), 200, 218

Dylan, Jesse (Dylan's
son), 1976, 199, 300,
368, 437

Dylan, Sara (Dylan's
wife), 115, 130, 268–9,
459, 464; meets Dylan,
101; and *Don't Look
Back*, 108–9; relation-
ship with Dylan, 133;
marriage, 151–2, 159;
children, 152, 173, 176,
188, 200; in Durango,
226; and 'Wedding
Song', 236–7; dislike
of tours, 241; separation
from Dylan, 244, 246,
254–5; and the Rolling
Thunder Revue, 277,
279–80, 284, 292–3;
divorce, 295–7, 301,
328; dispute over
custody of children,
295, 296, 298–301; in
Renaldo and Clara, 301,
303, 306

Dylan and the Dead, 420–
21

Dylan Liberation Front,
210

Eagles, The, 377
Earle, Steve, 449
East Village Other, 203,
213
Eat the Document, 164, 165,
174, 178, 179, 276, 415

Edwardson, Monte, 8
Electric Prunes, 422
Elektra label, 135
Eleven Outlined Epitaphs,
    84, 120
Elliman, Yvonne, 264
Elliott, Jack, 34, 258,
    259, 260, 271
Elliott, Marc, 192n.
Ellis, Terry, 111
Elwood, Philip, 347
Emergency Civil Liberties
    Committee (ECLC),
    80, 84, 86, 121
Emory University,
    Atlanta, 89
Empire Burlesque, 375,
    393–9, 402, 404, 410,
    412, 422, 423, 433
Epstein, Howie, 402
Esmond, Paul, 330, 369
Esquire, 175
Evening Standard, 95–6
Everett, Rupert, 413
Everly Brothers, 206
Evers, Medgar, 74, 75,
    263

Fabbro, Larry, 8
Faier, Billy, 70
Faithfull, Marianne, 114
Farina, Richard, 37, 40,
    63, 93, 101, 141, 287
Farm Aid, 401, 402–3,
    405, 406, 411, 416
Fass, Bob, 156
Fassbinder, Rainer
    Werner, 379
Feinstein, Barry, 119–20
Ferlinghetti, Lawrence,
    119
Fielding, Jerry, 227–8
Fig, Anton, 390
Fincher, Cynthia, 20, 28,
    29
Fire Island, New York,
    202
First Blues, 216
Fitzgerald, Ella, 417
Flanagan, Fiona, 413
Flint, Hughie, 116
Folklore Center, New
    York, 34, 51, 52

Folkways Records, 44
Ford, John, 304
Ford, Robben, 437
Forest Hills Stadium,
    New York, 145–7
Forman, Jim, 84
Foulk, Ray, 199
Fraboni, Rob, 235–6,
    237, 242
France-Soir, 166, 167
Franklin, Aretha, 339
Freewheelin', 56, 61, 67–
    8, 71, 73, 78, 95, 104,
    109–10, 115
Friedman, Steve, 11
Friends of Chile, 243,
    270
Froom, Mitchell, 428
Fuller, Jesse, 25–6, 36
Fulson, Lowell, 323

Gable, Clark, 407
Gabriel, Peter, 428
Gallo, Joey, 261–2
Garcia, Jerry, 363, 419,
    420–21
Garfield, Dave, 410
Garfunkel, Art, 204
Gargoyle, 87
Garnier, Tony, 448, 449,
    454
Gary, Bruce, 367
Gaye, Marvin, 422
Geffen, David, 234–5,
    238, 242, 247
Geffen Records, 391
Gerde's Folk City, New
    York, 36, 38, 40, 45,
    47, 53, 67, 71, 257, 274
Gerrette, Rosemary,
    161–2
Gershwin, George, 417
Getting to Dylan
    (Omnibus
    documentary), 414–15
Gibbons, Billy, 373
Gibson, Don, 449
Gilded Garter, Denver,
    24–5
Gillespie, Dana, 113,
    114–15
Gilmore, Mikal, 399,
    409, 410, 416

Ginsberg, Allen, 87, 112,
    113, 144, 157, 175,
    186, 215–16, 273, 278–
    9, 303–5, 307, 308,
    435
Gleason, Bob, 34
Gleason, Ralph J., 93,
    103, 209–10
Gleason, Sid, 34
Glenn, Glen, 448
Glover, Dave 'Tony', 20,
    22, 23, 28, 47, 48, 74,
    75, 85, 121, 143
Goddard, Donald, 262
Goddard, J. R., 34, 103,
    148
Gold Star Studios, Los
    Angeles, 368
Goldberg, Barry, 136–7,
    233, 310, 338
Goldberg, Michael, 347
Goldberg, Steven, 242
Golden Chords, 8–9
Goldfine, Linda, 269
Goldwyn Studios,
    Hollywood, Los
    Angeles, 309
Gooding, Cynthia, 29,
    70
Goodman, Steve, 219,
    221
Gottlieb, Bob, 220
Gottlieb, Stanley, 30
Gould, Ron, 63
Graham, Bill, 210, 235,
    238, 362, 382, 383,
    400–401, 402
Grammy awards, 356,
    357
Grandmaster Flash, 422
Grateful Dead, 219, 417,
    419–21, 460
Gravenites, Nick, 136
Graves, Robert, 76, 279,
    306
Gray, Michael, 252
Green, Al, 389–90
Green, Willie, 430
Greenbriar Boys, 38
Greenhill, Manny, 40,
    71, 106
Gregg, Bobby, 104, 131,
    144, 154

Griffin, Paul, 131, 251
Grossman, Albert, 45, 94, 113, 119, 168; influence on Dylan, 58–60, 66, 68, 70, 73, 106; house in Woodstock, 101; and *Don't Look Back*, 109, 111; Newport Folk Festival, 134–6, 139; and Edie Sedgwick, 150; 1966 world tour, 164; and the Bengali Bauls, 184; negotiations with MGM, 187; Dylan leaves, 191–2
Grossman, Sally, 101, 151
Gulliksen, Ken, 330, 332, 335–6, 341, 343, 361
Gunn, Elston (Bob Dylan), 9, 13, 16
Gunning, Sarah Ogan, 38
Guthrie, Arlo, 188, 243
Guthrie, Woody, 6, 20, 26–8, 31, 34, 38–9, 40–41, 48, 52, 53, 80, 81, 82, 84, 167, 188–9, 196, 304, 392, 423
Guthrie Memorial Concert, 188–9, 199

Haben, George, 9
Hall, Tony, 430
Halloween '64 show, New York, 122
Hammill, Peter, 255
Hammond, John, 37, 40, 45–7, 48, 50, 56, 58, 68, 249, 261, 270, 344
Hammond, John Junior, 46, 104, 145
Hard Rain, 291–4, 309
Harding, John Wesley, 186
Harris, Emmylou, 264, 266–8, 271
Harrison, George, 190, 193, 207, 217–18, 226, 424–7, 436, 461
Hart, Mickey, 421

Havens, Ritchie, 200
Hawkins, Ronnie, 145, 302–3, 305
Hawks, The, 127, 145, 153–4, 155–6, 162–3, 166, 180, 187, 289; *see also* Band, The
Head, Roy, 382
Heartbreakers, 257, 400, 402–3, 405–8, 409–10, 411, 412, 419, 423–4, 441, 445, 450
Hearts of Fire, 412–15, 418
Heffington, Don, 393
Hell, Richard, & the Voidoids, 257
Hellicar, Michael, 123
Helm, Levon, 145, 153–5, 180, 187, 201, 235, 243, 254, 255, 377, 383
Helstrom, Echo, 3, 9, 10, 11, 12, 16
Henshaw, Laurie, 111
Hentoff, Nat, 54, 71, 81, 97, 103, 125, 128, 148–9, 152, 277
Herman, Dave, 463
Hester, Carolyn, 37, 40, 42, 46–7
Hiatt, John, 406, 414, 418
Hibbing, Minnesota, 3–13, 38, 84
Hickey, Neil, 185
Highway 61 Revisited, 124, 125, 130–33, 142–3, 155, 156, 157, 158, 181, 201, 337, 452
Hilburn, Robert, 378, 455
Hill, Joe, 38
Hitchcock, Alfred, 304
Hoffenburg, Mason, 96
Hoffman, Gretel, 16, 20, 22, 23
Hoikkala, Leroy, 8, 9
Holly, Buddy, 446
Hollywood Bowl, Los Angeles, 147, 153
Holscomb, Roscoe, 38
Holzman, Jac, 44

Hooker, John Lee, 36
Hopkins, Nicky, 384
Horn, Jim, 343–4
Hornsby, Bruce, 436, 437
Hotel Americana, San Juan, 73–4
House, Son, 13
Houston, Cisco, 440–41
Houston, John, 304
Howard, Mel, 276, 278–9
Hubbard, Neil, 264
Hudson, Garth, 145, 157, 181, 182, 187, 240
Hughes, Howard, 460
Hughes, Karen, 358
Hunter, Ian, 271
Hunter, Robert, 417, 418

Iachetta, Michael, 177
Ian and Sylvia, 420
Infidels, 365, 369–70, 373–9, 381, 382, 383, 385, 390, 393, 394, 410, 416, 418, 431–2, 433, 440, 454
Ingber, Ira, 392, 393, 408–9
Inglewood Forum, Los Angeles, 240, 411
Inkspots, 416–17
Innocenti, Markus, 397–9
Intergalactic Studios, New York, 389–90
Iovine, Jimmy, 391
Isle of Wight Festival, 199–201, 204, 205

Jackson, George, 214–15, 219, 263
Jackson, Michael, 407
Jackson, Randy, 437
Jagger, Mick, 173n., 219, 460
James, Etta, 338
Jefferson Airplanc, 186
Jesting, Justin, 382
Jewish Defense League, 212
Joel, Billy, 422, 447

John, Elton, 436
John Birch Society, 52, 70–71
John the Divine, St, 334
John Wesley Harding, 74, 182, 183, 185–8, 189, 193, 195, 196, 197, 198, 237, 249, 252, 298, 337, 340
Johnson, Robert, 6, 37, 48–9, 55, 317, 446
Johnston, Bob, 132, 142, 156, 157, 202, 207, 208
Jones, Brian, 113, 173n.
Jones, Max, 87, 95, 120, 133
Jones, Mickey, 155, 166, 310, 383
Jones, Robert L., 37
Joseph, Anthea, 60, 62–4, 95–6, 111, 112–13, 162, 165, 167–8
Joseph, Miles, 457
Judson, Horace, 111, 415

Kael, Pauline, 314–15
Kahane, Rabbi Meier, 212
Kalb, Danny, 32
Kapralik, David, 68
Karman, Pete, 89, 91, 93n.
Kastel, Rabbi Kasriel, 369
Kaufman, Robert, 299
Keegan, Larry, 16
Keller, Martin, 370
Kelly, Dave, 343–4, 351, 356
Keltner, Jim, 229, 348, 367, 373, 383
Kemp, Louis, 10, 271
Kennedy, John F., 80, 83–4, 86, 153
Kerouac, Jack, 26, 303
Kibbutz Givat Haim, 213
King, Clydie, 349, 362, 365, 368, 391, 433, 458, 459
Kingston Trio, 20, 21, 34, 38, 39

Kirkland, Sally, 285, 458–9
Klein, Allen, 187
KMGX, 354
Knight, Sonny, 448
Knocked Out Loaded, 390, 393, 405, 408–11, 416, 418, 423, 437
Knopfler, Mark, 337, 338, 339, 340, 365, 371, 372–6, 407
Koerner, 'Spider' John, 20, 21, 22, 31, 75
Kokomo, 264–6
Konikoff, Sandy, 155
Kooper, Al, 130–31, 132, 134, 135, 136, 139–40, 142–3, 144, 145–6, 153, 157, 158, 207–10, 310, 367–8, 409, 437–8
Kornfeld, Barry, 94
Kornfeld, Dave, 81
Kortchmar, Danny, 364
Kramer, Daniel, 104, 105, 123, 148, 151
Kretchmer, Arthur, 39
Kristofferson, Kris, 223, 224, 226–7, 229, 230, 453
Krown, Kevin, 25, 32

Landau, Jon, 230–31
Landy, Elliott, 190, 192–3, 194
Lang, Don, 453
Langhorne, Bruce, 104, 105–6, 129, 144, 229
Lanois, Daniel, 428–31, 436
Lay, Sam, 136, 139
Leacock-Pennebaker Inc., 109
Leadbelly, 13, 21, 44, 361, 364, 423
Lee, David, 16
Lee, Peggy, 416
Lee, William E., 106
Leeds Music, 50, 55, 58
Lennon, John, 113, 118, 216, 253
Lenya, Lotte, 76
Let It Rock, 252

Letterman, David, 381, 383
Leventhal, Harold, 188, 212
Levy, Jacques, 260–61, 262–4, 265, 274, 418
Lewis, Ernest, 317
Lewis, Jerry Lee, 446
Lieberson, Goddard, 231
Life magazine, 4
Lightfoot, Gordon, 187, 206, 219, 448
Lindley, David, 344, 436, 437
Lindsey, Hal, 333–4, 335, 352, 353
Little Richard, 8, 10, 12, 20
Little Sandy Review, 75
Little Walter, 35
Little Willie John, 363
Live Aid, 400–401, 402, 403
Lloyd, Bert, 64
Los Lobos, 409
Lois, George, 379–80
Lomax, Alan, 22, 34, 43, 134–5, 138–9, 140, 364
Lone Justice, 391, 393
Lorimar Pictures, 415
Los Angeles Free Press, 104
Los Angeles Herald-Examiner, 399, 403
Los Angeles Times, 295–6, 310, 378, 403, 455
Lowndes, Sara *see* Dylan, Sara
Lowry, Ray, 174–5
Lubavitchers, 369, 377, 412
Lynch, Stan, 406
Lynne, Jeff, 424–7
Lyrics, 220, 404

McCartney, Paul, 253, 311, 432, 456, 460
MacColl, Ewan, 64–5, 153
McCoy, Charlie, 142, 156–7, 159, 187, 195, 205, 373
McCreary, Regina, 358

McFree, Farida, 296–300, 314, 328

McGhee, Brownie, 55

McGuinn, Roger, 216–17, 229, 233, 260, 261, 271, 363

McKee, Maria, 391, 428

MacKenzie, Eve, 52

McLagen, Ian, 384, 386

McLean, Jim, 62

MacLeish, Archibald, 208

Macmillan, 118–21, 173, 176, 179

Madness on Castle Street, 59, 453

Maimudes, Victor, 40, 89, 94, 102, 161, 461–2

Malka, 295

Manfred Mann, 183, 204

Mansfield, David, 271, 279, 280, 310, 313, 329

Manuel, Richard, 165, 182

Marcus, Greil, 206, 230, 320, 363

Margolis & Moss manuscripts, 82–3, 84, 87, 90

Marinac, Bill, 7, 8, 12, 29

Marisco, Tony, 382, 384

Markel, Bob, 118–19, 120–21, 173–4, 189–90

Marquand, Richard, 230, 412–13, 414

Mason, Dave, 264, 265, 363

Mayall, John, 116, 143, 373

Mayfield, Curtis, 182

Melamed, Vince, 393

Melanga, Gerard, 151

Melody Maker, 95, 110, 113, 120, 132, 320

MGM, 132, 187, 224–5, 229–30, 302

Midler, Bette, 221

Midnight Cowboy, 193

Minneapolis Tapes, 20, 28, 39, 47–9

Minnesota, University of, 13, 16–23

Mississippi River Festival, Edwardsville, Il., 199

Mitchell, Guy, 205

Mitchell, Joni, 285

Mitchelson, Marvin, 296, 299–300

Modigliani, Amedeo, 304

Monterey Folk Festival, 71, 93

Moore, Davey, 69

Morrisey, Paul, 150–51

Morrison, Jim, 232

Morrison, Van, 192, 320, 342, 417, 448, 449

Morton, Dave, 31

Mothers of Invention, 132

MTV, 372, 379, 399, 403

Muhoberac, Jaimie, 436

Muldaur, Maria, 141, 270, 363

Mundi, Billy, 207

Muscle Shoals studios, Memphis, 338, 340, 355, 364

Myers, Larry, 330, 335–6, 343

Nara, Chuck, 8

Nashville Skyline, 188, 192, 195–8, 201, 203, 204, 205, 207, 209, 253

National Association for the Advancement of Colored People (NAACP), 74

National Guardian, 77

NBC, 284, 289, 291–2, 294

Neely, Mary, 331–2

Neil, Fred, 35

Nelson, Paul, 75

Nelson, Ricky, 405–6

Nelson, Willie, 290, 401, 402

Neuwirth, Bobby, 37, 102, 106, 108–9, 111, 113–14, 116, 134, 139, 150, 164, 174, 177–8, 259, 262, 271, 276, 441

Never-Ending Tour, 436, 444–54, 456–7

Neville Brothers, 428, 430

'New Dylans', 219

New Morning, 206–10, 220, 237, 242, 248, 253, 322, 417

New Musical Express, 341, 367

New York Academy of Music, 218

New York Dolls, 382

New York Herald Tribune, 148

New York Post, 110

New York Times, 36, 37–8, 45–6, 69, 71, 146, 310

New York Town Hall, 68–9, 81

New Yorker, 97, 314

Newport Folk Festival, 71, 85, 100, 126, 133–42, 144

Newsweek, 77, 80, 83, 84, 96, 196

Nicks, Stevie, 407

Nico, 96, 151

Nietzsche, Friedrich Wilhelm, 124, 353

Night of the Hurricane I, 282–3

Night of the Hurricane II, 284–5

Nissenson, Jack, 39

Nixon, Richard, 239, 407

NRBQ, 436, 438

Ochs, Phil, 67, 149–50, 168–9, 243, 270, 286–7, 298

Odetta, 20–21, 23, 29, 60, 63, 137

O'Gorman, Ned, 46

Oh Mercy, 428–32, 433–4, 436, 437, 438, 439, 440, 447, 451, 453,

454, 456, 458, 462, 463
O'Hara, Frank, 87
Oldham, Spooner, 348
Oppenheim, David, 255
Orbach, Marty, 261
Orbison, Roy, 424–5, 427
Orlovsky, Peter, 215–16
Oswald, Lee Harvey, 86
Other End, The, New York, 257, 259, 260, 262, 270

Pageant, 123
Paine, Tom, 186
Pankake, Jon, 75
Paris, John, 390
Paris-Jour, 167
Parker, Christopher, 442–3, 446, 454
Parker, Junior, 409, 446
Parsons, Gram, 264, 266
Pat Garrett & Billy the Kid, 220, 222–31, 234, 302
Paul, Terry, 227, 229
Paxton, Tom, 68, 153, 188
PBS, 270
Peck, Gregory, 392
Peckinpah, Sam, 222–30, 302, 412
Pennebaker, Don, 59, 108–9, 111, 113, 115, 160, 162, 163–5, 173, 174, 175, 177–8, 180, 276
Pere Ubu, 257, 431
Perry, Fred, 164
Perry, Richard, 416
Peter, Paul and Mary, 58, 59, 71, 84, 128, 135, 140–41, 183
Petersen, Val, 8
Petty, Tom, 364, 400, 402, 405–6, 408, 409–10, 419, 423, 425, 427, 461
Planet Waves, 125, 235–8, 242, 247, 252, 395, 440, 454
Playboy magazine, 71, 148, 152, 308, 310

Porco, Mike, 45, 46, 257, 276
Power Station Studios, New York, 372, 376, 389, 394
Presley, Elvis, 12, 209, 219, 240, 298, 316, 318, 321, 404, 422, 448
Princeton University, 208
Prine, John, 219
Providence Journal, 100
Purple Onion, St Paul, 21, 28, 196

Q, 462
Quebec, Madelyn, 392, 403
Queens of Rhythm, 394, 410
Quinn, Martha, 348
Quintana, Charlie, 378, 381–4, 408

Raeben, Norman, 243–5, 246, 247, 304, 307, 331, 335
Raffedie, Judge, 296
Ramone, Phil, 242
Ramones, The, 257
Rawlins, Adrian, 31, 161
Ray, Dave, 28
Reagan, Ronald, 407
Real Live, 388
Record Plant, The, New York, 389
Red, Tampa, 317, 323
Redding, Otis, 339
Reed, Jimmy, 12, 36
Reed, Lou, 392
Renaldo and Clara, 244, 277, 279, 282, 295, 301–9, 312, 314–15, 317, 327, 392, 412, 415
Rice, Anne, 282
Richards, Keith, 400–401
Riley, Billy Lee, 317
Rimbaud, Arthur, 6, 37, 76, 87, 90–91, 124, 159, 168

Ripley, Steve, 364, 367
Rivera, Scarlett, 258, 264–6, 269–70, 271–2, 278, 280–81, 282, 287, 293
Rivers, Johnny, 446
Rix, Luther, 271–2, 281
Robbins, Paul Jay, 103–4, 123
Robertson, Robbie, 144–5, 153–5, 156–7, 161, 163, 178–80, 182, 187, 189, 233–4, 236, 237–8, 240–41, 253–4, 270, 383, 418, 428, 441
Robinson, Mark, 379
Rock & Roll Hall of Fame, 422–3
Rogers, Jimmy, 36
Rolling Stone, 183, 196, 201, 206, 207, 209–10, 211, 230, 252, 258, 270, 277, 308, 310, 320, 342, 349, 370, 403, 409, 431, 451
Rolling Stones, 97, 109–10, 113, 143, 156, 163, 186, 188, 198, 253, 432, 456
Rolling Thunder Revue, 255, 259, 270–73, 274–83, 284–5, 286–94, 295, 311, 440, 448, 450, 454
Ronson, Mick, 271, 275, 280, 289, 302–3
Rosato, Arthur, 367
Rosen, Jeff, 404
Rosenbaum, Ron, 308
Roth, Manny, 33, 35
Rothschild, Paul, 131, 132, 135–6, 138–9
Rotolo, Carla, 40, 42–3, 45, 72, 93–4, 96, 149
Rotolo, Suze, 42, 43, 45, 51–2, 55, 56, 60, 63n., 67, 69–70, 72–3, 76, 83, 89, 93–5, 96–7, 98, 106–7, 160, 463–4
Rowan, Pete, 158
Royal Albert Hall, London, 165–6

Royal Festival Hall, London, 91, 95, 96, 109
Rubin, Barbara, 150
Rubin, Judy, 11, 16–17, 18, 82–3
Rundown Studios, Santa Monica, 361, 364
Russell, Leon, 211

Saal, Hubert, 191, 196
Sager, Carole Bayer, 418
Sahm, Doug, 221, 285
Sainte-Marie, Buffy, 243
'St Paul Tape', The, 22, 27
Saltzman, Naomi, 191
Salut les Copains, 166
San Francisco Chronicle, 93
San Rafael, California, 419
Sandburg, Carl, 89
Santana, Carlos, 363, 387
Satin Tones, The, 10
Saturday Review, 242
Savakus, Russ, 131
Saved, 329, 349, 355–7, 359, 361–2, 364, 370, 372, 377, 433
Scaduto, Anthony, 3, 31–2, 83, 89, 148, 162, 200, 211
Schatzberg, Jerry, 149
Scheff, Jerry, 318–19
Schoenfeld, Sally, 72
Schrader, Paul, 397–8
Scorsese, Martin, 294
Scott, Roger, 341
Scratch, 208
Seay, David, 331–2
Sebastian, John, 104, 247
Sebastian, Lorey, 247
Sedgwick, Edie, 150–51
Seeger, Peggy, 64
Seeger, Pete, 20, 42, 52–3, 57, 60, 71, 137, 138, 139, 140, 243
Segal, Katie, 310
Self Portrait, 201, 203–7, 209, 248, 253, 410, 418, 441
Selvin, Joel, 347

Sex Pistols, 422
Sexton, Charlie, 378
Shadow Blasters, 8
Shafner, Gary, 462
Shakespeare, Robbie, 373
Shangri-La Studios, Malibu, 234, 285
Shankar, Ravi, 217
Shelton, Robert, 10, 31, 37–8, 42, 45–6, 89, 100, 103, 137, 146, 161
Shepard, John, 8
Shepard, Sam, 175, 276–8, 304, 392, 418
Sholle, John, 216
Shot of Love, 360–61, 364–6, 370, 372, 377, 384, 402, 433, 435, 454
Sibler, Irwin, 100, 153
Side One, 121
Siewell, Denny, 311–12
Signer, Ethan, 63–4
Silvers, Judy, 64
Silverstein, Shel, 323, 363, 414
Simon, Paul, 204, 420, 428, 454
Simon and Garfunkel, 132
Sinatra, Frank, 405, 416–17
Sing Out, 54, 60, 100, 103, 122–3, 153, 189, 190–91
Singers' Club, London, 64
Skyline Studios, Topanga, 408, 410
Slash, 436, 461
Sloman, Larry, 256, 272, 278–80, 282, 377, 379–80
Slow Train Coming, 335, 339–43, 344, 346, 351, 357, 359, 370, 372–3, 434, 440
Smith, G. E., 442, 443, 445, 447, 454, 457
Smith, Iain, 413
Smith, Jack, 77

Smith, Otis, 309
Smith, Patti, 257, 259, 276, 320, 342
Smith, Warren, 406
Smith, Willie, 348, 367
SNACK (Students Need Athletic And Cultural Kicks), 255
Snow, Hank, 406
Snyder, Gary, 87
Soles, Steven, 271–2, 310, 329
Solid Rock, 357n.
Solomon, Manny, 44
Songwriters Hall of Fame, 422
South, Joe, 157, 452
Special Rider, 404
Spector, Phil, 132, 218, 402
Spencer, Lena, 40
Spencer, Neil, 367
Spin, 397, 403
Spitz, Bob, 17, 31, 46, 89, 137, 138
Spoelstra, Mark, 42, 43
Springs, Helena, 317–18, 328, 338, 348–9, 355, 361, 365, 433
Springsteen, Bruce, 219, 253, 257, 320, 321–2, 366–7, 389, 395, 407, 422, 423, 427, 452, 453
Squeeze, 368
Stampfel, Peter, 39
Stanley Brothers, The, 38
Starr, Ringo, 207–8, 217, 365, 456
Stewart, Dave, 397, 399, 405, 412, 422
Stibal, Brian, 148
Stills, Stephen, 248, 285
Stone, Allen, 125
Stoner, Rob, 258–9, 265–6, 267–8, 269–70, 271, 272, 275, 281, 285, 286, 289, 292, 293, 309, 310–11, 312–13, 316, 317, 318, 373, 383
Stray Cats, The, 368

Street-Legal, 298, 315,
316, 319–21, 322, 327,
328, 338, 344, 417,
454
Studio Instrument
Rentals, New York,
270–71
Sugarman, Bert, 289–90,
292
Sullivan, Ed, 67–8, 70–
71
Sutton, Greg, 384, 386–7
Svedburg, Andrea, 77,
79, 80, 84
Sykes, Christopher, 414

Tackett, Fred, 348, 363
Talking Heads, 257
Taplin, Jonathan, 296,
380
Taplin, Rosanna, 296
Tarantula, 82, 85, 118–
26, 129, 151, 173–4,
179, 189–90, 220
Taylor, Mick, 373, 384,
385–6
Television, 257, 320
Ten O'Clock Scholar,
Minneapolis, 12, 16,
20, 21, 196
Tench, Benmont, 364–5,
384, 402–3, 423–3
Terkel, Studs, 70, 82, 84,
119
Terry, Sonny, 38
Thal, Terri see Van
Ronk, Terri
Thomas, Henry, 56
Thompson, Toby, 3, 185
Thornton, Terry, 73
Tiger, Edith, 86
Till, Emmett, 263
Time, 71, 111, 176, 403
Times, The, 96
Times They Are a-
Changin', The, 4n., 61,
78–9, 80–81, 97, 102,
120, 428
Townshend, Pete, 422
Traum, Artie, 216
Traum, Happy, 40, 67,
179, 190–91, 216–17,
249–50

Traveling Wilburys,
Volume One, 379,
425–7, 436, 451, 461
Travers, Mary, 119, 137,
246, 254
Troubadour, The,
London, 60, 63–4
True Confessions tour
(1986), 441
Truffaut, François, 277
Turner, Gil, 53, 54
Turner, Steve, 333

U2, 422, 428, 448
Under the Red Sky, 434,
436–9, 458, 460, 461
Underhill, Fred, 32, 33
Universal Amphitheater,
Hollywood, 320
Universal Studios,
Hollywood, 402
USA Today, 463

Valentine, Patty, 272n.,
341
Van Matre, Lynn, 238–9,
240
Van Ronk, Dave, 40, 42,
45–6, 76, 81, 84, 243
Van Ronk, Terri (Terri
Thal), 40, 44, 58, 81,
84
Van Zandt, 'Miami'
Steve, 389
Van Zandt, Townes, 448
Vaughan, Jimmy, and
Stevie Ray, 436
Vee, Bobby, 10, 13
Velvet Underground,
The, 132, 186, 187
Verlaine, Paul, 76, 168
Village Recorder Studio
A, Los Angeles, 235
Village Voice, 3, 71, 103,
258, 314
Villon, François, 76, 87
Vineyard Christian
Fellowship, 330–33,
335–6, 341, 348, 350,
369
24 Heures, 167
Von Schmidt, Eric, 37,
41–2, 48, 63–4, 71, 135

Wainwright, Loudon III,
219, 221
Waits, Tom, 430
Walk Down Crooked
Highway, 122–3
Wallace, Ian, 312, 318,
383
Wallace, Karen, 22
Wallace, Terri, 21–2
Warhol, Andy, 150–51
Warner Brothers, 231,
424, 425
Was, David, 436
Was, Don, 436–7, 438,
458, 462
Washington Post, 341
Waters, Muddy, 258
Wayne, John, 407
WBAI, 53
WBC-TV, 71
'We Are the World',
400–401
Weberman, A. J., 203,
210, 213–14, 218
Weill, Kurt, 76
Wein, George, 135
Weinberger, Sybil, 40,
43
Weintraub, Jerry, 311,
317
Weir, Bob, 419–20
Weissberg, Eric, 32,
249–50
Welles, Chris, 4–5
Welles, Orson, 314
Wenner, Jann, 132, 196,
201, 342
Wexler, Jerry, 221, 338,
339–40, 344, 355–6, 372
Weyl, Walter, 194
Whalen, Phillip, 87
Whitaker, Dave, 20, 22,
23, 26–7, 31, 35
White, Bukka, 13, 219
White, Josh, 35
Whitney Museum, New
York, 422
Who, The, 432, 456
Williams, Big Joe, 55
Williams, Don, 370
Williams, Hank, 6, 21,
38–9, 181–2, 298, 402,
412, 448

Williams, Paul, 434
Williams, Tennessee, 406–7
Williamson, Sonny Boy, 35, 382
Wilson, Tom, 68, 73, 104, 105, 116, 130, 131–2, 142
Withers, Pick, 338, 339
Witmark, 58
WNEW-TV, 71
WNYC, 44
Wolfe, Paul, 100–101
Wonder, Stevie, 285
Wood, Ron, 286, 365, 389–91, 396, 400–401
Woodstock, 192–3, 194, 197, 199, 201–2, 207
Words, 220
World Vision, 350

Writings and Drawings, 81, 120, 220, 396–7
WRVR-FM, 38
Wurlitzer, Rudy, 222–4, 226, 229
Wyatt, Lore, 77
Wyeth, Howie, 266, 267, 268, 269–70, 271–2, 281, 285, 288, 289–91, 310, 311, 329, 373, 383

Yarrow, Peter, 59, 101, 135, 139, 140
Yasgur, Max, 199
Yetnikoff, Walter, 276
Yevtushenko, Yevgeny, 396
Young, Izzy, 24, 26, 34, 44–6, 51, 52, 55, 58, 153

Young, Neil, 219, 255, 404, 422, 431
Yurchenco, Henrietta, 70

Zappa, Frank, 368, 373
Zimmerman, Abraham (Dylan's father), 4, 14, 212
Zimmerman, Beattie (Dylan's mother; née Beattie Stone), 4, 31, 78, 185
Zimmerman, David (Dylan's brother), 4, 7–8, 251
Zimmerman, Maurice, 31
Zuckerman, Sue, 42

READ MORE IN PENGUIN

In every corner of the world, on every subject under the sun, Penguin represents quality and variety – the very best in publishing today.

For complete information about books available from Penguin – including Puffins, Penguin Classics and Arkana – and how to order them, write to us at the appropriate address below. Please note that for copyright reasons the selection of books varies from country to country.

In the United Kingdom: Please write to *Dept. EP, Penguin Books Ltd, Bath Road, Harmondsworth, West Drayton, Middlesex UB7 ODA*

In the United States: Please write to *Consumer Sales, Penguin Putnam Inc., P.O. Box 12289 Dept. B, Newark, New Jersey 07101-5289*. VISA and MasterCard holders call 1-800-788-6262 to order Penguin titles

In Canada: Please write to *Penguin Books Canada Ltd, 10 Alcorn Avenue, Suite 300, Toronto, Ontario M4V 3B2*

In Australia: Please write to *Penguin Books Australia Ltd, P.O. Box 257, Ringwood, Victoria 3134*

In New Zealand: Please write to *Penguin Books (NZ) Ltd, Private Bag 102902, North Shore Mail Centre, Auckland 10*

In India: Please write to *Penguin Books India Pvt Ltd, 11 Community Centre, Panchsheel Park, New Delhi 110017*

In the Netherlands: Please write to *Penguin Books Netherlands bv, Postbus 3507, NL-1001 AH Amsterdam*

In Germany: Please write to *Penguin Books Deutschland GmbH, Metzlerstrasse 26, 60594 Frankfurt am Main*

In Spain: Please write to *Penguin Books S. A., Bravo Murillo 19, 1° B, 28015 Madrid*

In Italy: Please write to *Penguin Italia s.r.l., Via Benedetto Croce 2, 20094 Corsico, Milano*

In France: Please write to *Penguin France, Le Carré Wilson, 62 rue Benjamin Baillaud, 31500 Toulouse*

In Japan: Please write to *Penguin Books Japan Ltd, Kaneko Building, 2-3-25 Koraku, Bunkyo-Ku, Tokyo 112*

In South Africa: Please write to *Penguin Books South Africa (Pty) Ltd, Private Bag X14, Parkview, 2122 Johannesburg*

READ MORE IN PENGUIN

A CHOICE OF NON-FICTION

Jane Austen: A Life Claire Tomalin

'I cannot think that a better life of Jane Austen than Claire Tomalin's will be written for many years ... a truly marvellous book' *Mail on Sunday*. 'As near perfect a Life of Austen as we are likely to get ... Tomalin presents Austen as remarkably clever; sensitive, but unsentimental' *Daily Telegraph*

A Wavering Grace Gavin Young

'By far ... the most moving account of Vietnam to be written in recent years' Norman Lewis. 'This delicate, terrible and enchanting book ... brings the atmosphere of Vietnam so near that you can almost taste and smell it' *The Times*

Clone Gina Kolata

On July 5 1996 Dolly, the most famous lamb in history, was born. It was an event of enormous significance, for Dolly was a clone, produced from the genetic material of a six-year-old ewe. Suddenly, the idea that human beings could be replicated had become a reality. 'Superb' J. G. Ballard, *Sunday Times*

Huxley Adrian Desmond

T. H. Huxley (1825–95), often referred to as 'Darwin's Bulldog', became the major champion of the theory of evolution and was crucial to the making of our modern Darwinian world. 'Nobody writes scientific biography like Adrian Desmond, and this account of Huxley's progress ... is his best so far' *The Times Literary Supplement*

Cleared for Take-Off Dirk Bogarde

'It begins with his experiences in the Second World War as an interpreter of reconnaissance photographs ... his awareness of the horrors as well as the dottiness of war is essential to the tone of this affecting and strangely beautiful book' *Daily Telegraph*

READ MORE IN PENGUIN

A CHOICE OF NON-FICTION

Time Out Film Guide   Edited by John Pym

The definitive, up-to-the-minute directory of every aspect of world cinema from classics and silent epics to reissues and the latest releases.

Four-Iron in the Soul   Lawrence Donegan

'A joy to read. Not since Bill Bryson plotted a random route through small-town America has such a breezy idea for a book had a happier (or funnier) result' *The Times*. 'Funny, beautifully observed and it tells you things about sport in general and golf in particular that nobody else thought to pass on' *Mail on Sunday*

Nelson Mandela: A Biography   Martin Meredith

Nelson Mandela's role in delivering South Africa from racial division stands as one of the great triumphs of the twentieth century. In this brilliant account, Martin Meredith gives a vivid portrayal of the life and times of this towering figure. 'The best biography so far of Nelson Mandela' Raymond Whitaker, *Independent on Sunday*

In Search of Nature   Edward O. Wilson

'*In Search of Nature* makes such stimulating reading that Edward O. Wilson might be regarded as a one-man recruitment bureau for tomorrow's biologists . . . His essays on ants tend to leave one gasping for breath, literally speaking . . . Yet he is equally enchanting in his accounts of sharks and snakes and New Guinea's birds of paradise' *The Times Higher Education Supplement*

Reflections on a Quiet Rebel   Cal McCrystal

This extraordinary book is both a vivid memoir of Cal McCrystal's Irish Catholic childhood and a loving portrait of his father Charles, a 'quiet rebel' and unique man. 'A haunting book, lovely and loving. It explains more about one blighted corner of Ireland than a dozen dogged histories' *Scotsman*

READ MORE IN PENGUIN

A CHOICE OF NON-FICTION

Falling Leaves Adeline Yen Mah

'I am still haunted by Mah's memoir ... Riveting. A marvel of memory. Poignant proof of the human will to endure' Amy Tan. '*Falling Leaves* is a terrible and riveting family history ... It is also a story about endurance and the cost it can exact' *Daily Telegraph*

Anatomy of a Miracle Patti Waldmeir

The peaceful birth of black majority rule in South Africa has been seen by many as a miracle – or at least political magic. 'Essential reading for anyone interested in South Africa' *Literary Review*. 'One of the most authoritative reporters on the South African scene ... her analytical skills are deadly' *Sunday Times*

My Name Escapes Me Alec Guinness

'His diary for the eighteen months from January 1995 to June 1996 is a book of immense charm and the source of almost undiluted pleasure. Imagine a lucky dip where each entry comes up with a prize and you will have some measure of the writing' *Daily Mail*

The Feminization of Nature Deborah Cadbury

Scientists around the world are uncovering alarming changes in human reproduction and health. There is strong evidence that sperm counts have fallen dramatically. Testicular and prostate cancer are on the increase. Different species are showing signs of 'feminization' or even 'changing sex'. 'Grips you from page one ... it reads like a Michael Crichton thriller' John Gribbin

The Portuguese Marion Kaplan

This book records Portugal's rich and turbulent history and also ranges lightly across the issues, incongruities and paradoxes of Portugal today. 'Sympathetic, perceptive, lively and full of information' *The Times Literary Supplement*

READ MORE IN PENGUIN

A CHOICE OF NON-FICTION

Racers Richard Williams

'Where Williams really scores is in his evocation of the political chicanery and secret vendettas in Formula One' *Guardian*. 'Gets under the skin of this intelligent, sophisticated and cold-blooded sport ... the plot grips like Pirellis on a rain-slicked mountain pass' *Observer*

Floyd on Africa Keith Floyd

Keith Floyd's wonderful chronicle of cooking, eating and travelling around Zambia, Zimbabwe, Madagascar and South Africa is part safari and part recipe book. Inspired by the tropical fruits in the markets, the fish from sparkling lakes and the game from the bush, he conjures up some unforgettable meals.

The Way to Write John Fairfax and John Moat

While of direct use to the more practised writer, *The Way to Write* remains alive to the difficulties experienced by those who would like to explore their own creative writing but feel unsure of how to begin. This stimulating book takes you from the first confrontation with the blank page to the final manuscript.

The Little Book of Calm Paul Wilson

Feeling stressed? Need some help to regain balance in your life? The bestselling *The Little Book of Calm* is full of advice to follow and thoughts to inspire. Open it at any page and you will find a path to inner peace.

American Frontiers Gregory H. Nobles

'At last someone has written a narrative of America's frontier experience with sensitivity and insight. This is a book which will appeal to both the specialist and the novice' James M. McPherson, Princeton University

READ MORE IN PENGUIN

A CHOICE OF NON-FICTION

The Old Patagonian Express Paul Theroux

Beginning his journey in Boston, where he boarded the subway commuter train, Paul Theroux travelled the length of North and South America, to his destination in Patagonia. 'Fascinating, beautifully written ... a vivid travelogue described with the sensitive, richly observant pen of a born writer' *Sunday Express*

The Lions Diary Jeremy Guscott with Nick Cain

Packed with action from the pitch, the dressing-room and the heartlands, *The Lions Diary* is the complete insiders' account of the most successful tour in British rugby history. 'Hugely entertaining. If you want a book that tells it from the inside of a sweaty tracksuit after endless shuttle-runs, this is the one' *Daily Telegraph*

Michael Heseltine Michael Crick

'Michael Crick confirms his reputation as a superb investigator. He writes wittily and engagingly with a mastery of narrative pace as well as a shrewd political nose ... it should prove the definitive life' *The Times Literary Supplement*. 'Entertaining ... seems set to become the standard tome on his subject' *The Times*

Mornings in the Dark Edited by David Parkinson
The Graham Greene Film Reader

Prompted by 'a sense of fun' and 'that dangerous third Martini' at a party in June 1935, Graham Greene volunteered himself as the *Spectator* film critic. 'His film reviews are among the most trenchant, witty and memorable one is ever likely to read' *Sunday Times*

Fenland Chronicle Sybil Marshall

In *Fenland Chronicle* Sybil Marshall has collected together her mother's and father's remembrances of their childhood, marriage, family life and work in this traditional corner of England and drawn them into a vivid portrait of a time gone by.

READ MORE IN PENGUIN

A CHOICE OF NON-FICTION

The Penguin Opera Guide
Edited by Amanda Holden with Nicholas Kenyon and Stephen Walsh

'Remarkably comprehensive . . . The criterion for any guide is whether it can be read not only for reference but for entertainment, and Amanda Holden and her contributors pass this test with first-class honours' *The Times*

The 30-Minute Cook   Nigel Slater

'An inspired worldwide collection of quick and accessible dishes; robust and honest, they are constructed so the ingredients shine, the cooking is simple, and the results impressive . . . Go shopping with a copy and feast on the pleasure of real food' *Evening Standard*

The Pleasures of the Past   David Cannadine

'This is almost everything you ever wanted to know about the past but were too scared to ask . . . A fascinating book and one to strike up arguments in the pub' *Daily Mail*. 'He is erudite and rigorous, yet always fun. I can imagine no better introduction to historical study than this collection' *Observer*

Richard Feynman: A Life in Science   John Gribbin and Mary Gribbin

'Richard Feynman (1918–88) was to the second half of the century what Einstein was to the first: the perfect example of scientific genius' *Independent*. 'One of the most influential and best-loved physicists of his generation . . . This biography is both compelling and highly readable' *Mail on Sunday*

A Sin Against the Future   Vivien Stern

Do prisons contribute to a better, safer world? Or are they a threat to democracy, as increasingly punitive measures are brought in to deal with rising crime? This timely account examines different styles of incarceration around the world and presents a powerful case for radical change.